bc

7-353256

7-22-77

The Realm of the Extra-Human

# World Anthropology

*General Editor*

SOL TAX

*Patrons*

CLAUDE LÉVI-STRAUSS
MARGARET MEAD
LAILA SHUKRY EL HAMAMSY
M. N. SRINIVAS

MOUTON PUBLISHERS · THE HAGUE · PARIS
DISTRIBUTED IN THE USA AND CANADA BY ALDINE, CHICAGO

# The Realm of the Extra-Human

*Agents and Audiences*

*Editor*

AGEHANANDA BHARATI

MOUTON PUBLISHERS · THE HAGUE · PARIS
DISTRIBUTED IN THE USA AND CANADA BY ALDINE, CHICAGO

# General Editor's Preface

Religion, ritual, sacred belief — the subject matter of this and its companion volume, *The realm of the extra-human: ideas and actions* — are controversial in every sense. Where these elements or the concepts behind them lie in the human psyche; when, how, and why they came into the human experience; how we discover, describe, study, interpret them; what theorizing is valid; whether these are good questions: all these problems (and others) are dealt with differently by different scholars. Not only are the scholars influenced by differing private beliefs and scholarly traditions, but also by the differing cultures in which they are reared. The editor, who has his own views, describes the spectrum in his entertaining introduction to the two rich volumes by scholars with and without religion and from many of the changing world's cultural traditions, which show off contemporary work in all its variety. Like most contemporary sciences, anthropology is a product of the European tradition. Some argue that it is a product of colonialism, with one small and self-interested part of the species dominating the study of the whole. If we are to understand the species, our science needs substantial input from scholars who represent a variety of the world's cultures. It was a deliberate purpose of the IXth International Congress of Anthropological and Ethnological Sciences to provide impetus in this direction. The *World Anthropology* volumes, therefore, offer a first glimpse of a human science in which members from all societies have played an active role. Each of the books is designed to be self-contained; each is an attempt to update its particular sector of scientific knowledge and is written by specialists from all parts of the world. Each volume should be read and reviewed individually as a separate volume on its own given subject. The set as a whole will indicate what changes are in store for anthropology as scholars from the developing countries join in studying the species of which we are all a part.

The IXth Congress planned from the beginning not only to include as many of the scholars from every part of the world as possible, but also with a view toward the eventual publication of the papers in high-quality volumes. At previous Congresses scholars were invited to bring papers which were then read out loud. They were necessarily limited in length; many were only summarized; there was little time for discussion; and the sparse discussion could only be in one language. The IXth Congress was an experiment aimed at changing this. Papers were written with the intention of exchanging them before the Congress, particularly in extensive pre-Congress sessions; they were not intended to be read aloud at the Congress, that time being devoted to discussions — discussions which were simultaneously and professionally translated into five languages. The method for eliciting the papers was structured to make as representative a sample as was allowable when scholarly creativity — hence self-selection — was critically important. Scholars were asked both to propose papers of their own and to suggest topics for sessions of the Congress which they might edit into volumes. All were then informed of the suggestions and encouraged to re-think their own papers and the topics. The process, therefore, was a continuous one of feedback and exchange and it has continued to be so even after the Congress. The some two thousand papers comprising *World Anthropology* certainly then offer a substantial sample of world anthropology. It has been said that anthropology is at a turning point; if this is so, these volumes will be the historical direction-markers.

As might have been foreseen in the first post-colonial generation, the large majority of the Congress papers (82 percent) are the work of scholars identified with the industrialized world which fathered our traditional discipline and the institution of the Congress itself: Eastern Europe (15 percent); Western Europe (16 percent); North America (47 percent); Japan, South Africa, Australia, and New Zealand (4 percent). Only 18 percent of the papers are from developing areas: Africa (4 percent); Asia-Oceania (9 percent); Latin America (5 percent). Aside from the substantial representation from the U.S.S.R. and the nations of Eastern Europe, a significant difference between this corpus of written material and that of other Congresses is the addition of the large proportion of contributions from Africa, Asia, and Latin America. "Only 18 percent" is two to four times as great a proportion as that of other Congresses; moreover, 18 percent of 2,000 papers is 360 papers, 10 times the number of "Third World" papers presented at previous Congresses. In fact, these 360 papers are more than the total of ALL papers published after the last International Congress of Anthropological and Ethnological Sciences which was held in the United States (Philadelphia, 1956).

The significance of the increase is not simply quantitative. The input of scholars from areas which have until recently been no more than subject matter for anthropology represents both feedback and also long-awaited theoretical contributions from the perspectives of very different cultural, social, and historical traditions. Many who attended the IXth Congress were convinced that anthropology would not be the same in the future. The fact that the next Congress (India, 1978) will be our first in the "Third World" may be symbolic of the change. Meanwhile, sober consideration of the present set of books will show how much, and just where and how, our discipline is being revolutionized.

The present volume joins others in the *World Anthropology* series which deal with related cultural and psychological phenomena and well-being, and with related phenomena as they appear in various parts of the world through time.

*Chicago, Illinois*                                                        SOL TAX
*March 15, 1976*

# Table of Contents

# Introduction

AGEHANANDA BHARATI

In a survey of the state of the anthropological study of belief and ritual systems, I found to my surprise that no "school" had usurped suzerainty in this subfield in the same way that Chomskyan generative-transformational grammars have come to rule supreme, at this time, in linguistics; no one such school in this subfield has collected enough Brownie points to be able to lay claim to sole academic respectability. Conceivably, a formalist versus a substantivist school analogous to economic anthropology might have arisen. A strong rallying of Lévi-Straussians and anti-Straussians, or a binary opposition between quantifiers and humanists, etc. could have generated this kind of pecking order. Nothing of this sort happened. Instead, we found that the writing of the last decade represents a highly eclectic and remarkably nonpolemic stratum in anthropological writing. Those papers presented at the IXth ICAES Congress and now published in two companion volumes of *World Anthropology* (*The realm of the extra-human: agents and audiences* and *The realm of the extra-human: ideas and actions*) reflect that very wide, eclectic area, and for reasons of sheer editorial verve I felt that some structured opposition, some polarity, had to be supplied, where the totality of papers seen from the viewpoint of its authors may not warrant any polarization. As the Congress convened, it became clear to me and to my co-chairman Samarendra Saraf of Saugor University, India, that a considerable number of anthropologists, especially those who had backgrounds other than British or American, saw the study of origins of microsystems (e.g. shamanism, priesthood, sacrifice, etc.) as their chief professional commitment. In British and American anthropology, origins, or rather the study of the origin of a religion, has long been legislated out of training and research, and with reason. As we realized during the first hours of the event, colleagues from other parts of the world, some of them much more erudite than I, simply refused to argue this reason, or reasons, if not on ideological grounds, then certainly on logistic ones; they had written and prepared their papers long before the Congress began, and could hardly be expected to switch horses in midstream, even if the horses switched to were more powerful and effective. So while British- and American-trained anthropologists researching the realm of the extrahuman can be perfectly sanguine in attempting to trace the origin of one or the other microsystem, of one or the other kind of shamanism in one area, the ORIGINS of these phenomena in human pre-history cannot be studied as macrosystems, not because possible theories are bad, but because they are all equally good. Because no theory of the origin of the belief and manipulation of the extrahuman can be falsified, theses about these macro-origins cannot be scientific. They are often ingenious, always interesting, but not on a par with the dry, more arid research done in the field of the ethnography of religion and its theo-retical corollaries. Much more about this will have to be said in the preface to the companion volume, which deals with ideas and percep-tions, more amenable to enthusiastic speculations than are people and their audiences.

We had, then, an unplanned but clearly emerging line of conservative dissent, first pointed out by Lukas, in a suggestion that a separate session on history, ecology, and evolution in the anthropological study of religion should be convened. This turned out to be what most of my colleagues from America and Britain who were present at the meeting hoped it would not be — an attempted vindication of the early *Kultur-kreis* and the culture-historical approaches of Central European anthro-pologists of the turn of the century and early decades of the twentieth century.

In giving an overview of research on rituals, cults, and shamanism, we can see basically three types of scholars: the descriptivists, the psycholo-gists, and the historians. The descriptivists, who constituted the majority of the contributors to this session, can be subdivided into: the structurists (NOT "structuralists," because this term must be reserved for legitimate Straussians, but scholars who are concerned with structure rather than with process or function and who have some model in mind, inclusive of, but wider than, structuralist themes); the taxonomists (I class my-self in this category); and the "interesting-story tellers" (scholars who make elaborate statements about localized phenomena which fascinate them and which have nothing to do with anything else, unless linked by poetic analogy). All of these are, I think, anthropologically respect-able, including the story tellers, for as our Congress president said many years ago, "Anthropology is what anthropologists do."

The "interesting-story tellers" narrate what might concern fellow trav-elers who are attracted by similar sounds, smells, sights, and memories.

The "psychologists" include not only those who use psychological models in the narrower sense, such as those initiated by culture and personality proponents of the fifties, but also those who believe that the study of symbols and of symbolic systems other than language is relevant to the study of religious behavior. I profoundly disagree with these and insist that symbol talk is a perfectly eradicable and dispensable Jungian remnant, not needed in modern anthropological research; while symbol talk may do good things for the sophisticated discussion of Judaism and Christianity, it does nothing for the understanding of other ritual and belief systems which do not generate terms meaning "symbol" in their language.

By "historians" I mean not only *Kulturkreis* scholars such as those introduced in *The realm of the extra-human: actions and ideas*, but all scholars who believe that the ORIGIN of religion, as contrasted to the origins of various religious systems, can and should be studied. These historians are sequestered and numerous and they seem to hold the balance of production today in all British and American anthropological milieus. This and its companion volume contain a good number of papers which deal directly or obliquely with the question of origin. I do not like them, but they certainly produce permissible ethnological reports; some of them, though methodologically unsound, are nevertheless important because they deliver some ethnographic material which has not been presented before, or whose sources are inaccessible at this time, particularly in regions closed to Western anthropologists.

During my panel introduction, I requested that the participants should not read their papers or their abstracts. Rather I suggested that they should tell us what had not been said in their papers: that they should also voice their gripes about what had to remain unsaid, for one reason or the other, in their papers, and that they should voice their complaints about the current state of the art with special reference to the anthropological study of religious behavior and related areas. I exemplified this suggestion with my own paper. I had not stated in it that practitioners who are not established in any accepted hierarchy, who are pressurized or "marginalized" into a position of systemic censure, use instruments which are highly objectionable to the official religious hierarchy AND to the religious rank and file. This of course was meant as a cross-cultural suggestion, which had no place in my paper dealing with a regional set of complex phenomena. In a general overview, this is nothing new; we have it in a modified, though equally segmented, form in Gluckman's rites of rebellion or in my fellow panelist Norbeck's rites of reversal. In India, however, this opposition generated its own, highly sophisticated set of practitioners who developed their own code, opposed but parallel to the official one, and this part of the story is a historical peculiarity not replicated in other societies.

My gripes *vis-à-vis* the present state of the art are twofold: one technical, the other, if you will, ethical. The technical one was already mentioned in this preface, i.e. those anthropologists who use symbol-talk when there is no such talk in the emic corpus of the society studied — and this would be a criticism of some 90 percent of the audience, because most anthropologists working in the field of religion use symbol language at one time or the other. "Symbol," "symbolism," "symbolize," etc. are armchair categories generated by armchair scholars like the late C. G. Jung and the "Eranos" savants. Eliade, the most erudite among all "symbol" users in the study of religion, was very much on many people's minds, but he never appeared at the Congress in person, although he lives in Chicago. This technical gripe results from my insistence on the main precept of the "new ethnography," that is, the systematic separation between emic and etic strategies. Separation, not the mere awareness of the differences between those two corpuses, is what the "new ethnographer" has in mind. The difference between those categories generated by the cultural actor and those created by the investigator was known to Boas and rudimentarily even to Lewis Henry Morgan. When Lukas, one of the historians and scholars who suggested the subsession "History, Ecology, and Evolution," mentioned in passing that one of his teachers made a distinction between the emic and the etic, Lukas missed the point: it is not the acquaintance with the distinction between these two mutually exclusive modes that shows up the difference between traditional and new analyses, but the formalized separation of these two modes into separate and successive parts of description and analysis.

My ethical gripe was shared, in various forms, by many participants and, beyond the precincts of the Congress, by the majority of concerned anthropologists in the Western world. How much can the anthropologist tell about matters which are crucial to the understanding of an ethnological/anthropological situation but which the informants do not want discussed or publicized? Secret societies, clandestine religious cults, intimate initiations and other rituals, and the whole range of ritual things which constituted the bulk of ethnographic reporting over the past hundred years — there never was a moral justification for reporting such events without the subjects' permission, but now, when the informants are no longer colonized people, they have a say in

Peter takes for granted the obsolescent culture and personality dicta as codified by Geza Roheim (1947). Prince Peter and Geza Roheim do not heed the basic distinction between native and extraneously supplied medical and psychopathological categories. Does the oracle see himself as a psychopath or as an epileptic? Do his audiences see him thus?

Sharon's Peruvian *curanderos* and the Guyana Hindu shaman described by Singer et al. have in common a totally new potential in relation to curing in general. The increasing interst in therapy, so Singer observed at the American Anthropological Association meeting in New Orleans three months after the Congress, seems to involve more and more anthropologists who would join the ranks of the curers rather than the more conservative nucleus of observers: many more hitherto opaque family type resemblances between such unrelated practitioners as Singer's and Sharon's will be traced, and used, if Singer is right and anthropologists are indeed becoming curers in increasing numbers.

More about religious anthropologists taking THEIR religion as anthropology rather than doing anthropology of religion will have to be said in the companion volume's preface. Suffice it to say at this point, that the fact of an anthropologist's being a Hindu (or a Shintoist, or a Christian) does not permit him to imply the ideological superiority of his own ritual and belief system. There is a young, brilliant Brahmin anthropologist (not represented in this or its related volume) who happens to study the Zuñi. To him, the *kachinas* and the deities of the Southwest are in no way categorically different from the gods of the Hindu pantheon. This is as it should be, or else we are straight back to the days of anthropologists propounding Ur-monotheism as an archaic universal because they happen to be devout Christians.

It is one thing to say that the days of purely objective, personally and ideologically uninvolved anthropological reporting are gone and that no pretext should be made to having achieved, or even to trying to achieve, total objectivity, because there is no such thing in the tool-kit of today's field anthropologists. It is quite a different thing to draw one's methodology from one's religious conviction. The late Father Koppers, my first and soon rejected mentor in ethnology, used to get upset when it was suggested that faith was no warranty for success in the ethnographic reporting of religious phenomena. Koppers said (this is from a lecture note taken at Vienna in 1947), "a man who can build a canoe will be better qualified to talk about the Polynesian canoe builders than a man who does not master this craft." Canoes and outriggers are, however, of one kind, and religious behavior is of quite another. Canoes do not generate ideology, religion does. Gallus of Australia, a prominent plaintiff in the subsession on "History, Ecology, and Evolution," dealt with in the preface to the related volume, complained that the study of religion should not be primarily logical and objective, but that it must be religious — which is like saying that the study of emotion must be emotional. To the layman, the nonsensicality of the latter statement is immediately obvious; to the anthropologist and the philosopher and, in fact, to the methodologist of any science, that of the former is equally evident. Just as the discussion of emotion is not an emotional pursuit for the psychologist, the study of religion is not a religious pursuit for the anthropologist. In order to talk about shamans, there is neither the need to be nor even to feel like being a shaman, either by empathy or by some sort of privileged information which the Jung-Eliade continuum stipulates for the shaman. The inverse is true, too: no shaman is required to be an anthropologist. In fact, if he is, that is bad for the anthropologist, because he gets caught in the quandary of Marvin Harris' "well-informed informant" (1966), who talks anthropology and does not talk about what the anthropologist is looking for.

Statutory homage was paid to Eliade and to Lévi-Strauss, and this is as it should be. But whereas Lévi-Strauss' models are anthropological ones, however refutable, however criticizable, Eliade's work is not anthropological; it is that of an erudite, highly informed believer. An anthropologist might, and I am not being overly facetious, study Eliade as a sort of super-shaman or as a scholar among shamans; Strauss is not, notwithstanding McDougall's title — in fact, she would probably agree to this categorical dichotomy. Eliade's erudition often blurs the fact that he is indeed a scholar whose mainspring of information is a strong attachment to religious, specifically to mystic, modes. It is this, we believe, which bars his acceptance by professional anthropologists, in spite of the undoubtable fact that his knowledge of shamanism, trance, and other religious modes is superior to that of any other single anthropologist working with the practitioners and the phenomena involved. The quest for the origins of the shaman is inspired by a religious rather than a discursive input: every religion KNOWS, emically speaking, what the origins of the universe, of the gods, and of the priests and shamans were. The quest for the origin of religion is a religious quest, not an anthropological search.

That belief and involvement can be kept at bay in an analytical investigation of one's own religious convictions is well documented by Aiyappan, who hypothesizes that the monistic concept of Vedanta is a development from the tribal archetype of the man-god continuum exemplified in the mother-goddess complex of southern India.

Felicitas Goodman, in an anthropologically orthodox, modern mix of psychological and ethnological models, discusses the relation between such shamanistic syndromes as glossolalia and culture change under dislocation and rapid transition.

Some serious scholars investigated the connection of religious modes with basic human rights and other modernistic values (e.g. Oosterwal, Quarcoo, Salamone). The ideological underpinnings here are not always obvious, and some of the authors may not even be conscious of them. Choices between such contrasting options are NOT of a scientific, but of a moral, or perhaps, of a joint moral-*cum*-aesthetic order, well outside the scientific parameters of the sciences represented here.

A number of excellent papers deal with the ever-widening complex of sense-stimulation, particularly through psychotomimetic agents, in its religious dimensions. There is no doubt that the counter-culture at its peak generated serious scholarly interest as a spin-off, as it were. I am not thinking of the quasi-anthropology of the Castaneda literature (1968, 1971), but of such older works as Aberle's on peyote (1966), or Dobkin de Riós' recent book (1972) on ecstatic techniques using psychedelic agents among native South American populations. For good or bad, there is no trace in these contributions of the late Allan Coult's "psychedelic anthropology" (n.d.), which appears to be defunct since the untimely death of that tragic, amazing young anthropologist. Lex, Loeb, and Long are the contributors whose research centers on these techniques. There is a clear bifurcation here with regard to the incipient interest of the researchers. Some scholars obviously connect their findings with their one-time participant observation in the middle-class American drug culture of the sixties; others, of more conservative vintage, regard the ingestion of chemicals for religious purposes as being on a par with many other ritualistic techniques like trance acquisition in cross-cultural perspective. Marginal, cultist anthropology of the Castaneda type was not represented at this session, and I used my editorial privilege to reject four papers which clearly belonged to that genre. Those scholars who contribute serious studies here investigated individuals and their action patterns which were generated by the chemico-religious situation rather than the teachings, ideologies, and world view that result from psychochemical manipulations, both in religious and non-religious, i.e. pathological and rebellious (counter-establishment), settings. The reason for this scholary reticence must be obvious: the popular notion that psychedelics create a new world view is of lay provenance and is wrong.

It is quite impossible, of course, to review all the papers in this preface. Here, as well as in the companion volume, the contributions must speak for themselves, and the selection of the titles perused in this preface has to do with my own personal, thematic predilections. I am therefore not discussing more than one or two papers which belong to the "interesting-story" category, for I regard these as private, inviolable domains. Fotis Litsas's paper, although I would class it under the "interesting-story" rubric, has cross-cultural relevance; exhuming of the dead in a ritualistic setting is found in Thailand and possibly in other regions. A study clearly concerning the life cycle, including funerary rites, yields potential material for the Human Relations Area Files and *Ethnographic atlas* even if the author is not aware of it.

On the other hand, speculations on the analogy of purpose on the basis of artifacts found seems a much riskier prospect. Kralovánszky believes that the shawm-like instrument which he describes was used by the shamans and that it REPRESENTS the shaman through its human likeness, on the basis of analogies from the history of religion; this is inadmissible in my view, because there are not even any theoretical means of verifying or falsifying this proposition. As such, the paper belongs, albeit in a subtler manner, to the genre of origin studies of the early days of anthropological and comparative religion research.

Mahapatra's highly informative contribution feeds into ongoing research correlating extra-human personages in South Asia with caste structure. This is being done with great success by scholars not represented here, e.g. Beck (1969, 1972), E. Harper (1957), H. Gould (1967), and J. Mencher (1966), as well as with the current research of S. Wadley (1972), whose field report on possession in this volume provides powerful insight into binary types of spirit intrusion and spirit manipulation in village India.

McDougall's intriguing paper is grist to my own mill: the interpolation or imposition of "symbol" categories on "supernatural" phenomena insufficiently understood by the researcher or understood in a biased fashion is an anthropological syndrome which should be studied by anthropologists.

Nachtigall's title is, fortunately, misleading: his suggestions about the workings of shamans are not culture-historical ruminations, but are based on a sober statement of the actors' own beliefs as well as on observation of funerary ritual.

Newell's concept of "good and bad ancestors" is shared by Meyer Fortes in the *World Anthropology* volume, *Ancestors* (1976), yet it deserves a comment in this volume as well. Newell is justifiably concerned about the radical difference in the thematic and contextual structure of "ancestors" in West Africa and China, and he asks whether a redefinition of the role of ancestor may be needed to account for both these areas. Maybe. But doesn't ethnosemantics provide a more elegant guideline? If the native categories were checked out formally, if the semantic extensions of ancestor-words were listed, and if the functional overlap of these necessarily different taxonomies were compared as an afterthought, as it were, not with a prior commitment to the transcultural use of "ancestor," we might be better off than with a redefinition, because there is no guarantee that it will accommodate the full range of ancestor sememes in these two cultures, and *a fortiori* there is even less likelihood that it will accommodate yet other ancestral themes elsewhere. It is better, in my opinion, to forego or phase out terms created and fossilized by the anthropologists' Ur-vocabulary, when empirical data no longer justify their retention. "Ancestors," "ancestor," etc. might well be dropped just as "totemism" has been gently shelved in recent studies of phenomena that would have been bracketed under this caption in more optimistic and less rigorous days.

Though Patai's expertise lies quite outside my sphere, the discovery of mother goddesses and other officially unacceptable extra-humans in the Hebrew tradition is as enjoyable to the humanistically inclined anthropologist as is es-Shamy's statement about minor divinities in the *maghreb* (see preface to companion volume). This belongs in the British philosophers' category of "parson-skinning," a time-honored enterprise overtly or covertly pursued by some of the best anthropologists. It is pleasant to learn that Judaism does not contain only what the rabbi thinks it should, that Islam has more than the *ulama* doctors permit, or that Jesus might have been married to Mary Magdalen. As a tool for eliciting anthropological response, this research, when reintroduced into the field, generates what I call "cultural criticism": by telling the specialist informant that there are things in his tradition which he rejects or is ignorant of, one elicits, along with varying degrees of indignation, intensive response of an apologetic sort, response that leads to a more thorough understanding of the belief system involved.

Tu Er-wei's analysis of a Chinese deity ties in philological, classicist (i.e. Buddhologist), and other orientalist speculations with a hopefully observed or at least observable "primitive," i.e. non-Buddhist, non-Taoist, etc., belief stratum. The effort parallels that of Aiyappan in the South Indian context.

The survey of anthropological approaches to the study of religious behavior (*Biennial review of anthropology* [1972]), lists about one thousand titles and analyzes about eighty in some detail. However, close to 95 percent of the works listed and discussed in that publication were generated in English-speaking countries. This volume and its companion in *World Anthropology* present and combine a representative sample of the work that is being done inside and outside British and American anthropology. When the illuminati of the profession meet again in India in the latter part of this decade, a closer rapport between researchers is bound to appear — one that has crystallized, we would hope, on the basis and the merit of the gigantic undertaking that is *World Anthropology*. We hope in these two volumes to contribute richly to the business of knowing man and of transmitting this rapidly increasing lore to the next generation of people who would have their share in the enterprise.

## REFERENCES

ABERLE, D. F.
1966   *The peyote religion among the Navaho.* Chicago: Aldine.
BECK, BRENDA E. F.
1969   Color and heat in South Indian ritual. *Man* 4(4):553–572.
1972   *Peasant society in Konku.* Vancouver, B.C.: University of British Columbia Press.
CASTANEDA, C.
1968   *The teachings of Don Juan: a Yaqui way of knowledge.* Berkeley and Los Angeles: University of California Press.
1971   *A separate reality: further conversations with Don Juan.* New York: Simon and Schuster.
COULT, ALLAN D.
n.d.   "Psychedelic anthropology: people words play."
DOBKIN DE RÍOS, M.
1972   *Visionary vine: psychedelic healing in the Peruvian Amazon.* San Francisco: Chandler.
GOULD, H.
1967   Priest and counterpriest: a structural analysis of *jajmani* relations in the Hindu Plain and Nilgiri Hills. *Contributions to Indian Sociology* n.s. 1:26–55. New Delhi.
1964   "Ritual pollution as an integrator of caste and religion," in *Religion in South Asia.*

HARPER, E. N.
1957    Shamanism in South India. *Southwestern Journal of Anthropology* 13(3):267–287.

HARRIS, M.
1966    The cultural ecology of India's sacred cattle. *Current Anthropology* (7):51–66.

KOPPERS, W.
1947    Lecture notes taken in his course, "Allgemeine Völkerkunde." University of Vienna, Institut für Völkerkunde.

MENCHER, JOAN P.
1966    Nambudiri Brahmins: an analysis of a traditional elite in Kerala. *Journal of Asian and African Studies* 1(3):183–196.

MOORE, G. E.
1903    *Principia ethica.* London: Cambridge University Press.

NEWELL, WILLIAM H., *editor*
1976    *Ancestors.* World Anthropology. The Hague: Mouton.

ROHEIM, GEZA
1947    "Dream analysis and fieldwork in anthropology," in *Psychoanalysis and the social sciences,* volume one. New York: International Universities Press.

SIEGEL, B. J., *editor*
1972    *Biennial review of anthropology.* Stanford: Stanford University Press.

WADLEY, S. S.
1972    "Power in the conceptual structure of Karimpur religion." Unpublished doctoral dissertation, University of Chicago.

# SECTION ONE

# Neo-Hindu Acculturation: An Alternative to "Instant Chemical Religion"

ROBERT J. FORNARO

It was apparent with the publication of the 1967 Presidential Task Force report on drugs that the drug-abuse problem in this country had grown critical (President's Commission 1967). Many thousands of young people were actively experimenting with a wide variety of drugs for an even wider variety of reasons. The instances of drug abuse and drug addiction had increased dramatically. One factor behind these excesses was the attempt to establish "instant chemical religion" (Furst 1972: vii), i.e. to use drugs to induce a personal religious experience. The experiences gained through drugs were not readily applicable to American religious systems, so many turned to the alternative religious forms present in what Theodore Roszak calls "the counter-culture" (Roszak 1968). This discussion concerns itself with one of these alternate religious forms, neo-Hinduism, and the relationship it has with the drug problem. Germane to the discussion is the process of neo-Hindu acculturation, i.e. those changes in cognitive and behavioral patterns necessary for one to become a neo-Hindu.

The author is not a drug expert but a social scientist who seeks some insight into the relationship of drugs to neo-Hinduism and the behavioral changes implicit in that relationship. It is possible that what is presented here will stimulate others to investigate the relationship of drugs to the growth and development of the many other so-called "counter-culture" religious movements. This paper is simply a presentation of data and is not meant to be a definitive study of either neo-Hinduism or the drug problem.[1]

Under the financial auspices of a Ford Foundation Humanities Grant, information about neo-Hinduism was gathered over a three-year period from neo-Hindu literature and from a series of key informant interviews. Most of the data come from the many neo-Hindu societies in New York City. Random interviews were also conducted in Chicago and on several major college campuses.

[1]  For a more detailed account of neo-Hinduism, see Fornaro (1973).

## IMPACT OF NEO-HINDUISM

In the September 6, 1971 issue of *New York* magazine, Richard Levine asked the question, "Who is Hare Krishna and why are they doing all those strange things on Fifth Avenue?" Levine was witnessing the rather unique behavioral patterns of a neo-Hindu religious society. The term neo-Hindu refers to the newer post-Renaissance[2] institutional forms like the Arya Samaj, the Ramakrishna Vivekananda Mission, the Aurobindo Movement, the Divine Life Society, and many others. A conservative estimate would place the number of neo-Hindu centers in the United States at over one hundred (*The 1970 Directory of Light Centers*).[3]

The oldest neo-Hindu organization in America, the Ramakrishna Vivekananda Mission, opened in New York in 1932 and now has about fourteen centers throughout the country. More recent additions include the Integral Yoga Center, the Sivananda Yoga Vedanta Center, the SIMS (Students International Meditation Society), and the International Society for Krishna Consciousness. Each of these organizations also has multiple centers. Large urban areas like New York, Chicago, Los Angeles, and San Francisco have between ten and twenty centers each. The rate of growth and development of neo-Hindu societies varies, but generally most societies are now experiencing a period of rapid expansion.

The success of neo-Hinduism depends primarily on the talents and initiative of a bewildering array of sadhus, gurus, and swamis, who literally traverse the globe.[4] They are:

... those individual ascetics who cultivate the technique of Yogic concentration whether as their basic creed or as a routine or only as an adjunct to their ascetism, [and] have not only contributed to the spiritual life of the Indian people, but have also helped to create an abiding interest in the system of Indian religio-philosophical thought and practice among Euro-Americans by their achievements in this line, even more so than the few great expounders that have caught the Western imagination (Ghurye 1964: 226–227).

However, the swamis rarely represent themselves or their ideology as Hindu. Neo-Hindu ideology purportedly transcends mere religion. In actuality, the philosophical foundation of neo-Hinduism is VEDANTISM, one of the six traditional Hindu philosophical schools. The universalistic

---

[2]   This term refers to the religious revitalization movement known as the "Hindu Renaissance," a phenomenon that began in India in the early nineteenth century.
[3]   Careful cross-checking has shown the listing in *The 1970 Directory of Light Centers* to be fairly accurate. One should keep in mind that more centers have been added since 1970.
[4]   There are neo-Hindu centers in England, Australia, Canada, Ceylon, Denmark, Italy, France, Germany, New Zealand, and South Africa.

rhetoric of neo-Hinduism only masks the deep Hindu bias that all the swamis have. As one "instructor" of SIMS confided, "When you take the time to look into it, what is being offered is really Hinduism." The behavioral model the swamis present is, of course, very old to Hindu tradition. It is the model of the Hindu holy man who renounced the vanities of the world to achieve *moksha*, or release.

Of all the "great tradition" religions, Hinduism is generally believed to be nonproselytizing, i.e. both exclusive and communally based. Yet, with neo-Hinduism we are witnessing a Hindu religious form engaged in what can be described as rather successful "missionary" activity. A recent *Time* magazine article ("Searching again for the sacred," April 9, 1973) mentions the impact of the neo-Hindu religious societies and the role that they are playing in altering the behavioral patterns of thousands of Americans. A unique kind of acculturation is taking place, as neo-Hindu ideology and behavior patterns are diffused. Another and rather unique indicator of neo-Hindu influence and its relation to the drug problem was the passing of Resolution Number 677 by the State of Illinois House of Representatives. Following are some excerpts from that resolution:

WHEREAS, Transcendental Meditation offers an alternative to drug abuse and studies indicate that it shows promise of being the most positive and effective drug prevention program being presented in the world today; ... therefore, be it

RESOLVED, by the House of Representatives of the Seventy-seventh General Assembly of the State of Illinois, that all educational institutions, especially those under State of Illinois jurisdiction, be strongly encouraged to study the feasibility of courses in Transcendental Meditation and the Science of Creative Intelligence (SCI) on their campuses and in their facilities; and be it further

RESOLVED, that the Department of Mental Health of the State of Illinois, Drug Abuse Section, be encouraged to study the benefits of T.M. and insofar as the Drug Abuse Section deems it to be practical and medically wise, to incorporate the course in T.M. in the drug abuse programs; ... (State of Illinois 1972).

## SECULARIZATION OF AMERICAN RELIGION

To understand why so many Americans are turning to neo-Hinduism, it might be helpful to review Peter L. Berger's discussion of "the secularization process." According to Berger:

... secularization has posited an altogether novel situation for modern man. Probably for the first time in history, the religious legitimations of the world have lost their plausibility not only for a few intellectuals and other marginal individuals but for broad masses of entire societies. This [has] opened up an acute crisis not only for the nomination of the large social institutions, but for that of individual biographies. In other words, there has arisen a problem of "meaningfulness" not only for such institutions as the state or of the economy but for the ordinary routines of everyday life (Berger 1967: 125).

In response to the secularization process, the established religious institutions in the United States have themselves, in a manner, "secularized." In their haste to become "relevant" they unknowingly participate in the secularization process and accelerate it. The competing and contradictory ideologies and behavioral patterns of our pluralistic society are now readily being internalized by formerly highly "specialized" institutions. The American Jew, Protestant, and Catholic emerge from these institutions antiritualistic, antimystical, and somewhat antireligious. Rabbis, priests, and ministers engage in a multitude of "relevant" activities that tend to obscure their traditional religious identities.

To the youth engaged in elements of the various "counter-cultures," the traditional religious institutions and their practitioners are now part of what they derisively call "the establishment." Those who reject "the establishment" may in turn deny organized religion. However, the denial of institutional religion need not imply a rejection of all aspects of religion. The individual religious experience is rarely renounced, and many seek what they term a "spiritual lifestyle."

The "spiritual lifestyle," which at this level is usually self-defined, is hardly possible in religious institutions undergoing secularization. This is where the neo-Hindu religious societies have the advantage. They can and do provide for those seeking a "spiritual lifestyle." A devotee enters a neo-Hindu society as an individual, and his spiritual needs receive individual attention. As one of my informants stated, "Yoga makes me feel good — spiritual ... close to God ... secure."[5] And another said, "Yoga, unlike organized religion, is total involvement ... a total lifestyle."


INSTANT CHEMICAL RELIGION

Another response to the alienating forces of secularization was to seek the "spiritual lifestyle" through drugs — what Peter Furst terms "instant chemical religion" (Furst 1972: viii). Many have believed that the use of

[5] Unless noted otherwise, all quotes are taken from key informant interviews completed in April, May, and June of 1971. The surnames of some of the informants are withheld in view of the personal nature of some of the disclosures.

drugs could facilitate a mystical experience much like the one Aldous Huxley describes in *The doors of perception:*

My eyes travelled from the rose to the carnation and from that feathering incandescense to the smooth scrolls of sentient amethyst which were the iris. The Beatific Vision, Sat Chit Ananda, Being — Awareness — Bliss — for the first time I understood ... (Huxley 1954: 12–13).

The now-famous Timothy Leary proclaimed in 1963 a new religion based on drug enlightenment, which encouraged everyone to "turn on, tune in, and drop out." As Charles Winick states:

They have sought out the immanent and experiential, stressed the sensibility over the intellect, and otherwise pursued authenticity. Drugs are widely believed to provide a shortcut to the dimension of the non-rational and to the "wisdom of the East" which is often related to drug use (Winick 1973).

Even the Second Report of the National Commission on Marijuana and Drug Abuse observed the possible connection between drugs and mysticism:

The religious community must address the nature of the inner directed spiritual experience. Users of hallucinogenic drugs have reported religious or mystical experiences. These experiences cannot be dismissed simply by dogmatic refusal to examine the evidence: instead, both theologians and scientists must look at them closely (National Commission 1973: 394).

While the use of drugs is a common feature of many primitive religious forms, the mystical traditions of the great religions tend to negate the validity of a mystical experience brought on by drugs. The mystic states of the great tradition religions — Hinduism, Buddhism, Christianity, and Islam — are induced "naturally," i.e. using only the resources of the mind and body. However, there HAVE been attempts in the great traditions to induce the mystical state "artificially":

... there cannot be the slightest doubt that the Hindus and probably Buddhists of earlier days did regard the taking of psychedelic drugs as part of a wide range of *Sadhanas* [paths] which lead to ecstasy, albeit perhaps only in the preliminary stages (Bharati 1966: 287).

These attempts, of course, have never been accepted by tradition. Leary's message, which gained wide public notice, gave the impression that there was a causal and traditional relationship between drugs and Eastern mysticism.

In that eclectic confusion known as the "counter-culture," drugs were used in an attempt to transcend cultural and religious barriers. Because drugs are not viable transmitters of culture, a true understanding of what constituted a Hindu or Buddhist mystical experience has evaded the followers of "instant chemical religion." In many instances the quest for a drug-oriented mystical experience has only led to rapid physical deterioration and disillusionment. Alienated by their own religious institutions and disappointed by drugs, many have turned to alternative religious forms like neo-Hinduism.

## NEO-HINDU DEVOTEES

Each neo-Hindu center is run by a staff of "devotees." Usually under twenty-five years old, white, and middle-class, the devotees provided the key informant interviews. From the onset of the project the author let the milieu of the neo-Hindu society generate the modes of inquiry, i.e. participant observation and structured interviews. Participant observation allowed an overall look at how a neo-Hindu religious society functions, while the structured interviews provided data on drug use and behavioral change. In view of the antiestablishment orientation of the devotees, more vigorous gathering of quantified data was difficult and seemed inadvisable, inasmuch as it might have damaged the rapport that had been established with the informants.

Roughly 80 percent of the devotees interviewed reported that they had formerly used drugs. However, with a few exceptions, these individuals were what are termed "soft" drug users — drug-abuse, not drug-addiction, cases. The "soft" drug users usually began their drug experience by using amphetamines, i.e. dexedrine or "uppers" and tuinal or "downers." Amphetamines are readily available in many home medicine cabinets, and several of the informants reported that their parents were "hooked" on amphetamines. In the schools many of the informants had been introduced to marijuana or "pot."

The drugs most used in relation to some religious motivation are the hallucinogens or psychedelic drugs, i.e. lysergic acid (LSD), dimethyl tryptamine (DMT), and/or diethyl tryptamine (DET). According to Jordan Scher, Narcotics Specialist for the Narcotics Court of Cook County:

Opiate addiction is the modality of the intellectually less imaginative, the economically deprived, the Negro, and the Puerto Rican. The psychedelic is the agent of the middle and upper incomes, the artistic and jazz worlds, and more particularly the "avant-garde" and the cause-espousing college student. ... These are highly gregarious groups within the marijuana-psychedelic circle, and as evidence of their intellectual accomplishments and mystical leanings they tend to have literary gods and cultural guides. *The Tibetan book of the dead* is

for information on what to expect on "acid trips." Zen Buddhism, for religious
uplifting, is pursued in various adulterated forms particularly via Suzuki and
Alan Watts (Scher 1970: 34–35).

Many whom Scher calls the "marijuana-psychedelic" or "hippy circle"
(Scher 1970) come into contact with neo-Hinduism, because neo-Hindu
centers were established very early in hippy communities. Some individuals have been drawn into neo-Hindu activities by the sheer fact of
proximity. Others have seen in neo-Hinduism an opportunity to build on
the religious insights they felt that they had gained through drugs. One
typical case is that of a young man of twenty, now using the Hindu name
Sivadas, who said, "I began taking drugs for a spiritual reason." A young
girl, now using the name Aikya, stated, "My first acid trip made me
aware of God, another presence. I felt Christ. He meant something during
that trip." And still another young man, now called Dhinakaran, reported,
"When I took acid I felt most of my trips were religious experiences.
Maybe subconsciously we wanted religious experiences. Two of my
Catholic friends saw Mary and Jesus." All agreed, however, that use of
drugs could not sustain the religious experiences they had. Moreover,
because they were unable to relate these experiences to the religious
institutions in which they were reared, they turned to neo-Hinduism.

## NEO-HINDUISM AND DRUG REHABILITATION

Although most of the neo-Hindu devotees knew and used drugs, their
use of drugs was usually restricted to a time prior to their commitment to
neo-Hinduism. The neo-Hindu societies are decidedly antidrug, and in
their own special way, discourage drug use. The followers of Maharishi
Mahesh Yogi are instructed to cease the use of drugs fifteen days before
attempting "transcendental meditation." According to Guru Prem,
Addiction Specialist for the Addiction Services Center, City of New
York, "The Integral Yoga Center has helped thousands of drug-abuse
cases." Swami Ramananda of the Sivananda Divine Life Society claimed,
"Swami Vishnu helps young people with drug problems. They go to his
yoga camp in Canada." The neo-Hindu societies offer to help people
with their drug problems, thereby attracting those who want to get out of
the drug scene. The neo-Hindu attitude toward the user was summed up
by Balaram, a twenty-five-year old devotee of the Integral Yoga Center:
"You don't cure a drug addict, you offer him an alternative and hope
he'll take it."

Again it is important to note that the drug users who turn to neo-
Hinduism are usually white, "soft core" drug users from middle-class or

upper middle-class homes. The "hard core" addicts, usually black and Puerto Rican heroin addicts, are not attracted to neo-Hinduism. According to Steve Levy, a Horizon Center Director for the Addiction Services Center, City of New York, "These people [middle-class whites] took drugs for some spiritual reason. They are flower children. Black and Puerto Rican kids take drugs to survive." While somewhat successful with "soft core" abuse cases, the neo-Hindu societies have not significantly affected "hard core" drug addiction.

It is in the area of drug rehabilitation that neo-Hindu social consciousness surfaces; it is a special feature of the American centers. Although most of the centers carry on drug rehabilitation on an individual basis, some are engaged in societal and group programs. In New York the most active and aggressive in the area of drug rehabilitation is the Integral Yoga Center. Swami Satchidananda, founder of the center, appointed a young man, now called Balaram, as Community Services Director. Balaram coordinated Yoga programs designed to rehabilitate drug users. Yoga programs were instituted at the Bernstein Institute, the Payne Whitney Clinic, and at several Phoenix and Horizon Houses. On one occasion Balaram stated, "Part of our program here [at the Integral Yoga Center] is to fight the drug problem in this country."

One of the most active Yoga rehabilitation programs was directed by another of Swami Satchidananda's followers, a twenty-two-year old, now called Guru Prem. Guru Prem is an ex-drug user who believes Yoga is helping the drug-abuse cases in his charge, "For the most part everyone has made some sort of improvement."

A most successful case of rehabilitation was David, a young man of nineteen from a middle-class, Jewish family. At seventeen David started using marijuana, then graduated to LSD, then speed or metamphetamine (one of the most potent and dangerous of the amphetamines), and finally cocaine. He was sent to a psychiatrist, who referred him to the Integral Yoga Center and Guru Prem's program. David was the first "graduate" of Guru Prem's program and he made these observations, "Yoga has helped everyone in the program to some extent. Yoga helps people get in touch with themselves, get control of themselves. You don't have to stop drugs to start Yoga; however, use of drugs will gradually fall away."[6]

This was verified by another member of the group, Dan, a nineteen-year-old Oberlin College dropout, also from a middle-class, Jewish family. Dan stated, "Speed fucked me up. Yoga helps me dig what's inside my head, to know what's inside of me. I feel good without using

---

[6]  He is referring to those individuals who start Yoga by themselves and practice it from a book.

drugs. Yoga has brought a major change in my attitude, a positive change. I have confidence in myself."

Robert, nineteen years old, from a middle-class, Roman Catholic family, had tried almost every drug, including heroin, and stated, "What they offer me here is very constructive. I believe in Yoga philosophy. Yoga and the people here are helping me. I'm becoming more spiritual."

Paul, seventeen, another boy of Roman Catholic background, described himself as a "speed freak." Paul was pressured into the Horizon House program by the courts, and interestingly enough, he showed the greatest degree of internalization of neo-Hindu ideology. "Yoga sure has helped me, helped me realize myself ... my hangups. I was paranoid, always shy. Yoga is a way of life. It is living the truth, the union of mind, body, and soul. I am worshiping myself. At first I thought chanting was religious, but now I know it is not religious. It is a way of life."

However not all of the individuals in Guru Prem's program were responding. Billy an eighteen-year-old, said, "I've tried almost every kind of drug. I started the methadone treatment, but preferred Yoga. Without Yoga I would have O.D.'ed [died of an overdose] a long time ago, or I'd be out on the streets killing people." In spite of these sentiments, Billy was still using drugs and admitted that he "couldn't give it [Yoga] everything." He went on to say, "I can see Yoga now in a spiritual point of view. Superconsciousness is possible. I believe in God. Everything is God. All religions are true in theory, but they have become corruptions of true spirituality." Then, curiously, he said, "Yoga gets dangerously close to religion. ... You know, with the swami and all."

Another individual, who was forced by the courts into trying drug rehabilitation and chose Guru Prem's program, was David L., eighteen years old, from a middle-class home. His father was Jewish and his mother Roman Catholic. David L. started smoking marijuana at twelve, and at fourteen he was using speed. Unlike the others interviewed, David L.'s parents were also drug users, and he got his drugs from them. At sixteen David L. became a heroin addict, and by eighteen had failed to respond to several drug-rehabilitation programs. Guru Prem's program was his third, and he stated, "I'm off drugs now, but I don't think it will be a permanent thing. I took drugs for the sensual thrill ... the warmth of the dope ... the dope orgies."

Yoga was not working for Billy and David L. probably because neither really wanted to stop using drugs; both were forced by the courts to participate in a drug-rehabilitation program. Another factor was that Billy and David L. were heroin addicts, and Yoga and neo-Hinduism seem to have little effect on heroin addiction. However, neo-Hinduism does provide some help for the drug-abuse cases who voluntarily seek help.

## BEHAVIORAL CHANGE

It is really too early to tell what the long-range effects of neo-Hinduism will be on American society, but the information now available does point to some significant changes in the cognitive and behavioral patterns of those individuals identified here as devotees. Through some eighty extended interviews and participant observation, the following profile of cultural change began to emerge. The religious views of about 90 percent of those interviewed had changed considerably. When asked whether they believed in the Hindu concepts of *karma* and *samsara*[7] they answered in the affirmative. Their knowledge of *karma* and *samsara* came from neo-Hindu literature or from their respective swamis or gurus. A typical answer given was, "*Karma* and *samsara* certainly make more sense than ideas like heaven and hell and eternal damnation."

Although most of the informants did not identify themselves as Hindus, there were cases like Sivadas of the Sivananda Yoga Vedanta Center, "I am a Hindu now. I practice the Hindu religion. My *Isvara* [personal deity] is Siva, the meditative god. I stopped being a Jew because Hindu scriptures accept all other religions and tell you precisely how to come closer to God." Others had internalized the universalistic sentiments of neo-Hinduism. In the same center a boy called Harrell said, "Everything is the same. Jesus was a realized saint. He was like Krishna and Buddha." A young man named Kumar at the Integral Yoga Center put it this way, "I went from an atheist to a theist. All religions have got it. My travels around the world proved it to me. All ultimately describe the same goal in the same way." And, finally, Balaram, a devotee mentioned earlier, said, "All religions are but aspects of one total truth."

Attitudes toward the swamis, in several instances, amounted to worship. Devotees expressed themselves in this way, "I worship Parvati. I also worship Swamiji." "I pray to Swami Vishnu. I pray to Sivananda [founder of the Divine Life Society], for he is divine." "He guides me even when he is not physically present. To understand his powers I would have to be a 'Master' like him."

In most centers devotees readily engaged in neo-Hindu rituals, i.e. prostrating, chanting, offering food and flowers, in a kind of watered-

---

[7]   *Karma* is the law of action, the law according to which any action is the effect of a cause and in turn the cause of an effect. *Samsara* is the course of revolution or rebirth.

down *puja* worship.[8] The same kind of activity surrounded the swamis when they were present at these rituals.

The only individuals that seemed uneasy about the neo-Hindu rituals were those devotees who had been enculturated in Orthodox Christian and Orthodox Jewish homes. Raised in highly ritualized religious settings, these individuals recognize ritual behavior. One Greek Orthodox boy, however, sidestepped the issue by stating, "Ritual here is a state of mind. I don't worship an *Isvara*. I don't think in terms of forms. When I chant, I'm trying to set a state of mind."

Another area of cultural change was diet. Almost without exception, neo-Hindu devotees were strict vegetarians. Neo-Hindus consider meat eating extremely harmful, both physically and spiritually. No stimulants of any kind are allowed in the centers; even the use of spices is discouraged. Several devotees explained that their preference for a vegetarian diet is due to their commitment to *ahimsa*, or noninjury to any living thing. Most devotees, however, are vegetarians because their swamis are vegetarians.

Through acculturation, the American devotees gradually drop formerly learned patterns of behavior and begin emulating the cognitive and behavioral patterns of their gurus. Some devotees talk, act, and even write like their gurus; for example, I received this letter from a female devotee of the Krishna Consciousness movement:

I am happy to hear that you had the oppurtinity [*sic*] to read the nice phamphlet [*sic*] on the chanting of the Hare Krishna mantra. We have many books written by our spiritual master, His Divine Grace A.C. Bhaktivedanta Swami Prabhupad, which are translations of the transcendental knowledge handed down from the time when Lord Krishna himself appeared on this planet to display his pastimes 5000 years ago. This knowledge has been handed down from master to disciple, until it reached our spiritual master, Srila Prabhupad. In the Nectar of Devotion, one of the books which is from the Bhakti Rasamrita Sindhu by Srila Rupa Goswami, the example is given of the fruit of the mango tree, which is handed down from person to person, so that it is received intact, and does not become damaged or broken. Similarly, this fruit of Vedic wisdom has been handed down so that it remains in it's [*sic*] pure state, thru the disciplic succession.... If you are unable to come to our temple, then please just chant; Hare Krishna, Hare Krishna, Krishna Krishna, Hare Hare, Hare Rama, Hare rama [*sic*], Rama Rama, Hare Hare, and your life will be sublime.
In Service of Srila Prabhupada,
Kathy M.

Once committed to the neo-Hindu life-style, it is necessary to separate oneself from the American life-style, especially its emphasis on competition and materialism. No neo-Hindu seeks wealth or material pos-

[8]  *Puja* is a Hindu worship ritual.

session, and the popular goal of a higher education is looked upon as meaningless competition. As regards formal knowledge, neo-Hinduism is decidedly antiintellectual. Extensive reading, even of neo-Hindu works, is not encouraged. What a neo-Hindu needs to know will come directly from his guru, and all other knowledge is secondary.

Also, at a time when young people in our nation are beginning to share in the political process, the young people of the neo-Hindu religious societies remain apolitical. During the course of the study, the devotees never once mentioned politics. When the researcher tried to initiate a political discussion, the reaction was a kind of polite apathy. Neo-Hindu groups, at least in the United States, are not politically oriented, yet they do relate to politics in a negative way. Recently, the radical left was jolted when Rennie Davis, a leader of the peace movement and one of the Chicago Seven, joined the followers of the boy, Satguru Maharaj Ji. Davis renounced political activism and "is now dedicating all of his energies in serving the Lord" (*Divine Times*, May 1, 1973).

In an article entitled "Mystic politics: refugees from the New Left," Andrew Koplind observed:

> But anyone who looks around can see the force behind the spiritual, religious and existential cults that have developed in the spaces where political organizations are usually found. Gurus, Swamis, roshis, dervishes, gods and therapists are building impressive movements and extensive institutions while the traditional left sects contract in size and influence (Koplind 1973: 26).

Another area of difference from the overall American cultural style is the neo-Hindu attitude toward sex. Sex is viewed in these societies as negative, both physically and spiritually. It was interesting to hear young people at the height of their sexual powers saying things like, "Sex is not an expression of true love." "Sex is no big deal now. I just don't know what will happen." "Sex takes up too much energy. To do Yoga correctly there is no time for sex." "I'm still having sexual relations, but in an unattached way. Sex is really detrimental. It is wasting the vital force. With Yoga you don't have the energy or desire for sex. Sex really messes up my mind."

Sexual relations outside of marriage are strongly condemned by the neo-Hindu religious societies, and even married persons are enjoined to practice sexual moderation. One married female devotee stated, "I never want children. Children and the spiritual life don't mix. If we had children, we couldn't work full time for the institute. Swamiji says that you should limit your sex life. If you're serious about Yoga you must practice *brahmacarya* [self-control]. I would someday like to practice *brahmacarya*."

Sex and sexuality, even Hindu sexuality, play little role in the neo-

Hindu lifestyle. If, however, two devotees are persistent in their wish to marry, "the couples are married in the center, but, since the swami is not recognized as legal, couples first get a civil marriage ceremony, then wait for the swami to perform the 'real' marriage ceremony. About twenty couples have been married by the swami."

## CONCLUSION

The neo-Hindu religious societies are viable agents of acculturation. As adulterated as it may seem to the scholar of Hinduism, neo-Hinduism is now diffusing selected elements of Hindu culture around the world. The impact of neo-Hinduism in America underlines both Hinduism's new vitality and the present spiritual and cultural crisis in American society. The success of these societies is in no small measure due to their ability to relate to the problems of religious alienation and drug abuse. They represent a viable alternative to "instant chemical religion" by providing a "spiritual lifestyle" possible without drugs.

Neo-Hinduism changes young Americans by changing their cognitive and behavioral patterns. Individual alteration occurs in religious ideology, diet, sexuality, and political outlook. The devotees regard the swamis as "true" religious leaders, untouched by the process of secularization and worthy of emulation.

We are only beginning to feel the impact that neo-Hinduism is making in the American socioreligious sphere. This study represents just one approach in the examination of this unique phenomenon. The vast bulk of neo-Hindu literature still remains to be read, and new societies are continually emerging for examination.

## REFERENCES

ARNOLD, DAVID
1970    *Subcultures*. University of California: Glendessary Press.
BERGER, PETER L.
1967    *The sacred canopy*. Garden City, New York: Doubleday.
BHARATI, SWAMI AGEHANANDA
1952    "Radhakrishnan and the other Vedanta," in *The philosophy of Sarve-palli Radhakrishnan*. Edited by Paul Arthur Schilpp. New York: Tudor.
1966    *The Tantric tradition*. London: Rider.
DASGUPTA, SURAMA
1959    *Hindu mysticism*. New York: Frederick Ongar.

*Divine Times*
1973    May 1. *Divine Times*. Denver: Divine Light Mission.
EBIN, DAVID
1965    *The drug experience*. New York: Grove Press.
FORNARO, ROBERT J.
1973    Neo-Hinduism in America. *Journal of Social Research* 16. Bihar: Council of Social and Cultural Research.
FURST, PETER T.
1972    *Flesh of the gods*. New York: Praeger.
GHURYE, G. SADASHIV
1964    *Indian sadhus*. Bombay: Popular Prakashan.
HUXLEY, ALDOUS
1954    *The doors of perception*. London: Chatto and Windus.
KOPLIND, ANDREW
1973    Mystic politics: refugees from the New Left. *Ramparts* (July): 26.
LEVINE, RICHARD
1971    Article in *New York*. September 6.
MCGRATH, JOHN, FRANK SCARPITTI, *editors*
1970    *Youth and drugs*. Oakland, New Jersey: Scott Foresman.
MAHARISHI MAHESH YOGI
1968    *The science of being and the art of living*. New York: New American Library.
NATIONAL COMMISSION MARIJUANA AND DRUG ABUSE
1973    *Second report: drug use in America: problem in perspective*. March 22. Washington, D.C.: United States Government Printing Office.
PRESIDENT'S COMMISSION ON LAW ENFORCEMENT AND ADMINISTRATION OF JUSTICE
1967    *Narcotics and drug abuse task force report*. Washington, D.C.: United States Government Printing Office.
ROSZAK, THEODORE
1968    "The making of the counter culture: an invasion of centaurs," in *The sociology of youth*. Edited by Harry Silverstein, 272–280. New York: Macmillan.
SCHER, JORDAN
1970    "Patterns and profiles of addiction and drug abuse," in *Youth and drugs*. Edited by John H. McGrath and Frank R. Scarpitti, 34–35. Oakland, New Jersey: Scott Foresman.
SIVANANDA, SRI SWAMI
1958    *Sadhana*. Sivanandanager, India: Divine Life Society.
STATE OF ILLINOIS
1972    *House Resolution Number* 677, adopted May 24. Seventy-seventh General Assembly, House of Representatives.
WINICK, CHARLES
1973    "Some reasons for the increase in drug dependence among middle-class youths," in *The sociology of youth*. Edited by H. Silverstein, 433–436. New York: Macmillan.

# Lévi-Strauss in Fairyland

LORNA McDOUGALL

Structural analysis has received widespread acceptance as a formal method in a number of fields in recent years. In anthropology it serves a number of useful functions: it allows us to perceive an integrated world view, in all of its myriad associations; it reveals something of the methods of minds everywhere; it makes manageable materials which would otherwise seem too varied to have any connection.

The major drawback to the system lies in its very power to generalize mental capacities; it fails to distinguish cognitive systems from one another. Structuralism posits the ability of mind to create order out of chaos, to create patterns — "Every landscape offers, at first glance, an immense disorder which we may sort out any way we please" (Lévi-Strauss 1969: 59–60), but it also posits that any system of ordering is theoretically as good as any other. In *The savage mind*, the quality of tribal knowledge of the objective world of flora and fauna is never examined. We are told that systems are generated from an interest in knowledge for its own sake rather than for the sake of use. Though the thirst for objective knowledge is the most neglected aspect of primitive thought (Lévi-Strauss 1966: 3), any particular system is not necessarily equivalent to any other. Some systems bear up under empirical testing better than others. For instance, whereas the Roman system of numeration can be used to count any series of objects, it is unquestionably inferior to the Arabic system. Any formal arrangement may be better than none, and serve to ward off the anxiety of "not knowing," but some formal systems are better than others. The material basis of classification may be of greater interest than the fact that it can be construed as a part of a coherent system of knowledge. To those of us who inhabit the industrial world of no-smell, for example, classifi-

cation of plants and animals on the basis of smell may be more enlightening than classification by similitudes of form or structure. Information
about sensory experience can tell us more than information about cognitive processes, given that we are all faced with the task of living in the
world. If we accept the lack of cultural uniqueness in perceptual modes,
sensory experiences themselves become the doorways to understanding
of unique and varied world views.

Our eighteenth-century view of the "noble savage" has recently been
reconstituted into a Victorian picture of the "savage scientist," whose
thought process is quite rational and orderly. The time has now come for
us to begin to question the different orders of reality; to see which systems
correspond to empirical truths. In this task, we have to begin by enlarging our Western views as to what is pragmatically verifiable. The
realm of the scientist is generally considered to be "the natural world,"
and the application of mathematics is used to delineate this "natural
world" from its indefinable antithesis, "the supernatural." This happens
largely because no corresponding mathematics exist with which to describe or discuss "paranormal" phenomena. Sometimes it is even difficult
to tell whether experiences of the supernatural are "paranormal." The
"supernatural" is "natural" in a society which customarily allows its
members to have "paranormal" experiences.

To some extent we concede the reality of "supernatural" phenomena
such as witchcraft by recognizing their functional value in the social context in which they occur (Douglas 1971). But we are saying HOW witchcraft works in the social system rather than WHAT witchcraft IS, or even
what it means to the native. A short but disturbing article recently
appeared which suggested that the connection between reality and structure has never been tested in anthropology ((Hallpike 1971: 123–140).
Many societies describe witches in similar ways. Yet how do we know
that our concept of witchcraft which shows us these common elements
is in fact adequate? Have we shown that our terms and conditions are indeed related to actuality?

We have begged the most interesting question of all — are there indeed
people who possess certain witchlike powers? We have concentrated on
showing how a potentially disruptive force is harnessed to the ends of
social solidarity. Such mechanical explanations can always be fitted to societies which have not actually destroyed themselves. Yet the experience
of "witchcraft" remains untouched, likewise its impact on the native.

A parallel comes to mind in the studies of conflict. Since there are
many societies which continue to exist despite continuous conflict, anthropologists have sought to fit these ongoing conflicts into positive frame-

works. Although it is more reasonable to acknowledge that institution-alized conflict is symptomatic of social dysfunction which is not neces-sarily fatal to the parent society, the vogue since the publication of *The Nuer* (Evans-Pritchard 1940) has been to assign to conflict the same beneficial values which anthropologists are prone to discover in all social institutions. These findings are a disquieting instance of "doublethink." War is peace and conflict is socially adaptive, or at least an acceptable price for identity. We appreciate the irony of such a conclusion only in fiction.

The sociological "justification" of witchcraft is related to our concep-tion of it as "supernatural." Since Frazer or before, primitive beliefs in supernatural events have demanded some explanation. The explanation has been difficult because for Western man the supernatural pertains to the imaginary, not to empirical reality. Anthropologists generally feel no need to justify primitive beliefs which they themselves share.

We can begin to come to grips with the experiential nature of witch-craft and magic if we do not *a priori* categorize it as supernatural. Un-less an event falls outside the native concepts of what is natural, it is groundless prejudice to classify it as supernatural.

To a large extent, this paper is based upon observation of "supernatu-ral" experience among the natives of County Fermanagh, North Ireland. In the parish of Knockninny, by the shores of Lower Lough Erne, the main occupation is the rearing of cattle. Hay and oats are grown to sustain the livestock, and household supplies of food are also mainly from the farm — eggs, milk, chickens, cabbage, potatoes, perhaps carrots and onions. Farms are usually not above fifteen acres. Many houses still lack electricity and running water. They are often of traditional two-room construction, although recent government grants have permitted exten-sive renovations or rebuilding. The principal modes of transportation are still walking and bicycling, although the motor car is just beginning to alter patterns of recreation, especially drinking. It is not uncommon to see family outings to pubs now, though the pubs are traditionally male preserves.

One of the most striking observations at first is the very mundane quality of "supernatural" experiences. Ghosts are commonplace, as are visions of the dead. There is sometimes a feeling that one will be laughed at for being irrational, but people are quite firm in their own minds as to what they see when these experiences occur.

Beliefs in the spirit world of giants and dwarfs, magical animals, trees, flowers, birds and insects, ghosts, wraiths, poltergeists, and all manner of apparitions survive in Ireland today, even though people have become a little wary of admitting to them. These beliefs coexist, sometimes happily, sometimes unhappily, with the faith of the Catholic Church. Pagan and Christian beliefs sometimes fuse to the extent that a priest may be called upon to banish the evil wrought by a witch, to deal with the angry dead returning to haunt the living, or to bless stock dying as a result of the evil eye.

In order to give a brief account of this body of knowledge, I am going to describe the two major festivals of the Celtic year — May Day and November Night. Many of the injunctions as to correct behavior can be seen at these two times in paradigm form. They are in a sense the chief regulatory events in the year. The customs associated with the festivals are dying out now, but some remain in force. May Day and November Eve mark the major transitions in the year's cycle, and they represent the mysterious transformations of sunrise and sunset. As two Celtic scholars remark, "the alternation of day and night, light and darkness, had profound meaning for the Celts as it did for many other peoples" (Rees and Rees 1961: 83). The classificatory system has much to do with dualism. It is symbolically complete: light contains darkness, darkness contains light. May Day is a celebration of fertility, but presages barrenness and loss; November Eve is associated with the dead, but presages marriage and fertility. The parallel with yin-yang symbolism is perfect.

In past times May Day marked the beginning of the farming year. Young people took the cattle to the hills, a practice called *booleying*. November Night marked the feast of the harvest and fruition, and the end of the work of the farming year. At this time the cattle were brought down to the home farm from the mountain pastures, and young and old alike settled into an indoor existence again. November Night marks the beginning of the season of darkness, the period known in Scotland as *an Dudlachd* [the season of death revels], presided over by a king whose face is blackened, and whose emblem is a sword, scythe, or sickle (Rees and Rees 1961: 84).

Scholars are undecided as to the sequence the two half-years represent. *Sam* means summer and *Samain* is one of the names for November Eve, suggesting that winter may precede summer (Rees and Rees 1961: 85). In a cyclical system it scarcely matters. But there is a further interesting point. It is put forward also that the winter/summer arrangement of the seasons harmonizes with Caesar's testimony as to the precedence of night over day. "The Gauls," he says, "called themselves sons of the god of night and defined the division of every season, not by the number of days, but of nights" (Rees and Rees 1961: 85).

Most of the tales of visions do indeed take place at night. Night is the time of diminished visibility; the stress placed on night indicates the emphasis placed by this culture on the spiritual aspects of existence. Persons born during the hours of darkness are held to be able to see fairies, ghosts, wraiths, and ominous lights, which are invisible to those born during the day.

The relationship of sight to visions is an interesting one. Visions of the invisible take place during the time when we cannot see well. I am reminded of the theme of Oedipus, who had to lose his sight to gain INSIGHT.

At all events, night is the time of the spirits, and November Night more than any other. Hallow E'en, as November Night is now called in Fermanagh, due to English influence and the correspondence of the English and Irish festivals, is a night when the air is full of spirits. It is dangerous to walk abroad lest you disturb them. If you must walk out at night, you should follow the road, and on no account cut across the fields where you run the risk of encountering a "stray sod," and losing any sense of who or where you are. "Stray sods" are places set as traps for humans by fairies. They disorient the human and prevent him from entering the fairy domain.

The king of the fairies gives orders on this night for his subjects to move from fort to fort. The presence of mortals may disturb their journeys. The countryside in Fermanagh is peppered with these forts — raised mounds of earth, sometimes still surrounded by trees, either whitethorn (May bush) or mountain ash, both of which have regulatory powers in the spirit world. It is said that the fairy hosts travel in straight lines between the forts and that you will never see one of the mounds without seeing three. Fairy paths thus constitute an invisible network across the countryside. But they are just as important as the pathways marked on maps. It seems that beliefs of this sort about places where it is unsafe to go outlast more esoteric and dogmatic aspects of the belief system. They remain influential in determining how people move from place to place.

A recent article is of interest in this respect, entitled "The nonempirical environment of the Arctic Alaskan Eskimos" (Burch 1971). There are many similarities in the belief systems of Celtic and Eskimo origin. Both include the presence of giants and dwarfs. In both, settlements are constructed by reference to invisible coordinates rather than according to purely environmental considerations.

On Hallow E'en, houses are left open to admit spiritual visitors. One or two people still leave an extra place set at the table, and many set out plates of *boxty* for them. *Boxty* is a traditional Hallow E'en dish, made out of grated and mashed potatoes and butter. The feast is a fast day and meat may not be consumed. Every effort is made to make invisible guests feel welcome. In addition special care is taken to ensure that fairy dwellings — presumably in the ground, although I never actually heard them described — should not be damaged; water may not be thrown out of the house lest it run down upon them and spoil their furniture. Care must be taken to see that everything is left tidy upon retiring; that the household is "in order." Fairies have the ability to turn themselves into any animal form at will, and are particularly likely to change form on this night.

People stay at home on November Night to enjoy the comfort of the hearth, symbol of the vitality and "luck" of the household. It is an evening of *communitas* when master and servant join together to tell tales and to foretell the future. Divination of marriage is one of the primary activities of Hallow E'en, though the season also portends death. During this "falling" season of the year the sick, whether animal or human, are deemed unlikely to recover.

Bands of adolescents roam the countryside, setting the world awry — stealing gates, stuffing chimneys to smoke out fireside company, removing wheels from bicycles or the air from automobile tires, hiding farm implements. The youths walk the countryside without apparent fear of fairy retribution. Perhaps they are more at home with spirits. "Dressing up" seems to be occasionally practiced. In the past it meant wrapping up in a white sheet as a "ghost." There is some sense of cultural irony involved in this, as well as the traditional mocking of the old by the young. There is no "trick or treating" although apples, nuts, and sweets are frequently given to children and form part of the feast. Apples are the traditional symbol of fertility — even the darkest night of doom contains the light of birth to come.

Apples play a prominent role in many of the festivities and games. Hallow E'en is still known in some areas as "snap apple night" or "ducking night," after the games of the same name. Children duck for apples while older people play "snap apple." The traditional divinatory games are dying out now, but their number was once enormous. A game still played involves peeling an apple without a break and throwing the peel over the left shoulder, whereupon it will form the initial of the Christian name of the future spouse. Another involves placing a pair of hazel nuts, corresponding to a girl and boy, on the hearth in order to observe whether they jump together or apart when they heat up. If they move together, marriage will follow; if apart, it will not. Other kinds of divination require conjuring up the devil in different ways. The devil may appear in the form of the future spouse without fear of consequences on this night. Several games were intended to produce a VISION of the intended, or an apparition in a mirror (Irish Folklore 1943: 120).

November Night, as a night of transition between seasons, represents a rite of passage. Some proscribed things may be done with impunity, representing ritual license — the ridiculing of the old, dealing with "black powers," failing to distinguish master and servant. Other customs hold good for other nights too, sometimes in attenuated form — avoidance of "fairy paths," taking care not to annoy the spirit world. There is a similarity of tone between the Celtic beliefs in the return of life after the darkness of the year and the Christian doctrine of triumph over the tomb in eternal life, even though Catholic priests have been opposed to the idolatrous practices of divination associated with Hallow E'en.

May Day celebrations have few Christian overtones, and have fallen even more into disuse of recent years. The extant customs of May Day are specifics against witchcraft. The fertility motif in Fermanagh does not seem to have been pronounced even in the recent past, although traditional fertility rituals are reported from other parts of the country (St. Clair 1971: 40).

May Day is a time for delineating boundaries in an attempt to keep evil forces, whether human or otherwise, out. In some areas, it was customary to go around the boundary ditches and shake holy water upon them. There are many instances in which priests are effective in combating evil effects of the "wee people." It is believed that witches cannot cross water (Irish Folklore 1940: 98). Strangers are not welcome on your land on May Day; they may take away our "luck" or your property (Irish Folklore 1956). If you have a well — called a spa in Fermanagh — on your land, you protect it by strewing May flowers around it; likewise your house, where the flowers are strewn on the threshold. They are placed by children.

Children play a large part in communication with the fairy world. Fairies are prone to taking them away and leaving changelings. There are accounts of this within living memory. In many accounts, the fairies are said to be about the size of a six or seven year-old child.

The proprietor of a well ensures that no one will harm his person, family, stock, or crops during the ensuing year by being the first to draw water from the well on May morning. There are tales of people sitting up all night to be sure that they are the first to draw. If the owner were not, then the person who preceded him would have the power to take the butter from his cows for the whole year. This theme of taking the milk is central to the May Day customs, and we shall encounter it in some detail.

The giving of a coal from the fire is forbidden on May morning, as well as lending most other things. The household draws into itself and protects its own — health, well-being, and reproductive capacities are at stake. The isolation of the household in its struggle for well-being is clear. It is "unlucky" to have the first smoke up in the morning on the first of May (Irish Folklore 1956: 6); the fire is not to be shared. If you have the first smoke up, others may attempt to borrow "the seed of the fire" and put you in the embarrassing position of having to refuse. There is some feeling that your well-being is endangered by sharing. Wars of attrition and patience were once waged until some hapless soul was forced to give in.

Even known visitors are suspected of evil potential, if not of evil intentions. When butter was still churned at home, the visitor was obliged to take a "brash" at it, i.e. help to churn. A witch was expected to refuse.

One most requires protection from witchcraft on May morning, although it may take place at other times as well. Locally, the witch is called "Kitty the Hare." Kitty is an old woman who turns herself into a hare, runs across the fields and sucks the cows dry, or enters the byre and milks them dry there. The farmer, seeing the animal, gives chase, and either shoots at the hare or has his hound pursue the quarry. The hare cannot be killed with lead shot, however, only with silver; nor can the hound catch her outright. The gun may be taken out on a subsequent occasion loaded with a bent silver threepenny bit, or the hound may manage to take a bite out of the fleeing animal's hind parts. The hare usually disappears into a house, which when entered contains not a hare, but an old woman, whose foot or leg is bleeding exactly where the hare was wounded. One account tells how the hare was burned to death in the byre as she sucked the milk, and the next day the old woman was found dead in bed (Irish Folklore S. 1937: 55). Another way to deprive neighbors of their milk is as follows:

This is the way they used to take the milk — a rope pulled through the dew. Pull a rope through the grass and take the dew on a neighbour's land and then they'd hang the rope in their own kitchen and milk the rope the same as milkin' a cow and as they'd be milkin' they'd say "come all to me" (Irish Folklore 1956: 434).

When the perpetrators of the evil are identified, they are invariably your own neighbors or "friends," i.e. kin. Discovery itself is often enough to stop the thieves' activities. Alternatively, a cure may be sought from a priest, witchman, or witchwoman. Such a person always lives in another parish. Although legislation against witchcraft exists in Ireland (Byrne

1967: 27), it has not been invoked since 1711, when a number of Island Magee women were tried in Carrickfergus (Byrne 1967: 40–47). There have been few witchcraft trials in the whole of recorded Irish history and these trials are exceptional. They deal with forms of black art similar to those found in England or continental Europe, either a failure of the accused to partake of the sacraments of the Catholic Church, or performance of devotions and sacrifices to a demon of low degree (Byrne 1967: 18–19).

The story of the witch-hare is recorded as early as the twelfth century by Giraldus Cambrensis, who claims that the events related happened in England, Wales, and Scotland as well as Ireland (Byrne 1967: 72).

One of the tales about the witch-hare goes as follows: A hunt is in progress when the dogs suddenly come upon a hare injuring it before it escapes. After a long chase, the hare eventually dashes through the open doorway of a small cottage. The Master of the Hunt dismounts and goes inside the cottage. An old woman is bent over an open fireplace. The Master asks did a hare go inside, and the old woman, blowing and panting all the time, shakes her head. Then the Master notices that the old woman has an injury corresponding to that of the hare, and recognizes her as a witch.

The story is not merely a myth. Most reports give names and identify the time and place of the occurrence (Irish Folklore 1931: 167–168; 1937: 55; 1940: 103–104). What is involved is not fantasy or verbal creation, but experience. In each transformation, the tale deals not with culture-heroes but with real people. It is precisely this experiential aspect that structural analysis fails to consider, rendering it inadequate as a method of understanding this material.

Lévi-Strauss claims that "a myth is still felt as a myth by a reader anywhere in the world."

In the course of a myth anything is likely to happen. There is no logic, no continuity. Any characteristic can be attributed to any subject; every conceivable relation can be met. With myth everything becomes possible ... [yet] this apparent arbitrariness is belied by the astounding similarity between myths collected in widely different regions. Therefore the problem: if the content of myth is contingent, how are we going to explain that throughout the world myths resemble one another so much? (Lévi-Strauss 1963: 563–564).

Equating linguistics with the study of myth, Lévi-Strauss states: "... the arbitrary character of linguistic signs was a prerequisite for the acceding of linguistics to the scientific level" (Lévi-Strauss 1963: 563). This "arbitrary character" is a fundamental tenet of Lévi-Strauss' "science of myth." Linguists are now reconsidering the whole question of the arbitrariness of linguistic signs (Durbin 1971). I am going to take similar issue with what Lévi-Strauss calls the arbitrariness of myth.

Lévi-Strauss conceives of both a universal chaos of nature and a universal desire of the mind for order. Since the natural world is perceived as being without order, mind must "make up" the order which it imposes upon nature. The need for order is not discovered in the natural world, but invented.

The biases of structuralism reflect the personality of its founder. Mind is a disembodied *bricoleur*, endlessly reshaping "the ultimate discontinuity of reality" (Lévi-Strauss 1969: 62). Lévi-Strauss' consciousness is not of the "here and now" kind; even when he reaches his destination, he is somewhere else at some remove from the present. This characteristic is reflected in the "otherness" of his concept of mind. This quality is not to be regarded without sympathy, nor can it be; I think we recognize it all too well as a form of alienation:

No sooner had I mastered the men and the landscapes which I had travelled so far to see than they lost the meaning which I had hoped to find in them; and in place of these disappointing, though immediately present images, I found myself haunted by others which had remained in reserve from my past. Never, when they were part of the reality around me had I set any value upon them. But when I was travelling in areas which few had set eyes upon, and sharing the existence of people whose wretchedness was the price, paid by them of course — of my investigation into the distant past, I found that neither people nor landscape stood in the foreground of my mind. This was occupied, rather, by fugitive visions of the French countryside from which I had cut myself off, of fragments of music which were the perfectly conventional expression of a civilization against which I had taken my stand . . . (Lévi-Strauss 1969: 374–375).

This alienation recurs in the concept of mythic thought: "Mythic thought only accepts nature on condition that it is able to reproduce it. By so doing, it limits itself to the choice of those formal properties by which nature can signify itself . . ." (Lévi-Strauss 1970: 341).

References throughout *Tristes tropiques* stress the ultimate opposition of mind to nature, and in the jungles of Brazil, Lévi-Strauss encounters peoples by whom this notion is seemingly held: " . . . the face paintings [of the Caduveo] confer upon the individual his dignity as a human being; they help him to cross the frontier from Nature to culture, and from the 'mindless animal' to civilized man" (Lévi-Strauss 1969: 176).

He remarks upon the artificiality of Caduveo culture: " . . . characters they were, from some old romance of chivalry: wrapped up in their cruel make-believe of domination and prestige" (Lévi-Strauss 1969: 164).

He cannot avoid such a conclusion among a people who regard "natural" processes with such disfavor. "The idea of procreation filled them with disgust. Abortion and infanticide were so common as to be almost normal — to the extent in fact, that it was by adoption, rather than by procreation, that the group ensured its continuance" (Lévi-Strauss 1969: 162). In the thought of Lévi-Strauss, as well as in some of the cultures he studied, "complexities seem to spring from a delight in complication for its own sake" (Lévi-Strauss 1969: 200). Flagrant denial of the life processes necessitates elaborate mental gymnastics. "An entirely virgin landscape is so monotonous as to deprive its wildness of all meaning" (Lévi-Strauss 1969: 262).

The abstractive nature of the structural system is reflected in its interpretation of the philosophy of Karl Marx: "Marx followed Rousseau in saying — and saying once and for all, as far as I can see — that social science is no more based upon events than physics is based upon sense perceptions" (Lévi-Strauss 1969: 51). Its search is for models. I cannot help remembering the criticism of Abraham Maslow, that one trouble with classical science applied to psychology is that all it knows how to do well is to study people as objects, when what we need is to be able to study them also as subjects (Maslow 1966: 54).

We may be grateful for the extensive information about the author which *Tristes tropiques* contains. It deals with the ethical, personal, and spiritual problems of the anthropologist in a concise way. The frail nature of human life as Lévi-Strauss conceives it is central to the understanding of structuralism. Mind becomes an appetite for order which must be satisfied if we are to survive in the natural world; it represents our humanness, our unique need in the animal world. Mind is discontinuous with the natural world in Lévi-Straussian terms. To some extent, Lévi-Strauss is projecting the profoundly unnatural practices of modern man upon the natives of other cultures. It is possible to live in a modern city and know nothing of nature — either in the conventional "romantic" sense of wild waterfalls and remote canyons and deserts, or in the sense of the naturalness of one's own body and its needs, sexual or nutritive. The West provides us with a culture that inadequately nourishes the individual; but other sources show us that the wide variety of diets derived by native populations from intimate contact with the natural world are by and large nutritionally superior (Price 1969). It is we who have invented so much to put between ourselves and the natural world, and our failings should not be projected upon other cultures. The question must be asked of every culture: how much is in fact known about the natural environment? about natural processes? Objective knowledge may be pursued in the spirit of curiosity and not self-protection. It is clear from *The savage mind* that Lévi-Strauss knows that cultures do not use mind merely to combat nature, and that some native knowledge is based on fact and not on make-believe.

Why, then, should we assign a purely arbitrary significance to natural symbols? Because natural symbols are used for their positional and not their intrinsic value, replies Lévi-Strauss (1970: 56). Presumably this is why he does not deal with isolated symbols. But for natural symbols to be used in a systematic way, the inherent nature of their order must first be observed or discovered in nature itself. There is little evidence that mind functions in a vacuum, although facts discovered in the world of natural phenomena may be used for classificatory ends. Since "primitive" thought systems do not distinguish "real" and "imaginary" events, there is no reason for us to assume that the maybush of "myth" is any different from the maybush whose properties are known in mundane contexts. Nor must what seems *a priori* impossible therefore be invented.

It is apparent from the lengths that have to be gone to in structural analysis that its results are not obvious to the native in whose mind they are assumed to exist. Otherwise, he would tell us about them. How can we believe in the importance of resolving apparent "contradictions" when the natives couldn't care less? "With myth everything becomes possible" only because we have an unlimited view of myth as construct. Sometimes we rely heavily on the awkward premise that the outsider knows more about what the native is doing than the native does.

The structural approach disregards function altogether as the principal method for ensuring the comparability of cultures. Lévi-Strauss' anthropology "helps us to constitute a model to which no one society corresponds exactly" (Lévi-Strauss 1969: 390). Structuralism is searching for the broad formula, as is linguistics; while the meaning itself, at the level at which we encounter it in speech or "myth," remains particularistic. Logical transformations of the sort that Lévi-Strauss uses to show the universal functions of abstractive thinking cannot be invoked to explain "transformations" in the particular, such as we encounter in descriptions of witchcraft.

The data concerning witchcraft "transformations" are astonishingly similar regardless of the culture within which they occur. Even symbolic configurations differ only slightly. The witchlike characteristics most frequently found are association with animals, often animals or birds of the night; ability to change into animal form; ability to fly; dealings with the dead; perverse sexuality. To cite selections from ethnographic accounts of witches:

## Navaho — North America

Witches are active primarily at night, roaming about at great speed in skins of wolf, coyote and other animals (bear, owl, desert fox, crow) ... major features of witchery ideology. ... Night activity, were-animals, association with corpses and in incest, killing of a sibling as part of initiation, various points of technique ... (Kluckhohn 1967: 26–28).

## Azande — Africa

Witchcraft is like fire, it lights a light (Evans-Pritchard 1937: 34).

Nocturnal bird and animals ... are very definitely associated with witchcraft and are even thought to be the servants of witches. Bats are universally disliked, and owls are considered very unlucky if they hoot around a homestead at night. There is an owl called *gbuku* that cries *he he he he* at night, and when a man hears its cry he knows that a witch is abroad .... They say of a domestic cock which crows to welcome the dawn before men can see the first signs of its approach: "It sees the daylight within itself, it is a witch." Most feared of all these evil creatures is a species of wild cat called *andandara*. They live in the bush and are said to have bright bodies and gleaming eyes and to utter shrill cries in the night. Azande often say of these cats, "It is witchcraft, they are the same as witchcraft." The male cats have sexual relations with women who give birth to kittens ... (Evans-Pritchard 1937: 50–56).

## Trobriand Islands — Melanesia

These women [flying witches] have the power of making themselves invisible, and flying at night through the air. The orthodox belief is that a woman who is a *yoyova* can send forth a double which is invisible at will, but may appear in the form of a flying fox or of a nightbird or a firefly ... another variant of the belief about the *yoyova* is, that those who know their magic especially well, can fly themselves through the air .... They [potential *yoyova*] will be recognizable by their crude tastes, and more especially by their habit of eating raw flesh of pigs or uncooked fish ... a full bloom *yoyova* has to utter special magic each time she wishes to be invisible, or when she wants to fly, or acquire higher speed or penetrate darkness and distance in order to find out whether an accident is happening here ... she will often go at night to feed on corpses or to destroy shipwrecked mariners, for these are her two main pursuits ... she can "hear" as the natives say, that a man has died at such and such a place ... whenever the natives see a falling star, they know it is a *mulukwausi* on her flight (Malinowski 1922: 237–241).

## Lugbara — Africa

He [the witch] "walks at night" and enters his victim's hut silently "like a rat creeping over a wall." Often he may take the form of an animal, especially a leopard, wild cat, snake, jackal, owl or screech monkey, or any other night animal or indeed any animal seen suspiciously near a hut or seen by the victim in a dream ... or a witch may become visible as a light on the top of a hut, or as a light moving rapidly across fields, and it is a characteristic of all witches that they have a glowing light at their wrists and anus (Middleton 1967: 57–59). [Middleton continues that Logo, and Keliko witches share the same features.]

## Nahuatl (Tepoztlán) — Mesoamerica

The *nagual* [transforming witch] is a person who has the power to change into an animal, such as a dog or pig.

The transforming witch or *win* is ... a lazy and avaricious human being who magically metamorphosizes himself into an animal or bird at night and stealthily enters the houses of his sleeping neighbours to rob them of money and goods ... male rather than female ... in animal form may take sexual advantage of sleeping women — a heinous indignity since it combines bestiality and rape (Saler 1967: 79). [Saler also mentions that *naguales* are common among Zapotec (Mitla), Tzeltal (Amatenango), Maya (Chan Kom), Mam (Todos Santos), Kanhobal (Santa Eulalia), Tzutuhil (Santiago Atitlan) (Saler 1967: 72).]

## Cêwa — Africa

Techniques that sorcerers employ include ... attacking the victim while he is asleep; eating him while he is still alive, this being the Cêwa interpretation of tropical ulcers; belonging to a necrophagous guild; flying around in flat winnowing baskets ... and employing familiars, especially hyenas and owls (Marwick 1967: 107).

## Tzeltal — South America

The possessor of a nawal may, on whim but only at night, transform himself into the animal and roam the streets of the pueblo or travel the hills near the community. As the nawal he may converse with other nawales. The nawal is the source of power in medical practice, and all curers must have at least one nawal in their possession. A man is born associated with, or the possessor of a nawal. The nawal is revealed to him in a dream. He does not necessarily announce this to the community, or act any special way because he has an animal counterpart (Nash 1967: 127).

## Konkomba: Togoland — Africa

By transvection I mean the flying by night of a sorcerer to attack a sleeping victim. The flying sorcerer can be seen as a moving light that is known as *suonmi*, that is, "sorcerer fire." This belief, that flying sorcerers emit a light, was noted by Evans-Pritchard among the Azande, and it is found also among the Akan speaking peoples. ... A sorcerer is believed to be able to send snakes to lie in wait on a path until the victim comes along ... [or] sends his shadow to eat the victim's shadow (Tait 1967: 157).

## Cochiti — North America

The witches represent a vast conspiracy of ill-defined but definitely malignant beings that seek to destroy Pueblo civilization by attacking the health of its members. . . . They are of various types, appearing as humans, animals, and birds (especially owls) or as fireballs (Fox 1967: 264).

## Tswana: Bechuanaland — Africa

Among the activities attributed to these "night witches" is the exhumation of newly buried corpses. . . . It is believed also that they have special medicines that will enable them to throw the inhabitants of a homestead into a deep sleep, so that they may enter at will and do what they wish . . . associated with these "night witches" are various kinds of animal familiars. Foremost among them is the owl, which acts as their spy and whose hooting warns them that someone is approaching. . . . It is also said that, when the witches wish to go to a distant place, they ride on hyenas (Schapera 1957: 112).

## Fipa: South West Tanzania — Africa

A common image of a sorcerer is an old man who goes around his village naked at night, seeking to enter huts and remove head and pubic hair from their magically stupefied occupants, later using the hair to make noxious medicine. A more complex image consists of an old man and his wife, also naked, who carries her husband suspended upside down from her shoulders, while she clasps his lower legs to her breasts. . . . Sorcerers are said to have the means of turning their victims into zombies (*amasea*) which are then forced to work in their masters' gardens at night, sleeping on top of his hut by day. Certain experts in sorcery are said to have the power to metamorphose themselves (*ukusaangooka*) into the form of a ferocious animal, such as a lion or leopard, in which shape they attack and kill their human prey (Willis 1968: 185–186).

## Ngaju — South Borneo

The ancestor of the witches . . . appears in this world as a fishlike creature and misleads people who consume him, by which they not only become his property but are transformed into himself. . . . Witches capriciously harm their fellowmen. With their medicines (*ramon oloh* or *pulih* poison), which belong to so-called black magic, they cause numerous illnesses called by the term *penyakit lewu*, village illnesses. As young girls, they lead youths astray and suck their blood at night; they destroy the fruit in the womb and kill the pregnant. At night they detach their head from the body and fly about with the intestines trailing from it, stealing the livers of sleeping people or consuming corpses. They appear to people in the form of buffaloes and kill them if they stand on their shadow. . . . They do not only kill and destroy, but they also heal and bring alive (Schärer 1963: 50–52).

Among the strange facts that I and others before me have collected in Ireland are practically all of the supposed visible signs of witchcraft:

a. *Witches and Animals*   Witches are able to turn themselves into hares, tomcats, and foxes. The high rock near where I lived was intimately associated with "supernatural" visions, both Christian and pagan. Its cave is called "the foxes' cave." The summit, called the Moat, is the site of an ancient (prehistoric) grave. One man claimed to have heard the angels sing there, while others claimed visions of ghosts and wraiths there. "The foxes' cave" has been the site of supernatural occurrences for many centuries.

The association of cat — hare — fox is made on the basis of sound among other things. The howl of the banshee, which announces death in certain families, is said to resemble that of a tomcat, the shriek of a hare, or the bark of the fox. Cats are not allowed into the house. They are kept to curtail the activities of vermin, but they are not pets — except among old women.

b. *Flying Through the Air*   There are stories about witches with "flying hats." There are numerous accounts of lights seen traveling across bogs or lakes; also of people being in two places at once (out-of-body experience).

c. *The Dead*   Graves were once regularly ripped open and the hands cut off the corpses. A dead man's hand is particularly efficacious in churning butter, and there are accounts of people seen using one to scrape the butter from the churn, whereupon the volume of butter is increased (Irish Folklore 1941).

d. *Perverse Sexuality*   Despite common rumors that sex is unknown in Ireland, there is excellent archival material indicating the contrary. One account details a love charm which entails obtaining a pubic hair of the beloved, generally obtained during sleep (Irish Folklore 1951: 58). Such a charm is known by a person who has cures — who is seemingly different in Ireland from the one who bewitches, although there are some indications that these persons are one and the same.

e. *Hostility*   The hostility expressed in the customs of May Day is clear, likewise the destructive nature of the witch. The hare is an animal perfectly suited to the expression of sibling hostility: she separates her young and settles them in different locations in isolation. Sibling rivalry in Ireland is particularly marked in relation to land holding and accounts for much emigration. The fox is said to remove her young from the den after birth. The most interesting fact of all, if you believe native accounts of what has been seen, is that each aspect of witchcraft is empirically possible. The entire complex does not appear as witchcraft, but that may be due to the many invasions of Ireland and the disruption of the culture in the last thousand years.

There is an obvious conclusion. The reason for the universal similarity of witchcraft beliefs and supernatural powers is that what is being described is real, and is in each case the same thing. Our concern to make "primitives" as intelligent as ourselves has led us to overlook the special capacities of mind we have lost—possibly because we devote so much energy to theorizing and so little, as Huxley points out, to observation of the here and now (Huxley 1962). It is pure prejudice which tells us that in witchcraft we are dealing with a symbolic description, with "make-believe" rather than with reality.

We now come to the real problem. If we accept the phenomena described in accounts of witchcraft and other supernatural events as true, how do we understand them, and explain them? We have not yet begun. We shall have to come to grips with "out-of-body experiences"; with the nature of the energy transmitted by traveling lights; with communication during sleep (witches often visit victims during sleep, thus the testimony of the sleeper to the witching activity may be through accounts of dreaming); with the powers of the dead. The only bright spark in the situation is that these things may well be subject to the hard-core methods of the physical sciences. Then we can begin over, to see how differing societies develop and deal with what are evidently fearful powers of mind. We shall have to pay more attention to what animals know: in Ireland, you can see the supernatural "if you look between a horse's ears."

As to that difficult matter of transformation of human into animal, I am reminded of the report of Carlos Castaneda, who, after all, studied under a witch: " . . . to become a crow is the simplest of all matters [said Don Juan] . . . . It takes a very long time to learn to be a proper crow, he said, but you did not change, nor did you stop being a man. There is something else" (Castaneda 1969: 184 ff.).

## REFERENCES

BURCH, ERNEST S.
1971 The nonempirical environment of the Arctic Alaskan Eskimos. *Southwestern Journal of Anthropology* 27: 148–165.
BYRNE, PATRICK F.
1967 *Witchcraft in Ireland.* Cork: Mercier Press.

CASTANEDA, CARLOS
1969   *The teachings of Don Juan: a Yaqui way of knowledge.* New York: Ballantine.

DANAHER, KEVIN
1964   *Gentle places and simple things.* Cork: Mercier Press.

DOUGLAS, MARY, *editor*
1971   *Witchcraft confessions and accusations.* London: Tavistock.

DURBIN, MARSHALL
1971   "Non-arbitrary aspects of language." Paper read at Annual Meeting of American Anthropological Association, New York, November 20.

EVANS-PRITCHARD, E. E.
1937   *Witchcraft, oracles and magic among the Azande.* Oxford: Clarendon Press.
1940   *The Nuer: a description of the modes of livelihood and political institutions of a Nilotic people.* Oxford: Clarendon Press.

FOX, J. ROBIN
1967   "Witchcraft and clanship in Cochiti therapy," in *Magic, witchcraft and curing.* Edited by John Middleton, 255–284. New York: The Natural History Press.

HALLPIKE, C. R.
1971   "Some problems in cross-cultural comparison," in *The translation of culture.* Edited by T. O. Beidelman, 123–140. London: Tavistock.

HUXLEY, ALDOUS
1962   *Island.* New York: Harper and Row.

IRISH FOLKLORE
1931–1966   Unpublished manuscripts in the archives of the Folklore Dept., University College, Dublin. 1931:37; 1940:1248; 1941:782; 1943:952; 1951:1220; 1954:1348; 1956:1480; 1966:1697.

IRISH FOLKLORE S.
1937   Unpublished manuscript in the archives of the Folklore Dept., University College, Dublin. 1937:981.

KLUCKHOHN, CLYDE
1967   *Navaho witchcraft.* Boston: Beacon Press.

LÉVI-STRAUSS, CLAUDE
1963   "The structural study of myth," in *Reader in comparative religion.* Edited by William A. Lessa and Evon Z. Vogt, 561–573. New York, Evanston, London: Harper and Row.
1966   *The savage mind.* London: Weidenfield and Nicolson.
1969   *Tristes tropiques.* Translated from the French by John Russell. New York: Atheneum.
1970   *The raw and the cooked.* Translated from the French by John and Doreen Weightman. New York: Harper and Row.

MALINOWSKI, BRONISLAW
1922   *Argonauts of the Western Pacific: an account of native enterprise and adventure in the archipelagoes of Melanesian N. Guinea.* London: Routledge and Kegan Paul.

MARWICK, MAX
1967 "The sociology of sorcery in a central African tribe," in *Magic, witchcraft and curing*. Edited by John Middleton, 101–126. New York: The Natural History Press.

MASLOW, ABRAHAM H.
1966 *The psychology of science: a reconnaissance*. New York: Harper and Row.

MIDDLETON, JOHN
1967 "The concept of 'bewitching' in Lugbara," in *Magic, witchcraft and curing*. Edited by John Middleton, 55–68. New York: The Natural History Press.

NASH, MANNING
1967 "Witchcraft as social process in a Tzeltal community," in *Magic, witchcraft and curing*. Edited by John Middleton, 127–134. New York: The Natural History Press.

PRICE, WESTON A.
1969 *Nutrition and physical degeneration*. Monrovia, California: The Price-Pottenger Foundation.

REES, ALWYN, BRINLEY REES
1961 *Celtic heritage: ancient tradition in Ireland and Wales*. London: Thames and Hudson.

SALER, BENSON
1967 "Nagual, witch and sorcerer in a Quiché village," in *Magic, witchcraft and curing*. Edited by John Middleton, 69–100. New York: The Natural History Press.

SCHÄRER, HANS
1963 *Ngaju religion: the conception of God among a S. Borneo people*. Translated by Rodney Needham. The Hague: Martinus Nijhoff.

SCHAPERA, ISAAC
1952 "Sorcery and witchcraft in Bechuanaland," in *Witchcraft and sorcery*. Edited by Max Marwick, 108–120. Harmondsworth: Penguin.

ST. CLAIR, SHEILA
1971 *Folklore of the Ulster people*. Cork: Mercier Press.

TAIT, DAVID
1967 "Konkomba sorcery," in *Magic, witchcraft and curing*. Edited by John Middleton, 155–170. New York: The Natural History Press.

WILLIS, R. A.
1968 "The Kamkape movement," in *Witchcraft and sorcery*. Edited by Max Marwick, 184–198. Harmondsworth: Penguin.

# Gods, Kings, and the Caste System in India

L. K. MAHAPATRA

That the caste system in India is not purely a secular social order, but that religious values, rites, gods, and goddesses are important in it, has been known for a long time. We need only mention the well-known fact that cults of specific deities are associated with specific castes irrespective of status in the caste hierarchy. Hocart's view of a new caste emerging along with a new cult is derived from this (Hocart 1950: 59). Among others, Bouglé has stressed the importance of the sacrifice and the concepts of purity and pollution as distinctive characteristics of the caste order (Bouglé 1908: 81–82, 1958: 24–26). Hocart conceives of the caste system as a ritual organization, within which the individual castes have been assigned ritual duties or services to perform; the polluting services are relegated to the vassals or serfs (Hocart 1950: 17–18), who do not have a share in the public or state sacrifices and thus do not have communion with the Aryan gods. This viewpoint of Hocart has certain relevance to our theme, and we shall revert to him later. But, incidentally, it is important to note that Hocart has been neglected for various reasons (compare Dumont and Pocock 1958: 3 ff.).

Of late, Marriott has referred to Hocart while probing the link between the caste hierarchies of little communities and the great tradition of the greater community (1955: 189–190). Marriott notes the process of filtering down from great to little communities since later Vedic times, when there were two classes of sacrifices, simpler ones of the householders with the assistance of kinsmen and elaborate ones conducted only by kings with the help of professional ritual specialists. The royal sacrifices grew more elaborate, involving greater specializa-

tion of the ritualists. Similarly, he thinks that the villagers today practice more elaborate household sacrifices and employ a larger number
of specialists. He leans directly upon Hocart to trace the kinds of ritual
relationships among castes in villages from those once prevalent in the
royal palace among royal retainers. Hocart points out that "royal ways
filter down to the common people, sometimes slowly, sometimes with
astonishing rapidity, but naturally shorn of their pomp" (Hocart 1950:
155). Even a poor householder of Kishan Garhi, according to Marriott,
today retains six or seven servants of different castes "mainly to serve
him in ceremonial ways demonstrative of his own caste rank." Marriott
adds some other facts throwing light on such royal association:

Householders and their servants formally address each other by courtly
titles. Thus the Brahman priest is called "Great King" (*Maharaj*) or "Learned Man" (*Panditji*), the Potter is called "Ruler of the People" (*Prajapat*),
the Barber "Lord Barber" (*Nau Thakur*), the carpenter "Master Craftsman"
(*Mistri*), the Sweeper "Headman" (*Mehtar*) or "Sergeant" (*Jamadar*), etc.
About half of the twenty-four castes of Kishan Garhi also identify themselves with one or another of the three higher *varna*, thus symbolizing their
claims to certain ritual statuses in relation to the sacrifice or the sacrificer
of Sanskrit literary form. "Thus the apparent degradation of the royal style
becomes a step in social evolution" [Hocart 1950:155] (Marriott 1955:190).

However, the role of the Hindu kings in the evolution, functioning, and
maintenance of the caste system has been very rarely considered (Datta
1968; Bose 1949; Hutton 1951; Srinivas 1952, 1955, 1966; Maynard
1972; Sinha 1972; L. K. Mahapatra 1970). Hocart has given extensive
thought to it, but he goes so far when he considers the kings as gods,
having priestly functions and working with the Brahman to form a
sacerdotal pair, upholding the sacrificial organization for the good life
on earth, that he makes the state appear as a ritual organization, and
the king's palace, court, and complement of functional castes are duplicated in the God's temple, court, and ritual functionaries (Hocart 1927:
10–11; 1970: 93, 105). In fact, according to Hocart, "the Church and
the State are one in India. The head of this Church-State is the king"
(Hocart 1950: 67). "The temple and the palace are indistinguishable,
for the king represents the Gods" (Hocart 1950: 68). ". . . everyone likes
to imitate his betters, the big feudal nobles the king, the small nobles
the big ones, and so on . . ." (Hocart 1955: 155). We shall have to
examine Hocart's insightful ideas in some detail in the light of some
empirical data from Orissa.

Although implicit in Hocart's writings, the temple organization of
ritual and other services based on a caste division of labor and the

relation between the state deity, the divine kings, and the vassal kings, on the one hand, and the caste system at various levels, on the other, have not been expressly analyzed in terms of the relevant empirical data. We shall attempt to do that here within the limitations of space and data. However, it is felt that in analyzing the caste system of India, it is methodologically feasible and substantially profitable to begin with a particular cultural region because there is much truth in the statement that there is hardly a single caste system, but several, each specific to a linguistic-cultural region (compare Ghurye 1961). Orissa as a cultural region exemplifies, perhaps in an extreme fashion, the parallelism between the king's court, estates, and services, and those of the state deity. On the basis of this regional empirical study, further implications for understanding the interaction and interdependence between the gods, kings, and temples, on the one hand, and the caste system at the levels of the region as a whole, the princedoms, and the villages, on the other, can be identified and analyzed for India as a whole later on.

## GOD-KING IN ORISSA

Perhaps a little introduction to Orissa as a cultural region in this context is in order. Orissa had a checkered political history, although paradoxically its cultural continuity over a wide area in the ancient Kalinga or Utkala is significant. The cornerstone of this cultural continuity in the pre-Islamic past has been the cult of Lord Jagannath, the Lord of the Universe, identified as the penultimate incarnation of Vishnu in the form of Buddha, at Puri, Shrikshetra, one of the four most sacred centers of pilgrimage (*chaturdhama*) for the Hindus. Lord Jagannath is looked upon as the protector and even the sovereign of Orissa, and the Raja of Puri (formerly, of Orissa at Khurdha) officiates as his earthly deputy. The king is himself conceived as Vishnu, or Mobile Vishnu (*Chalanti Vishnu*). The institution of a state deity is perhaps as old as urban civilization itself, and we learn of it in the civilizations of Babylonia and Egypt. The Pharaohs were notably the Children of the Sun. So are many Rajput chiefs, as are also the chiefs in Orissa, who are "descended" from the gods, the sun, the moon, the ritual fire god, Agni, and even from the serpent-god, Naga. Such a conception of divine kingship was also quite widely prevalent for a long time in Southeast Asia, where Shiva, Vishnu, Harihara, Shiva-Buddha, Bodhisatva Lokeśwara of Mount Meru, or Indra were represented in the king on earth, his palace being the sacred microcosm of the kingdom (Heine-

Geldern 1942: 22ff.). In ancient Cambodia, the king was an incarnation of the God-King Devaraja, who was Lord Shiva himself (Heine-Geldern 1942: 22ff.). Similarly, the Raja of Puri, the descendant of the paramount sovereign of Orissa, is called *Thakur-Raja* [God-King], so much so that pilgrims used to have a *darshan* [audience] of the king before proceeding to the lord's temple. As such, he also functioned as the head ritual functionary of the Jagannath temple; "in the absence of other functionaries in cases of emergencies, [he can] . . . perform all ritual services except cooking and offering food to the Images" (Patnaik 1970: 88). Patnaik also refers to the similarities between the rituals of the temple and those of the palace. The palace was considered as a sacred place, the abode of the God-King and Mobile Vishnu; because of this none were allowed to enter the palace with leather footwear as in the case of a temple (Patnaik 1970). In the painted reliefs on the wall of the temple the king is seen performing the twelve important festivals in the manner that Lord Jagannath's are conducted (Mishra 1971: 114–115).

The king and the god underwent similar rituals at the time of waking up, bathing, receiving presents, eating breakfast, putting on clothes, giving audience, making offerings, and other daily rituals. Besides, the king had many special privileges, similar or homologous to those of Lord Jagannath himself, when he went to have an audience with the god. The king had vassal chiefs performing several services at the time of royal installation, coronation, and at the time of the temple visit. In the palace, the king's establishment had a vegetarian cuisine, and the queen was subject to no fewer ritual austerities (Mishra 1971: 114–115). Only Lord Jagannath and the king were addressed with the reverential terms, *Manima* or *Mahaprabhu*, not only at Puri, but also in other feudal princedoms, because feudal princes are conceived as minor gods in the image of the paramount king. The paramount Raja of Orissa, at least since the days of the Ganga dynasty in about the twelfth century, has made the Jagannath cult a state cult. It may be that this was gradually superimposed on the prevailing state cults of the feudal chiefdoms, where usually some form of *shakti* [tribal goddess] was the *ishta-devata* [patron-deity] of the royal dynasty (Bhattarika in Baramba, Sa-maleshwari in Sambalpur, Kila Munda in Ranpur, and Hingula in Talcher, etc.) (compare Kulke i.p.).

Lord Shiva has been worshiped almost everywhere in Orissa as *Mahadeva* [Great God] from time immemorial, and the Pashupat cult was in the ascendancy from the times of the fifth and sixth centuries. We may, therefore, visualize that Lord Lingaraj, the King of the Phallus, at Bhubaneswar Ekamra-Kshetra, was the state deity of Orissa by the seventh century, when the temple is said to have been constructed at Bhubaneswar by Yayati Keshari (Panigrahi 1961). But by the time of Shri Shankaracharya of the eighth century, who had visited Puri and whose monastery was established there to campaign in favor of the revival of Hinduism, the worship of Lord Jagannath and the cult center of Puri must have attained all-India importance and all-Orissa supremacy in the spiritual realm.

## STATE DEITY AND TEMPLE ORGANIZATION

At any rate, there is evidence that after the days of the Ganga Paramount King Aniyankabhima III (who had completed construction of the present temple of Lord Jagannath), the worship of Jagannath in Orissa was more intensified than during the previous kings' times. Traditionally, thirty-six functional castes were deployed to render services in the temple. It was this king who expressly regarded Purushottama [Lord Jagannath] as the real Emperor of Orissa, he himself ruling as his representative. Thus, by the early thirteenth century Lord Jagannath might have been well established as the state deity (*rashtradevata*) although according to Mishra (1971: 38), Purushottama [Jagannath] and Balabhadra were already regarded as *rashtradevatas* of Kongada and Toshali under the later Vaishnav Bhaumas by about the eighth century. Lord Jagannath was believed in so strongly as the lord and protector of Kalinga and Utkal, kingdoms of ancient Orissa (Mishra 1971: 43–44), that during the reign of Purushottama Gajapati, both Lord Jagannath and Lord Balabhadra rode horses and led the Orissa soldiers to victory, according to a popular legend painted on the temple walls. This identification of the god with the king of Orissa and the king's empire as the god's realm under his protective arms must have persuaded the feudal chiefs — in addition to the fact of military or political subjugation — to become willing tributaries of a divine King-God-State polity. In fact, there is an inscription in the temple of Lord Jagannath by the paramount king Purushottama Deva that enjoins the vassal kings of Orissa to obey his orders on proper attitude and approach toward Brahmans; transgression of these orders constitutes a great sacrilege and sin (*mahapataka*) against Lord Jagannath himself (S. N. Dash 1966: 264). At any rate, we find perhaps no princedoms in Orissa under British occupation where we do not come across the worship of Lord Jagannath, usually with his brother, Balabhadra, and sister, Subhadra, and where a complement of functional castes does not serve in the temple as they do in the palace nearby. There is some evidence that in order to legitimize their occupation of territory and curry favor with the Gajapati kings of Orissa, the vassal kings, like the king of Bolangir-Patna, constructed temples of Jagannath, Balabhadra, and Subhadra (S. P. Dash 1962: 253). Therefore, we may note that the Jagannath cult has been used for political purposes both by the emperor and the vassal kings, at least since the thirteenth century. Again, with political purposes of espionage and public propaganda in view, the Panda system was introduced by Aniyankabhima Deva III to court pilgrims from various parts of India, by learning their language and visiting them (Mishra 1971: 44). Lord Jagannath is invoked for permission to punish rebellious vassals (Mishra 1971: 49). In another inscription in the temple, the paramount king threatens, presumably on the authority of Lord Jagannath, that if the people do not work for the good of the sovereign and avoid the evil path, they will be expelled from the kingdom and all their properties will be confiscated (Mishra 1971: 50).

Let us now briefly consider the types of services and the number of functional castes engaged in serving in the two most important temples of Orissa, that of Lord Jagannath at Puri and of Lord Lingaraj at Bhubaneswar. The world-famous gigantic Sun Temple of Konarak, now in ruins and with no record of organized worship, need not concern us. Although it has been noted that the ritual and other services in the temple of Lord Jagannath were systematically organized in the thirteenth century, there is no justification to infer therefrom that the functional castes were not associated with the temple services much earlier, perhaps from the beginning of the temple worship in the legendary days of king Indradyumna, who, according to Skanda Purana, constructed the first temple of Puri. Even in the days of Indradyumna, as the legend goes (Mishra 1971: 82), the descendants of Savara chief Visvavasu, known as Daita, the descendants of Savara girl, Lalita, and the Brahman emissary, Vidyapati, known as Suara (Supakara), and third, the descendants of Vidyapati (by a Brahman wife?) were to serve as decorators and ministrants, as cooks, and as priests, respectively. Previous to the organization of services by Aniyankabhima Deva III, the local tradition has it that there were nine *sevaks* [servants]: (1) *Charu Hota*, (2) *Patra Hota*, (3) *Brahma*, (4) *Acharya*, (5) *Pratihari*, (6) *Puspalaka*, (7 and 8) *Dyatas* [the washerman and the barber], and (9) *Dvarapalaka* (Mishra 1971: 12–121).[1] It is highly probable that

---

[1] Some of the names of these nine *sevaks* cannot be translated exactly because they are proper names. Possible meanings are: (1) *Charu Hota* [the handsome head-

every time the temple was rebuilt, it became more complex and bigger, and the ritual services were further elaborated; the latter occurred also when dynasties changed. Again, just because there is a close parallel in the temple services in the Puri and Bhubaneswar temples, there is no valid reason to suspect that the services are wholly a carry-over from the temple at Puri to the Bhubaneswar temple. First, the Lord Lingaraj temple is probably 600 years older (compare Panigrahi 1961) and the cult center Ekamra-Kshetra is perhaps even older. King Indradyumna is said to have worshiped Lord Shiva there before Lord Jagannath in his present form appeared at Puri. Second, both Lord Jagannath and Lord Lingaraj are, as the legends run, gods of the Savara autochthones who had been recognized as some categories of temple functionaries. King Yayati Keshari, alleged to be a founder of the Lord Lingaraj temple, is said to have brought some Dravidian Brahmans (Bose, et al. 1958) as temple priests because, presumably, the local Brahmans were not well versed in Shaivism at that time, and he had to elevate the temple services from the tribal rites to Sanskritic ones.

The temple of Lord Jagannath engages temple servants performing 101 services or roles with their respective names, rights, duties, and perquisites (Mishra 1971). However, the actual number of castes is not ascertained from this, although castes from Brahmans to some untouchables, even to some descendants from tribal worshipers are known to be involved. Similarly, at the temple of Lord Lingaraj, somewhat less elaborately, in 1958 forty-one types of services were recorded (Bose, et al. 1958), involving twenty-two separate castes, ranging over almost the same ethnic spectrum. This has also been largely confirmed by M. Mahapatra (1972), who, however, gives a tally of thirty types of services. There is no doubt that there has been wide fluctuation in the total number of ritual services (roles), at least in the temple of Lord Jagannath. Those ritual services were recorded by British officers in 1807, soon after their occupation of Orissa after the Marathas, and the number was 219; apart from this there were 139 types of services connected with the management of the temple. In the 1950's the Orissa government compiled a record of ritual rites, which gave the number of ritual services as 140. Again the number of castes involved is not given, and it is seen that many of the priestly and other castes perform several roles at the same time. The fact that specific Rajas and even temple

---

priest], (2) *Patra Hota* [the priest in charge of vessels], (3) *Brahma* [the demiurge Brahma], (4) *Acharya* [preceptor], (5) *Pratihara* [garland-arranger], (6) *Puspalaka* [flower-arranger], (7 and 8) *Dyatas* [washerman and barber], and (9) *Dvarapalaka* [gatekeeper].

managers have been known to have introduced or discontinued specific services, offerings, and even fairs, etc. points to the prevalence of caste-centered core services in spite of the periodic fluctuations in the elaboration or proliferation of services. This is very clear from the stereotypical reference to *Chhatisha Nijoga* [thirty-six caste-centered ritual servants].

That almost all of the caste-centered ritual services performed in the temple of Lord Jagannath were duplicated in the palace of the King of Orissa may not be far from the truth, as indicated by Patnaik (1970) or by Mishra (1971: 44). Similarly, one may refer to the royal installation, attended by vassal chiefs in various roles, as bearing close similarity to the divine installation at Poushabhisheka in the month of Pousha when Lord Jagannath assumes *rajavesha* [royal attire] in a series of king-worthy rituals (*raja niti*). There is another divine installation in the month of Jyestha, known as *Rajendra-bhiseka*, auguring the proposal of marriage with Rukmini, as in the *Mahabharat*. Lord Jagannath assumes *rajavesha* again on the day of the full moon in the month of Phalgun. Not only that, the Lord holds his royal court on Sunian day in the month of Bhadra, when his servants and subjects (temple servants and peasants and other holders of temple lands) offer him loyalty and tribute. This Sunian is celebrated also in the Lingaraj temple, and this had been introduced by a former paramount king of Orissa, marking the beginning of an indigenous royal calendar of Orissa. But this should not lead us to expect absolute conformity of the royal services with temple services or *vice versa*. Each system of services has its own pattern of proliferation and development, although basically the same complement of castes renders more or less similar secular and ritual services in the temple as well as in the palace. With this limitation, we may properly appreciate the concept of TEMPLE COMMUNITY developed by M. Mahapatra (1972) under this author's guidance, wherein Lord Lingaraj is seen wielding both ritual and secular authority and performing other roles through kinship, kingship, and property institutions among gods and men in his Ekamra-Kshetra. The temple servants here, as at Puri, invite the God on the occasion of auspicious ceremonies in their families; the funeral pyre is ignited with fire from the temple, at least in the case of Brahman *sevaks*; and the *Daitapati* [descendants of Savara, worshiper of Lord Jagannath] perform "funeral rites" of the Lord when a new set of images is made every twelve years. Besides, the *Daitapati*, *sevaks* take charge of the Lord's decoration, worship, and offering of fruits, etc. from the day the Lord falls ill until the end of the *Car* festival. As the *Daitapati* are considered to be family members

of Lord Jagannath, they share the familial (*gyantisara*) dishes (Mishra
1971: 93–96). All of this very much corroborates Hocart's view that in
India the Church and the State are one (Hocart 1950: 67).

## STRUCTURAL CONSEQUENCES OF GOD-KING AND
## TEMPLE-STATE IDENTITIES

If we accept the implications of the observations made so far, we may
broadly agree with Hocart on the essential identity of the caste organization as mediated through the temple organization and through the
organization of services to the king's establishment. Our assertion is
that such identity is all the more pronounced in the case of state deities
of a kingdom, like Orissa, in which the deity is not monopolistically
owned (as, for example, the Brahman priestly families monopolize Lord
Pandurang of Maharashtra) and in which tribesmen abound, among
whom the caste system has yet to take strong roots. That the two ac-
claimed tribal deities came to be elevated as state deities, one after the
other, opens up a new field of promising research into the building of the
Hindu state, empire, and society in Orissa, much of which was part of
the Dandakaranya forests of the Ramayana era or of Jharkhand jungles
of medieval times; but this is not within the scope of our discussion.

At any rate, we may still consider the major structural consequences
of god-king and temple-state (or palace) identities. First, the caste system became well differentiated; rights and duties as well as hierarchical
relative positions became established with reference ultimately to their
ritual relevance and importance; caste regulations were not only backed
by state authority but also acquired the character of divine dispensa-
tion. This last development can be well documented from the temple
inscriptions or *Sanad* grants by various paramount kings wherein the
caste and other regulations were enjoined upon all including the vassal
chiefs and Brahmans, and which could be transgressed only at the cost
of committing a sin against Lord Jagannath. In this connection,
we may bring in here the supreme council of Brahman scholars at
Lord Jagannath's temple (*Mukti Mandap Pandit Sabha*), which sat in
judgement on caste matters and rituals, among other things. The present building for this *Pandit Sabha* was constructed in 1578. But the
institution appears to be much older than the buildings.

Second, the caste system, in its supposedly ideal differentiation and
elaboration at the temple of the state deity and the palace of the paramount king, became the model for emulation at the temples and palaces

of the vassal princes, with a *Pandit Sabha* of some sort to adjudi-
cate on caste matters. Everything was not necessarily an exact replica
of the model at the state capital and state temple. Actually, the roots
go deep into the Hindu society and polity, where the king is looked
upon as the authority in caste matters and is advised by Brahman
scholars, who together constitute the supreme authority on caste matters
in a princedom. Appeals from the level of the vassal chiefs lay before
the *Mukti Mandap Pandit Sabha,* which had derived royal authority
and divine ordination from the paramount king and the paramount
god, respectively.

Third, the superposition of the state deity, the paramount king, and
the paramount council of *pandits* on caste matters thus signified the
spiritual, political, and social leadership of the Vishnu-Mobile Vishnu
or god-king combination at the heart of the state and society in Orissa.
That the paramount kings derived political sustenance from this trinity
is without question, but that is outside the scope of the present paper.
However, we have seen how the state deity cult was used for political
purposes for achieving subjugation and integration of vassal princedoms
into an empire.


CASTE IN PRINCEDOMS

Although the above structural consequences have been cast in a static,
timeless frame, this is not at all the case objectively. Let us take the
second situation for a closer view, the one in which the caste order,
political setup, and the ritual organization at the level of the princedom
is shown as more or less modeled after the system evolved at the
political and religious centers of the state in Orissa. This author has
tried to throw some light in one of his national lectures (L. K. Mahapatra 1970) on the dual role of the Hindu king as the preserver of, and
also as the catalytic agent for change in, the caste order within his
domain. It can be argued, as Maynard (1972) has done, that in his
original role of maintaining the traditional order, the Raja gradually
also, driven by logic and pragmatism, became the authority to accord
recognition to the relative interactional status attained, in addition to
keeping the relative ascribed status of the castes (apparently) fixed.
This transition from fixity to flux gave the essential leverage to the
caste system insofar as individual castes or their sections could be recognized or not recognized as having this or that ritual or caste status
in a specific politically autonomous domain. It has also been this

author's thesis that in India, as in Orissa, such politically autonomous entities tended to behave as economically and socially autonomous units. This, at any rate, has been the situation in most of the former princely states and zamindaries of Orissa, where the political, economic, and social (caste interactions and status equivalence and hierarchy) boundaries tended to coincide in the recent past. If a caste or its subgroup attains a higher relative status in one princedom, perhaps because of its political or economic power or ritual purity or because of its value to the state or the king himself, this becomes the signal for the same caste or subcaste in other princedoms to claim such higher status. That the *Pandit Sabha* was not always obliging to the king or the castes in their claims is not very important. That this avenue was open to the castes, by going to the local king and *Pandit Sabha*, or by going over their heads to the *Mukti Mandap Sabha* for final judgement in matters of caste rituals and status determination, added an element of dynamism to the caste order. This is not so clearly evident from the traditional model of the caste system, whether in the Hindu scriptures or in early Western "scriptures" on Hindu society. This author has even come across cases of flouting of the decision of the *Mukti Mandap Pandit Sabha* in one or two princedoms. This happened during the late British regime, when the political hold of the descendant of the paramount king of Orissa was nonexistent and the local princes or their people did not need to fear any social or divine retribution, because of the prevalence of overwhelming secular trends towards social and economic freedoms in a countrywide democratic and capitalistic order.

## CASTE DUTIES AS RITUAL SERVICES

It is necessary now to point out two important things. First, in the temples and palaces of princedoms the caste organization did not exhibit as much differentiation and specialization as evidenced in the state deity's temple organization, where services were highly elaborate and sophisticated. In the variety and elaboration of caste-based services, the paramount king's palace and establishment appear to parallel closely the local Jagannath temple.

Second, the tasks allotted to particular families of particular castes in the temple, as well as in the palace, on a hereditary basis came to be invested with sanctity and privilege. It was one's religious duty as well as a privilege to perform the hereditary job, much as the "calling" was a religious duty in Christian medieval Europe. Hence the well-known

Sanskrit saying *Swadharme nidhanam shreyah, parodharmah bhaya-vahah* [one's own duty is the best to perform, others' duties are bound to give fear]. This elevated caste duties to what one might call ritual services. Therefore, transgression of caste duties in general came to be looked upon as sacrilege, not merely an act of criminality, to be punished by the King, the preserver of the social order. According to Hocart, these caste services were born of the sacrifices, especially the public or state sacrifices, whose elaborate, ritual requirements were functionally differentiated, coordinated, and mediated through the caste system. He says,

> ...the caste system is a sacrificial organization, ... the aristocracy are feudal lords constantly involved in rites which require vassals or serfs, because some of these services involve pollution from which the lord must remain free (Hocart 1950:17).

Again, "... the worthy or excellent castes are those which alone are admitted to share in the sacrifice, with whom alone the gods hold converse" (Hocart 1950: 18).

It is very difficult to pronounce on Hocart's theory of origin of caste. The only positive comment one may offer is on its plausibility. The state sacrifice to which he explicitly refers is a king's consecration or priests' installation ceremony. From what is known of such rituals in the palace of the present descendants of the paramount kings of Orissa, it appears that the services are not so elaborate or differentiated as in the temple of Lord Jagannath, although there is close resemblance. Apart from that, there are many vassal Rajas of the former princedoms who had been assigned services in the royal procession and other state ceremonies (Patnaik 1970: 62). One vassal chief was to hold a betel leaf container, another to hold a spittoon, and still others to hold swords, golden canes, or daggers as insignia of royal authority. Such services did not always conform to the royal roles, which the godlike Kshattriya Rajas were supposed to perform, had these services any caste nexus. On the other hand, in the daily and periodic ritual services at the state deity's temple, all the castes from the very low untouchable castes to the Veda-knowing Brahman had their assigned tasks and status inside or outside the temple. Hocart might not have attached importance to the temple organization; at the most important Temple of the Tooth in Ceylon (which he cites as an empirical source of his theory), he notes how all who officiated inside the sanctuary were Buddhist farmers. But inside the temples at Puri and Bhubaneswar several castes have ritual duties. Therefore, even if we do not accept his theory of origin of the caste from public sacrifices because there is a lack of adequate empirical evidence to support it, at least the continuing organization of temple services in Orissa and elsewhere may supply an important basis for his assertion that caste is born of ritual, or caste is a ritual organization. Further, we may, on the basis of the facets of equivalence of the palace and the temple, agree largely with him that,

... the temple and the palace are indistinguishable, for the king represents the gods. Therefore, there is only one word in Sinhalese and in Tamil for both (S. *maligava*; T. *maligai*). The god in his temple has his court, like the king in his palace: smiths, carpenters, potters all work for him (Hocart 1950:68).

Again, we may also go along with him (quite a bit) when he asserts:

... just as each clan has a chieftain, and the whole tribe a chief, so each clan has a temple and the whole tribe a state temple of the chief god. Thus as usual, the human organization reflects the divine, and vice versa, since the two are one.... (Hocart 1927:105).

Hocart, however, goes too far when he says that in India, "every occupation is a priesthood" (Hocart 1950: 16) because all craftsmen, including the dancing girl, worship the objects with which they earn their livelihood. While priesthood is meaningful in the context of a community, and family rituals are far from public ceremonies, we may concede that a degree of sanctity is ascribed thereby to the caste duties, to be performed with reference to their respective religio-ethical norms. But this is true of each caste taken INDIVIDUALLY; there is no clue to how A SYSTEM OF CASTES can be viably organized, put into execution, and maintained over a long period in a particular region.

## CASTE IN VILLAGES

Hocart, however, becomes very effective — as much as a true seer — when it comes to the functioning of caste at the village or intervillage level:

The king's state is reproduced in miniature by his vassals; a farmer has his court, consisting of the personages most essential to the ritual, and so present even in the smallest community, the barber, the washerman, the drummers and so forth (Hocart 1950:68).

Hocart identified the farmers, with much logic, with "feudal lords to whom the others owe certain services, each according to his caste"

(Hocart 1950: 8). If we find fault with him over his ill-chosen epithet, "feudal," what he actually means is clear from the following:

The gods of the farmers, the Maruts, act as Indra's bodyguard. Since divine society is a replica of human society, we must conclude that the farmers are the king's mainstay in battle. They are just as military then as the nobles (Hocart 1950:39).

But Hocart uses a back door to induct the farmers into the sacrificial organization thus: "The farmers . . . are the support on which the monarch and the priesthood rest, and their duty is to feed the sacrifice from their lands and cattle" (Hocart 1950: 39). In the state, which is a ritual organization, the others have other duties and if they cultivate, they do so only to feed themselves (Hocart 1950: 41). We may not agree with him wholeheartedly on the place of the sacrificial organization at the base of the caste system and especially on the role of the farmers *vis-à-vis* the sacrificial organization. For, this role of the farmer also agrees well with the view of the society as a military organization, which he himself pointed out.

However, there is substantive truth in what he says below:

This ritual organization has spread downward to such an extent that the poor cultivators in the jungle have their retainers to play the part which they alone are qualified by heredity to play at births, weddings, and funerals, but these are retainers of the community, the village, not of one lord (Hocart 1950:68).

We must again warn against absolute identities or replicas. The model is set by the court of the paramount king and the temple of the state deity, and the vassal chiefs and the temples, especially the Jagannath temple, in the princedoms largely follow suit. When we come to the village and intervillage level, this model is still valid and is looked upon as ideal, although the circumstances at the operational, interactional level do not allow for a 100 percent compliance. We shall discuss this below. But let us just recall how at the princedom level, representing the subregional organization of castes, the element of dynamism and flux has been as clearly evident in the variations of cirumstances of each caste as in the variations between princedoms. The caste organization at the state deity's temple and the king's palace seems immutable and sets the standard by which the caste status, activities, and norms are to be tested when in doubt or dispute. Thus, this apparent immutability and stability is an important structural aspect of the regional caste system of Orissa.

Let us examine briefly the social structure of villages in Orissa, in the first instance. A large multicaste village usually has a complement of functional castes: blacksmiths, carpenters, barbers, washermen, and Brahmans, with or without potters and astrologers, who have remained, in most cases until recently, in *Jajmani* relationships with the clean castes. In most villages of Orissa the cultivating caste (*Chasa*) or the militia-*cum*-cultivator caste *Khandavat* [the wielders of swords] were the landowning and economically powerful castes, which were served by all the functional castes. They conform to the significant features of DOMINANT CASTES. The *Khandavats* especially behaved like lords and held in many cases military service *jagirs*, although there are some villages whose owners and/or dominant castes were Brahman, braziers (*Kansari*), *Teli* [oilmen], or even fishermen, etc. The dominant castes or at least their representative, the headman of the village, who was appointed by and represented the king, exercised authority over the organization of caste-based services within the microcosm of the village. In many princely states or zamindaries in Orissa, the headman had the power to appoint or evict the village servants of functional castes, and he often took the initiative to bring a washerman or a barber to be settled on some *jagir* land under his control. He, or vicariously his (dominant) caste members, saw to it that the ritual services and other services, performed by the various resident and peripatetic members of other castes serving the village, were attended to properly, without conflict and disruption, and without intruding upon the privileges of other castes. He thus secured what is called by Srinivas VERTICAL SOLIDARITY in the village. We need not go into all the facets beyond pointing out the phenomenon. He also saw to it that all the important agricultural and related rituals and crisis rites for village welfare were performed and each section played its assigned role. In this sense, the headman and the dominant caste ensured the functioning of the village as a ritual, economic, and social organization. Hocart would give pre-eminence to ritual organization and derive the other facets from it. We may not grant him that; but this is not very important.

Although there may be a temple of the village goddess or other minor gods, the rituals are not elaborate and one or two castes (usually a non-Brahman, sometimes even a tribal priest) may be involved in the temple services. Thus, the services of the castes in the area cannot be readily invested with sanctity from their ritual relevance in the temple organization, and no public sacrifices are normally held on a large scale in the villages. But the chief deity is drawn into the caste disputes and into the village organization and well-being because the village assembly and the caste councils usually sit near the abode of the deity.

Thus, the deity's blessings are easily invoked to seal the decisions that are made, or the deity acts as divine witness to the oaths and contracts. There is a belief that the deity will punish a transgressor if case norms are violated. Therefore, although the caste services have their ritual character derived primarily from the temple-palace ritual network, this is also locally reinforced by the involvement of the main deity of the village. The close parallel between this situation at the village level and that at the state level with the state deity and king may easily be perceived.

The question as to why the functional castes are looked upon as village servants and not as servants attached to temporal or spiritual lords can be resolved simply. In the villages there are no such powerful or affluent lords as are available at the capitals of the state or of the princedoms. Basically the peasants have a subsistence economy and do not grow much beyond their needs; hence they have to pool their common resources, village land, or their individual resources to support the members of the functional castes (compare Hocart 1950: 155).

We may also briefly note that the caste headmen in a princedom in Orissa were invested with royal authority by the kings, who formally appointed them. Thus, we find how even at the village and intervillage levels, the gods and the kings have lent their authority and sanctity to the caste organization. It is not meant by this that there is only a filtering down of the great tradition from upper layers of the society or from their acknowledged centers. The very fact that minor gods, caste gods, various local cults and fairs, village headmen or Pargana-heads are of crucial importance in village India indicates that the vitality and importance of local traditions are not to be belittled.

## KING AND HINDUIZATION OF TRIBES

In fact, there is some evidence to show how the king has been instrumental in integrating minor tribal traditions and cults with the higher traditions and cults in a process identified by Marriott (1955) as UNIVERSALIZATION. Thereby the king has often taken some steps to make it easier for a hill tribe to become gradually accepted as a clean Hindu caste. We may consider one case from Orissa as an illustration.

A Hill Bhuiyan priest was worshiping Kanta-Kuanri, a goddess allegedly represented by a *tantrik yantra* found by chance in the area. The Raja of the Benai princely state came to learn of its importance in the Hill Bhuiyan lore and belief, and arranged the annual circuit of the goddess up to the palace temple of the state deity and back to the hill sanctuary. On the way the goddess was worshiped by all castes and tribes inhabiting the villages, where the ritual procession came to scheduled halts. Gradually the tribal goddess became allied to, and even identified with, a form of Durga, a Sanskritic goddess of the Great Tradition, and the Bhuiyan and other low priests of the goddess thus gained higher ritual and social status from the viewpoint of the Hindu society (compare Roy 1935: 104–117).

In the Hindu society of Orissa, there is a hierarchy of gods and goddesses, with the state deity, Lord Jagannath at the top, and the minor tribal gods and spirits at the bottom. The recognition of this hierarchy, as well as the several grades of purity and pollution attached to different occupations and ethnic communities, belongs to an initial phase of the process of Hinduization. To this we may add the other concessions granted by the king in his anxiety to woo the politically dominant tribal group in the region, the Hill Bhuiyan. Prominent among the concessions were that water from them was acceptable to Brahman and all other castes, as if the Bhuiyan were a clean Hindu caste and not *Mlechha*, and that the washermen might serve them at their life-cycle rituals, as in the case of clean Hindu castes. With this background and anchorage on the fringe of the Hindu society, it did not take long for the landholding, dominant, and long-settled cultivators among the Hill Bhuiyan, inhabiting the open plateaus in Bonai and other parts of Sundargarh, who sometimes owned zamindaries as vassals of the Rajas of princely states, to become accepted as a clean Hindu caste of cultivators. They sometimes even claimed status equivalent with the militia-cultivator caste of *Khandavat* (compare Khandavit Bhuiyan, Paik Bhuiyan, Praja Bhuiyan; Roy 1935: Appendix B, XI–XXIV). It is also not without significance that some Bhuiyan families continue to worship the local gods and goddesses as the only appropriate agents for the welfare of all castes. A similar process might have been at work in Bastar in elevating the goddess Danteswary beyond the tribal pale (compare Sinha 1962).

Therefore, the interaction between minor traditions and great traditions is a two-way process and is very complicated. This hierarchy of gods in the Hindu pantheon, the hierarchy of "feudal" lords in princely states in Orissa, and the locally dominant political power of tribal groups and their locally popular and — in the local imagination — also powerful cults of minor gods and goddesses have conjoined to open the avenues to integration with the Hindu castes and Hindu religion. (The Raja of Sambalpur had adopted the tribal goddess, Samalai, worshiped by the local Sahara [Savara], as the state deity, who came to the aid of the state during crisis [S. P. Dash 1962: 301, 303–304, 307–308, 342].) As we have seen above, the Rajas have played a significant role in the creation of new castes not only from among Hindus themselves, but also out of the tribal communities.

Sinha in his brilliant analysis of the state formation and Rajput myth in tribal areas of central India (1962) has thrown significant light on the role of the tribal Rajas and feudal overlords in the spread and intensification of Brahmanical tradition in tribal areas. The induction of ritual specialists and service castes was necessitated by the urge to follow the model of Rajput or Kshattriya rulers. This, in turn, resulted in the introduction of Hindu gods, rituals, festivals, ideas, beliefs, and values (Sinha 1958), besides effecting internal stratification based on grades of assimilation into higher Hindu caste culture and of interaction with higher Hindu castes (Sinha 1962). These processes must have gone on not only in Chhatisgarh and the former Gond states of Madhya Pradesh and in Manbhum areas among the Gond, Bhumij, and allied tribes, but must also have taken place in Orissa princedoms, where most of the princes were either themselves of tribal origin or adopted by the dominant tribal groups or heavily dependent on their tribal supporters.

To sum up, the state deity and the paramount divine king were served by a complement of castes, who attended to various ritual and secular tasks. But, because these tasks were performed for divinities, whether in temples or palaces, caste duties acquired the characteristics of ritual obligations. In this sense, the caste system may be conceived as a ritual organization. As the vassal kings also assumed divinity in the image of the paramount king and as the cult of the state deity spread to the princedoms, caste duties at the level of princedoms were similarly invested with ritual values. At the village levels we find the end point in the progressive decrease in elaboration of caste services, which nevertheless retained ritual character after the model of the paramount king and the vassal princes. The vassal chiefs often played a vital role in integrating the tribal peoples in the caste system by helping to "universalize" some local traditions centering around local gods and cults. These developments in Orissa have parallels elsewhere in India; Hocart's theoretical insights probably have been largely borne out by our empirical study in one cultural region of India.

Let me finish with an attempt to answer the question as to why it is that in the Orissa region, as perhaps nowhere else, the state deity has developed such an elaborate, sophisticated, and differentiated organization of caste-based services. Orissa, known in ancient times as Kalinga, was famous as a center of Jainism and Buddhism, and some merchants of Orissa were among the first disciples of Lord Gautama. It is well known how these two puritanical religions strove to usher in a caste-free (without *varna* and four *ashramas*) society. There must have been widespread, long-standing confusion of castes, anarchy in the performance of traditional duties, and economic disruptions, as pointed out by Maynard (1972), which brought, as a reaction, stiff, standardized norms and regulations to be enforced by the king. The *Kautilyashastra* recites the conventional form of duties of the four *varna* and then goes on to assert, "The observance of duty leads a man to bliss. When it is violated the world will come to an end owing to the confusion of castes and duties. Hence the king shall never allow people to swerve from their duties" (Maynard 1972: 90). This enhancement of royal responsibility to bring back the caste order to its normal efficacy is a plausible guess on the part of Maynard. In Orissa, well known all over India at least since Ashoka's days, it must have been felt that the tribal component of the population would become overpowering if allowed to remain too long outside the Hindu fold. And this could not be allowed because Orissa forms a continuous link with northern, eastern, southern, and central India. In this context it is not surprising suddenly to find Indradyumna, the legendary king of north India, with whom all the gods are pleased and who can go to *Brahmaloka* in his mortal body, coming to Orissa to elevate an unknown tribal god of the local Savara to the status of a supreme deity of the Hindus of India. Similar might have been the attempt by some other king to elevate the local Shiva Linga, worshiped by the Savara, to the status of a deity (Lord Lingaraj) of all-India importance. It is also significant that the great anti-Buddhist saint Shankaracharya is said to have visited Purushottama-Kshetra (Puri), one of the foremost sacred pilgrimage centers in the eighth century, and to have composed the famous *Jagannathashtakam*. A monastery (*math*) established by him was shifted to Puri in the ninth century where it assumed tremendous importance in the management of temple ritual (Mishra 1971: 151–152). The Shaiva King Yayati Keshari, perhaps the same as Mahashivagupta Yayati II of south Koshala, the doyen of the Somavamshi emperors of Orissa, is reputed to have built the Lord Jagannath temple at Puri and the Lord Lingaraj temple at Bhubaneswar, brought Veda-knowing Brahmans from north India, held a famous public horse sacrifice, and to have reestablished Brahmanism in Orissa in the tenth century. As a result, he is popularly designated Indradyumna II (Mishra 1971: 30–32).

The resurrection of Brahmanism was aided by the process of universalization which, it appears, must have been a very ancient and recurrent process in the orthogenetic growth of Indian civilization. But this was especially imperative and expedient in the region known as Dandakaranya or Jharkhand, which was the hinterland of the Orissa coast, where the spread of the Jagannath cult in the interior came in handy for holding up the caste services as ritual obligations, sacred and inviolable. To aid in this process, the Rajas, many of whom were tribal in origin, founded numerous Brahman villages in their princedoms. No wonder, therefore, that "in the Protected States of India few chiefs have retained their position as the paramount caste authority to such an extent as the chief of the Feudatory States of Orissa, a tract long isolated and untouched by modernizing influences" (O'Malley 1932: 64–65). Whether this speculation is valid or not, the fact remains that most of the numerous and powerful tribes inhabiting the northern, western, and southern hills and plateaus, the Bhuiyan, the Bathudi, the Gond, the Binjhal or Binjhwar, large sections of the Kond and Savara, the Bhumia, and the Amanatya, have come to be more or less assimilated to the Hindu peasantry, often considered equivalent in status to a clean caste. For once Elwin (1943) has been proved wrong, because Hinduization has not left the tribesmen in the dungeon of low menial status in Hindu society.

## REFERENCES

BOSE, N. K.
1949   *Hindu Samajer Gadau.* Calcutta: Viswa-Bharati.
BOSE, N. K., et al.
1958   Organization of services in Lingaraj Temple, Bhubaneswar. *Journal of Royal Asiatic Society* 24:2.
BOUGLÉ, C.
1908   *Essais sur le régime des castes.* Paris .
1958   "The essence and reality of the caste system." Introduction to *Contributions to Indian sociology* II. Translated and edited by Louis Dumont and D. F. Pocock. The Hague: Mouton.
DASH, S. N.
1966   *Jagannatha Mandira O Jagannatha Tattwa.* Cuttack: Friends.
DASH, S. P.
1962   *Sambalapura Itihasa.* Sambalpur: S. P. Dash.
DATTA, N. K.
1968   *Origin and growth of caste in India,* volume one (second edition). Calcutta: K. L. Mukhopadhyay.

DUMONT, L., D. F. POCOCK, *editors*
1958    "A. M. Hocart on caste," in *Contributions to Indian sociology*, volume 2. The Hague: Mouton.

ELWIN, VERRIER
1943    *The aboriginals.* Oxford: Oxford University Press.

GHURYE, G. S.
1961    *Caste, class and occupation.* Bombay: Popular Prakashan.

HEINE-GELDERN, R.
1942    Conceptions of state and kingship in South East Asia. *Far Eastern Quarterly* 2:1, 15–30.

HOCART, A. M.
1927    *Kingship.* Oxford: Oxford University Press.
1950    *Caste: a comparative study.* London: Methuen.
1970    *Kings and councillors.* Chicago: University of Chicago Press.

HUTTON, J. H.
1951    *Caste in India.* Oxford: Oxford University Press.

KULKE, HERMANN
i.p.    *Some remarks about the Jagannath trinity.* Heidelberg: South Asian Institute.

MAHAPATRA, L. K.
1970    "The role of the Hindu princes in the caste system in India." National lecture delivered at Ravishankar University, Raipur.

MAHAPATRA, M.
1972    "Lingaraj Temple: its structure and change, circa 1900–1962." Unpublished doctoral dissertation, Utkal University.

MARRIOTT, MC KIM
1955    "Little communities in an indigenous civilization," in *Village India.* Edited by McKim Marriott. Chicago: University of Chicago Press.

MAYNARD, H. J.
1972    Influence of the Indian king upon the growth of caste. *Journal of the Punjab Historical Society* 6:88–100.

MISHRA, K. C.
1971    *The cult of Jagannatha.* Calcutta: K. L. Mukhopadhyay.

O'MALLEY, L. S. S.
1932    *Indian caste customs.* Cambridge: Cambridge University Press.

PANIGRAHI, K. C.
1961    *Archaeological remains at Bhubaneswar.* Bombay: Orient Longmans.

PATNAIK, N.
1970    The recent Rajas of Puri: a study in secularization. *Journal of the Indian Anthropological Society* 5:1–2, 87–114.

ROY, S. C.
1935    *The Hill Bhuiyan of Orissa.* Ranchi: Man in India Office.

SINHA, S. C.
1958    Changes in the cycle of festivals in the Bhumij village. *Journal of Social Research* 1:1.
1962    State formation and Rajput myth in tribal central India. *Man in India* 42:1, 35–80.

1972   *A survey of research in caste.* New Delhi: Indian Council of
       Social Science Research.
SRINIVAS, M. N.
1952   *Religion and society among the Coorgs of south India.* Oxford:
       Oxford University Press.
1955   "The social system of a Mysore village," in *Village India.* Edited
       by McKim Marriott. Chicago: University of Chicago Press.
1966   *Social change in modern India.* New Delhi: Allied.

# Shamanism as a Profession

R. O. MANNING

A number of advantages would accrue if it were possible to analyze the role of the shaman as a profession. First, cross-cultural comparisons with other professions might become possible. Second, a better understanding of the position of the various professions and of entire professional systems as integral segments of cultures might be possible. Third, the establishment of a theory of the professions in which widespread confidence could reside might result. Fourth, a better conception of the professional-service needs of both individual clients and client populations might result. Finally, nothing less than new criteria for the relative development and progress of whole cultures *vis-à-vis* one another might be attainable, criteria which might be superior to the material-domination and nature-domination measures of today. Such criteria might somehow be human-nature oriented, that is, they might have a greater basis in human and social needs than do present measures. An understanding of cross-cultural professional development could lead the way to all of these desirable ends. Some major difficulties stand in the way of such an analysis, however. Foremost among these stands the current concept of profession itself.

## THE CONCEPT OF PROFESSION

The currently accepted concept of profession is an intricately wrought doctrine, the centerpiece of the sociological field of occupations and professions. It is probably unique among major sociological ideas in the manner in which its analytic employment has been restricted to situations of the European type. This has been unfortunate both for the other fields of the social sciences, where it might have proved useful, and for the development of the concept of profession itself.

For those unfamilar with the sociological field of occupations and professions, a brief introduction to the concept of profession may be useful. The term profession itself is old, going back to at least 1610 with reference to "a body of persons engaged in a calling" (*Oxford universal dictionary* 1955: 1593). In 1733 there were references to the professions of arms and acting. Traveling, some skill, and the existence of an occupational fraternity were early associated with the idea. In Germany some "journeymen" carpenters may still travel about the country for several years. Of course, there have long been references to prostitution as, "the oldest profession." The term profession continued into the twentieth century as a popular expression. As time wore on, it became increasingly associated with the prestigious roles of the lawyer, clergyman, and especially the medical doctor. To the twentieth-century layman, then, it became a "folk concept" (Becker 1962: 31) that implied esteem and prolonged formal training — except for the insistently continued, increasingly incongruous application of the term to prostitutes.

Scholarly interest in the social study of the professions began with the 1928 Herbert Spencer Lecture at Oxford by A. M. Carr-Saunders and especially the 1933 publication of *The professions* by A. M. Carr-Saunders and P. A. Wilson. Following Eliot Freidson (1970), we may quote Carr-Saunders and Wilson (1933):

> The system exhibits two principal features, the spontaneous coming together of the practitioners in associations, and the regulative intervention of the State .... It is the purpose of the professional associations to achieve, and of the State, where it intervenes, to grant, some degree of monopoly of function to the practitioners.

The emphasis upon a formal occupational association and licensing by government has continued. However, the sociological development of the concept of profession has increasingly come to focus upon the factors of prestige, public trust, and power, especially with regard to the practice of medicine in the United States, which is taken as the model of all professions everywhere. The fact that the sociological focus has so paralleled the twentieth-century "folk concept" of profession has had its problems. One of these is that nearly all occupations now seem to have formal associations and insist that they enjoy considerable public trust, and so there appears to be a coming, "professionalization of everybody," as a famous monograph has put it (Wilensky 1964). A second difficulty has been the jealous arguments of representatives of various occupational milieus that their occupation is a full and proper profession. The reply that sociologists have developed to these contentions is that BOTH the claims of occupational communities to professional status AND comparisons of relative professionalization are to be avoided, at least when possible (Vollmer and Mills 1966: vii). Sometimes, however, the intellectual worth of the claim of professional status has been so useful that it has not been possible to ignore the argument, e.g. the case of the social worker as argued by E. Greenwood (1957).

Finally, I have argued (1969) that the sociological concept of profession itself has developed into little more than an aggrandizing and legitimating argument for the entrenched professions; that the current concept of profession subtly justifies the prerogatives and power[1] of the leading professions through a circuitous argument. The definition implies that the professions are esteemed because they are so benevolent and that, indeed, they ought to be esteemed because of this benevolence, or:

... in a misleading argument "profession," defined on a basis of prestige and formal education, has been equated with the exercise of power. Instances of "professions" were then defined as having formal, legally recognized "professional" organizations, which is an additional means by which "profession" is equated with power, for such interest groups as have formal organizations ... possess considerable political leverage. The argument then concluded with the observation that these "professions" are also conspicuous for their altruism, their concern for the interests of the general public. There evolved an implicit admonishment to respect and revere the "professions," i.e., the individual practitioners who are possessed of power, education and prestige, and who are also profoundly solicitous of the common good. It now appears that this concept of profession evolved simultaneously as the legitimatory argument for these entrenched interests evolved. The capstone would seem to be the association which a number of writers see between "the professions," as earlier conceived, and as critically reviewed here, and democracy, freedom, or both (Manning 1969).

More to the point as far as shamanism as a profession is concerned (Manning 1969) is an alternative theory of profession, one which invites comparisons of professionalization and of professional relations, both within and across cultures. This theory of the "proto-profession and

---

[1] The American doctor's median salary was reported by the *New York Times* (1971: 27) to be $40,550. The high salary of medical doctors is especially incongruous since so many scholars stress the utter absence of a "pecuniary motive" in the professions (Fichter 1961; Flexner 1915; Gilb 1966: 17; Key 1950: 141; MacIver 1922: 7; Tawney 1921; Vollmer and Mills 1966: 45, 154, 247; Wardwell 1955). Attention is especially drawn to John W. Gustad's remarks (1959: 209; 1960) that the choices by medical doctors of their careers are made "rationally," rather than as a function of personality.

matrix (originating) culture," stresses that a true profession, or PROTO-PROFESSION, to distinguish it from contemporary sociological usage, possesses five attributes. These are discussed next.

## THE ATTRIBUTES OF A PROFESSION

1. *The particular professions presuppose the existence of culture-wide, transcending, professional communities of peers.* Like all communities, the transcending professional communities have their norms, both specific and abstract "values." The boundaries of a particular professional community are usually identical with those of its MATRIX CULTURE. By "matrix culture" is meant the originating or base culture in which a profession is found, in other words, the specific culture which gave birth to that profession. The practice of acupuncture, for example, is coextensive with Chinese culture (or was until recently), and it has not yet been able to extend beyond the boundaries of its matrix culture.

The fact of the coextensiveness of the transcending community and its matrix culture is of some importance. It has not been generally recognized, nor even broached in an analytic approach. This should be no surprise, since neglect of the study of professions OUTSIDE Western society, that is, the anthropological study of the professions, is part and parcel of the relative neglect of the study of nonprestigious and organizationally unimportant professions WITHIN Western society. The earlier definition of profession, i.e. Carr-Saunders' definition, tended to insist that the professions were a uniquely European development, just as earlier generations had insisted that culture itself was uniquely European.

We may indicate briefly the significance of the coextensive character of the transcending professional community and its matrix culture (or sub-culture) by noting several implications. First, support for the hypothesis of the existence of proto-professions is adduced by the fact that a primary postulated attribute, viz. coextensiveness, may be established as a cultural universal. Second, the institutional character of the professions (in the sense of being constructive and continuous and functional) is affirmed by the manner in which the matrix culture and its professions are intertwined. For a basic way in which a culture is conceived is as a *modus operandi* of coping with a given social and physical environment. Professions have a key role in the manner of this coping. Third, a specific ethos will entail particular socialization procedures. The fact that specific professions usually coincide with specific cultures implies that professional socialization must be considered to be a cultural attribute, and not merely as a program of socialization and instruction for practitioners alone. Fourth, many authors have stressed the transcending professional community's independence of the local subcultural community. But unless there is also a clear recognition of the ultimately dependent relationship between the transcending community and its matrix culture, it is implied that the transcending professional community is rather more "free," "scientific," "universal," (Hughes 1963: 667, 668), and generally more impressive than it actually is. This is an additional aggrandizing reference that has occurred in the earlier definition of profession.

2.   *A control of time is afforded the professional practitioner.* The ability and right to control the use of one's time is a necessary, but not a sufficient, attribute of a true profession, that is, a proto-profession. Language is a guide here, for persons in a non-proto-profession are indeed "occupied" (that is, engaged in an "occupation," rather than a "profession"). A nurse's time is certainly not at her discretion in the way that a lawyer's, a physician's, or a prostitute's time is. Certainly a factory worker's fixed hours inhibit his activities in many ways, especially when compared with those of, say, a clergyman, lawyer, professor, etc.

Many persons in clearly non-proto-professional work roles possess this desirable discretion, for example, the self-employed. In the proto-profession, however, it is more than an incidental convenience. It is of very great importance in connection with certain other attributes.

3.   *The true profession is practiced at the edge of extant knowledge.*[2] Informed opinion and proficient technique are the best resort that is available at this point in human knowledge.[3] "Professions," i.e. opinions, are thus as good as may be had. The precise character of this precipice at the temporary terminus of knowing, however, varies greatly with the particular proto-profession. The generality entailed by this theoretical proposition may be difficult to grasp. It is compounded by drastic differences in the rates of growth at these ends of knowledge. The profes-

---

[2]   If I remember correctly, I am indebted to Professor Erwin O. Smigel for first suggesting this.

[3]   This seems at once obvious and difficult to document, but I suspect that many students of the professions will agree with it. See Smigel (1964: 325) on the fact that, "The longer the man on the make stays with the firm and the more responsibility he is given, the closer he comes to areas of legal practice WHERE LAW IS NOT DEFINITE" (emphasis added). Cogan (1953: 36) notes the involvement of the professions with the most basic concerns of man, and H. L. Wilensky (1964: 149–150) writes on the mysteries traditionally associated with esoteric occupational skills. Of course, one sense of "mystery" is the knowledge of craft. Many writers equate the professions with possession of knowledge of the esoteric.

sions apparently randomly comprehend a portion of the arts and a portion of the sciences.[4] Particular professions in the sciences tend to extend knowledge in their fields more rapidly than do others. The ways in which this affects the various contending scientific transcending proto-professional communities is especially well treated in T. S. Kuhn's *The structure of scientific revolutions* (1970). Taken together, those in the sciences may appear to extend knowledge in their areas more rapidly than do those in the arts, but the fact is that "knowledge" is defined differently by the various transcending communities. Radically different conceptions of knowledge imply different techniques of "contributing to" or augmenting the respective fields.

It is the nature of theoretical formulations to be comprehensive, to provide broad generalizations. This is why the full implications of the contention that the proto-profession is practiced at the edge of extant knowledge (and that this varies with the particular proto-profession), may

[4]   For our purposes the arts are distinguishable from the sciences by the manner in which they each acquire knowledge in their respective areas. The arts advance their knowledge by ACCUMULATION, i.e. by preserving, perfecting, and adding new techniques and new insights. The sciences augment their knowledge by THEORETICAL REVISION, i.e. by continually replacing inferior working theories by superior working theories, as indeed is attempted in this paper on the proto-profession. The adjective "working" is useful here to distinguish those theories which are seriously entertained and from which hypotheses are derived, from the prior "theories" which are no longer regarded seriously. Theoretical superiority thus involves (a) greater simplicity and (b) greater comprehensiveness. The objects of scientific theories are explanation and prediction. T. S. Kuhn (1970) deals in detail with these theoretical revisions. What I term "working theories" here, he rather unfortunately called "paradigms," a term which has evoked much criticism and confusion. Kuhn's main point, that professional communities become interest groups supporting particular working theories ("paradigms"), is excellently established.

For several reasons it seems appropriate to introduce a clear distinction between the arts and the sciences. Not the least of these is the common insistence that "professions" are almost uniquely possessed of "theoretical" knowledge (e.g. Barber 1963: 672, 682; Carr-Saunders and Wilson 1933; Cogan 1953: 49; Foote 1953; Goode 1960: 903; Greenwood 1957; Kornhauser 1962: 11; Murray 1909; Reiss, Jr. 1955; Slocum 1966: 123; Vollmer and Mills 1962; Whitehead 1935: 297).

Most social scientists discuss theoretical knowledge and science in a manner that is congruent with the definition given above. However, a number of writers appear to identify the practice of a profession with the arts, rather than with the sciences (e.g. Greenwood 1957; Hughes 1958: 159-160; Reiss, Jr. 1955: 73-74). There is some confusion as to how an art may be theoretical, given the sense of "theoretical" that is understood by most social scientists. The "theoretical" knowledge postulated to be in the possession of the "professions" is vague, nebulous, and appears to be at odds with the usual understanding of the term "theoretical." If the mere existence of a great deal of information is intended (which some writers deny), then many occupations not normally admitted to be professions would qualify as such.

In connection with our thesis that the contemporary treatment of "professions" is aggrandizing and legitimating, it should be pointed out that theory is today associated with science, and that few fields are more impressive in the mind of the general public.

not be readily apparent. It is perhaps best to provide an instance of this attribute in the practice of one profession. Since prostitution has been the age-old example of a profession, we may look to it for confirmation. The prostitute practices at the edge of knowledge since the problem of attaining sexual satisfaction is (a) closely related to the psychology of the individual client, and (b) has only recently been understood, even as a physiological event. Finally, (c) sexual satisfaction is a problem of concern to certain other professions as well, i.e. psychology, psychiatry, medicine, and physiology.[5]

4. *A profession is practiced under a protecting normative umbrella.* The normative system of the transcending professional community entails norms which function to protect the practitioner in several ways (Caplow 1954; Hughes 1937, 1951a, 1951b, 1952). The effect of these is subtle, however, and many apparently commonplace attitudes and beliefs are invested with moral sanctions that actually make the procedures that they imply mandatory. For example, successful practice is usually defined in such a way that persons outside a transcending professional community have few indices of its attainment (Carr-Saunders 1955: 286–287; Fichter 1961; Hughes 1951b, 1963: 656; Meigh 1952). While clients have objectives which they desire to achieve through the good offices of the practitioner, his normative umbrella provides guarantees that the attainment of clients' goals cannot be equated with successful practice. Thus, professional practitioners never guarantee "success," at least not in lay terms. The reasons for this are, first, the norms of the transcending professional community prohibit guarantees of this sort, and second, as noted above, successful practice is defined in such a way that it is virtually untranslatable into clients' goals.

Besides creating a barrier that prevents lay evaluation of success, the protecting normative umbrella guards the practitioner from the inadequately socialized client. The inadequacy of socialization referred to is not the general socialization of the culture or the society in question. This is rather the particular socialization that prospective clients of a proto-profession should, but may not, have acquired as part of their more general socialization experience. This will hereafter be referred to as

---

[5]   Many academic disciplines, especially those that may require elaborate organizational support in their research activities and that do not normally consult with clients or patients, are not *per se* proto-professions. To be rigorous about it, these constitute proto-professions only insofar as they may also be professed in a university, i.e. when the other attributes enumerated here tend to be present. Thus, the existence of a privileged relationship with clients or other such persons (students, in the case of university professing) is necessary.

EXTERNAL SOCIALIZATION, or client-preparation socialization, as opposed to INTERNAL SOCIALIZATION, or practitioner-preparation. It should be noted that a major reason that anthropologists have neglected native proto-professions is that their EXTERNAL SOCIALIZATION for these professions has not been sufficiently adequate to admit them into the client relationship.

The contribution of particular professions to the general societal and cultural socialization procedures, i.e. the significance of EXTERNAL socialization efforts, has not usually been appreciated. This has been touched upon in the discussion of the coextensiveness of the transcending professional communities and their matrix culture. However, when one seeks to establish a client relationship with a proto-professional practitioner, it is apparent that many of the customary introductory procedures have the underlying function of screening those who apply to become clients or patients. In consulting a physician in our own society, for example, the prospective client-patient demonstrates by his responses to a number of essentially trivial stipulations that he has been suitably (i.e. minimally) prepared to enter into the relationship.[6] He demonstrates that he may be expected to follow "doctor's orders" by appearing at the appointed time. He waits to be examined, then follows instructions to disrobe, and so forth. Should he or she abrogate these procedures or otherwise show signs of being inadequately prepared for the client role, the practitioner is free to reject him. *The professional practitioner nearly always retains the prerogative to refuse a client.* This has been explicitly denied by a number of writers, who take pains to stress that not turning away any client is an element in the eminent altruism of the professions: the professions, they claim, are universally bound to give service to whoever may request it (Greenwood 1957; MacIver 1922).[7] This contention ignores the fact that the manner of "requesting" professional attention itself constitutes a test of the external socialization of the prospective client. A stress upon the eminent altruism of the professions has been part of the legitimating argument which followed from the earlier concept of profession.

Clearly there is a relationship between the claim of altruism (the "service orientation") and the statement that those in need of professional

---

[6] Once the relationship has been entered into, it is the responsibility of the practitioner to continue the client's socialization until it reaches the requisite level (Henderson 1935).
[7] This is not to say that the various transcending proto-professional communities do not take whatever steps are possible and convenient to see that their services are reasonably AVAILABLE. The public has been educated to believe that these services are virtually indispensable, and not to see that they were minimally available, as a matter of policy, would be self-defeating. For another author's stress on AVAILABILITY as a central attribute of all professions, see Freund (1963: 693).

services are never rejected. However, close examination shows that the decision as to such need or the possible usefulness of services, if rendered, lies within the discretion of professional competence. It is not that the practitioner as an individual has any special "right" to refuse a client. It is rather that as an adequately socialized professional, he is bound to follow the norms of his transcending professional community.

The effect of these norms is to protect the practitioner (and thus the entire transcending community) from situations in which action can be taken without a reasonable chance of success, as "success" is defined by the profession. Similarly, lawyers may or may not "take a case," and a prostitute may exercise a righteous measure of "self-respect" in reserving the "right" to refuse a prospective client. A physician may insist that professional ethics prohibits his "touching" a case, or that there is "really nothing that he can do" for the person in question. As in the case of "success" of treatment, laymen are not competent to judge otherwise.

It has been pointed out frequently that the professional practitioner is protected in the event of client dissatisfaction. But such protection does not reside merely in the absence of practical formal recourse in law. More certain safeguards are provided by the protecting normative umbrella: he OUGHT not be accepted as a client if he does not conduct himself as he OUGHT. And if he conducts himself as a client (of this profession) should, then no doubt he will understand that he also ought not to seek INFORMAL recourse (personal retaliation, reprisal, abuse, disrespectful acts) nor FORMAL recourse, in the event of dissatisfaction.

The above observations are most conveniently confirmed in an alien culture and an unfamilar proto-profession. The writer well recalls, for example, the elaborate procedures, assurances, and indications of adequate external socialization that were required upon the visit of an Occidental man to a Japanese geisha house.

The protecting normative umbrella also creates the "privileged" client relationship. This usually involves a structured kind of primary-group relationship, but it seems better to conceive of this as the simple development of solidarity between the practititoner and the client, rather than as a primary-group relationship alone. For, in addition to a personal intimacy such that the sanctions of norms peculiar to the relationship may be communicated with fullest facility, there is also an element of hierarchical structuring, with the practitioner exercising control. Of course, the entire "privileged" client-practitioner relationship is an artifact of the norms which the process of professional socialization implants in both the practitioner and the client.

The client-professional relationship is said to be "privileged" because it appears to grant customarily certain immunities and rights, formal (e.g. legal) and informal, depending upon the profession. Perhaps the most important of these is PRIVACY. This centrally important common denominator of the "privileged" relationship does more than simply permit and facilitate confidential information. Privacy, like secrecy (see Simmel 1950), builds solidarity. Thus, it is an important functional constituent in the client-professional relationship. However, insofar as it places the client further under the influence of the practitioner, it also protects the professional and his transcending professional community. For while the professional practitioner is protected by the particular professional socialization of both himself and his client (i.e. by both the internal and external socialization), the intense character of the "privileged" relationship allows the practitioner to further the external socialization of his client.

In an endeavor to distinguish the privileged client relationship from other relationships, it has been contrasted with the customer-salesperson relationship (Greenwood 1957). While this is but one of many situationally defined relationships with which a contrast is possible, emphasis upon this contrast is especially misleading. It is misleading in the same manner in which other aspects of the study of professions have been misleading. "the customer is always right" (Ditz 1968). The status of the professional practitioner is thus contrasted with a status of sharply limited prestige. This leads to the inference that professional practitioners are NECESSARILY persons of high status, which we question.

No doubt some individuals possess more ability, personal power, and greater social honor than others. This is irrefutable. Our objection is simply that these desirable attributes are not uniquely associated with professional work, provided that the nature of this is properly understood. To restate a major contention, it appears likely that the reason that the emphasis on prestige is perpetuated in sociological writings on professions is that it is a premise in an argument the function of which is an unwitting legitimation, justification, and defense of the status quo.

5. *Proto-professional practices are socially licensed.* This licensing is largely of an INFORMAL rather than a FORMAL character. Indeed, the study of exclusively formal instances of licensing may be misleading. Formal licensing is the legalistic consequence of the measure of social recognition granted a particular profession (Caplow 1954: 139–140; Cogan 1953: 47; DeLancy 1938; Hughes 1952, 1955, 1958; Kornhauser 1962: 11; Ross 1923: 477; Slocum 1966: 122; Vollmer and Mills 1966: 13, 247). Licensing is often instituted wherever the society requires the presence of the

elements of a profession, in cases where a mature transcending professional community has not yet evolved. Such formal licensing provides a
temporary expedient in marginal cases where a society's or a culture's
manner of coping with its physical and social environment requires this
development.

A major function of licensing is to define the relationship between
individual practitioners and the general public. Formal licensing is a
formal (legal) normative act with formal and informal normative consequences. The precise nature of licensing is determined by the societal
and cultural norms that were being violated in the absence of the proposed
licensing, or prior to its establishment. Licensing, formal or informal, is
thus essentially accomodative. Its objectives usually entail the creation of
one or more of the four main attributes of the proto-profession already
discussed. Thus, if the mere existence of persons whose skills are proto-
professional in nature is the problem, then the aim of licensing is usually
the establishment of the transcending professional community. Once this
exists, under conditions which permit it to flourish, it will automatically
provide for recruitment. In the reverse situation, where the need is for
persons of non-proto-professional skills, then entirely different social
measures are undertaken, for the problem is much simpler. Appropriate
educational programs alone might suffice. There is no need to create,
encourage, support, and recognize a transcending proto-professional
community. Simpler remedial measures, in the form, say, of enabling
legislation, might accomplish the needed reform. However, a shortage of
practitioners in a particular proto-profession is an inherently more
complex problem. The complexity of the proto-profession requires
correspondingly complex normative innovations. For example, a licensing
board manned either by recognized members of the particular proto-
profession, or, in the absence of these, by members of other acknowledged,
and especially allied, professions, might be the first step. Ideally, of course,
the board would be manned by members of the particular transcending
community. This major step in support of the specific transcending
community would lend the prestige of local or regional authority to the
professional community and its members.

Licensing need not be of a formal and direct kind, however, and the
legitimating authority need not be that of the "State," as A. M. Carr-
Saunders and P. A. Wilson have stressed. For example, the fact that
during the Middle Ages many professions were practiced by persons in
religious orders would seem to indicate that in such cases the informal
licensing authority was, in fact the Church (Carr-Saunders and Wilson
1933: 289–294).

The professions differ from the nonprofessions in their normative intricacy. This revised concept of the profession, the proto-profession, is not intended to be either a model, an archetype, or an ideal type. It is rather a description of one side of the dichotomy dividing labor in a society or culture. It is not to be equated with social honor and education, for some professions fully in possession of the normative intricacy discussed here lack both these. Criminal professions, for example, have highly developed socialization procedures (for prospective clients as well as for practitioners), which are largely informal. This does not mean that they are any less involved or less intense than those found in other professions. Insofar as criminal and exploitative proto-professions and their norms involve greater conflict with the general normative system, the internal socialization task in these milieus must be more formidable. In other words, if "education" is conceived of broadly as socialization, and not as limited to formal, and especially university training, then such professions as that of the safecracker and the prostitute require more "education" than do "respectable" ones.

## THE PROFESSION OF SHAMANISM

Our object in this section is to compare the various ethnographic accounts of shamanistic practice with the conception of profession developed earlier (Manning 1969) and described in the previous section. It will be our contention that the major features of shamanism parallel those found in professions of the European type. With one recent and notable exception, there has been a great neglect of cross-cultural studies of the professions, especially where so-called primitive cultures have been concerned.

The recent and notable exception, Eliot Freidson's 1970 work, *The profession of medicine*, explicitly compares Zande shamanism and medicine as practiced in the United States. Using the conventional model of profession, stressing prestige, social standing, benevolence and the possession of scientific knowledge, he is able to affirm the superiority of American medicine and the relatively weaker power position of shamanistic practitioners among the Zande. Although Freidson is properly critical of many aspects of American medicine and his study is excellent as MEDICAL SOCIOLOGY, as a contribution to the study of occupations and professions it is disappointing. This is not surprising, considering the ethnocentrism of his notion of profession.

The chief point in our concept of the proto-profession is that on a continuum of normative intricacy some "truly professional" roles appear in most cultures. To examine this we may compare the five attributes of the proto-profession with accounts of shamanism. First among these is the attribute of coextensiveness of most professions with their matrix or originating culture. It has been noted that this appears to be a culturally universal fact in itself. That is, most professions have some specific culture as their origin and for some historical period the profession has not been practiced beyond the limits of that culture. Perhaps this has been so obvious as to require no direct comment but there has been sufficient indirect comment to remove any doubts of the validity of the notion. For example: "For each society in which divination is practiced there is, to be sure, a proper list of its occasions" (Park 1967: 234); "the Chinese diviner in Singapore does not receive the same pattern of cases as does the Zulu" (Elliot 1955: 159ff.); "nor has European contact failed to change (by enlargement) the scope of the institution among the Plateau Tonga" (Colson 1958: 79–80). Needless to say, the specifically proper occasions are culturally-defined and bounded. In another place Park notes:

The "field" of ritual in time and space is indefinitely extended to the borders of the social world known to its congregation. By contrast, the "field" of the diviner's séance is restricted, centering upon an immediate problem, and dissipating as distance and time rob the problem of reality" (Park 1967:242).

A second facet, the control by the professional of his time, is easier to establish in non-European societies than in European societies, where rigorous adherence to work schedules is the rule for professional workers. Most recorded instances of shamanism have occurred where individuals may have far more control over the times of their comings and goings than do average Americans or Europeans. The major point here is that the shaman has even greater freedom to depart from schedules and expectations as to his comings and goings. Claude Lévi-Strauss (1967: 25–28) recounts the unusual disappearance in September 1938 of the sorcerer of a band of Nambicuara Indians in central Brazil. Despite rumors that there were political reasons for the sorcerer's convenient disappearance from tribal life at that time, his account that he had been carried off by a thunderstorm could hardly be questioned. The point is not that a fabrication was required in order to gain a leave of absence but that the professional prerogatives of the shaman's life afforded him this measure of freedom and control over his time.

The third attribute of a proto-profession practice at the edge of knowing, is attested by a great wealth of evidence. Both shamanism and magic *per se* are practiced at the edge of knowledge. Indeed, Malinowski's famous theory that magic is resorted to whenever received knowledge disappears is very pertinent. Although referring to the magic used by non-proto-professionals — that is, ordinary people — Malinowski's theory has especial relevance for those whose vocation is magic.

George C. Homans has tried to reconcile Malinowski's theory of magic and Radcliffe-Brown's criticism of the theory. He has done so by suggesting that in any case the ends of knowing are foci of anxiety, and that both Malinowski and Radcliffe-Brown agree about this. It is just that:

Malinowski is looking at the individual, Radcliffe-Brown at society. Malinowski is saying that the individual tends to feel anxiety on certain occasions; Radcliffe-Brown is saying that society expects the individual to feel anxiety on certain occasions ... both statements are true (Homans 1941: 168).

The shaman, as a professional practitioner at the edge of knowledge, is much involved with magic. The anxiety that Homans associates with the positions of both Malinowski and Radcliffe-Brown is encountered by the shaman in his clients or patients. The fact that he works at the temporary terminus of knowing is not concealed from his clients. It is part of the protective normative umbrella upon which all proto-professional practitioners rely. As J. Robin Fox notes, "The doctors maintain that they can only do their best and that the issue is very much in doubt" (Fox 1967: 268). Fox's remark was in reference to Cochiti therapy.

A remark in E. E. Evans-Pritchard's paper on the morphology and function of magic may be quoted here

... new magic is constantly being created, and that it is created by successful men influenced by the rumors of magic which attend their success, and that whilst magic gives men confidence in their undertakings, it also represents a record of man's actual achievement. Primitive man is not a romantic but a practical hardheaded being, even in his magic, and there is no magic to attempt the impossible (Evans-Pritchard 1967:19).

George K. Park feels that working at the edge of knowledge is so important that it virtually defines divination, or as he puts it, "Divination is always, I think, associated with a situation which ... seems to call for decision upon some plan of action which is not easily taken" (Park 1967). Claude Lévi-Strauss also deals with the psychology of the shaman and his awareness of his working with the unknown. In the spiritual crisis during which he became a shaman he "must have been on a journey to the beyond" (Lévi-Strauss 1967: 35-36).

The protective normative umbrella, the fourth attribute of the proto-profession, is connected with the client's knowledge that the practitioner is working at the end of knowledge. The client understands in advance that no guarantees of cures or of the efficacy of the magic can be given.

Too much is unknown. The client's own faith in the practitioner and his magic may well figure in the success of treatment or action taken. Lack of faith is entirely relative and beyond ascertaining.

Thus, the greatest protection the practitioner has is the external socialization of his client. The client's conception and his faith in the practitioner are often crucial to a happy conclusion, but these are but two aspects of external socialization. Another element that is equally powerful is the definition of successful treatment or of action taken. Since a client cannot really judge the efficacy of the treatment, he cannot conclude that it has failed. It merely did not come up to his hopes — which were no doubt ignorant and ill founded, considering the complexities of his case. A well-schooled client also has enough fear of the practitioner or "respect" for him — even one who he might feel has failed him — to reject the idea of taking reprisals or making demands for restitution of the fee he paid.

Like any true professional, the shaman is licensed, the fifth attribute of a proto-profession. He is licensed to depart from the usual norms which govern behavior in his culture. This LICENSING OR AUTHORITATIVELY APPROVED DEVIANCE may be formal or informal. The use of a Roman Catholic title ("Lego") in the case of one of the *curanderos* [medicasters] discussed by Irwin Press, and the presence of religious statues in the offices of other *curanderos* (1968a: 7, 8), implies authoritative approval of their conduct.

George K. Park, similarly, sees the culturally authorized indulgence and toleration of divination as a species of licensing, "As a legitimating procedure, divination in the folk world has much in common with what we may call the 'licensing and certifying complex' in the contemporary urban world" (Park 1967: 252). The measure of formality or explicit social process that is involved in the licensing of shamanism varies with the culture and the particular shamanistic role under consideration. For just as societies of the European type possess hierarchical professional struc-tures, so also do many folk societies (MacDonald 1890: 294–295; Balicki 1963).

Finally, the presence of professional associations may be established in the case of shamanistic pactitioners, as well as among European prac-titioners. These societies, guilds, or cults have their own norms and, if anything, enforce them more strictly than is done in developed societies. Manning Nash notes the case of "a curer who was killed by the rest of the curers for what essentially was a violation of guild rules" (Nash 1967: 132); E. E. Evans-Pritchard, too, notes the significance of the secret societies of Zande practitioners (Evans-Pritchard 1967: 17).

Certainly greater study of the proto-professions of folk societies would show further similarities. For example, the pattern of illicit professions in folk societies parallels the existence of illegal professions in modern society. The most common illicit profession is that of witchcraft, a great blight (Kennedy i.p.), and the object of much shamanistic practice.

## A TYPOLOGY OF PROFESSIONAL RECRUITMENT

The recruitment of both clients and practitioners has long been a prime concern in the sociology of occupations and professions. The application of a revised conception of profession (the proto-profession) appears to shed light on this subject in such a way as to be profitable to both sociologists and anthropologists.

It will be recalled that two kinds of socialization have been distinguished, INTERNAL SOCIALIZATION (or practitioner-preparation) and EXTERNAL SOCIALIZATION (or client-preparation). Remembering that recruitment is intimately related to socialization, we may distinguish similarly between INTERNAL RECRUITMENT (i.e. of practitioners) and EXTERNAL RECRUITMENT (i.e. of clients). The study of shamanism as a profession is helpful here because in the total absence of formal, university-type training, greater attention naturally evolves about the role of socialization in the recruitment of both clients and professions. Thus, recruitment tends to be seen more as an act of intellectual persuasion, involving values and commitment, rather than demographic change. A fourfold table of the two kinds of professional socialization and the two kinds of professional recruitment is helpful here (see Table 1).

Table 1.    Professional socialization and recruitment

|  |  | Resulting Recruitment | |
|  |  | Internal | External |
| --- | --- | --- | --- |
| Type of professional | Internal | Type I | Type II |
| Socialization |  |  |  |
| Causing the recruitment | External | Type III | Type IV |

Type I recruitment describes the recruitment of professional practitioners through the stimulus of internal socialization itself. It may be termed HIERARCHICAL RECRUITMENT, since it especially figures in the upward movement of practitioners within the transcending professional community. This type of recruitment also bears a resemblance to Edwin H. Sutherland's theory of differential socialization (1947) into criminal life. Sutherland's theory itself bears a remarkable resemblance to W. I.

Thomas's statement of 1901, "The gaming instinct." This type of internal recruitment has received a great deal of scholarly attention in sociology. It is potentially applicable to the study of shamanism and other professions of folk societies (Martin and Grigg 1970).

Type II is the PUBLIC-EDUCATION RECRUITMENT of clients, which is an obligation or norm in most professions.

Type III we may term EVANS-PRITCHARDIAN RECRUITMENT, in that it is the mode of practitioner recruitment which he discusses as being particularly common among the Zande (Evans-Pritchard 1967: 19). Claude Lévi-Strauss (1967: 32) also deals with this type of practitioner recruitment. It follows from the external socialization of the specific profession: rumors, incitements, or encouragements nudge the layman into the professional role, or into training for the role. Recruitment results from the fact that the general public through a thoroughly adequate program of external socialization, has come to have an excellent conception of the nature and character of practitioners and candidate-practitioners. On the basis of this knowledge, the public itself urges suitable candidates into the profession. In Western societies this may occur most frequently in the case of candidates for the priesthood, where the public has been made well aware of the importance of "vocations." There has been some attention to this mode of recruitment with regard to professions of the European type, but the sources of external socialization that have encouraged internal recruitment have been limited to parents and teachers (Feldman: 1972).

Type IV external recruitment may be termed DIFFUSION RECRUITMENT, because it follows from the general cultural diffusion of ideas concerning a particular profession and the wisdom of seeking its advice and aid.


CONCLUSION

In its four parts this paper has attempted (1) to present and criticize the currently accepted notion of profession, using the point of view of the sociology of sociology as a point of departure. (2) An alternative theory of profession (or proto-profession, as it has been called) has been offered. (3) Materials on shamanism have been examined with a view to demonstrating the existence of proto-professional practitioners in folk societies, as well as in "developed" ones. A final section (4) has dealt with the interrelated recruitment procedures of clients and practitioners, presenting a fourfold table of socialization and the recruitment resulting from this socialization. The study of shamanistic recruitment, both internal and external, has raised a number of points that are useful to consider in studying professional relations in developed countries. The comparative significance of Type III, or Evans-Pritchardian recruitment, is a particularly interesting concern. Perhaps overreliance on this type of recruitment is to be associated with a disappearance of practitioners. A cycle of Type II (public-education recruitment) and Type IV (diffusion recruitment) may offer the best means of assuring the growth of specific proto-professions. There is recent evidence of this in the case of psychoanalysts, where the mere presence of a practitioner assures an increase in the demand for consultation, so that the demand can never be fully met. Of the four types of recruitment distinguished, only one, Type I, or hierarchical recruitment, has received adequate attention in the sociological studies of internal (practitioner) recruitment in the United States. The fact that Type III, or Evans-Pritchardian recruitment, is especially noted as a means of internal (practitioner) recruitment in the folk world suggests that this deserves further attention in studies elsewhere. In general, there appears to have been a marked neglect of the interrelations between Types I and III, and Types II and IV, or between the respective recruitment procedures for clients and for practitioners. The fact that several writers (Lévi-Strauss 1967: 36; Fox 1967; Messing 1967: 288) stress that a demonstrated competence of external socialization is a prerequisite for internal recruitment makes this look especially promising as an area of research in either modern or folk cultures.

## REFERENCES

BALICKI, ASEN
  1963  "Shamanistic behavior among the Netsilik Eskimos," in *Magic, witchcraft, and curing*. Edited by John Middleton, 191–209. Garden City, New York: Natural History Press. (Originally published 1963 in *Southwestern Journal of Anthropology* 19:380–396.)
BARBER, B.
  1963  Some problems in the sociology of the professions. *Daedalus* 92: 669–688.
BECKER, HOWARD S.
  1962  "The nature of a profession," in *Education for the professions*. Edited by N. B. Henry, 27–46. Chicago: National Society for the Study of Education.
CAPLOW, T.
  1954  *The sociology of work*. Minneapolis: University of Minnesota Press.
CARR-SAUNDERS, A. M.
  1933  "The Herbert Spencer Lecture, given at Oxford in 1928," in *The professions*. Edited by A. M. Carr-Saunders and P. A. Wilson. Oxford: Clarendon Press.

1955    "Metropolitan conditions and traditional professional relationships,"
        in *The metropolis in modern life*. Edited by R. M. Fisher. New York:
        Doubleday.

CARR-SAUNDERS, A. M., P. A. WILSON
1933    *The professions*. Oxford: Clarendon Press.

COGAN, M. L.
1953    Toward a definition of profession. *Harvard Educational Review* 23:
        33–35.

COLSON, E.
1958    *Marriage and family among the Plateau Tonga*. Manchester: Manchester University Press.

COTTRELL, L. S., E. B. SHELDON
1963    Problems of collaboration between social scientists and the practicing
        professions. *The Annals of the American Academy of Political and
        Social Science* 346:127–131.

DE LANCY, F. P.
1938    *The licensing of professions in West Virginia*. Chicago: Foundation
        Press.

DITZ, G. W.
1968    "The salesman's multidimensional mobility and its relation to the
        operational structure and occupational status." Paper presented at
        the Annual Meeting of the Midwest Sociological Society, April 18.

ELLIOTT, A. J. A.
1955    *Chinese spirit-medium cults in Singapore*. London.

EVANS-PRITCHARD, E. E.
1967    "The morphology and function of magic: a comparative study of
        Trobriand and Zande ritual and spells," in *Magic, witchcraft, and
        curing*. Edited by John Middleton, 1–22. Garden City, New York:
        Natural History Press. (Originally published 1929 in *American
        Anthropologist* 31:619–641.)

FELDMAN, SAUL D.
1972    "The fate of Howard S. Becker in survey research: survey research
        and the study of socialization in graduate school." Paper presented
        at the Annual Meeting of the Pacific Sociological Association, April
        10–13.

FICHTER, J. H.
1961    "What determines success?" in *Religion as an occupation, a study in
        the sociology of professions*. Edited by J. H. Fichter, 176–180. South
        Bend, Indiana: University of Notre Dame Press.

FLEXNER, A.
1915    Is social work a profession? *School and Society* 1: 901–911.

FOOTE, N.
1953    The professionalization of labor in Detroit. *American Journal of
        Sociology* 58: 371–380.

FOX, J. ROBIN
1967    "Witchcraft and clanship in Cochiti therapy," in *Magic, witchcraft,
        and curing*. Edited by John Middleton, 255–284. Garden City, New
        York: Natural History Press. (Originally published 1964 in *Magic*,

faith, and healing: studies in primitive psychiatry today. Edited by A. Kiev, 174–200. New York: Free Press of Glencoe.)

FREIDSON, ELIOT
1970   *The profession of medicine.* New York: Dodd, Mead.

FREUND, P. A.
1963   The legal profession. *Daedalus* 92: 689–700.

GILB, C. L.
1966   *Hidden hierarchies: the professions and government.* New York: Harper and Row.

GOODE, W. J.
1960   Encroachment, charlatanism, and the emerging profession: psychology, sociology, and medicine. *American Sociological Review* 25: 902–914.

GREENWOOD, E.
1957   Attributes of a profession. *Social Work* 2:44–55.

GUSTAD, J. W.
1959   The march to a different drummer: another look at college teachers. *Educational Record* 40:209.
1960   *The career decisions of college teachers.* Atlanta: Southern Regional Education Board.

HENDERSON, L. J.
1935   Physician and patient as a social system. *The New England Journal of Medicine* 212:404–413.

HOMANS, G. C.
1941   Anxiety and ritual: the theories of Malinowski and Radcliffe-Brown. *The American Anthropologist* 43:164–172.

HUGHES, E. C.
1937   Institutional office and the person. *American Journal of Sociology* 43: 404–413.
1951a   "Work and the self," in *Social psychology at the crossroads.* Edited by M. Sherif and J. H. Roher, 313–323. New York: Harper.
1951b   Mistakes at work. *Canadian Journal of Economics and Political Science* 17:322–325.
1952   Psychology: science and/or profession. *The American Psychologist* 7: 441–443.
1954   Professional and career problems of sociology. *Transactions of the Second World Congress of Sociology* 1:178–185.
1955   The "Gleichschaltung" of *The German statistical yearbook:* a case of professional neutrality. *The American Statistician* 9:8–11.
1958   *Men and their work.* Glencoe, Illinois: Free Press.
1963   Professionals. *Daedalus* 92:655–668.

KENNEDY, J. G.
i.p.   Psychosocial dynamics of witchcraft systems. *International Journal of Social Psychiatry.* Paper presented at the Annual Meeting of the Pacific Sociological Association, 1968.

KEY, V. O.
1950   *Politics, parties, and pressure groups.* New York: Crowell.

KORNHAUSER, W.
1962   *Scientists in industry: conflict and accomodation.* Berkeley: University of California Press.

KUHN, T. S.
1970   *The structure of scientific revolutions.* Chicago: University of Chicago Press.

LÉVI-STRAUSS, C.
1967   "The sorcerer and his magic," in *Magic, witchcraft, and curing.* Edited by John Middleton, 23–41. Garden City, New York: Natural History Press. (Originally published 1963 in *Structural anthropology.* By C. Lévi-Strauss. New York: Basic Books.)

MAC DONALD, JAMES
1890   Manners, customs, superstitions and religions of South African tribes. *Royal Anthropological Institute of Great Britain and Ireland* 19:264–296.

MAC IVER, R. M.
1922   The social significance of professional ethics. *Annals of the American Academy of Political and Social Science* 101:5–11.

MALINOWSKI, B.
1948   *Magic, science, and religion, and other essays.* Boston: Beacon.

MANNING, R. O.
1969   "Proto-profession and matrix culture: a theoretical analysis of the concept of profession." Paper presented at the Annual Meetings of the Eastern Sociological Society, April 19, the Midwest Sociological Society, May 2, the Pacific Sociological Association, April 26, and the Central States Anthropological Society, May 1.

MARTIN, P. Y., C. M. GRIGG
1970   "Choice among professions: a comparative study of medicine, law and college teaching." Paper presented at the Annual Meeting of the American Sociological Association, September.

MEIGH, S. D.
1952   The implications of membership in a professional body. *British Management Review* 12:126, 133–140.

MESSING, S. D.
1957   "The Highland-Plateau Amhara of Ethiopia." Unpublished doctoral dissertation, University of Pennsylvania, Philadelphia.
1967   "Group therapy and social status in the Zar cult of Ethiopia," in *Magic, witchcraft, and curing.* Edited by John Middleton, 285–293. Garden City, New York: Natural History Press. (Originally published 1958 in *American Anthropologist* 60:1120–1126.)

MURRAY, J. A. H., *editor*
1909   *The new English dictionary,* two volumes. Oxford: Clarendon.

NASH, MANNING
1967   "Witchcraft as social process in a Tzeltal community," in *Magic, witchcraft, and curing.* Edited by John Middleton, 127–133. Garden City, New York: Natural History Press. (Originally published 1961 in *American Indigena* 21:121–126.)

PARK, GEORGE K.
1967   "Divination and its social contexts," in *Magic, witchcraft, and curing.* Edited by John Middleton, 253–254. Garden City, New York: Natural History Press. (Originally published 1963 in *Man: Journal of the Royal Anthropological Institute* 93:195–209.)

*New York Times*
1971   Article on American doctors. *New York Times* (September 13).
PRESS, IRWIN
1968a "Which doctor? MD's, curers and patient preference in Bogotá, Colombia." Paper presented at the Annual Meeting of the Central States Anthropological Society, May 2.
1968b "Urban illness: symptoms and causality among curer and hospital patients in Bogotá." Paper presented at the Annual Meeting of the American Anthropological Association, November 22.
RADCLIFFE-BROWN, A. R.
1933   *The Andaman Islanders.* London.
REISS, A. J., JR.
1955   Occupational mobility of professional workers. *American Sociological Review* 20: 693–700.
ROSS, E. A.
1923   *Principles of sociology.* New York: Century.
SIMMEL, GEORG
1950   "The secret and the secret society," in *The sociology of Georg Simmel.* Edited and translated by K. Wolff, 307–379. Glencoe, Illinois: Free Press.
SLOCUM, W. J.
1966   *Occupational careers: a sociological perspective.* Chicago: Aldine.
SMIGEL, ERWIN O.
1964   *The Wall Street lawyer.* New York: Free Press.
SUTHERLAND, E. H.
1947   *Principles of criminology.* Philadelphia: Lippincott.
TAWNEY, R. H.
1921   *The acquisitive society.* New York: Harcourt, Brace.
THOMAS, W. I.
1901   The gaming instinct. *American Journal of Sociology* 6: 750–763.
VOLLMER, H. M., D. L. MILLS
1962   Nuclear technology and the professionalization of labor. *American Journal of Sociology* 45: 863–869.
VOLLMER, H. M., D. L. MILLS, *editors*
1966   *Professionalization.* Englewood Cliffs, New Jersey: Prentice-Hall.
WARDWELL, W. I.
1955   Strain in a marginal social role. *American Journal of Sociology* 61: 23–25.
WHITEHEAD, A. N.
1935   *Adventures in ideas.* New York: Macmillan.
WILENSKY, H. L.
1964   The professionalization of everyone? *American Journal of Sociology* 70: 137–158.

# Religion and Human Play

EDWARD NORBECK

The expansion of the scope of science in modern times has brought to scholarly consciousness a skein of questions and topics of investigation that could not have existed earlier. As the new topics arise progressively, we are often struck by our blindness in failing to see them earlier. Among the subjects on the horizon of anthropological investigation is the study of human play, a topic which the social sciences and particularly anthropology have either neglected or studied only in part and with restricted goals, generally of bringing some sort of improvement in conditions of social life. Thus, articles on certain facets of the study of human play, such as the play of children and the psychological value of recreation, have been relatively abundant. Only rarely, however, has play been discussed within a wider scope; only very rarely has its intimate connection with religion among historically known societies been a subject of concern. I have elsewhere (Norbeck 1971:48-53) discussed probable reasons for our tardiness in regarding human play as a subject worthy of investigation, and I shall here limit my concern principally to play in its relationship with religion and the bearing upon other subjects of anthropological interest of both play and religion.

As a preliminary step it is necessary to define play and to discuss briefly what appears to be its general significance in human life. Play may be distinguished from other behavior by a distinctive combination of traits. It may be defined as voluntary, in some way pleasurable behavior, that is separated from other activities in time and most markedly separated by a quality of make-believe or transcendence of ordinary perception and ordinary psychic states. The keynote of play is then transcendence, a departure from ordinary states of being to another realm of perception or existence. Its transcendental qualities range from only a slight change from the ordinary to dramatically different behavior and perception. So defined, play includes activities conventionally or often defined as play: games, sports, and other recreational activities, song, dance, wit and humor, and theatrical performances and other forms of mimicry. Also embraced by this definition are all other branches of aesthetics, such as visual art. An especially noteworthy inclusion is psychic transcendence in the forms of fantasy, trance, religious ecstasy, and transcendental states induced by drugs or other means, such as alcohol, hyperoxygenization, and bodily deprivation. Remarkable psychic states of these kinds have probably seldom been regarded as play, but let us note an exception. Conventionally included among the activities of play of children are states of vertigo sought by the children through physical acts such as being swung rapidly by their hands in a circle.

Play is characteristic of the entire mammalian class and among the mammals is so distinctive and, presumably, so biologically fundamental that it is recognizable interspecifically. Like threatening and fearful behavior, acts of play may be perceived as such by members of different species, and actual play sometimes occurs between representatives of species widely separated evolutionally. Human beings, for example, play with dogs, cats, and other domesticated animals, and these animals of different species sometimes play with one another. Among all of the forms of mammalian life, man appears to be the most outstanding player, an animal species that plays from birth, and perhaps earlier than birth, until death, and plays more frequently and in a wider variety of ways than other mammals.

Like all other human behavior, the play of man is uniquely distinctive from the behavior of nonhuman mammals because it is conditioned by culture. Forms of human play differ from society to society in congruence with other aspects of their cultures and in ways of which the members of a society, the players, may be conscious, semiconscious, or wholly unconscious. In the Western world, for example, play has been an evil or, at the least, a foible, a weakness in which we "indulge." We have been thoroughly familiar with this attitude, which is not shared by many non-Western societies, because Christian religious beliefs strongly and explicitly sanctioned work as virtue and play as vice. We have scarcely been aware that the very religion which so labeled play has often at the same time promoted and exalted as acts of piety certain forms of play which, in other guise, it prohibited.

Before proceeding to the main concern of this paper, it is useful to say a few words about the biological and evolutionary significance of play. We have noted that play is characteristic of all mammals. Its incidence or intensity appears to mount in accord with the chain of evolutionary progression leading to *Homo sapiens*. Among mammals, the various species of the order Primates are the foremost players, and man, the pinnacle of our homocentric depiction of evolutionary development, is the greatest player of all. Following the theory of biological evolution, we are obliged to infer that play is innate behavior vital to the existence of mammals and that it has survival value for them. Moreover, since the incidence and intensity of play appear to correlate with the position of species in the evolutionary sequence leading to man, the survival value of play for the species concerned appears also to mount with the position on the evolutionary tree.

Without speculating further about the nature of the biological meaning of play to human beings, we may return to the unspeculative statement that play is universal human behavior, abundantly evident in every society. Its forms are quite sharply limited and, as our earlier brief inventory shows, they may be placed under a small number of categories. These circumstances may be interpreted as one of the many lines of evidence pointing to the essential psychic unity of all races and varieties of human beings.

Let us note especially that during all recorded history until recent times and in all ethnographic accounts of nonliterate societies, play has been intimately associated with religion in a variety of ways. Like the relationship between religion and morality, the connection between play and religion is not necessary or inherent. Modern play is, of course, primarily secular. Morality, play, and religion may all be seen as independent entities, although all three have often been associated in varying degrees. The association of religion with play during most of history is a reflection of the former importance and pervasiveness of religion in human life. Until modern times, horticulture, fishing, hunting, the curing of disease, or any other human activity of importance included beliefs and acts of supernaturalism. As with most ideas and practices of medicine until recent years, these fundamentally secular activities were sometimes identified as religious. These circumstances may be described in the statement that religion has an ancient history of providing for any important activity an interpretation that is often both a validation or motive for performance and also a mantle that permits, fosters, and controls the activity.

The special significance of religion with reference to play has been its role as a permissive-controlling agency, especially of forms of human play that are particularly attractive to human beings but at the same time potentially dangerous to social harmony and individual well-being. The weakening or disappearance of this functional aspect of religion, without replacement by secular institutions fostering an equal degree of social harmony and individual psychic well-being, may be regarded as one of the costs of the transition to modern civilization.

During most of man's history, religion has been the primary vehicle for man's forms of play. Although seldom so recognized or acknowledged by our scholars of religion, whose views of the world remain strongly conditioned by attitudes incorporated in traditional Judaeo-Christian thought, a principal function of religion throughout the world has been the providing of entertainment. The occasions for play throughout the year have been the days of religious events, the annual ceremonial cycle, and the religious events themselves have strongly incorporated acts of play. If all societies of the world are considered, we may say that every form of play, including games, wit and humor, and violent ecstatic states, has been religious behavior. Religion has also been the primary vehicle for painting, sculpture, music, song, dance, drama, and all other forms of aesthetics. In the Western world and among the culturally elaborate societies of Asia, it is only recently that the arts in their most highly developed forms left the patronage of religion. In the Western world, wit and humor lost the sponsorship of religion long ago. So, in ideal or interpretation, if not in actuality, did various other forms of play. Protestant Christianity has been remarkable in the world for its attempts to stamp out any behavior called play for the reason that it was seen as inimical to the Church or to attainment of the goals of virtuous and godly life as defined by the Church. But the Protestant prohibition of play was never complete, for certain forms of play were interpreted as religious activities. Some forms of aesthetics were permitted or fostered, and one form of play that may be seen as potentially disruptive to the social order, ecstatic transcendence, was encouraged and given special approval as an act of piety. As a pious Christian, one might with strong social approval enter states of ecstatic transcendence far more violent and dramatic than those of the young people of today who, illegally and with strong social disapproval, take secular trips induced by drugs.

Few other societies have so strongly attempted to control forms of play. In common with Protestant Christianity, however, many have permissively controlled the potentially dangerous forms of play. The two outstanding examples are states of ecstasy and a class of religious acts, which I have called "rites of reversal," that includes many and sometimes all forms of play.

Ecstasy as an act or phenomenon of religion has a long but uncharted history and has been described as existing in mild or extreme form in probably every society of which we have detailed descriptions of religious behavior. Ecstatic transcendence, identified variously as possession by spiritual beings, vision, revelation, or a psychic state of otherworldliness, has been consciously and unconsciously sought as a religious goal in countless societies. The ability to enter trance has often been a requirement for religious specialists, young men entering social manhood, and for those who are thought to need supernatural aid or approval. As in modern Bali, the entire adult population may sometimes be permitted or encouraged to enter states of trance as a ritual event conferring spiritual benefit. In some societies, transcendence must come "naturally," without adventitious aids. Suggestion and autosuggestion are doubtless always important aids, but in many societies clear-cut mechanical procedures are followed for attaining psychic transcendence. These prominently include bodily deprivation, various extreme forms of self-torture, violent motor behavior such as frenzied dancing, and the ingestion of substances which alter the sensibilities. The taking of drugs derived from plants to reach religious goals of ecstasy is an ancient human custom, particularly well developed among Indians of South America. The use of marijuana in a similar religious context is an ancient custom of India, alive today, where marijuana is prepared and used in many forms, solid, liquid, and as an ingredient of what might be called a cuisine.

In none of these societies has ecstasy, however induced, been viewed as a social problem, and it seems reasonable to think that its socially supportive aspects have outweighed its negative or disruptive effects — under the cultural conditions of the societies concerned. It seems reasonable also to think that transcendence is most frequently, if unconsciously, sought for its own sake, as a form of play with physiological import. Where the ability to enter trance has been a requirement of religious specialization, the trancer must learn to control ecstasy, turning it on and off at will. Without this ability he cannot be a religious specialist of value to the rest of society, but is simply someone in need of the services of a qualified man of religion. Religion may here be seen as interpreting ecstasy, allowing and controlling it, and putting to social use psychologically unstable individuals, themselves psychotherapeutically aided by their calling.

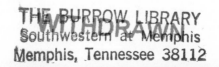

Where psychic transcendence is the privilege or expectation of all members of society, the role of religion seems very clear as a channel for the controlled expression of human behavior that might otherwise be disruptive. Balinese trance dancers are told exactly when and how to enter trance, what to do while entranced, and when to leave trance. It is the same with the taking of marijuana in India and of plant drugs by South American Indians. The opportunity for transcendence is presented, made socially acceptable as an act of religion, and the actors are told precisely when to begin, when to stop, and how to act. At no time is the entranced looked upon as socially deviant.

Rites of reversal similarly include acts that, as everyday events, are potentially dangerous. These rites constitute a large class of acts, mostly regarded as religious events, which have as their keynote the reversal of behavior prevailing at other times. The theme of reversal probably exists in the concepts of every society, and, most frequently, it has been incorporated into religious beliefs and practices. Reversals range from acts that reverse ordinary, colorless procedures of everyday life to which, in their ordinary form, no special significance may be attached. Examples are walking, talking, and dancing "backwards," the wearing of clothing inside out or with the directions the reverse of normal, wearing the clothes of the opposite sex, and prohibitions against ordinary activities of work such as hunting, cultivating plants, fishing, or eating certain foods.

Although no more common than the foregoing acts, another distinguishable subclass of reversals is far more striking, because it has obvious moral import, both to the anthropological observer and to the people concerned. These are customs that expect or require violations of the normal rules of etiquette and morality or constitute a make-believe reversal of the social hierarchy. In some societies many or all of the normal rules of propriety are suspended. Examples are rites of reversal of many societies of Africa and aboriginal North America, the Holy Festival of India, the grand orgiastic festivals of ancient Greece and Rome, and Mardi Gras or Carnival of Europe in its ancient forms. In some societies, theft, bodily assault, obscenity, lewdness, and sexual license were all permitted or expected, and one might with impunity assault verbally or physically his social superiors. Relatives in positions of social conflict, such as young married men and their mothers-in-law or husbands and wives might berate or mock each other without fear of later retaliation, and commoners might, or might be required to, deride rulers for their failings. Incorporated among the rites of reversal are many of the conventional forms of

play, of which derisive wit and humor and mimicry stand out. Transcendence through ingestion of drugs or alcohol might also be included, and the rites throughout are transcendental forms of play in having an aura of make-believe.

The inferable functional significances of rites of reversal are multiple, and I shall here concern myself with them only within the range of the topic of this paper. In these rites, the significance of religion with reference to play may once again be seen as permissive control. In the reversals with moral import, one sees the rites as safety valves, mock or make-believe acts that allow behavior otherwise prohibited, such as the venting of resentment, hostility, or other hateful feelings engendered by social conflict. Expression of these sentiments is done in controlled ways that bring no later social disruption and might well operate to promote future or continued social harmony by inversely sanctioning the norms applying on all except these special occasions. We may note that the most common "reversal" of normal social behavior in sub-Saharan African societies consists of mutual assaults, mock battles, between relatives of a new bride and groom. The assaults are traditional at the time of the wedding, when the bride is "captured," and they may also occur at festive occasions of any other kind for some time after the wedding. The two sets of opponents here are people who at other times must and do preserve harmonious relations but among whom some conflict of interest exists.

The foregoing examples of the role of religion with reference to human play and our interpretation of this role as permissive control may be seen as part of a generalization about religion which has been made many times and in various ways — without reference to play. Religion is seen to interpret human behavior, seemingly, or in fact, to prescribe the behavior, and certainly to motivate, guide, and control it. Except for play, all of the biologically based forms of behavior innate to man have been seen as linked with religion in these ways in numerous societies. Examples are sexual intercourse (of a sexually reproducing species), human sociality (of an inherently social animal), and economic activities (of a species of mammal requiring food and protection from the environment and enemies). It is appropriate to add to this list the biologically based human proclivity to play. In substantiation of our opening statements we may, then, say that until recent times play has also been closely linked with religion.

The relationships of religion and play have various other aspects of anthropological interest. One of these concerns the nature of religious ecstasy and ecstatic states in general. Cultural anthropologists have for many years contributed to our knowledge of the distribution and local variations in forms of religious ecstasy. Such information has long been sufficiently abundant to allow us to state that, like other forms of play, the religious thrill represents the expression, in culturally modified form, of an innate proclivity of man. As a religious act, and in the form peculiar to a given society, ecstasy may or may not be attractive to individual members of that society. In general, however, where religious ecstasy is valued, the number of religious ecstatics is large. Where, as in our own society today, religious ecstasy in extreme form is generally disfavored, its incidence is accordingly low. It appears to be difficult or impossible to distinguish physiologically between religious ecstasy induced by suggestion and auto-suggestion and secular states of transcendence induced by drugs or whatever other means. This circumstance has obvious implications relating to current social and psychological problems connected with the illegal use of so-called psychedelic drugs in our increasingly secular society.

A related question, as yet scarcely voiced in anthropology, concerns the forms of human play, asking about the circumstances that foster the flourishing of certain forms and the discouragement of others. A partial answer may be given by cultural anthropologists by comparing and contrasting the forms of play of various societies and relating them to other aspects of the cultures of these societies (see, for example, Norbeck 1968), as is suggested in the foregoing remarks concerning religious ecstasy in the modern United States. A fuller answer to the question requires the aid of biologists and neurophysiologists who can shed light on the biological significance of play, and thereby also deal with differences among individuals in activities of play.

The connection between religion and play has scholarly and practical implications of still another kind of which hints appear here and there in the preceding pages. This concerns the relationship of work to play, and thereby also concerns a number of scholarly subjects, such as the Protestant ethic, motivation toward achievement, and social problems of our own nation in connection with activities of play. These social problems may be briefly described as difficulties stemming from the inhibition of play which Christianity, particularly Protestantism, has sanctioned. These subjects are interrelated in complex ways and cannot be dealt with satisfactorily in this brief discussion. It is worthy of note, however, that a knowledge of all three subjects — play, work, and associated religious values and customs —

is useful and probably necessary to allow us to gain clear understanding of the subjects as they apply to our own or any other society.

Questions that spring to mind concerning the relationships of religion and play and their connection with scholarly and social issues have no end. I shall mention in conclusion one additional topic of very lively current interest for which information on one common form of religious play may have especially great value. A large group of modern anthropological studies known by various names, including cognitive anthropology, French structuralism, and the study of symbols and symbolism, have included among their stated goals, or have important bearing upon, attempts to delineate modes or structures of human thought that are assumed to be fundamental and panhuman. A recurrent element in many of these studies has been the pointing to examples of binary opposition among societies of the world as a common or universal way of conceptualizing. Most of the examples used to date have been of binary opposition of secular concepts. As I have previously suggested (Norbeck i.p.), transcendental versus ordinary psychic states may be regarded as an example of binary opposition. More important to the goals of these studies is the fact that binary opposition appears to exist in the ideas and practices of religion of most and perhaps all societies of the world. The largest, but as yet essentially untapped, body of information on actual customs of binary opposition is provided by the numerous accounts of rites of reversal among societies of the world of all levels of cultural complexity, rites which most frequently are based upon concepts of opposition of which the actors are often fully conscious. Information available on African societies alone constitutes a massive body of data (for a partial compilation, see Norbeck 1967). Perhaps it may be useful also to regard play and nonplay as being in some sense a pair of psychic-physiological states in binary opposition.

To gain understanding of the nature of human play and religion and their relationships to other aspects of human life as suggested by the various topics and issues mentioned here, the comparative data of cultural anthropology promise to contribute greatly. Yet it seems amply clear that the services of physical anthropology, which has already presented a substantial amount of information on the play of lower primates, and of other scientific specialties, including biology, neurophysiology, psychology, and the various other disciplines of the social sciences, are also necessary.

# REFERENCES

NORBECK, EDWARD
1967    African rituals of conflict. *American Anthropologist* 65:1254–1279. (Reprinted in *Gods and rituals, readings in religious beliefs and practices*. Edited by John Middleton. New York: American Museum of Natural History.)
1968    Human play and its cultural expression. *Humanitas* 5:43–55. (Also available on tape. Behavioral Science Associates Sound Seminars. New York: McGraw-Hill.)
1971    Man at play. *Natural History* (December): 48–53.
i.p.    "Rites of reversal in cross-cultural perspective."

# The Akan Stool Polity: A Political Organization

ALFRED KOFI QUARCOO

In terms of the rather simplified dichotomy of the indigenous West African political systems that we find in the anthropological literature, the political style typified by that of the Akan of modern Ghana is called a "centralized" one. That is, there are centralized, specialized or autonomous political roles and institutions. Such systems existed for example in Benin, old Oyo and Dahomey where the sociopolitical systems are centralized and highly differentiated. In Benin, the *Oba* [king] is at the head of an elaborate political structure with hierarchically arranged court officials, hereditary and appointive positions (see Fortes and Evans-Pritchard 1940; Bradbury 1957; Lloyd 1960). Opposed to this is the situation in which the mechanisms of government are not readily visible or differentiated as among the Lega or the Konkomba (Middleton and Tate 1958).

The Akan statecraft which we call the STOOL POLITY in this essay was highly developed in Asante, and King Osei Tutu, at the instance of his priest friend Okomfo Anokye, gave a special place to the lineage stool as a symbol of chieftainship. Through their efforts a new Asante state evolved where the segmentary social organization of the newcomers in the matrilineage was reflected in the segmentary character of the new state that came into being after the war of liberation with Denkyira (Wilks 1967).

Akan political organization therefore developed by stages, although the overall pattern derived from a basic one with essentially the same structure. It is a form of chieftainship – a system of leadership which is by no means restricted to Ghana. Akan chieftainship is, however, a structure which centers around lineage stools and the sociopolitical competence of these stools. This style of government we designate the AKAN STOOL POLITY, because it grew around, and in relation to, the use of an object of art – the *asesedwa* – a type of Akan stool, as a symbol of office.

The *asesedwa* is crucial not only in government, but in the whole culture. Indeed, its position in the institution of government derived from its various other social roles. Political stools were attached to kin groups in the first instance, but further development accommodated in the system stools that attached to kinship only. The male stools, *mmammadwa*, which developed later in the Akan political system are examples of the expansion we refer to and the dynamism of the system (Quarcoo 1970).

The main feature of the system as it developed is that there were established what might be described as concentric circles of political power or competence rising from lineage levels to community and state aggregations, but there was one center. Smith describes this pattern as one of corporation aggregates related to each other and represented in the corporations' oneness. That is, the "stools" in combination form the structure (Smith 1956: 68).

The Akan of Ghana are the numerically dominant ethnic group in Ghana. A glance at the geographical distribution of ethnic groups clearly indicates this position (see Map 1). Brong Ahafo, Asante, the Western and Central Regions of Ghana are officially Akan. In the Eastern Region, of course, live the Akuapim. Although the Akan generally inherit matrilineally, there are patrilineal groups like the Kyerepongs, the people of Mamfe and Mampong in Akuapim. Male stools, to which a more detailed reference will be made, are of course inherited patrilineally. All Akans claim to be related through a clan system. There are eight well-known matri-clans and eight patri-clans (see Boahen 1966). Table 1 gives a diagrammatic presentation of the principal clans, their moieties, and their symbols.

At various periods in history, Denkyira, Akwamu and Akyem were great political powers among the Akan. Akwamu was at its height around 1681 and so was Akyem (Wilks 1957; Field 1940; Danguah 1928). Before 1700, Denkyira was a very outstanding nation but its power was broken by one of its subordinates – the Asante. By 1730, the most renowned Akan power was Asante. All of these states developed the political structure we call the stool polity, but it is Asante that expanded it. It might be said that the case history of Asante is better known because many of the early documents on the Akan were on

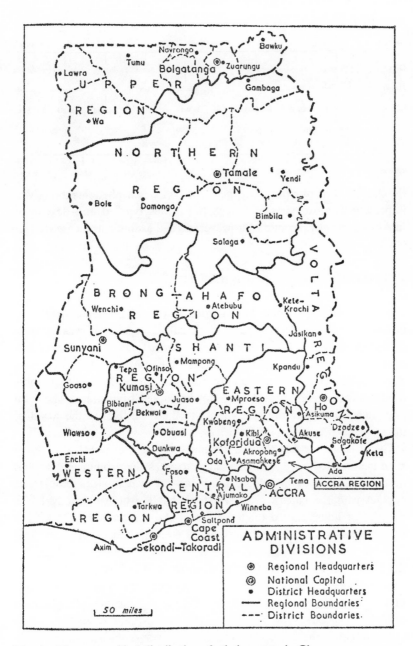

Map 1.  The geographical distribution of ethnic groups in Ghana

Table 1.   Clans of the Akan

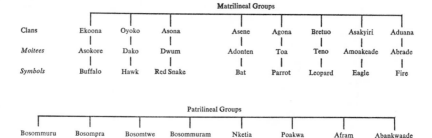

| | | Matrilineal Groups | | | | | | |
|---|---|---|---|---|---|---|---|---|
| Clans | Ekoona | Oyoko | Asona | Asene | Agona | Bretuo | Asakyiri | Aduana |
| Moitees | Asokore | Dako | Dwum | Adonten | Toa | Teno | Amoakeade | Abrade |
| Symbols | Buffalo | Hawk | Red Snake | Bat | Parrot | Leopard | Eagle | Fire |

| | | Patrilineal Groups | | | | | |
|---|---|---|---|---|---|---|---|
| Bosommuru | Bosompra | Bosomtwe | Bosommuram | Nketia | Poakwa | Afram | Abankwaade |

the Asante. For our purpose, the stool polity is a phenomenon which is present in most parts of Ghana but it was typified and developed in Akan generally. Asante is, however, a good example as a case study.

## THE *ASESEDWA* IN AKAN CULTURE

The *asesedwa*, which may be regarded as one of the most significant objects of art in Akan culture, is so called because it was initially carved from the *osese* tree *(Fruntumia elastica)*. *Dwa* means stool and *osese* is the *tree*; thus *asesedwa* means the *osese* stool. Today only chief's stools are carved principally from *osese* trees. Many other stools used in other social context need not be carved from *osese*. The term *asesedwa* today therefore refers more to the form than to the wood of the stool.

Every *asesedwa* has three main parts: the *animu* [seat], the *annan* base is so called because that section touches the ground and gets in or *mfinifini* [leg or middle section] and the *wiaboo* [the base]. The contact with the earth's crust. A stool that is whole normally has a number of holes carved on the sides of the shorter parts. There are usually *pua* [knobs] below the upward flaring sides of the seat. The social significance of these features now is unfortunately not clear, but the knobs act as handles for the stool when it is being lifted. Of the three sections the middle part continues to be very important in terms of the aesthetic, historical and sociological significance. This section often bears specific symbols with definite meaning and function.

Historically, the *asesedwa* type of stool was known and carved in Akan long before King Osei Tutu of Asante placed a special premium on it and made it the principal symbol of political office. A story is told that after the conquest of Denkyira, the people of modern Ahwia, who now live only six miles from Kumasi, the Asante capital, introduced the art from Denkyira. Investigation into the origins of the art suggests that the various stories we get are legendary and in some cases even mythical. History, however, seems to establish the fact that it was the Asante that popularized its use in politics and government.

Generally, the *asesedwa* is an art object which is nevertheless utilitarian. Its importance is domestic as well as societal. It was apparently first used as a seat, but institutions grew around and in relation to this object of art to make it the most socially significant material object of the culture. Stools vary in design, size and social importance. There are children's stools, female stools, bridal stools, men's stools, priest's stools, and chief's stools. Each kind has a number of divisions. Kyerematen's summary of the social function of the *asesedwa* is very crisp and adroit. He writes:

Among the settled peoples of the South, acquisition of a stool was regarded as a prime necessity. The first gift to be made by a father to his child when the later began to crawl was a stool. Crawling signified that the child had come to stay. A young girl undergoing the rite to mark her attainment of puberty was placed on a stool and it was customary for a husband to present his newly married wife with a stool to make sure of keeping her. It was on a stool that a deceased person was bathed before being laid in state. Because of this close association between a person and his stool — there is a saying that there can be no secrets between a man and his stool — it was believed that his spirit inhabited the stool which he regularly used and this persisted even after death. Hence one was expected, when vacating one's stool, to tilt it on its side, to prevent some one else's spirit or evil from occupying it. (Kyerematen 1964: 11–12).

## PERSONAL LINEAGE STOOLS

It appears that the stool, which in time became the first item of an inheritance or legacy, built around itself a special significance. As lineages grew one may assume that personal stools of certain individuals became correspondingly important. Heads of lineages might pass down their stools to their posterity, and such stools helped to present and preserve the presence of the departed elders. Elsewhere, I have suggested that the importance of such inherited stools is related to the importance of the matrilineal bond in the social structure. Similarly, the patrilineal groups trace descent from the patrilineal ancestor or "stool." Therefore, crucially, *succession to political offices normally went down to those who inherited chiefs' lineage stools.* Like other lineage stools, chiefs' stools gave the right to inheritance, but the chief's lineage stools also legitimized the authority the occupant exercized over the people, or rather this authority was symbolized by the stool. The lineage, therefore, is an important social unit and lineage stools — which as a rule began as personal stools — are the principal symbols of office. The offices that the incumbents of the stools hold are stool offices. When one stool becomes the *primus inter pares*, the other stools in the Akan system in time align themselves in a pattern with specific competences in a governmental structure. Once a lineage stool has been accepted as the stool of the collectivity, it becomes something like the stool for investing political power to successive heads. Successive heads however continue to have specific personal stools which may be kept as monuments in remembrance of them. So that although the purport is specific it allows this usage which helps to present historical charters of past leaders and the periods in which they lived.

The lineage stools therefore represent discrete collectivities. They remind the living of the ancestors and provide symbols of group identity and solidarity. Some light is thrown on the process by which lineage stools graduate to the status of town or state stools by Danguah.

A family stool, by means of the influence and process and intelligence, or sagacity of its occupants can become a town stool, tribal stool, provincial stool, and at last the paramount or national stool. Having attained this pinnacle of success by gradual evolution, the paramount stool comes to be looked upon as endowed with supernatural powers and consequently no power on earth should attempt to undo what the gods have brought to perfection. It becomes sacred to the nation or tribe. It becomes an object of worship. The spirit of their history, the soul of their ancestry and tradition come to be enshrouded and enshrined within it (Danguah 1928: 114).

The point of stools attaining or being given specific places in a polity is important. Each lineage stool symbolizes and embraces the spirits of all the dead and living of that unit, and the apex stool is regarded as embracing the whole community of lineages. The stool occupant is the link not only between the living and the dead but also with the yet unborn. Each lineage is a political unit (Busia 1958: 2) and elders of the lineages may be counseillors of the lineage chiefs who in turn will be councillors of the village or town or constituent chiefs of a kingdom. The political structure, therefore, is made up of tiers of lineage stools and stool offices with a resultant complex system of rights and interactions.

Reviewing the Akan political system in an essay comparing English, Gold Coast, Akan, and Fanti laws relating to absolute rights of individuals, W. E. G. Sekyi, a lawyer, philosopher and politician suggested that the political community may be compared with concentric circles of people around a founding ancestor which make definable corporate bodies. We may say that, more appropriately, the pattern is one of foci of stools and stool offices which represent aggregations of ancestors in specific political juxtaposition to founding or dominant ancestors and other ancestors (Sekyi n.d.). Rattray made a similar analysis of the situation when he pointed out in his *Ashanti law and constitution* that tiers of stools represented peoples over whom the stools had jurisdiction (Rattray 1929: 63).

Aggregations through migrations were also believed to have helped to form political groups around stools. Busia illustrates this pattern by his material on the Wenchi people of Ghana (Busia 1958: 4). Villages were supposed, in some cases, to have formed around the supreme chief or rather stool, because those villages also grew around the stools, the general pattern therefore being lineages taking particular political positions over a period of time.

There are a few stools in Akan, however, that were supposed to have appeared suddenly, and these stools have mythical or legendary stories to back their competences. In the main, such stools tended to be the lineage stools of the dominant lineages within a defined political community. Hence the *Abakandwa* – meaning *abakan-* [that which came first] and *dwa* [stool], the stool that came first – was the supreme stool of the Denkyira power which was supplanted by the Asante power. The Asante, of course, had the famous Golden Stool which came into being after their successful overthrow of Dwenkyian during the early part of the eighteenth century.

In Denkyira, stools were specially arranged as were people in the political organization, and this was also the arrangement of their combat forces in war. The apex stool was the *Abakandwa*. On the right side of the king whose throne was the *Abakandwa*, was the *Nifahene* [the right-wing chief]. His stool was the *Kyerefem* stool. The left-wing chief had the *Akumatire* stool. That of the chief of the advance guard was called the *Adonten*. The rear guard chief was known as the *Kyidom* [the back army]. The *Twafo* stool was the stool of the scouts (Kuma 1965). The respective positions were kept in war and this formation has been referred to as the *Pesua* [the horseshoe strategy].

This kind of wing chief system persisted in all Akan political structures and is a feature of the framework of the balance of political power which is the main feature of the Akan stool polity. Akwamu and Akim are the other Akan groups in which the Akan stool polity was most visible. In the case of Asante the coming of the Golden Stool was one of the greatest landmarks in Akan political history. The stools of the states of Jueben, Manpong, Nsuta and Bekwai which initially came together for the war of independence against Denkyira had their distinct stool polities (see Busia 1958: 85). They formed the Asante union. To reduce the individual and strong allegiances to their respective states called the *amantoo*, the Golden Stool was created as a symbol of the federation. There are on record cases of attempted secessions at different periods by some members of this federation which were curbed by other members of the union who saw fame in their togetherness.

The Golden Stool provided, therefore, a definite POLITICAL THEORY, although the incident did not create the theory. The event nevertheless enlarged upon the idea of the *asesedwa* in politics which had already developed. The stool did not usher in a Republican Constitution. It gave a new dimension to a known monarchical system in which the ruler was not above but under the law crystalized in that object of art — the stool. Social and criminal laws were promulgated by the incumbent and the Oyoko lineage based in Kumasi continued to supply the incumbents of the stool (see Kyerematen 1969). What happened was a shifting of an overall national allegiance to a stool, so it was regarded as one in which all the others were subsumed. This was the point of the submission of all the stools of the other constituent states to be processed and absorbed into the Golden Stool of the new Asante nation. The Golden Stool was to DOCUMENT AND WITNESS the event of the political union. In this instance, the Golden Stool was also the charter that was signed to establish the union. It became the coronation stool of the kings of Asante from that day.

In most of the Akan states of Ghana, there is or are stools which serve in this capacity. In Akin Abuakwa and Akwamu the paramount stools are also regarded in the same light.

## CREATION OF OTHER STOOLS IN THE STOOL POLITY

Akan stool politics have been dynamic. Lineages may develop by accretion or by addition effected through migrations. As there were increases in lineages, stool offices increased. Later, another dimension of office emerged to augment the process of government. As the political domain of Asante grew, elders in constituent states could be asked to oversee lands far away from their areas. Eventually, some levels of offices became free of matrilineal lineage attachments, while, for example, the military organizations of the *amantoo* [constituent states] continued to be largely lineage based. The later military organization of Kumasi began to give way to groups not based on lineages but on military considerations and powers. Instead of lineages, there were *fekuo* [parties] composed of different clan members with leaders who were titled *asafohenfo* [chiefs of groupings or captains] (Busia 1958: 90). With this developed the male stools or *mmammadwa*. This also enhanced the Asante political administration – the administration which was present in other Akan states. *Mmammadwa* attached to kinship only and not offices. The way some of the stools were inherited gave some early observers the notion that the Akan political stools would become patrilineal. Indeed, some patrilineal stools are very important in Akan. Hence the *Abontendomhenedwa* of Kyebi is normally ranked with the next highest stools after the supreme stool of Akyem Abuakwa stool polity. *Mmammadwa* and other offices therefore helped to enlarge the system of government which was essentially lineage based.

## STOOLS AND LEGITIMIZATION OF AUTHORITY

We recall that the Akan *asesedwa* is the highest symbol of political office and that it is by means of a stool that the political authority of a chief is legitimized. At all the levels of political leadership in a given community, chiefs were nominated, elected, and installed or enstooled. The enstoolment is a process by which the elected incumbent is ritually placed on the *animu* of the stool making sure, however, that his buttocks do not touch the stool (see Danguah 1928; Busia 1958: 13; Quarcoo 1970: 105-112). Chiefs swear to their elders and to their people that they will live by their oath of office, the content of which is clearly known but again stated to them on the day they make their declaration. Subordinate chiefs swear to their higher chiefs and, in each case, it is essentially to the stool, which stands for the collectivity, that they swear. The elders also swear to the chief that they will uphold him so long as he lives up to expectations. If he fails in the future to respect his oath, he is destooled. That is, he is dismissed from office. So that, imbedded in the constitution of the stool polity is destoolment.

In Akan, it is a female official called the queen mother who nominates a candidate from the ruling lineage of which she is female head. She becomes the king's principal adviser. Failure to do this may end in her own destoolment, because she too, like the king, holds a stool office. There are qualities which are expected of a good candidate. Among these, he is expected to be respectful, he should be without any physical blemish, he must be temperate in all things, and must respect other people's rights.

By the enstoolment of a leader, he, it is supposed, inherits the social personality of all the chiefs that have gone before him. He is referred to as *Nana*, that is, "grandfather" or "ancestor," regardless of his age. He receives the reverence due to grandfathers or ancestors by all. Indeed, he becomes the bridge between the dead ancestors and the living people over whom he is set. The late Ghanaian lawyer and philosopher Mr. W. E. G. Sekyi is known to have paralleled what happens at enstoolment with the idea of apostolic succession of the Christian Church. By the same object of the stool, the new chief's power is held in check and this is what the stool is meant to embody – a political theory and constitutional norms.

## THE STOOLS AS HISTORICAL CHARTERS

Apart from the coronation stools, chiefs usually have personal stools, which after their deaths are treated and kept as monuments to their memory. Not all chiefs get their stools so preserved. Personal stools of chiefs are preserved by blackening them with egg yolk and soot, if the chiefs died while still the incumbents of their respective stools. Destooled chiefs have normally no black stools. That is, their historical charters are excluded from what we may call the library of physically recorded history. The so-called black stools are not objects of worship as gods. For one thing, the ancestors are part and parcel of the collectivity or community, so they cannot be worshiped. Since they are spirit, however, they can be used, according to the belief system, as intermediaries. The black stools are therefore sociologically essentially records of people's activities and history. They are objects of reverence, although the reverence given to them may be seen in some cases almost as worship of these objects. Whether or not ancestral stools are objects of worship is not the issue with which we are particularly concerned here. The aspect which is unknown or very lightly stressed, if at all, is what we underscore, namely, that such stools are historical records. Thus, although the language of the symbol is specific, stools allow for a number of usages including preservation of history and retention of contact with the departed leaders.

Of course, the leaders were linked with the people they led and, by this fact of association, the ancestors as a whole receive their due respect and remembrance. It is because of this special place of the stool that chiefs who break their promises are dispossessed of their authority, and their stools are not preserved in this special way. For example

King Kofi Karikari was set aside in 1874 and Osei Kwame in 1800. King Karikari was supposed to have been rude to his elders who occupied some of the constituent state stools. For being drunkards, chiefs Kwabena Aboagye of Asumegya, Kwabena Bruku, and Kwasi Ten were destooled. It is interesting to note that gluttony was regarded as being bad enough in a leader to warrant his destoolment. One chief named Kwame Asona was dealing in obnoxious charms and medicines, and so he was stripped of his office. For having an abusive tongue and being disrespectful to his elders and their advice to him, Akuamca Panyin lost his office. Other interesting incidents of destoolment include the cases of Osei Yaw Akoto who suffered destoolment because he was prone to disclosing or referring to people's slave ancestry and the dethronement of Mensa Bonsu for being excessively cruel (Busia 1958: 21–22). Such chiefs would normally not have black stools and their place in history is notorious rather than famous.

One point that may be added is that a chief could not be removed unless he had been impeached by his elders and subchiefs, if he had any, and found guilty. Naturally, relationships between the impeachers and the impeached get strained. In the interest of future good government, therefore, restraint is exercised before anyone is impeached, if he is impeached at all. In the Akan stool polity, therefore, these historical records operate apart from the coronation stool or stools. We talk about stool or stools because while in some Akan states only one of the stools so kept is the coronation stool, in others any one of a selected few may be used. The former is true of the union of Asante – that is the Asantehene and the latter, of Akropong Akuapim in the Eastern Region of Ghana.

A group in the Akan political system whose voice must be heard either in enstoolment or destoolment is the *mmerante* [the young men]. They are also called the *nkwankwaa* [the commoners]. They formed part of the *asafo* [military companies]. Some few years ago, this kind of group was rather too powerful in Akyem Abuakwa, again in the Eastern Region of Ghana (Danguah 1928).

Constitutionally, the Akan stool polity abhors tyranny. The chief is under the law and not above it. This is why he ceases to be the people's ruler if and when he disrespects his oath of office. A politically inactive group is that which tolerates a leader who fails them. Every one in an Akan political community has a kind of political representation through lineage stools. Political representation becomes a matter of course through one's membership in a lineage which is represented in the polity by a stool. Of course, as we have outlined, the apex stool tends to be only a *primus inter pares*, and the lineage-based nature of the stools does not, it would seem, make the political structure necessarily undemocratic. At each level of the polity, the pattern is one in which the chief is under the law although he is, at the same time, the representative of the ancestors as a whole.

## LINEAGE STOOLS AND CONTEMPORARY GHANA

We have attempted so far to trace the development of what we have called the stool polity in Akanland of Ghana, but at this point, we must indicate that this kind of political organization is universal in all but the Northern and Upper Regions. Even in these two regions the framework of political organization is similar. Here the "skin" (that is types of animal skins) replaces the stool of the south as the principal symbol of authority or political power. Chieftainship continues to be an important institution of government. It is still lineage based. Lineage heads, or rather representatives of lineages which are today political aggregations, are elected to councils which are sometimes referred to as councils of natural rulers. The resilience of the stool polity as an institution is remarkable. Through the process of friendship, conquest or acculturation the ways chiefs are chosen and installed are similar throughout Ghana. While among the Akan, the queen mother continues to be the prime nominator of a chief, a class of officials called stool fathers developed to become king makers in patrilineal communities such as those among a majority of the Ga and Dangbe of Ghana. There have been some changes in some institutions and items of the stool complex. By the stool complex, we mean the supporting regalia and personnel servicing the stool polity. Attachment to a stool continues to give usufruct rights in land although usufruct rights can now be purchased or leased.

An African king [here, more appropriately an Akan chief] is not an ordinary despot, or other irresponsible person, but as a matter of fact, the first among his equals, and controlled by them in council which represents the people and expresses their will. (Alicoe n.d.: 1).

This description of a Ghanaian chief is still valid and the balances and checks in the institution, theoretically at least, still operate. The voice of the commoners must be heard. Although it is lineage based, it is a democratic institution.

At different points in the history of chieftainship in Ghana the institution went through a number of crises. The educated "elite" tried during the second half of the nineteenth and the beginning of the twentieth centuries to relegate the institution to the background. Some contemporary politicians today have tried to dismantle the institution. Sooner or later any one of the contemporary politicians who tried to destroy the institution learned that he was somehow cutting against the grain; for the institution continues to symbolize or rather EPITOMIZE, the culture. The stool polity is still a very effective machinery for government and communication. Under the dominion status and also after independence, in the First Republican Constitution of Ghana, the place of chiefs was guaranteed. The position was the same under the army regimes of 1966 and 1972. The interregnum government under the Second Republican Constitution enshrined the place of chieftainship as an aid to the government of Ghana.

Under Articles 153-155 of Chapter sixteen of the 1969 Republican Constitution of Ghana, the place of chiefs was actually spelled out. Article 153 states that the institution of chieftaincy together with traditional councils as established by customary law and usage is hereby guaranteed. The political history of Ghana indicates that chieftainship has had many trials, difficulties and inadequacies in contemporary Ghana. However, the institution has, at the same time, proved a very viable, most widely understood and utilized and stable institution. The triumph of chieftainship over many strains and stresses in modern Ghana makes its scientific and detailed study important. It is significant to note that the respect, for example, that the king of Asante receives in this day and age is similar to that which his predecessors had in the past. It is likely that the sentiment which aroused the people of Asante to go to war in 1900 is still there among the Asante for their supreme stool.

It is noteworthy that the first prime minister and president of modern Ghana encouraged the introduction of stool art into the parliament house. The presidential chair in parliament was a combined kind of *asesedwa* with a *hwedom* [a chair-with-back type of stool]. The mace of Ghana is silver and gold with a head molded in the form of a bird — the eagle. It rests perpendicularly and not horizontally on the table.

CONCLUSION

It is significant that the machinery of political administration provided by the stool polity continues to be very relevant to urban and especially rural Ghana. Lineage stools are therefore still important. The full force of the institution of chieftainship tended to be absent in very cosmopolitan towns where the restricted norms of the indigenous populations are not enforceable. Chieftainship on Cape Coast waned during the early part of the twentieth century, but the picture seems to be different with the spirit of cultural revivalism which swept over Ghana a few years ago. In Kumasi, however, the picture is different in spite of the mixed composition of the population. Asante chieftainship remains an example of the strong and virile nature of the stool polity. Indeed, in most parts of Asante and Akanland generally, the institution of chieftainship is the kind of government that is understood and the effective means of communication at the community level. The overall picture, however, appears to suggest that the institution is more effective in rural than it is in urban Ghana. At present, of course, it is difficult to categorize Ghana strictly into rural and urban, and the rural-urban dichotomy is unreal. In some cases what are generally designated as urban conditions do not exist at all in places so styled.

When it comes to interpersonal problems and civil suits against one another, the chiefs continue to be preferred by most people to the courts of the present central administration. A case study of Mampong in Asante undertaken recently confirms this observation. There, the chief was approached for arbitration in different cases ranging from quarrels and fights between husbands and wives and rival wives to land cases and even cases of a criminal nature. What he did with criminal cases, or cases he found were above his jurisdiction as stated by the present law of the land, was to pass them on to the magistrates' courts. In the past however, most of such cases would have been dealt with by him as the occupant of the supreme political lineage stool in Mampong.

The impartial observation of the political style which we have called the STOOL POLITY suggests that it might well be disastrous to relegate the institution forcibly to the background. This is so because it appears the stool polity is not an obsolete and anachronistic institution yet in the Ghanaian context. This is not a suggestion that it should be retained even if and when it becomes decadent. It is not a moral pronouncement but a suggestion that in the present circumstances the stool polity is sociologically a significant institution. A recent trend among highly literate persons to be willing to accept stool offices is very significant. A few years ago the feeling probably was that chieftaincy was a dying institution, especially with the new militant political elite and universal adult suffrage as practiced in the Westminster style of government. Paradoxically, the study of the family in Ghana appears to need more critical attention in relation to its sociopolitical importance. The stool polity — the kind of centralized political system that was described in books about Asante and Akan, and later about other parts of Ghana — has been dynamic, but the central core of it has been the same. That the system has been resilient and sociologically significant through many years makes a more detailed study of it desirable, and the study will be greatly illuminated by way of the examination of this material culture — the *asesedwa* as a symbol of office, and the stool complex as supplementary art and personnel of the stool office.

## REFERENCES

*References Cited in the Text*

AKUFFU, B. S.
1945    *Ahenfie Adesua*. Studies in Akan Customs and Institutions 1. Exeter.
ALICOE, THOMAS
n.d.    *Evolution of Gold Coast chiefship*. Sheffield: Sheffield Telegraph and Star.
*Basel Church Notes*
n.d.    By courtesy of Nene Akrobetto, Paramount Chief of Yilo Krobo, Ghana.
BLAKE, J. W.
1960    *European beginnings in West Africa, 1454–1578;* 1:56. London: Longman Green.
BOAHEN, ADU A.
1966    The origin of the Akan. *Ghana Notes and Queries* 9:3–10.
BONSU, OSEI
1938    Wood carving by the wood carver of Asantehene. *Teachers' Journal* (Gold Coast) 18:3, 269–270.
BOSMAN, W.
1705    *A new and accurate description of the Guinea*. (Translated from the Dutch). Published in Wolf (1958).
BRADBURY, R. E.
1957    *The Benin kingdom and the Edo speaking peoples of western Nigeria*. Ethnographic Survey of Africa: West Africa 13. London: Oxford University Press for the International African Institute.
BUSIA, K. A.
1958    *The position of the chief in the modern political system in Ashanti*. London: Oxford University Press for the International African Institute.
DANGUAH, J. B.
1928    The culture of the Akan. *Africa* 22:4.

DUA AGYEMAN
  1964   *Ashanti stool histories.* Source material in the library of the Institute of African Studies. Legon, Ghana.

FAGE, J. D.
  1961   *Ghana historical interpretation.* Madison: University of Wisconsin Press.

FIELD, M. J.
  1940   *Social organization of the Ga people.* London: Crown Agents for the Colonies.

FORTES, M.
  1969   *Kinship and social order: the legacy of Lewis Morgan.* Chicago: Aldine.

FORTES, M., E. E. EVANS-PRITCHARD
  1940   *African political systems.* London: Oxford University Press.

KUMA, J. K.
  1965   "Denkyira 1600–1617." Unpublished master's thesis, I.A.S. Legon. (See also *Ghana Notes and Queries* 9.)

KYEREMATEN, A. A. Y.
  1964   *Panoply of Ghana.* London: Longman Green.
  1969   The royal stools of Ashanti. *Africa* 39:1.
  1970   *Kingship and ceremony in Ashanti.* Kumasi: U.S.T. Press.

LLOYD, P. C.
  1960   Sacred kinship and government among the Yoruba. *Africa* 30:3, 221–237.

MIDDLETON, J., DAVID TATE
  1958   *Tribes without rulers.* London: Routledge and Kegan Paul.

MORTON, WILLIAM P.
  1960a  Ogboni cult. *Africa:* 362–363.
  1960b  The Oyo government. *Africa.*

QUARCOO, ALFRED K.
  1965   "Processes of social control among the Dangme (Shai)." Unpublished master's thesis, University of Ghana, Legon.
  1966   The phenomenon of ancestor cult. *Institute of African Studies Research Review* 3:1. Legon.
  1970   "Oral traditions of Denkyira." Unpublished thesis.

RATTRAY, R. S.
  1923   *Ashanti.* London: Oxford University Press.
  1927   *Religion and art in Ashanti.* Oxford: Clarendon Press.
  1929   *Ashanti law and constitution.* Oxford: Clarendon Press.

REIDORF, CARL, REV.
  1895   *A history of the Gold Coast and Ashanti.* Kumasi: Basel Mission Book Depot.

SARPONG, P. K.
  1967   The sacred stools of Ashanti. *Anthropos.*

SEKYI, W. E. G.
  n.d.   "Comparison of English, Gold Coast, Akan, relating to absolute rights of individuals." Archives Cape Coast, Ghana.

SMITH, M. G.
1956    Segmentary lineage systems. *Journal of the Royal Anthropological Institute* 76:2, 54–55, 67.

SUTHERLAND, D. A.
n.d.    *State emblems of the Gold Coast.* Accra: Government Printing Department.

WILKS, IVOR
1957    *The rise of the Akwamu empire.* Transactions of Historical Society of Ghana 3.
1964    "The growth of Akuapim state," in *The historian in tropical Africa.* Edited by Jan Vanisa, Raymond Maudy, and L. V. Thomas. London.
1967    "Ashanti government," in *West African kingdoms of the nineteenth century.* Edited by D. Forde and P. M. Kabberry. London: Oxford University Press for the International African Institute.

WOLF, FREDA
1958    *Pageant of Ghana.* London: Oxford University Press.


*Further References*

ADU, A. L.
1949    *The role of chiefs in Akan social structure: an essay.* Accra: Government Printing Department.

AGYEMAN, E. A.
1966    A note on the foundation of the Gyama kingdom. *Ghana Notes and Queries* 9:36–39.

AKROFI, C. A.
1962    *Twi mmebusem* [Twi proverbs]. London.

AZU, ENOCH
1925    Adangme historical and proverbial songs. *Gold Coast Review* 1925–1927.

BALMER, W. T.
1926    *A history of Akan peoples of the Gold Coast,* p. 208. London: Atlantis Press.

BASCOM, WILLIAM
1962    African arts and social control. *African Studies Bulletin.* New York: African Studies Association.

BOAHEN, ADU
1964a   The decline of Ashanti. *Ghana Radio and T.V. Times* 5:10–13, 16.
1964b   The rise and growth of the Ashanti empire. *Ghana Radio and T.V. Times* 5:2, 5, 7, 15.

BREFFIT, G. W.
1960a   Ashanti's living legend: the history of the sacred stool of Ashanti. *West African Review* (November): 40–43.
1960b   The golden stool of Ashanti. *Gazette of John Lewis partnership* (August 6).

BROKENSHA, D.
1962    Kinship residence in a Guan town. *Proceedings of the Nigerian Institute of Social and Economic Research.*

CLARK, E.
1930    Sociological significance of ancestor worship in Ashanti. *Africa* 3:4, 431–471.
DAAKU, K. Y.
1966    Pre-Ashanti states. *Ghana Notes and Queries* 9:1–13.
FORTES, MEYER
1950    "Kinship and marriage among the Ashanti," in *African systems of kinship and marriage.* Edited by A. R. Radcliffe-Brown and Daryll Forde, 252–284. London: Oxford University Press for the International African Institute.
FULLER, SIR FRANCIS C.
1921    *A vanished dynasty, Ashanti.* London: J. Murray.
LYSTAND, ROBERT A.
1958    *The Ashanti — a proud people.* New Brunswick, New Jersey: Rutgers University Press.
NAHN, MILTON C.
1956    *The artist as creator: an essay on human freedom.* Baltimore: The Johns Hopkins Press.
NKETIA, J. H.
1957    *Funeral dirges of the Akan people.* Achimota: University College Gold Coast.
OZANE, PAUL
1968    "The archaeological contribution to Asante Abakosem." Unpublished manuscript, Department of Archaeology, University of Ghana, Legon.

# Religious Change in a Northern Nigerian Emirate

FRANK A. SALAMONE

A number of scholars (Herskovits 1943: 394–402; Aquina 1967: 203–219; Guiart 1970: 122–138) have argued recently for a more processual approach to the phenomena of conversion. Such an approach stresses the active roles of the convert in responding to a proselytizing agent. Geertz (1968), for example, made the important observation that Islam is neither an independent variable nor a monolithic entity. His point is that it is idiosyncratic in every sociocultural system in which it is found and therefore cannot be used as an explanatory model in itself. Rather, Islam itself must be explained as part of a process of interaction which we can call Islamization.

The particulars of Islamization may vary because of local sociocultural elements, but the etic features used by all Muslims to distinguish themselves from non-Muslims are rather consistent and so allow comparisons to be made, which then allow us to separate sociosyncratic responses from more universal ones. Barkow (1970) offers a Nigerian example, the Hausa-Maguzawa relationship, that aptly illustrates the advantage of this approach.

Like Islam, Christianity has a well-developed etic code of belief and behavior that in practice allows for great variation. Recent research (Sahay 1968) has indicated some ways in which this process occurs. In any event, it is clear that the convert is not a passive recipient of a pre-

This paper is based on research conducted during the summer of 1970 and in 1972. I also wish to acknowledge my debt to the theoretical inspiration of Dr. Jerome Barkow, who in his writings states clearly what I have only stuttered. I also wish to thank Dr. M. Estellie Smith for her corrections and suggestions. Responsibility, of course, lies with me for any errors.

packaged faith, as early acculturation theory tended to suggest. Rather, the convert chooses to identify himself as a Christian or a Muslim because of emically perceived advantages. Conversion is, emically at least, a very rational process. Whether the advantages in any particular case are real is a matter for further empirical research, as I have discussed at greater length elsewhere (1972). In fact, many of the disadvantages that may accrue from conversion result just because conversion is a process and not an event; i.e. it takes place over a period of time and requires constant learning of "Christian" behavior. A convert often discovers after conversion that such behavior conflicts with internalized values or society's norms (Sahay 1968; Guiart 1970; Salamone 1972; Luzbetak 1970).

It is important to point out that Christianity is no more a monolithic entity than is Islam. It is also important to make clear that there is no "typical" convert or "typical" missionary approach, unless we are talking about stochastic relationships. Unfortunately, no one has yet supplied us with the data needed to produce these mathematical models. As a step toward gathering that data I would like to offer the following research approach and then to give an example of its application.

An important research strategy is first to discover what kind of people are learning what kind of Christianity. I grant that this should be stating the obvious, but the literature is filled with examples that prove that this is not an obvious statement (Heiss 1970: 49–53). Too often stereotypic views of missionaries replace solid empirical research. Therefore, solid analysis of the entire missionary situation and its ecological texture is sorely needed. Barkow (1970) has already indicated how an approach combining that of Le Vine and Barth (1970) can advance our understanding of cultural change. Such an approach emphasizes conversion as a process, in fact as a number of processes, rather than as an event. It has the further advantage of working out from the individual without sacrificing the overall framework.

The northern area of Nigeria provides a laboratory rich in ethnic diversity, an area that provides adequate data to illustrate the approach I suggest. Barkow has clearly analyzed, for example, methods used by two subcultures of the Hausa to distinguish themselves from one another. The most minute differences are overplayed and large similarities are ignored, in much the way Goffman (1959) predicted that groups attempting to preserve separate identities would behave. Groups which, at one level are etically similar, will, because of the differences in the environment, be emically different. The desire to preserve these differences may greatly influence the responses made to similar ecological changes, and the presence of Christian missionaries in an area is an ecological change of great importance. Groups, then, that appear to outsiders to be mere "variants" of one another are frequently to insiders "foreign" people, simply "not like us, at all."

This is exactly the case in Yauri Emirate, Nigeria, for the Dukawa and Gungawa. Harris (1930), among others has suggested that these "tribes" are subgroups of one another, but Gunn and Conant (1960: 10) point out incisively that the "traditional ability of the peoples of the middle Niger region to adjust to one another within larger political units may constitute their chief significance for Nigeria as a whole." If we dwell on the more sophisticated Barthian approach, we shall understand better how ethnic groups operate rather than be bogged down in outmoded theories of biological transference of culture. As Harris (1930) makes clear in his excellent detailed descriptive account of the Gungawa in Yauri, the Gungawa and Dukawa, whatever the truth of their common "origins" may be, have in Bateson's terminology a different ethos.

The above point has been, perhaps, somewhat labored, for I wish to show that the two groups I have chosen to discuss from the Yelwa area are indeed two distinct ethnic groups. That is important because part of my research strategy consists of studying the ways in which two different ethnic groups use ethnicity in exploiting different ecological niches in the same general area and how this then conditions their response to two variants of missionary influence. Unfortunately, in the past the tendency has been to forget the importance of differences among groups in an area as small as Yauri.

A number of other considerations may have justified such an approach in the past, but this can no longer be the case if we wish to avoid the pitfalls of both the grossly macrocosmic approach of too much social science and the microcosmic approach of our own past that too often ignored interaction between groups in a fruitless search for the "pure" structure unpolluted by "culture-contact." In the real world, as Barth and his disciples (1970) have so clearly shown, groups do interact and change because ethnic boundaries are permeable. It makes anthropological work complicated, but it also makes it much more interesting.

This paper presents a discussion concentrating on the advantages that conversion to Christianity might have for members of two particular ethnic groups as they see it. Insofar as possible, the total context of the missionary contact is at least sketched. The differential response of two groups in the same area to two different missionary strategies is presented, viz. that of the Gungawa to a United Mission Society (U.M.S.) approach and the Dukawa to a Dominican Catholic approach. To make the comparisons clearer only one aspect of the ethos of each group will be considered, i.e. values regarding women.

A logical next step would be to take the same ethnic group and discuss the responses of its members to two different religions as Ottenberg (1971: 231–260) does for the Igbo. In the Igbo case he found that the major variable operating was wealth-prestige. The Gungawa offer a case in Yauri of people choosing between Islam and Christianity.

## YAURI DIVISION

Although not all Dukawa and Gungawa live in the Yauri Emirate, there have been Dukawa and Gungawa there for at least 200 years (Harris 1930). The people I am comparing live in two villages that have been in the Yauri area for at least 200 years and show little difference from Dukawa and Gungawa outside the Yauri area, at least as described in the works of Gunn and Conant (1960). Father Ceslaus Prazan, O.P., has done a great deal of ethnographic work among the Dukawa. His manuscript is currently in press, and he has assured me that there are no significant differences between the Dukawa I studied and those outside Yauri (personal communication). Insofar, then, as any segment of a larger group is typical of that group, the two groups compared here are typical of Dukawa and Gungawa settlements.

Both the Dukawa and Gungawa fled to Yauri, long a haven for those forced to seek refuge. Both seem to have come from the Kontagora region to escape Fulani slave raids. If one believes the myths of origin, both are of the same "stock" (Harris 1930: 291–321). Today, however, they are culturally distinct ethnic groups who use their alleged genealogical ties as a means of ordering their mutual relationships in the complex interethnic world that is Yauri. Whatever the facts of their common cultural origin, each group has become a distinct ethnic group by emphasizing different cultural traits and values, values that have a high "survival" role in the complex Yauri world. By first describing that world briefly and then focusing on one set of values, responses to two groups of missionaries are made more clear.

Yauri is one of a number of emirates in what, under British rule, was Northern Nigeria. More specifically it was part of Sokoto Province. Today it is a small emirate and division in the Northwestern State of Nigeria. It has an area of 1,306 square miles and is located along the Niger River. Its total population is 72,000, or about 58 persons per square mile. Yelwa, population 8,000, is its largest city. Most of the inhabitants of

Yelwa identify themselves as Hausa and look down on the totally non-Hausa rural inhabitants. Unlike other emirates, Yauri has no rural Hausa farmers, except for Gungawa Muslims who identify themselves as "Hausa."

This scorn for the rural people enables the inhabitants of Yelwa town to verify to themselves their own Hausa identity. This verification is necessary in the face of the scorn shown to them by more sophisticated Hausa from Katsina or Sokoto whom they encounter on their many trading expeditions and who occasionally pass through Yauri. Barkow (1970) has done an excellent job in describing the psycho-cultural processes involved in maintaining and establishing self-identification in striving to achieve a "more perfect" ethnic identity.

In northern Zaria, Muslim Hausa (both rural and urban) and the pagan Hausa (the Maguzawa) established patterns of behavior that served as boundary markers. Those in the lower-ranked groups, the rural Hausa and Maguzawa, borrowed behavior traits from the urban Hausa. The rural Hausa, however, were torn by events, for they feared identification with the pagan Maguzawa Hausa yet felt strong emotional pulls to the Maguzawa way of life. The Maguzawa served for the rural Hausa as living proof of their Hausa identities, for they were all that a good Hausa was not. They were pagans. They were drunks. Their women worked in the fields, etc. The Maguzawa played up to and exaggerated the stereotypes held of them by the Hausa.

The same process is at work in the Yauri area even though the ethnographic details are different. The minority groups in Yauri are not subgroups of the Hausa. They are separate groups. While in northern Zaria Barkow's three groups form part of a continuum on a scale measuring "Hausaness," at Yauri the situation is one of ethnic pluralism. At Yauri, the Hausa regard the pagan minority groups as inferior and emphasize their differences from them. Individuals may now and then pass as Hausa, but even after Islamic conversion it would be hard for groups to pass through the Hausa ethnic boundary in Yauri.

A full discussion of the reasons for this fact would fill a separate paper. In brief, the town Hausa need other ethnic groups to exploit the many ecological niches in Yauri. They fear that for themselves to do so would cost them their self-identification as true Hausa, an identification often endangered because of their alleged Kanuri and "mixed" Gungawa origins. To people in Katsina and Kano the inhabitants of Yelwa are bushmen or "hicks."

The majority of Yauri's peoples are, therefore, politically "minority" groups, i.e. they have less access to power than do the ruling Hausa-

Fulani. The minority peoples live either in the bush, like the Dukawa, or on islands like many Gungawa. Decisions made in town are sent to the bush via representatives of the rulers. These representatives carry on all business in Hausa, the *lingua franca* of the area.

In a number of ways, the Hausa-Fulani impress on minority peoples their inferior status *vis-à-vis* themselves. Since the Hausa, by definition are Muslims, the minority people tend to identify Islam, Hausaness and power as interchangeable entities. All do not, however, perceive Islam as a means to power for themselves, for Islam has long been the religion of their oppressors. The fact that the current Emir is a wise and generous ruler means less to them than the fact that Muslims enslaved people and are still their tax collectors.

The road to power in the Northwestern State of Nigeria is via Islam. The Yauri division is no exception to the general rule. Every member of the government is a Muslim. Every merchant of importance is a Muslim. In short, anyone of any real importance is a Muslim.

The recent political reforms, begun in 1970, curbed the power of the old native authority but not of Islam. They, in fact, strengthened it by bringing Muslims from outside Yauri into the division to fill positions of power. The divisional secretary and executive officer, for example, are both Nupe from Kwara state. All the members of the government must attend the mosque regularly or else risk censure. Since the Emir of Yauri is the *de facto* spiritual leader of his emirate, such activities increase his religious prestige. Thus, the loss of political power to the newly consti-tuted division has not led to a loss in religious power. Nor does it seem likely to do so since the government leaders in Yauri are eager to point out the Islamic basis for their rule.

It is in their interest that the pagan population of Yauri be given daily reminders of the power and prestige of Islam, for the larger the per-centage of Muslims, they believe, the less will their power be questioned. While this may seem to contradict the earlier assertion that whole groups will find it difficult to cross ethnic barriers, it does not. The government leaders are generally from outside Yauri. Further, there was no assertion made that any conscious barriers were placed to the conversion of whole groups. It should be mentioned that the converts try to "pass" as Hausa, but the Hausa continue to refer to them by their original ethnic name.

Within this complex interplay of ethnic groups, the Dukawa and Gun-gawa must survive. Each group has chosen (in Barth's phraseology) to exploit a different ecological niche and has entered into symbiotic rela-tionship with other groups. If Christianity or Islam has adaptive and ex-ploitative potential it will be chosen to the degree to which it interacts with other elements of Dukawa and Gungawa life. The Dukawa, for example, have adapted to the area as horticulturalists who are also the best hunters and leather workers in the area. The primary work team for all these activities is male.

Moreover, all the male members of the work team are tied together primarily through having done bride service together. They are tied together in a relationship cemented by female links. Each man feels closest to those who have helped him perform his *gormu,* bride service. Those who have formed *gormu* teams hunt together and farm together. Logically, then, women are the external signs of male solidarity in Dukawa society and divorce is never permitted. Adultery is rare and Dukawa informants consider it a crime that strikes at the very fiber of Dukawa society. Anything, therefore, that might interfere with the organization of male work teams would be resisted, for it is through these work teams that the Dukawa defines himself *vis-à-vis* other ethnic groups (Salamone 1972).

For the Dukawa male, *gormu* service, a seven-to-eight-year project, functions as a rite of passage. It is never performed alone, but always with the assistance of one's age mates. Young work teams travel from place to place working on gardens in widely scattered parts of "Dukawaland." Such teams, obviously, perform many functions, not the least of which is tying the acephalous Dukawa together by affirming their ideals openly and facilitating communication and contact among the small compounds.

The Dominicans threaten the Dukawa ethos in a number of ways not at first patently obvious. Certainly, the Dominicans cannot help but admire the chastity of Dukawa women. They do realize the vital importance of the institution of *gormu* in cementing Dukawa ties. They have, however, alienated the Dukawa by insisting that potential converts adhere to the Catholic definition of marriage. By that they mean that no sexual intercourse is permissible before the performance of the exchange of vows.

While the missionaries have ingeniously patterned the Catholic ritual after the Dukawa ritual, they have failed to realize the importance of the Dukawa distinction between "having a wife" and "being married." Any young man doing *gormu* HAS a wife. He is not MARRIED however, until the completion of his bride service. In fact, he will not complete his bride service until he is sure that his marriage is sexually satisfying, a fair precaution in a society that strongly prohibits adultery. Usually, he also demands proof of his wife's fertility before becoming fully married, another reasonable precaution in a society with a low incidence of polygyny, for only 50 percent of the Dukawa in Yauri have more than one wife. To tamper with the institution of the *gormu* in any way threatens to change it significantly.

While the incidence of polygyny is low, it does exist and its most frequent type is leviratic. The levirate, as anthropologists have stressed for some time, serves a number of functions. It maintains alliances; it provides for widows and their children; it serves various religious purposes, etc. The Dukawa, like other people, consider it a secondary form of marriage, i.e. no one is expected to have only a wife obtained through the levirate. But Christianity forces one to have but a single wife. The convert, therefore, who has a wife would have to refuse to honor his solemn obligation should the levirate situation present itself. The convert doing *gormu* and facing the necessity of the levirate would have to withdraw from Dukawa society since he would be forced to cancel his bride service contract lest he have two wives.

So long as the Catholic emphasis is on individual converts and demonstrable knowledge of the faith, the individual will learn, often after conversion, that he is somehow "less" a member of his society than he was previously. If the advantages in remaining a convert are high enough, enough other members of one's society may become converts to effect changes in Christianity that will make the convert more comfortable. A wiser missionary approach among the Dukawa would be to emulate that used among the Gungawa.

Whatever their "ancestry" the Gungawa of Shabanda are today one people with a widely uniform culture, as the following quotation from Harris (1930: 291) makes clear:

One would have expected to find much greater differences seeing that offshoots of several differing tribes — Shanga, Kambari and Bussa — are to be found in the islands, having been driven there during the raids from Kontagora in the 19th century. The position appears to be that whatever a man's tribe may have been, once he has joined the island community his children become islanders both in name and custom.

What Harris is describing, of course, is the cultural basis of "descent" and the formation of new ethnic groups to adapt to new environments. The Gungawa are different in significant ways from any of the other ethnic groups from whom they draw their members. They are different because they must retain their distinct ethnic identity to exploit their particular niche in the wider milieu.

The Gungawa are horticulturalists, and their onion farming is of major importance to non-Gungawa as are their fishing activities. The Gungawa, who are remarkable for their "fearlessness of the Niger," supply a valuable source of needed protein to members of other ethnic groups.

While male work teams are the basis for the work organization, unlike the Dukawa situation, women and their chastity do not form the valuable tie linking men together. The Gungawa form their male work teams on a patrilineal-patrilocal basis, with a chain of authority highly articulated on a kinship basis from the most minor of officials to representatives of the Hausa emir.

The chastity or lack of it of Gungawa women only becomes important if a question of paternity should arise. No Gungawa family is willing to lose any potential members. A woman who leaves one of its members while pregnant or who appears pregnant shortly thereafter is a cause of concern, for there is danger that the child will be lost to the kinship group of the man she left. By prohibiting divorce and proclaiming the sanctity of the family, Christianity strengthens Gungawa social organization. It does so by reinforcing its underlying principles. The need for families to remain together was recognized by the first United Mission Society missionaries to the area in the early 1950's.

The approach used was that of converting entire families or large sections thereof. Since the Gungawa do not have either the *gormu* or the levirate and since polygyny is relatively rare, there was little to interfere with the U.M.S. stress on monogamy. They do have a four-day bride service that a man and his young male kin perform immediately after his first marriage. But the lengthy service of the Dukawa is foreign to them. Gungawa bride service stresses the solidarity of the patrilineage and the acceptance by one's patrilineage of one's spouse. The emotional tie of the Dukawa is missing in the Gungawa service.

Furthermore, the Gungawa found much to gain from the U.M.S. religion. From the first, the Gungawa preached the faith to other Gungawa. Indigenization was thus facilitated since one did not have the barrier of European presentation. Unlike the Dominicans' case with the Dukawa, outside ethnic groups were not brought in to preach as catechists. The Gungawa ran their own church in Shabanda. They have translated parts of the New Testament into Gunganci after first creating a written language.

The practical advantages of a written language for a trading people became readily apparent. The advantages of having some members practice the old faith and others practice Christianity seem readily apparent also. While Christianity continues to grow in Shabanda, a sizable number of people remain traditionalists in religion. Many families have both Baptist and traditionalist members and live in perfect harmony with one another. Lately, Islam has begun to spread in Kwanji district, of which Shabanda is part.

Because Shabanda was not directly part of the Kainji Dam project, none of its people were forced to relocate, and traditional farming methods of shifting horticulture continue to be practiced. No part of Yauri, however, escaped the results of Kainji completely. One result of the dam was the opportunity to give frequent examples of Islamic power to re-settled Gungawa, and most of the 44,000 people resettled were Gungawa. While these resettled Gungawa have been the prime targets of prose-lytizing efforts by Muslims, the strengthening of Islamic conversion methods has had a "spill-over" effect, i.e. other groups are being preached to by well-trained *mallams*.

The *mallams* are trained through a government-sponsored agency, the Islamic Education Trust. The I.E.T. was founded in Nigeria by Sheik Ahmad Lemot and is affiliated with the International I.E.T centered in Mecca. Its main Nigerian office is in Sokoto. There, post-secondary-school students are trained for three months to instruct local *mallams* in "modern methods" of conversion. These students are hired by the local authorities during their vacations to supervise in-service training for local *mallams*. The student assigned to Yauri, Musa Abarshi, has appointed a *mallam* to keep a constant watch on all other *mallams*. This *mallam*, Mallam Hamaidu, had been an Arabic teacher at the Gebbi Primary School, one mile from Shabanda. The choice was by design, not accident.

Suffice it to say that the training is rigid; the *mallams* are tested care-fully on their knowledge of Islam and methodology of conversion. The government supplies the *mallams* with motorcycles and permission to settle in the villages. Government approval is one key to their success. Another is the fact that the resettled Gungawa underwent a major eco-logical change.

They no longer live on islands or along the banks of the Niger. They find it difficult to irrigate their onion plants by traditional methods and find instead that they must irrigate them with Lister pumps available only through the government. It is no surprise that while there were few Muslims on the islands there has been a tremendous increase in the number of Muslims since the resettlement was completed in 1968. The resettled Gungawa are finding it to their political and economic advantage to convert to Islam.

Those Gungawa who live in Shabanda have traditionally been re-nowned for their rapid acceptance of "modern methods." They have, in short, been willing to adapt to survive. In the present situation in Yauri it is not surprising to find the people of Shabanda living in peace with one another while some are Muslims, some are Christians, and some are traditionalists, for this reflects a rather wise adjustment to reality that enables people to maximize the opportunities available for each group. Outside Shabanda, the number of converts to Islam is increasing so rapidly (Roder 1970) that if the rate continues almost all resettled Gungawa will become Muslims.

One interesting result of the Gungawa conversion to Islam in large numbers is the phenomenon of schismogenesis it presents. Outside Shabanda the newly converted Gungawa try to dissociate themselves as much as possible from the pagan Gungawa. In turn, pagan Gungawa mock them rather openly. Since the Hausa refuse to acknowledge these new Gungawas completely, one can predict that the Muslim Gungawa may form a separate ethnic group, exploiting a different ecological niche from pagan Gungawa and embracing radically different values.

Shabanda, it must be stressed, is important because it offers a special setting for Islamic and Christian conversion, because it combines traditional and modern elements.

Its people travel the seven and one-half water miles to the Dominican hospital for preventive checkups while other ethnic groups will not travel there from down the road for serious illness. People from Shabanda send large numbers of students to institutions of higher learning. For example, ten young men were in universities and teacher training schools in 1970. No other minority group in Yauri had even one in an institution of higher learning. The elementary school on Shabanda is a major reason for the success of its young people.

In its way Shabanda is a model of how change was able to come to the Gungawa without the major ecological wrenching consequent on forced resettlement.

## SUMMARY

Individuals will become converts to those religious systems that enable them to better adapt to their ecological niches. The U.M.S. have aided the Gungawa of Shabanda by emphasizing the kinship bases of their authority structure and providing an easy access to literacy. Christianity has failed to make many converts among the Dukawa because of the dissonance between the value system of the Dominican missionaries and those values that bind Dukawa society together. The U.M.S. have striven for mass conversions in an effort to make the convert feel at ease in his new role. The Dominicans have treated the individual and thus isolated the convert and vitiated their chances for further conversion.

The U.M.S. first gained a foothold in Shabanda by reinforcing family ties. It did so in a way compatible with Gungawa society. That it has other advantages for the inhabitants of Shabanda became rather evident as time has passed. The converts learned of these advantages after conversion. But their successes served as positive feedback to other Gungawa who in about twenty years have made the island one of the major centers of Christianity in northern Nigeria.

The Dominicans, by stressing individual commitment and by cutting converts off from ties formed by the *gormu* complex, have tended to isolate their converts from their ethnic groups. It is granted that the Dominicans and U.M.S. faced different problems, but the Dominicans have failed to set up an indigenous clergy and have demanded a high initial knowledge of Christianity from Dukawa converts. As negative feedback is sent to the Dukawa system by converts, one can predict a low conversion rate, at least so long as the *gormu* complex remains adaptive for Dukawa social organization.

The recent resettlement of Gungawa consequent on the building of Kainji Dam has given impetus to an Islamic conversion movement. The resettled Gungawa, faced with adapting to a different ecological niche, have been turning to Islam for its greater economic and political advantages. The government-sponsored effort has made inroads at Shabanda.

Finally, Shabanda with its Christians, Muslims and traditionalists provides a unique setting for the study of religious change in a more traditional Gungawa setting.


## REFERENCES

AQUINA, SISTER MARY
    1967    The people of the spirit: an independent church in Rhodesia. *Africa* 203–219.
BARKOW, JEROME
    1970    "Hausa and Maguzawa: processes of group differentiation in a rural area of North Central State, Nigeria." Unpublished doctoral dissertation, University of Chicago.
BARTH, FREDRIK, *editor*
    1970    *Ethnic groups and boundaries.* New York: Little, Brown.
GEERTZ, CLIFFORD
    1968    *Islam observed: religious development in Morocco and Indonesia.* New Haven: Yale University Press.
GOFFMAN, ERVING
    1959    *Presentation of self in everyday life.* Garden City: Doubleday.

GUIART, JEAN
    1970   "The millenarian aspect of Christianity in the South Pacific," in *Millennial dreams in action.* Edited by Sylvia Thrupp, 122–138. New York: Schoken Books.

GUNN, HAROLD D., F. P. CONANT
    1960   *Peoples of the middle Niger region in northern Nigeria.* London: International African Institute.

HARRIS, PERCY G.
    1930   Notes on Yauri (Sokoto Province), Nigeria. *Journal of the Royal Anthropological Institute* 60: 283–334.

HEISS, DAVID R.
    1970   Prefatory findings in the sociology of missions. *Journal of the Scientific Study of Religions* 6 (Spring, 1970), 49–63.

HERSKOVITS, MELVILLE
    1943   The Negro in Bahia, Brazil: a problem in method. *American Sociological Review* 8: 394–402.

LUZBETAK, LOUIS
    1970   *The church and cultures.* Techny: Divine Word Press.

OTTENBERG, SIMON
    1971   A Muslim Igbo village. *Cahiers d'Études Africaines* 11, Number 2.

PRAZAN, FATHER CESLAUS
    n.d.   "The Dukawa." Unpublished manuscript.

RODER, WOLF
    1970   *Kainji Lake research project, New Bussa, Nigeria.* FAO.

SAHAY, KESHARI
    1968   Impact of Christianity on the Uraon of the Raipur Belt in Chotanagpur: an analysis of its cultural processes. *American Anthropologist* 70: 923–942.

SALAMONE, FRANK A.
    1972   Structural factors in Dukawa conversion. *Practical Anthropology* 219–225.

# SECTION TWO

# Deified Men and Humanized Gods: Some Folk Bases of Hindu Theology

A. AIYAPPAN

Whether the gods and human spirits are a continuum or two distinct though interacting categories seems to have been a matter of some interest to formulators of world views. In the part of India to which this article relates, namely Kerala State, the subject is occasionally discussed by rural philosophers, but the question is phrased differently. It is asked this way: Is the god X a man who became a god or was he a real god? Was Rama a good king elevated to the rank of a god or was he an incarnation of Vishnu?

Except for the extreme rationalists, no one questions the ranking of Vishnu, Shiva, etc. as high gods, but the question arises about deities at the intermediate levels. The most ancient Vedic tradition seems to have been DUALIST insofar as it kept the gods and ancestral spirits in two categories. Later, Ramanuja, the dualist philosopher, also maintained the separation of the human soul from God. Hindu myths contain dozens of stories of human beings aspiring through the performance of austerities (*tapas*) to the position of Indra, the leader of gods in the Hindu heaven.

Likewise, in the stories and beliefs about yoga, humans gain superhuman power (*siddhis*) annihilating the distance between man and the Supreme Being. The underlying "mood and motivation" (Geertz 1966: 4) in all these mythical and ritual activities seem to be an assertion of man's will to power in contrast to the absolute surrender (*sarana:gati*) of the dualists.

Shankara, the chief protagonist of the *advaita* [nondualist or monistic Hindu theology], viewed the human spirit and the divine as identical — as a unity. Shorn of his dialectics, Shankara would appear to an anthropologist almost Tylorean! Shankara was a Nambudiri Brahman of Kerala in the eighth to ninth century A.D. A student of Kerala society cannot but be interested in Shankara's catholocity of view which gave ready acceptance to folk religions and their rites as stages in man's spiritual development.

One of the things I have attempted in this paper is to give some hints about the probable nature of popular religion in Kerala in the centuries preceding Shankara. Such a reconstruction as I have attempted is necessary, as Kerala has no history or literature worth the name until after the tenth century A.D. Even a rough idea of the sociocultural milieu in which Shankara's basic personality structure was laid out would be of interest to a wide range of scholars.

The concept of *avatar* [the incarnation of gods as human beings or animals] is the second aspect of the man-god continuum which is central and crucial in Hindu religion and mythology. I refer to this transformation as the process of humanization of gods. In order to deal properly and adequately with spiritual beings they have to be given forms. Hence the term *mu:rti* [that which has taken or been given a shape] for spiritual beings and also for their icons.

The Upanishads and mythologies (*pura:na*) of the Hindus are works of the elite, mostly Brahmans, and they are in the Sanskrit language. Through Brahman propagandists and through translations into other languages the ideas concerning their ancestor cults, gods, *avatar*, and yogic practices have spread widely among the upper non-Brahman castes, but only in an extremely vague, diluted form among the lower castes and least among the tribal communities of India.

I propose to examine the nature of the spiritual beings, but more particularly ancestral spirits among a tribal community of Kerala. On the basis of this examination, I present the hypothesis that the germ of the idea of monism, namely the continuity of man with god is likely to be found among the primitive substratum of India's population.[1] Anyway,

---

[1] After this paper was drafted, I came across the following paragraph in which Dr. Pauline Kolenda discusses a possible line of evolution of monistic thought among the Sweepers of Khalapur: "Another category are all those supernaturals who have gained a measure of autonomous power from God through mortifications, or devotion either to him, or to another of these same autonomous creatures. Supposedly, during the *Satyug* (ancient age of pure morality), the important mother goddesses and male godlings were devout mystics who died in religious trance. Through their austerities and closeness to God, they gained power from him, but power independent of his will. Thus, it is explained, there is monism in supernatural power. All power is God's, but nevertheless these creatures who take their power from him are independent of him" (Kolenda 1964: 76–77).
The Gond of Mandla have a collective ceremony to UNITE the life spirits of their

the idea could not have been a sudden discovery of the Upanishadic philosopher but should have been vaguely in the popular mind at its sensitive, creative, myth-making level.

The same broad spectrum of religious beliefs and practices is found in Kerala as in other regions of southern India, with slight local variations matching with the specialities in the social structure and history of the Hindus of the state. The Brahmans of Kerala — the Nambudiri Brahmans — being more exclusive in religious matters than their counterparts elsewhere share very little of their Vedic specialities with the non-Brahmans. The result of this Brahman attitude is that most of the non-Brahman transition and calendric rites have been more or less without the intervention of Brahman ritualists. The number of Siva or Vishnu temples are few in Kerala compared to the large number of those dedicated to the Mother Goddess Bhadrakali.

The worship of Sasta or Ayyappan at Sabarimala, of Subrahmanya or Palni in Tamil Nadu, of Vishnu at Guruvayur and of Bhadrakali at Kodungallur is of statewide importance. The worship of ancestral spirits and the propitiation of spirits concerned in sorcery and diseases are extensively practiced, though their popularity is declining among the educated sections of Keralites who are exposed to the neo-Vedantism popularized by Swami Vivekananda. Like all people burdened with a syncretic growth of religion, most Keralites have now to divide their attention between different and occasionally contradictory worlds of faith and thought.

Until about the fourth century A.D. (on a rough estimate) ancestral cults associated with urn burials and megaliths such as cists played a very great part in the religious life of Kerala. The evidence for this is found in the very large number of urn burials, cists, etc. found all over Kerala (Aiyappan 1933: 299–314). When the Nambudiri Brahmans, with their very great and superior prestige, began their cultural conquest of Kerala, their impact influenced first the chieftains and the ruling classes. The degree of Sanskritization of rituals, modes of worship and of spoken Malayalam was closely correlated with the closeness of the local people to the prestigious Brahman immigrants.

As adequate historical research has not been made into the dynamics

---

dead with Baradeo, their supreme god. The expression "unite" which they use in this context is significant. It may be incipient monism. The object of the ceremony is to get rid of the spirits effectively and forever. There is no thought of helping them in their postmortem life as in the Indo-Aryan *shraddha*. The Gonds erect cairns in honor of their distinguished dead and it is considered an act of merit to add a stone to the cairn (Fuchs 1960: 343–354).

of Sanskritization in Kerala, we are not in a position to get a correct picture of the manner in which pre-Nambudiri culture, and more particularly the religious institutions, were changed by the Brahmans. There is no doubt that massive changes took place and during the process the Nambudiris themselves made several adaptations, some of a radical nature.

Of all the local rituals, those connected with the treatment of the dead and ancestral spirits by the non-Brahmans underwent the maximum amount of change. The honoring of the dead by urn burial and the construction of megalithic cists gave place to the Brahmanical type of funeral and *shra:ddha* ceremonies. An example of a cult which the Brahmans took over from the pre-Aryan culture of Kerala is the cult of serpents. They not only accepted it but became high priests of the cult at two centers in Kerala while the non-Brahman specialists, reduced to Untouchable status, continued their serpent rituals in their own style.

As regards the cult of ancestors, the Nambudiri Brahmans, naturally, and the highly Sanskritized clans of ruling chieftains such as the Zamorin Raja and the Rajas of Cochin follow the Indo-Aryan practices *in toto*. Except for the *shra-ddha* ceremonies, they do nothing else for their ancestors. The non-Brahman castes led by the Nayars, however, have not become Sanskritized to such an extent as to be able to give up their old practice of making shrines for their ancestral spirits and worshiping them as though they were minor gods and communicating with them through mediums. In northern Kerala the shrines for ancestral spirits are called *kottam*. Anyone who is not able to build a special shrine uses a room in his dwelling to keep the symbols of the ancestral spirit — a stool or an image. Or he keeps a piece of stone under a tree as the symbol of the departed to be worshiped on prescribed occasions. The same shrine room or open tree-shaded shrine may be used as a shrine for family gods by the non-Brahman castes from the high-ranking Nayars down to the low-caste Pulayas.

For a social anthropologist who has set for himself the difficult task of analyzing the belief and religious systems of a complex society with a population of over twenty million, the study of tribal communities of the region offers some tactical assistance. He can contrive an experimental field situation with fewer variables to be handled at a time.

In Kerala I have had the good fortune to study an intensely traditional, religious-minded tribal community, the Kurichiyas of Wynad, who have been isolated in a hilly tribal pocket of the Kerala State with minimal contacts and communication with the plains people until recent times. The Kurichiyas number now about 11,000 and are believed to have migrated to their present habitat as farmers. Though it is not possible to date their migration exactly, the probabilities are that it was prior to the fourth or fifth century A.D., when the influence of the Brahmans was slight or even absent, the caste structure and economic differentiation had not assumed their present morphology and the basic matrilineality of Kerala society was strong.

The Kurichiyas consider themselves equal in status to the Nayars, yet they tap palm wine, which is at present the diacritical occupation of an inferior caste, the Izhavas (Aiyappan 1944), who are now untouchable to both the Nayars and Kurichiyas. The social distance between the Nayars and Izhavas has been growing over the centuries, the initial impulse for this having come, in all likelihood, through the intervention of the Brahmans.

The Kurichiyas, in my view, represent an ancient section of Kerala society from which the matrilineal northern Kerala Nayars and the Tiyyar (Izhavas) branched off. The Nayars, as a matter of fact, are not one caste, but a cluster of castes set apart to perform various services for the Brahmans and the ruling families, the services ranging from administration and fighting to various forms of ceremonial assistance and menial work.

The religion of the Kurichiyas may also be taken to represent a broadly archaic form of the faith and practices of the pre-Nambudiri Keralites, more specifically the Nayars and Izhavas. Several centuries of peripheral contacts with advanced groups, Brahmans and Nayars, who came later to Wynad have had some impact on the Kurichiyas, but their effect is indeed slight. Siva, Vishnu, Rama, Krishna and other gods and goddesses of the Puranic Hindu pantheon mean almost nothing to the Kurichiyas. In none of their shrines do they have any icons.

The Kurichiyas believe that they had 108 named matrilineal sibs of which the names of only sixty-six are remembered and of these nine became extinct within living memory. The fifty-seven clans are grouped into two exogamous phratries, marriage within the phratry being strictly prohibited. They live in large matrilineages of the type described for the northern Malabar coast Nayars by Gough (1962: 385–404).

The Kurichiyas believe in a Creator who in their prayers is referred to as I:svara or Peruma:l'. He created the various gods, goddesses and innumerable evil spirits. Ranking just below Peruma:l', are the Four Mothers or great Mother Goddesses to whose world the dead are believed to go. The most pervasive and active god of the Kurichiyas is Malaka:ri.[2] Their myths describe him as a great hunter armed with bow

[2] The word Malaka:ri means "Kari of the Hills." Kari is a very old Dravidian

and arrows. He established his supremacy over Wynad by subduing another god Pul'l'aya:ran and a ferocious bloodthirsty goddess Karimpili whom he reduced to a pacific character, placed in charge of the welfare of women and children, and also made the goddess of graveyards. Vadakkatti is the Kurichiya goddess of dry farming; Vet't'aka:l'an of hunting, fishing, and the making of bridges and rafts; Gul'ikan of guarding the threshing floors and cattle. A male deity, Atira:l'an, also called the Mediator god (*Mu:nna:n teyyam*) looks after the interpersonal relationships in the large Kurichiya lineages and is the main channel of communication between men and gods. Atiralan is a close spiritual equivalent of the secular functionary, Munnan.[3] Each sib has a tutelary god or goddess (some of whom are major gods) as its special guardian. No segment of a sib can attain independent social status without a shrine established for its tutelary deity. True to their matrilineal organization, twenty-seven out of their total number of forty-six deities are female.

The Kurichiyas build small temples for their mother goddesses about which they share cults and beliefs with the rest of the Kerala Hindus. However, for Malakari, Atiralan, Vettakalan, etc., they build only cairns, which is a very old Dravidian tribal practice (Fuchs 1960: 343–354). Each sib may have shrines and cairns for three to seven gods in a special enclosure not far from the cluster of dwelling houses. In a room in the best of these houses, the ancestral shades of the clan have their place. A lighted lamp or a simple low stool of wood is the material symbol for the shade. When new households are established, the presence of a shade is essential before it can be called a house. A house without an ancestral shade is regarded as only a shed (*pandal*). In the

---

personal name surviving now in backward areas as a personal name of lower-caste men in Kerala. The Malayalam word for cairns which represents the seat of Malakari and other Kurichiya gods is *tad'angay* [a structure which retains (things)]. Hill gods in backward areas of central Kerala have cairns, to add a pebble or piece of rock to which is considered to be an act of merit. As cairns are associated in prehistoric southern India with funerary rites, I wonder if Malakari may, after all, be a deified culture-hero. This question requires far more probing than I have been able to undertake. For the present, in the absence of other cultural clues, I have desisted from discussing this matter and accept the views of my Kurichiya informants.

[3]   The Mediator god, or Mu:nna:n god, is sociologically speaking a most interesting deity providing a Durkheimian proof for Kurichiya religion as a projection of society. For details about the equivalent of this social functionary among the Nayars and Izhavas, see Gough (1962: 327). Her "Enangar" is spelled as "Inangar" by me (Aiyappan 1944).

kitchen block a female ancestor-spirit (*pe:na*) is believed to be present. She is symbolized there at the time of ceremonies by a lighted lamp.

The Kurichiyas call their male ancestral spirits *nizhal,* a word which literally means 'shadow." The Kurichiyas have a simple burial ceremony with none of the elaborations noticed among the nontribal Keralites. After the burial, care is taken to observe ritual pollution and then to remove it. The dead are believed to go to the world of the Four Mothers. Only a very small number of outstanding men who were considered able and efficient during their lifetime are, on request, permitted by the Creator and the Four Mothers to return to the earth and be with their kin.[4]

The living have to seek the help of the old shades of the clan, the Mediator god and Malakari to bring them down from the spirit world and conduct elaborate rites spread over two to three years. When a shade comes down, its medium, now possessed, rolls down on the ground. This is characteristic of this class of superhumans. In the final act of the drama, while the shade's medium is still in trance, the shaman of the senior shade requests the shaman of the Mediator god to lead the new shade to the shrine room of the household. The Mediator god leads the new shade by the hand to the room where he remains forever or until transferred to another branch household.

The position of the shades in the hierarchy of superhumans is at the lowest level, but their functions are more numerous and diverse than those of any other member of the superhuman group, except perhaps the Mediator god. Though the shades are housed separately, offerings of food, etc. are given to them side by side with other superhumans at the time of the New Rice ceremony. The shade is believed to make the seeds germinate properly and the plants thrive, to discipline the members of the household, to receive fines from the head of the household if he is guilty in any respect and to watch the storage bins of cereals against pilferage.

When the head of a lineage goes out on important business, he formally seeks the permission of the shade. Instances are known of the shade punishing failure on the part of heads of families to observe this rule. In all respects the shade acts as a superior family head. The shade of a sib with administrative functions for a village, in like fashion, exercises control over other sibs in the territory.

The spirits of ancestresses, less numerous than those of male ancestors, are called *pe:na.* (This is an old Dravidian word used exten-

---

[4] Persons who have died of smallpox may become shades and have to be ritually disposed of.

sively among the Gond tribe for their goddesses.) For the rest of the Malayalis, pena means "ghost," "spirit," or "devil." The Kurichiyas refer to her respectfully as *pena mutta:chi* [spirit grandmother]. It is interesting to find that the Kurichiyas use this word in its old Dravidian sense. The place for the *pena* is a corner of the "northern" house which is used as the kitchen and dining hall of the household. When offerings are to be made to the *pena*, she is represented by a lighted brass oil lamp. She is believed to be concerned with the affairs of the women of the household. When the women quarrel, the Mediator god is believed to appeal to the *pena* to intervene and punish the guilty. Punishment usually takes the form of sickness.

Gough (1959: 240–272) has described in detail the way in which the cult of the dead is organized among the Nayars and I have described the same for the Izhavas (Aiyappan 1944). The role of the ancestor spirits in the affairs of the living has been routinized and narrowed down in the case of the Nayars and the Izhavas while the funeral ceremonies involving the services of priests and specialists have grown enormously. Unlike the punitive Nayar ghost, the Kurichiya shade is a constant presence, generally beneficent and used as an important channel of communication with the gods.

The Nayars, Izhavas and Kurichiyas agree, however, in making very little difference between the gods and shades. The Nayars and Izhavas regard the shades of some sorcerers to be as powerful as some of the minor gods. It is, however, difficult to generalize about the Nayars and Izhavas, as their culture and social structure are heterogeneous and complex compared to the homogeneity and simplicity of the Kurichiya social structure and culture. The Kurichiyas are more egalitarian and less authoritarian than the Nayars, and the differences in the roles of their respective ancestor spirits have to be seen against this background.

The Nayars and Izhavas who perform *shra:ddha* ceremonies of the Indo-Aryan pattern primarily as a filial duty to assist the *preta* [ghost] in its progress further away from the earth and only marginally for the benefit of the living are not conscious of the contradiction in the continued practice of their ancestor worship which, unlike the *shra:ddha*, is a response to the wish, in the ritual drama, of the spirit to return to the earth. The Kurichiyas are clear in their minds about what they are doing. They have no categories corresponding to the *preta* and *pitris* and a still higher category of gods. The Kurichiya ancestral spirits and their gods are alike in being denizens of the world of the Four Mothers.

Kurichiya experts in mythological lore are agreed that seven of their deities are humans who became gods. My best informant went to the extent of claiming the Bhagavati of Vallu:rka:vu as an ancestress of the Kurichiyas who was unjustly killed by her mother's brother. In the light of this claim, the legends about this temple and its rituals require close study. The deities with legendary human origin are: (1) Pra:ntan Pul'l'a Teyyam, (2) Cha:ntampili, (3) Da:rampili, (4) Vel'anilattu Bhagavati, (5) Kal'l'amvet't'i Bhagavati, (6) Atiral'ichi and (7) Kalliyot Mutta:chi. The first of these is believed to have been a weaver attached to the temple of Teytal Amma. I have been able to collect very little information about the second and third. The fourth is said to have been a Kurichiya girl, a flawless person or "full person," as the Kurichiyas believe, and was selected for a foundation sacrifice but was miraculously saved by Vettakalan. The fifth Kallamvetti Bhagavati, was a Kurichiya woman who guided the god Pullayaran in the Vemom area. The sixth, Atiralichi, was a Kshatriya woman stolen by the god Pullayaran and given away to the Kannolan sib. Kalliyot Muttachi was a young woman whose honor was miraculously saved by a rock splitting and engulfing her. An eighth god, Vettakalan stands on a somewhat different plane. What is of interest to us here is the firm belief of the Kurichiyas that men and women are potential gods and goddesses.

To say definitely which of the Kurichiya deities are their cultural inventions and which are adaptations from the general Kerala types will be a worthwhile task which I wish to attempt later in my full-length study of the Kurichiyas. It is obvious that they brought with them the analogues of several of their deities but modified their roles to meet their needs in Wynad. Earlier I have mentioned their god Vettakalan. This is the god of hunting and of war in Kerala, but the Kurichiyas have given him an additional role as the god of public works.

The myth about this god worked out by Kurichiya myth makers gives Vettakalan a new incarnation as a Kurichiya youth and then as a somewhat different god. The story in bare outline is as follows: A good Kurichiya was working under a Nambiar chieftain. As he was overworked, the chief gave him his young daughter and niece as assistants. The niece became pregnant and asked her Kurichiya lover for palm wine and meat. Malakari at this time wanted the god Vettakalan to remain in Wynad to help the Kurichiyas. So he asked that the pregnant woman be given the palm wine and meat sacralized by having been offered to him. The baby boy she gave birth to had miraculous powers and vanished in various forms: as a bird, butterfly, etc. Ultimately, he attached himself as the divine manager of the goddess, Bhagavati, of the Tondernad temple. The motif of the miraculous generative powers of sacralized food in this story is found elsewhere in Kerala, but its incorporation in a myth to transform the role of Vettakalan appears to me suggestive of a germinal theory of *avatar* [incarnation of gods], crude though it may be.

The Kurichiyas are generally illiterate. They refused to go to schools, because it meant getting polluted. They are more pollution-purity conscious than even the Nambudiri Brahmans of Kerala. Only now do we get a few of the first generation to attend school. The concepts I have been talking about — monism, dualism, man-god continuum, incarnation of gods, etc. — would all be strange to them. The distinguishing feature about them is their strong commitment to their gods and rituals and to the values which keep their matrilineages, clans and community well knit and integrated. While modernity confuses and confounds them, their tradition is clear to them. If I were to tell them in monistic language, "You are that," they might not understand me, but if I put the idea in another way, "Your shades are as good as your gods," they would all agree. About *avatars* in the Kurichiya belief system, I am not sure; nor are they.

# REFERENCES

AIYAPPAN, A.
    1933    Rock-cut cave-tombs of Feroke, S. Malabar. *Quarterly Journal of the Mythic Society, Bangalore* 33:219–314.
    1944    *Iravas and culture change*. Bulletin of the Madras Government Museum. Madras: Government Press.
FUCHS, S.
    1960    *The Gond and Bhumia of eastern Mandla*. Bombay: Asia Publishing House.
GEERTZ, C.
    1966    "Religion as a cultural system," in *Anthropological approaches to the study of religion*. Edited by M. Banton, 1–46. London: Tavistock.
GOUGH, KATHLEEN
    1959    "Cults of the dead among the Nayars," in *Traditional India: structure and change*. Edited by Milton Singer, 240–272. Philadelphia: Folklore Society.
    1962    "Nayar: North Kerala," in *Matrilineal kinship*. Edited by David M. Schneider and Kathleen Gough, 384–404. Berkeley: University of California Press.
KOLENDA, PAULINE MAHAR
    1964    "Religious anxiety and Hindu fate," in *Religion in South Asia*. Edited by Edward B Harper, 71–81. Seattle: University of Washington Press.

# Shamanism in Central Asia

V. BASILOV

The researchers of shamanism still do not pay enough attention to Central Asia, although shamanism is a phenomenon common to a broad range of peoples. This is largely explained by the lack of factual material. Although over 100 works contain data on shamanism (moreover, one-third of them are rather detailed), these data are still insufficient. In addition, they have not yet been summarized and are scattered in various editions, some of which are almost unavailable. Meanwhile, an analytical review of shamanism cannot be considered comprehensive without material on Central Asia. Thus it is time to summarize the available data, although I shall not cite all the descriptive material here. My assumption is that specialists are acquainted with the literature.[1]

In Central Asia, as in other places, people believed that shamans possessed the ability, mostly inherited, to contact spirits — their helpers. Usually, contact with spirits occurred in a state of ecstasy achieved with the accompaniment of some musical instrument. At the end of the eighteenth century the basic functions of shamans were: curing diseases caused, as was believed, by evil spirits or sorcery; finding lost articles; and telling fortunes. These common characteristics can still be applied to the concrete manifestations of shamanism in all parts of Central Asia. However, many differences can be observed in these forms among various Central Asian peoples and groups. Even the local name for the shaman was not uniform: *porkhan* (Turkmen, Karakalpaks), *parkhon* (Uzbeks of Khorezm), *baksy* (Kazakhs), *bakshi*

---

[1] An incomplete bibliography of works on shamanism, mostly on Kazakh material, was compiled by I. Chekaninskij. See volume one of Chekaninskij (1929).

(Kirghiz, some Uzbeks, Uighurs), *folbin* (Tajiks, Uzbeks from the Zeravshan valley and the Tashkent oasis). In a number of places, along with these popular terms, people also use other names. Thus Uzbeks of Ferghana valley, Uzbeks and Tajiks in Samarkand and Ura-Tyube sometimes called shamans *parikhon*, and Uzbeks in Khorezm called them by the less-used term *folbin*.

While analyzing the shaman rituals, attributes, and beliefs, one can identify two spheres characterized by different features of the shaman traditions. Kazakhs, Turkmen, and Karakalpaks come into one sphere, with northern Kirghiz close to them. The other sphere comprises Tajiks, from valleys, and Uzbeks, mostly sedentary. There is no clear-cut borderline between the two areas. Thus mixed traditions of shamanism exist in Khorezm. Strong Uzbek-Tajik influence has been noted in southern Kirghizia. In eastern Turkestan various forms of Central Asian shamanism are closely intertwined.

What are the features of these two forms?

## "TURKIC" OR "CATTLE-BREEDER" COMPLEX

1. Only men become shamans (Kazakhs, western Turkmen, Karakalpaks), or generally men (Turkmen of Khorezm).

2. For musical accompaniment stringed instruments are used: *kobyz*, more seldom *domra, dutar*; sometimes pipes were used by Turkmen and *kobys* — by Karakalpaks, *komyz* by Kirghizians, mostly in the north.

3. There is no uniformity in the names of the spirits who help the shaman. Kazakhs usually use the Arabic term *jinn*, Turkmen call them *jinns* or *pari*, a Kazakh shaman also asks a *pari* for help. Kirghiz call the shaman's spirits *chymyn* [a fly] or *jinns*, while *paris* to them are not shaman's allies, but enemies to humans. Kazakhs and Kirghiz call the spirits *devs*. There are no data on Karakalpaks, because little research has been done.

4. Often the spirits helping the shaman are imagined not only as human beings but as animals (Turkmen, Kirghiz and Uzbeks of the Khorezm oasis who came from the Aral region). Judging by the texts for summoning spirits similar images are not alien to Kazakhs.

5. A performance of shamanism usually takes place after dusk (Kazakhs, Turkmen, and Kirghiz).

6. The shaman uses a lash to whip spirits which cause harm (Kazakhs, Turkmen, Karakalpaks, and Uzbeks from Khorezm).

7.   Shamans use sabres or knives to show their ability to neutralize the effect of sharp metal objects. This ritual is found mostly in Turkmen villages: a barefooted shaman jumps on the blades of two sabres held on their shoulders by four persons. Sometimes the handles of the sabres are stuck into the ground and sometimes one sabre is placed on the ground blade up. The shaman walks on the sabres without cutting his feet. A Turkmen shaman is known to have stabbed himself with a sabre or asked somebody from the public to hammer the sabre into him with a wooden hammer. Many people have seen the blade penetrate the flesh, after which the shaman has removed the sabre, leaving no wound. On rare occasions a dagger has been substituted for a sabre. Sometimes shamans prick a patient with the knife and the patient remains uninjured. Shamans jumping on sabres lifted from the ground have been recorded in Karakalpak and Kazakh villages as well as in the villages of Uzbeks in Khorezm. Kazakh shamans more often use knives, pretending to pierce themselves and patients with them. Kirghiz shamans pierce their own and their patients' chests with knives. It is alleged that a certain shaman has cut off a patient's head and afterwards attached it to the body.

8.   Shamans use red-hot iron articles, taking them in their hands, putting them into their mouths, licking them, and walking on them barefooted (Kazakhs, Turkmen, Karakalpaks, and various groups of Khorezm Uzbeks and Kirghiz).

9.   Kazakh shamans, while performing, strike their heads and become enraged. Karakalpak shamans strike their heads against a door. In western Turkmenia some shamans strike the door with such force that the whole *yourta* [nomad's round tent] is shattered. Kazakh and, as it is said, Karakalpak shamans beat their heads and chests with the butt of an ax.

10.   During the performance shamans climb up a hanging rope and reach the *yourta*'s roof (Turkmen, Kirghiz).

11.   During the performance the shamans' actions are supplemented by movements resembling a sort of dance (Kazakhs, Turkmen, Kirghiz, and Karakalpaks of the Ferghana valley).

12.   Shamans, during the performance, strike the patient with the lungs of a sacrificial animal (Kazakhs and Kirghiz).

13.   After a collective meal when the meat of a sacrificial animal is eaten, its bones are collected and thrown away. It is believed that together with the bones the spirits which caused harm to the patient are also thrown away (Kazakhs, Turkmen, Karakalpaks, and Kirghiz). This ritual is also known among Uzbeks of Khorezm and the Ferghana

valley, but there it is not connected with shamanism. Kirghiz also believe that this ritual can be performed without a shaman.

14.   In some cases shamans transfer the spirits which caused disease to the skull of a horse or a dog (Kazakhs and Kirghiz; Turkmen in western regions practice this ritual very rarely).

## "TAJIK" OR "AGRICULTURAL" COMPLEX

1.   Shamans are, as a rule, women (Tajiks and Uzbeks of the Zeravshan valley, Tajiks of Ura-Tyube, and Uzbeks of the Tashkent oasis, southern Kazakhstan, and the Ferghana valley).

2.   Tajik and Uzbek shamans use a tambourine for musical accompaniment, without a drumstick. Karakalpak shamans in the Ferghana valley also use tambourines.

3.   Spirit-helpers of the shaman are almost always called *paris*. In the Zeravshan valley (Tajiks and Uzbeks) spirit-helpers are also called *momo*. A small group of Uzbeks in southern Kazakhstan, known as Sarts, call the patron spirit of a woman shaman *mama*.

4.   As a rule, the shaman's spirits are imagined in the shape of a human being. Only rarely are they imagined as animals.

5.   It is believed that the shaman (man or woman) has sexual intercourse with a patron spirit of the opposite sex (Tajiks and Uzbeks of the Zeravshan valley, Tajiks of Ura-Tyube, and Uzbeks of Khorezm). In the Turkic complex one finds only a feeble reflection of this belief, and in a number of cases, as in southern Kirghizia, it can be explained by the Tajik influence.

6.   During fortune-telling in all the above-mentioned regions, people use a cup of water into which a piece of cotton wool is usually put.

7.   The performance is held, as a rule, during the daytime.

8.   During the performance, lamps are lit for spirit-helpers.

9.   During the performance, flour and food made of flour are used as a ritual snack of which spirits also partake (Tajiks and Uzbeks of the Zeravshan valley, Tajiks of Ura-Tyube, and Kirghiz of southern Kirghizia).

10.   A bundle of withes is used for treating a patient (Uzbeks of the Ferghana valley, the Khorezm and Tashkent oases). A woman shaman touches the patient with the withe.

11.   At the end of the performance a woman shaman shows an article which was allegedly bewitched and found by her spirits. This object presumably inflicted harm on the patient (Uzbeks of the Fer-

ghana valley, Tashkent and Khorezm oases as well as Turkmen-Choudurs in the Khorezm oasis).

12.   During treatment a woman shaman covers the patient with white cloth (Uzbeks and Tajiks of the Zeravshan valley, Tajiks of Ura-Tyube, Uzbeks of the Ferghana valley, Khorezm oasis and southern Kazakhstan, and Kirghiz of southern Kirghizia).

13.   The shaman sprinkles or smears the patient with the blood of a sacrificial animal (Uzbeks and Tajiks of the Zeravshan valley, Tajiks of Ura-Tyube, Uzbeks and Karakalpaks of Ferghana, Uzbeks of Khorezm and southern Kazakhstan, and Turkmen-Choudurs of Khorezm).

14.   In a number of places, along with small cattle, a chick or a cock is used.

15.   During treatment a shaman ties knots in threads, thus depriving evil spirits of their ability to cause harm (Tajiks and Uzbeks of the Zeravshan valley, Tajiks of Ura-Tyube, and Uzbeks of Ferghana and southern Kazakhstan).

16.   During the performance a shaman's dance is either absent or not a characteristic feature.

Further accumulation of factual material will add new features to the above-listed complexes, will make clearer the borderlines of the areas of determining features, and may possibly reveal that some of the elements enumerated above are characteristic of both forms of Central Asian shamanism. However, the conclusion about the existence of two different complexes will not be revised.

Close ties between the peoples of Central Asia are accompanied by mutual cultural influence. That is why in regions where the features of one complex are predominant one finds features characteristic of another complex. Thus, in the Zeravshan valley one sometimes finds shamans using *dutar*, lash, or crook. In some regions of the Ferghana valley there are shamans who perform to the accompaniment of the *dutar*. In the regions of Samarkand and Ura-Tyube shamans perform mostly at night and during the ritual the bones of sacrificial animals are used. Kirghiz and Uzbeks of Khorezm have women shamans along with men.

Still, the geographical boundaries of various versions of shamanism coincide in general with the boundaries of settlement of Central Asian peoples. Peculiar local features of shamanism are connected with certain ethnic strata and the differences between the two forms are in many respects explained by the features of the ethnic history of the peoples inhabiting the two regions. The "Turkic" or "cattle-breeder" version preserved a connection with Siberian shamanism which is reflected in the similarity of a number of features: a lash is used, the

shaman dances, and tricks with red-hot articles and knives are performed. In this area of interest there are still some little-studied
stories of wonder-horses on which a shaman allegedly traveled to
another world during performances. Thus, Kazakh shamans sometimes used to run out of the *yourta*, jump on a horse, and ride to the
steppe, chasing away evil spirits. A Turkmen-Chouduri shaman rode
on a horse to a distant well where a bewitched article was allegedly
hidden. One Turkmen-Gyoklen shaman during the performance saddled
a she-goat and rode on it in the *yourta*. "Oh, my horse!" cried a
Kazakh shaman during the ceremony of summoning spirits described
by A. Divayev.

The vanished idea of the shaman's trip to another world on a
wonder-horse has left its traces not only in the ritual. In legends about
the founders of a group of Turkmen *khwajas* who adopted all the
functions of shamans, a Khan of Khiva summons a *khwaja* and tells
him: "Cure my son without dismounting the horse." Why did the
Khan prohibit the *khwaja*, who had an army of spirit-helpers, from
dismounting? This detail, unjustified by common norms of behavior,
is also a reminder that a horse is necessary for the performance. As we
know from another legend about the same Turkmen *khwaja*, this was
not a common horse. When returning from Khorezm to Nokhur the
*khwaja* turned part of a clay wall into a horse and a snake into a
whip. Certain Kazakh rituals lend perspective to these legends: Kazakh
shamans sent their *kobuz* to outrun the fastest horses; in Central Asia,
as in Siberia, the shaman's musical instrument acts as a wonder-horse.
The summoning of spirits by Kazakh, Kirghiz, and Altai shamans has
common features which can be explained only by genetic kinship.
Kirghiz' ties with the Altai are especially evident, as Kirghiz alone
divide their shamans into black and white.

Only twenty years ago it was believed that shamanism was brought
to Central Asia by waves of Turkish immigrants. But with the accumulation of new material (Sukharëva 1962; Snesarev 1969) it was
suddenly revealed that many essential features of shamanism derived
from ancient local belief connected, primarily, with the culture of
peoples speaking the Iranian language. This continuity with local
traditions is especially evident in the "Tajik" version. It can also be
traced in the Iranian names of spirits (*pari*, *momo*, *dev*) and shamans
(*porkham*, or, more correctly, *parikhon* and *folbin*) and in the details
of ritual. Snesarev, while looking for an explanation of the shamans'
custom of using withes during the performance, pointed to the use of tree
branches in the cult of Zoroastrians. A tambourine is a definite feature

of Siberian influence, but it has long been known in Central Asia and it functions as an element of culture created by a region's population speaking the Iranian language. An ancient Central Asian custom is to tell fortunes with the help of a mirror or a cup of water as well as the use of a chicken for sacrifice. Even transvestism, the traces of which have been noted only in Khorezm and in the Ferghana valley, can be explained by local traditions.

"Turkic" shamanism also adopted the traditions of the Iranian-speaking world, and left a strong impression on Central Asian shamanism as a whole. Among the Turkic-speaking peoples Uzbeks stand out as having received the strongest influence from shamanism and the religious practices of ancient Iranian-speaking peoples. Thus, only some features of Central Asian shamanism reveal genetic ties with Siberia, which weakens the position of those researchers who consider shamanism as a purely Siberian phenomenon.

Despite the existence of two forms of Central Asian shamanism, there are common features which make it possible to consider shamanism as a single historico-ethnographic phenomenon. Source testimonials dating earlier than the eighteenth century are not available, and by then Central Asian shamans did not use ritual clothing. Everywhere in Central Asia, shamanism, to some degree, was influenced by Islam. In general, similarities between the two forms of shamanism can be explained by the common fate of former religions after the establishment of Islam and not by a long-standing cultural interchange.

Central Asian shamanism of the nineteenth and twentieth centuries is interesting not only as a local version of this widespread phenomenon, but as a special version, characteristic of the later stage of shamanism under complete domination by monotheistic religion. This is evidently a relic of shamanism which acquired its peculiar makeup as a result of the spread of Moslem ideology. The most characteristic feature is that a Central Asian shaman does not travel to another world. The concept of a special world populated exclusively by spirits is also absent. A shaman feels ecstasy and loses his senses, which is explained by his relations with spirits, but nobody imagines him as being transferred to another sphere or land. Unlike a Siberian shaman, who is possessed by spirits or who himself rides to the world of spirits on his tambourine-horse, a Central Asian shaman instructs his spirit-helpers to go and find evil spirits or an evil-causing object. This feature of Central Asian shamanism is a result of rigid Moslem editing. To explain an illness by saying that spirits stole the man's soul is not accepted in Islam; that is why the task of finding the patient's soul is beyond the scope of the spirit-helpers of a Central Asian shaman. Along with his spirits a shaman also calls popular Moslem saints for help. More examples of the dependence of the shaman cult on Moslem ideology could be cited easily.

This dependence poses a question: how is the specificity of the shaman ideology proper expressed? In our opinion there is no such specificity in Central Asia since all the concepts underlying shamanism were borrowed from popular beliefs. Even the spirit-helpers in Central Asia (as well as in Siberia) are not specifically shamans' spirts, since it has been recognized that all other people can contact these spirits. That is why the Central Asian material does not allow us to speak of a special shaman ideology.

In general, from the point of view of a researcher in the history of religions, local specific forms of Central Asian shamanism lack originality: its rituals, beliefs, and practices are characteristic not only of the Central Asian peoples, but also of other peoples and, moreover, are often not connected originally with shamanism. Thus, some features of Central Asian shamanism were discovered far from Central Asia, including sexual intercourse between a man and the spirit reflecting him, spirits passed down as a legacy, men wearing women's clothes, spirits attracted by music, spirits fed with blood, a shaman pointing to the color of a sacrificial animal, the bones of a sacrificial animal preserved and buried, spirits depicted as dolls, a shaman looking into a mirror or a cup of water during fortune-telling, spells combatted by locking a lock or tying knots, and a shaman manipulating red-hot iron articles or coals.

In this connection the still widespread opinion that shamanism is a special form of religion is wrong. Shamanism is a special form of performance of religious rites. Playing the role of middleman between spirits and people, a shaman resembles a sorcerer, and actually shamanism and sorcery are so close to each other that it is difficult to draw a clear-cut line between them. Both shaman and sorcerer represent an early form of priesthood, characteristic, in general, of religions of the preclass and prestate periods. With the emergence of developed religions a new type of priesthood emerged, organized and acting in accordance with a codified ritual. Shamanism, or sorcery, remained as an unofficial cult, pushed into the background and without its former significance and function. It is in this form that shamanism remained in Central Asia, experiencing the influence of Islam, but retaining traces of its original state.

# REFERENCES

ABRAMZON, S. M.
  1971  *Kirgizy i ikh étnogeneticheskie i istoriko-kul'turnye svjazi* [The Kirghiz and their ethnogenetic and historico-cultural ties]. Leningrad.
BAJALIEVA, T. D.
  1972  *Doislamskie verovanije i ikh perezhitki u kirgizov* [Pre-Islamic religious beliefs and the vestiges of them among the Kirghiz].
BASILOV, V. N.
  1970  *Kul't svjatytkh v islame* [*The cult of saints in Islam*]. Moscow.
CHEKANINSKIJ, I. A.
  1929  Baksylyk. Sledy drevnikh verovanij kazakhov [Baksylyk. Traces of ancient Kazakh religious beliefs]. *Zapiski Semipalatinskogo Otdela Obshchestva izuchenija Kazakhstana* I. Semipalatinsk.
SNESAREV, G. P.
  1969  *Relikty domusul'manskikh verovanij i obrjadov u uzbekov khorezma* [Relics of pre-Moslem religious beliefs and rites among the Uzbeks of Khorezm]. Moscow.
SUKHARËVA, O. A.
  1962  *Islam v Uzbekistane* [Islam in Uzbekistan]. Tashkent.

# Shaman and Priest in Yucatán Pentecostalism

FELICITAS D. GOODMAN

Various forms of Pentecostalism are at present spreading in Latin America with remarkable rapidity. Lalive d'Epinay (1968) speaks of a Pentecostal explosion in Chile, and an article in the *New York Times* in December, 1972, estimates that by the end of the century, at the present rate of growth, every fifth Brazilian will be Pentecostal. The situation is similar in other Latin American countries.

In Mexico, the Apostolic church, a branch of the Pentecostal movement, has gained considerable prominence. The Apostolics differ from the Pentecostals in their emphasis on the unitary aspect of the Trinity. As they put it, the Pentecostals believe in three gods; they believe only in one. Mexicans came in contact with the sect in the first decade of the century in the United States, and by 1914 several congregations of the church were active in northern Mexico (Gaxiola 1964). In Mexico, as elsewhere in Latin America, the period after the Second World War saw a sudden spurt of growth in the various Pentecostal churches, bringing with it increased missionary effort. In 1959 this missionary effort was also expanded to the peninsula of Yucatán, which until then had been a somewhat neglected area in the backwater of this development. During the short history of the Apostolic movement in this part of the Republic of Mexico, congregations of varying size sprang up, mostly in rural areas. No statistics are available, but estimates made in the summer of 1972 enumerate and describe nineteen active congregations.

"A cross-cultural study of dissociational states," in which I participated, was conducted by Dr. Erika Bourguignon of the Department of Anthropology at the Ohio State University. It was supported entirely by Public Health Service Research Grant MH 07463.

This figure is quite unreliable, however. The reason is not so much that no proper records are kept. All the congregations I came to know during my fieldwork in the area possess a carefully written baptismal registry of their (adult) baptisms. Rather, the uncertainty about the status of the congregations arises from the fact that they evidence a curiously erratic pattern of growth. Under a system where the ministers rotate in an arbitrary sequence, with new ones insinuated into the circuit occasionally as they emerge from the local congregations, these groups show a puzzling waning and waxing of membership. There may come a sudden, often phenomenal increase, alternating with a period where the membership melts away, possibly disappearing entirely. In the latter phase, members either join other congregations, most frequently the Pentecostals proper, or they become entirely indifferent and return, as the Yucatecan parlance goes, to the *plaza,* that is, to secular life. This "glowworm" effect seems to correlate directly with the type of minister in charge of the particular congregation. A few case histories may elucidate the point.

Felipe, for instance, was the minister of the congregation at Utzpak (all names of persons and places have been changed) when I started my fieldwork there in 1969. He was born in a Maya backwoods village and had lived in Utzpak for more than ten years. He was considered kind, had a fine singing voice, played the guitar well, and did not demand any tithing from his desperately poor parishioners. In his sermons he offered simple, straightforward exegesis from a wide selection of topics from the New Testament. His prayers were gentle leadings, his orations for the "baptism of the Holy Spirit," evidenced by tongue speaking, were couched as gentle reminders of the power of the Lord and of the promise of the Holy Spirit to the believers. During his ministry, which lasted, with some interruptions, from 1965 to 1969, only two men acquired the capacity for speaking in tongues. The once promising congregation nearly disappeared. The services were often attended only by Felipe's parents and by the old *hermano* [male member] on whose land the temple was built. Nor was his failure restricted to Utzpak. In the summer of 1969, he attended a Bible Institute for three months and was then sent to evangelize on the island of Cozumel. The group there consisted of six adult members. Half a year later, none was left.

The problem was not, apparently, that Felipe was of peasant stock. Xavier, another minister, born and raised in the town of Campeche, was a housepainter by trade. Without any formal schooling, he had learned to read in the church. He knew the Bible well and again preached on a rather comprehensive range of topics. He was put in charge of a growing village congregation some distance from Utzpak, under the supervision of the very successful new minister at Utzpak. When the latter congregation suddenly began to grow under this man, Xavier was left to his own devices. Although an impressive tongue speaker — he had acquired the behavior only a few months previous to his assignment — not a single member of his congregation started speaking in tongues. Within a very short time, the group dissolved.

The urban congregations are also dependent on the minister in this manner. In the fall of 1969, the very effective pastor of the congregation in Mérida, the capital of Yucatán, was sent to a Bible Institute for a year. His place was taken by a man similar in approach to Felipe. When the Mérida minister returned in July 1970, his fine church was nearly empty. A week after his arrival I saw him preach to a congregation of four women, one of them his mother, the second his brother's wife, and the other two also members of his own household.

By contrast, the successful ministers are often personally brusque and make considerable financial demands on their congregations. They are not interested in wide-ranging exegesis, but rather concentrate single-mindedly in their sermons on two main topics: the imminence of the Second Coming of Christ and the importance of speaking in tongues. They hammer away at arguments supporting the prophecy that the millennium is just around the corner and the Kingdom of God will be established on earth. Since the Lord's wrath will destroy everything except his church, meaning the Apostolic one, it is vitally important to be a full member of it. For this, one needs a baptism by water, to wash away the accumulated sins, and, much more importantly, baptism by the Holy Spirit, as evidenced by tongue speaking, without which there is no access to salvation, the Kingdom of God, or heaven. Since these are the two traits that mainly distinguish the successful from the unsuccessful minister, we will have to analyze what their relative merits might be for the congregations in question.

It is easily understandable that people should rally to a sect preaching about the end of the world, when they are locked into painful, sudden, cultural dislocation. That the populations of Latin America are in this manner traumatized needs no elaborate proof (Wolf and Hansen 1972). In such a situation the imminence of the millennium is a tremendously attractive doctrine. This is especially so, as the emphasis is on the DESTRUCTION of the present world, represented by the oppressive dominant society, and one's own survival within the chosen church. But I would contend that this alone does not suffice to explain the attraction the successful minister holds. And, in fact, this is not what the people flocking to his services identify as the salient attraction either. While expressing appreciation for a fiery speaker, what informants point out as truly important is "the joy of the Lord" they are seeking — and receiving — in these services. And this joy comes with the speaking in tongues. It is this behavior then that we should scrutinize more closely.

The successful minister is highly adept in teaching the behavior of tongue speaking to his congregation. To this end, he marshals important aids, outstanding among them rhythmic manipulation. He guides the congregation into loud and very rhythmical singing; he demands rhythmical hand clapping and provides other means of accenting the beat of the singing, such as rattles and guitar music; he teaches the congregation *coritos* [short hymns of rousing melodies, easily learned by heart] which often directly ask for the "gift of tongues"; he also institutes rhythmical shouting of certain formulas, such as "*séllalos, séllalos*" [seal them, meaning seal them with your power, Holy Spirit]. The supplicant for the "gift" is often completely surrounded by this type of acoustic effect, which also contains a great deal of tongue speaking by those already in possession of the behavior. As a result of this kind of intense manipulation, speaking in tongues does, in fact rather quickly ensue in most subjects.

What then is this tongue speaking? As I have pointed out elsewhere (Goodman 1972), speaking in tongues, or glossolalia (from the Greek, *glosso* [tongue] and *lalia* [speech] can go from rather mild speech automatisms (such as often evidenced by members of the various charismatic movements and enthusiastic churches in the United States, when the typical statement is, "I just opened my mouth and it flowed out") to very intense utterances which may seem to the naive observer nothing more than a loud jumble of shrieks. They are not that, as power spectograms of these utterances clearly reveal. What in fact these utterances are might be termed, whether high or low intensity is represented, as definitely structured energy discharge episodes. And cross-culturally and cross-linguistically, they reveal similar features.

These features are mainly the strictly regular rhythm of the utterance, its striking "pulsing," which goes from muscle constriction (expressed as a consonant, frequently a glottal stop) to release (as vowel), over and over again, and particularly its intonation curve. This intonation rises, in the speaker, from the middle range to a clearly discernible and very brief peak, and then drops to levels below that of the onset. In the "jumble of shrieks" mentioned above, the power spectogram shows a rapid, highly contracted series of such peaks. I have transcribed and analyzed glossolalia utterances from such diverse linguistic and cultural environments as an Appalachian tent revival in Ohio; an Evangelical temple in Indiana; a Streams-of-Power congregation on St. Vincent Island in the Caribbean; an Apostolic church in Mexico City, where the native tongue was Spanish, and on Yucatán, where it was Maya; a nondenominational sect on the island of Nias in Indonesia, with Niasian as the native language; and others. Yet in each instance the diagnostic traits of glossolalia emerged with unfailing regularity.

I would therefore propose that this agreement is only possible because the behavior is based on and in turn determined by a common physiological substratum. Observations on the subjects while they are uttering glossolalia give us some clues as to what this common base might be. These findings support the conclusion that the speaking takes place in a more or less intense, aroused state of dissociation, varying from mild "trances" resembling daydreaming to very intense loss of contact with the environment and its stimuli. This altered mental state or trance, then, is the common base present in this behavior.

It goes without saying that we need to distinguish this insight into the neurophysiological process from the cultural interpretation of the resultant behavior. In the Pentecostal churches, and also in other denominations, glossolalia is INTERPRETED as evidence of a possession by the Holy Spirit. In anthropological terms, we are thus dealing with a form of possession trance, with the Holy Spirit held to be the possessing spirit. Approached from this angle, the successful minister then is the one who induces the trance state and by virtue of this capability appears to have spiritual power. He emerges as a shaman.

It is customary in the literature to distinguish between two types of religious practitioners, the SHAMAN and the PRIEST, and to correlate these with societal structure. In this scheme, the shaman correlates with loosely organized food-gathering societies, the priest with elaborate, food-producing agricultural ones. But we may also conceive of the difference, as has been done extensively in the literature, as arising from a distinction between behavioral components of the specialists themselves: the shaman is the medium for spirit possession, the priest the ritual specialist. Using concepts that emerged from the research of our group (Bourguignon 1972) we may say that the shaman uses altered states of consciousness (trance, hyperaroused conditions of dissociation) in his religious armamentarium as the outstanding behavioral feature; the priest is indifferent to this aspect and concentrates rather on learned ceremonial, ritual elaboration and theology.

Viewed on this higher level of generalization, societal structure may not always be the factor determining whether the religious practitioner present is the shaman or the priest. Both may, in fact, be simultaneously available as possibilities, latent, as it were, in a group, as I tried to show above on the basis of the examples from the Apostolic congregations in Yucatán. Depending on the social, cultural and environmental situation of a group, one or the other type of specialist is given preference, according to the overriding needs arising from the group. In the Apostolic congregations of Yucatán, the "practitioner of choice" is the shaman. We may now want to ask, what are the needs inherent in the present situation of the society in Yucatán that select for the shamanistic approach to religious experience and against the theological one, and how far does what the shaman has to offer meet those needs?

I would suggest that the rapid culture change foisted on this society from the outside is perceived as unmanageable and intensely painful by certain sectors of the Yucatecan society, specifically the peasantry. What people need in such times is some psychological strategy for relieving the anxiety, stress and tension, characteristically produced by situations of overwhelming cultural distortion. This is precisely what the shaman-minister is making available to his congregation. He teaches ways in which "the joy of the Lord" may be experienced, and more than that. "After we speak in tongues, our troubles are troubles no longer," say the informants.

To use our own vocabulary, the trance behavior which they learn as they engage in tongue speaking offers a possibility for releasing stress. Typically, hyperaroused trance episodes are followed by euphoria, a feeling of happiness, a relaxation. The peaking and subsequent attenuation, which, as we saw when discussing the glossolalia utterance, is the evolution of such an event on the neurophysiological level, is an effective tension-release mechanism. This property of the behavior has been used extensively in healing practices around the world in non-Christian contexts (see, for instance, Zempleni 1966). The resultant euphoria does not eliminate the memory of the conditions that produced the stress, and thus it is incorrect to refer to the behavior as an escape mechanism. Rather, it blunts the cutting edge of those conditions. The stresses are reduced to manageable proportions, they are placed in a different perspective. They have been internalized, in a manner of speaking, and in that way made familiar and bearable. Trance behavior thus emerges as an important mechanism for adaptation to "catastrophic" culture change. It is for this reason that the shaman-minister eclipses the priest — the theologian — in the present cultural situation of these populations.

# REFERENCES

BOURGUIGNON, ERIKA, *editor*
   1972   *Religion, altered states of consciousness, and social change.* Columbus Ohio: Ohio State University Press.
GAXIOLA, MACLOVIO L.
   1964   *Historia de la iglesia apostólica de la fe en Cristo Jesús de México.* Mexico City: Librería Latinoamericana.
GOODMAN, FELICITAS D.
   1972   *Speaking in tongues: a cross-cultural study of glossolalia.* Chicago: University of Chicago Press.
LALIVE D'EPINAY, CHRISTIAN
   1968   *El refugio de las masas.* Santiago, Chile: Editorial del Pacífico.
WOLF, ERIC R., EDWARD C. HANSEN
   1972   *The human condition in Latin America.* New York: Oxford University Press.
ZEMPLENI, A.
   1966   "La dimension thérapeutique du culte des rab," in *Rites de possession chez les Lebou et les Wolof*, 295–439. Psychopathologie Africaine 2.

REFERENCES

# Sense Stimulation and Ritual Response: Classifying the Religious Symbolism of the Persian and Yemenite Jews

LAURENCE D. LOEB

It is not uncommon to hear Jews described, in popular parlance, as some monolithic entity, an ethnoreligious population sharing most traits in common. Jewish scholars, however, have long been aware that this represents, at best, a simplistic postulation. While, in reality, there is a remarkable degree of conformity to focal cultural patterns and values among traditional Jews throughout the dispersion, the explanation for these similarities is to be sought in a literate Jewish GREAT TRADITION, whose core — the Bible, Talmud, and Midrash — are known, in some measure, by all Jews. Propagation of the Jewish great tradition was not left to the largely illiterate masses, but to the educated, who fulfilled a leadership role in interpreting the tradition for others.

It is not my intention here to explore and delineate the similarities of custom and behavior traditional to diaspora Jewry, but to evaluate, instead, variation in Jewish culture. For centuries Jewish scholars have noted extensive local variation in the ritual behavior of Jews all over the world, precisely in those artifacts and activities where one might expect the greatest conformity to the carefully codified Jewish great tradition. Indeed, the codifiers themselves always took this into account, for the Talmud, the main sourcebook of Jewish law, is essentially a discussion of, and opinions about, Jewish local LITTLE TRADITIONS. Sa'adyah Ga'on, Moses Maimonides, and Joseph Karo, among others, sifted through the variations, postulating those which they considered most appropriate. However, there has never been an authority who could enforce his decisions throughout the Jewish world. Thus, the Yemenites tend to follow Maimonides, the Persians, until some 200 years ago, appear to have followed Sa'adyah Ga'on, the Jews of Spain and their descendents chose the code of Jacob ben Asher and Joseph Karo (*Shulkhan Arukh*), while the Jews of Europe heeded the substantial revisions to this last code proposed by Moses Isserles. Jewish scholars tend to view their world as divided between the ritual traditions of Spain (Sephardic) and those of northern Europe (Ashkenazic). More recently there has been some appreciation of the "Oriental" Jewish tradition, but in Israel, where the consequences of such classifications are of daily import, only two chief rabbis are recognized: one Ashkenazic and one Sephardic.

"Custom annuls *halakha* [law]" (Montefiore and Loewe 1963:668) is one Talmudic maxim which serves to validate diverse Jewish rituals. Variation, often necessitated by the vicissitudes of the local environment, was viewed as potentially enriching, provided that it was not in diametric opposition to the great tradition. The importance of little traditions should not be underestimated in the survival of diaspora Jewry.

Despite the otherwise careful scholarship noting and describing the Jewish little traditions, the classification of them into Ashkenazic, Sephardic, etc. is clearly *ad hoc*. To the best of my knowledge, no METHODICAL classification of Jewish ritual variation is extant. Parameters for ordering and categorizing Jewish ritual symbols and manifest behavior with regard to them have yet to be offered. The best collections of local custom are haphazard (Ben-Jacob 1966), making comparison exceedingly difficult.

While researching the religious tradition of the Persian Jews of Shiraz,[1] I was struck by a pattern of response to generally acknowledged customary Jewish symbols which seemed to differ from that of Jews elsewhere. Having spent most of my life among Ashkenazim from both Western and Eastern Europe and lesser periods among Spanish-Portuguese Sephardim and Yemenites, I noted, in particular, a distinctive variance in the diversification of the sense stimulation prompted by these symbols, as well as qualitative and quantitative alteration with regard to each of the five senses.

It occurred to me that the relative sense stimulation produced by each symbol could provide one set of parameters for methodically comparing Jewish ritual behavior. Rating each symbol in terms of the five senses does not suffice to present a valid profile of the total com-

[1] Fieldwork was done in Iran in 1967–68 with grants furnished by the Memorial Foundation for Jewish Culture, Cantors Assembly of America and a New York State, Herbert Lehman Fellowship.

munity experience for comparative purposes, for it covertly assumes universal equivalency of importance, frequency of occurrence, and type of participation for each symbol. Rating itself is usually a tricky approach to social data and is the source of considerable controversy. (A case in point is Alan Lomax's Cantometric/Choreometric project.) But if the error can be kept to a minimum, the graphed score may provide a valuable visual expression of social factors, i.e. a profile of a LITTLE TRADITION.

In order to test the utility of this approach it was decided to compare two communities. I chose to contrast the tradition of Shiraz, Iran, with that of Sana, Yemen. The Shiraz data are my own. Because the Sana data are too limited for purposes of this study (Kafih 1963), I was compelled to use data from other localities (Brauer 1934; Nahum 1962; Sapir 1951). Hence, I refer to this community as "Yemenite."


## COMPILATION OF DATA

In this study, forty-five ritual objects, places, and activities were selected.[2] Each was assigned a clearly arbitrary meaning by the Jewish great tradition, hence they may be designated "symbols" or "symbolic." Many could be further subdivided into smaller components whose evaluation would be more precise and accurate than that of the gross composite symbols presented here. However, as this is merely an initial probe into the utility of this approach, these forty-five symbols more than suffice.

During field research in Iran, I noted a range of ritual observance from extremely meticulous to extremely lax. This personal deviance from the ideal no doubt occurred in the past as well and is reported for other Jewish communities (Zborowski and Herzog 1962). Nowadays, observance of traditional Shirazi custom is on the wane due to acculturative pressures of modern Iranian life on the one hand, and inroads made by the Sephardic (mainly Baghdadi) tradition on the other. It was deemed desirable to choose an instant in time preceding these pressures, to evoke material more indigenous than found at present. The year 1949 was selected, as I had appropriate data for that period. Furthermore, a compromise between real and ideal observance was struck by comparing the behavior and attitude of the very pious with more typical, tradition-minded Shirazis.

[2] Refer to the *Encyclopaedia Judaica* or the *Jewish encyclopaedia* for their explanation.

Table 1.   Rating Shirazi and Yemenite symbolism

| Ritual Object/Place/Activity | Shirazi | | | Yemenite | |
| --- | --- | --- | --- | --- | --- |
| | F.I.P. | a b c d e | | F.I.P. | a b c d e |
| 1. Amulet [a] | 2 4 4 | 4 0 3 0 1 | | 2 4 4 | 4 1 3 0 0 |
| 2. *Halla* (priest's share) | 0 - - | - - - - - | | 4 3 3 | 3 2 1 2 3 |
| 3. *Mzuza* | 5 3 3 | 4 0 4 0 1 | | 5 4 3 | 4 0 3 0 1 |
| 4. *Pe'ot* (side-locks) [b] | 5 1 3 | 5 0 2 0 0 | | 5 5 3 | 5 0 3 0 0 |
| 5. *Seder* plate | 1 5 4 | 5 3 3 2 4 | | 1 5 4 | 5 3 3 2 4 |
| 6. *Siddur* (prayer book) | 4 2 2 | 5 2 3 0 0 | | 5 4 3 | 5 3 3 0 0 |
| 7. *Sukka* (tabernacle) | 2 5 4 | 5 2 3 3 2 | | 2 5 4 | 5 2 3 4 3 |
| 8. Synagogue | 4 5 4 | 4 5 3 2 1 | | 5 5 3 | 4 5 3 3 3 |
| 9. *Tora* | 4 5 4 | 5 3 4 0 0 | | 4 5 3 | 5 5 3 0 0 |
| 10. *Tsitsit* (fringes) | 4 5 3 | 5 2 4 0 1 | | 5 5 3 | 5 1 3 0 1 |
| 11. *Aliya* (pilgrimage/Israel) | 1 5 2 | 5 4 3 2 2 | | 1 5 2 | 5 4 3 2 2 |
| 12. *Aliya* to (read) Tora | 3 5 3 | 5 4 3 0 0 | | 3 5 3 | 5 5 3 0 0 |
| 13. Animal Sacrifice | 3 5 4 | 5 4 1 1 1 | | 0 - - | - - - - - |
| 14. *Bar Mitsva* | 1 2 2 | 4 5 1 1 1 | | 0 - - | - - - - - |
| 15. *Brakha* (general blessing) | 5 5 3 | 3 5 1 1 1 | | 5 5 3 | 4 5 2 1 1 |
| 16. *Brakha* on food | 4 4 3 | 2 3 2 4 5 | | 5 4 3 | 2 3 2 3 4 |
| 17. Burning leaven | 1 3 2 | 5 1 1 3 0 | | 1 5 2 | 5 1 2 2 0 |
| 18. Circumcision | 1 5 4 | 5 4 4 0 2 | | 1 5 4 | 5 3 4 1 3 |
| 19. Covering head | 4 3 4 | 4 0 3 0 0 | | 5 3 4 | 5 0 3 0 0 |
| 20. Fasting | 2 5 4 | 1 1 2 2 4 | | 2 4 4 | 1 1 2 3 5 |
| 21. *Hannuka* candle lighting | 2 3 3 | 5 2 1 1 0 | | 2 4 3 | 5 1 2 1 0 |
| 22. *Havdala* (Sabbath separation) | 4 3 3 | 4 3 2 4 4 | | 4 3 3 | 3 4 2 4 4 |
| 23. Honoring the dead | 4 5 4 | 3 4 2 2 3 | | 4 5 4 | 4 4 2 2 2 |
| 24. *Hoshannot* beating | 1 2 3 | 4 2 5 0 0 | | 1 3 3 | 4 1 4 0 0 |
| 25. *Kashrut* (general) | 5 5 4 | 3 0 1 1 4 | | 5 5 4 | 4 2 2 2 4 |
| 26. *Lulav* and *etrog* waving | 2 5 4 | 5 2 4 3 0 | | 2 5 3 | 5 3 4 2 0 |
| 27. *Matsa* baking | 1 4 2 | 3 1 3 3 0 | | 2 5 3 | 4 1 4 1 0 |
| 28. *Matsa* eating | 2 5 4 | 3 1 4 2 5 | | 2 5 4 | 3 1 2 1 5 |
| 29. *Mgilla* reading | 1 5 4 | 2 5 1 0 0 | | 1 5 3 | 3 5 0 0 0 |
| 30. Pilgrimage | 1 5 4 | 5 4 3 1 1 | | 1 5 4 | 5 4 3 1 1 |
| 31. Priestly blessing | 5 5 4 | 3 5 4 0 0 | | 5 4 3 | 2 5 1 0 0 |
| 32. Private prayer | 2 2 2 | 2 3 2 0 0 | | 5 5 4 | 4 3 2 0 0 |
| 33. Public prayer | 4 5 4 | 4 5 3 2 2 | | 5 5 3 | 5 5 3 2 2 |
| 34. *Qiddush* (sanctification) | 4 3 3 | 4 3 2 3 5 | | 4 4 4 | 3 4 2 2 5 |
| 35. Ritual handwashing | 4 3 3 | 3 1 5 1 0 | | 5 4 3 | 3 2 5 1 1 |
| 36. Ritual immersion (female) | 3 5 3 | 2 1 5 1 1 | | 3 5 3 | 2 1 5 1 1 |
| 37. Ritual immersion (male) | 1 2 2 | 2 1 5 1 1 | | 1 3 3 | 2 1 5 1 1 |
| 38. Ritual slaughter | 4 5 2 | 3 1 1 1 1 | | 4 5 2 | 5 1 3 1 1 |
| 39. Sabbath candle lighting | 4 4 3 | 5 0 1 1 0 | | 4 4 3 | 5 1 2 1 0 |
| 40. *Seder* (Passover meal) | 1 5 4 | 5 4 3 2 5 | | 1 5 4 | 5 4 3 2 4 |
| 41. Separation of meat and milk | 5 3 4 | 5 0 1 2 4 | | 5 5 4 | 5 1 1 3 4 |
| 42. Sermonizing | 4 5 3 | 3 5 0 0 0 | | 4 4 3 | 3 5 0 0 0 |
| 43. *Shofar* blowing | 2 5 4 | 3 5 2 0 1 | | 3 5 4 | 3 5 2 0 1 |
| 44. Study | 4 3 2 | 3 5 0 0 0 | | 4 5 3 | 5 4 2 1 1 |
| 45. *Tashlikh* (casting out) | 1 3 3 | 4 1 2 0 0 | | 0 - - | - - - - - |

Table 1 (continued)

*Key*

| | | |
|---|---|---|
| F - Frequency of occurrence | I - Importance | P - Extent of participation |
| 0 - does not occur | 0 - unknown | 1 - single individual |
| 1 - once per year or less | 1 - minimal importance | 2 - select group |
| 2 - several times per year | 2 - somewhat important | 3 - males only/females only |
| 3 - at least once per month | 3 - important | 4 - entire community |
| 4 - at least once per week | 4 - very important | |
| 5 - every day | 5 - maximal (critical) importance | |

| Senses | Sense involvement |
|---|---|
| a - sight | 0 - no apparent involvement |
| b - hearing | 1 - minimal involvement |
| c - touch | 2 - slight involvement |
| d - smell | 3 - medium involvement |
| e - taste | 4 - high involvement |
| | 5 - maximal involvement |

a  An amulet does not, strictly speaking, belong in the great tradition, but it is such a widespread phenomenon, that it is not inconsistent to include it for our purposes.
b  *Pe'ot* have not been worn in Shiraz for more than 50 years; the figures are projections of the old tradition, which could not have been an especially important one.

Having to rely largely on literary sources for the Yemenite data, I attempted, insofar as possible, to balance the ideal, as set forth for Sana, with practices reported for the villages. The Yemenite congregation I observed in Jerusalem in 1960–1961 was a mixed one, thereby increasing the difficulties of evaluation.

The scaling selected was quite arbitrarily fixed at 0 to 5 for: Frequency of occurrence (F), Importance (I) and Sense involvement; it was set at 1 to 4 for: Extent of participation (P). (F) and (P) factors were determined empirically and are objective; (I) and Sense involvement were the subjective impression of the author as observed or based on interviews in the Shirazi situation, or as interpreted from the literature in the Yemenite case.

## ANALYZING THE DATA

Table 1 is a presentation of the raw data which, upon appropriate computation, yield the figures found in Table 2. The resulting numbers represent the relative impact of each symbol in terms of sense stimulation, weighted for frequency of occurrence, importance, and extent of participation. They range from a minimum of zero to a maximum of 500.

Table 2.  Sensory involvement: comparative score for Yemen and Shiraz

| Ritual Object/Place/Activity | Shiraz | | | | | | Yemen | | | | | |
|---|---|---|---|---|---|---|---|---|---|---|---|---|
| | a | b | c | d | e | Total | a | b | c | d | e | Total |
| 1. Amulet | 128 | 0 | 96 | 0 | 32 | 256 | 128 | 32 | 96 | 0 | 0 | 256 |
| 2. Halla | 0 | 0 | 0 | 0 | 0 | 0 | 108 | 72 | 36 | 72 | 108 | 396 |
| 3. Mzuza | 180 | 0 | 180 | 0 | 45 | 405 | 240 | 0 | 180 | 0 | 60 | 480 |
| 4. Pe'ot | 75 | 0 | 30 | 0 | 0 | 105 | 375 | 0 | 225 | 0 | 0 | 600 |
| 5. Seder plate | 100 | 60 | 60 | 40 | 80 | 340 | 100 | 60 | 60 | 40 | 80 | 340 |
| 6. Siddur | 80 | 32 | 48 | 0 | 0 | 160 | 300 | 180 | 180 | 0 | 0 | 660 |
| 7. Sukka | 200 | 80 | 120 | 120 | 80 | 600 | 200 | 80 | 120 | 160 | 120 | 680 |
| 8. Synagogue | 320 | 400 | 240 | 160 | 80 | 1,200 | 300 | 375 | 225 | 225 | 225 | 1,350 |
| 9. Tora | 400 | 240 | 320 | 0 | 0 | 960 | 300 | 300 | 180 | 0 | 0 | 780 |
| 10. Tsitsit | 300 | 120 | 240 | 0 | 60 | 720 | 375 | 75 | 225 | 0 | 75 | 750 |
| 11. Aliya to Israel | 50 | 40 | 30 | 20 | 20 | 160 | 50 | 40 | 30 | 20 | 20 | 160 |
| 12. Aliya to Tora | 225 | 180 | 135 | 0 | 0 | 540 | 225 | 225 | 135 | 0 | 0 | 585 |
| 13. Animal Sacrifice | 300 | 240 | 60 | 60 | 60 | 720 | 0 | 0 | 0 | 0 | 0 | 0 |
| 14. Bar Mitsva | 16 | 20 | 4 | 4 | 4 | 48 | 0 | 0 | 0 | 0 | 0 | 0 |
| 15. Brakha (general) | 225 | 375 | 75 | 75 | 75 | 825 | 300 | 375 | 150 | 75 | 75 | 975 |
| 16. Brakha on food | 96 | 144 | 96 | 192 | 240 | 768 | 120 | 180 | 120 | 180 | 240 | 840 |
| 17. Burning leaven | 30 | 6 | 6 | 18 | 0 | 60 | 50 | 10 | 20 | 20 | 0 | 100 |
| 18. Circumcision | 100 | 80 | 80 | 0 | 40 | 300 | 100 | 60 | 80 | 20 | 60 | 320 |
| 19. Covering head | 192 | 0 | 144 | 0 | 0 | 336 | 300 | 0 | 180 | 0 | 0 | 480 |
| 20. Fasting | 40 | 40 | 80 | 80 | 160 | 400 | 32 | 32 | 64 | 96 | 160 | 384 |
| 21. Hannuka candle lighting | 90 | 36 | 18 | 18 | 0 | 162 | 120 | 24 | 48 | 24 | 0 | 216 |
| 22. Havdala | 144 | 108 | 72 | 144 | 144 | 612 | 108 | 144 | 72 | 144 | 144 | 612 |

| | a | b | c | d | e | Total | a | b | c | d | e | Total |
|---|---|---|---|---|---|---|---|---|---|---|---|---|
| 27. *Matsa* baking | 24 | 8 | 24 | 24 | 0 | 80 | 120 | 30 | 120 | 30 | 0 | 300 |
| 28. *Matsa* eating | 120 | 40 | 160 | 80 | 200 | 600 | 120 | 40 | 80 | 40 | 200 | 480 |
| 29. *Mgilla* reading | 40 | 100 | 20 | 0 | 0 | 160 | 45 | 75 | 0 | 0 | 0 | 120 |
| 30. Pilgrimage | 100 | 80 | 60 | 20 | 20 | 280 | 100 | 80 | 60 | 20 | 20 | 280 |
| 31. Priestly blessing | 300 | 500 | 400 | 0 | 0 | 1,200 | 120 | 300 | 60 | 0 | 0 | 480 |
| 32. Private prayer | 16 | 24 | 16 | 0 | 0 | 56 | 400 | 300 | 200 | 0 | 0 | 900 |
| 33. Public prayer | 320 | 400 | 240 | 160 | 160 | 1,280 | 375 | 375 | 225 | 150 | 150 | 1,275 |
| 34. *Qiddush* | 144 | 108 | 72 | 108 | 180 | 612 | 192 | 256 | 128 | 128 | 320 | 1,024 |
| 35. Ritual handwashing | 108 | 36 | 180 | 36 | 0 | 360 | 180 | 120 | 300 | 60 | 60 | 720 |
| 36. Ritual immersion (female) | 90 | 45 | 225 | 45 | 45 | 450 | 90 | 45 | 225 | 45 | 45 | 450 |
| 37. Ritual immersion (male) | 8 | 4 | 20 | 4 | 4 | 40 | 18 | 9 | 45 | 9 | 9 | 90 |
| 38. Ritual slaughter | 120 | 40 | 40 | 40 | 40 | 280 | 200 | 40 | 120 | 40 | 40 | 440 |
| 39. Sabbath candle lighting | 240 | 0 | 48 | 48 | 0 | 336 | 240 | 48 | 96 | 48 | 0 | 432 |
| 40. *Seder* | 100 | 80 | 60 | 40 | 100 | 380 | 100 | 80 | 60 | 40 | 80 | 360 |
| 41. Separation of meat and milk | 300 | 0 | 60 | 120 | 240 | 720 | 500 | 100 | 100 | 300 | 400 | 1,400 |
| 42. Sermonizing | 180 | 300 | 0 | 0 | 0 | 480 | 144 | 240 | 0 | 0 | 0 | 384 |
| 43. *Shofar* blowing | 120 | 200 | 80 | 0 | 40 | 440 | 120 | 300 | 120 | 0 | 60 | 600 |
| 44. Study | 72 | 120 | 0 | 0 | 0 | 192 | 300 | 240 | 120 | 60 | 60 | 780 |
| 45. *Tashlikh* | 36 | 9 | 18 | 0 | 0 | 63 | 0 | 0 | 0 | 0 | 0 | 0 |
| Totals | 6,493 | 4,707 | 4,307 | 2,036 | 2,789 | 20,332 | 8,101 | 5,561 | 5,001 | 2,466 | 3,371 | 24,500 |
| Percentages | 31.9 | 23.2 | 21.2 | 10.0 | 13.7 | = 100% | 33.0 | 22.7 | 20.5 | 10.1 | 13.8 | = 100.1%[a] |

*Key*

a - sight, b - hearing, c- touch, d - smell, e - taste

[a] Rounding off to the nearest tenth is responsible for this discrepancy.

Figure 1 is a graphic representation of Table 2, arranged by sense. Figure 2 compares the relative impact of eight selected symbols in graphic form.

The evidence indicates some important divergence in the impact of great tradition symbols among Shirazis and Yemenites. The Yemenite tradition appears to be considerably more intense in each sense category and overall (about 20 percent). However, the proportion of sensory impact in each sense category is roughly the same for Yemen and Shiraz. The graphs reveal that, for the most part, the sense stimulation provided by the symbols has a similar effect in both communities, but that the degree of involvement varies. Shirazis and Yemenites differ most in their visual and tactile responses, and appear most similar with regard to taste.

The profile graphs found in Figure 2 illustrate, on a microlevel, the different impact of several symbols. Examples 31 (priestly blessing) and 44 (study) are markedly dissimilar in the two communities, while 34 (*qiddush*) and 35 (*ritual handwashing*) are only slightly less so. Public prayer (33) has a very similar impact in both communities, though by no means identical. Examples 16 (*brakha* on food), 26 (*lulav* and *etrog* waving) and 10 (*tsitsit*) show crossing of the plotted points; this demonstrates alternation of impact; for example, *tsitsit* has more visual impact in Yemen, but greater auditory and tactile impact in Shiraz. Some symbols, e.g. 44 (study), involve total sensory participation in one community, but not in the other.

## IMPLICATIONS

Analysis of the data suggests that this kind of profile analysis will indeed be of help in comparing various Jewish little traditions. There are indications that the great tradition provides an adequate baseline for comparative purposes. Both of these premises require some elaboration.

There are several important weaknesses in the method explored in this paper. The ratings with regard to importance (I) and sense involvement are subjectively derived and thus require careful handling and the development of means of verification. This implies that a proper comparison of this kind would require expertise in the traditions to be compared. The assumption underlying the weighting of input factors, i.e. that they are of the same order, is more than likely incorrect. In measuring sensory impact or sense-stimulation, this assumption tends to favor regular, frequent activities over less common ones. In truth,

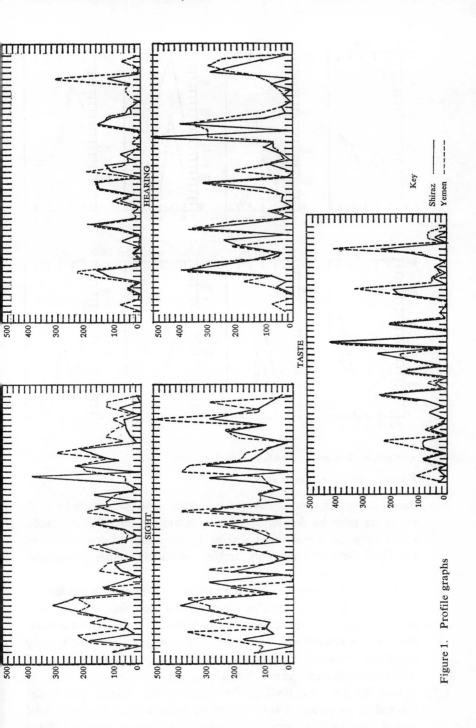

Figure 1.  Profile graphs

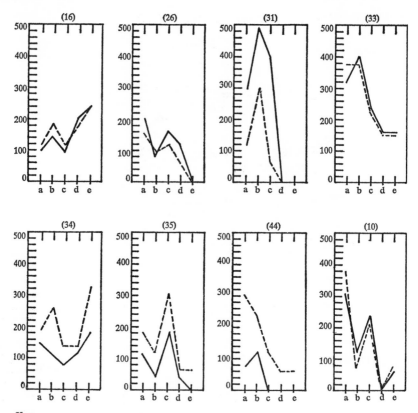

Key

a - sight, b - hearing, c - touch, d - smell, e - taste

Figure 2.   Profile graphs by symbol

the more contact with a symbol, the less the impression made by it. A technique must be developed to compensate for this. Objectification might be made considerably simpler by reducing the comparison to the ideal little tradition only and/or substituting other parameters for the five senses.

Despite these shortcomings, the method of comparison outlined in this paper has several positive aspects. Data are coherently classified and quantified. Differences between traditions are clearly noted qualitatively and quantitatively, and through graphing they may be quickly visualized. While the number of symbols must be expanded to several hundred, this presents no problem whatsoever.

Utilizing the great tradition baseline, we can observe differential cultural development. Thus, in Yemen, study is strongly emphasized among Jews (as it is among their Muslim neighbors), far beyond the great tradition norm; in Shiraz religious study falls far short of that norm. In Yemen, the priestly blessing is performed knowledgeably, conforming to the great tradition. In Shiraz, the local tradition ignores the great tradition expectation of finger deployment by the priests, but tacks on a coda ceremony, including a personal blessing to each male by each priest as well as physical extension of the blessing by extending, touching, and kissing *tsitsit* [fringes] in an exchange gesture. Why this ritual activity has been developed to so high a level of sensory involvement is not yet known.

It is hoped that by using symbol profile analysis with sense-stimulation as a parameter, it may be possible to construct a typography of Jewish little traditions.

## REFERENCES

BEN-JACOB, ABRAHAM
  1966   *Yalkut minhagim.* Jerusalem: Government Printer.
BRAUER, ERICH
  1934   *Ethnologie der jemenitischen Juden.* Heidelberg: Carl Winters.
KAFIH, JOSEPH
  1963   *Jewish life in Sana.* Jerusalem: Ben-Zvi Institute.
MONTEFIORE, C. G., H. LOEWE
  1963   *A rabbinic anthology.* New York: Meridian Books.
NAHUM, YEHUDA LEVI
  1962   *Matspunot yhude teyman.* Tel Aviv.
SAPIR, JACOB
  1951   *Sefer masa' teyman.* Jerusalem: Lewin-Epstein.
ZBOROWSKI, MARK, ELIZABETH HERZOG
  1962   *Life is with people.* New York: Schocken.

# Characteristics of Sisala Diviners

EUGENE L. MENDONSA

## SISALA SOCIAL STRUCTURE

The Sisala live mainly in the Tumu District in northern Ghana. The environment is African savanna, which is primarily bush, due to the relatively low population density. The Sisala show cultural uniformity with the other tribes of the Ashanti hinterland, that is, they are patrilineal, with a social structure of the Guinea type, and they practice hoe horticulture to produce a subsistence diet of millet, sorghum, maize, yams, and rice. Cattle are kept in small numbers for sacrificial purposes and bridewealth.

Agnatic descent is the keystone of Sisala social structure. Their society is divided into a number of patri-clans (*-viara*), which form localized ritual units having a common interest. The clan is an exogamous unit made up of several villages or sometimes village segments. The village (*tang* or *jang*) is the important focal point of identification for an individual. Patrilocal residence dictates, therefore, a divided sense of identification for the women, while men remain firmly rooted in their natal villages. A village is normally divided into a series of lineages (*jechiking*) which are arranged to form two reciprocal burial groups — that is, the village is divided in two. While the entire village considers itself to be one body of kinsmen,

I carried out ten months of fieldwork in northern Ghana in 1971–1972 while a research student at the University of Cambridge. I would like to acknowledge the financial support of the British Universities Student Travel Association; the Ling Roth Fund and the Anthony Wilkin Fund, Faculty of Archaeology-Anthropology, University of Cambridge; and the Smuts Memorial Fund, University of Cambridge. I also wish to thank my supervisor, Professor Meyer Fortes, and Professor Jack Goody for their encouragement and support.

kinship increases in intensity as the units of the segmentary system become smaller, and therefore the reciprocal burial groups are felt to be "brother" groups. The lineage (*jechiking*) is the important corporate unit. It is the subsistence-residential homestead or walled enclosure normally inhabited by an agnatic extended family. This unit is further divided into compounds or yards (*kaala*) made up of joint families who farm together. Each *kaala* is divided into houses (*diasang*) and rooms (*dia*). In this segmentary system the developmental cycle is a continual enlargement of the single room (*dia*), through marriage and childbirth, into higher-order units which may eventually result in fission and a repetition of the process.

Today the Isalung-speakers are governed by a paramount chief (the *Tumukuoro*) and various village chiefs (*kuoro*), of whom twelve are divisional chiefs. This system was initiated by the British during their colonial efforts in northern Ghana, and although these political units did not correspond to traditional ones, they have since become realities. The most important precolonial political unit was the village (*jang*), under the leadership of the village *tinteintina* (custodian of the earth) and the elders (*nihising*). Because there were no "chiefs," the *tinteintina* wielded politico-ritual power based on his control of the ancestral shrines. Today the village chief (*kuoro*) has taken on the political functions, while the *tinteintina* has remained concerned with ritual matters such as the fertility of the earth and the fecundity of women.

Sisala society is a gerontocracy, and life is a series of age-based stages or grades. There are two important rites of passage for a man or woman, namely, marriage (*jaanung*) and death (*suunung*). The first allows the passage from the status of small boy (*henmie*) or girl (*hantolowie*) to adult (*niwang*). This transition is further enhanced when the marriage produces living offspring. The second rite of passage comes at a person's death, necessitating the performance of elaborate funerary rites marking passage from the status of elder (*nihiang*) to that of a remembered ancestor (*lelung*).

## KINDS OF SISALA DIVINATION

For the Sisala, divination is not so much a way of knowing the future, as a way of knowing *fa fa* — that is, knowing which occult entity has afflicted them — although it can also be used to determine whether affliction lies ahead. There are five major ways in which this is accomplished: (1) necromancy, (2) ordeal, (3) throwing cowries, (4) fairy-calling, and (5) traditional divination.

NECROMANCY If a death is thought to be due to witchcraft, the members of the family in which the death has occurred may perform necromancy at the funeral. In former times this involved three men carrying the dead body on their shoulders; it was thought that as the men wandered around the crowded funeral, the body would point out the dead person's killer. However, during colonial times the British stressed immediate burial of the body, and now the Sisala have substituted for the body a bundle of ebony sticks tied with the cover cloth of the dead person. If this bundle does not point out an individual who is responsible for the death, it may point to a shrine. This type of divination is practiced infrequently, and is most likely to be performed when the person has died mysteriously, e.g. by drowning or in the bush.

ORDEAL    Ordeals are infrequent, possibly owing to the low level of witchcraft accusation but also because the Sisala prefer a less public means of sanction. Many times I noticed that persons would avoid taking their grevances to a public forum or ordeal. At first I thought this was a function of their guilt, but soon I learned that the Sisala prefer private means to public means. One day I was sitting with the *nihiang nihiang* [oldest man] of Bujan, and we were discussing the fact that his son's wife had had one *cedi* stolen while at the Tumu market. I suggested that she swear by the rain (*gmiese duong*) in order to punish the thief or force him to come forward, but everyone present was shocked at the suggestion. The *nihiang nihiang* explained that the Sisala do not like to do such things, and when I asked why this was so, he related a story:

A long time ago in Kasana [a Kasena village to the north] an old woman had just pounded some *dawa-dawa* flour, and a woman of another lineage came and took part of it. When the old lady returned to discover the theft, she swore by the rain, calling it to kill the thief. Meanwhile the thief had put some of the flour in every cooking pot in her lineage. Every lineage member ate of it except one man who had just gone to the farm. The rain sent the lightning and killed all the lineage members except the one man at the farm. This is why we now hesitate to swear by the rain, although we don't taboo it. The Kasena still do this frequently, but we do not. Even if a chicken were to eat some of the flour, the rain would kill it. Many innocent people can die from such an act.

Nevertheless, some people do swear by the rain to discover a hidden thing, since doing hidden things (*luore*) is considered bad and is akin to witchcraft — as indicated by the word *luore*, which is cognate with the word for stomach, *luorung*, which is the seat of witchcraft. Since witchcraft is such a bad thing, some people feel justified in swearing by the rain to find a witch, but more commonly a sacrifice will be made on the earth shrine to determine whether a given individual is a witch.

The scorpion ordeal is another form of divination. It is usually used to divine a petty theft or some other minor delict — e.g. a man may determine which of his wives put her hand into his compound granary (*viribalung*). Suspects are lined up and the scorpion is allowed to crawl over their arms, and the sting is both the proof and the punishment. When persons are accused of a petty crime, they often expose themselves to a kind of ordeal. When confronted, a person may deny the deed and add, "If I am guilty, let a snake bite me." The Sisala greatly fear the bite of a snake, and also believe that such a bite is often a punishment by the ancestors.

Although these institutions have judicial functions, they can be viewed as divinatory devices as well. Reynolds (1963: 121) has pointed out that an ordeal can be considered a legal device when administered to one person, whereas it is a divinatory device when several persons are involved. Yet there is an element of divination even in an accusation of witchcraft. A ritual formula is followed to stimulate an answer from the occult world, and this is precisely what the traditional diviner does when he divines. When looking at divination, one should therefore consider the entire range of devices used to receive feedback from *fa fa* [the occult world].

THROWING COWRIES   Diviners who throw cowrie shells (*vuge ari mowribie*) are also known and consulted, but this practice is not indigenous to the Sisala and has probably diffused into the Sisala area from the Islamic peoples to the north. There are relatively few Sisala who actually practice this kind of divination. Mostly cowrie-shell-throwers are found in the northwest section of Sisala-land, which is more heavily influenced by Islamic culture, and they are strangers who practice as wandering diviners. Many of the Sisala who practice throwing cowries are innovators who have made several earlier attempts to achieve prestige by nontraditional means. In my experience, the same individuals who have tried throwing cowries have also tried calling fairies — which is also a practice that has been borrowed from the neighboring Awuna and Kasena to the north. Pagan Sisala who consult traditional diviners tend to look down on cowrie-throwing as less reliable than traditional divination, and traditional diviners have told me that if their verdict was too different from that of a cowrie-thrower, the latter would die from ancestral anger. Cowrie-throwers are sometimes consulted if they happen to be passing through the village — e.g. when a Wangara cowrie-thrower came through Bujan,[1] many persons consulted him merely because he was there, and they hoped

[1] Bujan is the village where most of my fieldwork took place. It has about four hundred people, and is relatively isolated and traditional.

he would tell them something good. In general, however, when a Sisala suffers an affliction, he will seek out the traditional diviner to ascertain the occult cause. Cowrie-throwers are not viewed as being in the same class. One informant (a diviner) told me the following story, which is biased, but nonetheless reflects a general feeling:

The divining bag [of the traditional diviner] came from God. It was here prior to those who throw cowries and who only profess to see things. Anyone can become a cowrie-thrower by going to another cowrie-thrower and asking to share his medicine. His face is washed with the medicine after he pays a fee, and he can start throwing cowries.

FAIRY-CALLING    The fairy-caller (*kantonngo yirang*) is a relatively recent introduction from the neighboring Awuna-Kasena peoples. There are only a few Sisala men who have learned this technique of divining, and the technique does not seem to be gaining much ground. Of the 272 Sisala males I interviewed about their consulting habits, only 7.3 percent had ever been to a fairy-caller in their entire lifetime, while 86 percent had consulted a traditional diviner at least once in the month prior to the interview. It is commonly held that Sisala men do not know the proper technique for calling fairies, therefore those who wish to consult a fairy-caller often make a rather long journey across the border into Upper Volta to do so. Some of the Sisala fairy-callers have fallen into outright disrepute as fakes and charlatans, and the people speak of them with contempt. They are usually individuals of some drive, who greatly desire public recognition, but who lack any traditional role in the public eye. Some fairy-callers even try throwing cowries as well.

The Sisala say that in former times (*fa fa*)[2] there were no fairy-callers among them, although there have always been fairies (*kantonngo*). Fairies are beings of the wild, that dwell in trees or in the rivers of the bush. They are perceived as having access to both *fa fa* and *lele* [ancestors], and they can communicate with God and bring these messages back to man. At times they capture a man while he is walking through the bush and teach him secrets of one kind or another. But the Sisala have never had any way of initiating contact with the fairies, and have remained in a position of passively waiting for the fairies to communicate with them. The Awuna-Kasena, on the other hand, have developed a technique whereby the diviner calls the fairies, who then communicate by voice with assembled clients. Several persons consult such a diviner each night, and he calls the fairies to come into a dark room and speak to each of them about their

---

[2]    This term has a temporal, as well as a spatial aspect. It refers to the past, but it is also the occult world where the ancestors dwell (see Mendonsa, i.p.).

troubles or wishes.[3] The fairy-caller is the link between man and the fairies, and the fairies are the link with God (*Wia*), whereas the traditional diviner is a link with the ancestors (*lele*).

The institution of calling fairies is most widespread among those Sisala who live to the north and border on the Awuna-Kasena; Sisala people there tend to consult fairy-callers more often, and Islam is more entrenched there. Moslems use fairy-callers as a means of divining the wishes of Allah. Most of the Sisala men who have attempted to learn to call fairies live in these northern clans. The institution does not greatly affect the Sisala to the south — for example, the Crocodile Clan[4] forbids any of its members from becoming a fairy-caller, although it is not taboo to consult one. Needless to say, traditional diviners are quite scornful of fairy-callers, and one frequently hears a diviner make reference in the course of his divining to "those fairy-callers who make so much noise."

TRADITIONAL DIVINATION   A traditional diviner (*vugura*) is a man who occupies an accepted, traditional status in Sisala society. Neither the fairy-caller nor the cowrie-thrower has such a status. The office of diviner was instituted by God for the sake of the ancestors, who have perpetuated divination as a means of maintaining control over the living and thereby insuring the continuity of the moral order. It is the link *par excellence* with the occult world, and is the method most used when affliction strikes.

## MYTH OF ORIGIN

The first diviner was thought to have descended from God shortly after man descended to earth via the baobab tree. God gave shrines to men, but men did not understand what their function was nor did they know how to sacrifice on them, therefore affliction abounded in those first days (e.g. children were continually sick, wives died in childbirth, crops failed). God saw that man was confused, and sent down the diviner to help man in the proper use of shrines.

The first diviner was the chief of all diviners, the black ant (*chung-chusunung*), which today remains a symbol of divination. The black ant is seen as being similar to God, and therefore serves as a link with God. When a diviner tells someone that he must "apologize to God" or to "pray to God," the person will be instructed to take items (e.g. three kola

---

[3]   I had the opportunity to attend such a séance in Upper Volta, and wish to thank D. L. Kanton for his help in making this possible.
[4]   Bujan is situated in the Crocodile Clan parish.

nuts and fifty cowries) to do so. If the decision is left to the client, he can do one of two things: he can take the objects to a black anthill and leave them on top of it, or he can take them to a real diviner. Also, when people purchase medicine from a medicine man (*dalusungtina*), they must throw away any remaining medicine on a black anthill — which is symbolic of returning the medicine to God. Black ants are like God because both are omnipresent, and both are dangerous if certain precautions are not taken. Black ants never sleep, and anyone who has walked through the African bush at night with a torch focusing on a black anthill has noticed that the ants are busy at work. Black ants are also very strong, and can destroy an entire millet harvest in one night if it is not properly protected. One informant made the following statement:

Black ants are like God and Moslems. Have you ever seen a pile of millet after black ants have finished with it? They enter, and leaven othing but the chaff. That is what Moslems do, too.

Myth (*namaka*) explains that it was God who sent down the black ant to instruct the first human diviners in the beginning, and black ants taught the diviners to teach the people the purpose of their shrines. Man had received the blacksmith shrine prior to the divining shrine, and yet he did not know how to use it to prevent affliction; because he had no way of knowing when to sacrifice on it, affliction was rampant in the land.

Myth relates that God gave the divining shrine to man so that he could have a link with the occult world. It allowed man to communicate with *fa fa*, and provided a feedback mechanism. When affliction struck, man had some way of knowing the occult reason behind the affliction, and, more importantly, he had a mechanism for ameliorating the affliction through shrine sacrifice. The Sisala verbalize this as a link with God (*Wia*), but it must be emphasized that this is somewhat misleading, because when they say this they are using God as a general symbol of *fa fa* — an occult mythical state which includes not only *Wiajang* [God's village], which is in the sky, but also *lelejang* [the ancestors' village], which is in the earth, as well as the "mystical" side of all shrines, rivers, rocks, trees, and farms. The diviner deals with the whole range of occult entities, but most consultations reveal an ancestral cause of affliction. The Sisala do not always verbalize about the ancestors as causative agents, but will do so if pressed; and they may substitute the word "God" or "shrine" — e.g. "a shrine has afflicted me," or "God has done it."

## THE POWER OF THE ANCESTORS

Almost every consultation deals directly or obliquely with the power of the ancestors as guardians of the moral order. Much of the work of Meyer Fortes among the nearby Tallensi has pointed to this power in the daily lives of the living.[5] Cultures in northern Ghana exhibit a pattern of ancestor worship, and the Sisala are no exception. The following two cases illustrate the importance of the ancestors and the belief in their power.

My informant said:

In the village of Pulima a man named Baton decided to go to Tumu. He went to the lineage of Tokurojang and told lies, saying that he was asked by the elders of his compound to collect twenty *cedis* in bridewealth from Baduong. He collected this money and went home, but when he returned home he did not inform anybody, and spent the whole amount himself.

In about three months' time, when the people of Pulima came to collect the bridewealth *(hajarikiaa)*, they were told that Baton had already collected it. The members of Tokurojang informed the Pulima party that Baton had said that the Pulima elders had sent him to fetch the money for them. The Pulima elders returned immediately to their village and confronted Baton with the facts. They asked him if he had done this thing but he denied it. The elders could not prove him guilty, so they dropped the matter. Not long afterwards Baton became seriously ill, and his parents went from place to place trying to find medicines to cure him. None of the medicines worked, and they finally took him to the government health center in Tumu where he was given many injections, but he still did not recover. On the way home from the health center he died, and his body was taken home and buried.

The elders came together and called in a diviner. They consulted to know the cause of death. They asked if he was killed by the ancestors because he went to Tumu and told lies. It was determined that this was the case, and Baton's father was required to bring a cow, goat, and sheep to sacrifice at the ancestor *(lele)* shrine. If they had not done this, the ancestors would have brought great harm to the family (lineage) of Baton in the future. Because he told lies, he was killed by the ancestors.

Another informant related the following account:

At Tuorojang in Tumu there was a young man named Cedu. He caught a goat that was for the ancestor of his house *(dia)*, and killed it to sell the meat. When the day came for the sacrifice, the elders searched for the goat so that they could kill it at the lele shrine. They could not find it, and asked to know who might have caught the goat. They could not decide who had taken the goat, so they caught another and used it for the sacrifice instead. During the sacrifice, the elders begged the ancestors to forgive them for not sacrificing the proper goat. The elders asked the ancestors to find and punish the thief. After the sacrifice, when all the elders had gone to their various houses, they heard that Cedu had

[5]   See especially M. Fortes "Pietas and ancestor worship" (1970), "Some reflections on ancestor worship in Africa" (1965), and *Oedipus and Job in West African religion* (1959). Also, Goody (1962) shows how the ancestors figure centrally in the redistribution of roles and property among the neighboring LoDongaa.

died. They summoned a diviner to determine the cause of death, and found that Cedu had been the thief. He had been killed by the ancestors because he was the person who stole the goat which belonged to the ancestors. Cedu's father was required to bring a cow to be sacrificed to the ancestors so that they might not do further harm to the family in the future.

These two cases clearly illustrate that the Sisla believe the ancestors have the power of affliction. When an individual goes contrary to the moral order, he stands the chance of suffering the wrath of the ancestors. In both of these cases a wrong was discovered and the ancestors were called upon to afflict the deviant. When a serious affliction befell a person who might have been the culprit, the elders consulted a diviner to determine whether this had been the case. Divination is the only method whereby the living can determine the actions of the ancestors, and by linking an affliction and a delict, divination reinforces belief in the power of the ancestors.

## AFFLICTION AND DEATH DIVINATION

In both of the above cases, death divination revealed that the ancestors had been the cause of death. Other afflictions, such as illness and accident, can also be caused by the ancestors, but death is the ultimate affliction.

After death, two consultations take place. The first is called *vuge na yoho* [literally, "divine to see the funeral"], and takes place before the funeral, as soon after death as possible; but since it is best to call a diviner from another village in cases of death determination, sometimes a day passes before this divination takes place. If the deceased was the lineage elder, his heir will consult; if not, the *jechikintina* will consult just outside the lineage gateway (*peke*) in the shade area (*biling*). This is the only divining session that is held out of doors, as a public affair which anyone may attend, although, unless the death was an unusual one, usually only the family and close friends do attend. The primary function of this consultation is to determine whether the upcoming funeral will be free from conflict and quarrel — that is, whether it will be a "cool funeral" (*yoho fiala*). At this time the family may also ask the occult cause of death (although most omit the question until the second consultation after the funeral); this is usually done only if the family suspects witchcraft or poisoning. In any case, the main reason for this initial consultation is to determine whether any sacrifices need to be performed prior to the funeral to ensure that no conflict will erupt there. After the funeral, a second consultation takes place, which is called *vuge ne wi la siti suung suri* [literally, "divine to uncover the truth about death"]. This usually takes place shortly after the funeral. Some persons postpone making the second consultation for a week or so, but it should not be put off for long. Whereas the first consultation is public, the second is private, and is attended only by the lineage elders of the death lineage. Again, the *jechikintina* calls in an outside diviner and consults to know the occult cause of death, which nearly always involves the ancestors — that is, some delict is uncovered and used as a rationale of death. It may be determined that the ancestors became enraged at some breach of the norm and caused the death. Once the cause of death is known, it is determined what ritual remedies and sacrifices need to be performed. In addition, the lineage consults to know whether the death has "brought anything our way" — e.g. has the soul of the dead man decided to come back into a newborn child of the lineage; has the funeral been pleasing to the ancestors; has any shrine been defiled during the course of the funeral; has the soul (*dima*) of the dead man been successfully incorporated into the village of the ancestors (*lelejang*)? In essence, then, this consultation is performed to clear away any lingering ritual obligations resulting from the death, and to provide an explanation of the death, as well as a means of rectifying any wrongdoing.

## REASONS FOR CONSULTING A DIVINER

The harshness of life leads people to consult diviners quite frequently, although most clients go to a *dalusuntina* [owner of medicine] first, and only when "medicine" fails is a diviner contacted.[6]

Table 1.   Number of times a diviner was consulted in the previous month

| Consultations | 0 | 1 | 2 | 3 | 4 | 5 | 6 | 7 | 8 | 9+ | Totals |
|---|---|---|---|---|---|---|---|---|---|---|---|
| No. of clients | 37 | 71 | 90 | 36 | 22 | 6 | 3 | 2 | 1 | 3 | 271 |
| Percent | 14 | 26 | 33 | 13 | 8 | 2 | 1 | 1 | 0 | 1 | 100 |

Table 1[7] shows that the modal number of consultations during the month prior to the interview was two, and only 14 percent of the population had not consulted a diviner during that period.

In an environment where almost no scientific medicine exists, it is not surprising that one of the main concerns of the Sisala is health. Table 2

[6]   Kiev (1964: 14) also found that the normal consultation order was first herbalist, then diviner.
[7]   The data in Table 1 and the tables which follow were taken from an interview schedule administered to 271 Sisala males throughout Sisala-land.

Table 2.   Reasons for consulting a diviner

|  | No answer | Jour-ney | Mar-riage | Child-naming | Ill-ness | Insom-nia | Child-birth | Dreams | Wife infertility |
|---|---|---|---|---|---|---|---|---|---|
| No. of clients | 25 | 32 | 33 | 4 | 102 | 12 | 18 | 3 | 7 |
| Percent | 9 | 12 | 12 | 1 | 38 | 4 | 8 | 1 | 3 |

|  | Death | To see future | Conflict in compound | Death of animals | To foretell outcome of harvest | General trouble | Total |
|---|---|---|---|---|---|---|---|
| No. of clients | 3 | 3 | 4 | 1 | 1 | 10 | 271 |
| Percent | 1 | 1 | 1 | 0 | 0 | 4 | 100 |

shows that the modal reason for consulting a diviner is illness. Of the sample interviewed, 38 percent said that illness was their motivation, while another 15 percent of the troubles that led to consultation (e.g. insomnia, childbirth, infertility, and death) were health-related. Clearly over half of the persons who consult diviners do so because of a health problem which is occurring at the time of the consultation. The Sisala say, "We do not consult by heart," meaning that a Sisala man does not consult a diviner unless there is an affliction, and the affliction is usually an immediate one.

The belief in occult causation, and especially in the power of the ancestors, is the primary motivation to consult and the *raison d'être* of divination. These beliefs exist in a milieu where scientific medicine is difficult to obtain, and where traditional medicine is often ineffective. The majority of the population takes refuge in traditional divination, which provides them with a ritual outlet when empirical ones are lacking or fail. Many Sisala admit the superiority of the "white man's medicine" and readily use it when it is available, but when it is not, or when it and/or their own medicines fail, they consult to determine the occult cause of the affliction. Once that is determined, they are provided with a ritual course of action, whereas they had no course of action before.

## FALLIBILITY OF DIVINATION

The Sisala have a saying: "Diviners tell lies and people die, and they tell lies and the people live," which indicates that there are powers greater than divination. Diviners are fallible because fate (*Wia ne longe* — literally, "what God brings down") is something that a diviner cannot always know. One informant explained that diviners may tell you certain things to do "to have life," but when a person's time to die comes, diviners are useless.

Several factors enter into the belief in the fallibility of diviners. First, it is common knowledge that some diviners are better at their art than others and can communicate with the occult world more effectively. Bascom (1941 : 52) also notes this tendency in Ifa divination when he says:

The diviners themselves admit that some of their number may not be able to answer all questions, and it is to be noted that in placing the blame on the individuals lack of knowledge of Ifa, they shift it from the system itself.

Second, some diviners are believed to tell outright lies to get gain. Third, a diviner's shrine may lose power (*dolung*)[8] if he does not sacrifice on it periodically, or if one of the ancestors who previously owned it is angry with him. Fourth, tradition relates that diviners have been imperfect even in the past, and since *fafa* is a pattern for the present, even imperfection in *fafa* is carried into the present world of the living.

Diviners are well aware that people do not consider their pronouncements as final, and they often add a rider to the pronouncement, such as: "If I have spoken the truth, you will hear of a funeral soon" (a very ambiguous statement, and a highly probable event to predict in western Africa). I have many times heard Sisala, by circular, *ex-post-facto* thinking, justify a diviner's pronouncement because such an event transpired. Because a diviner is not considered infallible, more than one is consulted about an important matter. The second consultation is a check on the first, and if the first diviner's edict is confirmed by a second consultation, it is considered to be valid, so that no more divining is needed. However, if the second diviner contradicts the first one, then the client seeks a third diviner to try and match up the third edict with one of the other pronouncements, in which case the inconsistent one will be ignored. In fact, most clients use an institutionalized technique called *dachevung* to test a diviner's edict. Although I was unable to find a suitable translation for the word *dachevung*, roughly it means "he heard some things." Once a client has "heard some things" from one diviner, he does not have to go through another complete consultation to check the validity of the proclamation. He may merely go to a diviner and tell him that he wants to have *dachevung*. This method of divining is much quicker than a normal consultation, and is used only to confirm or reject another diviner's edict, because with *dachevung* the diviner does not have to open his bag and go through all of its contents; he merely uses a wand. This method is also called *a ga purung* [literally, "to steal the bag"]. The client squats before the diviner and presents silent alternatives in the form of

---

[8]   The occult power lies behind all life. It is the power which runs the universe and comes from *Wia*.

marks on the floor or in the dirt. The diviner points the wand toward one mark or the other without knowing what they mean. For example, if the first diviner has told the client that his affliction was due to a quarrel with his elder brother, he will present that as one possibility. If the second diviner chooses that possibility (without knowing what it is), the client will be satisfied that the first diviner was telling the truth and the *dachevung* will come to an end. The following is an account of a *dachevung:*

The client entered the room of the diviner and indicated that he would like to have a *dachevung* conducted. He squatted before the diviner and made two marks on the dirt floor. In his mind he had assigned the edict of the first diviner to one of the marks, while the other mark stood for the negation of that edict (he told me this afterwards). When he made the marks he said: "What has brought me from the house this morning?"

Diviner: "This." (The wand pointed to one of the marks.)

At this point the client made several more marks in silence and said: "What is inside it?"

Diviner: "This."

Client (making new marks): "I've put it down."

Diviner: "No!" (This was an attempt on the part of the client to get the diviner to contradict himself.)

Client: "I've stolen it."

Diviner: "This is what you have stolen."

This type of consultation takes only a few minutes, whereas a normal consultation can take up to an hour.

Although the Sisala are aware that, for one reason or another, diviners do not always tell the whole truth, they view divination as the only legitimate mechanism whereby they can receive feedback from the ancestors. Since diviners are not infallible, and since they are considered the best means of receiving such feedback from the occult world, a client wishing to consult about an important matter may travel some distance to consult an alien, and therefore unbiased, diviner (see also Colson 1970). This diviner is alien only in the sense that he is a stranger, and hence is thought to be less prejudiced than a local diviner. He is normally a Sisala diviner, although Kasena diviners and fairy-callers are also consulted. In any case, he operates within a similar cultural framework as a local diviner.

Divination is a powerful mechanism for the release of anxiety in Sisala society. In a society where illness is unchecked by modern medicine, where wells can go dry or water holes dry up, where crop success is at the mercy of the elements, divination provides answers in a world of questions. Even Moslems, Christians, and the educated elite find it difficult indeed, when faced with affliction, to resist the "concreteness" of divination. More than once I have been sitting with a diviner and had an educated Christian enter the room to consult. In one case I had had a conversation the previous week with this very Christian in which he had passed divination off as a mere superstition of "uneducated pagans," yet when faced with the severe illness of his wife, he resorted to the ways of his forefathers. I have seen men who were very depressed at the onset of the consultation leave happy and content with what they had learned. On the other hand, a consultation may increase one's anxiety, as in the case of a man whose worst suspicions are confirmed. But there is almost always a ritual outlet provided by divination for the release of anxiety. Almost no consultation ends without the client having been instructed to avoid a "danger" before consulting the diviner, but only afterward does the client have means to avoid it. Therefore, even though many consider diviners to be fallible, it is the traditional method *par excellence* of dealing with dangers, problems, and affliction. Also, the internal structure of the institution of divination is ordered so that it copes with this fallibility. Indeed, the belief in fallibility may be partly responsible for the continued existence of divination. Concerning the repeated consultation of many diviners, Horton (1967: 167) says:

What is notable in all this is that the client never takes his repeated failures as evidence against the existence of the various spiritual beings named as responsible for his plight, or as evidence against the possibility of making contact with such beings as diviners claim to do. Nor do members of the community in which he lives ever try to keep track of the proportion of successes to failures in the remedial actions based on their beliefs, with the aim of questioning these beliefs. At most, they grumble about the dishonesty and wiles of many diviners, whilst maintaining their faith in the existence of some honest, competent practitioners.

In spite of the belief in fallibility, it must be pointed out that diviners themselves consult each other frequently. In fact, Table 3 shows that they

Table 3.   Number of consultations by diviners in the month prior to the interview

| Consul-tations | 0 | 1 | 2 | 3 | 4 | 5 | 6 | 7 | 8 | 9 | 10 | 11 | 12 | 13 | 14 | 15 | 16 | Total |
|---|---|---|---|---|---|---|---|---|---|---|---|---|---|---|---|---|---|---|
| **Diviner** | | | | | | | | | | | | | | | | | | |
| Number | 12 | 1 | 6 | 10 | 8 | 1 | 5 | 0 | 1 | 0 | 1 | 0 | 9 | 4 | 2 | 0 | 2 | 62 |
| Percent | 18 | 2 | 10 | 16 | 13 | 2 | 8 | 0 | 2 | 0 | 2 | 0 | 15 | 6 | 3 | 0 | 3 | 100 |
| **Sisala male** | | | | | | | | | | | | | | | | | | |
| Number | 37 | 71 | 90 | 36 | 22 | 6 | 3 | 2 | 1 | 3 | 0 | 0 | 0 | 0 | 0 | 0 | 0 | 271 |
| Percent | 14 | 26 | 33 | 13 | 8 | 2 | 1 | 1 | 0 | 1 | 0 | 0 | 0 | 0 | 0 | 0 | 0 | 100 |

do so more frequently than the average pagan male. Sisala diviners, like their Yoruba counterparts (Bascom 1941: 52–53), believe in divination as a means of communicating with the occult world, and regularly perform postdivinatory sacrifices in an effort to appease the ancestors and thereby avoid or eliminate an affliction.

## DIVINER CHARACTERISTICS

Persons who become diviners tend to be traditional, conservative individuals who are oriented toward the past and who adhere to the ways of the ancestors — the true path (*wenbiing titi*). A comparison of shrine ownership by diviners as against pagan males highlights this conservatism (see Table 4).

Table 4. Shrine ownership by diviners and by pagan males

| Number of Shrines | 0 | 1 | 2 | 3 | 4 | 5 | 6 | 7 | Total |
|---|---|---|---|---|---|---|---|---|---|
| Diviner | | | | | | | | | |
| Number | 0 | 7 | 10 | 12 | 25 | 5 | 4 | 0 | 62 |
| Percent | 0 | 12 | 16 | 19 | 39 | 6 | 6 | 0 | 100 |
| Pagan male | | | | | | | | | |
| Number | 62 | 25 | 29 | 59 | 78 | 6 | 6 | 6 | 271 |
| Percent | 23 | 9 | 11 | 22 | 29 | 2 | 2 | 2 | 100 |

Also, diviners appear to be more conservative in that they utilize other diviners more often than do nondiviners (it is also true that they do not have to pay the fee). Table 3 shows that Sisala males have a mode of two consultations per month, whereas the diviners have a mode of three consultations, and many consult as often as twelve times per month.

Diviners also appear to have traveled slightly less than nondiviners (see Table 5). Disinclination to travel is an indication of conservatism.

Table 5. Farthest city visited by diviners and by nondiviners

| | No answer | Tumu | Wa/Bolga | Tamale | Kumasi | Accra | Total |
|---|---|---|---|---|---|---|---|
| Diviner | | | | | | | |
| Number | 0 | 11 | 12 | 6 | 24 | 9 | 62 |
| Percent | 0 | 18 | 19 | 10 | 39 | 15 | 100 |
| Nondiviners | | | | | | | |
| Number | 6 | 15 | 55 | 54 | 98 | 33 | 261 |
| Percent | 2 | 6 | 21 | 21 | 38 | 13 | 100 |

Most diviners are males, but some very old women, who "are like men because they can no longer bear children," do practice divination (see Table 6).

Table 6.   Sex of diviners

|  | No response | Male | Female | Total |
|---|---|---|---|---|
| Number of respondents | 1 | 54 | 7 | 62 |
| Percent | 2 | 87 | 11 | 100 |

My sample included no diviners below the approximate age of twenty, and the greatest number of diviners were between the ages of thirty and forty (see Table 7).

Table 7.   Age of diviners

|  | 20–30 | 31–40 | 41–50 | 51–60 | 61–70 | 71–80 | 81–90 | Total |
|---|---|---|---|---|---|---|---|---|
| Number of respondents | 12 | 21 | 15 | 8 | 1 | 3 | 2 | 62 |
| Percent | 19 | 34 | 24 | 13 | 2 | 5 | 3 | 100 |

Divining is not a full-time occupation (see Table 8). Most diviners are full-time farmers, who take clients in the early morning hours before they go to their farms, and sometimes (but rarely) at night.

Table 8.   Occupation

|  | None* | Farmer | Trader | Hunter | Laborer | Educated | Total |
|---|---|---|---|---|---|---|---|
| Diviner |  |  |  |  |  |  |  |
| Number | 8 | 51 | 2 | 0 | 0 | 1 | 62 |
| Percent | 13 | 82 | 2 | 0 | 0 | 2 | 99 |
| Nondiviner |  |  |  |  |  |  |  |
| Number | 7 | 224 | 2 | 3 | 26 | 6 | 268 |
| Percent | 3 | 83 | 1 | 1 | 10 | 2 | 100 |

* The "None" category largely contains old men, most of whom were farmers when young.

## SUMMARY

While the Sisala have other kinds of divination, the traditional method predominates. The institution of divination provides a customary way of communicating with the ancestors who control the power of the universe. Ancestors use this power to afflict the living, and divination allows the living to determine the cause and to remedy this affliction. Most diviners are males, and the rest are old women and therefore have shown their support for the gerontocratic order. Diviners appear to be traditionalists who have inherited a position in the social order which functions to orient the Sisala toward the "true path" of the ancestors. Divination, therefore, acts as a social control mechanism. Deviant behavior is handled in the context of affliction-divination-sacrifice. Affliction leads a client to consult a diviner, who provides an institutionalized occult cause, as well as a sacrificial remedy, to his problem. Thus, divination is a conservative mechanism which reinforces the established social order, and it is not surprising to find that ordinarily Sisala diviners are older males who own a higher than average number of shrines, who have had little travel experience, and who tend to engage in farming rather than nonfarming economic pursuits.

# REFERENCES

BASCOM, W.
 1941   The sanctions of Ifa divination. *Journal of the Royal Anthropological Institute* 81(2):43–54.
COLSON, E.
 1970   "The alien diviner and local politics among the Tonga of Zambia," in *Man makes sense: a reader in modern cultural anthropology*. Edited by W. Simmons. Boston: Little, Brown.
FORTES, M.
 1959   *Oedipus and Job in West African religion*. Cambridge, England: Cambridge University Press.
 1965   "Some reflections on ancestor worship in Africa," in *African systems of thought*. By M. Fortes and G. Dieterlen. London: Oxford University Press.
 1970   "Pietas and ancestor worship," in *Time and social structure and other essays*. By M. Fortes. London: Athlone Press.
GOODY, J.
 1962   *Death, property and ancestors*. London: Tavistock.
HORTON, R.
 1967   African traditional thought and Western science (in two parts). *Africa* 38:50–71, 155–187.
KIEV, A.
 1964   "The study of folk psychiatry," in *Magic, faith and healing: studies in folk psychiatry today*. Edited by A. Kiev. Glencoe, Ill.: Free Press.
MENDONSA, E.
 i.p.   The divinatory process and temporal-spatial concepts among the Sisala of northern Ghana. *Journal of African and Asian Studies*.
REYNOLDS, B.
 1963   *Magic, divination and witchcraft among the Barotse of Northern Rhodesia*. London: Chatto and Windus.

# The Goddess Cult in the Hebrew-Jewish Religion

RAPHAEL PATAI

## THE CANAANITE AND ISRAELITE PANTHEON

Before embarking upon a rapid survey of the history of a female deity in the Hebrew-Jewish religion — spanning almost three thousand years — it should be pointed out that from the Israelite settlement in Canaan (thirteenth century B.C.) to well after the capture of Judah by the Babylonians (586 B.C.) there existed side by side two different types of Hebrew religion. One was the Yahwistic religion fought for by some early Hebrew leaders (the so-called "Judges"), taught by the prophets, and embraced by the authors and editors of all the books which make up the Hebrew Bible. Within this religion a definite theological progress can be discerned from the relatively primitive tribal Yahwism of the Patriarchs to the lofty, universal, ethical monotheism of Isaiah or Jeremiah. However, this doctrinal development was not paralleled by a growth in popular acceptance. On the contrary, exclusive Yahwism remained the religion of a minority, so that the Yahwist point of view represented in the Biblical books could rightly be termed "a minority report" (Eakin 1971: 209).

The majority of the Hebrew people followed not this prophetic religion, but a different one which can be termed popular and which either did not include the worship of Yahweh, or consisted of his worship together with that of a number of other deities. As a critical perusal of the Biblical sources will readily show, in villages and cities the simple folk and their leaders (often including the kings and their entourages) persisted in serving gods and goddesses, i.e. in following a religion which did not differ substantially from that of the neighboring

Canaanites (Albright 1968: 199).

In the Canaanite pantheon, as well as in the religions of other ancient Near Eastern peoples, there were four central deities who formed something like a tetrad, at least in the sense of intensively interacting with one another (Patai 1967: 164–170). In Ugarit in the fourth century B.C. the four most prominent deities were El, the father god, called the Begetter of Creatures or *Bull El*; his wife Athirat (Asherah) whose full name was Lady Athirat of the Sea, and who was also called *Qudshu* [Holiness], the Maid Athirat, or She Who Gives Birth to the Gods (Pope and Röllig 1965: 246–249, 279–283; Albright 1968: 121–122); their son Baal; and their daughter Anath. Baal is an appellative meaning "Lord"; the son-god's personal name was Hadad, and he was also termed Prince, King, Rider of Clouds, *Aliyan* [Triumphant], and Majesty, Lord of the Earth. He was the god of the storm and rain, and of fertility, who periodically died and then came back to life (Pope and Röllig 1965: 253–264; Albright 1968: 124–126).

Anath, the sister and consort of Baal, was known as the Maiden Anath, the Virgin, the Girl, Mistress of Kingship, Mistress of Dominion, Mistress of High Heaven and, at least in Ascalon, as *Derketo* [Dominion]; in Carthage she was styled "Radiance of the Presence of Baal" (Pope and Röllig 1965: 235–241; Albright 1968: 128–130). She was the goddess of war and the hunt, and of female fecundity, and loved gods, men, and animals. On one occasion, while she assumed the shape of a heifer, Baal lay with her "seventy-seven — even eighty-eight times" (Patai 1967: 61–62; Albright 1968: 128). Yet Anath remained the "Virgin." She thus united in herself the contrasting features of virginity and promiscuity, and of motherliness and bloodthirstiness.

The Hebrew Bible speaks of El, or in its fuller form, Eloah or Elohim. In Israeli tradition Elohim had early become identified with Yahweh [shorter forms: Yahu, Yah], who consequently was often called Yahweh-Elohim. Occasionally the two names appear in parallelism (Albright 1968: 171). In the Song of Moses, dating from the thirteenth century B.C., the names Yahweh, Yah, El, and Elohim appear together (Exodus 15:1-2). Other ancient names for God were Shaddai (Numbers 24:4) and Elyon (Isaiah 14:14). The worship of this male god had been well established among the Israelite tribes by the time they settled in Canaan. When they became acquainted with the Canaanite Baal, it was inevitable that they should identify the two deities. How the relationship between Yahweh and Baal developed is a crucial issue in the early history of Hebrew religion. The two gods may have been combined, they may have competed for the loyalty of the Hebrews or they may have been served alternately. As far as we can judge from the Biblical sources, the separate identity of Baal and El in Canaan went unnoticed by the Israelites who by their own desert traditions were predisposed to consider El (Elohim) as the appellative of Yahweh.

Following their settlement in Canaan the Israelites acquired agricultural skills from their indigenous neighbors. This also meant that they came under the influence of the Canaanite goddesses who were in control of vegetation as well as animal and human fertility. Since their own nomadic religion included no female deity, when the Hebrews adopted the worship of the Canaanite goddesses they retained their Canaanite names. The result of this syncretistic development was that from the time of the Judges the religion of the Hebrews centered on a modest pantheon which consisted of Yahweh-Elohim and/or Baal, and the goddesses Asherah and Anath. Astarte was but an appellative of Anath, just as Elath was of Asherah, and Baal of Hadad in the Canaanite pantheon, and Elohim of Yahweh in the Israelite religion.

## ASHERAH

Of the three Canaanite names of goddesses — Asherah, Anath, and Astarte — Asherah is most frequently mentioned in the Bible. Occasionally, especially when used in the masculine plural, Asherim, the term seems to refer to trees or groves sacred to Asherah. The other Canaanite name of Asherah, Elath, appears in the Bible only in the sense of *elah* [terebinth] (Albright 1968: 189). Thus in the Israelite environment both names of this Canaanite goddess assumed a dendritic connotation.

The historical basis for the frequent mention of Asherah in the Bible is the rapid spread of her worship among the Israelites. No sooner did they settle in Canaan than "the Children of Israel . . . served the Baals and the Asherahs" (Judges 3:5–7), and studded the countryside with *bamoth* [high places] or, as Albright argues, *stelae*, or standing stones (Albright 1968: 205). At the time this happened the worship of Asherah had been largely replaced among the Canaanites by that of her daughter Anath (Astarte), so that the spread of Asherah's worship among the Israelites can be regarded as a cultural lag. The archaeological evidence is clear on this point. In numerous sites excavated in Palestine, the layers dating from the Middle and Late Bronze (circa twenty-first to thirteenth centuries B.C.), when the sites were inhabited by Canaanites, abound in Anath (Astarte) statuettes. From the beginning of the Iron

Age (twelfth century B.C.) to the destruction of Judah in 586 B.C., when many of the same sites were settled by Israelites, the equally large number of statuettes found show Asherah. The two goddesses are represented in two types of figurines which differ so markedly that confusion between them is impossible.

The Asherah figurines show the goddess with a horizontal hairline across her forehead and a hairdo that hugs her head tightly all around. She has protruding breasts, often pushed upward by her two hands. From the waist down her body is not shown; instead, a cylindrical column with a flaring base is substituted. The frequency with which these Asherah figurines turned up in excavations of Hebrew sites in Iron Age Palestine indicate that the worship of Asherah played a role in Israelite houses corresponding to that of the *lares et penates* in ancient Rome. Her role as giver of fertility and facilitator of childbirth assured her a primary place in the home cult. A seventh-century B.C. Hebrew incantation text found in Arslan Tash in Syria invokes the help of the goddess for a woman in delivery (Reed 1949: 80–81, 87).

Just as Asherah was city-goddess of Tyre and Sidon (Pope and Röllig 1965: 247), so she became a publicly venerated goddess in Israel. As early as in the twelfth century B.C. the town of Ophrah had a public sanctuary in which there was an altar of Baal and a wooden statue of Asherah, both attended by a priest, Joash. When Joash's son, Gideon (Jerubbaal), under the influence of a vision of the Lord Yahweh, destroyed this holy place, the townspeople wanted to put him to death and he was saved only by his father's plea (Judges 6:25–32).

Three centuries later, soon after the death of Solomon, the Yahwist prophet Ahijah of Shiloh reproaches Israel for serving other gods, but the only ones he mentions by name are the "Asherahs" (1 Kings 14:15). Some fifty years after the secession of Israel from the Davidic dynasty, King Ahab (873–852 B.C.) of Israel "made an Asherah" (1 Kings 16: 33) and thus incorporated her worship into the royal court ritual. The Biblical historian notes that "450 prophets of the Baal and 400 prophets of the Asherah ate at the table of Jezebel" (1 Kings 18:19), the wife of Ahab who was the daughter of Ethbaal, King of Sidon. After the miraculous victory of Elijah over this legion of prophets, he had the 450 Baal prophets slaughtered, but, remarkably, no harm befell the Asherah prophets — at least the Biblical account does not mention them. Subsequent half-hearted reforms carried out by Ahab's successors also only proceeded against the worship of Baal, who was regarded by that time as a competitor of Yahweh, but not against Asherah, who was considered his consort and complement (Patai 1967: 40ff.). The worship of Asherah continued in the Kingdom of Israel until the Assyrians put an end to it in 721 B.C. The southernmost outpost of Asherah worship in Israel was Beth-El (some ten miles north of Jerusalem) which contained a *bamah* dedicated to her. Here her worship continued for another hundred years until King Joshiah of Judah (639–609 B.C.) took the city and put an end to her reign.

In Judah, the worship of Asherah was introduced into the Jerusalem Temple itself by Maacah, the wife of Solomon's son Rehoboam (928–911 B.C.), who wielded great influence over her husband (2 Chronicles 11:21–22). She, we are told rather enigmatically, made a *mifleset* [obscene object] for Asherah (1 Kings 15:13; 2 Chronicles 15:16). From this time on, as the Book of Kings shows, the worship of Asherah remained part of the cult of the Jerusalem Temple for 236 years, or almost two-thirds of the 370 years during which the Solomonic Temple functioned in the capital of Judah. Only three times in those 370 years did a Yahwist king remove the Asherah figure from the Temple; but each time the goddess was soon restored to her place at the side of Yahweh by one of the king's successors (Patai 1967: 45–50).

## ANATH-ASTARTE

The Bible does not contain a single direct reference to the worship of the goddess Anath. Only in place names, such as Beth Anath and Anatoth (the plural of Anath), and in personal names such as Shamgar son of Anath, Anatoth, and Antothiya, did her name survive.[1] However, the reason for this silence is not the absence of the worship of Anath in Israel and Judah, but the fact that this name of the goddesss was supplanted by her appellative, Astarte, just as Hadad was by Baal. In the entire fourteenth-century Ugaritic literature the name Athtart (Astarte) appears very rarely and, when it does, the context makes it probable that it was the appellative of Anath.[2] Between the fourteenth and the twelfth centuries the use of the name Anath declined and the

[1] Albright (1950–1951: 28–29) proposed that the Hebrew text of Psalm 68:24 be slightly amended to read "Why, O Anath, dost thou wash thy feet in blood, the tongues of thy dogs in the blood of the foes?" See also Albright (1968: 187–188).
[2] One point should be mentioned concerning the identification of Astarte with Anath. In the Ugaritic epic of Keret all the gods are typically referred to by both of their current names in strict parallelism. Thus, when Anath and Astarte are mentioned in the same manner, the two names almost certainly refer to the same goddess. In any case, whether Anath and Astarte were identical or not makes no appreciable difference in our understanding of the worship of Astarte among the Israelites.

use of Astarte increased. In any case, in the days of the Hebrew Judges (twelfth to eleventh centuries B.C.), Astarte simply meant "Lady," in the sense of "the Goddess," just as Baal meant "Lord," or "the God."

The nature of the Biblical references to non-Yahwistic worship is such that it is almost impossible to establish whether the two goddesses Asherah and Astarte were served simultaneously or whether Asherah was supplanted by Astarte, as she had been among the Canaanites (*Encyclopedia Miqrait* 1971: 407). The two phrases "the Baals and the Asherahs" and "the Baals and the Astartes" — both denoting foreign gods in general terms — appear in turn in the historical books of the Bible (Pope and Röllig 1965: 250; *Encyclopedia Miqrait* 1971: 408).

Archaeological evidence indicates that the cult of Asherah was more popular than that of Astarte: compared to the abundance of Asherah figurines, Astarte statuettes are relatively rare from the Israelite period. Those found show a naked woman with two large spiral locks framing her face and neck (occasionally also two horns adorn her head) and with the breasts and pubic area strongly emphasized.

Another appellative of Anath, by which she was known at the latest from the Late Bronze Age on, was "Queen of Heaven." Several Egyptian inscriptions, among them a stele erected in the twelfth century B.C. in Beth Shean, Palestine, refer to Anath as "Lady of Heaven." Similarly, Assyrian inscriptions call Ishtar, Anath's Mesopotamian equivalent, "Queen of Heaven," and other documents attest to the use of this appellative elsewhere (Patai 1967: 98; Albright 1968: 272; *Encyclopedia Miqrait* 1971: 316). The Israelites adopted this appellative only in the seventh century, perhaps during the reign of Manasseh (698–642 B.C.). At any rate, the only Biblical book referring to the Queen of Heaven is Jeremiah, from whom we learn that prior to the great Yahwist reform of King Josiah in 621, the people of Jerusalem and other Judaean cities, led by their kings and princes, worshiped the Queen of Heaven by burning incense, pouring out libations, and offering her cakes (Jeremiah 7:17–18; 44:15–19). The last-named rite was performed in Babylonia as well in honor of the Mesopotamian Queen of Heaven. The sacrificial cakes offered to her were called *kamanu*, possibly the origin of their Hebrew name *kawwan* (Schrader 1902–1903: 441–442, 425).

The Judaean exiles who found refuge in Egypt in 586 B.C. continued to worship the Queen of Heaven (Jeremiah 44:15–19), and their descendants persisted in this practice in the Jewish military colony in Hermopolis (160 miles south of modern Cairo) at least until the fifth century B.C. In another Jewish military colony, on the Island of Elephantine (Yeb) in Upper Egypt, the worship of the goddess under the combined name Anath-Yaho or Anath-Bethel continued to the end of the fifth century B.C. (Patai 1967: 99).[3]

Outside of the Jewish communities Anath survived into Hellenistic times, when she was called Qudshu-Astarte-Anath [Her Holiness Astarte-Anath], and became known under the composite name Atargatis, that is, Astarte-Anath, the *dea Syria* of Lucian (Pope and Röllig 1965: 236, 244–245). Among the Jews in the Talmudic period some of her features became incorporated into the image of the Shekhina, the "Presence" of God.

## THE CHERUBIM

In the Solomonic Temple the goddess Asherah, as represented by her statue, was physically present, but no attempt was made to introduce her into the Second Temple, which was completed by Judaeans returned from Babylonian exile in 516 B.C., and remained the center of Jewish worship until it was destroyed by the Romans in A.D. 70. However, a representation of the feminine element was not lacking in the Second Temple. The only statuary to which even the strictest anti-iconic Yahwist never took exception was that of the two Cherubim, winged human figures, placed in the Holy of Holies, as the innermost sanctuary was called. According to Biblical tradition, the Cherubim in both the desert Tabernacle and the Temple of Solomon stood on both sides of the Holy Ark, which was shielded by their outstretched wings. While no mention is made in the Bible of the sex of the Cherubim, small ivory plaques from Egypt, Israel, and Syria, dating from the fifteenth to the ninth centuries B.C., show them in the form of winged feminine genii. From this evidence it can be concluded that the Cherubim in the Temple were also female figures, and that when the Second Temple was built the new Cherubim placed in it were of similar appearance. However, there is some circumstantial evidence that in the first half of the third century B.C. they were replaced by statuary which depicted a male and a female Cherub in sexual embrace (Patai 1967: 126–131). The festive crowds which thronged the Temple courtyard on the pilgrimage festivals would be allowed to catch a glimpse of these

[3]   Albright (1950–1951: 18–19; 1968: 138–139, 143, 187, 248) finds the traces of one more feminine deity in the Bible: he considers *Kosharot* of Psalm 68:7 as a reference to the midwife-goddesses called in Ugaritic, as well as in Canaanitic, by this name. The singular form in Canaanitic, *Koshart*, designated the goddess of childbirth.

Cherubim and were told: "Behold, your love before God is like the love of male and female!" When Antiochus Epiphanes, king of Syria (175–164 B.C.), sacked the Temple, his henchmen dragged the sacred statuary out into the market place of Jerusalem and derided the Jews as pornographers: they ". . . occupy themselves with such things!" (Patai 1967: 123).

The sources which refer to the embracing Cherubim date from several centuries after the events they report. We thus have no contemporary interpretations of the two Cherubim. In the Talmudic and Midrashic passages describing the embracing Cherubim, dating from the third and fourth centuries A.D., the idea of erotic statuary in the Holy of Holies of the Jerusalem Temple was so foreign that it verged on sacrilege. The least doubt concerning the authenticity of this tradition would therefore have induced the sages to suppress it; that it was reported means that it existed. We can likewise accept as authentic the rabbinic interpretation of the Cherubim: the male Cherub symbolized God, and the female the community of Israel.

There is some circumstantial but contemporary evidence concerning the presence of male and female Cherub statuary in the Second Temple. The Alexandrian Jewish philosopher Philo (circa 15 B.C. to A.D. 45) interpreted the two Cherubim as representing the two aspects of God: one Cherub symbolized God (Elohim) as father, husband, begetter, and creator, with the qualities of reason, goodness, peacefulness, gentleness, and beneficence; the other Cherub symbolized the Lord (Yahweh) as mother, wife, bearer, and nurturer, with the qualities of wisdom and sovereignty and the power to legislate, chastise, and correct. These two groups of divine powers, says Philo, were "mingled and united" — perhaps a reminiscence of the intertwined male and female Cherubim whom he may have seen if he had made the pilgrimage to Jerusalem (Patai 1967: 111–116). The view that one Cherub was male and the other female became a basic tenet of the Kabbala.

## THE SHEKHINA

In Babylonia, where the bulk of the Jewish community lived after 586 B.C., the worship of the goddess apparently disappeared. At least no traces of it were left in the meager historical sources relating to the early postexile period. Before long, however, a remarkable development occurred which ultimately resulted in a return of the female divine principle to the Jewish religion. This process originated in the growing

feeling that the numerous Biblical anthropomorphisms and anthropop-
athisms conveyed a much too physical and human-like picture of God.
This resulted in a number of hypostases, i.e. conceptualized agencies or
agents, acting as intermediaries between God and the human perception
of this manifestation. Actually, this tendency emerged as early as 400
B.C., when the latest Biblical books, Proverbs and Job, were written.
In them *Hokhma* [Wisdom] appears as such a hypostasis, a personage
separate and distinct from God. About the same time, the Targums, or
Aramaic translation-paraphrases of the Bible, began to use with considerable consistency the term "Shekhina" whenever the original Hebrew
text was felt to be too anthropomorphic. Shekhina means literally 'act
of dwelling', but it can best be translated into English as 'presence',
Like many abstract nouns in Hebrew it has the feminine gender. To
mention a single example, the Biblical verse "I will dwell among the
Children of Israel" (Exodus 29:45) is rendered in the Targum of On-
kelos "I will let my Shekhina dwell among the Children of Israel."

Gradually the Shekhina assumed a more and more physical or tan-
gible character. The end result of this process can be seen in those
Talmudic passages (dating from A.D. 200 to 500) which describe the
Shekhina as, for example, keeping the infant Moses company while he
lay in the ark of bulrushes, being carried in a casket by the Children of
Israel in the desert, and dwelling in the Tabernacle, the Temple of
Jerusalem, and certain synagogues in Babylonia. She is said to have
announced her presence by producing a tinkling sound like a bell,
shown herself to humans and animals, walked with the brokenhearted,
and rested between husband and wife. At the same time her radiance
was said to have been such that even the angels had to shield themselves with their wings so as not to see her (Patai 1967: 140–147).

In the Talmudic period the Shekhina and the related concept of the
Holy Spirit were used synonymously (Marmorstein 1950: 130–131).
From about A.D. 300 on we have testimony to the effect that the Holy
Spirit was considered an independent entity that could confront and
even admonish God (Patai 1967: 148).

The feminity of the Shekhina is implicit in all the statements about
her simply because the noun is of the feminine gender in contrast to
the divine names Elohim, Yahweh, Elyon, Shaddai, etc., all of which
are masculine. In addition, however, the Shekhina assumed an unmistakably feminine role in her relationship to both men and God. Thus
we read that when Moses died, the Shekhina carried him on her wings
to his distant burial place, which act of kindness duplicates what Anath
did for her brother-husband Baal. The Shekhina caressed and kissed

the walls and columns of the Temple. When the patriarchs died, she took their souls in a kiss. She is the love aspect of God, but also represents the divine punitive power (Patai 1967: 152–153), which again is reminiscent of the same two contrasting roles of Anath some two thousand years earlier.

## THE MATRONIT

With the emergence of the Kabbala, the great mystical trend in Judaism, in the thirteenth century, the Shekhina was given a new name, Matronit (from the Latin *matrona*), and became both the sister and the wife of God who, in relation to her, was styled "the King." The *Zohar* [Splendor], the most important book of the Kabbala, written around 1286 by Moses de Leon in Castile, Spain, contains an almost incredibly sensuous myth cycle about these two divinities.

Their origin can be traced to an earlier divine pair. The divine Father brought forth the Supernal Mother, or the "Female." "She spread out from her place and adhered to the side of the Male (the Father), until he moved away, and she came to unite with him face to face. And when they united they appeared as veritably one body" (*Zohar* III: 296a). The union between the Male and the Female is both complete and ceaseless. Thus when his "seed is about to be ejaculated, he does not have to seek the Female, for she abides with him, never leaves him, and is always in readiness for him. His seed flows not save when the Female is ready, and when they both desire each other; and they unite in a single embrace, and never separate . . ." (*Zohar* I:162a-b).

Out of this union were born the Son, also known as the King, and the Daughter, or Matronit. The Father and Mother loved their children exceedingly, adorned their heads with many crowns, and showered blessings upon them. However, the Father loved the Daughter more, while the Mother's favorite was the Son. In fact, the Father constantly kissed and fondled the Daughter until the Mother suffered pangs of jealousy and demanded of the Daughter that she cease beguiling the Father (*Zohar* I:156b, Sitre Torah). As to the Mother's love of the Son, she expressed it by giving him her breast most generously and continuing to suckle him even after he grew up and married his sister, the Daughter or Matronit (*Zohar* III:17a).

The marriage between the Son (the King) and the Daughter (the Matronit) was licit, because "above on high there is no incest" (Tishbi 1961: 623) — an archaic concept that again reminds us of the absence of incest in Ugaritic and other ancient Near Eastern myths.

The Temple of Jerusalem, built by King Solomon, served as the wedding chamber of the King and the Matronit, and as their bedroom thereafter. However, the marriage was marked by many quarrels, bitter separations, and tempestuous reunions. The reason for these vicissitudes was that the Matronit became closely associated with the People of Israel (this is why she is often referred to by the name *Kneset Yisrael* [Community of Israel]) and whenever Israel sinned the marriage of the King and the Matronit was disrupted. Otherwise, the sacred union between them took place in the Temple-bedchamber every midnight, or, according to another version, once a week, on the night between Friday and Saturday. This intensive love-life of the King and the Matronit is reminiscent of the heightened sexuality of the ancient Canaanite gods, King Baal and the Maiden Anath. The issue of the union between the King and the Matronit are the human souls and the angels. When Israel sins, Samael (Satan), who in the form of a serpent or riding a serpent lurks at all times near the private parts of the Matronit, gains power, glues himself to her body, and defiles her. When this happens, the King departs from her and withdraws into the solitude of his heavenly abode. This unhappy state continues until the Day of Atonement when the scapegoat is offered to Azazel (Satan). Attracted by the offering, Satan lets go of the Matronit and she then can reunite with her husband the King (*Zohar* III:79a; I:64a).

The destruction of the Temple of Jerusalem was the ultimate tragedy for the King and the Matronit. The Matronit remained homeless and accompanied her children, the People of Israel, into their exile, where she is constantly being violated by other gods. The issue of these involuntary submissions are the souls of the gentiles who are able to suck from the Matronit, just as the Children of Israel did while the Temple still stood (*Zohar* I:84b). The Matronit suckling her children is an image reminiscent of Asherah and Anath suckling their offspring in Ugaritic mythology.

The King, unable to endure solitude, let a slave-goddess, Lilith, take the place of his true queen, and thus it is now Lilith who rules over the Holy Land. This act, more than anything else, caused the King to lose his honor (*Zohar* III:69a).

## MYSTICISM AND MYTHOLOGY

As a rule, the Kabbalistic authors represent the nature of God and the various persons comprised in him in the form of mystical interpretations of passages, expressions or single words contained in the Bible.

Thus, the four persons in the deity, the Father, the Mother, the Son (the King), and the Daughter (the Matronit), are derived from the Tetragrammaton, the most sacred four-letter name of God, YHWH (Yahweh). The letter Y is called the Father and stands for Wisdom; the first H is the Supernal Mother, called Understanding; the W is the Son; and the second H the Daughter (*Zohar* III:290a-b; 65b). However, even if we accept these statements at face value, three considerations indicate that much in Kabbalistic theology is not the result of mystical speculation but belongs to the realm of mythology. One is the striking similarity between the Kabbalistic tetrad and several ancient Near Eastern tetrads. These similarities are so numerous and detailed that they can only be explained by borrowing, despite the considerable time lag between them.[4]

The second consideration is that, quite apart from these affinities, the concrete details given about the four persons in the deity and the relationships among them are unmistakably mythological. The Kabbalistic authors stress that the Father, Mother, Son, and Daughter are but four attributes, aspects or *Sephirot* (as the Kabbalists term the divine emanations) of the one God, and are mystical symbols of his Wisdom, Understanding, Beauty, and Sovereignty. However, the stories about the four divine persons, their loves (couched in most explicitly sexual terms), jealousies, joys, sorrows, extramarital unions, separations, etc., are myths and must have been perceived as such by all readers, with the possible exception of a few with rigorously mystical minds and an unusual capacity for rigidly controlled, abstract-symbolic thought.

The third factor is the specific power relationship the Kabbala assumed to exist between human actions and the vicissitudes that befell the divine-Son-King and Daughter-Matronit. When the pious of Israel copulate with their wives on Friday night, this, it was taught, brings about a joyous union between the King and the Matronit. In fact, the human sexual act causes the King to emit his seminal fluid from his divine male genital and to fertilize the Matronit who thereupon gives birth to angels and human souls (*Zohar* I:12b). When the same pious and learned men keep apart from their wives during the six days of the week, the Matronit joins them and couples with them (*Zohar* I:49b–50a). When there is strife in the world, the male Cherub and the female Cherub, representing the King and the Matronit, turn away from each other and thus their nakedness is revealed (*Zohar* II:176a; III:59a).

Such a close correspondence between human and divine acts would

---

[4]    This subject is discussed in some detail in Patai (1967: 164ff).

only make sense to the followers of the Kabbala (the majority of Jews from the fifteenth to the eighteenth centuries) if it was based on a solid mythical belief in actual human-like sexual relations between the King and the Matronit. Even if the Kabbalistic authors originally understood them to be abstract-mystical symbols of two "emanations" of God, by the time their explications reached the average Kabbalist the mystical concept had turned into concrete mythical image. The spread of this popular-mythical, as opposed to the scholarly-mystical, view of the Matronit and her relationship to the King and to men was facilitated among the Jews who lived in Christian countries by the presence of a popular Mariolatry.

In any case, in the Kabbalistic development of Judaism, the female deity, who was tenaciously worshiped by the Israelites in Biblical times, again came to occupy an important place in popular Jewish religious consciousness. In the old days Yahweh had his female counterpart or consort[5] in either Asherah or Anath-Astarte-Queen of Heaven; in the later Middle Ages he — now styled the Son, the King, or the Holy One, blessed be He — had his wife, mate or consort in the Matronit-Shekhina. Of course, in Biblical times the goddess was worshiped with elaborate rites, none of which were carried over or revived for her later successor, the Matronit. From the days of the Second Temple of Jerusalem God monopolized all ritual expression of worship in both private and public. Since the sixteenth century, however, on Friday nights, homage was paid in home and synagogue to Queen Sabbath, in whose tenderly erotic image one can detect but a faint echo of the more passionate Matronit.

This lack of ritualism for the Matronit contrasts strangely with the important role she played in the mythical belief system. Unlike the *deus absconditus*, she remained on earth, accompanied her children into exile, and continued to be keenly and emotionally concerned with their welfare. She thus supplied the psychologically important divine mother-and-wife figure in Judaism, just as her predecessors Asherah and Anath had in Biblical times. Her essential identity with Asherah, the very thought of which would have met with general horror and revulsion, was recognized, in a remarkable insight, by one of the greatest sixteenth century Kabbalists, Moses Cordovero of Safed (Cordovero 1780: 120c).[6]

---

[5] This was argued by Hugo Gressmann (1920: 64–65) and Morgenstern (1940: 121, n. 98; 1945: 95, n. 159, 96, 107, 111).

[6] Cordovero (1780: 120c) says: "It is explained in the *Zohar* that Sovereignty, i.e. the Matronit, is called Asherah, since she sucks from Beauty (the King) who

# REFERENCES

ALBRIGHT, WILLIAM F.
1950–1951   "A catalogue of early Hebrew lyric poems," in *Hebrew Union College Annual* 23(1):1–39.
1968   *Yahweh and the gods of Canaan.* New York: Doubleday.

CORDOVERO, MOSES
1780   *Pardes Rimmonim.* Koretz: Z'vi Hirsh ben Arye Leb and Sh'muel ben Yissakhar Ber.

EAKIN, FRANK E., JR.
1971   *The religion and culture of Israel.* Boston: Allyn and Bacon.
*Encyclopedia Miqrait*
1971   Volume six. Jerusalem: Mosad Bialik.

GRESSMANN, HUGO
1920   *Die Lade Jahwes.* Berlin: W. Kohlhammer.

MARMORSTEIN, A.
1950   *Studies in Jewish theology.* Oxford: Oxford University Press.

MORGENSTERN, JULIAN
1940   "Amos studies III," in *Hebrew Union College Annual* 15.
1945   *The Ark, the Ephod and the "Tent of Meeting."* Cincinnati: Hebrew Union College.

PATAI, RAPHAEL
1967   *The Hebrew goddess.* New York: Ktav Publishing Company.

POPE, MARVIN H., WOLFGANG RÖLLIG
1965   "Syrien: Die Mythologie der Ugariter und Phönizier," in *Wörterbuch der Mythologie*, volume one. Edited by Hans Wilhelm Haussig, 219–312. Stuttgart: Ernst Klett.

REED, WILLIAM L.
1949   *The Asherah in the Old Testament.* Fort Worth: Texas Christian University Press.

SCHRADER, EBERHARD
1902–1903   *Die Keilinschriften und das Alte Testament* (third edition). Revised by H. Zimmern and H. Winkler. Berlin: Reuter and Reichard.

TISHBI, ISAIAH
1961   *Mishnat HaZohar,* volume two. Jerusalem: Mosad Bialik.

---

is her husband, inasmuch as he is called Asher. He is Asher and she Asherah (author's translation). In fact, the passage of the *Zohar* (I:49a) referred to by Cordovero, while it speaks of Asher and Asherah, does not identify the latter with the Matronit. Thus this identification is original Cordovero.

# Tibetan Oracles

H. R. H. PRINCE PETER OF GREECE AND DENMARK

Oracles in Tibet are called *Chos-sKyong* or *Chos-rGyal* and sometimes also *Chos-dje*, which is a more popular form. Before the Chinese occupation of Tibet they coexisted with the Lamaist Church and were shown both popular and official esteem. They never really came into conflict with Buddhism although high-ranking dignitaries tended to look upon them as remnants of a bygone age and the expression of popular credulity. Oracles were to be found distributed all over the country, the minor ones in villages and populous centers while major ones (including the most important one, the State Oracle, about which more will be said later) were found in some of the larger monastic institutions. This shows that they were well integrated in Tibetan society and that although their personalities were generally the result of psychic abnormalities, they were rarely looked upon as sick but, in a society imbued with the faith in a spiritual world, were taken seriously as mediums of the gods. The Dalai Lama, in a conversation with Günter Schüttler (Schüttler 1971), is quoted as having said:

This has nothing to do with Buddhism. The oracles are absolutely without importance. They are only small tree-spirits. They do not belong to the three treasures of Buddhism. Relations with them are of no help for our next incarnation. They should be looked upon as a manifestation of popular superstition which is deleterious to the health of human beings.

This pronouncement can be compared to those of high-ranking bishops of the Greek Orthodox Church when they condemn the practice of the fire-walking *Anasteriadides*, a ceremony that they disapprove of but are bound to accept because of popular pressure.

Today, since the Chinese occupation of Tibet, many oracles have taken refuge in India. In Dharmsala, Himachal Pradesh, northern India, there are in exile together with the Dalai Lama, four high-ranking oracles, among them the Netchung State Oracle, and in refugee camps throughout the country there are minor oracles, who are still avidly consulted by their fellow Tibetan refugees.

## HISTORY

The origin of the Tibetan oracles is mysterious. All that we can say is that they are certainly of great antiquity and antedate Buddhism, which was introduced into the country in the seventh century A.D. They are usually considered to be related to the Central and Arctic Asian shamans, whose geographical proximity makes this hypothesis plausible. What makes this theory, in my opinion, doubtful, however, is the fact that they act rather as mediums for the gods and do not claim to behave in the classical way that shamans do. The shaman, when he goes into a trance, sees his soul leaving his body to visit the world of the spirits in a long, arduous, and sometimes painful trip, returning when it is finished, carrying the message which those who consulted him are expecting. In contrast with this procedure a medium acts as a mouthpiece for the gods or spirits who possess him and speak through him, very often without his own knowledge of what is being said, answering directly the questions of those who consult him. I think, despite the pronouncement of His Holiness quoted above, that this shows an affinity with Indian spiritual practices and India, the country from which Buddhism also entered Tibet. Thus it is recorded that, shortly after the Lord Buddha's death, roughly in the seventh century B.C., *Iddhi* [the control over supernatural forces] very quickly penetrated Buddhism. A work of the first century A.D., the *Saddharma Pundarika*, deals with this question. Again, in southern Buddhism, *Parita* is a magical ritual which the great Indian Buddhist sage, Nagasena, says in the *Milinda Panna* (discussions with the Hellenistic Punjab general and ruler, Menander) was accepted and recognized by "the Blessed One." The practice of magic was not alien to Lamaist practices in pre-occupied Tibet, as is witnessed by those institutions which in Lhasa dealt exclusively with it: the monasteries of Moru, Ramoche, and Karmäs in Lhasa.

Oracles came to Tibet together with the early religion of the country, Bön, and from it were carried over to Buddhism. Tradition tells us that the Indian sage, Padmasambhava (Guru Rimpoche), founder of the Samye monastery in central Tibet, installed oracles there. We are told

Plate 1.  The ritual paraphernalia and uniform of a Tibetan oracle

Plate 2. The heavy helmet (*Tsen-sha*) worn by Tibetan oracles, with the breast-piece (*melong* [mirror]) in front; the *toli* ([sun] of the Arctic shaman?) in front, the scarf (*khatag*) and red loop for catching spirits on the right

Plate 3. Lhag-pa Thöndrup dressing for the séance

Plate 4.  Seated on a chair, concentrating himself while a lama attendant plays a drum and cymbals

Plate 5. A calm face before the trance

Plate 6. Concentrating

Plate 7. The spirits taking possession of the oracle

Plate 8. Going deeper into the trance

Plate 9.   Prophesying under possession

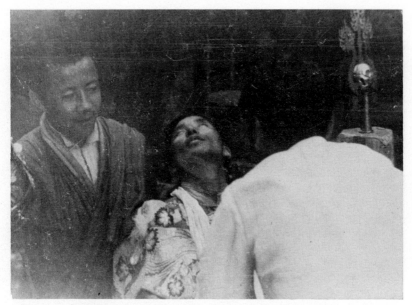

Plate 10. Collapsing after the trance is over, the attendants busying themselves with relieving the oracle of his helmet and clothes

Plate 11.   Another trance — that of the *Ge-nyen* or *Jo-wo Ching-karwa* demon of the Amne-Machen range in Amdo (note the Amdo nomad's headgear worn during the trance)

also that these were recognized by Tsong Khapa, the reformer of the Lamaist Church, and later recognized officially by the great fifth Dalai Lama. He was the first to institutionalize the State Oracle of Netchung, as we shall see.

Oracles are described in the Tibetan book *sKu Nga rGyalpo kang-sag* [confessions of the five sacred kings]. The five kings (*rGyalpo sKu Nga*) are: in the east, Samye, where the Body is incarnate; in the west, Netchung, where the Word is incarnate; in the north, Norbu-gang or Karmasar, where Deeds are incarnate; in the south, Gah-dong, where Wisdom is incarnate; in the center there are further places of incarnation such as Lhamo or Tsang-karpo.

Austin Waddel (1895) sees a connection between these five sacred kings and the five brothers of Ch'ad-duning in Mongolia, which, in his view, establishes a connection with Central Asia.

## GRADATION OF ORACLES

Village oracles are of various categories; they are known as *Lha-ka, Ku-tempa, Nak-pa*, etc. Their popular name is *Chos-dje*.

In Kalimpong, on the northern border of West Bengal, I had the opportunity of studying the local *Chos-dje*, Lhag-pa Thöndrup, who served the needs of 3,500 Tibetans resident there. He is the same man described by Günter Schüttler (1971), although his study took place some years later and after Lhag-pa Thöndrup had gone through a harrowing period. I have described my study in *Folk* (1961), and I include here some photographs taken at the time (see Plates 1–11). Subsequent to my interviews with Lhag-pa Thöndrup, he abandoned the profession and sold me his uniform, which is now a prize exhibit of the Tibetan collection in the National Museum of Copenhagen. The reason he did this was that while being possessed by the spirit of Dorje Chung-den, one of the protective deities of Tibetan Buddhism, he nearly died of suffocation while swallowing a *khatag* [silken presentation scarf]; this was the horrible way in which the person whose spirit possessed him was assassinated by enemies.

It seems, however, that he was not able to remain very long outside the profession and returned to it with a new set of clothes. In a séance which I filmed and sound-recorded, the Kalimpong *Chos-dje* was possessed in one afternoon by no less than four spirits, a very exhausting performance as I could see. Questions were put to him, and he answered them somewhat indistinctly and certainly ambiguously as seems to have been the practice of all good oracles ever since the Delphic Pythia. In order to induce a trance, a drum and cymbals, played by a lama, were used. It should be noted that the oracle himself does not handle the instruments as a shaman would. He concentrates himself very visibly, and the trance comes upon him surprisingly quickly. When questioned about what he made use of to induce a trance, he first said that he used nothing more than drumming and concentration; he later admitted (although reluctantly because, as he said, it is prohibited) that in some cases as a prelude he took a mixture of red pepper and hashish. Schüttler mentions other inducements such as monotonous praying, autosuggestion, deep breathing that changes the metabolism, and the strangulating effect of the tightness of the chinstrap of the heavy helmet that he wears, all of which certainly play a role.

Some oracles of a higher grade are the following: *Tsin-marpo* at the monastery of Samye who wears a red-brown mask (hence his name), which he keeps with him in a box; he has a locked room in which he operates where Tibetans believe he hacks souls to pieces. *Dzasa-marpo* [the red Dzasa] is a Lhasa nobleman who made an enemy of Pehar (or Pekar), a pre-Buddhist devil by whom he was killed; he was enthroned after his death at Samye, the original seat of the demon, by his servants who wished to avenge their master. *Karma-shar*, the oracle of the Sera monastery in Lhasa, is known also as "the king of the body"; he goes ceremoniously in procession through the city in the seventh month of the Tibetan year accompanied by the outcast Tibetan disposers of the dead (the *Ragya-pa*). The prophecy which he delivers on this occasion is written down and is nailed to the door of his temple for all to read. The *Gadong Chos-dje* is the companion of Pehar known also as "the wooden bird." The *Lubug Tshu-shi* oracle specializes in the cure of madness; he proceeds by searching the body of the insane with a *melong* [a mirror], then using an arrow he "takes" a piece of flesh out (a piece of meat which no doubt he had up his sleeve) which is supposed to contain the devil that is harrassing the victim; he chews the piece of meat, then spits it out into a vessel containing liquid and drinks the whole to effect the cure. At Sera there is a female oracle, the only woman oracle, who is intimately connected with the order of militant lamas, the *Dop-dop*. The *Lung-tö* oracle in central Tibet, a money-lending oracle, when he is consulted, vomits coins while in a trance; the money has to be paid back later, and reimbursement is effected by the oracle covering the coins with saffron powder and swallowing them one by one again while in a trance.

I come now to the State Oracle of Netchung who is the best known and at the apex of the hierarchy. He is now in exile together with the Dalai Lama, and I would very much like to have an interview with him. He is the incarnation of the pre-Buddhist devil, the three-headed and six-armed Pehar. Waddel (1895) suggests that he may be another form of the "white overcast sky demon" of the Turki and suggests that the reason the saga of King Kesar of Ling cannot be recited at the monastery of Drepung, which is close to the place where the Netchung oracle has his seat, is that King Kesar conquered the Turki. Here again we find a pre-Buddhist connection with Central Asia. The oracle is said to have been brought to Tibet in the reign of the Tibetan king Thi sRong Detsan by Padmasambhava and enthroned in the monastery of Samye as its guardian. Originally, the incarnation was not a lama but a layman who could marry and have children. This is given as a reason why he refused, as we shall see, to live within the precincts of Drepung monastery.

Under the fifth Dalai Lama, Pehar is said to have left Samye for Tsheltung Th'ang, which lies approximately three miles southeast of Lhasa. Here he came into conflict with a Lama named Z'ang. This Lama forbade the decorator of the monastery to paint a fresco of Pehar in the temple. Whereupon Pehar turned himself into a young assistant to the painter and got the latter to paint a monkey with a torch in his hand instead. The picture came to life and the monkey set fire to the monastery. Lama Z'ang was very angry and, having contrived a *dö* [devil trap], caught Pehar in it and put him into a wooden box, which he threw into the *Kyi-chu* [the river of Lhasa]. The box floated down to Drepung where the fifth Dalai Lama noticed it and ordered it to be brought to him. The abbot of Drepung did this and, as he was carrying the box on land, it got heavier and heavier. Unable to continue, he stopped and opened it to see what could be inside it. Whereupon Pehar flew out in the form of a dove and settled on a tree, which the Dalai Lama accepted as the abode in which he had chosen to live.

Netchung, which means "the small dwelling" and is located some six miles from Drepung, was built around the tree and has remained the habitat of the State Oracle ever since. The temple has three doors with a large painting of Dorje-chang on the middle one. It is always locked because that Buddhist deity is considered to be Pehar's successor. The building has three floors and a golden roof. The original tree still stands in one of the rooms. In another room the State Oracle sits on a throne to prophesy. Behind him is a large statue of Padmasambhava. Once a year on the second day of the first month of the Tibetan year, the Netchung oracle goes in procession to Lhasa accompanied by the Drepung magistrate. He sets himself up in a special temple east of the Lhasa cathedral, the *Jo-khang*, where he now makes prophecies for the whole year. Apart from this ceremonial appearance, he is regularly consulted by the Tibetan government on questions of policy. He can also be consulted privately by anybody but, curiously, against payment. His prophecies are in the name of Pehar, whose spirit possesses him, but he is, notwithstanding, responsible for what he says and can be penalized for false utterances! At his death, a successor is found among candidates in competition. The winner must be able to bend a sword "which eighteen men cannot bend." One of my Tibetan teachers in Kalimpong, Lobsang P'hüntsok Lha-lung pa, was the son of a Netchung oracle (the one before the last) who had married and founded a family. During the flight of the Dalai Lama to Yatung in the Chumbi valley at the time of the invasion of Tibet by the Chinese armies in 1950, the Netchung oracle was consulted repeatedly as to what course of action the Tibetan ruler should take. Should he take refuge in India or should he stay in Tibet? Twice the oracle said that he should stay in Tibet despite attempts by the government to get him to say the contrary. It is said that it was eventually discovered that he had been bribed to deliver his message by the pro-Chinese monks of Sera, who also occupied the passes to Sikkim with armed guards to keep the Dalai Lama from escaping abroad.

In conclusion, I will say that this is a somewhat sketchy and incomplete account of Tibetan oracles but I hope that, however imperfect, it will stimulate discussion of this subject.

# REFERENCES

LUC DE HEUSCH
   1962   *Cultes de possession et religions initiatiques de Salut en Afrique,*
          Tome 2. Brussels: Annales du Centre d'Étude des Religions de
          l'Université de Bruxelles, Institut de Sociologie.
NEBESKY-WOJKOWITZ, RENÉ
   1955   *Wo Berge Götter sind.* Stuttgart.
PETER, PRINCE OF GREECE AND DENMARK, H.R.H.
   1961   The trances of a Tibetan oracle. *Folk* 3.
SCHÜTTLER, GÜNTER
   1971   *Die letzten tibetanischen Orakelpriester: psychiutrisch-neurolo-
          logische Aspecte.* Wiesbaden: Franz Steiner.
STADLING, J.
   1912   *Shamanismen i Norra Asien.* Stockholm: P. A. Nordstad and
          Sönner.
WADDEL, L. AUSTIN
   1895   *The Buddhism of Tibet or Lamaism.* London: W. H. Allen.

# Breaking Ties with Deceased Spouse

PAUL C. ROSENBLATT, R. PATRICIA WALSH, and
DOUGLAS A. JACKSON

In many societies there are death customs which either eliminate reminders of a deceased spouse or increase psychological distance from a deceased spouse. These customs include destroying, giving away, or temporarily putting aside personal property of the deceased, observing a taboo on the name of the deceased, changing residence, and fearing the spouse's ghost. Of what use are these customs? We believe these customs serve to break ties with the deceased spouse and, as a consequence, to facilitate establishment of a new relationship in which the pattern of rights and obligations resembles that in the marriage that was ended by the spouse's death. Such tie-breaking would be especially useful if the new relationship is between people who formerly had to inhibit marital response to one another, that is, between people who formerly knew one another and who did not have a marital relationship.

Reminders of a deceased spouse may stimulate responses that are likely to interfere with a new marital or quasi-marital relationship. Consider a widower living in the dwelling he shared with his deceased wife and surrounded by her possessions. If activities such as sharing a meal or having sexual relations with some other woman were improper and inhibited in this setting before his wife's death, they will continue to be more difficult to practice than if the setting were changed. Further, the familiar setting will remind the man of previously well-learned behavior specific to the marriage ended by the death, or motivate him to engage in

This research was supported by grants to Paul C. Rosenblatt from the National Institute of Mental Health (MH 18453) and the University of Minnesota Agricultural Experiment Station.

such behavior, perhaps a routine morning conversation or a going-to-sleep routine that requires the presence of the deceased wife. Such residual dispositions may block resumption of a normal, productive life by promoting grief and denial (Averill 1968). We believe that spouse-specific response patterns cued by reminders of the spouse are modal cross-culturally. Hence, we believe a common condition of bereavement around the world is that something resembling marriage to a new person is difficult in the presence of reminders of the previous marriage.

From a cue-conditioning perspective (e.g. Estes 1959), the disposition to respond in a manner inconsistent with a new marital relationship would be reduced by elimination of cues to respond as one did while the spouse was still alive and by learning of new responses to the old cues. Thus, removal of the wife's personal possessions or changing one's feelings about her through fear of her ghost will both reduce old response dispositions.

In addition, others in the environment of the widow or widower will retain response dispositions toward the widow or widower that are cued by reminders of the deceased person and that make it difficult for the surviving spouse to enter a new marital routine with someone else. For these other people it would also be easier to accept a new marital relationship of widow or widower if reminders of the deceased are reduced and if psychological distance from the deceased is increased by such devices as fear of the deceased's ghost. From this discussion follows the first of three hypotheses considered in this paper: (1) *Remarriage rates are positively correlated with the practice of tie-breaking customs.*

Initially we did not think of the levirate and sororate as likely to require inhibition of previously learned response dispositions. Our naive assumption was that many levirate and sororate arrangements for widows and widowers are with people toward whom sexual and domestic interactions had been marital in spirit. But that does not seem to be a supportable assumption. First of all, many levirate and sororate marriages are with affinal kin who may have been outside any category of sexual privilege. Second, reports of privileged sexual relations with spouse's "siblings," relations which might be most productive of ease of moving into a new marital relation, are not very common. In our sample of 78 societies we could not get reliable ratings of special intimate relationship with a possible replacement spouse; however, one rater thought it present in only 12 cases, the other in only six. In contrast, raters agreed that sororate remarriage was present in 23 cases and levirate remarriage in 43 cases. In Murdock's *Social structure*, sex relations were rated as freely or conditionally permitted with brother's wife in 34 of 250 societies and with wife's sister in 28 of 250 (Murdock 1949: 270). In contrast, brother's wife marriage was rated as permitted in 153 societies and sister's husband marriage as permitted in 133 societies (Murdock 1949: 270). Although one could argue that privileged sex is so interesting to Westerners that it would be reported in literature on almost any society in which it commonly occurs, it seems safer merely to say that there is no evidence that privileged sex antecedes levirate or sororate remarriage at all commonly. Considering that levirate or sororate remarriage is common, while there is no evidence that privileged sex is common, it does not seem likely that people will have acquired marital response dispositions to the spouse's "sibling." Rather, we would expect in many cases inhibition of sexuality and domestic activities. Consequently for levirate and sororate remarriage, the problems of old response dispositions may be even more severe. Not only does the couple face the generalized inhibitions of the surviving spouse, they may have specific inhibitions to each other. They will have had more likelihood of developing habitual nonmarital patterns. Furthermore, each may have been learned by the other as a cue to making old responses to the deceased. If so, each could be a cue to grief and to dispositions that block acquisition of a new marital pattern. Thus, tie-breaking customs may be even more necessary for sororate and levirate remarriage.

This leads to two more hypotheses: (2) *Where levirate or sororate remarriage is present, tie-breaking customs are more likely to be present.* (3) *The rate of remarriage is more strongly associated with the practice of tie-breaking customs where remarriage is a sororate or levirate remarriage than where it is not.*

Before going into a presentation of our research methods, there are two issues we must discuss — the problem of independent identification of tie-breaking customs and the definition of remarriage.

In a sense, this is a bootstrap operation. We are testing hypotheses assuming we know what tie-breaking customs exist, but we also must somehow identify tie-breaking customs independently of their correlations with our remarriage measures. We have done this through reading ethnographic reports of societies not in our research sample and making inferences about what seemed to be serving as tie-breaking customs. The list of customs and beliefs was modified somewhat by the winnowing out of customs which we could not measure validly. This process led to measuring these customs in our research: fear of ghosts (two measures); disposal, giving away or putting aside for a substantial amount of time some personal property of the deceased (two measures); temporarily or permanently abandoning the dwelling or a room of the dwelling in which survivors and deceased lived together; temporarily or permanently abandoning the campsite or community in which the survivors lived with the deceased; and practicing a temporary or permanent taboo on the name of the deceased.

Defining marriage and remarriage for comparative study is notoriously difficult. We were willing, however, to operate with an imperfect working definition in order to get at the psychological and social phenomena of interest. We considered remarriage to be either what the ethnographer calls marriage, whether he gives a qualifying statement or not (rarely were they given), or a relationship that is both heterosexual and co-residential.

## RESEARCH METHOD

### Sample

A sample of 78 societies was drawn from the universe of societies defined by Murdock and White in their "Standard cross-cultural sample" (1969). The Murdock and White standard sample was drawn to minimize cultural diffusion artifacts and to maximize the use of well-described societies. However, we had to shop among their list of 186 societies to find ones that seemed to have adequate descriptions of death customs, and that met our requirement that no society be used in the sample which had been a source of ideas in the original research proposal, or in the identification of tie-breaking customs. Ten of the 78 cases are substitutes from the same culture areas as societies in the Murdock and White sample. These substitutions were made because they provide a good description of death customs, whereas the ones they replace in the Murdock and White sample do not. That these societies were in fact in the appropriate culture areas was determined by consulting Murdock's (1968) catalog of culture areas and the *Ethnographic atlas* of the journal *Ethnology*. For every society we tried to focus on a particular time period and a particular community or type of community, and in some cases we used sources different from or additional to those listed by Murdock and White. A bibliography of sources used is available from the authors.

### Rating Procedures

Ratings were usually made from extracts, generally photocopied pages and chapters, of materials relevant to death customs and the other variables of interest in the study. All variables in this study were related by at least two raters working independently of one another, and different variables were rated by different rater pairs or groups. The raters of the key variables in this paper were Terrichristine Hall, Merrie Norman Harrison, Paul C. Rosenblatt, Elizabeth A. Syme, R. Patricia Walsh, and Richard Walz. The levirate and sororate ratings were made by TH and PCR, ratings of fear of ghosts by TH, MNH, RPW and RW, ratings of widow remarriage by PCR and RPW, ratings of almost all tie-breaking customs other than fear of ghosts by MNH and PCR, and one rating of property destruction by PCR and EAS. TH, MNH, EAS, and RW were completely ignorant of the theoretical analysis of tie-breaking customs; all raters worked in ignorance of the status of the societies they were rating on variables other than the ones they were rating.

Variables were included in final analysis when they obtained high reliabilities, were measurable in a substantial number of cases, and were not too strongly correlated with variables that they shouldn't be correlated with, including sex of ethnographer(s) and order in which raters rated the material. Furthermore, we used Campbell and Fiske logic (1959), which requires in the case of ratings that a rater's ratings of something generally correlate best with the other rater's ratings of the same variable.

We attempted to measure the percentage of widows who practice any form of levirate, percentage of widowers who practice any form of the sororate, and presence or absence of levirate and sororate. Levirate was defined as the marriage of a widow to any male member of her deceased husband's family, lineage, or clan; sororate as a marriage of a widower to any female member of his deceased wife's family, lineage, or clan. The measures of presence-absence and of percentages were intended to be of actual occurrence; however, it is likely that those ratings are contaminated by norm statements that appeared to be statements about actual behavior. How we handled the definition of marriage and remarriage has been discussed in the introduction to this article.

In defining various tie-breaking customs we defined a ghost as a spirit, apparition, or other manifestation of a specific deceased person, capable of being perceived or perceived as acting in the world of the living. Name taboos were rated on a three-point continuum from absent to present but temporary to present and permanent, and raters were instructed to use a broad definition of taboo, one that would include in the category of taboo a norm that it is in bad taste to mention the name of the deceased person. The disposal of personal property of the deceased was rated with two items. One item asked for ratings of "some personal utensils or prized objects of typical dead adult disposed of with corpse or given to other groups or put out of sight and use for substantial amount of time." The other assessed destruction of potentially usable personal property of the deceased on a four-point continuum from absent to present but symbolic, to present and substantial, to present and total. The combined ratings of the two property disposal items correlate with each other .55, N = 49, p < .0005. Desertion or destruction of the dwelling or a room of the dwelling of the deceased was measured and considered present whether it was present temporarily or permanently. Temporary or permanent camp or village abandonment was the other of the key variables. All the tie-breaking and remarriage measures were of typical adults, excluding royalty, slaves, or other atypical social categories.

Combined ratings of variables reported in this paper represent simple adding or averaging of variables with adequate reliability coefficients. For variables rated on presence-absence by two raters, cases of disagreement were deleted. In combining ratings of presence-absence by four raters, a case was used only if three or four of the four raters agreed. A combined rating of degree of fear of ghost was automatically recorded as 00 if there was a combined rating of absence on the presence-absence measure. The Appendix to this article lists all societies in the sample and their ratings on the key variables in this report.

Table 1.   Tie-breaking customs and remarriage

| | Percent widows who remarry | | Percent levirate marriage | | Levirate present | | Sororate present | | Inter-rater correlation | |
|---|---|---|---|---|---|---|---|---|---|---|
| | r | N | r | N | r | N | r | N | r | N |
| Disposal of personal objects | .14 | 21 | .56* | 15 | .56** | 33 | .79** | 20 | .71 | 55 |
| Useful property destroyed | .41** | 32 | .80** | 21 | .45** | 43 | .60** | 22 | .51 | 71 |
| Name taboo present | .11 | 18 | .51* | 14 | .38* | 29 | .28 | 15 | .93 | 46 |
| Dwelling or room abandoned | .35* | 25 | .44* | 15 | .08 | 31 | .29 | 19 | .82 | 63 |
| Camp or village abandoned | .16 | 25 | .50* | 16 | .11 | 34 | .09 | 18 | .65 | 68 |
| Fear of ghosts present | .68** | 19 | .48* | 18 | .35* | 28 | .68** | 17 | .35a | 30a |
| Degree of fear of ghosts | .56** | 17 | .10 | 18 | .16 | 28 | .58** | 17 | .41a | 47a |
| Inter-rater correlation | .74 | 34 | .61 | 24 | 1.00 | 47 | .69 | 25 | | |

\*   p < .05
\*\*   p < .01
a   Medians for correlations generated by four raters.

Table 1 contains interrater correlations for the variables discussed in detail in this paper. The two rows of figures in Table 1 dealing with ghost fear are based on ratings of four raters. These were ratings made in our first batch of ratings, when instructions were not well written and raters were inexperienced. Although the average inter-rater correlations for these two measures of ghost fear are rather low, all inter-rater correlations were positive, and the pooling of ratings by four raters gives a stability comparable to pooling more frequently agreed-on ratings by two raters. The reliabilities of the two measures of percentage of widowers remarrying were too low. For percentage of widowers remarrying the inter-rater correlation was .41 (N = 22); and for percentage of widowers remarrying by the sororate the inter-rater correlation was .37 (N = 13). Because of these low reliabilities the two measures are not discussed further in this paper. All other measures achieved at least tolerable reliability.

For most of the variables discussed in this paper there is a substantial case loss from the original seventy-eight. This is largely due to the limitations of the ethnographic literature and the magnitude of our theoretical ambitions. Our hope is that future ethnographic research will more often provide a grain of description dealing with death and bereavement that will enable comparative research on more representative groups of societies. Case loss makes generalization problematic, though we doubt that we have systematically lost cases discrepant from or consistent with hypotheses.

*Diffusion Analysis*

We tested for the possibility that culture traits that we hypothesized to be functionally related might diffuse jointly. We found that percentage of widows remarrying through levirate is distributed nonrandomly on an arc running north through Oceania, into Asia and then south through the Americas. Of the variables hypothesized to correlate with it, only one, the destruction of usable personal property of the deceased, may be similarly nonrandomly distributed. We say "may be" because there is significant nonrandomness only with some opportunistic rearranging of societies on the arc. However, when we attempted a matched pairs analysis of joint diffusion, following method four of Naroll and D'Andrade (Naroll 1962), there was no difference in support for functional and diffusional hypotheses. The fact that there is no evidence for diffusion on the other property disposal item further reduces concern about diffusional artifacts.

## RESULTS AND DISCUSSION

Table 1 summarizes the crucial intervariable correlations. For percentage of widows practicing levirate remarriage, six of the seven crucial tie-breaking customs are significantly correlated. For presence-absence of levirate four of seven correlations are significant, and the same number is significant for presence-absence of sororate. The evidence indicates that tie-breaking customs may well facilitate remarriage.

Two of the tie-breaking variables, destruction of useful personal property and fear of ghosts present are related to all four remarriage variables. These two tie-breaking variables seem the best candidates for tie-breaking available to any society. In contrast, there is one tie-breaking variable that is related to only one of the remarriage variables, temporary or permanent camp or village abandonment. The difference between the two variables that are tied to all four remarriage variables and the single variable that is related to only one remarriage variable is an understandable one. Destroying personal property of somebody else or fearing his ghost both seem easier behaviors to engage in than abandonment of dwelling or living area. Abandonment of dwelling or living area would be costly in terms of effort, economics, and perhaps psychological disruption, especially in societies with difficult-to-build dwellings. In addition, it might inconvenience many people who are not very bereaved. Destroying the deceased's personal property is considerably easier in that it is likely to be duplicated among the possessions of others. However attractive someone else's things are, they are not likely to be necessary for survival. We realize that the concept of personal property is not present in some societies, but we think our analysis makes sense for the many societies in which it is present in some form. Ghost fear, like destroying personal property, costs much less economically and requires much less physical effort than dwelling abandonment. Moreover, ghost fear builds on normal cognitive processes following a death. It seems normal for people to believe in ghosts. In our data, a belief that the ordinary dead adult has a ghost was rated as present in 65 of the 66 societies for which our raters could make ratings.

An examination of relative frequencies of community abandonment, ghost fear, and property destruction indicates that community abandonment is in fact much less popular than the other two tie-breaking customs. Our raters rated fear of ghosts as present in 33 of 44 societies and disposal of personal property of the deceased as present in 42 of 50 societies, whereas community abandonment was rated present in only 7 of 62 cases.

Five of the seven tie-breaking variables are more strongly correlated with percentage of widows remarrying by levirate than with percentage of widows remarrying whether or not by levirate. Although this difference is not significant, it is in the direction of supporting our idea that tie-breaking would be more facilitative of a levirate remarriage than of a nonlevirate remarriage.

In attempting to understand the role of name taboos we added an additional measure — a measure of whether the name taboo, if present, "applies primarily to behavior of close relatives of the deceased adult and/or to behavior in the presence of close relatives of the deceased." If a key function of name taboos is to break ties for the spouse(s) of the deceased, then it seems to us that name taboos would relatively often apply primarily to close kinsmen of the deceased or to people in their presence. In fact, for 14 of the 18 societies that we could rate on this variable this was the case; the name taboo DID apply primarily to close relatives or to people who were in their presence.

There are three negative correlations among the seven tie-breaking customs. Presence of ghost fear correlates $-.04$ ($N = 61$) with destruction of useful personal property. The great surprise, however, is that tie-breaking by means of name taboo correlates $-.37$ ($N = 25$) with presence of ghost fear and $-.42$ ($N = 24$) with degree of ghost fear. Although there is some clustering among the tie-breaking items, name taboo and ghost fear seem the only culture traits that may be functional alternatives. It is a bit surprising that these should be functional alternatives, since an *a priori* guess would be that there would be a number of societies in which mentioning a person's name would summon his ghost. Perhaps that is in fact the case, and societies in which a name taboo is practiced appear low on fear of ghosts only because ethnographers working in these societies were not in a position to discuss ghosts of specific people. Or perhaps the two culture traits represent incompatible dynamics, one of denying or avoiding threats and one of meeting them head-on with intense emotion.

*Deviant Case Analysis*

Analysis of deviant cases often is instructive in probing the limits of theory. In this study, such an analysis is illuminating. There are seven cases in our sample which (1) lack any tie-breaking belief or custom or have only token disposal or destruction of personal property of the deceased, and (2) have either levirate or at least some percentage of re-marriage of widows. We lack any deviant cases with sororate present. How the deviant cases handle widow remarriage is of interest. By our theory they should either have some kind of tie-breaking for remarrying widows or they should have troubled remarriages.

Our seven deviant cases are the Gheg, Kafa, Katab, Koreans, Santal, Tikopia, and Zapotec. One problem in discussing them is that they are not strongly described in the area of tie-breaking. For our seven measures of tie-breaking customs, they lack reliably ratable information on an average of 4.28 items, while the other 71 societies lack reliably ratable information on an average of 2.00 items. Thus, our deviants may only be deviant because they are poorly described. Nonetheless, examination of ethnographic descriptions of widow remarriages in the seven deviant cases is interesting. For five of the seven, widows who remarry change residence, whereas widows who do not remarry usually stay in the residence they were living in before the death of the husband. The five are the Kafa (we infer residence change from Huntingford 1955: 114–115), Katab (Meek 1931: II, 37), Koreans (Brandt 1971: 132), Tikopia (Firth 1936: 175), and Zapotec (Parsons 1936: 68). It should be noted that the Brandt reference we cite for the Koreans is not the one providing the death custom extracts we rated. However, the source of our extracts, Osgood (1951), was unclear about residence for remarrying widows. We thought it safe to use Brandt because on points that both Osgood and Brandt discussed there was considerable overlap. Another difference, however, is that Brandt reports substantial fear of ghosts (200–201). Thus, had we used Brandt the Koreans would not have been a deviant case.

Of the remaining two cases, we lack residence data on the Santal, where at any rate remarriage rates are very low (Culshaw 1949: 146). For the Gheg, widow remarriages, which are usually leviratic, ordinarily do not involve change in residence. Often Gheg remarriages are seriously troubled (Durham 1928: 171). Although Durham's discussion suggests that a principal source of the problem is lack of freedom of choice for widows, it may well be that underlying the freedom of choice problem is a deficiency in tie-breaking.

Our deviant case analysis has augmented our theorizing by suggesting that change in residence for remarrying widôws is a functional alternative to other means of tie-breaking. Residence change fits our theoretical conception of what is necessary for a custom to be tie-breaking, involving as it does, a change from the stimulus setting of the marriage ended by death. Further, the one deviant case for which residence change does not seem to occur is the one deviant for which we have reports of troubled remarriages. The epistemological status of residence change as a tie-breaking custom is, of course, very low. No conclusions can be drawn without examination of the relationship of residence change to the remarriage variables in the entire sample of societies.

## Alternative Interpretations

One possible alternative interpretation of the relationship of tie-breaking customs to remarriage is that the destruction of personal and other property, and the abandonment of dwelling or community increase the dependency needs of surviving spouses. With home and subsistence-getting tools destroyed remarriage is more desirable. There are, however, some deficiencies in this alternative. One is that it cannot account for the results involving name taboo and fear of ghosts. Another is that there are many alternatives to marriage that would be possible, particularly returning to family of consanguineal kin, taking up residence with same-sex unmarrieds, or becoming dependent on spouse's kin but without a marital relationship. Another alternative is that house and property destruction are easier where remarriage is more likely or easier. However, that interpretation also fails to account for the ghost-fear and name taboo data.

## Cultural Context of Remarriage

If anthropology has produced any immutable truth it is that culture traits come in packages, that various aspects of culture are tied together. Thus, in seeking understanding of our data, it is necessary to look beyond the variables we focused on to see if there are other variables related to the ones studied that can provide interesting insights into cultural constraints on the phenomena we have been discussing here.

One finding of interest in our data analysis is that polygyny is related to remarriage of widows. The *Ethnographic atlas* ratings of polygyny correlate significantly with percentage of widows remarrying ($r = .32$, $N = 34$, $p < .05$) and percentage of widows practicing the levirate ($r = .36$, $N = 23$, $p < .05$). That would suggest that polygyny puts a premium on women, making it less desirable that a widow stay single. If people come to value the remarrying of widows, it would seem that they would be under pressure to develop customs that will facilitate widow remarriage. With widow remarriage, in a polygynous society there is less likelihood that some men will be single well on into maturity, which would put more pressure on social control systems to deal with their sexuality. Alternatively or additionally, polygyny may be associated with a pattern of rights of women that makes widow remarriage by levirate a common event. The relationship between percentage of widows remarrying and polygyny may then be an artifact of the relationship between percentage of widows remarrying and percentage of widows remarrying by the levirate.

All four remarriage measures are negatively associated with mean size of local community as rated in the *Ethnographic atlas*. Percentage of widows remarrying correlates $-.39$ (N = 29, p. < .025), percentage of widows remarrying by the levirate correlates $-.71$ (N = 20, p < .0005). For levirate present or absent the correlation is $-.45$ (N = 28, p < .005), and for sororate present or absent the correlation is $-.48$ (N = 18, p < .025). That may mean that in small-scale societies there are less often structures alternative to a marriage-based familial relationship in which to subsist and function, or it may mean that sexual division of labor is more crucial in small-scale societies so that each adult needs the labor of someone of the opposite sex in order to subsist. Conceivably it is in small-scale societies where remarriage alliances are more frequently of great importance. If so, it may be of value to maintain an alliance beyond the death of one of the persons whose marriage knitted the alliance. Remarriage of the surviving spouse by means of levirate or sororate would be of value then.

### Applications to the Urban Areas of the United States and Europe

Our results suggest that remarriage in the urban areas of the United States and Europe could be facilitated by customary disposal of the personal property of the deceased, customary change of residence, and customary name taboo. It seems unlikely that fear of ghost could become customary. If surviving spouses in the urban United States and Europe continue to be left on their own about moving, disposal of personal property of the deceased, and how to treat their memories of and past relationship with the deceased, we can expect remarriage for them to be difficult. Moreover, without the force of custom to engage in the tie-breaking acts, the acts may seem to be disrespectful to the dead or selfish or frivolous. Thus, the acts are potentially of use, but are unlikely to be used by many if they are left as mere options advocated by counsellors and the popular literature on dealing with bereavement.

# APPENDIX: RATINGS OF KEY VARIABLES

Ratings of key variables in this study are listed in this appendix, grouped by type — marriage (columns 1–7), ghost fear (columns 8–10), property destruction (columns 11–13), and other tie-breaking variables (columns 14–17). For all variables, higher numbers mean more of the property being measured. The specific variables given in each column are as follows:

1–2   Percentage of widows remarrying by the levirate.
3      Levirate present or absent (1 = present).
4      Sororate present or absent (1 = present).
5–7   Percentage of widows remarrying (the sum of two raters' ratings, hence scores range from 000 to 200).
8      Ghost fear present (1 = present).
9–10  Degree of ghost fear.
11–12 Extent to which useful personal property of the deceased is destroyed.
13    Some personal property of the deceased destroyed, given away, or put out of sight and use for a substantial lenght of time.
14    Dwelling or room of the dwelling of the deceased destroyed or deserted at least temporarily (1 = present).
15    Name taboo or norm against using name of deceased.
16    Name taboo, if present, applies primarily to close relatives or behavior in presence of close relatives of the deceased.
17    Temporary or permanent abandonment of camp or village at death of typical adult (1 = present).

| Society | 1–7 | 8–10 | 11–13 | 14–17 |
| --- | --- | --- | --- | --- |
| Abipon | ······· | ··· | 111 | 1800 |
| Ainu | ··1···· | 117 | 061 | 0800 |
| Andamanese | 7711··· | 117 | 041 | 1401 |
| Aweikoma | 6011150 | 125 | 071 | ···· |
| Azande | ··1···· | ··· | 101 | ·810 |
| Balinese | ······· | ··· | ··· | 0··0 |
| Thai peasants | ······· | ··· | 02· | 0··0 |
| Basques | 0000··· | 000 | 000 | 00·0 |
| Carib | ······· | 000 | 08· | 18·· |
| Kaihsienkung village, China | ··1···· | 108 | 04· | 00·0 |
| Chippewa | ··1·175 | ··· | 061 | 0810 |
| Comanche | 6311155 | 115 | 081 | 1810 |
| Copper Eskimo | ······· | 125 | 051 | 10·1 |
| Cubeo | ····040 | 000 | 041 | 08·0 |
| Eastern Timbira | ···0··· | ··· | 000 | 0··0 |
| Egyptian Fellahin | ······· | ··· | ··0 | 00·0 |
| Eyak | ······· | ··· | 081 | 00·0 |
| Ganda | ····105 | 112 | 00· | 06·0 |
| Garo | ··11126 | ··· | 040 | 0··0 |
| Gheg (Albanians) | 621·175 | ··· | 02· | ···0 |
| Gros Ventre | ··1·160 | ··· | 061 | 00·· |
| Haitians | ······· | 122 | 00· | 0··0 |
| Hausa (Muslims) | ····155 | 110 | 000 | 0810 |
| Hidatsa | ··11120 | ··· | 041 | 00·0 |
| Hill Maria Gond | 731···· | 112 | 081 | 12·· |
| Huron | ······· | ··· | 021 | 0610 |
| Ibo | ······· | ··· | 020 | 0··0 |

| Society | 1–7 | 8–10 | 11–13 | 14–17 |
|---|---|---|---|---|
| Ifugao | ······· | 122 | 00· | ·0·0 |
| Japanese villagers | ······· | ··· | 021 | 00·0 |
| Javanese villagers | ····110 | 112 | 000 | 0··0 |
| Jivaro | 701·190 | 120 | 061 | ···0 |
| Kafa | ··1·095 | 000 | 02· | ···0 |
| Kapauka | ····160 | 1·· | 02· | ···0 |
| Kaska | ··11140 | 120 | 061 | 10·0 |
| Katab | 451·140 | ··· | ··· | ···0 |
| Klamath | ··11··· | 123 | 101 | 1610 |
| Koreans | ····055 | ··· | 00· | 0··0 |
| Lapps | ····165 | 1·· | 04· | 10·· |
| Lepcha | 6511180 | 120 | 061 | 02·0 |
| Lolo | 701·200 | 122 | 04· | 0··· |
| Manus | 0001105 | 125 | ··· | 10·0 |
| Marshallese | 1011··· | 122 | 00· | 0··0 |
| Masai | ······· | ··· | 061 | 081· |
| Mbundu | ······· | ··· | 021 | ·0·0 |
| Mbuti | ······· | 000 | 07· | 18·1 |
| Mende | ······· | ··· | ··· | ·0·0 |
| Micmac | ··1·100 | ··· | 061 | ···0 |
| Miskito | 7011··· | 123 | 051 | ·81· |
| Murngin | 9411197 | 113 | 08· | ·0·· |
| Nicobarese | ······· | 120 | 081 | 0··0 |
| Burmese villagers | ······· | ··· | 02· | 0··0 |
| Omaha | ··11090 | ··· | 071 | 0··· |
| Orokaiva | 541···· | 120 | 061 | 00·0 |
| Papago | 7011155 | 120 | 071 | 1·1· |
| Pawnee | ··1···· | ··· | 081 | ·40· |
| Samoa | ··1···· | 123 | 00· | 0··0 |
| Santal | ··1···· | ··· | ··· | ·0·· |
| Semang | ······· | 122 | 081 | 1··1 |
| Seniang | 2311··· | 117 | ··· | ···0 |
| Shavante | ······· | 000 | 081 | 0··0 |
| Shilluk | ··1···· | 113 | 061 | ···· |
| Siriono | 971·155 | 115 | 081 | 1··1 |
| Siwans | 000···· | ··· | 02· | 00·0 |
| Thonga | ··11160 | 127 | 071 | 10·0 |
| Tikopia | 000·030 | ··· | 00· | 00·0 |
| Todas | 731···· | ··· | 040 | ·810 |
| Trobriand Islanders | ··1·170 | ··· | 001 | 00·0 |
| Trukese | ··11··· | 000 | 061 | 07·0 |
| Tswana | ··11150 | ··· | 021 | 0··0 |
| Tupinamba | 971·130 | 120 | 071 | ···· |
| Twana | 7011··· | 118 | 061 | 0410 |
| Vanua Levu Fijians | ······· | 117 | 04· | 0··0 |
| Vedda | ······· | 113 | 001 | 1··1 |
| Walbiri | ··1·175 | ··· | 04· | 1811 |
| Western Apache | 6111173 | ··· | 081 | 181· |
| Wukchumni | ··11··· | ··· | 041 | ···0 |
| Yurok | ··11··· | 113 | 041 | 0410 |
| Zapotec | ····040 | ··· | 02· | 00·0 |

# REFERENCES

AVERILL, J. R.
  1968   Grief: its nature and significance. *Psychological Bulletin* 70:721--748.
BRANDT, V. S. R.
  1971   *A Korean village between farm and sea.* Cambridge: Harvard University Press.
CAMPBELL, D. T., D. W. FISKE
  1959   Convergent and discriminant validation by the multitrait-multimethod matrix. *Psychological Bulletin* 56:81–105.
CULSHAW, W. J.
  1949   *Tribal heritage, a study of the Santals.* London: Lutterworth.
DURHAM, M. E.
  1928   *Some tribal origins, laws and customs of the Balkans.* London: Allen and Unwin.
ESTES, W. K.
  1959   "The statistical approach to learning theory," in *Psychology: a study of a science,* volume two: *General systematic formulations, learning, and special processes.* Edited by S. Koch, 380–491. New York: McGraw-Hill.
FIRTH, R.
  1936   *We, the Tikopia.* London: Allen and Unwin.
HUNTINGFORD, G. W. B.
  1955   *The kingdoms of Kafa and Janjero.* London: International African Institute.
MEEK, C. K.
  1931   *Tribal studies in northern Nigeria.* London: K. Paul, Trench, Trubner and Company.
MURDOCK, G. P.
  1949   *Social structure.* New York: Macmillan.
  1968   World sampling provinces. *Ethnology* 7:305–326.
MURDOCK, G. P., D. R. WHITE
  1969   Standard cross-cultural sample. *Ethnology* 8:329–369.
NAROLL, R.
  1962   *Data quality control.* Glencoe, Ill.: Free Press.
OSGOOD, C.
  1951   *The Koreans and their culture.* New York: Ronald.
PARSONS, E. C.
  1936   *Mitla: town of the souls.* Chicago: University of Chicago Press.

# The Spirit "Rides" or the Spirit "Comes": Possession in a North Indian Village

SUSAN S. WADLEY

The relationships among men and supernaturals are a continuing theme in discussions of Hindu religious practice. The types of communication which are believed to exist between man and god are one aspect of man-god relationships. Here we deal with possession, one form of communication between men and spiritual beings which plays an important role in village religious practice throughout India. Possession as communication from god to man complements communication by priests and other specialists from man to god.

I will be particularly concerned with the interplay between the form of communication and the type of supernatural involved. My contention is that there are "rules" concerning the type of communication which men choose to use in communicating with particular spirits. Through a close examination of a snake possession rite which occurs in the villages of Mainpuri District, Uttar Pradesh, some of the rules underlying these choices can be formulated.

## HINDU PATTERNS OF POSSESSION

Initially I would like to distinguish two broad patterns of possession which are defined by the nature of the spiritual beings causing posses-

This paper is based on research conducted in Karimpur from December 1967 to March 1969. I am grateful to the National Science Foundation for sponsoring this research. To Charlotte Wiser, who provided me with a ready-made family in Karimpur and to the villagers themselves, I remain forever in debt. And I wish to thank Dr. David K. Jordan and Bruce W. Derr for their many useful suggestions on earlier versions of this paper.

sion, the type of specialist, if any, involved, and the institution through which contact is obtained.[1]

Possession rituals, like other Hindu rituals, often require the services of specialists. The role which these specialists play is crucial to understanding the relations between man and god which are being expressed in these rituals. Dumont and Pocock (1959) deal with one type of specialist concerned with possession — the oracle. They claim that throughout India, as we all know, there are priests, specialists who worship the gods, who know the sacred sayings and steps in the rituals which are necessary to keep the gods happy and not to anger them. But in anthropology and Indology, there has been an overriding emphasis on Brahmanic religion and thus on priests. Another specialist, whose role complements that of the priest, has been ignored. Dumont and Pocock's argument is that complementing the institutionalized function of the priesthood is that of the oracle:

Apart from the priest, there is another person who plays a fundamental role. At least, this is what we shall attempt to show from the literature. All over the country there are people who, in certain circumstances and especially in festivals, are believed to be possessed by one deity or by several deities or spirits in succession. The god speaks through man ... who incarnates him or upon whom he alights. This person is referred to in the literature under a great variety of names, such as "oracle," "shaman," "magician," and native terms (1959: 55–56).

Thus possession of the oracles[2] complements the function of the priesthood, the oracle being the mouthpiece of the deity, the priest making offerings to the deity.

There are, however, other specialists concerned with possession rituals, correlated to different types of possession. Dumont and Pocock say that there is a:

... distinction to be maintained between the institutional possession of the specialist and the occasional possession of persons by evil spirits or "demons" which are exorcized, most often by the "oracle" himself (1959: 56).

[1]  I believe that both types of possession occur throughout India. Also Berreman's statement (1964: 56) that Pahari shamans are unlike plains shamans but like South Indian ones (Harper: 1957) is incorrect, perhaps because of an inconsistency of terminology. What Opler (1958) calls shaman is really an exorcist (as exists among the Paharis) and on the plains the oracle (shaman to Berreman) also exists.
[2]  Using the terminology of Eliade and Dumont, I will differentiate shaman from oracle. Eliade defines shamans as those individuals who travel to another world while in a state of ecstasy. An oracle exists when the spiritual being inhabiting another world comes to the chosen individual and resides in him. Thus I will be speaking only of oracles, never of shamans. There is some justification aside from Eliade's definition for not using shaman: shaman has been used in the literature

Contrary to Dumont and Pocock, I believe that the occasional possession of persons by evil spirits is as much an "institution" as possession by the specialist or oracle and that we must include in the category
"possession," possessions both of the specialist and of the "victim."
Furthermore, there is a ritual specialist concerned with the occasional
possession of victims — the exorcist.

Here it is necessary to differentiate oracle from exorcist. This separation is somewhat complex because an exorcist may also be an oracle;
however, on functional grounds there is a difference and I hope that
the relevance of this difference will soon become clear. Basically, an
oracle is possessed by a spirit and speaks while possessed; the exorcist
causes a possessing spirit to leave his victim, often by using *mantras*,
"magic," and the power of other spirits. In most cases, the exorcist
himself is not possessed and therefore is not an oracle. In North India,
the native terms for oracle are *baki* (Berreman 1963) and *bhagat*. The
native terms for exorcist include *jharnewala* (Berreman 1963) *ojha*,
*mantravidh*, and *mativah* (Planalp 1956).

These two types of specialists are concerned with two different categories of spiritual beings. Recently Babb (1968) has analyzed popular
Hinduism partly in terms of two aspects of divinity. Divinity, *paramātma*,
becomes active in the affairs of men only when differentiated into concrete supernatural beings. There are two basic aspects or permutations
of divinity: benevolence or malevolence; or, as I will use the concept,
two broad categories of spiritual beings, benevolent and malevolent
ones — the good guys and the bad guys. There are various levels of
goodness and badness represented by Hindu supernaturals, but in terms
of possession these differences are not usually critical. Rather, primarily
good spirits possess oracles and primarily bad spirits possess victims.

There are, then, two basic categories of possession rituals. The first
category of possession includes possession of a victim by ghosts or
other malevolent spirits that cause illness or psychological disturbances
(Freed and Freed 1962; Opler 1958; Berreman 1963; Planalp 1956).
These spirits "ride" or "adhere" to their victims. In these possessions,
anyone may be possessed and a specialist, an exorcist, is called to
communicate with the spirit causing the illness and induce it to depart.

The second category of possession includes those by a harmless
deity who is attracted by drums and dances to his oracle (Berreman

---

on Indian religion to designate numerous individuals having a variety of functions
— so that shaman as used by one author indicates an exorcist, by another it indicates oracle. Seldom does it mean shaman in Eliade's sense of the word (see
Harper 1957; Opler 1958; Planalp 1956; Berreman 1963, 1964).

1963) or possesses a particular devotee (Freed and Freed 1962). Another type of possession by a harmless deity occurs when there is an oracle who can voluntarily induce a personal familiar spirit to possess him and to speak to clients through him (Berreman 1964; Harper 1957). These spirits "come to" their oracles. These spiritual beings are generally benevolent, though feared, and leave voluntarily. The possessed is usually a specialist or particular devotee of the spiritual beings causing possession.

The patterns relating to these two types of possession are shown in Table 1:

Table 1.   Patterns of possession

| Situation | | Specialist | |
| --- | --- | --- | --- |
| | Oracle | Exorcist | Victim |
| Good spirit | + | — | — |
| Bad spirit | — | + | + |
| Possessed | + | — | + |

In this table the nature of the spirit, good or bad, benevolent or malevolent, causing possession is correlated with the type of specialists involved, either oracles or exorcists, and the presence or absence of victims and thus the institution through which contact is attained. This difference is clearly seen in the terminology related to possession — the spirit "rides" or the spirit "comes." These two patterns of possession are relevant in comprehending what may be considered an anomalous rite of possession which occurs in parts of North India. This rite, which requires both an oracle and an exorcist is described below. By examining it in detail, it is possible to gain further insight into the nature of the Hindu peasant's communication with his supernaturals.

## *DANK:* SNAKE POSSESSION IN KARIMPUR

Being somewhat familiar with possession in India, I was rather startled (and pleased) after six months in Karimpur[3] to find an elaborate and ritualized possession occurring. I had known of people being possessed by ghosts and being cured. I had seen men try to cure snakebite victims by reciting *mantras* and playing a special kind of music.[4] Also I

[3]   For the sake of continuity I have retained the appellation "Karimpur" given this village by William and Charlotte Wiser (1971).
[4]   I also had in my possession a collection of folklore materials collected by the Wisers in the 1920's and provided to me by Norvin Hein. This collection contains

had seen goddess-possession at a yearly ritual when the village is rid of illness. All of these fit the facts that I had previously learned.

Sometime in July, knowing my interest in such things and liking my "radio" (the tape recorder), people started saying "Wait until Snake's Fifth (*nāg panchme* — Saven 2:5). Ragubar plays snake very well." So on the morning of Snake's Fifth, when I heard the music associated with snakebite, I went to find it, tape recorder on my shoulder. What I found astounded and perplexed me.

The ritual of possession that I saw on Snake's Fifth is *Dank*, a snake-bite curing rite also used to cure other illnesses and to cause possession of an "oracle" of the snake king. I am concerned here with the possession of the oracle, not snakebite.[5] On Snake's Fifth, *Dank* is played throughout the day, with the snake king's oracle repeatedly becoming possessed and answering questions from the villagers gathered around. *Dank* as translated by the villagers means "snake", though the word also refers to the whole rite. I will use the expression "playing *Dank*" as a direct translation of the village expression *Dank khelte hai*, or, if you wish, "snake playing".[6]

*Dank* is usually conducted during the monsoon season, when Snake's Fifth occurs and snakebite and boils are most common. It is a rite

---

ten *mantras* associated with curing snakebite. But as I discovered in Karimpur, these *mantras* [magical ritual sayings], are of varying sorts designating parts of the rite itself.

[5] When *Dank* is played for snakebite, the victim becomes actively possessed by the snake and his cure is named. If the victim does not become possessed, he was not actually bitten. Another common snake-caused ill is boils, which are thought to be the poison of a snakebite in a previous life erupting in this one. In this case, *Dank* is played as for actual snakebite to cure the boils. If none of this works, i.e. the victim is not possessed but the illness continues, the oracle is called. *Dank* will be played for him and he will become possessed and thus be able to answer questions concerning the cure. It should be noted here that in most of Uttar Pradesh snakebite really is the snake's psychic possession of the victim's body and therefore the snake must be exorcized to save the individual (Briggs 1920; Planalp 1956). Meanwhile, the snake cannot be killed because then the victim will surely die.

In one case in Karimpur in the summer of 1968, a farmer boy of about twelve years was working in the fields when a snake appeared and tried to bite him. The boy raised his stick and beat it, but shouted loudly that a snake had bitten him. Apparently at this point, he became unconscious as if actually bitten. In order to cure the boy whose mind was controlled by the beaten snake, the oracle was called. Eventually it was established that the boy should be taken to bathe in the Ganges (about forty miles away) on a certain Monday two weeks hence and then he would be all right.

[6] *Khelnā* literally "to play" is used to designate possession elsewhere in North India. It identifies an active and extreme possession which is manifested by the physical activity of the possessed; *khelnā* is also used to indicate goddess possession in Karimpur.

conducted by men alone, although it can be played for a woman if she is bitten by a snake. Women are allowed to be present at the far edges of the crowd or on nearby housetops, but no pregnant woman is allowed near the site of *Dank* as she might anger the snakes. Actual participation in the playing of *Dank* is limited to those who know the ritual songs, but the audience is composed of any interested man or boy who happens along.

### The Participants

*Dank* as played on Snake's Fifth requires a variety of participants. The two most important are the oracle himself, who is also considered a *bhagat,* and the leader or master, who is in actuality the exorcist.

The snake king's oracle is a young farmer, an extroverted, active man who is famous as well for his storytelling. According to village legend, this man was bitten by a snake three or four years before and recovered after being possessed by the snake king. They also say that when he was first bitten by the snake, he instantly leaped upward to a tree limb and nearly died.

Some time after his first possession, the snake king came to him in a dream and said that he should take food for two and put aside the first serving for the snake king. Then he could eat the second. Also, he must not eat from others' pots and must never sit in a chair. If he follows these rules, he will become rich. The village folk conclude this telling of his dream by saying that a similar incident happened in another village and the man there became rich.

I also heard several times that the oracle does not follow the rules laid down by the snake king and therefore his powers are decreasing due to his misbehavior. Nevertheless, there is always a snake over him (*us ke ūpar sānp hamesha hai*).[7] And in his words, he "plays snake very well."

The master is a shepherd of about thirty-five years. He became the master (*astīk*), for the Karimpur area at the death of his *gūrū,* a water-carrier from Karimpur, some years ago. He believes that he, too, will one day take on disciples and be a *gūrū,* but he is still too young for that position. His *gūrū* taught him the *mantras* for *Dank* and other curing rites. After learning them, he went to the Ganges where, putting

---

[7]   This expression indicates that a snake is always riding on him. The same phraseology is used in a common village expression, "worries are always over my head" (or *parīshānī mere sir ke ūpar hai* [riding on me]).

his head in the sacred waters, he said each of them, thus guaranteeing their power.

In addition to the master and oracle, a group of men called *baigī* are necessary to play the drums and sing the songs of *Dank* — songs which please the snake king and prompt him to possess his oracle. Untouchables are not allowed to be part of this group, but all other men are eligible once they have learned the songs.

The men of Karimpur also play *Dank* in nearby villages, usually for curing illness, not for snakebite. They play outside of Karimpur primarily because of the snake king's oracle, who is well known in the area. And men from other villages come to question this oracle on Snake's Fifth. The oracle can tell how to cure illness of humans or beasts, name thieves and provide other kinds of information.

## The Setting

*Dank* occurs outdoors and any large open area is suitable. On Snake's Fifth, it occurred in the open area in front of a potter's house. A large new clay pot like those for cooking milk is brought to the site. One side of it is rubbed with *ghii* after which ashes from a milk stove are sprinkled upon it and seven to nine snakes are drawn in the ashes. Twenty annas and some leaves from a betel nut tree are put inside of it "to make it work truly." The pot is then set upon a flour sieve and a brass tray is placed upside down on top of the pot.

During the rite itself, the tray is treated as a drum and sets up a fierce ringing din. The snakes are drawn so that the oracle will see them and feel pleased. Meanwhile, a small brass pot is filled with water and *nīm* leaves and a *ghii*-filled clay lamp is placed on its top. A folded blanket is placed on the ground with the clay pot-tray in front of it and the water pot to one side. Barley seeds are then sprinkled on the blanket.

As the men gather, they align themselves to the two sides and back of the pot-tray combination. No one is allowed to sit to the front of the pot-tray because the snake king enters from that direction. In addition, the opening to the front must always be toward the Ganges. And there is a constant battle to keep observers at the sides near the front so seated as not to block the passage. Those who know the songs of *Dank* sit along the sides of the blanket, the oracle between them, seated cross-legged on the blanket, the master to his right. One of the men has a drum and another a wooden stick with which to beat the pot-tray combination.

## The Rite

After much commotion, discussion and shoving around, the singers begin *kārikh*, songs to make the snake king happy, and come and possess the oracle. First the men to one side sing, then those on the opposite side repeat the line. Gradually the drum player begins and the man by the pot-tray begins to beat it on the top with one hand and on the side with the wooden stick, setting up a fierce ringing din rather like a collection of cymbals being beaten continuously.

The song continues until the oracle is possessed by the snake king or until the end of the song. If possession does not occur, the singers will rest briefly, then begin again. The oracle sits motionless staring straight ahead. When he does become possessed, he begins a circular movement with the upper half of his body, slowly at first with little forward movements, then faster and faster until his hair lock is standing straight out due to his speed and his head is almost touching the ground on each forward movement (one or two men sit behind him to catch him if he should topple over that way).

Suddenly, he collapses onto the ground, bent forward from his hips. The song stops and the master takes over, beginning with a prayer (*prāthnā*) at the same time dipping a piece of barley in the *ghii* of the lamp and throwing it at the possessed oracle. From now until the end of the rite, the oracle is addressed as *Maharaj* [Great King].

The master then recites a series of *bācā*, ritual sayings which praise the gods. Next he recites a series of ritual questions (*pūchonī*) which establish the real identity of the spiritual being possessing the oracle. The possessed oracle is required to answer these questions. After the identity of the possessing deity is established, questions are asked by the men gathered around and the oracle answers them.

The men asking the questions give one or two rupees to the oracle after their answer is given (the oracle is told the amount and if it is not enough he will demand more). One or more questions are asked during each possession, with the master periodically asking the oracle if he is tired and wishes to stop.

The oracle's answers are discussed by the audience and further verification is often required. When the questions are over, the master again dips a piece of barley in *ghii* and throws it at the possessed, at the same time reciting an *uThonī* or ritual saying to bring the oracle out of possession.

The oracle at this time has two possible actions. He may sit up and stare about in a dazed manner. Or he may go into a kind of spasm, leaping (with a very rapid movement) to his feet to be caught by five or six men standing ready behind him (the oracle may warn them before the *uThonī* that he will require this service and in any case they are prepared).

Covering his mouth, ears, and nose with a cloth and holding his feet down and his body securely, they shout *khūn*, sayings to make the snake king return home.[8] The people of Karimpur say that at this moment the possessed oracle may die; that his spirit is with the gods and if they do not hold him securely, his body will fly heavenward. At this point, the oracle has a completely rigid arched body and in his spasmodic movements is capable of moving the group of men holding him two or three feet in any direction.

One or more *khūn* may be necessary before the snake king leaves and the unpossessed oracle relaxes and drops into a sitting position on the ground. The *khūn* are of different types, some being more powerful than others and I have seen it take ten minutes of *khūn* before the spasm ceases.

The whole cycle takes from fifteen to forty-five minutes, depending upon the number of songs necessary to induce possession, the number of questions asked, and the number of *khūn* required to force the snake king to leave. On Snake's Fifth, the whole cycle is repeated again and again until all the questions are asked or everyone is exhausted.

## THE ORAL COMPONENTS OF *DANK*

*Dank* is composed of the following named oral components which structure the events of the ritual: *kārikh* [songs to make the snake king happy and come and possess his oracle], a *prāthnā* [prayer], *bācā* [ritual sayings invoking various gods], *pūchonī* [ritual questions], *uThonī* [sayings to cause the possessed oracle to rise], and *khūn* [sayings to make the snake king leave]. Of these, the first and last are known and recited or sung by a group of men, usually of middle-ranked castes. The other four are known by the master and can only be used by him. The functioning of these components is intricately tied to relationships between the various supernatural beings involved and the purpose and

---

[8] There are two explanations as to why these body openings are covered. One is that the snake king is forced to leave through the openings of the snakebite. The other is that then no oxygen can get in his blood to combine with the poison of the snake king — the combination of the poison and the oxygen creating a gas which causes unconsciousness. This latter explanation comes from several high school boys and may be the more "modern" explanation.

structure of the rite as a whole. To comprehend *Dank* fully it is necessary to examine closely the texts of the various named oral components.


## *The* Kārikh

The *kārikh* are the songs to make the snake king happy; *kārikh* is probably derived either from the word *karish* [to draw or pull] or from *karita* [to cause to occur]. There are many songs called *kārikh*: these songs deal with two topics — songs specifically about Raja Basuk, the snake king, or songs about Zahir Pir, a regional god who controls snakes.

Basuk is a derivation of the name Vasuki, King of the Snakes, or Nāgas, Lord of the Nether World, in the Sanskritic literature. In the *Mahabharata* and *Puranas*, Vasuki is listed second, after Sesha Naga, in the catalogue of snakes:

But as Sesha, the first-born among the snakes is absorbed by his ponderous duty of carrying either the earth or the supreme deity, it is Vasuki who acts as the sovereign ruler of the serpent tribe whenever an active leadership is required (Vogel 1926: 199).

So it is Vasuki (Basuk), the great king, who is appealed to for possession and who does possess — rather than Sesha Naga, who does not actively participate in mundane affairs.

Zahir Pir is also known as Gugga. He is known and worshiped in Punjab and western Uttar Pradesh. He is an intermediary god, one who mediates between the high gods and the world of men; by analyzing his various legends, we see that his powers are derived from Shiva, via his *gūrū* Gorakhnath. He is known for being a warrior and a loving husband, but most important is his power over snakes — because he gained control over them they now serve him as they serve in Sanskritic works the great god Shiva (Wadley 1967).

Neither the songs about Raja Basuk nor about Zahir Pir are fully comprehensible to the outsider until the local stories about these two figures are known. In a rather cryptic fashion, the songs relate to, or refer to, incidents in the legends of these two supernaturals. Although not specifically songs of praise, they are about Basuk and Zahir Pir. And certainly the change in meaning from *jas*, songs sung to the same melody and for the same purpose for Devi (the Goddess) to *kārikh* is relevant. By *jas* is meant "fame" or "praise"; *kārikh* means "to pull" or "to cause to occur" — Devi is made happy by the singing of *jas* and thus possesses her oracle; Raja Basuk is made happy and is also induced to possess his oracle. The songs about Zahir Pir can be understood in light of his controlling the snake king; if he is pleased by *kārikh*, he can make Raja Basuk possess the oracle.

## *The* Prāthnā

The prayer, or *prāthnā*, which follows the possession of the oracle is often omitted in the cycle of *Dank* and is not particularly important or enlightening. Essentially it is a reminder to the higher, more powerful gods of their presence at *Dank*. Much of the message of the prayer is repeated in the *bācā* which follow.

## *The* Bācā

The *bācā*, literally "saying", is the first step in gaining control of the possessing deity once he is "riding" on his oracle. The *bācā* begin with the master saying:

Master:  Oh God, as Bavan you deceived Bali
　　　　 Becoming Krishna [you] destroyed Kans
　　　　 Har Nar Khush was killed.[9]
　　　　 Being Ram, Ravan was ridden.
　　　　 The black (snake) was subjugated.
　　　　 Mathura was full of light.

The *bācā* then make reference to god (*gusain*), in this case specifically Vishnu, whose exploits in various *avatars* are mentioned, concluding with Krishna's subjugation of the black snake and Mathura's deliverance. The master, having praised the god by listing his various conquests of evil beings, goes on to deal with the snake king.

Master:  Do you hear the words of the master?
　　　　 Oh Basudev, say yes.[10]
Oracle:  Yes.

Note that the master asks the snake king if he has heard this recitation of the dominance of Vishnu. The master continues:

Master:  Yes the snake comprehends.
　　　　 The companions met and sang *mangal*.[11]
　　　　 Ganga, Gauri, Gayatri, the three gave blessings.[12]

[9]  In the Wiser's version (n.d.) of *bācā*, this line translates: "Taking the form of Narsigh, [you] killed Harina Kush."
[10]  There is one variant of this line used sometimes: rather than Basudev, god Basu, the snake king is referred to as *bishdev*, or "poison god".
[11]  In this line, the "companions" are female. The *mangal* are one kind of song in praise of god.
[12]  Gauri refers to Parvati; Gayatri is Saraswati.

> The snake is safe.
> Very happy is the snake.

As the master continues to gain control of the snake, he clarifies the snake's understanding of the situation and then notes the blessings of the goddesses — blessings which, it seems, aid in making the snake safe.

The master then goes on to verify his assumption:

Master:   King Basuk who is here, the king is happy?
Oracle:   Yes.
Master:   His horse is happy?
Oracle:   Yes.

Now the master knows that the possessing deity is well and that the oracle, or body, is also fit. Note that the image is that of riding, as seen in the use of horse for the oracle himself. This series concludes the *bācā*.


## *The* Pūchonī

At this point, the master moves immediately into the *pūchonī*, literally "questioning." These, again, are memorized, required *mantras* and the questioning gives the master further control of the snake king. He says:

Master:   You are fine, I am fine, the horse is fine.
            These things are true things.
            Why is there such laziness in your head that you bite this man?
            I am asking you why.
            Why do you not put out your hand?
Oracle:   Am putting out hand.
Master:   The king is giving his hand for one
            second or for all life?
Oracle:   For life.
Master:   Extending my hand, catching your arm,
            I'll repeat to you the words of the *gūrū*.
            To you the *gūrū*'s words, the warrior's word, the strong words.
            If you hide your *jat* [caste], you will become a leper.
            King, who are you?
Oracle:   Black.

In this series of exchanges, the master forces the snake king to show cooperation by stretching out his hand so that the master may hold it while repeating the *gūrū*'s words. The *gūrū* refers to Gorakhnath or some other *gūrū* associated with Zahir Pir and the warrior is Zahir Pir himself. Again, the use of more powerful supernaturals allows the master control of his possessing spirit. And it must be remembered that these *mantras* are believed to be powerful in themselves, as sanctified by the waters of the Ganges.

After the *pūchonī*, the real business can commence — the questions for the snake king. Questions from the men in the audience are related to the snake king via the master who repeats the snake king's answer. However, during this questioning period, the master not only asks the snake king for advice, but also about his behavior during possession of the oracle and his desires. Although not using *mantras* during this section of the rite, the master attempts to maintain his control. At times he even scolds the snake king. For example:

Master:   Great King, today you have given much trouble.
          You took much *khūn* today.
          What is wrong?
Oracle:   Nothing.
Master:   There is something. You are angry with me.
Oracle:   Yes.
Master:   Speak the truth.
Oracle:   You did not give thirteen *khūn*. [Thirteen is the most powerful *khūn*.]
Master:   If thirteen *khūn* you would be oversatisfied. So many words all together at one time will burst out. So why are you again and again giving trouble? Thirteen is nothing.
          Great King, you are not angry?
          How many times will you play?
Oracle:   Many.
Master:   So we should bring milk, Great King?
          Will you drink milk?
Oracle:   Yes, will drink.
Master:   Will drink?
Oracle:   Yes, will drink.

[The oracle is questioned further to discover whether he will drink during play or during the questions or after the whole cycle is over. He chooses to drink during "play."]

Master:   OK. I am giving *uThonī*. Don't do *khūn*. Don't cheat. Take my words. When I say them, then. You deceive me, then I will become angry.

Thus we see that during the more informal (not bound by ritual sayings) portion of the ritual, the master coerces and controls the snake, now Maharaj, the Great King. However, there is some feedback from the oracle — his words are believed and he is pacified with milk, which is given him during "play" as he had requested. After the question period is completed, the master returns to the use of his magical formulas.

## *The uThonī*

The *uThonī*, literally "lifting," is used to make the oracle rise. There is only one and it goes like this:

A bangle of conch shells
A garland of pearls.
Feel like a lotus,
Lanka was destroyed.
The ditch of Lanka was as wide as the sea.
Get up, snake,
Hanuman the Great's decree.

Here again, the master uses the power of another supernatural to control the snake king.

## *The* Khūn

As noted previously, the cycle may end with the *uThonī*. However, the oracle may require *khūn*. This *khūn* can mean "blood," but more likely means "murder," that is, the removal ("murder") of the snake king from the oracle's body. With the master leading, the men shout the *khūn*, repeating each line twice.

It is necessary to shout the *khūn* until the oracle comes out of his spasm. There are a variety of *khūn*, their efficacy being dependent in part on the supernaturals referred to in them. It is best not to use a powerful *khūn* unless it is absolutely necessary to remove the snake king and return the oracle to life. All of the *khūn* end with the same two lines:

If life is in the edge of nails or cells of hair,
Arise, awake, be conscious.

And in about half the occurrences of *khūn*, these two lines are followed by a third:

Shri Guru Param Hans. Ram says.

The rest of each *khūn* is concerned with episodes from the mythological repertoire of the North Indian villager and with references to various supernaturals. In the following frequently used *khūn*, the episode is a favorite for the Karimpur storytellers and the god is, though Muslim, still powerful:

Earthen pot, clear water, golden spout.
So Raja Basuk's daughter filled.
Taking the pot in the hand, all poison was removed.
That poison Mahmada cleansed.
Make without poison, Khuday.
If there is life in the edge of nails or cells of hair,
Arise, awake, be conscious.

*Dank* functions, then, because of the powers of particular spiritual beings that are brought to bear on the snake king. With the help of these powers, men are able to control the snake king when they call him to earth to possess his horse. The snake king remains dangerous, he does ride his victims and his oracle, and he does not "come" to them as do benevolent supernaturals. But through the recitation of the various ritual sayings (the *mantras*) by the master this dangerous aspect of the snake king's possession can be controlled. Control is necessary at all times, however, as seen in the above descriptions of the components of *Dank* — there is control for causing possession, cessation of possession, and control during the rite itself. At no point is there lack of control, through the mediation of the master, by some other more powerful and more benevolent spiritual being.

## DISCUSSION

The rite which I have described is contrary to the normal possession patterns. The first anomaly is the presence of both an oracle and an exorcist. Secondly, the nature of the possessing spirit is itself unclear. It is almost as if the snake king is a good guy, but yet is not. And in fact, this is the case.

Possession of an oracle is normally by a benevolent or harmless deity who can be and is often worshiped regularly by the oracle. The deity comes at the oracle's call and goes willingly — it is not necessary to force it to leave. In Karimpur this pattern of possession is found in goddess possession. The goddess is first worshiped, often with the aid of a Brahman priest. A few men sing *jas*, songs in praise of the goddess, songs which should please her and make her want to dance in her oracle.

But there are many differences between goddess possession and *Dank*: the songs do not stop with the oracle's possession; little structure of events is evident; the goddess' identity is not checked, nor is she forced to leave. No *mantras* are recited at the possessed at any time.

The men singing *jas* are not near the oracle and pay little attention to him — they just keep on randomly singing.

Possession by a malevolent spirit, on the other hand, is normally of a victim who becomes ill. In Karimpur, snakes are treated in many respects as ghosts and other malevolent spirits who possess victims. In fact, snakes are believed to possess their victims, and cure of snakebite requires that the snake be forced to leave his victim. *Dank* is played to make the snake actively possess his victim (and admit his possession) so that the master can compel it to depart in the same manner that he compels the snake king to leave his oracle.

However, there are some essential differences in nature which separate snakes from ghosts. Snakes are worshiped on a fixed day in the annual calendar; ghosts are rarely worshiped and even more rarely in a fixed rite. Furthermore, snakes are considered to be a kind of "god" as the term Basudev illustrates: Basu refers to Basuk and *dev* is a term for supernaturals who are at least somewhat better than the totally malevolent ghosts. But like other malevolent spirits, snakes are not worshiped for gain, but for appeasement.

In Karimpur they are not worshiped for rain, sons, litigation, etc.; rather one begs them to be satisfied with the offerings and to stay out of one's home and away from one's children. In contrast, benevolent spirits are supplicated: they are worshiped for gain (material and spiritual) as well as propitiated. Priests, in their role as priests, do not worship snakes in Karimpur, or, as one informant put it, "snakes are like gods, but we would never cry out to them on our deathbed. We have no love for them."

These characteristics of snakes indicate that they are indeed malevolent spirits, although not as malevolent as some other spirits. It is this element of malevolency which necessitates an alteration in the usual pattern of oracle possession. Because the snake king is a malevolent spirit, his possession of the oracle must be carefully controlled.

Therefore, although singing and drumming are not unusual in causing possession, what follows is. Because the spirit is potentially bad, an exorcist is required to control him. The master functions as this controlling agent and as an exorcist. The *uThonī* and *khūn* are the tools that the exorcist uses to force the spirit to leave his victim. The *bācā* and *pūchonī* enable the exorcist to have control of the possessing spirit at all times.

All possessing spirits, good or bad, are dangerous — the extreme danger possible with the snake king is reflected in the attempt to control him while he possesses the oracle. The variation on the normal possession patterns noted earlier is that *Dank* is an induced possession of an oracle by a bad spirit, thus an exorcist is required to control the spirit and eventually to compel it to leave. This variation is diagramed in Table 2.

Table 2.   Patterns of possession (with addition)

| Situation | Specialist | | |
|---|---|---|---|
| | Oracle | Exorcist | Victim |
| Good spirit | + | — | — |
| Bad spirit | — | + | + |
| Possessed | + | — | + |
| *Dank* | + | + | — |

The character of the supernatural who possesses his oracle or victim is a crucial factor in the choice of specialists for the rite itself. Once a given supernatural's position in the power structure of the pantheon for a given area is understood, the factors underlying the organization of possession rites become clear.

There are "rules" governing man's communication with his supernaturals and one of the primary factors in these rules is the nature of the possessing supernatural. *Dank* is an anomaly which can be understood only if the nature of snakes in Karimpur is understood. Yet although *Dank* represents a peculiar pattern of possession, the attributes of snakes in Karimpur make this peculiarity sensible.


CONCLUSION

The above discussion of *Dank* also provides an insight into the basic paradigm of Hindu communication with supernaturals. Possession is one form of communication between man and spiritual beings — and in the case of possession by malevolent spirits, communication is with malevolent spirits. In discussing man's relationships with spiritual beings, we cannot eliminate those with ghosts and other malevolent spirits, nor can we treat them separately. Communication between man and good spirits cannot be understood apart from that between man and bad spirits.

Ignoring for a moment the special case of *Dank*, possession of the oracle complements that of the victim: if a good spirit, it's an oracle; if a bad spirit, a victim. This complementation recalls Dumont and

Pocock's argument — the function of the priest complements that of the oracle. They state that the priest mediates from man to the deity; the oracle from the deity to man. But although Dumont and Pocock recognize the possession of victims by "evil spirits or 'demons'," they do not regard demon possession as an "institution." Likewise, they ignore another specialist whose function also complements that of the priest. In fact they are guilty of the charge that they have brought against others — that of too much emphasis on Brahmanic religion and on priests.

If the priest mediates from man to the deity and the oracle from the deity to man, surely the exorcist also mediates from man to the deity and the victim from the deity to man. Priests are specialists who worship gods, who know the sacred sayings and steps in the ritual necessary to keep the gods happy and not to anger them. Exorcists are specialists who expel spirits, who know the sacred sayings and steps in the ritual necessary to keep the spirits under control and to force them to leave.

Both the words of the priest and those of the exorcist are called *mantra* by the natives. And the priest is trained for his role by another priest; the exorcist is also trained for his role by another exorcist.

Man can speak to the spirits two ways — through two specialists, the priest and the exorcist. And the spirits can speak to man in two ways — via the oracle or the victim. Or to put the argument in another form, given a good spirit, the function of the priest complements that of the oracle; given a bad spirit, the function of the exorcist complements that of the victim. Likewise, given communication from man to spiritual beings, the function of the priest complements that of the exorcist; given communication from spiritual beings to man, the function of the oracle complements that of the victim (see Table 3).

Table 3. Function of specialists in communication between man and spiritual beings

|  | To | From |
| --- | --- | --- |
| Good spirit |  |  |
|  | priest | oracle |
| Bad spirit |  |  |
|  | exorcist | victim |

I have offered two general patterns for comprehending not only possession, but communication between man and spiritual beings in North India. However, *Dank* was an aberrant pattern. The patterns offered are dependent upon the opposing categories "good" and "bad." However, "good" and "bad" are ideal types and the characters of

Hindu supernaturals are variable — some being less good than others, some being less bad than others. Only by comprehending the nature of the spiritual being involved do the moods and motivations underlying a specific ritual appear not only realistic, but logical and correct.

## REFERENCES

BABB, LAWRENCE A.
  1968 "Systemic aspects of Chhattisgarhi religion: an analysis of a popular variant of Hinduism." Unpublished doctoral dissertation, University of Rochester.
BERREMAN, GERALD D.
  1963 *Hindus of the Himalayas.* Berkeley: University of California Press.
  1964 "Brahmins and shamans in Pahari religion," in *Religion in South Asia.* Edited by Edward B. Harper. Seattle: University of Washington Press.
BRIGGS, GEORGE W.
  1920 *The Chamars.* London: Oxford University Press.
DUMONT, LOUIS, D. POCOCK, *editors*
  1959 *Possession and priesthood.* Contributions to Indian Sociology 3:55–75.
FREED, RUTH S., STANLEY A. FREED
  1962 Two mother goddess ceremonies of Delhi State in the great and little traditions. *Southwestern Journal of Anthropology* 18:246–277.
HARPER, EDWARD B.
  1957 Shamanism in South India. *Southwestern Journal of Anthropology* 13:267–287.
OPLER, MORRIS E.
  1958 "Spiritual possession in a rural area of northern India," in *Reader in comparative religion.* Edited by William A. Lessa and Evon Z. Vogt. Evanston, Illinois: Row, Peterson.
PLANALP, JACK M.
  1956 "Religious life and values in a North Indian village." Unpublished doctoral dissertation, Cornell University.
VOGEL, J. PH.
  1926 *Indian serpent lore.* London: Arthur Probsthain.
WADLEY, SUSAN SNOW
  1967 " 'Fate' and the gods in the Punjabi cult of Gugga: a structural semantic analysis." Unpublished master's thesis, University of Chicago.
WISER, WILLIAM H., CHARLOTTE V. WISER
  1971 *Behind mud walls, 1930–1960,* with a sequel: *The village in 1970.* Berkeley: University of California Press.

# The Shamanistic Element in Taiwanese Folk Religion

MITSUO SUZUKI

By shamanism I mean a kind of magico-religious practice, whose adherents, in the area under the influence of Chinese civilization, are generally denoted by the word *wu* ( 巫 ). The distinguishing features of *wu* [a shaman of East Asiatic type] are:

1. He becomes possessed voluntarily by various spirits — those of deities, of the dead, etc.
2. He indicates with his own actions and speech the will, judgement, and emotions of those spirits.
3. He discloses, through the help of the spirits possessing him, the hidden causes of diseases and other misfortunes, and thus gives advice to clients.
4. He makes his living by answering the questions, as mentioned above, of his clients.

If we used such a definition of shamanism, fruitless — at least in East Asia — discussion concerning the distinction between genuine shamans and false ones could be evaded. It would suffice if people believed, or acted as if they believed, in the efficacy of a shaman's séance and let him carry out a certain magico-religious function defined traditionally in their society.

We find such shamans in all three East Asian countries: Japan, Korea, and Taiwan. However, *dangki* (童乩) [Taiwanese male shamans], with whom I am chiefly concerned here, have a distinctive inclination toward exaggerated frenzy and sometimes bloodshed. This element is not conspicuous in Japanese or in Korean shamanism; therefore it deserves some detailed description. A kind of "division of labor," which is recognizable between shamans and Taoist priests on the occasion of temple festivals, is another point of interest. We notice similar structural peculiarities in the total framework of folk religion in Japan and Korea as well, but in somewhat different directions. The problem must be rooted in the characteristics of religio-historical development in each country, especially in the relationship of shamanism or other archaic beliefs with higher religions imported later from outside.

During my stay in Taiwan from 1969 to 1970 I had opportunities to observe various festivals. Some of them featured the participation of male shamans. I have selected three cases and shall analyze them to find out the basic roles played by the shamans in those ceremonies.

*Case A: Festival of Mazu Temple in Keelung Harbor*

This temple is situated on a small island in Keelung Harbor, the original inhabitants of which were supposed to be fishermen. Mazu ( 媽祖 ) [the female protective deity of navigators and fishers] was perhaps worshiped by the fishermen at first. As time passed, however, the island became closely connected with Keelung City, and fishermen now constitute only a small part of the island's inhabitants; accordingly, various deity images — almost ten including that of Mazu herself — are now honored in the temple without any meaningful (hierarchic and so forth) relationship traceable between them as is generally the case in Taiwanese temples.

The festival of the temple was held on the fifteenth of June in the lunar calendar. Its main event was an inspection by Mazu around the district. The area included sea (part of Keelung Harbor) as well as land. First the deity images were transported by ship, and later by portable shrines.

Before the inspection by land started, a male shaman appeared in the vicinity of the temple; he was suddenly possessed, took off his shirt, shouted loudly, and knocked strongly at a desk in front of the altar. He then ran toward a corner and hit his own shoulder with a sword, causing some bloodshed. In the same frantic manner he wrote many magical letters on papers.

Meanwhile people were tightly binding the deity images with red cloth to the shrines, thus making preparations for the procession. But before the procession began the carriers suddenly started to run around with the shrine as if possessed by a furious spirit.

During the procession the shaman rode on a shrine with a black flag in one hand and a sword in the other. People of the district, old and young, waited for the procession before their houses, made obeisance to it as the shrines passed before them, and received kindled incense sticks and sheets of paper charms. The procession entered almost every side street; therefore the supernatural inspection around the district seemed perfect.

As his frenzy was probably meant to indicate, the shaman was possessed by Mazu, and, as an embodiment of the deity, he made an inspection tour of the district under her protection.

When the procession returned to the temple, the shaman got off his shrine and stealthily disappeared without receiving a greeting or a word of comfort from the people. The sharp contrast between the importance — logically at least — of his presence as an incarnated deity in the procession and such careless treatment of him personally is surprising and worthy of notice. It seems that the shaman was employed on the occasion only for his technique of being possessed. Complete disregard for his religious personality exists hand in hand with probable disdain for his social status, which belongs to "nine lower classes" (下九流), according to traditional Taiwanese standards.

## Case B: Festival of Ongya Temple in Tainan

The temple is situated in Xigang (西港), an old port town near Tainan City. The town seems to be a kind of religious center of the area; this is inferred from the fact that on its triennial festival, deities representing more than seventy surrounding villages visit the town to pay homage.

The historical growth of the temple seems very complicated; the composition of the festival shows, on analysis, many different elements. The primordial core which led to the construction of the present temple is, however, supposed to be the belief in Ongya (王爺) [epidemic deity].

Before modern preventive medicine was introduced by the Japanese colonial government, the Taiwanese people often suffered from rampant epidemic diseases of a tropical as well as subtropical nature. At that time they had no other means of saving themselves except by placating Ongya, who is the king of various epidemic spirits and therefore can protect human beings from those diseases. It is because of this that temples dedicated to Ongya are very numerous, especially in the southern part of the island where only the land deity has more temples.

The diffusion of the Ongya belief was accomplished through the custom of building and sending Ongya ships. On the festival of Ongya people make a beautifully decorated ship for Ongya, and, after satisfying the deity with good food and drinks, send him out to sea never to return. However, the whim of the currents and winds sends the Ongya ships back to land from time to time; then the unexpected as well as unwelcome visit of the deity must be received with the utmost care and courtesy. A small shrine is usually built for the Ongya newcomer, thus gradually, under favorable conditions, a new center for the worship of the epidemic deity develops.

It is generally said that *dangki* [the Taiwanese male shamans] have a special connection with Ongya. Some people even stress that Ongya is their patron deity. Such a belief probably arose in olden days out of the helpless situation of the people who had only shamans to rely on to save them from the incessant danger of epidemics, which is the very essence of the awe-inspiring personality of Ongya.

During the festival, which lasted three days, Taoist priests observed secret ceremonies in the inner corner of the temple. The general public was not allowed to approach that corner; the public, however, showed no interest in the elaborate Taoist practices, and the attractive power of the festival for them was centered in the procession of village deities visiting the temple, which featured the shamans' frenzy and bloodshed.

It is not so clear why the village deities of the surrounding district visited the temple on this occasion. But various sources seem to suggest that through direct contact with the spirit of Ongya, which is especially powerful during the festival, it was hoped that the "spiritual energy" of village deities would be strengthened. Generally a portable shrine, but sometimes a horse without a rider, constituted the core of the procession of each participant village. Besides invisible deities supposed to be in the shrines or on horse back, one or two male shamans accompanied each shrine or horse and were evidently playing the role of visible representatives of village deities.

Except for red cloth bands on their heads and sometimes also around their waists, shamans wore only short pants. They were noteworthy also for the blood which was on their foreheads, shoulders, and backs. To extract the blood various tools are employed, such as a wooden rod implanted with long nails. I also observed a shaman showing a long needle pierced through his mouth from right to left. They say that thanks to the divine power possessing shamans, bloodshed causes them no pain.

The people were excited and cheered at the sight, making the blood-stained shamans the heroes of the festival.

*Case C: Celebration of the Completion of a New Temple Building for the Land Deity in Shinzhu*

In Mayuan ( 麻 園 ) village near Shinzhu ( 新 竹 ) a new temple building for the land deity ( 土 地 公 ) was completed and a special festival celebrating the occasion was performed; "passing over fire" ( 過 火 ) by male shamans was its main event.

The newly built building was magically decorated by Taoist priests; they put up magical letters and symbols drawn on paper in the four inner corners of the building. Especially important for the occasion was a heap of rice which symbolized a "dragon" ( 龍 ), a mythical water animal resembling a huge serpent. The claws of the dragon were depicted on several eggs and his scales were suggested by coins which were neatly set on the rice heap.

A dragon was a representative of good power; he occupied the holy inner space of the temple during the festival, while a "tiger," symbolizing the wicked power of the world, had been expelled the night before by the magical practices of Taoist priests.

"Passing over fire" is an extremely fascinating spectacle for the general public, and it is often performed by male shamans on festive occasions. In the ceremony, a great quantity of charcoal is kindled and spread on a dry rice field beside the temple.

While a Taoist priest of low status ( 法 官 ) continued a long series of chanting and magical gestures, asking the deity to descend, two male shamans, brothers, gradually became more and more pale and began to vomit frequently, a symptom of a true trance. Then the shamans suddenly took off their shirts, and, aided by the people, put on heavily decorated ritual garments. They also bound red cloths around their heads. After madly brandishing swords and demonstrating that they were fully possessed, they began to walk on burning charcoals, which had been spread like a road about fifty meters long. Following them, a group of enthusiastic devotees, led by a few carrying deity images in their hands, dared to walk into the charcoal fire too.

Thus purified by fire, the deity images were then deposited on the altar inside the temple.

In this case, two kinds of Taoist priests participated in the ceremony: (a) a higher Taoist priest, who prepared the temple for the festival and performed routine chanting of Taoist sutras, etc. and (b) a lower priest, who assisted shamans who were possessed by the deity. According to some sources it is not rare that one and the same Taoist priest performs all these functions. Whether a lower priest participates or not, we can clearly distinguish two different parts in the organization of the ceremony: a part played by Taoist priests and a part played by male shamans. The former draws heavily on Taoist written documents, sutras, cosmological dogmas, etc., all of which are the mixed products of the higher religions of Chinese civilization. On the other hand, the latter does not rely on any such literary tradition; male shamans are just possessed, become frantic, brandish swords, and sometimes cause bloodshed.

If we examine all three cases, we perceive a common structural contrast in the process or organization of the ceremonies concerned: Taoist priests with their sophisticated, civilized tradition differ drastically from shamans with nothing but their simple archaic technique of being possessed.

It is of profound interest that the people show little interest in the former but are easily enchanted by the latter. For them the essence of a festival is not so much the elaborate ceremony performed by Taoist priests as the direct fusion of a human being with things divine; this fusion is enacted by the person of the male shaman. It is for this reason that one aspiring to be a male shaman usually makes his debut on the occasion of a temple festival. He suddenly jumps out in delirious manner before the crowd and shows himself as possessed by the deity of the temple, for whose birthday the festival ceremony is then being observed. The more frantic he becomes the better, because that is what testifies to the public that he is truly possessed by the deity. Once he has been widely accepted as a male shaman representing the deity, he can administer superhuman therapy for various diseases as well as bring in happiness and dispel misfortune. People of the district call upon him chiefly to get divine information regarding the cause of a difficult malady. On request he becomes possessed by his protector spirit (the deity of the temple) and gives the client an appropriate medical prescription.

When compared, shamanism in the three East Asiatic countries reveals interesting similarities and differences. The main social function of shamans is almost the same from country to country: to provide cures and remedies for diseases and other misfortunes with the help of spirits. They care for that section of each society which lies beyond the reach of modern medicine.

The strong inclination toward a bloody frenzy distinguishes the Taiwanese male shamans sharply from their counterparts in Japan and Korea. If I am justified in stressing that this inclination is characteristic of Taiwanese shamanism — therefore also of the shamanism of South China — it ought to be possible to trace some cultural linkage between them and certain archaic cultures of Vietnam and Thailand.

The tradition of *wu* ( 平 ) [shaman] in Chinese civilization seems to be traceable into its very ancient phase. As is well known, the full bloom of shamanism occurred in South China during the period of Warring States. We could mention, for example, that great classic of shamanistic literature *Chuci* ( 楚辞 ). Incidentally, the Chu Kingdom on the midstream of the Yangtze River was built by a people speaking a language which shows a marked resemblance to the Thai language.

On the other hand, the culture of North Chinese origin, which gradually penetrateding and culturally assimilated the southern areas, seems characterized by a nonshamanistic or even antishamanistic ideology. Confucius' famous words: "I decline to discuss such things as strange phenomena, ghosts, and deities" is a concise summary of the attitude typical of this culture. In a society dominated by Confucianism, the official doctrine of the series of succeeding Chinese empires, shamans could never be given any high or respectable status. But old written documents testify to the high prestige shamans enjoyed in ancient kingdoms. Their gradual degeneration through ages into a pariahlike status must have been precipitated not only by some inevitable historical tendency toward "rationalization" but probably also by the oppressive influence from the Confucian antishamanistic culture, which later became the mainstream of unified Chinese civilization.

It is generally agreed that South China, homeland of the Taiwanese people, was originally the habitat of various peoples related to present-day inhabitants of Vietnam and Thailand. It would be safe, therefore, to postulate that a highly shamanistic tradition existed there before the advent of northern culture, which probably inflicted continuous cultural damage on the former with the result that the shamanistic tradition could only survive among illiterate people at the bottom of the social scale. The role played by the Taiwanese shamans in temple festivals can best be explained as the ultimate product of such a historical development.

A sketchy comparative glance at the Japanese as well as the Korean situations is useful here. The antishamanistic influence of Confucianism is naturally discernible in Japan and Korea, because both countries received Confucianism as an official ideology at some period of their histories.

The native religious belief of ancient Koreans is supposed to be the shamanism of North Asiatic origin. In ancient times the status of shamans in Korean society must have been very high, so much so that in the beginning of the Silla Kingdom, the first unified kingdom of the peninsula, the names of kings can be deciphered as signifying "shaman." The tradition, however, was severely damaged first by Buddhism, the state religion of the Koryo Dynasty, and then fatally by Confucianism, the official ideology of the Yi Dynasty.

At present, Korean shamans are treated as a kind of pariah; the thought of marrying one of them would be abhorred by ordinary people. Notwithstanding, it is not unusual even in Seoul, the capital of Korea, and among intellectuals that a *mudang* (巫 堂) is called to officiate at a *kut* (굿), [séance] in cases of emergency like severe illness. It is with such admirable vitality that native belief has survived suppressive influences of higher, foreign religions.

In Japan, too, ancient records are full of the names of great (female) shamans, whose important political function readily reminds us of the first kings of ancient Silla, mentioned above. Then came the overwhelming influx of foreign religions which, however, had slightly different consequences from the Korean case. It might be on account of the geographical isolation of Japan from the Asian mainland that the archaic shamanistic beliefs evaded the direct intervention of higher religions; when the two came into contact, the result, unlike that in Korea where the confrontation was drastic and total, turned out to be gradual and mild. Both elements fused together; especially remarkable was the shamanization of foreign Buddhism as well as the influence of Buddhism on native shamanism. The influence of Confucianism on the Japanese people was never so great as in Korea during the Yi Dynasty. Its direct influence was limited to the *samurai* class; religious beliefs, particularly among peasants, received nothing but negligible influence from Confucianism.

A comparison of the structural peculiarities in the total religious framework of Japan, Korea, and Taiwan (South China) would be useful not only for the proper understanding of shamanistic elements in each country, but also for an analysis of some critical problems presently confronting each country, facets of which I hinted at in my essay: "The structure of folk society in Korea: a viewpoint of Japan-Korea comparison in modernization."

## REFERENCES

SUZUKI, MITSUO
    n.d.    "The structure of folk society in Korea: a viewpoint of Japan-Korea comparison in modernization," in *The characteristics of the modernizing process in Japan.* Edited by Kamishima Jiro. Tokyo: Azia-Keizai-Kenkyujo.

# The Study of Shamanism among the Peoples of Siberia and the North

I. S. VDOVIN

The shamanism of the peoples of Siberia and the North attracted the attention of scholars and travelers a long time ago. An extensive body of literature began to accumulate about shamanism starting with the eighteenth century. However, it was mostly confined to descriptions of the purely external aspects of shamanism as practiced by different peoples in Siberia and the North (Popov 1932).

The orderly scientific study of the field did not begin until the last quarter of the nineteenth century when the first programs for the collection of information about shamanism were published (Potanin 1880; Agapitov 1883). These programs were also mainly oriented toward study of the external forms in which shamanism manifested itself (descriptions of the shamans' performances, regalia, the ceremonies over which they regularly presided, and so forth). As a result, studies of the religious beliefs of the peoples of Siberia "which dealt with shamanism and the shamans, dwelt exclusively on externals and viewed the teachings of shamanism as a lot of crude and silly gibberish born of abysmal ignorance" (Mikhajlovskij 1892: 4).

In Soviet times, the shamans and their activities also excited the interest of investigators and the local population. This was primarily because the natives themselves, and particularly the youth, were coming out in opposition to the shamans and their activities. They did not want to abide by the conservative customs and the whole way of life the shamans were preaching and defending. The shamans were opposed to all the new things coming into their lives, the schools and medical centers being opened, the Soviet self-governing bodies and local courts, and so on. The shamans' attitudes brought down on their heads the sharp criticism of the younger people. They were correctly regarded as men who stood in the way of the social, cultural and political advancement of the local population as well as the latter's acceptance of the new Soviet forms of production, culture, and life in general. Protests were voiced in many articles and reports that appeared in various publications at the end of the 1920's and during the 1930's and 1940's. Those were the years of growing conflict between the bearers of the old traditions (expressed by the shamans) and those who were striving for enlightenment and the establishment of a modern base for their economic (collective farm), cultural, and political life.[1]

Meanwhile the search was going on for ways of ensuring a comprehensive scientific interpretation and study of shamanism as a form of the religious ideology of the peoples of Siberia — a study pursued from the positions of historical and dialectical materialism. That implied a complete investigation of shamanism and its place in the spiritual life of the masses and not merely descriptions of the shamans' performances (Kosakov 1930).

That shamanism should be studied as a religion was acknowledged and repeatedly stressed by Bogoraz-Tan, the distinguished student of the culture and life of the peoples of Siberia and the North. In 1932 he pointed out that antireligious work in the North was being directed against the shamans, whereas the struggle against religion as a world outlook had been relegated to the background (Bogoraz-Tan 1932: 144). He also bemoaned the fact that "our information about shamanism is still of a futile nature. It presents a disorderly array of material of varying authenticity."[2]

For a broad and comprehensive interpretation of shamanism as a definite religious ideology there had to be fresh material, exhaustive studies, and descriptions of its particular manifestations. More data had to be collected about the social role of shamanism in the life of the Siberian peoples, their system of religious ideas, the content of their cults, and so on. That work was begun and is still under way. Its results have been summed up in special papers (Suslov 1931; Zolotarev 1934) and numerous articles published in different journals, largely by the Institute of Ethnography of the USSR Academy of Sciences.[3]

---

[1]   A large number of such articles and materials was carried by the collections of Buryat studies, *Zhizn' Burjatii* [Life of Buryatia], by local papers, the issues of *Tajga i tundra* [Taiga and tundra] published by the Institute of the Peoples of the North, and so on.
[2]   Arkhiv AN SSSR [Archive of the Academy of Sciences of the USSR], f. 250, op. 1, d. 15, l. 1.
[3]   *Sborniki Muzeja Antropotogii i Etnografii (MAE)* [Collections of the Museum

Attempts were made as early as the 1930's to study shamanism as one form of religious ideology of preclass society. But the methods and approach adopted in studying the phenomenon were not always consistent, nor were they very effective (Zelenin 1935; Bogoraz-Tan 1932: 153–155).[4] The fact remains that many ethnographers, especially among the older generation, were just beginning to master materialist dialectics and the Marxist methodology of historical materialism. Consequently, the dependence of the shamans' functions on different stages in the social development of different peoples was hardly investigated. The shamans and their practices were often viewed in isolation rather than in relation to the social and economic conditions of the society that produced them and that they served. There were also objective obstacles to the study of the problem. No written histories of the peoples of Siberia and the North existed; their contemporary level of social development had hardly been examined at all.

Shamanism is a concrete historical phenomenon with features peculiar to a given people; these features depend not so much on historico-cultural factors as on the social and economic development and history of the given people.

In that respect the work of the well-known Soviet ethnographer and historian of religion, Anisimov, merits particular attention. Anisimov spent many years studying the history of Evenk clan society (Anisimov 1936) before undertaking the study of the history of the evolution of their religious ideas, cults, and shamanism in the light of the social development of Evenk society. In his investigations he consistently applied, broadly and deeply, the method of dialectical and historical materialism to problems of the history of the religion of a particular people (Anisimov 1958) and of the peoples of Siberia as a whole, the latter being a field to which he has contributed a broad historico-

---

of Anthropology and Ethnography] 1918, vyp. 1, t. 5; 1925, vyp. 2, t. 5; 1927, t. 6; 1929, t. 8; 1930, t. 9; 1949, t. 10; 1949, t. 11; 1949, t. 12; 1951, t. 13; 1953, t. 14; 1955, t. 16; 1958, t. 17; 1961, t. 20; 1971, t. 22; *Trudy Instituta etnografii* [Transactions of the Institute of Ethnography] 1936, vyp. 3, t. 14; *Trudy Instituta etnografii. Novaja serija* [Transactions of the Institute of Ethnography. New series] 1947, t. 1; 1947, t. 2; 1951, t. 14; 1952, t. 18; 1957, t. 25; 1959, t. 51; 1961, III, t. 64; 1961, t. 66; 1962, t. 75; 1962, IV, t. 78; 1963, V, t. 84; articles in the journal *Sovetskaja etnografija* [Soviet ethnography]; *Ezhegodnik Muzeja istorii religii i ateizma* [Yearbook of the Museum of the History of Religion and Atheism] 1957, vyp. 1; 1958, vyp. 2; 1959, vyp. 3; 1961, vyp. 5; 1962, vyp. 6; *Voprosy istorii religii i ateizma* [Question on the history of religion and atheism] 1950; 1958, vyp. 5; 1960, vyp. 8, and so on.

[4]  On these pages the author presents his theory of stages in the development of shamanism corresponding to certain stages in the development of primitive society.

genetic approach (Anisimov 1959, 1967, 1969).

The study of shamanism among the different peoples of Siberia and the North is now being pursued by scientific institutions. The important thing about this study today is that young scientists who themselves belong to the national groups studied have been drawn into the work. This is seen as a guarantee of great success in the study of shamanism among the peoples in question. The young scientists know the history, customs, and culture of their own people, and it is much easier for them to understand all the fine points and peculiarities of the cults of the groups of which they are members. Proof of their success abounds in the published studies (Mikhajlov 1962, 1965, 1968a, 1968b; Alekseev 1966, 1967, 1969; Taksami 1968, 1969, 1971; Patachkov 1968; Biche-ool 1968; Satlaev n.d.). Nevertheless, many problems remain and require further consideration and interpretation.

Proper criteria have still not been established for the definition of the concept of shamanism (its scope and content); neither have general views on the method of approach to this form of social consciousness been worked out. Different authors view shamanism from different angles. In spite of the relatively large amount of material published on the subject, special summarizing works on shamanism among the peoples of Siberia and the North have not appeared. In view of this it seems useful to define certain general approaches to the study of shamanism as a whole.

Every social phenomenon — its social nature, functions, and content — can be successfully analyzed with the help of the methodology of dialectical materialism and its corresponding techniques. Shamanism is a form of religious consciousness which was found everywhere in the past among the native inhabitants of Siberia and the North who stood at different stages of the dissolution of the primitive communal system and transition to class society. As to the forms and content of shamanism and its social functions among the different peoples, they showed substantial differences. Like all other forms of ideology, shamanism did not stand still; it was not an unchanging or fixed phenomenon but developed and altered together with the social, economic, and cultural development of the particular people. The whole system of religious ideas, beliefs, and cults of the peoples of Siberia and the North is usually viewed as a separate entity without regard to the social and economic development of the people or their history. The concrete historical study of shamanism as practiced by a particular people, its historical development and its connections with other social phenomena was not even attempted. The one exception was the work of

Anisimov. Attention was not directed to its ideological essence or its role in the life of the people at different stages of their history.

Besides the religious ideas they shared in common, essential differences existed from one people to another in Siberia and the North. The characteristic features of the shamanism of the peoples of Siberia and the North include: (1) animism, which is fundamental to their view of the world; (2) dualism, or the notion of the material and nonmaterial substance of man, of evil and good things or beings surrounding man, of the world as consisting of several spheres; (3) the existence of special practitioners of their cults, or shamans; and (4) certain other common traits.

At the same time, marked differences existed between the shamanism of different peoples. These were determined not so much by ethnocultural traits as by the level of socioeconomic and general cultural development attained by a given people. The shamanism of the Buryats is one thing, that of the Chukchis quite another. The religious system of the Buryats was characterized by a complex hierarchy of all kinds of gods whose numbers ran to many dozens. That system directly and indirectly reflected the level of social and economic relations the Buryats had attained in actuality. Other features of their religious practices were: (1) the belief in "white" and "black" shamanism; (2) the high professional level of the shamans; (3) the complicated initiation customs; (4) the broad sphere of their social functions; and (5) the existence of established prayers, chants, and so on.

Shamanism among the Chukchis was of a simpler sort. They did not have the same complex and numerous pantheon. Though they shared many of the same religious ideas, the observation of their rites and ceremonies took place within the confines of the patriarchal-family community and was administered by the head of the community. Their cults were focused on nature, ancestors and sacred places. To their shamans they assigned the function of medicine men, charmers of the weather and seers. Their shamans were not professionals like those of the Buryats. Every Chukchi family could have a drum, which was the special attribute of the shaman alone among the Buryats. Evidently, at different stages of the history of preclass society, religion combined with its foundation — the socioeconomic system — in different ways. Hence the need for a concrete historical approach to the study of shamanism in all its manifestations as one of the aspects of the history of a particular people. Knowledge of history in general and the history of social and economic development in particular is an essential requirement of the dialectic-materialistic method of studying all social phenomena, including religious ideologies. Shamanism can only be correctly understood and its social function properly assessed if it is examined in relation to the history of the people. With respect to the end of the nineteenth and beginning of the twentieth centuries, researchers must also take into account the colonial policy of the Russian autocracy and the influence of Christianity, Lamaism, and Buddhism on the peoples of Siberia and their religious ideas.

Here are a few relevant examples. At the end of the eighteenth century, all the Itelmen and sedentary Koryaks on the eastern and western coasts of Kamchatka were Christianized. The dogmas of the Greek Orthodox Church were persistently and systematically drilled into them, especially the idea of one god who was almighty and all-seeing, and the virtue of humility and submission in this world as a guarantee of peace and happiness in afterlife. All of this left a peculiar stamp on the religious creeds of the Itelmen and their neighbors, the Christianized Koryaks.

The colonial oppression of the native population of Kamchatka was always marked by cruelty and unbridled exploitation of the natives who were deprived of all human rights. As a result, feelings of helplessness and hopelessness became the ingrained moods of the Itelmen and Koryaks by the middle of the nineteenth century. Their helpless despair was intensified by the decline in their basic occupations, the spread of disease, the high mortality rate, the burdensome taxes and other levies, their unpayable debts to tradesmen, unrelieved poverty, and their whole semistarved existence. All of this provided fertile soil for the acceptance of messianic ideas and their adaptation to fit local beliefs. Their messiah was not Christ; they endowed their mythical culture-hero, Kutkh (or Kutkynnyaku among the Koryaks), with the role of deliverer.

Traveling in Kamchatka in 1848, I. G. Voznesensky made this entry in his diary: "The Koryaks and the Kamchadals (Itelmen) of the Ukinsky (eastern) coast are waiting for the appearance of Kutkh and expect him to come any day."[5] At that time, people who had traveled along the western coast of Kamchatka informed Voznesensky that "the Koryaks are all gathering at one place and heading north to meet Kutkh. . . . They have abandoned their pastures and fishing and hunting tools and some of their worn outer garments and have let their reindeer herds scatter."[6] They said: "Kutkh is walking on the earth and his wife

[5]   Arkhiv AN SSSR [Archive of the Academy of Sciences of the USSR], f. 53. op. 1, d. 5, l. 96.
[6]   Arkhiv AN SSSR [Archive of the Academy of Sciences of the USSR], l. 99.

under the earth, and therefore there will be earthquakes and the earth will cave in." [7]

Never before in the mythology of the Itelmen or Koryaks had Kutkh or Kutkynnyaku appeared in the role of a messiah. He acquired that function as a result of the remarkable way the local people revised the Christian preachers' stories of the judgment day and second advent of Christ and other Christian fables and reworked them in their minds. The local myths combined with the legends spread by the Christian preachers in odd ways. This example shows quite clearly how the body of Koryak and Itelmen religious beliefs was augmented, and the ideas of Christianity worked into the stories of the native population about their mythical heroes. The same example proves that the religious beliefs of the peoples of Siberia and the North were flexible and in process of change and by no means as resistant to outside influences as is sometimes claimed. Other examples may be given to illustrate religious transformations of a deeper and more fundamental nature under the influence of social and economic development and changed conditions of life.

For instance, a new cult — the cult of the spirit of Heri Mapa — gained a broad following among a section of the Nanai between 1870 and 1911. The story is told in great detail by I. I. Koz'minskij (1927). The old and new spirits were believed to be in conflict, and the spirit of Heri Mapa defeated all the other spirits. An interesting touch was that to explain how the spirit managed the world and participated in the affairs of men, the Nanai invested the spirit with the power to use all the new means of transportation then being introduced along the Amur. Thus, Heri Mapa was alleged to travel by sea, land and airborne ships. In fact, the cult revealed some new features: although the Nanai had never practiced blood sacrifices before, they now began to buy pigs and cocks from the Russians and use them as offerings to Heri Mapa. Obviously, very serious changes must have taken place in the life of the Nanai to produce such radical changes in their religious ideas. At the same time, they did not give up their old ideas, cults, and shamanistic rituals. The appearance of the new cult must be considered a growth in the direction of greater complexity of their religious ideas.

Here is another example. In 1904 a religious movement started in the Altai country among the Altai-Kizhi. The movement, known in the literature as Burhanism, had extremely complicated social and political roots. Even more complicated were its religious foundations and its orientation on "the Lamaist cult, Buddhist ideology and elements of

[7]  Arkhiv AN SSSR [Archive of the Academy of Sciences of the USSR], 1. 96 ob.

shamanistic ceremonial" combined (*Religioznye verovanija narodov SSSR*, 1931: 201–202). The external stimulus to the appearance of Burhanism was Russia's defeat in the Russo-Japanese War.

These examples justify us in claiming that the religious ideas, beliefs, and cults of the peoples of Siberia and the North changed radically as marked changes took place in their social and economic development as well as in their political and legal status in the empire. The process was also influenced by the culture and religious systems of neighboring peoples. The same examples show how, under the primitive communal system, economic and social changes were directly reflected in the religious consciousness of the people. In a society with a primitive communal way of life, where there are no classes and consequently no purposefully directed activities to conserve the old forms of religious consciousness, we do not find conflicts between different religious trends. Such a society is still free of the dominating role of the ruling classes, for the latter do not yet exist. Therefore, their religious ideas, beliefs and cults under the primitive communal system change in form and content more easily and spontaneously than under a class society.

Shamanism, like every religion, possesses a number of definite traits peculiar to that form of social consciousness. Most prominent are its religious ideas about nature, natural phenomena, society, and man. In the course of their struggle for existence, the people of the era of primitive communal society were constantly aware of their dependence on the elements and the forces of nature. They were not able to explain those natural phenomena scientifically, and therefore they explained everything in fantastic ways which constituted their first naive religious concepts. The fantastic, unscientific content of those concepts found expression in their mythology, which served at the same time as the soil on which these concepts fed and maintained their historical stability. The mythological basis of their religious concepts also nourished the other main elements of religious experience such as religious feeling (moods) and acts of religious worship (cult) (Plekhanov 1957: 303).

According to Engels, in the religious concepts of preclass society, alongside the forces of nature, there also operate social forces — forces which stand opposed to man in a capacity just as foreign and at first just as inexplicable as the forces of nature, and, like the latter, dominate him with the same apparent natural inevitability. The fantastic images which originally reflected only the mysterious forces of nature now also assumed social attributes and became representations of historical forces (Marx and Engels 1930: 328–329).

The social content of its ideas and cults changes as the given society develops and its socioeconomic relations change. That confirms the importance of a concrete historical approach to the study of the people's religious consciousness in general as well as the individual aspects of that consciousness. It is quite imperative to define the social functions of that consciousness and its content and orientation, and to elucidate the social role of the shamans as it changes and becomes more complicated in pace with the development of society.

The shamans and their practices are only one manifestation of shamanism. They are the product of their society and of the development of social relations and religious ideology. By studying the role of the shamans in the religious observances of the peoples of Siberia and the North, we can follow the gradual clarification and extension of their functions as administrators of the people's cults. Their emergence coincides with the growing separation of mental and manual labor. The deeper the decay of the primitive communal foundations of the given people and the greater the material inequality of its members, the augmentation of private property and manifestations of social differentiation, and hence formation of class relations — then the broader and more varied are the social cults and religious functions of the shamans, their professionalism and attributes. And contrariwise, the less the primitive communal foundations of the people's life are affected by decay, the lower the level of material inequality and private property relations — then the narrower are the social functions of the shamans and their role in the religious observances of the people.

In their social and economic development, the Buryats of Siberia were far ahead of the small peoples of the North, among them the Koryaks. The formation of class relations among the Buryats was already clearly defined by the eighteenth century (Zalkind 1970: 303). But the Koryaks were still at the stage of the dissolution of the patriarchal-family community as late as the end of the nineteenth century. Their highest social organizations were the villages, which were associations of neighbors and relatives, embracing several patriarchal-family groups. Not infrequently these villages had special traditions and even a special dialect of their own.

The different levels of development of the productive forces, production, and social relations of the Buryats and Koryaks were matched by different levels of development of religious ideas and differences in the social role and functions of the shaman.

For instance, the Buryats practiced public worship, with several thousand people participating and collective sacrifices offered. The shamans officiated during these functions. They also offered clan sacrifices to different gods, and performed ceremonies attendant on birth and death. Buryat shamans went through a period of special training; there were "white" and "black" shamans, and a cult of shamans. They preserved the traditions of shamanism, their legends, genealogies, hymns, and incantations. The Koryaks did not practice public worship of the Buryat type. Their shamans chiefly served a patriarchal-family community or group of communities (the village). Their main tasks were to heal the sick and predict the future and the prospects of the hunt. They did not have to make sacrifices to the ancestors of the patriarchal-family communities, the patrons of the family's welfare, or the forces of nature, or the spirits that guarded the fishing and hunting grounds. These duties were performed by the heads of the patriarchal-family communities if they did not have their own shaman. Under ordinary conditions, the shamans engaged in fishing and other occupations alongside the other inhabitants of the village or encampment. The Koryaks did not have professional shamans.

The dependence of the types and forms of shamanism on historical conditions is apparent. Consequently, its study calls for a concrete historical approach which takes into consideration all the facts of the people's history. First, the shamanism of separate peoples must be studied; then we can proceed to broad surveys and generalization about the development of the people's religious consciousness under the conditions of the dissolution of the primitive communal system and transition to class society.

Shamanism is not only a Siberian phenomenon. In one form or another it is evidently characteristic of all peoples standing at the threshold of the formation of class society.

Exchange of experience in studying different forms of religious consciousness, among them the shamanism of the native inhabitants of Siberia, North America, certain regions of southern Asia, and the island world of Oceania is very much on the agenda of the day. It will help to disclose the laws of development of the religious forms of ideology of preclass societies, a field which so far has been poorly explored.

# REFERENCES

AGAPITOV, N. N.
1883   Opyt programmy dlja izuchenija verovanij inorodtsev [An attempted program for the study of the religious beliefs of non-Russians]. *Izvestija Vostochno-Sibirskogo Otdelenija RGO* 14(3).

ALEKSEEV, N. A.
1966   Materialy o religioznykh verovaniiakh jakutov kak istoriko-etnograficheskij istochnik [Materials on religious beliefs of the Yakuts as a historical-ethnographic source]. *Sovetskaja Etnografija* 2.
1967   "Traditsionnye religioznye verovanija jakutov XIX–XX vekov" [Traditional religious beliefs of the Yakuts in the nineteenth and twentieth centuries]. Unpublished dissertation, Moscow.
1969   Kul't ajyy — plemennykh bozhestv pokrovitelej jakutov [The cult of *ajyy* — tribal patron deities of the Yakuts]. *Etnograficheskij Sbornik*, vyp. 5. Ulan-Ude.

ANISIMOV, A. F.
1936   *Rodovoe obshchestvo evenkov (tungusov)* [Tribal society of the Evenks (Tungus)]. Leningrad.
1958   *Religija evenkov* [Religion of the Evenks]. Moscow, Leningrad.
1959   *Kosmologicheskie predstavlenija narodov Severa* [Cosmological conceptions of the peoples of the North]. Moscow, Leningrad.
1967   *Etapy razvitija pervobytnoj religii* [Stages in the development of primitive religion]. Moscow, Leningrad.
1969   *Obshchee i osobennoe v razvitii obshchestva i religii narodov Sibiri* [General and individual features in the development of the society and religion of the peoples of Siberia]. Leningrad.

BICHE-OOL, S. I.
1968   *Religioznye perezhitki tuvintsev i puti ikh preodolenija* [Vestiges of religion among the Tuvinians and ways of overcoming them]. Ulan-Ude.

BOGORAZ-TAN, V. G.
1932   Religija kak tormoz sotsstroitel'stva sredi malykh narodnostej Severa [Religion as a brake on socialist construction among the minority peoples of the North]. *Sovetskij Sever* 1–2.

KOSAKOV, I.
1930   *K voprosu o shamanstve v Severnoj Azii* [On the question of shamanism in North Asia]. Moscow.

KOZ'MINSKIJ, I. I.
1927   Vozniknovenie novogo kul'ta u gol'dov [The emergence of a new cult among the Golds]. *Sbornik Etnograficheskikh Materialov* 2.

MARX, K., F. ENGELS
1930   *Sochinenija* [Works], volume 20.

MIKHAJLOV, T. M.
1962   *Burjatskoe shamanstvo i ego perezhitki* [Buryat shamanism and its vestiges]. Irkutsk.
1965   *O sovremennom sostojanii shamanstva v Sibiri. Kritika ideologii shamanizma i lamaizma.* [On the contemporay state of shamanism

in Siberia. A critique of the ideology of shamanism and Lamaism]. Ulan-Ude.

1968a O metodike izuchenija sovremennogo sostojanija shamanizma [On the methodology of the study of the contemporary state of shamanism]. *Trudy burjatskogo instituta obshchestvennykh nauk,* vyp. 2. Ulan-Ude.

1968b *Opyt klassifikatsii shamanskogo fol'klora burjat* [Attempt at a classification of the shamanist folklore of the Buryats]. Moscow.

MIKHAJLOVSKIJ, V. M.

1892  *Shamanstvo (sravnitel'no-etnograficheskie ocherki)* [Shamanism (comparative ethnographic essays)], vyp. 1. Moscow.

PATACHKOV, K. M.

1968  Iz opyta raboty po preodoleniju religiozno-bytovykh perezhitkov u khakasov [From an experimental paper on overcoming vestiges of everyday religion among the Khakass]. *Voprosy preodolenija perezhitkov proshlogo i stanovlenija novykh obychaev i traditsij.* Ulan-Ude.

PLEKHANOV, G. V.

1957  *Izbrannye filosofskie proizvedenija* [Selected philosophic works] 3. Moscow.

POPOV, A. A.

1932  *Materialy dlja bibliografii russkoj literatury po izucheniju shamanstva Severo-Aziatskikh narodov* [Materials for a bibliography of Russian literature on the study of shamanism among North Asian peoples]. Leningrad.

POTANIN, G. N.

1880  *Programma dlja sobiranija svedenij o sibirskom shamanstve* [A program for the collection of information on Siberian shamanism]. Irkutsk.

1931  *Religioznye verovanija naradov SSSR* [Religious beliefs of the peoples of the USSR] 1. Moscow.

SATLAEV, F. A.

n.d.  *Kocha-kan: starinnyj obrjad isprashivanija plodorodija u kumandintsev* [Kocha-kan: an ancient ritual for soliciting fertility among the Kumandins].

SUSLOV, I. M.

1931  *Shamanstvo i bor'ba s nim* [Shamanism and the struggle against it]. Moscow.

TAKSAMI, CH. M.

1968  "Features of the ancient religious rites and taboos of the Nivkhi (Gilyaks)." *Popular beliefs and folklore tradition of Siberia.* Budapest.

1969  Pervobytnorodovye otnoshenija i religioznye verovanija u nivkhov [Primitive tribal relationships and religious beliefs among the Nivkhi]. *Strany i narody Vostoka,* vyp. 8. Moscow.

1971  K voprosu o kul'te predkov i kul'te prirody u nivkhov [On the question of the cult of ancestors and the cult of nature among the Nivkhi]. *Religioznye predstavlenija i obrjady narodov Sibiri v XIX–nachale XX veka.* Leningrad.

ZALKIND, E. M.
  1970   *Obshchestvennyj stroj burjat XVIII i pervoj poloviny XIX veka*
         [Social structure of the Buryats in the eighteenth and first half of
         the nineteenth centuries]. Moscow.

ZELENIN, D. K.
  1935   Ideologija sibirskogo shamanstva [Ideology of Siberian shaman-
         ism]. *Izvestija Akademii nauk SSSR. Otdelenie obshchestvennykh
         nauk* 8.

ZOLOTAREV, A.
  1934   *Perezhitki totemizma u narodov Sibiri* [Vestiges of totemism
         among the peoples of Siberia]. Leningrad.

# SECTION THREE

# Altered States of Consciousness in Northern Iroquoian Ritual

BARBARA W. LEX

Although the ritual uses of dreams and dreaming in Northern Iroquoian societies are well documented and analyzed (Wallace 1956, 1958, 1966, 1970a; Blau 1963, 1969; Tooker 1964, 1970; Trigger 1969; and Shimony 1961 are but a few examples), recent scientific research into altered states of consciousness suggests that dreams constitute only one type of possible dissociational state (Bourguignon 1968, 1970, 1972; Goodman 1971, 1972; Wallace and Benson 1972). Descriptions of historical and contemporary Northern Iroquois rituals present ample evidence of a variety of mechanisms employed to achieve such dissociational states, suggesting an approach which treats ritual as only one of the many means for achieving altered states of consciousness. This study places the Northern Iroquoian, particularly the Huron and New York Onondaga Iroquois, rituals in a new perspective.

Beginning with a general discussion of dissociational states, scientific treatments of this topic are presented. Selection of particular populations for study is explained, and rituals selected for analysis, and the functions of these rituals are then explored, identifying the preconditions which give rise to dissociational states and the behavioral characteristics of such states. Finally, an exploratory examination is made of the importance of dissociational experiences in tribal-level societies.

In 1966 the author conducted fieldwork at the Onondaga Reservation. Research was supported by the Phillips Fund of the American Philosophical Society. From 1965 to 1968 fieldwork was carried out intermittently. Orthography employed follows the conventions of the authors whose references are cited.

## DISSOCIATIONAL STATES

Anthropologists have long been aware of institutionalized usages of dissociational states, variously termed "altered states of consciousness" (Tart 1969, 1972), "altered awareness" (Naranjo and Ornstein 1971), and "peak experiences" (Maslow 1962, 1968, 1970) by psychologists. Using Murdock's *Ethnographic atlas* (1967), Bourguignon identified institutionalized forms of dissociation in 437 societies, 89 percent of the 488 societies for which relevant data were available (1972: 418). Indeed, Goodman, who uses "altered states of consciousness" and "dissociation" synonymously to refer to a person divorced "from awareness of the ordinary reality surrounding him" (1972: 59–60), asserts that "we are dealing with a capacity common to all men" (1972: 70). Nevertheless, despite this ubiquity, systematic study of altered states of consciousness has been hampered by a lack of consistently utilized terminology. In his discussion of this topic, Lewis (1971: 13) points out that "anthropologists are still dazzled by the unique attributes of particular customs, or complexes of institutions," effectively precluding comparative studies. Goodman (1972: 59) states:

The conditions into which the glossolalist or the meditating person places himself are known by many different terms in the literature: ecstasy, frenzy, trance, delirium, somnambulistic or hypnotic states, and so on. The reason for the confusing proliferation of designations (although, for some writers, they do have quite specific meanings) is because, as Ludwig (1968:69) points out, this "relatively uncharted realm of mental activity has been neither systematically explored nor adequately conceptualized."

The lack of precise definitions is not the only factor which hampers comparative research. Behaviorist psychologists have criticized the study of subjective experience, termed "private events," on the grounds that "private experience is not available for scientific observation" (Aaronson and Osmond 1970: 12). Anthropologists have been "absorbed in often quite pointless debates as to the genuineness or otherwise of particular trance states" (Lewis 1971: 26). Ecclesiastics of the Christian church have viewed "ecstatic experiences" and "the reality of visions" with suspicion (Cox 1969: 76). Specialists of all these three Western philosophical traditions have manifested distrust of these states; lacking a basis for an evaluation of "trickery" in the reports of observers, scientifically trained or not, accusations of "pathology" are made. Hence, concluding her review of traditional approaches, Goodman concludes: "The problem boils down to the question of whether altered states *per se* are to be considered pathological" (1972: xxii).

In this study it is assumed, after Selye (1950) and Wallace (1959, 1966, 1970a), that dissociational states are but one segment of the ordinary individual's stress response repertoire. Furthermore, because Goodman's definition implies a knowable, fixed, concrete reality "out there" from which the individual is somehow estranged, Tart's definition, "a qualitative alteration in the overall pattern of mental functioning, such that the experiencer feels his consciousness is radically different from the way it functions" (1972: 1203), is employed. It must be remembered, however, that the reports of certain scientific researchers shed light on various aspects of the physiological states of individuals experiencing dissociation.

In the psychologist Barber's discussion (1970: 129) of yoga and hypnotism, he concludes:

... attempts to denote these states of consciousness independently of the subject's verbal report have not proved successful; a critical scrutiny of the observable phenomena that are popularly associated with the term[s] ... tends to divest them of the mystery with which they have been enveloped; some of the assumptions regarding the factors effective in producing the phenomena have failed to be validated by empirical studies; and several conclusions drawn from the past studies of the phenomena are invalidated by methodological errors.

Apparently unaware that fire handling and fire walking is a widespread shamanistic practice (Eliade 1964), reports of yogic thermal control are either dismissed or given explanations from classical physics (Barber 1970: 124–125). The physiologists Wallace and Benson (1972: 125), however, state:

... there are in fact several ways in which an individual can control his physiological reactions to psychological events. Among the claims for such control the most notable have come from practitioners of meditation systems from the East.

Results of their study of experienced users of the "transcendental meditation" technique of Maharishi Mahesh Yogi indicate manifestations of a "wakeful, hypometabolic state" in which occur:

... reductions in oxygen consumption, carbon dioxide elimination, and the rate and volume of respiration; a slight increase in the acidity of the arterial blood; a marked decrease in the blood-lactate level; a slowing of the heart beat; a considerable increase in skin resistance, and an electroencephalogram pattern of intensification of slow alpha waves with occasional theta-wave activity (1972:130).

Having pointed out that hypnosis patterns have no resemblance to meditation, but rather "visceral adjustments in a hypnotized person merely reflect the suggested state" (ibid.), they also note that although meditation produces a complex of responses, the operant conditioning of "biofeedback" (Di Cara 1972) can produce learning in the automatic nervous system such that "a specific visceral response to a given stimulus" is generated (Wallace and Benson 1972: 131).

Ornstein, a psychologist, has identified the basic component in the methods of meditative systems:

The strong common element seems to lie in the actual restriction of awareness to one single, unchanging process. It does not matter which actual physical practice is followed; whether one symbol or another is employed; whether the visual system is used or body movements repeated; whether awareness is focused on a limb or on a sound or on a word or on a prayer. This process might be considered in psychological terms as an attempt to recycle the same subroutine over and over again in the nervous system. The instructions for meditation are consistent with this; one is instructed always to rid awareness of any thought save the object of meditation, to shut oneself off from the main flow of on-going external activity and attend only to the object or process of meditation. Almost any process or object seems usable and has probably been used. The specific object of meditation is much less important than maintaining the object as the single focus of awareness over a long period of time (Naranjo and Ornstein 1971:161).

One sufficient, if not necessary, meditation object appears to be some sort of utterance or activity, lacking semantic content, literally non-SENSE upon which the practitioner's attention is fixed. Because of the learning process as well as man's continual striving to attach meaning to sensory inputs, however, the meditation object becomes identified with the meditative state itself.

Because of the apparent lessened rates of physiological activity, meditation has been placed at one end of a continuum of mental states (Goodman 1972: 60); the two poles are termed, respectively, hypoaroused and hyperaroused (Goodman uses "trance" synonymously with "hyperarousal," not noting that meditating yogis are sometimes popularly said to "be in a trance"). Further, in her study of glossolalists, Goodman has identified "driving" behaviors, that is, techniques used to facilitate the onset of the hyperaroused state in which glossolalia appears (1972: 60).

Although no method INEVITABLY induces a dissociational state (Goodman 1972: 74), numerous strategies have been used to prepare, physiologically and psychologically, for dissociational states. In laboratory experiments "rhythmically spaced sound and light signals" have been employed, producing effects in cortical response patterns (Goodman 1972:

60, 74), but laboratory studies of glossolalists are lacking. Nevertheless, some of the driving behaviors reported in her study are suggestive of physiological changes. Use of musical rhythms is suggested as one widespread means by which dissociational states are achieved (Wallace 1966: 54–55). Certain words, although in the general, nonesoteric vocabulary, are imbued with special meaning and employed as cues to trigger glossolalia. Loud, fast hymns are sung, producing hyperventilation. Glossolalic utterances, themselves nonsemantic, are elsewhere employed by "guides" who assist those "seeking the Holy Spirit" to achieve the dissociational state in which glossolalia can occur (Kildahl 1972).

Lewis (1971: 39) provides a rather thorough overview of the driving behaviors of hyperaroused states:

As is well known, trance states can be readily induced in most normal people by a wide range of stimuli, applied either separately or in combination. Time-honoured techniques include the use of alcoholic spirits, hypnotic suggestion, rapid over-breathing, the inhalation of smoke and vapours, music and dancing; and the ingestion of such drugs as mescaline or lysergic acid and other psychotropic alkaloids. Even without these aids, much the same effect can be produced, although usually in the nature of things more slowly, by such self-inflicted or externally imposed mortifications and privations as fasting and ascetic contemplation (e.g. "Transcendental meditation"). The inspirational effect of sensory deprivation, implied in the stereotyped "mystical flight" into the wilderness, has also been well documented in recent laboratory experiments.

Furthermore, the religious historian Cox, having compared the "hermit's cell of the old style mystic" with "acid rock" music played amid the stroboscopic light of the modern discotheque, concludes: "All this suggests that disciplined sensory deprivation as experienced by the classical mystics, and the modern experience of calculated sensory overload, do produce some markedly similar results" (1969: 110).

In short, dissociational states have been and can be observed in individuals behaving in particular cultural contexts; moreover, laboratory experiments on the physiology of dissociational states are beginning to close the gap between speculation and knowledge. Therefore, as with any nonidiosyncratic human behavior, patterns of dissociational behavior are learned, socially transmitted, and observable.

## THE NORTHERN IROQUOIS

In 1962, William N. Fenton, dean of modern Iroquoianists, commented: "So much has been written about the Iroquois that their combined ethnological and historical literature rivals that of any primitive people, being exceeded only in the bibliography of North America by the Eskimo and Navaho" (1962: v). Since that time the information explosion has further increased the scope of the Iroquoian ethnologists' analytical tasks. This plethora of literature precludes exhaustive, systematic sifting of every existing description or analysis of Northern Iroquoian cultures for evidence of dissociational states.

Furthermore, rituals are performed on a number of the Iroquois reservations in both the United State and Canada. Adherents of the traditional religion, revitalized by the Seneca prophet, Handsome Lake, are commonly termed "the Longhouse people" or "Longhouse believers." The label is derived from the structure, modeled somewhat after the aboriginal house type, in which public religious ceremonies, as well as political activities, take place at Allegheny, Cattaraugus, and Tonawanda (Seneca) Reservations in western New York, the Onondaga Reservation in central New York, the Six Nations and Oneida Reserves in western Ontario, the Caughnawauga Reserve (Mohawk) in Quebec, and the St. Regis (Mohawk) Reservation on the border between Canada and the United States (Tooker 1970: 1). Descriptions of ceremonial practices at several longhouses are available: Sour Springs Longhouse at Six Nations Reserve, Coldspring Longhouse at the Allegheny Reservation, Newton Longhouse at the Cattaraugus Reservation, Tonawanda Reservation Longhouse, and Onondaga Reservation Longhouse (Tooker 1970). Tooker has noted: "With increased knowledge of Iroquois ceremonialism came increased recognition that ritual practice in the various longhouses differed" (1970: 5), and Fenton has observed: "To the extent that acute observations of local patterns of behavior may be observed to hold for several communities they may be considered pan-Iroquois culture norms" (1951: 9). Because of these observations, certain Onondaga rituals have been selected for this research, meeting the criterion of representativeness of a locally diverse tradition as well as being "pan-Iroquoian" as defined by Fenton.

Writing about the Onondaga Longhouse, Blau (1965: 251) explains:

The Longhouse as an institution is functionally integrated into almost every aspect of Iroquois life. Due to its prominent role in fulfilling so many varied needs of the community, its contribution to cultural solidarity is immeasurable. The people regard it as the focal point of their community and have given it a central location on the reservation, easily accessible to all.

Further, Blau has identified ten factors which have provided for Onondaga cultural stability; eight of these pertain to prestige, the other two to territorial security. In Iroquois Confederacy traditions, for example, Onondagas are "instrumental in the formation of the Iroquois League,"

Central Fire-Keepers of the Confederacy, "guardians or watchkeepers of the League." They functioned as "Keepers of the Laws and Wampums of the Confederacy," as Nation of "the culture hero Hyenwatha" who "figures prominently in origin legends of the League," holders of the title of *Thadodaho,* "Grand Sachem or chief arbitrator of the fifty *Rodiyaner,* or Lords of the Confederacy." They were holders of the largest number of chieftainship titles of the League and witnesses to the death of Handsome Lake, the Seneca prophet who died there in 1815 (Blau 1965: 252–255). Onondagas have never been displaced far from the lands they held aboriginally and their reservation today is relatively isolated from urban encroachment, despite proximity to the city of Syracuse, New York (Blau 1965: 255–256). Blau (1969: 7) states: "The Onondaga language is still spoken, and eight major ceremonials are still observed, including a fifteen-day Midwinter Festival." Hence, recent observations of Onondaga rituals are an appropriate choice.

The Huron, Iroquoian speakers who lived in the vicinity of the southern end of Georgian Bay when encountered by the French in the first half of the seventeenth century, are the Iroquoian peoples best known to us from the early descriptive writings of French explorers and missionaries. Two modern ethnographies of the Hurons (Tooker 1964; Trigger 1969) are based on three primary sources: "Samuel de Champlain's account of the winter (1615–1616) he spent in Huronia; Gabriel Sagard's account of his winter visit in 1623–1624; and the yearly *Relations* of the Jesuits who began intensive work among the Huron in 1634" (Tooker 1964: 3). Although biased by their zealous drive to convert the pagan Huron, the *Jesuit relations and allied documents* (edited by Thwaites 1896–1901) are the most extensive of these records and, therefore, most useful to anthropologists because they reflect long-term observation of the Huron.

Because the Jesuits were primarily interested in religion, their narratives, which were written partially to persuade pious Frenchmen to contribute funds to missions, devote considerable attention to the ritual practices of the native peoples whom they encountered. The greatest value of these documents lies in their descriptions of Huron culture, which was virtually destroyed by 1649, and although the descriptions of rituals are not the product of meticulous note-taking ethnographers, they give an idea of the aboriginal Huron culture. Furthermore, remnants of one Huron Nation, the Arendahronon or Rock People, were forced to flee after the predations of the Iroquois in 1649, and joined the Onondaga. For these historical reasons, certain Huron rituals will also be examined for evidence of altered states of consciousness.

## NORTHERN IROQUOIAN RITUALS

The selection of specific rites for study is somewhat complicated by the confounding effects of the teachings of Handsome Lake, the Seneca prophet whose visions, beginning on June 15, 1799, formed the basis for a revitalized Iroquois religion: "This religion is a compound of old Iroquois and Christian religions with some unique elements added" which "quickly supplanted the older form of Iroquois religion" (Tooker 1964: 72). However, one significant area of nonconformity to the Code of Handsome Lake today is related to the proscription of the many medicine societies and their activities. The rationalization that "tobacco wasn't burned" by the nineteenth-century ritualists who were officially to dissolve the societies, as required by Handsome Lake, indicates that one requirement of prescribed ritual behavior — tobacco burning — is recognized, but another — the proscription of medicine societies as emphatically stated by Handsome Lake — is ignored.

The importance of the medicine societies to the Iroquois cannot be discounted. Through the ministrations of medicine societies, individual illness became a group concern: participation in these societies reinforced traditional Iroquoian patterns of mutual aid, alleviated anxieties attending illness, and the recruitment pattern by which persons thus cured became members tended to increase knowledge of and participation in the traditional culture (Lex 1966: 9). Because Tooker has observed, "The 17th-century French descriptions of Huron religion emphasize the ceremonies given by an individual to cure his illness or, in general, to obtain good fortune in his endeavours or to prevent illness or other ill fortune and virtually ignore the communal calendric ceremonials" (1964: 72), rituals which include the "Dream and Curative" complex identified for the Onondaga by Blau (1969: 45–55), some components of which are public performances of the False Face Society, will be analyzed.

Tooker has also observed that "In the 19th- and 20th-century descriptions of Iroquois religion . . . the rituals concerned with individual crises have been most often ignored and calendric ceremonials described in length" (1964: 72). She suggests that such changes do not indicate a radical shift of emphasis in Iroquoian religion, but rather that early observers found the communal calendric rituals less flamboyant. It is also possible that during the reservation period, communal calendric rituals emphasizing group solidarity might have become more socially important to the maintenance of group ties, that a shift from communal living in longhouses to residence in free-standing homes might make performance of individual-centered rites less publicly noticeable (to casual observers and ethnographers alike), or that certain elements present in these rites are felt to warrant concealment from potentially disapproving outsiders.

If evidence for the use of altered states of consciousness can be found via the analysis which follows, scholars may legitimately question the belatedness of such a discovery. Although it is possible that the present viewpoint is in error, it is also possible that use of altered state might be concealed from observers, or that observers might be unaware that such states are, or have been, used in ritual contexts for several reasons (e.g. because masks which conceal the face are used by certain medicine societies), including the lack of legitimacy of such states in Western cultures. As discussed previously, interpretations of dissociational states as either "trickery" or "pathology" have influenced anthropologists as well as other observers. Similarly, the Jesuit Fathers often refer to shamans as "sorcerers," "jugglers," "charlatans," or "soothsayers" (Thwaites 1896–1901: VIII, 125, 255, 257, 261; and X, 197 are a few examples).

Wallace has proposed thirteen minimal categories of religious behavior: prayer, music, physiological exercise, exhortation, recitation of the code, simulation, *mana*, taboo, feasts, sacrifice, congregation, inspiration, and symbolism comprise his "rough and ready classification of the kinds of actions that most observers recognize as religious" (1966: 53). For present purposes the second and third categories are of immediate relevance. In his discussion of music, which is said to be almost universally present in ritual, Wallace (1966: 55–56) comments

... musical media are preferred because of their effect upon the human performer and his audience and that sometimes, as in "voodoo" dancing and drumming, the participants are consciously aware that musical performance facilitates entry into a desired state of heightened suggestibility or trance in which possession and other ecstatic religious experiences can be expected to occur.

With regard to "physiological exercise: the physical manipulation of psychological state" Wallace asserts:

Efforts to induce an ecstatic spiritual state by crudely and directly manipulating physiological processes are found in every religious system. Such manipulations may be classified under four major headings: (1) DRUGS; (2) SENSORY DEPRIVATION; (3) MORTIFICATION OF THE FLESH by pain, sleeplessness, and fatigue; (4) DEPRIVATION of food, water, or air.

Having presented several cross-cultural examples, he continues:

The effectiveness of these procedures in inducing psychological change has been demonstrated, even in a nonreligious setting, by clinical experimentation in the effects of sensory deprivation and in the various "brainwashing" or "thought reform" techniques practiced by agencies of social control in both Western and Communist countries. Physical discomfort produced by torture, prolonged sleeplessness, and fatigue, whether self-applied or imposed by others, can alto be effective in inducing cognitive change. Similarly, the deprivation of food, of water, and of normal atmospheric air to breathe, can, with varying speeds, produce extreme states of disorientation, dissociation, or euphoria.

In sum, then, one may say that physiological manipulation of the human body, by any means available, to produce euphoria, dissociation, or hallucination is one of the nearly universal characteristics of religion. The ecstatic experience is a goal of religious effort and whatever means, singly or in combination, are found to be effective in reaching it, will be employed by, or on behalf of, at least some communicants (1966:55–56).

Of the twenty-seven Onondaga rites he identifies, Blau includes eleven different rites under the "Dream and Curative" rubric; however, six of these directly involve public performance of a medicine society, the False Face Society, and shall be treated as a unit. Others are the Bowl Game, Stirring Ashes Rite, Dream Guessing, and *Ohgiwe* or Feast of the Dead.

For dreams and cures to be placed under a single complex is natural to Iroquois philosophy because dreams can cause illness when spirit forces who manifest themselves in this manner are not properly satisfied. The rites of this complex are among the oldest Iroquoian traditions and are well documented in the early literature of the Eastern Woodlands, especially in the *Jesuit relations* (1969:54).

Chafe, in his article "Linguistic evidence for the relative age of Iroquois religious practices," finds unanalyzable Seneca roots in terms for several ceremonies, songs, dances, and ritual paraphernalia, and certain specific roots "associated with varied aspects of shamanism" (1964: 280). The assumption here is that the unanalyzable forms are older (1964: 279). Recommending a guarded interpretation of these data, Chafe nevertheless points out that "Negative evidence is available in the fact that with the exception of the Midwinter Ceremony, which contains a large portion of shamanistic elements, all of the calendric ceremonies have clearly analyzable, descriptive names" (1964: 281). Unanalyzable roots are found in the Seneca terms for Feast of the Dead, the Bowl Game (as well as the Feather Dance, both included in the Four Sacred Rituals), and the Midwinter Ceremony (Chafe 1964: 280).

Blau places the individual chant or *adǫ́we* (another of the Four Sacred Rituals) in his "Thanksgiving Complex," although it "formerly functioned as a personal death song whenever a warrior's death seemed imminent" and originally belonged in the older, now obsolete War

Complex (1969: 49–50). The individual chant is one of the Four Sacred Rituals. At Onondaga today, "Individual chants may be performed as a distinct rite, or they may be sung in appreciation for a religious event which has just transpired" (Blau 1969: 112). These are usually sung by the individuals to whom they belong, males whose fathers' or mothers' lineage held them (Fenton 1936: 16; Speck 1955: 735–737; Tooker 1970: 26). Hurons employed songs as a preparation to meet death in war, particularly if tortured, as well as at home by natural causes (Thwaites 1896–1901: X, 61, 267; XV, 67; XXIII, 173–175). Indeed, the fact that "the Huron believed that those who died in war . . . had no communication in the after life with other souls" (Thwaites 1896–1901: XXXIX, 31; Tooker 1964: 132), denying to these individuals the Feast of the Dead may be due to the lack of opportunity to sing songs in the case of violent death. Tortured prisoners, if they did not do so voluntarily, were compelled to sing (Thwaites 1896–1901: VIII, 23; XIII, 55–71; Trigger 1969: 48–49).

Individual chants today contain "burden" or nonsense syllables as well as words; for example, utterances such as *hé, hé, hé, hé, wiiiiii, hiya, ho ho ho ho ho*, are commonly used by the Onondagas in ritual contexts. Physiological experiments suggest a consequence of these practices. Bunn and Mead, in a recent experiment, have demonstrated that texts with "a preponderance of consonants containing large volume increments (e.g. letters *h* and *s*) produced hyperventilation in all of their subjects" (1971: 870). Indeed, one subject experienced apnea (temporary stopping of breathing) which lasted up to eighteen seconds after reading aloud. This evidence from a laboratory experiment suggests that certain phonations may be more conducive to the onset of hyperventilation than others; nonsemantic utterances of Onondaga rituals appear to meet this criterion.

Huron songs were particularly efficacious for transcending other potentionally painful experiences:

Some have, besides, a secret or a charm which has been declared to them in a dream with the song to be used before going, for example, to the fire feast, after which they can handle the fire without hurting themselves (Thwaites 1896–1901:XVII, 197).

Fire handling is an integral portion of the curative rites of the False Face Society: *Hadijistagáya* [they handle the fire] is the name given to a ritual wherein:

After a dramatic entrance the False Faces attempt to break through the guards at the stoves [four men at each stove, one group from each moiety] at either end of the Longhouse. If successful, they may "juggle" live coals in their bare hands and scatter ashes on the congregants. After much excitement and an occasional skirmish the masked supernaturals are pacified with tobacco. They greedily stuff their pockets with the tobacco collected from the congregation prior to the rite. The supernaturals are requested to abstain from upsetting the stoves or harming anyone. The False Faces dance, displaying their joy (Blau 1966:568).

"False Face dancers prefer a fast tempo and short songs" (Fenton 1962: 107). Fenton (1937: 228–229) reported:

A peculiar form of hysterical possession formerly occurred among women at Tonawanda. An informant states that it was confined to certain nervous women who became possessed of the False Face Spirits whenever the masked men appeared. On hearing the rumpus of whining [described in Blau (1969:192) as "whinney-like staccato sounds"] and rattles, which marks their approach, one woman would fall into spasms, imitate their cry and crawl toward the fire, and, unless she was restrained, plunge her hands into the glowing embers and scatter the fire as if she were a False Face hunting tobacco. Someone always grabbed her, while another burnt tobacco, imploring the masked men to cure her. The ritual usually restored her normal composure. Other women became possessed of the tutelaries of the Bear or Buffalo Societies. My informant used to think women became possessed to show off. Some of these women were clairvoyants. Another informant remembers a man who became possessed, thirty years ago at Newton, for resisting a Door-Keeper [ritual guard at the Longhouse door]. When the masked ritual conductor nudged him with his rattle, he obstinately refused to join the round dance. They struggled and the man, overcome with fear, fell into a spasm and cried like a False Face. They had to blow ashes on him. Afterward, the man did not remember his behavior. In all cases, the form of the hysteria was prescribed by the culture.

Early French writings about Huron rituals are full of descriptions of fire handling and fire walking; reports of the *awataerohi* curing dance, performed to cure a disease of the same name (Tooker 1964: 103), yield evidence of ritual uses of dissociational states as well as the use of rituals to bring dissociational states under control (cf. Fenton 1937: 228–229). Symptoms often resulted from particular dreams (Thwaites 1896–1901: X, 183; XIII, 233; XX, 151–155).

Tooker (1964: 103) states: "It is tempting to equate this ritual with that of the Iroquois I'dos Society." According to Parker (1909: 172), writing on the Seneca:

The head singers of the *I'dos* are two men who chant the dance song. This chant relates the marvels the Medicine Man is able to perform, and as they sing he proceeds to do as their song directs. He lifts a red-hot stone from the lodge fire and tosses it like a ball in his naked hands; he demonstrates that he can see through a carved wooden mask having no eye-holes, finding various things about the lodge. . . ."

At Onondaga, only members of the False Face (*hondo?i*) and Husk Face (*hadiʒiso*), but never the I'dos Societies, appear publicly, particularly at certain junctures in the fifteen-day Midwinter calendric ceremonial. Blau (1966: 576; 1969: 194) comments

. . . this traditional mode of behavior is so outstanding that the rite is called *hadijistagáya*, they handle the fire. Wearing a doctor mask imbues one with the power to handle live coals and ashes with immunity, as well as to withstand extreme cold, cure the ill, drive out evil and see clearly.

Speck (1955: 91) has labeled one aspect of this ritual as the "fire ordeal." According to Blau (1967: 258–259):

Although not an ordeal in the sense of determining guilt or innocence, it is, however, regarded as a test of faith, and not all members of the False Face Society will be so daring or demonstrative when handling fire.

Much has been written about False Face masks, and several typologies and systems of mask classifications have been suggested by researchers; however, informants do not subscribe to these (Blau 1966; Hendry 1964). For example, Blau (1966: 567) states:

Nevertheless, little evidence has indicated that particular masks are always utilized in particular rituals or have specialized functions. Fenton's Seneca dichotomy of the "common faces" or "beggars" and the "great doctor" or "leader" masks is not based on mask type. Any mask that acquires a reputation for curing accumulates power over a period of time and may "graduate" from the class of common faces to the role of "leader." The wearer of this mask is then said to portray *Shagodowe' hgo:wa*, the "Great Defender," or "Great World-Rim Being," a Seneca prototype. At one Iroquois Longhouse the leader of the False Faces may be a mask of the crooked mouth type, at another Longhouse it may be the "spoon mouth blower" type. In view of this, it seems fruitless to attempt to classify masks in relation to ritual function since masks of all types might appear in any ritual of the False Face Society, save the separate rites utilizing wooden faces as opposed to husk faces.

That Onondagas use some other schema is shown by Blau's report (1966: 567) of a private curative rite in which only black masks were worn, "in obedience to a dream"; although rare this usage is "based upon the 'natural' dichotomy of wooden false faces, red and black" (ibid.)

Efficacy, or "power," appears to be a significant criterion for Onondagas' classification of masks. Much attention has been devoted to the more plastic features of False Face masks, particularly noses and mouths. One Iroquoian myth attaches significance to "broken-nosed" masks —

these are symbolic of the contest between the Great Rim Dweller and the Creator in which the latter crushed the former's nose with a mountain. Furthermore, the various facial contortions are said to represent "agonized" visages.

However, an alternate interpretation, employing the concept of dissociational states, suggests that these simulacra are stylized representations of individuals in HYPERAROUSED DISSOCIATIONAL STATES. Although great attention has been paid to noses and mouths, little interest has been manifested in the less plastic eyes. In hyperaroused dissociational states, if the eyes are not closed it can be seen that the pupils are clearly constricted. Eyes in False Face masks are usually represented by relatively flat pieces of metal, with a small hole pierced through both metal and wood. Hence, the expanse of metal, possibly representing the cornea, is large; the hole, which represents the pupil, is comparatively small. False Face masks, therefore, may simulate hyperarousal. By wearing such an aid, which may be seen as a form of driving (Goodman 1972), the dissociational state may be reached.

Blau (1966: 577–578) cites Thwaites (1896–1901: XIII, 263) as the

... earliest mention anywhere of Shamans demonstrating the hunchback posture and probably indicates that the others [imitating a deceased powerful Shaman the first fifteen days after his death] were imitating his affliction in order to emulate this once powerful and respected Shaman.

He further suggests that this is a prototype of the False Face Society which was diffused as a result of the dispersal of Huron refugees among the Iroquois. Trigger (1969: 99) considers this highly speculative. Another interpretation notes the motor behaviors which are apparent in hyperaroused dissociation. Métraux (1972: 122) in his study of Haitian voodoo describes persons ridden by various *loa*:

His chaotic leaps and gestures are like the bucking of a wild horse, who feels the weight of a rider on his back; she might have been thought to have fainted, had she not thrown her head from side to side and had her body not been subject to mild spasms, gradually reaching her shoulders which she shook rhythmically.

That motor behavior in hyperaroused dissociation is subject to cultural patterning is well documented by Goodman (1971, 1972). Hence the "crawling" so characteristic of False Face sickness and the performance of False Faces, whatever its original model, can be interpreted as a manifestation of dissociation. Onondagas refer to the False Face Society as *hondo' i* [hunchbacks], although Senecas and other Iroquoian people use the label *gagohsa* ["mask" or "face"]; Onondagas seem to place an emphasis on behavior, rather than appearance.

Barber (1970) has dismissed reports of thermal control as lacking in scientific rigor. Coe, a chemist, finds fire walking and fire handling valid and comprehensible: "No paranormal explanation is necessary." (1957: 110). Nevertheless, he also tells us: "I will never forget the fear that shook me, the first time I decided to touch red-hot iron with my fingers" (1957: 107). Yet under certain conditions, explicable by classical physics, he was able to do so. Coe overcame his fear through a belief in "scientific" explanation. Possibly Northern Iroquoian peoples have overcome theirs by believing in the efficacy of certain measures, among them the use of powerful masks, simulating visages of persons in hyperarousal. Zitnik et al., physiologists, in their study of temperature effects on cutaneous venomotor reflexes in man, discovered that reflex venoconstriction could be abolished by taking a deep breath, performing mental arithmetic, or inhaling ammonia (1971: 507). The aspirate phonations of False Faces may effect changes in oxygen level; the analogue of mental arithmetic may be the concentration on certain chants. Applied physiological studies are just beginning to yield evidence that internal control of the body is indeed possible. Hence, whether explanations from human physiology or classical physics are applied, singly or in combination, such "feats" become less mysterious and no longer is this practice "an enigma to modern ethnology" (Blau 1967: 260).

Nevertheless, a description of the Midwinter Ceremonial observed at New Coldspring Longhouse at Allegheny Reservation (Seneca) by Fenton (1972: 106) indicates that dissociational states are falling into disuse:

As the False Face crawled and stooped toward the women's fire, I noted that their behavior lacked enthusiasm. Only Herb Doody, who was properly raucous, and Ham Jimerson, who danced while scooping hot ashes, moved the patient's head on its axis, and pumped her arms, came up to expectations. ... I thought that audience participation was quite limited: I saw no frightened children and no cases of hysterical possession; nor did anyone crawl to the fire.

The author has observed that members of the Onondaga False Face Society, although not unenthusiastic in their ritual performances, comment to one another about the heat of the coals which were handled. Indeed, the struggle between men and *hondo'i*, before the two stoves of the Onondaga Longhouse, may symbolize a conflict about the usage of these states. The hunchbacks are "bought off" with tobacco, and retire, although in recent years the stove HAS been toppled. Such license impressed the Jesuits, who likened the unbridled behavior at ceremonies, including strewing of fire, to that of Mardi Gras (Thwaites 1896–1901:

XLII, 155), but no similar public, symbolic struggles are reported by them. In view of Western attitudes toward dissociation, modern ambivalence may be indicative of changing values.

Nonetheless, elements of a belief system tend to reinforce one another. Onondagas "stress the power that becomes theirs when the Mask Spirit appears to them in a dream" (Blau 1967: 260). Dreams, themselves one form of dissociational state, are important in several other Onondaga rituals.

Tooker writes: "In a sense, much of Huron and Iroquois ritual for the maintenance of health and good luck rests on this principle of reenactment of dreams" (1964: 90). Dream Guessing, one of the rites of Blau's "Dream and Curative" complex, was witnessed at Onondaga by the Jesuits in 1671 (Thwaites 1896–1901: LV, 61):

The ceremony is held either for the cure of some person of wealth and station; or before their hunting expedition, to obtain good success therein; or when they are about to adopt some important war plans. It will sometimes last four or five days, during which all is in disorder, and no one does more than snatch a hasty meal. All are at liberty to run through the cabins in grotesque attire, both men and women, indicating — by songs, or by singing in enigmatical and obscure terms — what they have wished for in their dreams; and this each person tries to divine, offering the thing guessed, however precious it may be, and making a boast of appearing generous on this occasion.

The name applied to this ritual, *onoharoia*, "is cognate to one of the names now used by the Iroquois to refer to the Midwinter Ceremonial" (Tooker 1970: 85).

Blau has identified seven components of the Dream Guessing Ritual, using field observation at Onondaga as well as evidence in the *Jesuit relations*. He also notes the statement of an informant: "*Hodinowh áyata* [dream guessing], is what Midwinter Rites are all about" (1963: 233). Speaking of the general significance of dreams, their functions are diverse:

... a vehicle for attaining membership in Medicine Societies. They may reveal methods utilized in curing illness. They may reveal predictions of important events, or the outcome of a particular event. Power from animal and nature spirits are bestowed upon people through dreams. Dreams are a way of communicating with the Dead (1963:245).

The Jesuits noted that for the Huron these rites were "the prop and maintenance of their whole state" (Thwaites 1896–1901: XVII, 193). Today Dream Guessing at Onondaga is more elaborate than at any other Iroquois Longhouse (Blau 1963; Tooker 1970). The therapeutic value of dream interpretation in Iroquois culture has been fully explored by

Wallace (1958).
Indeed, Blau (1963: 245) asserts:

The Dream Guessing Rite is a method of satisfying the underlying Iroquois need to have their desires fulfilled, and to act as agents in fulfilling the desires of others. Their dreams MUST be guessed, because these represent a disturbing element. The people MUST help in fulfilling the desires of others, because of *Hadáenidáseh*, the cooperative spirit of helping one another, a cardinal principle in Iroquois society.

Dreams also play an important part in the Bowl Game ritual, which is associated with the sun. Blau relates the customs of pregame preparations, designed to "effect an influence over the six peach stones," which include an injunction to "watch their dreams" and to "report any significant dream the next morning" (1969: 159). He witnessed just such a report, the narration of a dream which was predictive of the Bowl Game's outcome. The blanket from the bed in which the dream occurred was placed under the ritual paraphernalia in the Longhouse, and the game was played atop this "powerful" piece of cloth (Blau 1969: 159–160).

Pregame rites and the actual play itself involve use of songs and charms, and generate much enthusiasm on the part of players and spectators alike. If not used for predictive purposes, the game is played for curing purposes, in which case, "the harder you play, the better the medicine" (Blau 1969: 154).

The *Jesuit relations* include references to the "game of dish" (1896–1901: X, 187). It was played for curative purposes (ibid, 201). Father La Jeune and others disapproved of the practice of gambling in general, but took note of the cheerfulness of both winners and losers.

Enthusiasm, excitement, and vigorous activity are all components of the Skin (Thanksgiving) Dance and the Great Feather Dance (which, along with the Bowl Game and the Individual Chant comprise the Four Sacred Rituals). Dancing combines Wallace's second and third ritual components, music and physiological exercise. Tooker (1970: 27) remarks: "In the Feather Dance, the two musicians sit straddling a wooden bench and pound the edge of the rattle on the bench in front of them. The sound so produced is so loud it is often difficult to hear the song." Furthermore, the special nature of these rituals is manifested by the requirement that "Indian costume" ought to be worn for them (Tooker 1970: 29).

In the Skin Dance at Onondaga, eighteen spirit forces are enumerated. When the Great Feather Dance is performed all participate, for not only is it "the Creator's own Dance," but also it is performed at the same time in the Sky World.

"Even the weak and elderly attempt to arise and dance, if only for a stanza or two" (Blau 1969: 101–102). An elderly informant, despite infirmities, often participated actively in dances, claiming: "It makes me feel better."

Dances, and accompanying songs, are integral to the *Ohgiwe* or Death Feast, conducted at Onondaga in April, "when the ground begins to thaw." This elaborate cycle of songs and dances, at Onondaga seventy-six (which may then be repeated), is a "Communal Memorial" (Fenton and Kurath 1951: 145) for all the dead, which lasts all night. Shortly before dawn (and the end of the ceremony), the women of the *Ohgiwe* Society hold baskets of ribbons over their heads; these are snatched by others, symbolizing communication with the spirits of the dead of the community. Whether or not the dead are dancing among the living and snatching at ribbons at dawn in Onondaga Death Feasts is a scientists' debate: informants believe they are; for them these rituals are still efficacious.

Singing and dancing the *Ohgiwe* continues through the night, ending at dawn. Unique to this community ritual is the singing of certain women's songs in a falsetto voice, and the reversal, from counterclockwise to clockwise, of the circuits of dancers and of feast food distribution. By dawn everyone is quite fatigued, so that preconditions for hallucinations might be engendered by thinking about the dead, noting the presence of characteristics peculiar to recognition of the dead, and observing or participating in long sequences of dances and songs.


CONCLUSION

Although this analysis is far from an exhaustive treatment of the complete roster of Northern Iroquoian rituals, hyperaroused dissociational states, or at least attenuated symbolic forms of behavior previously associated with the facilitation of such states, have been identified. In addition to those rituals discussed, six additional dances might be added to this list, as could be the Stirring Ashes Rites. But it is clear even from this discussion that Northern Iroquoian rituals prove to be no exception to Wallace's rule: "ecstatic experience is phrased for the individual and the group as possession by the divinity or as communication with the divinity" (1959; 1966: 55) via the two categories of religious behavior Wallace has termed physiological exercise and music.

Furthermore, in certain rituals the features of license and reversal have been observed. Although some anthropologists have viewed these behaviors as ritualized expressions of political significance, manifested via sanctioned channels for the therapeutic release of hostility, these deviations can also be viewed as a stereotyped form of risk taking, which some social psychologists see as a mode of seeking excitement (Klausner 1968).

Indeed, risk taking can be seen as the *raison d'être* for warfare among the aboriginal Northern Iroquoians. Trigger's excellent historical ethnography brings the Huron into focus as a tribal-level society. Elman Service has observed, in his discussion of the external polity of tribal societies, that it is at this level of sociocultural integration that "terrorization or psychological warfare, seems to be at its highest development" (1962: 104). In tribes, atrocities have more impact than the waging of actual combat.

Today the Onondaga reject identification with their seventeenth-century cannibal ancestors. Nevertheless, the *Jesuit relations* is replete with tales of elaborately conducted tortures, designed to destroy the victim systematically as painfully as possible over a period of hours or days: both Huron and Iroquois used similar practices and shared similar beliefs about war, its purpose, causes, and dangers.

Furthermore, young men prepared themselves by holding hot coals between their arms (Thwaites 1896–1901: XXXVIII, 259), for example, so that they might gain courage (Trigger 1969: 44). Doubtless, such practices also gave individuals practice in transcending pain, for if captured, the goal of the victim was not to cry out when tortured, while the goal of the conquerers was to apply every possible technique to cause the victim to disgrace himself with cowardly vocalizations. Certainly the mortifications of the flesh which young men used to prepare themselves for war and the death songs sung by captured men are indicative of dissociational states. Perhaps, too, Northern Iroquois saw death itself as a peak experience, a conclusion supported by the recently published findings of the psychiatrist Russell Noyes, Jr. (1972).

Frequent and common usage of dissociational states, including those facilitated by risk taking, may also explain the Iroquois' predilection for alcoholic beverages. The term for brandy — "fire-water" (Thwaites 1896–1901: XXII, 241) — suggests an association with fire handling in dissociational states. That the Hurons experienced pleasure in drunkenness, rather than drinking (ibid.: IX, 205), and their "furious craving" for liquor for which they had had "at first a loathing" (ibid.: XLVIII, 61–63), provides additional supporting evidence: the end, not the means, is important.

From another perspective, use of dissociational states may also explain the enigma of cultural retentions. Many Onondaga rituals bear strong resemblance to those described in the mid-sixteenth-century reports of the Jesuits. Noting the extent to which missionaries have tried to terminate performances of the more exuberant rituals, it is suprising to many, including Iroquoianists, that so much of the traditional culture persists. Informants, cognizant of Christian missionaries' attitudes toward ecstatic religion, firmly assert "they pray, WE DANCE." Some persons, at least, have not been dissuaded from carrying out traditional rituals. Although attenuation has occurred (cf. Fenton 1972), perhaps the rediscovery and legitimization of aboriginal therapies, a trend already begun with the award of a grant to support the services of a medicine man as instructor of Navaho medical students (*New York Times*, October 14, 1972), will give new life to the spark which has been nurtured in rituals which have persisted through three centuries of contact with whites.

## REFERENCES

AARONSON, BERNARD, HUMPHRY OSMOND
   1970   *Psychedelics: the uses and implications of hallucinogenic drugs.* New York: Doubleday.
BARBER, THEODORE X.
   1970   *LSD, marihuana, yoga, and hypnosis.* Chicago: Aldine.
BEAUCHAMP, WILLIAM M.
   1888   Onondaga customs. *Journal of American Folklore* 1:195–203.
   1893   Notes on Onondaga dances. *Journal of American Folklore* 6:181–184.
BLAU, HAROLD
   1963   Dream guessing: a comparative analysis. *Ethnohistory* 10:233–249.
   1964   The Iroquois White Dog Sacrifice: its evolution and symbolism. *Ethnohistory* 11:97–119.
   1965   Historical factors in Onondaga Iroquois cultural stability. *Ethnohistory* 12:250–258.
   1966   Function and the False Faces: a classification of Onondaga masked rituals and themes. *Journal of American Folklore* 79:564–580.
   1967   Onondaga False Face rituals. *New York Folklore Quarterly* 23:253–264.
   1969   "Calendric ceremonies of the New York Onondaga." Unpublished Ph.D. dissertation, New School for Social Research, New York.
BOURGUIGNON, ERIKA
   1968   *A cross-cultural study of dissociational states.* Columbus: Ohio State University Research Foundation.
   1970   "Hallucination and trance: an anthropologist's perspective," in

*Origin and mechanisms of hallucinations.* Edited by Wolfram Keup. New York: Plenum Press.

1972 "Dreams and altered states of consciousness in anthropological research," in *Psychological anthropology* (second edition). Edited by F. L. K. Hsu. Homewood, Illinois: Dorsey Press.

BUNN, JACK C., JERE MEAD
1971 Control of ventilation during speech. *Journal of Applied Physiology* 31:870–872.

CHAFE, WALLACE L.
1964 Linguistic evidence for the relative age of Iroquois religious practices. *Southwestern Journal of Anthropology* 20:278–285.

CLARK, J. V. H.
1849 *Onondaga,* two volumes. Syracuse.

COE, M. R., JR.
1957 Fire-walking and related behaviors. *Psychological Record* 7:101–110.

COX, HARVEY
1969 *The feast of fools: a theological essay on festivity and fantasy.* New York: Harper and Row.

DI CARA, LEO V.
1972 "Learning in the autonomic nervous system," in *Altered states of awareness: readings from* Scientific American. San Francisco: W. H. Freeman.

ELIADE, MIRCEA
1964 *Shamanism: archaic techniques of ecstasy.* Translated by Willard R. Trask. New York: Bollingen Foundation.

FENTON, WILLIAM N.
1936 *An outline of Seneca ceremonies at Coldspring Longhouse.* Yale University Publication in Anthropology 9. New Haven: Yale University Press.

1937 The Seneca Society of Faces. *Scientific Monthly* 44:215–238.

1940 *Masked medicine societies of the Iroquois.* Smithsonian Institution Publication 3624:397–430. Washington: United States Government Printing Office.

1941 Tonawanda Longhouse ceremonies: ninety years after Henry Lewis Morgan. *Bulletin of the Bureau of American Ethnology* 128:140–168. Washington: United States Government Printing Office.

1951 "Introduction" in *Symposium on local diversity in Iroquois culture.* Smithsonian Institution, Bureau of American Ethnology, Bulletin 149. Washington: United States Government Printing Office.

1962 "Introduction," in *League of the Iroquois.* By Lewis Henry Morgan. New York: Corinth Books.

1972 "Return to the Longhouse," in *Crossing cultural boundaries: the anthropological experience.* Edited by Solon T. Kimball and James B. Watson. Scranton, Pennsylvania: Chandler.

FENTON, WILLIAM N., G. P. KURATH
1951 "The Feast of the Dead or Ghost Dance at Six Nations Reserve, Canada," in *Symposium on local diversity in Iroquois culture.* Smithsonian Institution, Bureau of American Ethnology, Bulletin

149:139–166. Washington: United States Government Printing Office.

GOODMAN, FELICITAS D.

1971   "Disturbances in the Apostolic Church: case study of a trance-based upheaval in Yucatán." Unpublished Ph.D. dissertation, Ohio State University.

1972   *Speaking in tongues: a cross-cultural study of glossolalia.* Chicago: University of Chicago Press.

HENDRY, JEAN

1964   *Iroquois masks and maskmaking at Onondaga.* Smithsonian Institution, Bureau of American Ethnology. Bulletin 191, Anthropological Papers 74. Washington: United States Government Printing Office.

INGALLS, A. G.

1939   Fire-walking. *Scientific American* 163:135–138.

KILDAHL, JOHN P.

1972   *The psychology of speaking in tongues.* New York: Harper and Row.

KLAUSNER, SAMUEL Z., editor

1968   "The intermingling of pain and pleasure: the stress-seeking personality in its social context," in *Why man takes chances: studies in stress-seeking.* Garden City, New York: Doubleday.

KURATH, GERTRUDE P.

1954   Onondaga ritual parodies. *Journal of American Folklore* 67:404–406.

LEWIS, I. M.

1971   *Ecstatic religion: an anthropological study of spirit possession and shamanism.* Harmondsworth, England: Penguin Books.

LEX, BARBARA W.

1966   "Some aspects of False Face Society membership." Unpublished manuscript.

LOUNSBURY, FLOYD G.

1953   *Oneida verb morphology.* Yale University Publications in Anthropology 48:111.

LUDWIG, ARNOLD

1968   "Altered states of consciousness," in *Trance and possession states.* Edited by Raymond Prince. Montreal: R. M. Bucke Memorial Society.

MASLOW, ABRAHAM H.

1962   Lessons from the peak-experiences. *Journal of Humanistic Psychology* 2:9–18.

1968   *Toward a psychology of being.* New York: Litton Educational Publishing.

1970   *Religions, values, and peak-experiences.* New York: Viking.

MÉTRAUX, ALFRED

1972   *Voodoo in Haiti.* Translated by Hugo Charteris. New York: Schocken Books.

MORGAN, LEWIS HENRY

1962   *League of the Iroquois.* New York: Corinth Books.

MURDOCK, GEORGE P.
1967 Ethnographic atlas: a summary. *Ethnology* 6.

NARANJO, CLAUDIO, ROBERT E. ORNSTEIN
1971 *On the psychology of meditation.* New York: Viking.

*New York Times*
1972 "HEW grants 4.7 million five year grant to University of New Mexico." October 14.

NORBECK, EDWARD
1967 "African rituals of conflict," in *Gods and rituals: readings in religious beliefs and practices.* Edited by John Middleton. Garden City, New York: The Natural History Press.

NOYES, J. RUSSELL, JR.
1972 The experience of dying. *Psychiatry.* May.

PARKER, ARTHUR C.
1909 Secret medicine societies of the Seneca. *American Anthropologist* 11:161–185.

PARKER, CHIEF EVERETT, OLEDOSKA PARKER
1972 *The secret of No Face (an Ireokwa epic).* California: Native American Publishers.

SELYE, HANS
1950 *The stress of life.* New York: McGraw-Hill.

SERVICE, ELMAN R.
1962 *Primitive social organization: an evolutionary perspective.* New York: Random House.

SHIMONY, ANNEMARIE ANROD
1961 *Conservatism among the Iroquois at the Six Nations Reserve.* Yale University Publications in Anthropology 65. New Haven: Yale University.

SMITH, DE COST
1888 Witchcraft and demonism of the modern Iroquois. *Journal of American Folklore* 1:184–194.
1889a Additional notes on Onondaga witchcraft and Hon-do-i. *Journal of American Folklore* 2:277–281.
1889b Onondaga superstitions. *Journal of American Folklore* 2:282–283.

SPECK, FRANK G.
1955 *The Iroquois: a study in cultural evolution* (second edition). Cranbrook Institute of Science, Bulletin 23. Bloomfield Hills, Missouri: Cranbrook Press.

TART, CHARLES T.
1969 *Altered states of consciousness: a book of readings.* New York: Wiley.
1972 States of conciousness and state-specific sciences. *Science* 176: 1203–1210.

THWAITES, REUBEN G., editor
1896–1901 *Jesuit relations and allied documents,* seventy-three volumes. Cleveland: Burrows.

TOOKER, ELISABETH
1964 *An ethnography of the Huron Indians 1615–1649.* Smithsonian Institution, Bureau of American Ethnology, Bulletin 190. Wash-

ington: United States Government Printing Office.

1970   *The Iroquois ceremonial of midwinter.* Syracuse: University of Syracuse Press.

TRIGGER, BRUCE G.

1969   *The Huron: farmers of the North.* Chicago: Holt, Rinehart and Winston.

WALLACE, ANTHONY F. C.

1956   Revitalization movements. *American Anthropologist* 58:264–281.

1958   Dreams and wishes of the soul: a type of psychoanalytic theory among the seventeenth-century Iroquois. *American Anthropologist* 60:234–248.

1959   Cultural determinants of response to hallucinatory experience. *American Medical Association Archives of General Psychiatry* 1:58–69.

1966   *Religion: an anthropological view.* New York: Random House.

1970a   *Culture and personality.* New York: Random House.

1970b   *The death and rebirth of the Seneca.* New York: Alfred A. Knopf.

WALLACE, ROBERT KEITH, HERBERT BENSON

1972   "The physiology of meditation," in *Altered states of awareness: readings from* Scientific American. San Francisco: W. H. Freeman.

ZITNIK, RALPH S., ETTORE AMBROSIONI, JOHN T. SHEPHERD

1971   Effect of temperature on cutaneous venomotor reflexes in man. *Journal of Applied Physiology* 4:507–512.

# Shamanism, Trance, Hallucinogens, and Psychical Events: Concepts, Methods, and Techniques for Fieldwork among Primitives

JOSEPH K. LONG

> In every village, some ... diagnose the patients'
> sickness.... While any success enormously enhances
> their reputations as healers, failure does not neces-
> sarily diminish the people's trust in their powers.
> It is easy to find an excuse or to blame the stars if
> something goes wrong with the treatment.
>
> STEPHEN FUCHS [1]

By using a logic identical to this, anthropologists have virtually refused
to give any recognition to psychical events, or the subject matter of parapsychology; little progress has been made in the past three decades (cf.
Humphrey 1944). Recently, forced by Castaneda's work (1968, 1971,
1972) and student pressure (Tart 1972: 1203), anthropologists and
psychologists have been forced to yield somewhat and at least admit the
possibility that "psi," or paranormal events, may be active ingredients of
cultural phenomena.

Scientific objections to parapsychology do not come from deficiencies
of proofs. The various methodological and statistical problems of parapsychology as introduced by the laboratory techniques of J. B. and
Louisa Rhine have been reviewed (Schmeidler 1969; J. B. Rhine and
Brier 1968; J. B. Rhine 1971). Challenges to methods and statistical
results have been answered. Indeed, it is by now quite impossible to
dismiss the evidence for telepathy, clairvoyance, precognition, and
psychokinesis.[2] And, one is reminded, scientists still regarded hypnosis
as a form of magic as late as 1900.

---

[1] In Magic, faith, and healing, page 122.

[2] Clairvoyance is a person's perception of the condition of material objects without the aid of the usual or so-called known senses (i.e. it is extrasensory perception
[ESP]). Telepathy, another form of ESP, is person-to-person communication. Tech-

*Objections to Parapsychology*

The objections to parapsychology involve two processes, one logical and one irrational. The first is that the events of parapsychology may not be explained by present theories or principles of physics. Recent work by Dr. Thelma Moss of the U.S. National Institutes of Mental Health and the University of California Los Angeles Neuropsychiatric Institute indicates that this objection may shortly be removed through Kirlian photography and biofeedback encephalography (Moss and Johnson 1972, i.p.).[3] Even then, a problem will remain. No existing theory can place paranormal phenomena within a comprehensive (e.g. biosocial-evolutionistic) framework. I submit that via the holistic, interdisciplinary approach of anthropology such a theory might be generated;[4] alternatively, we are left with theological speculation.

The second objection to parapsychology relates to the personality of the scientist and the growth of science *vis-à-vis* Western religion, wherein principles of evolution are opposed by those of divine creation. In this context, paranormal events are illogically associated with the supernatural by theologians and scientists alike, and dismissed as superstition by the latter. Honigmann (1963: 342-343) suggests that this is a communication problem inherent in the language of science. This is true, but the fear of producing a proof for supernatural entities, etc. remains among scientists, irrespective of linguistic barriers. In any case, it is not necessary to argue for the existence of psychical events, the need for

---

nically, it is often difficult to determine whether a given event represents telepathy or clairvoyance, or, if the former, how many persons are involved in the transmission. Precognition is the perception of events before they happen. We have come no closer to rational explanation for this than Einstein's theory of relativity, and that was not very close. Retrocognition, or perception of past events — which would be less difficult to accept cognitively — is virtually unsupported by laboratory experimentation. Psychokinesis, which is not necessarily ESP, is movement of objects, as in the "poltergeist" phenomenon (which differs culturally but not physically in different societies), without electromagnetic or direct contact. Electromagnetic causes have been ruled out for all of these phenomena, which have been tested in Faraday cages.

[3] Neher's physiological experiments (1962) on the relationship of brain waves to music, or rhythm, suggest that biofeedback encephalography may eventually explain a variety of ethnomusicological and possession phenomena. Among the Kumina of Jamaica, alteration of rhythm and tone is utilized by drummers to reverse the regression of trance states (Long 1972).

[4] Such comprehensive theories would by no means be new (cf. Myers 1903; James 1936; Jung and Pauli 1952; Murphy and Dale 1961), but only more updated; at the time most general theories were being formulated, parapsychology was an infant science, without laboratory controls, and the nature of psychical events was not so well understood as is presently the case.

scientists to study them, or the irrelevance of theology to parapsychology. A more relevant question is whether, accepting the above assumptions, psychical events are a legitimate concern for anthropologists who are interested in mythology, structuralism, and social organization.[5]

## Psychopathology versus Reality: The Cross-Cultural Problem

Jensen (1963: 230), speaking of psychical healing and the use of psychical powers in shamanism, says that "there can be no doubt that man actually possesses such abilities," but whether, in any given case, the ability is psychical or simply due to suggestion "does not matter very much." With this I must vehemently disagree. To begin with, this evades the issue of reality, a problem that is discussed later. It is already widely assumed in ethnography that that which cannot be "explained" by direct observation must therefore be dismissed as an example of suggestion, superstition, etc. For a given ethnography, patently erroneous data may not make much difference. But where does this take us theoretically in terms of long-range perspectives about cross-cultural patterns?

Ackerknecht (1971: 28), speaking of shamanism cross-culturally, reflects the position of many anthropologists in noting that "psychopathology plays an important role in the life of certain groups of medicine men," implying that this might be a general characteristic for shamanistic practitioners. Prince (1968; see also Long 1972) indicates that Ackerknecht's example from the Siberians is perhaps far from the norm cross-culturally: "mystical experiences often result in states of placidity and well-being which sound very much like good mental health." In fact, because of the usual assumptions made in studying shamanism, evidence is probably insufficient to establish either view. On the other hand, if one assumes that paranormal events have no basis in reality, then one must logically take the position that perception of paranormal events reflects, at best, hallucination, and at worst, insanity. By usual psychiatric definitions, then all who have nonpharmacogenic visions would be classed as psychotic.

[5] Elkin (1938: 197–232, 256–281, 320–329), a primary source on Australian Aborigines, has devoted an entire book to the subject (Elkin 1944). Rose (1952, 1955, 1956) has continued the Australian work, using laboratory procedures borrowed from parapsychology (for a review, see Rhine and Pratt 1957: 109–111). Devereux (1953, 1961: 288) and La Barre (1959: 23–29, 57, 61, noting various accounts by Hoebel, Spier, and Beals) have studied psi in American Indians. Swanton (n.d.) no doubt observed many psi events among Indians, but apparently refused to admit his belief in the reality of them until after his retirement.

## Social Organization

It may be argued that such an untenable position is merely the sort of trap one falls into semantically with psychological anthropology. What effect could this inadequacy of data have upon social anthropology? Male role and status among the Plains Indians was based largely on visions (Lowie 1922, 1935). Lowie (1924: 228), being subject to hallucinations in a fully awake condition, was sufficiently cautious to realize that visions were not *ipso facto* evidence for psychosis; indeed, among the many cross-cultural instances of visions and divination cited (Lowie 1924), it is never clear whether he regards them as psychical or delusional. He concludes that those whose visions are "best" (most accurately predictive) are those most esteemed, who thus have the highest status. This is surely correct, but is it a complete explanation? The structuralist would argue that we have explained nothing until we understand what underlying process was reflected in the role in which "best" visions, and thus esteem, were generated. Was the underlying process predictive ability based on an understanding of "natural" phenomena, or pure psychical ability, as so often suggested by Neihardt (1932)? Surely the answer should make a vast difference in our interpretation of Plains Indian culture. One way, social organization is based on precise intellectual judgments, so that the vision is but a vehicle; the other way, it is based on the ability to distinguish between true psychical visions and mere hallucinations. In either case, the acquisition of vision itself was probably of secondary importance, and it is at this point that Lowie's interpretations are ambiguous. Ultimately, it may not be the success of the vision quest *per se* which is important, but the getting and proper interpreting of the correct (i.e. genuine, extrasensory) vision. How much difference the correct acknowledgment of psychical phenomena may make to social anthropology remains to be seen, but the care that role-theorist Linton took in distinguishing between psychical and delusional phenomena (see Linton and Wagley 1971: 86–93) suggests it is of some considerable importance.

## Intelligence and Sorcery

The mental health of shamans and related practitioners aside, psychical ability is no respecter of intelligence, as parapsychologists have noted for many years (J. B. Rhine 1947: 134–135), although in general those of very low intelligence quotient (IQ) are without psychic abilities. Intellectual and extrasensory development may, in fact, be at odds. Jensen (1963: 230–231, 234–235) makes the familiar suggestion that for purposes of magic primitive peoples cannot distinguish between fact and trickery. Erasmus (1961) gives innumerable examples of how primitives indeed make "frequency interpretations" (probability estimates based on inductive inference from experience) and act accordingly. If this were the case, then the most intelligent of a society — those best able to make accurate frequency interpretations — would be the shamans, sorcerers, and healers. But examples of consistently high intelligence among these are lacking. Similarly, among the laboratory-tested and "proven" psychics of our own culture, the often conflicting "professional predictions" reveal both poor frequency interpretations and an inability to distinguish between precognition and hallucination.[6] Thus, we must conclude that practitioners depend more on psychotherapeutic or true psychical abilities than on frequency interpretations. Even where "faith healing" occurs, it is important to distinguish between the effects of suggestion (faith, or psychotherapy) and psychical energy (Long 1972).[7]

*Psychical Energy, Healing, and Kirlian Photography*

Photography developed in Russia (Kirlian and Kirlian 1961) may prove to be a major breakthrough in understanding psychic phenomena. Americans have only recently succeeded in replicating Kirlian's technique (Moss and Johnson i.p.), wherein the photographs are made by exposing film to an object in a high-frequency electrical field. This reveals "flares" of various sorts which, interestingly enough, appear to have specific relationships to acupuncture points (Worsley 1972).[8]

[6] The life of Cayce, who is the best documented psychic healer (Carter and McGarey 1972), was a comedy of errors (Sugrue 1942); certainly, even had he wanted to dupe the naive, he would not have been intellectually capable of doing so. The ambiguities of his precognitive dreams notwithstanding, his autohypnotic healing sessions and their highly technical and intellectual content must surely prove to be essential data for Jung's theory (1924) of the "collective unconscious."

[7] It should be understood that "faith healing," as the term is used by religious groups in some parts of the United States, denotes what psychologists consider to be suggestion, or perhaps a form of hypnosis, which may indeed have beneficial results with psychogenic diseases. "Psychic healing" does not necessarily denote involvement with faith healing; in fact, some psychic healers claim that faith is entirely unnecessary to the cure. In "laying on of hands," some religious groups combine "faith" with the psychical.

[8] This and similar articles on Kirlian photography, acupuncture, and diagnosis, such as that by Dean De Loach (1972) in the October issue of *The Osteopathic Physician*, should be taken seriously, even though they are not highly technical. Osteopathy, being less scientifically rigorous than some other fields, tends to allow

Flares of ill persons are dim and irregular, whereas those of some psychic healers are regular and large. Radical changes take place in these characteristics following healing. In conjunction with this, we note that Rosicrucians claim to heal by methods identical to, but with quite different origins from, those shown in the anthropological film *Pomo Shaman* (Heider 1970: 88–89). We may expect to find such phenomena in nonpsychic types of healing, such as faith healing: La Barre (1962: 39) gives an example of apparent but unexpected (even by the practitioner) psychokinesis in such a context, and this is recorded on film.[9]

Anthropologist Joan Halifax-Grof (n.d.), working with Cuban refugees in the University of Miami Florida Medical School hospital, has recently discovered what may prove to be another dimension of psychical healing. About five terminal cancer patients have been released indefinitely, their disease being arrested or dissipated. Following agreement by several physicians that death is imminent, members of patients' families are notified. They visit the patient and appear to "talk him out" of dying. This is sociocultural, of course, but may also involve psychical activity.[10] "Voodoo death" (cf. Clune 1973: 312; Lester 1972) may represent a similar phenomenon in reverse, in some cases or to a certain degree.

## Dreaming, Possession, and Meditative States

Anthropology has considered dream states (cf. Opler 1959), but with unimpressive results and very little concern with psychical aspects. Carefully controlled laboratory experiments on dreams and other altered states of consciousness at Maimonides Medical Center in New York indicate that dreams may present the most usual and vivid sources of psi

publication of articles on innovative materials more readily than do more conservative sciences. Articles in this issue at least serve to outline the technique of Kirlian and demonstrate how it may be set up for further experimentation.

[9]   La Barre (1962: 136) also attributes the ability to handle snakes with impunity to some form of psychokinesis. Herpetologists would probably question this, for there is a definite art to handling snakes. Another film showing a snake handler actually being bitten (Adair 1967; Mead 1968) suggests that this ability, in religious context, may be a function of the rhythm of music and a corresponding brain wave (electroencephalograph) pattern, perhaps involving both handlers and snakes (again, see Neher 1962).

[10]   Roger Lauer (personal communication), of the National Institutes of Mental Health, has reported the discovery that a blood chemical just isolated causes constriction of arterioles at the periphery of tumors, thus cutting off the blood supply and arresting cancerous growth. The reason for the presence of this chemical in some individuals is not known.

events, including precognition (Krippner 1971, 1972; Krippner, Honorton, and Ullman 1972; Krippner, et al. 1972; Honorton 1967; Honorton and Krippner 1969). We know little about paranormal events during possession states, such as trance in primitive ritual (cf. Prince 1968; Bourguignon 1968), although supposed events are frequently reported in such contexts (e.g. Huxley 1966). The work of Neher (1962) in conjunction with that of Fischer (1971) and Grof (1972) suggests that psi may eventually be found in the context of possession and meditation.

## Psychopharmacology and Shamanism

Castaneda (1968, 1971, 1972) has raised more forcibly than previously the issue of psychical events induced, or at least facilitated, by hallucinogenic drugs. Despite his initial attemps to discriminate between reality and hoax by ethnosemantic and traditional verification procedures (cf. Honigmann 1968), he was led to discuss apparently psychical phenomena as "a separate reality."[11] In fact, the "separate reality" probably represents a complex juggernaut of psychical events, exaggerated by the sorcerer Don Juan, and thus confused by Castaneda, due to his fixation on disbelief in the reality of psychical events (as opposed to suggestion or hypnosis). In several cases Don Juan, another sorcerer named Don Genaro, and Castaneda simultaneously "see" clearly impossible events (e.g., the precipitation of an auto out of thin air) together, thus anthropologically "verifying" them. In another case Don Juan makes different sorcerers' apprentices see him simultaneously, but with each person seeing him dressed in completely different costumes. In neither case is the question whether these events are real, but at what level they are real. In both cases Don Juan was probably exhibiting extremely powerful telepathic abilities, in the latter case projecting different images to each apprentice. The physical manifestations of some of Castaneda's

---

[11] The "separate reality" concept is perhaps legitimate, and certainly convenient, because it fits so well within the new field exemplified by the *Journal of Transpersonal Psychology*. Although some or all of the board members of this journal are known to believe in the reality of paranormal events, the use of terms such as "altered states of consciousness" (Tart 1969, 1972; Teyler 1972; Ornstein 1972) appears to be a *deus ex machina* allowing discussion of altered states with relatively infrequent reference to psychical events. In fact, it seems that such usage magically precludes the need for a distinction between the real and the unreal. This field has at least been productive in terms of demonstrating the logical fallacies of scientific logic in "straight" psychology. But it introduces more confusion than revelation in discussion of psychical events for anthropology.

events do not detract from this argument, for they may represent psychokinetic events.[12]

An extensive study of lysergic acid diethylamide (LSD) in psychotherapy of terminal cancer patients has been conducted at the Maryland Psychiatric Research Center and the Johns Hopkins medical centers. Summaries of some aspects of this work (Pahnke, et al. 1970; Grof 1972) indicate that LSD is not only potentially therapeutic but is highly conducive to psi events. In fact, events reminiscent of retrocognition or reincarnation (both of these may be explained alternatively as forms of clairvoyance), precognition, clairvoyance, cosmic consciousness, archetypal experiences, and astral projection (clairvoyant "dreaming"?) have all been observed. Of course, most of these are difficult to verify when mixed with the total range of LSD hallucinogenic content, but they do suggest that anthropological research along these lines among primitive people as well as with modern mystics may prove productive.

*Anthropology and Modern Occultism*

Modern occultists abound in the United States. It is estimated that more than 200 occult groups of ten to thirty persons each are active in Dallas. Even for anthropologists uninterested in making detailed studies in modern societies, these provide interesting study situations by which problems of psi verification may be examined. Many modern occultists can indeed demonstrate psychical abilities (Krippner, Honorton, and Ullman 1972), although the great majority cannot.

*Summary: Potentials in Fieldwork*

Problems of studying psi during fieldwork are caused by: (1) disbelief in psi until after the fact, event; (2) problems of reality verification for psi events because of inadequate fieldnotes; and (3) insufficient knowledge of how to verify psi during fieldwork. The last is the crux of the whole problem of relating anthropology to parapsychology. Until acceptable verification is relatively common, it will be impossible to go far toward a general theory of anthropology of the paranormal.

[12]  Innumerable examples similar to this may be gleaned from ethnographic reports on the use of hallucinogenic drugs, as well as from discussions of divination and possession. Unlike Castaneda, most anthropologists have not taken the trouble to attempt verification, so that the significance of such reports is seldom clear.

The most obvious anthropological approach to the study of psi is that of direct observation (cf. La Barre 1959: 25), wherein the anthropologist checks out predictions (and frequency of hits versus misses) and the validity of current images (telepathy, clairvoyance). Films may be used to verify psychokinetic events, such as moving objects like pencils across a stationary table (La Barre 1962: 39; Ullman 1971).

Indirect evidence may lend weight to events that are subject to trickery. In a study of herbalists in Jamaica (Long 1972), one shaman gave repeated evidence of telepathy out of context of religious practices. (During diagnosis, as she related to the investigator later, she usually faked her "visions.") Telepathic events were so natural that they escaped observation until the shaman's roadside attendants expressed occasional surprise when the observer appeared without the shaman's having predicted the time of his appearance. As visits were usually timed randomly and "at the moment," and there were no telephones or lookouts, this appeared to represent telepathy, especially as the shaman CLAIMED psychical powers only during diagnosis. Another indirect support in this case was that the shaman eventually confided that, although she frequently treated people for *duppies* [ghosts], she does not really believe they exist, except "in the mind"; that is, she has little regard for the "supernatural," and does not, apparently, consider telepathy to be an example of such.

Another test procedure is to take parapsychological laboratory methods, such as "ESP cards," into the field and test the abilities of the shaman or sorcerer. An inexpensive manual, with cards and record sheets, is available (L. Rhine 1966). It alerts the beginner to potential hazards of testing and provides tables for quick estimates of statistical probabilities with only a few test runs, in order to determine whether the person is apt to be strongly psychic. One hazard is that some persons who are strikingly psychic in occasional instances or specific situations may never score significantly in laboratory situations.

Lastly, mechanical devices may eventually be taken into the field to "measure," as it were, the substance of psychical events. Grof (personal communication) has just identified by electroencephalograph monitoring a specific brain wave pattern, roughly midway in the LSD intoxication, that appears to represent a brief period of near-perfect psychical ability. If he continues to find replication of this brain wave type, then (1) it may possibly be identified in nonintoxicated individuals using psi, and (2) it may be used to train LSD patients or other subjects, through biofeedback techniques, to produce psi at will (presently, an extremely rare phenomenon). Similarly, Kirlian devices may soon be adapted for fieldwork in areas where electricity is available. Thus, psychical healing and perhaps other psychical phenomena may be measured, or at least photographed, directly.

Of these various means, the first two are no more difficult than current field techniques and can easily be achieved without interference with work directed toward other specific problems, as in applied anthropology. In fact, the "mystic symbols" of ESP cards may actually be used in a sort of parlor game to enhance rapport with shamans of any culture, as the cards are independent of language and, to a degree, culture free. Hopefully, ethnologists will soon exert the minimal effort necessary to produce reliable data on the psychical abilities of people in non-Western cultures. Such data may prove more significant for the understanding of the sum of human behavior than those data already obtained in the field of parapsychology.

## REFERENCES

ACKERKNECHT, ERWIN H.
1971    *Medicine and ethnology.* Edited by H. H. Walser and H. M. Koelbing. Baltimore: Johns Hopkins University Press.
ADAIR, PETER
1967    *Holy Ghost people.* New York: McGraw-Hill/Contemporary Films.
ASHBY, ROBERT H.
1972    *Guidebook to the study of psychical research.* New York: Samuel Weiser.
BOURGUIGNON, ERIKA
1968    *Cross-cultural study of dissociational states.* Bethesda: National Institutes of Health.
CARTER, MARY E., W. MC GAREY
1972    *Edgar Cayce on healing.* Virginia Beach: Association for Research and Enlightenment.
CASTANEDA, CARLOS
1968    *The Teachings of Don Juan.* New York: Simon and Schuster.
1971    *A separate reality.* New York: Simon and Schuster.
1972    *Journey to Ixtlan.* New York: Simon and Schuster.
CLUNE, FRANCIS J.
1973    Comment on Voodoo deaths. *American Anthropologist* 75:312.
DEAN, E. D., ETHEL DE LOACH
1972    What is the evidence for psychic healing? *The Osteopathic Physician* (October):72–136.
DEVEREUX, GEORGE
1953    *Psychoanalysis and the occult.* New York: International University Press.
1961    *Mohave ethnopsychiatry and suicide.* Bureau of American Ethnology Bulletin 175. Washington, D.C.: U.S. Government Printing Office.

ELKIN, ADOLPHUS P.
  1938   *Australian Aborigines.* London: Angus and Robertson.
  1944   *Aboriginal men of high degree.* Sidney: Australasian.

ERASMUS, CHARLES
  1961   *Man takes control.* Minneapolis: University of Minnesota Press.

FISCHER, ROLAND
  1971   A cartography of the ecstatic and meditative states. *Science* 174: 897–904.

FUCHS, STEPHEN
  1964   "Magic healing techniques among the Balahis in Central India," in *Magic, faith, and healing.* Edited by Ari Kiev, 121–138. New York: Free Press.

GROF, STANISLAV
  1972   Varieties of transpersonal experiences: observations from LSD psychotherapy. *Journal of Transpersonal Psychology* 4:45–80.

HALIFAX-GROF, JOAN
  n.d.   "Terminal cancer in Cuban refugees."

HEIDER, KARL
  1970   *Films for anthropological teaching.* Philadelphia: Temple University Program in Ethnographic Film.

HONIGMANN, JOHN J.
  1963   *Understanding culture.* New York: Harper and Row.
  1968   "Verifying ethnographic facts," in *Festschrift in honor of Morris E. Opler.* Edited by Mario D. Zamora, J. Echols, and J. Mahar.

HONORTON, CHARLES
  1967   Creativity and precognition scoring level. *Journal of Parapsychology* 31:29–42.

HONORTON, CHARLES, STANLEY KRIPPNER
  1969   Hypnosis and ESP performance. *Journal of the American Society for Psychical Research* 63:214–252.

HUMPHREY, BETTY M.
  1944   Paranormal occurrences among preliterate people. *Journal of Parapsychology* 8:214–229.

HUXLEY, FRANCIS
  1966   *The invisibles: voodoo gods in Haiti.* New York: McGraw-Hill.

JAMES, WILLIAM
  1936   *Varieties of religious experience.* New York: Modern Library.

JENSEN, ADOLF E.
  1963   *Myth and cult among primitive peoples.* Chicago: University of Chicago Press.

JUNG, CARL G.
  1924   *Psychological types.* New York: Harcourt, Brace.

JUNG, CARL G., W. PAULI
  1952   *Naturerklärung und Psyche.* Zurich: Rascher.

KIRLIAN, S. D., V. KIRLIAN
  1961   Photography and visual observations by means of high-frequency currents. *Journal of Scientific and Applied Photography* 6:397–403.

KRIPPNER, STANLEY

1971    Implications of contemporary dream research. *Journal of the American Society of Psychosomatic Dentistry and Medicine* 18: 94–140.

1972    "Experimentally-induced effects in dreams and other altered conscious states." Paper presented at the Twentieth International Congress of Psychology, Tokyo, August, 1972.

KRIPPNER, STANLEY, CHARLES HONORTON, MONTAGUE ULLMAN

1972    A second precognitive dream study with Malcolm Bessent. *Journal of the American Society for Psychical Research* 66:269–279.

KRIPPNER, STANLEY, JAMES HICKMAN, NANETTE AUERHAHN, ROBERT HARRIS

1972    Clairvoyant perception of target material in three states of consciousness. *Perceptual and Motor Skills* 35:439–446.

LA BARRE, WESTON

1959    *The peyote cult.* New York: Schocken Books.

1962    *They shall take up serpents.* New York: Schocken Books.

LESTER, DAVID

1972    Voodoo death: some new thoughts on an old phenomenon. *American Anthropologist* 74:386–390.

LINTON, ADELIN, CHARLES WAGLEY

1971    *Ralph Linton.* New York and London: Columbia University Press.

LONG, JOSEPH K.

1972    Medical anthropology, dance, and trance in Jamaica. *UNESCO Bulletin of the International Committee on Urgent Anthropological and Ethnological Research* 14:17–23.

LOWIE, ROBERT H.

1922    Religion of the Crow Indians. *Anthropological Papers of the American Museum of Natural History* 25:309–444.

1924    *Primitive religion.* New York: Boni and Liveright.

1935    *The Crow Indians.* New York: Farrar and Rinehart.

MEAD, MARGARET

1968    Review of *Holy Ghost people. American Anthropologist* 70:655. (See Adair 1967.)

MOSS, THELMA, K. JOHNSON

1972    Is there an energy body? *Osteopathic Physician* (October):27–43.

i.p.    "Bioplasma or corona discharge," in *The galaxies of life: papers from the First Western Hemisphere Conference on Kirlian Photography, Acupuncture, and the Human Aura.* New York: Gordon and Breach.

MURPHY, GARDNER, L. DALE

1961    *Challenge of psychical research.* New York: Harper and Row.

MYERS, F. W. H.

1903    *Phantasms of the living.* London: Longmans, Green.

NEHER, ANDREW

1962    A physiological explanation of unusual behavior in ceremonies involving drums. *Human Biology* 34:151–160.

NEIHARDT, JOHN

1932    *Black Elk speaks.* Lincoln: University of Nebraska Press.

OPLER, MARVIN, *editor*
1959    *Culture and mental health.* New York: Macmillan.
ORNSTEIN, ROBERT
1972    *Psychology of consciousness.* San Francisco: W. H. Freeman.
PAHNKE, WALTER, A. KURLAND, S. UNGER, C. SAVAGE, S. GROF
1970    Experimental use of psychedelic psychotherapy. *Journal of the American Medical Association* 212:1856–1863.
PRINCE, RAYMOND, *editor*
1968    *Trance and possession states.* Montreal: R. M. Bucke Memorial Society.
RHINE, J. B.
1947    *Reach of the mind.* New York: William Sloane.
RHINE, J. B., *editor*
1971    *Progress in parapsychology.* Durham, North Carolina: Parapsychology Press.
RHINE, J. B., ROBERT BRIER, *editors*
1968    *Parapsychology today.* New York: Citadel Press.
RHINE, J. B., J. G. PRATT
1957    *Parapsychology.* Springfield, Illinois: Charles C. Thomas.
RHINE, LOUISA
1966    *Manual for introductory experiments in parapsychology.* Durham, North Carolina: Institute for Parapsychology.
ROSE, RONALD
1952    Experiments with ESP and PK with aboriginal subjects. *Journal of Parapsychology* 16:219–220.
1955    A second report on psi experiments with Australian Aborigines. *Journal of Parapsychology* 19:92–98.
1956    *Living magic.* New York: Rand McNally.
SCHMEIDLER, GERTRUDE, *editor*
1969    *Extrasensory perception.* New York: Atherton.
SUGRUE, THOMAS
1942    *There is a river.* New York: Holt, Rinehart and Winston.
SWANTON, JOHN R.
n.d.    "Open letter to 'Fellow Anthropologists.' " Newton, Massachusetts.
TART, CHARLES T.
1969    *Altered states of consciousness.* New York: John Wiley.
1972    States of consciousness and state-specific sciences. *Science* 176: 1203–1210.
TEYLER, TIMOTHY J., *editor*
1972    *Altered states of awareness.* San Francisco: W. H. Freeman.
ULLMAN, MONTAGUE, *editor*
1971    Film on psychical events in Russia. New York: Maimonides Medical Center.
WORSLEY, J. R.
1972    Using the aura as a diagnostic aid. *Osteopathic Physician* (October):47–59.

# The Culture-Historical Origin of Shamanism

HORST NACHTIGALL

According to Ohlmarks, Shirokogorov, Eliade, and other competent authors, shamanism is distinctly characterized by the following two phenomena: spirits and the ecstatic journey of the soul. A survey of the cultural and geographical distribution of shamanism shows that it is found chiefly among hunting cultures in all parts of the world, among the central and north Asiatic nomads, and also in Asiatic advanced cultures of ancient Iran, China, and Tibet and sporadically among agricultural cultures all over the world.

Since contemporary shamanism gives no definite answer as to its place of origin, many different theories have been proposed as to where it might have first been developed. Authors, such as Bogoras, Jochelson, Ohlmarks, and Eliade find the origin of shamanism in hunting cultures; on the other hand, Shirokogorov, and especially the anthropologists of the Vienna School, see its origin in the agrarian cultures.

Among the elements which make up shamanism, the training of the would-be shaman and his burial appear to me to be of great importance. Therefore, these periods in the life of a shaman deserve some critical examination. Most of the reports about the would-be shaman indicate that he is a sick person, often in bad physical condition, and suffers from epilepsy. Despite his frequent attempts, he cannot evade the spirits whose demands oppress human beings everywhere. He therefore finds himself in an inextricable condition: suffering from a mental disease. The affected person is faced with two alternatives: either he dies or he rescues himself by accepting the function of a shaman. His vocation can mean passing through a difficult mental test as well as healing himself of his deep psychosis.

An important characteristic of the shaman is his ability to shift his level of consciousness while he is in a trance. His normal consciousness is blocked and scenes from the mythology and religion of his people appear in his subconscious. Often, when he regains consciousness, he is unable to remember what happened to him during the séance.

Just as in the vocation and the training period, so in reality is his work as shaman a repetition of his self-healing. With the aid of shamanism the collective psyche of a group of people is brought together, and they are confident they can overcome their own psychoses. It is well known that shamanism is found chiefly in subarctic regions. Ohlmarks, therefore, spoke of an arctic hysteria, a kind of psychosis which may be caused by the extraordinarily difficult geographical and climatic conditions of the subarctic regions with their long and dark winters (see also Devereux 1961; Silverman 1967). But such almost unbearable conditions in the arctic and subarctic regions, even though important, are just one aspect of the causes of shamanism. The other aspect, and doubtless the most fundamental, is the spiritual outlook found mostly among hunting cultures around the world: the belief in souls and spirits which we call animism.

Basic to our understanding of shamanism is the following view: from a very weak position the human being must try to assert himself in exceptionally inimical surroundings. When he realizes that human beings as well as things are separable into physical and spiritual components, he must try from the subordinate physical position of his body to get spiritual power beyond that of his surroundings. But the intercourse with spirits or souls is dangerous, since the food human beings eat, i.e. plants and animals, also have souls. This requires one to have special regard for every animal which one kills for food or for clothing, since every being has a soul.

Extraordinary ability and experience are needed therefore to be in contact with the spirits and souls. However, one cannot acquire these experiences directly. They are acquired through abstinence, suffering, and loneliness. The ultimate success in controlling spirits is not attained through will, but rather when high powers inflict pain on the one concerned as a sign that he has been chosen by the spirits themselves. This occurs through revelation which generally comes through dreams. Later he experiences some physical troubles which make the would-be shaman a somewhat sick person; he never becomes a simply healthy person.

The causes of some of the difficulties in life, such as sickness, death, and unsuccessful hunting, are attributed to the violation of taboos. It seems that a wretched and sick person is more able to reduce violation of taboos in his society than the normal healthy one who is more apt to violate sexual or hunting taboos. It is often reported that shamans are sick, stammering, and deformed, and are at a disadvantage because of their bad health. They are often said to be sexually abnormal or to be people with a "double sex" (Baumann, following Ehrenberg, 1955).

According to earlier reports, the origin of shamanism lies in the belief that every human being must find ways of getting out of the dangers of life (Eliade 1957: 22 ff.; Lommel 1965: 31 ff.). In early times every person was not only the conjurer of his own spirits, but also his own doctor. It is said that not until the time when famine broke out did the first Eskimo decide to travel to the mistress of animals in the sea in order to appease her so that she might again send rich booty to human beings. People wondered about this. It is said that the spirits helped the first shaman because he had previously met them alone on the outskirts of the village and made an agreement with them.

Since then shamans have been capable of talking to the spirits in jargon — a language which no one else understands. Benedict (1922) and Bogoras (1930) wrote of the importance of visions and dreams in connecting human beings, especially rising generations, with the spiritual world. It is Benedict (1923) who created the concept of the "guardian spirit." Both phenomena, visions and spirits, are not only the determining factors for the hunting cultures, but also characterize individual totems. Furthermore, they are a distinguishing mark of the shaman among whose auxiliary spirits a main or a protecting spirit plays a special role (Eliade 1957: 89 ff.). This similarity alone leads to the conclusion that there is a strong relationship between the economics of hunting people and shamanism.

Of particular interest is the experience of skeletonization of the shaman during his period of training. Gahs (1926) has already written about this. Gahs relates the shaman's experience of dismemberment to the myths portraying human sacrifice among agricultural peoples and some rituals of secret societies. After a special study of the mythology of dismemberment among agricultural peoples, Jensen (1948) worked out the "religious outlook of the early agricultural peoples." These myths are about the dismemberment of a mythical being of ancient times from whose body all useful plants were believed to have originated. It was also the same way in which death is thought to have made its first appearance in the world. This event is repeated on the occasion of human sacrifices among agricultural peoples.

It has been pointed out that the purpose of the initiation ceremonies, during which occasionally the initiates symbolically die and then, like the moon, are resurrected, is to dramatize the mythology of the moon. In Jensen's (1933) comprehensive monograph on initiation ceremonies among agrarian cultures, we learn that often the boys are made to put on maidens' dresses and are not permitted to be in men's attire until the initiation ceremonies have ended. According to other reports the initiates lose their memories while camping in the bush. After the initiation they no longer remember their previous life and must therefore learn everything from the beginning. They walk backwards; they cannot find the way to their parents' houses anymore; they hold the cutlery the wrong way and must be fed like babies. The new names which the initiates often get after the initiation ceremonies as well as the strong prohibition against their relatives calling them by the names they were given at birth, also emphasize the notions that the initiation means the loss of all memories of their previous lives as well as the extinction of their previous individuality. The initiated person becomes an entirely new person.

Let us now compare the initiation ceremony in the agrarian cultures with the experiences of a would-be Siberian shaman during his dismemberment (see Friedrich and Buddruss 1955: Eliade 1957: 77ff.; Lommel 1965: 32 ff.). The Yakutian shaman, for example, must undergo the ceremonial procedures of skeletonization for seven days. During this period he lies in his tent. His body is covered with blue welts as well as blood. It is during this period that the spirits come, and he imagines the spirits cutting off his head and placing it on the upper board of the tent. Both of his eyeballs are then removed by the spirits and placed near the head. With these eyes he observes the whole process of cutting his body into pieces: the spirits dismember his joints with iron axes and clean his bones by scraping the flesh and removing the intestines out his body. They then cut the flesh into tiny pieces and distribute them among the spirits of sickness. All must have their share because the future shaman can heal only the diseases caused by the spirits who have eaten parts of his body. Then the spirits come to rearrange the bones and place the eyeballs in their original sockets in the head. Thereupon they cover the skeleton with new flesh and transform the candidate into a new shaman.

Another report says that if the spirits eat some flesh from the shaman's leg, he will be capable of curing sicknesses affecting the leg; if they eat some of his ears, he is able to cure sicknesses of the ears; if they eat from his shoulder, he will be able to cure ailments affecting the shoulders, etc. Those young candidates unable to endure such spiritual trials usually say: "My bones and my flesh were not sufficient — that is why the spirits turned away from me."

Still different reports say that good shamans had to go through this dissection ceremony three times and the bad ones only once. The one whose flesh was not sufficient for all the spirits was not able to cure the sicknesses caused by these spirits. And still other reports say that the flesh of the shaman candidate is distributed on the different paths frequented by the spirits.

Among the Samoyeds, the shaman candidates narrate that a smith from the underworld cuts their bodies into pieces and boils the different parts in a pot till the flesh dissolves before it is given to the spirits. The smith frames the head of the shaman on an anvil while giving him instructions about how diseases are to be cured and souls to be saved. He then sews the bones together with iron wire and covers them with flesh.

In the mythology of the Buryats the spirits of deceased shamans carry the candidate into the upper world. There, they cut his body into pieces, bale him, and cover his skeleton with new flesh while giving him instructions. Quite similar is the concept of the Tungus who believe that ghosts of former shamans skeletonize the new candidate, eat his meat, and drink his blood before they cover his bones with a new cover of flesh. The Yakut-shamans believe that the bones must be counted first. In case of a missing bone, a member of his family has to die. According to some accounts, the whole family may die during the development of a great shaman. For every single bone of the shaman the spirits demand a human tribute from the members of his family.

If one compares the initiation ceremonies in agrarian cultures with the skeletonizing rituals of the shamans, one notes that the initiates of the agrarian cultures die symbolically and are reborn as new human beings. Then they have to learn the simplest work of everyday life again. They know neither parents nor relatives; rather, they behave like new-born babies. The shaman candidate, however, who is subject to this skeletonizing ceremony, does not lose any of his former abilities. In addition he obtains new and more powerful qualities. In both situations it is necessary to die in order to achieve perfection. The agrarian initiation ceremonies, however, regard death as perfection. Quite often the process of dying is dramatically demonstrated through the use of a devouring monstrous being. After that the initiate is reborn as a new person. From this very instant he becomes an adult member of his tribe with equal rights. It is believed that he is now capable of marrying and having children to contribute to the propagation of his kinship group.

The shaman candidate, on the contrary, suffers a pseudo type of death. In his skeletonized condition he is able to observe everything happening to him during the spiritual ceremony. He is not reborn, but is rather resuscitated to a new and stronger life after his bones have been joined together and covered with flesh. I put special emphasis on the difference between the agrarian conception of rebirth of a new being analogous to a new plant germinating from a seed and the hunters' conception of the revival of the original bones. There is no need for the shaman to relearn the familiar skills and capabilities of his childhood and youth; rather he acquires new and stronger powers after the skeletonizing ceremonies.

These events or imaginary experiences, which are crucial in the lives of young initiates in agrarian cultures as well as shaman candidates, were not "invented" to serve as a trial to qualify one into a new epoch of life. Neither were they calculatedly devised for the sake of having a ceremony to perform, which could easily have taken a completely different form. On the contrary, they grew from beliefs which are rooted in the emotional life of the people.

Jensen, in his review of the religious life in agrarian cultures, speaks of a central idea which makes mankind understand everything as a unity, resulting from the transient culture and the environmental conditions in which man lives. Death and procreation, the fate and rebirth of human beings, animals, and plants, all are part of the religious view in agrarian cultures.

In the same way the hunter, in his spiritual outlook, identifies himself with the most impressive experience in his world, i.e. with the animal he hunts. But there is nothing which coincides with the symbolism of plants in their life and extinction. Corresponding to the hunter's basic attitudes, the booty, especially big game and even fish, should be reincarnated. That is why hunting tribes especially honor the killed animals. Their bones are not thrown away, but are arranged together in the correct order on a scaffold. They are given a burial similar to that given to human beings, because, as my thesis (Nachtigall 1953) has shown interment on platforms or in trees is a typical form of burial among hunting peoples all over the world.

This is related to the universal belief in the heavenly land of souls. The foundation of this attitude is the belief in revival, as contrasted with rebirth, of man and animal from the skeleton stage. A number of myths indicate that this kind of reanimation could not take place because, out of carelessness or for other reasons, the bones were no longer complete; thus revival either remained incomplete or the particular man or the animal limped, or else a substitute for the missing bone had to be found. Another relevant event, which may be of some interest in this very context, is that described by Bogoras (1930). He tells of a Yukaghir shaman who had been killed twice by someone and whose bones had been scattered. Each time, the shaman revived. Not until the man had killed the shaman for the third time and had burned his bones was revival no longer possible.

To sum up, it may be stated that the idea of skeletonization of the would-be shaman and his revival by the assembling of his bones which are covered with new flesh, is analogous to that of hunting peoples' idea of revival of big game animals from their bones. During this ceremony, as we are told, the shaman candidate dies, but it is an incomplete death. He observes everything, i.e. his own dissection, and also receives instructions relevant to his later practice. His flesh is eaten by those spirits from whom he will later get his power. The original skeleton of the shaman is then provided with new flesh; he himself is given new qualities and revived in his old individuality. Thus this fundamental experience of the shaman during his development has to be associated with the spiritual concept of the hunting culture. Therefore the culture-historical origin of shamanism could be regarded as belonging to the culture-historical period of hunting peoples.

## REFERENCES

BAUMANN, H.
   1955   *Das doppelte Geschlecht*. Berlin: Reimer.
BENEDICT, R. F.
   1922   The vision in Plains culture. *American Anthropologist* 24.
   1923   *The concept of the guardian spirit in North America*. American Anthropological Association Memoirs 23.
BLEIBTREU-EHRENBERG, G.
   1970   Homosexualität und Transvestition im Schamanismus. *Anthropos* 65:189–228.
BOGORAS, W.
   1930   "The shamanistic call and the period of initiation in Northern Asia and Northern America," in *Twenty-third Congress of Americanists*, 441–444. New York.
DEVEREUX, G.
   1961   Shamans as neurotics. *American Anthropologist* 63(5):1088–1090.

ELIADE, M
1957   *Schamanismus und archaische Ekstasetechnik.* Zurich and Stuttgart: Rascher.

FRIEDRICH, A., G. BUDDRUSS
1955   *Schamanengeschichten aus Sibirien.* Munich: Otto Wilhelm Barth.

GAHS, A.
1926   "Blutige und unblutige Opfer bei den altaiischen Hirtenvölkern," in *Internationale Woche für Religionsethnologie,* 217–232. Mailand.

JENSEN, A. E.
1933   *Beschneidung und Reifezeremonien bei Naturvölkern.* Stuttgart: August Schröder.
1948   *Das religiöse Weltbild einer frühen Kultur.* Stuttgart: August Schröder.

JOCHELSON, W.
1910–1926   *The Yukaghir and the Yukaghirized Tungus.* The Jesup North Pacific Expedition 9. Leiden.

LEHTISALO, T.
1937   Der Tod und die Wiedergeburt des künftigen Schamanen. *Journal de la Société Finno-Ougrienne* 48:1–34.

LOMMEL, A.
1965   *Die Welt der frühen Jäger, Medizinmänner, Schamanen, Künstler.* Munich: Callwey.

NACHTIGALL, H.
1952   Die kulturhistorische Wurzel der Schamanenskelettierung. *Zeitschrift für Ethnologie* 77:188–197.
1953   Die erhöhte Bestattung in Nord- und Hochasien. *Anthropos* 48: 44–70.
1972   *Völkerkunde.* Stuttgart: Deutsche Verlagsanstalt.

OHLMARKS, A.
1939   *Studien zum Problem des Schamanismus.* Lund and Copenhagen.

PARK, W. Z.
1938   *Schamanism in western North America.* Chicago: Northwestern University Press.

SHIROKOGOROV, S. M.
1935   *Psychomental complex of the Tungus.* London.

SILVERMAN, J.
1967   Shamans and acute schizophrenia. *American Anthropologist* 69: 21–31.

STERNBERG, L.
1925   "Divine election in primitive religion," in *Twenty-first Congress of Americanists,* 472–512. Göteborg.

# The Role of Women in the Male Cults of the Soromaja in New Guinea

GOTTFRIED OOSTERWAL

I.   The Soromaja are a dual-organized tribe in the Upper Mamberamo area of West-Irian. They subsist upon sago, the production of which is almost exclusively a female affair. Hunting and fishing are the domain of the men, but their significance is social and embedded in myth and ritual rather than in the economy. Hunting contributes very little to the food production, except in the form of catching piglets. But the raising of these piglets is, again, the exclusive task of women. This means that in these marginal societies where food shortages are often very severe, the existence of the tribe depends on the work of the women. And because it is also the women who bear the children, not only the existence, but the very continuity of the tribe depends on them. Women are frequently referred to as "life-givers," especially when they are industrious. But the title does not stand only for prestige and high social status, it also expresses male admiration and envy.

The position of the men in these small-scale, semi-nomadic societies is rather precarious, and they know it. Often they will say: "How can we men live without the women?" Of course, they will never admit their dependent position to the women. "These women of ours think already that they are more powerful than we are." But the men's role in war and as transactors in exchange of goods does not give them enough power and prestige to balance the tremendous economic position of the women or to establish a relationship of reciprocity. Much of the group consciousness and solidarity among the men, the tensions between the male group and the female group, the envy and antagonism as well as the violence with which the men defend their secrets and their position go back to this economic weakness and dependence on

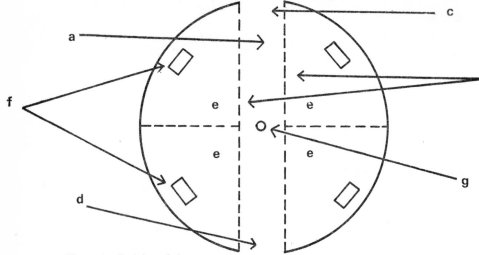

Figure 1.   Interior of the *cone*

the women. This precarious position is experienced as a threat causing anxieties and uncertainty. The religious ceremonies of the Soromaja are an attempt to counteract this threat: they are an all-male affair.

Soromaja religious life centers in the *cone*: a huge, circular culthouse with an overhanging conical roof (see Figure 1). Its interior is divided into three sections: the middle is a corridor (a) about six feet wide, which is formed by two parallel rows of posts (b). These run from the northern entrance (c) through which only men can enter to the female entrance (d) in the south end. On either side of that corridor (a space for males only) is found an open area (e) which is considered female. In every quadrant of the circular floor is a square opening (f) which serves as a fireplace. During the *cone* festivities the men dance in the corridor, whereas the four quadrants are reserved for the women. An elderly man seated at each of the posts that make up the corridor sees to it that no man steps — intentionally or unintentionally — into the space where the women are or *vice versa*. That would cause utter chaos, whereas the ceremonies, as a repetition of the mythic past, are intended to recreate the good order.

In the center of the *cone*, reaching from the top down to the bottom, hangs a long pole (g) which the Soromaja call *tome* [penis]. The *cone* festivities begin when this penis is screwed off by six or eight of the strongest men of the tribe. This is a thrilling moment. All noise and hilarity cease. It is evidently a very significant act upon which much depends. At that moment, only the screeching sound of the sacred flutes is heard as they are played in a little house standing near the *cone*.

Women and children are absolutely forbidden to be present at this occasion, or even hear the sound of the flutes. Because the *cone* very often stands in the middle of the village — an indication of its central importance to the life of the villagers — a number of men stand guard at various strategic places in and around the village to chase the women away, if necessary by brutal force. People believe that if the women hear the sound of flutes or see these first events, a great flood will suddenly destroy their village, and all the people on earth will perish. The custom is, however, that at the moment when the six or eight men are about to "screw off" the *tome*, two elderly women make their way to the *cone*. The guards react furiously. The women are chased with burning sticks out of the village and deep into the jungle where the other women and children are waiting full of "fear and trembling."

Immediately after the flutes have been stored away, and the six or eight strong men have ended their wild dancing with the "screwed off" *tome* between their legs, the other men and the women crowd into the culthouse. The fires are lit, filling the whole house with smoke. Night after night, as long as the supply of food which was prepared prior to the ceremonies lasts, the men and women dance and sing in the *cone*. They sing to the bats, the moon, the phallus, the vulva, and the many other symbols of "creative power" that are represented all over the culthouse, to do their work: to plant sago and to give the people many pigs; to give power and fertility, health and new births; to counteract the evil forces that are causing floods and earthquakes, death and disease, etc.

At a signal from the men sitting at the posts that separate the men in the corridor from the women dancing in the open spaces of the *cone*, some elderly women push themselves through the throng into the corridor. This action represents the chaos out of which good order is expected to come again. However, it is after these elderly women have been pushed out of the *cone* that the chaos reaches its climax: the normal rules and taboos regulating sexual relationships between men and women are abandoned. Any man can now invite any woman — and *vice versa* — to leave the *cone* for a "secret rendezvous." In recent years, with the great shortage of women in these societies (Oosterwal 1959: 829–838), this reenactment of the primordial chaos has been extremely strenuous for the women. For many days afterward, the women — and even some of the men — complained that they felt "rather sore," and that they (the women) were so exhausted that the ceremonies had to end prematurely because they were too tired to prepare the food in the daytime while the men slept.

Myths and songs describing the coitus of the ancestors who created the *cone* and the present order of things and whose deeds are reenacted in the *cone* rituals are the foundation and the justification of the Soro-maja's religious promiscuity. Perhaps "sacred prostitution" would be a better term here, as it is mainly the men who demand and "use" the women, whereas the role of the women is to please and to serve out of compulsion. The myths "explain" that it is because of a woman (or two women) that the chaos came about. By their rituals the men "re-create" the cosmic order and make it continue. This is accomplished by the blowing of the sacred flutes.

On a certain night, which is determined by the conjunction of the moon and the stars and the success of the men responsible for hunting and preparing the ceremonial "flute-pig," the leader of the ceremonies gives the signal that all women must leave the *cone*. This first signal is completely ignored. In fact, some of the women who, tired of dancing, sacred prostitution, and the preparing of sago for the hungry crowds, have already left the *cone*, return at this signal and crowd into the smoke-filled culthouse again. After this first signal a whole new atmosphere takes over. Everybody is aware that something very important is about to happen. A second and a third signal follow the first one. By this time, however, most of the women have indeed left the *cone*. At midnight, when the first strong men in charge of the flute ceremonies appear at the male entrance of the culthouse, holding the notched flutes in their hands, only four (or two) elderly women are still in the *cone*. Then, suddenly, the sound of the flutes is heard. They are blown first in the little house standing close to the *cone*. Later, they are ceremoniously carried around the *cone*, and blown at each of the six ceremonial fires lit outside the culthouse. The flutes are blown in pairs: a male flute and a female flute.

When the men appear again at the north entrance, after having made the full circle of the *cone* and ready to carry the flutes into the *cone*, they suddenly pretend to see the four (or two) women still dancing inside. A tremendous furor is raised. There is shouting, scolding, and screaming everywhere. Some men get a piece of burning firewood and furiously chase the women out of the culthouse. The women, with their hands covering their faces, flee from the place, pursued by a number of wildly enraged men waving sticks and burning pieces of firewood. From this moment on, the *cone* has become forever (that is, until the following *cone* festival) the possession of the men, and here the sacred flutes are blown and kept. No woman is henceforth allowed to come near the place, let alone to touch it. And when the men blow the flutes, no woman is allowed to remain in the village or its immediate neighborhood.

In contrast to the elaborate *cone* festivals, which take place irregularly and usually as a result of a severe crisis threatening the whole existence of the Soromaja tribe, a flute ceremony occurs at least once a week and often more frequently. This depends largely on the success of the men in the hunting of a "flute-pig." The elaborate flute ceremonies cannot be described fully here, but they include the ceremonial hunting of a "flute-pig," sacrificial offerings, the "feeding" of the flute, elaborate cleansing, and other personal preparations, etc.

Whereas the big *cone* festivals have tremendous social and political implications and involve many other tribes (Oosterwal 1961: 213–239), these flute ceremonies are entirely a tribal affair and are the exclusive prerogative of the men. Suffice it to mention that to the question "Why are the flutes blown?" the men always answer "But we must live," or "But we must eat." The flutes are believed to possess vital strength, fertility, and the power of growth, which is believed to be transmitted to people, animals, and plants. The flutes are blown when death and disease have struck or when the sago acreages are exhausted; they are blown when the women are out to prepare the sago or before the men go out hunting; when it has not been raining for a while or when a woman is about to give birth; and so forth. The blowing of the flutes is believed to ensure the good order of things and to guarantee the continuation of life. Neglecting to do so would cause chaos and death. The flutes, in fact, are considered "life-givers." So strong is this belief that if a man does not have a sister or a cousin to give in exchange for his wife (sister exchange is a rule by which marriages are contracted) the lineage of the bride is willing to accept a flute (i.e. its name and power) in exchange for the girl it is giving away in marriage. The same is reflected also in the ceremony of the "reviving of the spirit": at the end of the initiation ceremonies, when the boys (aged fourteen to sixteen) are considered "killed," they become alive only after their fathers have blown the flutes. Thus, the young men come to believe that the flutes are life-givers indeed, and that life, fertility, health, power, status, prestige, and the good order of things, all depend upon the men and their blowing of the flutes.

II.   The exclusion of the women from the most important religious ceremonies is characteristic of nearly all the societies of New Guinea and Melanesia as it is, indeed, of many other areas of the world. It comes as a surprise, therefore, that so very few social scientists and historians of religion have given attention to this phenomenon in a more systematic way.[1] This is all the more striking as a vast bibliography exists about the exclusively male initiation and puberty rites, male (and female) secret societies, and the sexual antagonism in New Guinea and Melanesia. (See, for example, Allen 1967, Langness 1967 and Stagl 1971). It is true that in general some of the explanations offered for the exclusion of women from the cults apply also to the male initiation ceremonies, and many of the factors that are at the root of the strong sexual antagonism in Melanesia are also basic to the exclusion of women from the cults. Yet, this latter phenomenon also clearly stands on its own. And though it is part of the whole social and economic structure, it definitely deserves more careful and systematic attention by itself. The *cone* rituals of the Soromaja may serve as a starting point and, in their own way, throw some light on this rather widespread phenomenon.

A first conclusion is that in the case of the Soromaja, the exclusion of the women from the cults is not primarily a result of a patri-clan structure, as Schlesier maintains, for all of New Guinea and Melanesia (1958: 318 ff.), or of a change from a matrilineal and uxorilocal structure to a patrilineal and virilocal one (Stagl 1971: 38, 39, 95–97).[2]

A second conclusion is that rather than being merely a form of sexual discrimination, an expression of male envy and a reflection of the existing sexual antagonism, the exclusion of women has very positive functions for both the men and the women. *It is precisely in their exclusion that the women fulfill an important role and make significant contributions to the whole order of Soromaja life and society:*

A. The flute ceremonies, like most religious ceremonies, need an "audience," which has to be impressed or convinced, which profits from them or admires, applauds, and stimulates the "transactors." In these small-scale societies where the only significant criterion of distinction and segmentation is that of sex, this role can be fulfilled only by the women. It is true that the uninitiated children are also usually kept away from the flute ceremonies, but the men did not object when

---

[1]  A notable exception is Erhard Schlesier (1958), who devoted a whole chapter to the "religious and social foundations of the exclusion of the women from the cults in Melanesia."

[2]  Due to the brevity of the description of the *cone* ceremonies and to the absence of data concerning the social and economic structure of the Soromaja, some of the conclusions may not be immediately apparent. The reader is therefore referred to more elaborate studies of these cults and societies of the Mamberamo area, such as J. van Eekhoud (1962), A. C. van der Leeden (1956), and G. Oosterwal (1961, 1967).

children heard the sound, touched the flutes, or when they peeped into the *cone* while the flutes were blown.

The Soromaja know of certain patrilineages, but these distinctions lose their significance in all matters pertaining to the whole community, such as wars, intercommunal relations, trade and exchange, and religion. The men nearly always act as one group, characterized by equality, solidarity, and a rather strongly developed group consciousness. And since the flute ceremonies are community affairs, only the women can fulfill the important role of "audience." And they do it well.

B.   As a result of the strong position of women as "life-givers," the social balance between male and female is broken. Yet, all good relations in Soromaja society — as indeed in most others — depend on "reciprocity," in which each group gives as well as receives. The exclusion of the women from the cults turns the men into givers — otherwise they are only receivers; whereas the women, who always give, here fulfill the important role of receivers. And they fulfill this role graciously, and usually voluntarily.

C.   Possession of the flutes also counterbalances the strong economic position of the women and their role as "life-givers." Believing that the flutes give them "creative power," the men used to say: "Our women can only work on the things that we have created." The flute cults thus give the men an equal status as "producers," restoring the necessary balance in society.

It cannot be denied that the men greatly envy the women for their strong position as life-givers and sustainers. And the flute cults are indeed an overt expression of male sex envy, as Bettelheim (1962) has shown for many male puberty rites. The men emphatically stated over and over again: "The flutes are life-givers." And their whole attitude and behavior attest that belief. It is in the possession of the flutes, then, that men become the equals of women in their role as life-givers: producing food and giving birth to children. In these marginal, atomistic societies, where the threat of extinction is always present, nothing contributes more to a person's power and prestige than being a "producer" of life and food. Envy and the fear of losing their important position explain the genuine anger of the men when they storm at the women who approach the sacred flutes too closely. In spite of the element of "make believe," the men's fury and excitement are very real. And the women, understanding what is at stake, play their role beautifully.

D.   "Male" and "female" are considered the representatives of the two halves of the cosmos (Oosterwal 1967). In this dualism, each of the two halves is a unit, a totality of its own, with its own specific roles and functions. The good order is maintained only when each unit fulfills its own assignments, in rigid separation from the other, thereby at the same time complementing the work of the other. Crossing or blurring the boundaries between the two halves, putting together what does not belong together or acting the role of the other will cause chaos, death, and disease. No man will touch the instruments used for the production or the preparation of sago or touch anything else considered female. The men say that the resultant "pollution" will do them great harm, and in the end even kill them. But the opposite is also true. A man's presence at the "female" sago acreages would spoil the sago and ruin the food supply. In the same way, no woman would ever dare to touch a bow and arrow, typical male attributes.

The whole of life, from the economy to dancing and singing, is thus divided into a male and a female part or sphere. The circle of houses closest to the *cone* is called *peejawoom*, the rows farthest away, *tawanawoom*. The first row of houses is where the married people live, whereas the second row is reserved for the unmarried, the uninitiated, the strangers (guests), and for women in childbirth or during their monthly retreats. The upstream section of the river is called *peejawoom* whereas the downstream part is *tawanawoom*. Therefore, the men always bathe in the upper part and the women in the lower part of the river. For the men represent the *peejawoom* half of the universe and the women the *tawanawoom*. The sky, the sun, hunting, the right hand, etc., are *peejawoom*; the earth, the moon, the sago, the left hand, etc., are *tawanawoom*. The cults reflect and validate these principles of role differentiation and identification. The flute ceremonies cannot be shared by male and female alike. This would cause disorder and destruction. "The flutes would lose their power," the men say. It is therefore in their exclusion from the cults that the women can best help to maintain their own role-identity and make their contribution to the whole of Soromaja life and society.

E.    Though the *peejawoom* and the *tawanawoom* must be kept separate, life is impossible without the cooperation of the two. Each unit needs the other and in turn complements the other. The Soromaja say: "As a child needs both a father and a mother, so we exist by the cooperation between *peejawoom* and *tawanawoom*." The separation and cooperation, conflict and complementarity, with the unavoidable tensions between the two, are reflected in nearly every aspect of the Soromaja's life: in the economy, at meals, in the upbringing of the children, in personal contacts; in kinship and marriage, in dancing and feasting; in childbirth, initiation, and even at death. But, again, it is in religion and myth and especially in the rituals connected with the *cone*, that this conflict and cooperation, separation and complementarity, most clearly come to the fore, and that this dualism finds its foundation and justification: the *cone* has a male and a female entrance; the different parts of the building are either male or female, and so are the symbols in the *cone*. In their cooperation they produce the result the Soromaja hope for.

There are male flutes and female flutes. When they are blown, the men stand in two rows opposite each other. One row of men holds the female flutes; the opposite row their male counterparts. The female flutes are blown first, then the male. The men holding the male flutes are very strong and muscular. They have to "outblow" the female flutes (the conflict). But, neither the male nor the female flutes can produce the melody independently. Only in the cooperation of the two is a melody born that will give life and fertility to the community.

The whole *cone* festival expresses this conflict and cooperation between male and female. And they complement each other only when each fulfills its own assigned role. The men begin to sing that it was Adjaw, a male culture-hero, who "in the beginning created the rivers and fishes, the birds and the trees." It was Adjaw who created man and who gave him pigs and tobacco and who built the first *cone*. After he finished his "work of creation," so the songs continue, Adjaw wanted to have intercourse with his wife, Jowesso. But she refused. At that moment, the women dancing and singing in their part of the *cone*, begin to shout that it was Jowesso who gave the rain, the sago, and the fruits, and who built the first *cone*. Now a real contest begins, in dance and in song, about who built the first *cone* and gave it to mankind; for that ultimately determines the status and the power among the Soromaja.

The conflict is "settled" when the flutes are brought into the *cone* and the last women are often literally thrown out of the culthouse. But this happens only after the chaos has reached its climax. At first, some of the elderly women push themselves into the corridor where the men are dancing. Now the men, imitating Adjaw, urge the women in song and dance and by symbolic signs to have intercourse with them. But, like Jowesso the women first refuse. However, life can continue only if both halves of the cosmos cooperate. And, the women now willingly do so. Nearly all the taboos regulating sexual behavior are cast aside. This is the chaos out of which life and the good order will be born again. Not only the women sense this "sacred prostitution" as a chaos; the men do as well. They experience it as contamination and pollution, a weakening of and a threat to their virility. Order is restored when the last women have been chased out of the village and the flutes have been blown in the *cone*.

F.   It is noteworthy that nearly all the myths tell that the *cone* originally belonged to the women, and that two women (often two sisters; sometimes also a mother and her daughter) discovered the power of the flutes. At that time, these myths tell us, the men were excluded from the rituals. Then, the men put up a real fight, and with the help of supernatural power they stole the flutes and by force took the *cone*. From that time on the women have been excluded from the cults.

These myths are known all over New Guinea and the Melanesian island world. But rather than being merely a "fancy" explanation of present conditions (etiological myth), these myths, it seems, express historical truths and are of great psychological significance. The role of the Soromaja women in today's cults seems closely related to these controversies in the existential relations between the sexes, rather than being merely the result of a more or less accidental historical development.

The age when women were the owners of the *cone* was the age of chaos: everything was just the opposite of what is considered good and normal and holy today. According to these myths, men and women could not even have normal sexual intercourse, and sago and pigs were rare or did not yet exist. Often, these myths speak about a tyrannical giant with a long penis who made life miserable. Only when two men "screwed off" the tyrant's penis and took over the *cone* did life become normal as it is today.

It seems that attributing the discovery of the *cone* and the flutes to the women, who are now excluded from it, makes the women rather content with their particular role in the ceremonies. To the men it asserts that, as the women invented the flutes, they now can truly fulfill the role which nature has assigned to women: the giving of life. At the same time, giving women the honor of having discovered the flutes relieves the men of the guilt feeling for the exclusion of women from the cults. These myths, indeed, mean a great "psychological liberation."

G.   Finally, the exclusion of the women has the very important function of making the cults secret. And secrecy is always a very significant aspect of the cultic life. It contributes to making the ceremonies more important.

The women themselves play their role of pretended ignorance marvellously. For it is indeed a "pretended ignorance." They know the secrets, the myths, and the supposed power of the flutes. It is simply impossible to keep that a secret. Yet, the women show real fear. Their actions show how dependent they are upon the creative activities of the men and how helpless in the face of exclusive male control of the flutes, with their dominant powers in society. It is the women who through their exclusion, fulfill the role of the true believers and who thereby make the rituals real. In acting out their role, the women convince the men of the great importance and the truth of the men's role: the power to create new life, to make the sago grow and the good order continue. There is ample evidence that when the women no longer act their role, or when they publicly announce their knowledge of the secret, the religious ceremonies disintegrate and even disappear, and with them the whole fabric of society. The role of women in the male cults of the Soromaja is clearly important and positive.

## REFERENCES

ALLEN, M. R.
  1967   *Male cults and secret initiations in Melanesia.* Melbourne: University Press.
BETTELHEIM, B.
  1962   *Symbolic wounds.* New York: Collier.
COHEN, Y.
  1964   *The transition from childhood to adolescencce: cross-cultural studies of initiation ceremonies, legal systems and incest taboos.* Chicago: Aldine.
LANGNESS, L. L.
  1967   Sexual antagonism in the New Guinea highlands: a *bena-bena* example. *Oceania* 37:161–177.
MEGGITT, M. J.
  1964   Male-female relationships in the highlands of Australian New Guinea. *American Anthropologist* (special publication) 66:204–224.
MURPHY, R.
  1959   Social structure and sex antagonism. *Southwestern Journal of Anthropology* 15.
OOSTERWAL, G.
  1959   The position of the bachelor in the Upper-Tor Territory. *American Anthropologist* 61:829–838.
  1961   *People of the Tor.* Assen: Van Gorkum.
  1967   "Muremarew: a dual-organized village on the Mamberamo," in *Villages in Indonesia.* Edited by Koentjaraningrat, 157–188. Ithaca: Cornell University Press.
REIK, T.
  1946   *Ritual: four psychoanalytic studies.* New York: Grove.

SCHLESIER, ERHARD
1958    *Die Melanesischen Geheimkulte.* Göttingen: Musterschmidt.
STAGL, J.
1971    *Der Geschlechtsantagonismus in Melanesien.* Acta Ethnologica et Linguistica 22; Oceania 4. Vienna: Institut für Völkerkunde.
STRATHERN, M.
1972    *Women in between: female roles in a male world; Mt. Hagen, New Guinea.* New York: Seminar Press.
VAN DER LEEDEN, A. C.
1956    *Hoofdtrekken der sociale struktuur in het westelijk binnenland van Sarmi.* Leyden: Ydo.
VAN EEKHOUD, J.
1962    *Ethnografie van de Kaowerawedj.* The Hague: M. Nijhoff.
WHITING, J. W. M., *et al.*
1958    "The function of male initiation ceremonies at puberty," in *Readings in social psychology.* Edited by E. E. Maccoby, T. M. Newcomb, and E. L. Hartley. New York: Holt, Rinehart and Winston.
YOUNG, F. W.
1962    The function of male initiation ceremonies. *American Journal of Sociology* 67:379–396.

# Certain Aspects of the Study of
# Siberian Shamanism

L. P. POTAPOV

Siberian shamanism is a subject in which ethnographers have long evinced an unflagging interest. For two and one-half centuries it has engaged the attention of Russian researchers in particular. The accounts of early travelers who observed it initially out of sheer curiosity gave rise to an interest that persisted right up to the 1917 October Revolution and led to efforts to describe and explain shamanism as a distinct feature of the culture and life of the Siberian peoples. A great deal of concrete material was collected about it. This was summarized in various publications, arranged in collections by local and central museums, and made the subject of special monographs devoted to Siberian shamanism in general and the various forms shamanism took among different Siberian peoples (Mikhajlovskij 1890; Harva 1938; Ohlmarks 1939; Bouteiller 1950; Findeisen 1957; Eliade 1951, 1957; Banzarov 1896; Troshchanskij 1902; Shirokogorov 1919; Anokhin 1924). In the Soviet period, interest in the problem of shamanism has grown keener and deeper. The study of Siberian shamanism has branched out into a number of new lines. Concrete material already at hand has been subjected to analysis while the search for new material has continued. Siberian shamanism has been examined from a theoretical angle to develop a scientific definition of shamanism that would fit into the general framework of the history of religion, while at the same time taking note of its distinctive features. Another aspect under consideration is the genesis of shamanism: the time, locale, and causes of its appearance; its stages of development; and the development of a historical classification of Siberian shamanism in its various stages.

Further study of shamanism, with emphasis on its specific features, will make it possible to establish an ethnographic classification of Siberian shamanism. This aspect can be linked with others: the evaluation of shamanism as an element of the culture and life of a given Siberian people; its place and importance in the people's life; the social role of shamans and their position in society; and their influence on social and home life.

There are many possible approaches to the subject, but there is great value in studying the source materials and making a comparative study of separate elements of shamanism. Many conclusions may thus be drawn concerning the origin, ethnic history, cultural history, and even general history of various Siberian peoples. There are many indications of ethnocultural and ethnogenetic ties between the peoples of Siberia and other peoples now living far beyond the confines of Siberia.

Although a great many attempts have been made to formulate a scientific definition of Siberian shamanism, to describe its essential features, explain its origins, and so forth, not one of them can be considered more than conjectural. Whether Siberian shamanism represents a distinct religion is still an open question. Some researchers do not consider shamanism a religion at all; others regard it as a special kind of religion found exclusively in Siberia and northern Asia. (Among those who do not regard shamanism as a religion are: Eliade 1951; Roux 1962: 8; Grebner 1924; Ohlmarks 1939.) Still others see in shamanism a universal religion which existed in one form or another among all peoples (Tokarev 1964). There is also a hypothesis that shamanism represents a definite stage in the evolution of religion (Bogoraz 1910; Mikhajlovskij 1890). Yet no exact criteria on which to base an interpretation of Siberian shamanism as a religion have been accepted.

The same lack of agreement characterizes the literature on the question of the factors that gave rise to shamanism and the time of its emergence. It is not clear, for instance, whether shamanism spread from a single center or sprang up in different regions.

The most common view is that there is a connection between the appearance of shamanism and the healing role performed by the shamans, themselves almost psychopathic individuals. The philosophical basis of shamanism is accordingly derived from the notion that illness is caused either by an evil spirit entering the body of the sick man, or his soul departing from his body. The idea of an evil spirit entering the body was deduced from the observation of pregnant women (Zelenin 1936), but this explanation is not very convincing or valid.

Nor do matters appear any clearer with respect to the initial appearance, or dating, of shamanism. A number of researchers proceed from a global chronology of stages, based on the socioeconomic periodization of society. Some relate "early" shamanism to the primitive communal system in general, and "later" shamanism (Siberian shamanism in the nineteenth and twentieth centuries) to the religions of class society (Zelenin 1936). Others place the appearance of shamanism in the middle of the period of barbarism and spread its existence over the whole era of the clan system (Tokarev 1964).

The study of shamanism consists primarily of the examination of the shaman's cult and paraphernalia, specifically, his garb, drum, symbolic objects, and other items used in the administration of his cult and the types of performance, plus the explanation of their functions, symbolism, and the semantics of their terminology. Nor are the shaman's ideas about nature and man, his dogmas, canons and taboos to be overlooked. In that connection it is appropriate to delve somewhat deeper, on the basis of my own experience, into the study of source material.

The most significant point relates to the detailed study of the shaman's drum — its type, construction, functions, symbolism, design, and various parts. Particularly important are the names of the drums and their parts, for the semantics of such names contain valuable hints as to origins.

At the close of the 1920's I personally studied the drums with the help of shamans still active among various peoples of southern Siberia, and noticed a number of very curious things (Potapov and Menges 1934). It had long been known that the shaman's drum was called either by the Mongolian name *tuur* (*tungur*) or *chalu*, the Turkic name. However, it appeared that in addition to the generic name, the drum was also referred to by different names during the shaman's séances. What is more, these other names often differed even among kindred tribes and peoples.

The explanation offered was that during the séance, the drum was supposed to symbolize the shaman's mount on which he made his trips to the spirits, and so he gave his drum a more concrete and suitable name. How did he choose the name? From my observations that the drum symbolized the animal whose hide was drawn over it (this is confirmed by the ceremony of the "animation" of a new drum as the "animation" of the animal whose hide was used), I expected that the name of that animal would serve as the symbolic name of the drum (Potapov 1947). Among all the ethnic Altai groups, the skin of the elk or reindeer bull, the Siberian stag, or the roebuck was most often used for the drum. Exceptions to this general practice rarely occurred.

Surprisingly, however, it was discovered that the symbolic names by which the shamans referred to their drums bore no relation at all to the names of the above animals, even though the shamans insisted that they were "riding" those very animals. The names designated for the drum among the various peoples were recorded as follows (Potapov 1970): Teleuts — *ak adan* and *ak chagal*; Shortsi — *gegri-adan* and *chagal*; Chelkantsi — *ak adan, yer bodan, yer pagych* (*pagys*); Kumandintsi — *ak adan*; Tubalars — *ak adan*; Telengites — *ak adan*.

What was even more surprising was the fact that the shamans uttering these symbolic names could not explain them. They could not say why drums made of the hides of elks or Siberian stags and "animated" as these animals were designated by other names which bore no relation whatever to the usual names for those animals.

The answer emerged later, after a comparative study was made of the names that were most interesting. It was learned, for instance, that the most widespread name, *adan*, was what the southern Altaians, Touvinians, Kirghiz, and other peoples commonly called the double-humped, gelded camel on which they rode. *Gegri-adan* means a single-humped camel, while *yer bodan* refers to the colt of the camel, a term still used by the Touvinians and Kirghiz. Eventually deciphered also was the word *ak chagal* (sacred *chagal*): that is what the Uighurs, Yakuts, and Mongols call the dappled horse with black and red spots on its head and chest. *Chagal* is not the generic word for horse; it applies only to this kind of dappled horse. Finally, the term *yer pagych* (*pagys*) was deciphered as elk bull. As applied to the elk, the term, altered to *bagysh*, survives among the Kirghiz of Soviet Central Asia, where it has been preserved in the nomenclature of the large clan and tribal groups of the Kirghiz (*sari bagysh, chon bagysh*), although there are no elks in Kirghizia. On the other hand, the elk is regularly hunted in northern Altai, especially by the Chelkantsi and Shortsi. Yet its ancient name has gone out of daily use, probably because of the great ethnic merging of northern Altaians with all kinds of newcomers. It has survived only in the religious terminology of the Chelkantsi, a sort of linguistic relic whose meaning has been forgotten, even by the shamans.

Consequently, all the symbolic names of drums listed above can be explained as the names of the domesticated animals on which the shamans rode, but not as the names of the wild animals whose hides were drawn over the drums. The only exception is the Chelkantsi word for elk; for these people did use elk skin to make drums. The symbolic naming of the drum as the shaman's untamed mount (the Siberian stag *Cervus elaphus xanthopygus*, and so on) was practiced among the Touvinians, Khakass, and Tofalars (Karagas).

One may ask: what is the epistemological significance of this material? The fact that in their ceremonies the Shortsi, Chelkantsi, Kumandintsi, and Tubalars, those ancient hunters on foot and dwellers of the mountain taiga, spoke of the drum as *ak adan* [camel mount] shows that there were steppe or (depending on where they lived) alpine and steppe elements familiar with camel breeding in their ethnic composition, for there were no camels in the taiga. As the culture and domestic habits of the newcomers were assimilated and spread in the ethnic milieu of the aboriginal hunters of the alpine taiga, their traditional notions about the shaman's drum gained currency, only to lose their original meaning with time under the influence of both the shaman's teachings and the changed economic and natural conditions.

Thus, the symbolism of the shaman's drum, expressed in the animation of the local wild animal whose hide was used, proved to be contaminated with imported ideas of the drum as a camel mount. The drum was traditionally referred to as *adan* during the séance, although the real meaning of the word, camel mount, had been forgotten, obliterated by time. The newcomers to the northern Altai were the Teleuts, as attested by either written historical records, linguistic data or abundant additional ethnographic material. They came here under the press of political events from the Irtysh steppes, where they were breeding camels as late as the first half of the eighteenth century (Potapov 1969).

Among the modern Teleuts, other evidences of camel worship persist. The patron or "master of the drum" of the Teleut shaman was *Ak-Tailak* [the sacred young camel], a calf two or three years old. That corresponds to the custom of some Kirghiz shamans (*bakshi*) to take the young camel, *Ak-Tailak*, as their guardian spirit. Other Kirghiz *bakshi* made Buura their guardian spirit, visualizing him as a camel with "feet of ice." The Altai shamans had an analogous spirit called "cloudy-eyed Pura-Khan with feet of ice." The remarkable similarity of these shamanistic elements cannot be anything but a reflection of the ancient ethnogenetic ties of the Altaians and Kirghiz, today substantiated by a wealth of other material (Abramzon 1971).

We need hardly point out what a valuable ethnogenetic signal is present in the Chelkantsi's symbolic name for the drum, *yer pakych* (*pagys*), which bears directly on the ethnic history of the Turkic-speaking peoples of Altai and the Kirghiz of Central Asia. The term *chagal* is singularly revealing. Its analysis discloses a whole realm of time-rooted ethnogenetic ties between the peoples of Siberia, Central Asia, and eastern Turkestan, and helps us to elucidate the ethnic composition and origins of a number of Turkic-speaking peoples, among them the Yakuts, Altaians, and Uighurs. It is also interesting as a reflection of the ancient custom of the Turkic nomads to call their mounts by the color of their hides, a vivid illustration of which can be found in their heroic epics.

The term *chagal* and similar symbolic names for the drum were used not by isolated shamans, but by all the shamans of the given ethnic group, whether Teleuts, Shortsi, or others. We meet this word among the modern Yakuts, not in its ritualistic sense, but rather as an echo of the historic past. Soviet specialists in hippology have proved the Central Asian origin of the modern Yakut horse, which reached far north thanks to the migrations of cattle breeders who were the historical ancestors of the Yakuts (Lapping 1937). As proof we might mention that the dappled Yakut horse is called *tsagyl-jagyl*, meaning "horse with large brown spots on its crest and withers", by the Yakuts, *jagal* by the Mongols.

Dappled horses were indeed bred in the early Middle Ages by the nomads of the eastern part of Central Asia, including one of the groups of the historical ancestors of the Yakuts, referred to in the written Chinese sources as the *Kulikang* and in the Turkic runic texts as *kurykan*.

Since *chagal* is a Uighur word which came into north Altaian shamanistic usage via the Telengit-Teleuts, its presence in the local shamanistic lexicon attests to Uighur, Teleut, and Yakut ethnogenetic ties. The ancestors of the Telengit (Telengit-Teleuts) belonged to the confederation of Tele tribes headed by the Uighurs during the Turkic khanates of the sixth to eighth centuries.

In that remote historical period the symbolic name of the drum, *chagal*, was based on reality, for the dappled horse was indeed bred and its hide indeed drawn over the drum. It is an interesting detail that the Teleuts who brought the name *chagal* with them to the Altai permitted raw horsehide to be used for the shaman's drum; in this they differed from the other Altai tribes.

The etymology of the word *chagal* [dappled or spotted horse] evokes an association with another Turkic-speaking people or tribe of early medieval nomads called the *Ala-at* (or, in the Chinese sources, the *Po-ma*) meaning "dappled-horse breeders". The historical connection between the dappled-horse breeders and the ancient Hsienpi-Koochü ethnic milieu[1] has already been pointed out. During the Turkic khanates, the dappled-horse breeders lived in Sayan-Altai under the rule of the Uighurs (Potapov 1970: 92). The historical and ethnographical layers in which the drum's symbolic name of *chagal* is imbedded go very deep.

Material of no less scientific importance can be found in the shamanism of the other Siberian peoples. The following was ascertained in a certain Yakut group: the drum, which is also regarded there as the shaman's mount, was symbolically called *Kulan-at* or "wild horse" (*Equus hemionus*) (Okladnikov 1955: 230). The fact that the name of that wild inhabitant of the Central Asian steppes served as the symbol of the drum attests once more to the southern origins of the Yakuts. In that connection it is well to remember that some Central Asian nomads sporadically tamed and rode the wild horse even in remote antiquity (at the time of the Huns, for instance).

Yakut and Sayan-Altai ethnogenetic ties are reflected in other ways. The iron cross piece by which the Yakut drum is held is called *baryk*; the vertical handle on the inside of the Altai drum is known as the *bars* or *mars*. Under the hide of the Yakut drum, along the rim, there are little protuberances called "horns," which strongly resembled the crossbands on the antlers of the *teke* [mountain goat] or the *arkhar* [mountain ram]. Among the southern Altaians such horns on the rim of the tambourine are simply called *arkhars*. The Touvinians carved a likeness of the wild mountain goat (*te*) on the vertical handle of the drum. The shamans called it their personal mount, *Te-holge*; that is, the kind of horse that on the death of his master was buried with him.

The great antiquity of the historical and ethnocultural ties of the Yakuts, and particularly the Uighurs, is borne out in the Yakut word for shaman — *oiyun*. Among the Uighurs of eastern Turkestan, the Kirghiz of Central Asia and the Khorezm Uzbeks, the same word

---

[1]   In the fourth century, the Tele tribes were designated in the Chinese sources as "Koochü."

designates the shaman's séance (Troshchanskij 1902; Ol'denburg 1918; Snesarev 1969: 48; Bajalieva 1972: 147). Not considered here is the interesting and often amazing material on south Siberian shamanism, including the material bearing on the shaman's drum which testifies to ancient historical contacts and even ethnogenetic bonds between the remote ancestors of the Turkic-speaking peoples of Sayan-Altai and such distant peoples as the Saami (Lopari), the Samodiytsi (Selkups and others), the Mongols and so forth (Klements 1890; Manker 1938; Emsheimer 1948; Dioszegi 1963). It is noteworthy that similar relations can be discerned among the above-mentioned peoples with regard to certain of their ritualistic foods and dishes used in the shaman's ceremonies, or the ritualistic wedding clothes they use, or their material culture. All this heightens the importance and authenticity of the new type of source material presented here.

## REFERENCES

ABRAMZON, S. M.
  1971  *Kirgizy i ikh etnogeneticheskie i istoriko-kul'turnye svjazi* [The Kirghiz and their ethnogenetic and historical-cultural ties]. Leningrad.
ANOKHIN, A. V.
  1924  *Materialy po shamanstvu u altajtsev* [Materials on shamanism among the Altaians]. Petrograd.
BANZAROV, D.
  1896  *Chëhnaja vera ili shamanstvo u mongolov* [Black magic or shamanism among the Mongols]. St. Petersburg.
BAJALIEVA, T. D.
  1972  *Doislamskie verovanija i ikh perezhitki u Kirgizov* [Pre-Islamic beliefs and their survivals among the Kirghiz]. Frunze.
BOGORAZ, V. G.
  1910  K psikhologii shamanstva u narodov Severo-Vostochnoj Azii [On the psychology of shamanism among the peoples of Northeast Asia].*Etnograficheskoe Obozrenie* 1, 2.
BOUTEILLER, M.
  1950  *Chamanisme et guérison magique*. Paris.
DIOSZEGI, V.
  1963  Denkmäler der Samojedischen Kultur im Schamanismus ostsajanischen Völker. *Acta Ethnographica* 12. Budapest.
ELIADE, MIRCEA
  1951  *Le Chamanisme et les techniques archaïques de l'extase*. Paris.
  1957  *Schamanismus und archaische Ekstasentechnik*. Zürich-Stuttgart.
EMSHEIMER, E.
  1948  Eine Sibirische Parallele zur lappischen Zaubertrommel. *Ethnos*

FINDEISEN, H.
 1957  *Schamanentum*. Stuttgart.

GREBNER, F.
 1924  *Das Weltbild der Primitiven*. Munich.

HARVA
 1938  *Die religiösen Vorstellungen der altaischen Völker*. Helsinki.

KLEMENTS, D. A.
 1890  Neskol'ko obraztsov bubnov minusinskikh inorodtsev [A few models of the drums of the non-Russian natives of Minusinsk]. *Zapiski Vostochno-Sibirskogo Otdelenija Russkogo Geograficheskogo Obshchestva* 2, vyp. 2.

LAPPING, V. D.
 1937  Jakutskaja loshad [The Yakut horse]. *Konevodstvo* 6.

MANKER, E.
 1938  *Die lappische Zaubertrommel*. Stockholm.

MIKHAJLOVSKIJ, V.
 1890  *Shamanstvo* [Shamanism] 1. Moscow.

OHLMARKS, AKO
 1939  *Studien zum Problem des Schamanismus*. Lund and Copenhagen.

OKLADNIKOV, A. P.
 1955  *Istorija Jakutskoj ASSR* [History of the Yakut ASSR] 1. Moscow, Leningrad.

OL'DENBURG, S.
 1918  Kratkie zametki o peri-khonakh i duakhonakh v Kuchare [Brief observation cn the *peri-khon* and *duakhon* in Kuchara]. *Sbornik MAE* 5, vyp. 1. Petrograd.

POTAPOV, L. P.
 1947  Obrjad ozhivlenija chamanskogo bubna u tjurkojazychnykh plemën Altaja [The ritual of animating the shaman's drum among the Turkic-speaking tribes of the Altai]. *Trudy Instituta Etnografii AN SSSR. Uovaja serija*. 1. Leningrad.
 1969  *Etnicheskij sostav i proiskhozhdenie altajtsev* [The ethnic composition and origin of the Altaians]. Leningrad.
 1970  K semantike nazvanij shamanskikh bubnov u narodnostej Altaja [On the semantics of the names of shaman drums among the Altai nationalities]. *Sovetskaja Tjurkologija* 3.

POTAPOV, L. P., MENGES
 1934  *Die Herstellung der Samanentrommel bei den Sor*. Mitteilungen des Seminars für Orientalische Sprachen zu Berlin.

ROUX, JEAN-PAUL
 1962  *Revue de l'histoire des religions*. Paris.

SHIROKOGOROV, S.
 1919  *Opyt izuchenija shamanstva u tungusov* [An attempted study of shamanism among the Tungus]. Vladivostok.

SNESAREV, G. P.
 1969  *Relikty domusul'manskikh obriadov i verovanij u uzbekov Khorezma* [Relics of pre-Islamic rituals and beliefs among the Khorezm Uzbeks]. Moscow.

TOKAREV, S. A.
1964   *Rannie formy religii i ikh razvitie* [Early forms of religion and their development]. Moscow.

TROSHCHANSKIJ, V.
1902   *Evolljutsija chërnoj very u jakutov* [The evolution of black magic among the Yakuts]. Kazan.

ZELENIN, D. K.
1936   Ideologija sibirskogo shamanstva [The ideology of Siberian shamanism]. *Izvestija AN SSSR. Otdelenie Obshchestvennykh Nauk.* Moscow, Leningrad.

# Learning of Psychodynamics, History, and Diagnosis Management Therapy by a Kali Cult Indigenous Healer in Guiana

PHILIP SINGER, ENRIQUE ARANETA, and JAMSIE NAIDOO

## THE EDUCATION OF THE HEALER

The "education" was a process of interaction among three men, during which it was often not clear who was the psychiatrist, who was the healer-informant, and who was the anthropologist. Indeed, the healer has now visited the United States four times as a result of the anthropologist's and psychiatrist's initiatives. In 1970 and 1973 he came as a visiting lecturer to the anthropologist's university. In 1969 he was invited to participate in an Agency for International Development conference in Wisconsin on the problem of gaining cultural acceptance for unconventional high-protein foods. In 1967 he spoke before the American Academy of Psychotherapy on religious healing.

By now, the role of anthropologist and informant, psychiatrist and healer, are so blurred that one may justifiably ask "Who is the anthropologist, and who is the informant?" This in turn raises serious questions about the nature not only of anthropological ethical behavior "in the field" (where is that?) but of medical ethics as well. But these questions will have to be dealt with in another place.

Cooperation between the Mental Hospital in Guiana and the East Indian Kali healers, most notably Jamsie Naidoo, began in 1963, when the anthropologist lived at a Kali temple located about fifteen miles from the Mental Hospital. The psychiatrist-director of the Mental Hospital, or "The Mental" as it is locally known, was Dr. D. Panday, himself a Guianese of East Indian origin and trained in London's Maudsley Hospital. He was succeeded as director in 1964 by Dr. Araneta. During the years 1963-1966, until Dr. Araneta left, a great deal of cooperation developed between the anthropologist, healer, and psychiatrist.

In 1963, all diagnoses, as far as the healer was concerned, were "working" diagnoses, involving reality problems and treatment. The diagnostician-healer is very concerned with the motivation of the patient and his sincerity in coming for treatment. Little or no attention is paid to the differential subtleties of diagnosis as regards the patient's behavior. This is because outside of motivation, PROGNOSIS does not depend upon diagnostic shadings in Kali work, which is basically concerned with functional-emotional disorders. These differentiating symptoms are the equivalent of scientific detail for the Western psychiatrist. For the Kali healer it was foolishness because he already knew, as a member of the culture, what could go wrong with persons in the culture.

The Goddess Kali, or the Divine Mother, is believed to have originated among the pre-Aryan Dravidians as they changed from food gatherers to cultivators. All growing things were regarded as representing the female principle, and the earth mother gradually became the Mother Goddess.

Psychologically, Freudian-oriented psychiatrists believe Kali represents a derivative of an infantile, ambivalent image of the mother, that her grotesque endowments are the expressions of aggressive feelings derived from anal, urethral, and phallic phases of psychosexual development, and that the gnashing teeth, protruding tongue, and blood coursing down the cheeks relate to cannibalistic wishes of the child to the mother figure. Further, the blackness of the skin is an overall "investment" of the mother figure with cruelty and ill-feelings. These are derivatives of the anal-sadistic phase of development, etc.

The Kali healer-pujari's explanation is as follows:

He holding head because when de country was all shake up, de *rakshasa* come, he cut off de neck. [There is no consistent gender in local patois.] That show he destroy all the evil people. At that time he show no sympathy for anybody at all. He have four hand to show you are a man, you have two hand, so he have four, double amount you strenth. One hand hold cutlass, one holds *tirsul* [trident] one holds head, one holds *udkay* [drum]. When he wants to enjoy, he plays drum. When he stick out tongue, he have power to kill.

Diagnostic categories were always related to specific, stereotyped dreams. This type of stereotype is similar to the symbolism of the orthodox analyst. The ability to produce a particular dream for a particular therapist is also a common phenomenon in Western psychiatry, although not interpreted as such.

The diagnosis bears the name of two major dreams:

1. Kateri. (This is the Madras name. The Hindu name is Churyl.) The Kateri may be a man or a woman and is associated with negative aspects of sexuality. A pregnant woman often has a particular dream, followed by spontaneous abortion. Sometimes the Kateri "can take a man shape" which "dreams her." When the Kateri "interferes" with a man, there are usually sexual problems, including impotence.

2. Dreaming Dutchman. (This is more common among men.) Here the assumption is that the individual has rested or napped in a spot where a Dutchman was buried, or where he buried his wealth after the British defeated the Dutch. The healer says:

The Dutchman hold you because you don't give anything, not even a little rum. Den you get fever. Go to doctah. Doctah do injection, medicine, tablets etc. De Doctah say he can's manage, "me no find you complaint." Neighbors tell go see priest. Me go devote de mudder. Me ask: Can you remember where this bai go shot or where go walk and so on: Whilst me talk, Dutchman come and start to play pon de bai. Den me put some *babut* [sacred ash] on he forehead and me telle he what work he got to do.

The healer's therapy, which basically has not changed over the years, consists of having the patient come to temple, or church, for a designated number of Sundays. This is because everyone, including the healer, works six days a week in the sugar fields, and Sunday is the free day.

In brief, although there are different kinds of "work" to be performed, all have the following elements. Preparations by the patient-devotee before going to church. This includes abstaining for three days before Sunday, from all "rank," i.e. rum, fish, meat, and sex. Clean "garments," (and sometimes new ones depending on the case) are also required, along with new cooking utensils. The patient will also bring *prasad* [food that will be blessed and offered to the deities (*deotors*)]. This includes sweets and all varieties of fruits. Sometimes sacrificial animals (ram-goat, fowl-cock) are offered (for a fuller description of the therapy, see Singer, et al. 1967: 103–113).

The most significant innovation over the years has been the most recent one (1973) introduced by the healer, which is that the patient-devotee may now speak DIRECTLY to Kali Mai (Mother Kali) herself ("played" in trance by a healer) IN ENGLISH; formerly it was necessary to have a translator who would speak the sacred language (a South Indian dialect "Gouri") and "interpret" to the patient from the Kali trance-healer-diagnostician and back again. Jamsie Naidoo justifies this innovation on the grounds that people want to know directly, and in English, what is being said to them, without the need of an "interpret."

However, over the years of contact with the psychiatrist, the healer observed that the psychiatrist would always ask the patient, "What will you do when you get better?" Initially, there was resistance to asking or answering this question. Patients would interpret it as meaning, "What are you going to give me in return for my making you better?" They would reply, "Doctah, me nah got nothing. You like fowl, you like sheep, fish? Me nah got no money." The healer eventually put the question in the following form: "Doctah want to know, what you going to do to make youself happy. What kind of work you like to do?" Of equa! importance was not only the "translation" of the question, but the fact that it came from the healer and not the doctor. Sick people are all too used to doctors demanding fees before service.

After the healer finally learned the importance of the question in relation to the concept of motivation, that, for example, a patient might not want to get well because of the attention the sick role was providing him, he incorporated it into his own therapy. This awareness has resulted in his insistence that Kali work be consciously FAMILY-oriented, instead of just culturally family-oriented, which it largely was. Today the healer tells his patients, "You cannot get well unless you live good with each other."

An example of the healer's growing awareness of behavior is seen in the case of a fifty-six-year-old widow who practiced money-lending. She was postmenopausal and suffered from headaches (head-a-swing, head-worry), insomnia, general weakness, and depression. The healer recommended electric shock (after having seen its effect in cases of depression in many instances) saying:

I don't think she can get well because she wants love and nobody loves her. She has too much money but she will not help any relatives. That's why you must take money. Give electricity, she will feel a little better and if she feels better, she might get some friends. This person loves money more than people.

After five treatments of electroconvulsive therapy [ECT], the woman's depression lifted, although she had continued spells of severe depression. The healer's comment was that "she doesn't want to live again, because she doesn't want to give up money."

*Dream Work*

The healer has also increased his understanding of dreams and has enlarged his dream repertoire beyond that already discussed. Although he would always ask the patient about his dreams and expect one of the standard replies, he noticed that the psychiatrist would sometimes ask in cases of patients with repressed hostility: "Do you dream as though a lot of people are fighting each other, or meeting accidents?" This would often result in the patient describing dreams of those sorts.

In anxiety cases, the psychiatrist would ask whether the individual had "running" dreams, or "falling from heights," or "being late for the work bus." There would usually be positive responses with personal detail.

The healer, after observing this for some weeks, asked the psychiatrist why he would ask for such dreams instead of the Kateri or Dutchman dreams. It was explained to him, with many examples, that many persons have a great deal of anger which they are not able to express openly. Some familiar examples would be a young man complaining of headaches who was facing the prospect of an arranged marriage he did not want. Now, when the healer asks for dreams and does not receive the usual cultural response or is told that the person did not dream at all, he probes for hostility and anxiety dreams involving falling and violence. Dreams of violence have been integrated with the Dutchman dream, requiring Dutchman work (therapy). Retroflexed rage dreams are also incorporated into the Dutchman diagnosis.

*Electroconvulsive Therapy [ECT]*

Although the healer had witnessed many cases of ECT successfully applied to cases of depression, he did not make it part of his own therapeutic, recommended armamentarium until he was personally involved in a special case. A twenty-six-year-old man was brought to him by a well-known family. The patient had been married four months and was showing paranoid schizophrenic behavior. He had poorly systematized delusions and auditory hallucinations. There was no previous history before the onset. The healer brought the young man to the psychiatrist who hospitalized him. The patient refused to stay and escaped on several occasions returning to his family, which, in each case, brought him back to the hospital. Finally a series of five ECTs was administered. After the fifth treatment, the family, accompanied by the healer, came to the psychiatrist and requested release of the patient who was showing marked improvement. The psychiatrist told the healer that the patient had indeed improved, but required additional treatment. Against advice, the patient was discharged. Two weeks later, the patient was returned, and was given another course of ECT (six treatments) until a degree of memory loss ensued. He was then released into the healer's Kali care, improved steadily, and has maintained himself without problems since.

The therapeutic formula evolved here between the psychiatrist and the healer was that in severe psychotic cases not amenable to Kali cultural reinforcement, ECT would be administered up to memory loss, then reintegration would proceed via Kali reenculturation. Later, the psychiatrist developed the technique of unilateral ECT without resulting loss of memory.


## REASON FOR COLLABORATION

Having accepted a new country as one's milieu for psychiatric investigation and therapy, a psychiatrist cannot but commit himself to the values and culture of the population; otherwise he would suffer culture shock. This is because he cannot escape the fact that "mental disorders" or syndromes can only be adequately defined, recognized, evaluated, and appreciated through the understanding of the functional interrelatedness of the environment with the inner motivation of the individual and the "accepted" community goals. In other words, "mental disorders," have meaning only in the society in which they manifest themselves. In view of this, the opportunity of forming a working relationship with the local Kali healers, initiated by the anthropologist, was a most welcome recourse in the efforts to identify the problems, define goals, and conceive plans for a mental health program of the host country (British Guiana). The working relationship was therefore initially sought with the following objectives in view: (1) It supplied the psychiatrist with the means of learning the cultural patterns, the existing social institutions and organizations along which he might direct his (patient) therapy, which perforce must take cognizance of the attitudes of the community to be effective. (2) The fantastic inadequacy of the psychiatric facilities (one psychiatrist for the whole country) was such that the reorganization of this exploration was an inescapable, if not frantic, move to meet the psychiatrist's own desparate plight. (3) It showed promise of evolving methods of evaluating techniques of community psychiatry, while at the same time, discovering, testing out, and articulating psychodynamic principles that may be operating in the Kali healing methods, affording an invaluable, preexistent laboratory and calling for no additional responsibility from the psychiatrist. (4) The relationship also afforded the psychiatrist a chance to introduce Western psychiatric concepts where he felt these might be of help to the healer in dealing with mental disorders. (5) To prepare the community, it afforded a chance for the psychiatrist to effect such change in cultural awareness and attitudes in coping with the anticipated cultural impact of increasing Western infiltration into the socioeconomic structure of the country. (6) The prospect of utilizing the healer's help for specific psychiatric syndromes, in which the anthropologist had reported amazing results, offered the desired resource for the already impossible work schedule of the psychiatrist. (7) The need to control the operations of the healer, who had no training in the recognition of somatic disorders, demanded the relationship as an urgent humanitarian medical responsibility. (8) The collaboration also offered a social rehabilitation facility, which had been nonexistent up to the time of the psychiatrist's involvement with the service. (9) The establishment of a liaison with the leaders of the communities, among whom the Kali healers involved were found to be most influential, afforded the mental health service an opportunity to evolve into a culturally modifying institution that contributed to allaying the social ills of the community. (10) With such an evolution, it was hoped that insights could be gained into preventive measures against mental illness through the elucidation in greater depth of the personal and environmental interrelationships that were predisposed to regression.


## THE WORKING RELATIONSHIP ESTABLISHED WITH THE KALI HEALERS

A series of visits to the Kali temples and observations of the healing rituals, followed by discussions with the healers on the theories behind their practices, was undertaken. After a solid personal relationship (which is the only meaningful relationship in the personality-oriented, rather than object- and role-oriented Western pattern of culture) was established, the healer was invited to assist in the evaluation of new cases at the Corentyne clinics and the Mental Hospital. This consisted of having the healer help in the history taking, which was a tremendous asset because of his mastery of the peculiarities of the idiom characteristic of the district. A conference on the emotional needs of the patients, as brought out in the interviews followed, and a comparison of the theories of management that were felt to be indicated was then undertaken. This provided the psychiatrist with insights into the patterns of cultural expectations, the traditions and myths that underlie the "accepted" community goals, and the functional interrelatedness of the environment and the inner motivations of the individual; it also shed some light on the factors that predispose to functional regression.

The healer also made periodic visits to the Mental Hospital to bring patients for evaluation (a) as to whether or not organic problems existed, or (b) as to whether his methods had or had not produced the desired results on "mental" cases. In these instances, diagnostic and management conferences were undertaken, wherein the healer was afforded some insights into signs of organic disturbances and also some information on how drug therapy, used in the clinic, could assist the patient in responding better to the healer's predominantly cultural reinforcement therapy (directed at bringing about order and organization out of emotional chaos). In these visits, the healer also was enabled to follow up cases that he had referred for admission, and the therapeutic procedures employed in the hospital were explained to him. The unilateral electroconvulsive therapy to the nondominant hemisphere of the brain, which proved more effective in calming patients than the conventional bitemporal placement was developed and had dramatic effects in that it involved no memory impairment. This afforded the patient the continuation of the value-reinforcing therapy of the healer, through "devotion."

The healer's collaboration with the psychiatrist also took the form of management conferences for cases to be followed by the Kali healer and for cases that were ready for discharge.

Another form of collaborative therapeutic effort consisted of cases on which the psychiatrist had used drug and supportive psychotherapy but had then referred to the Kali healer because, being deficient in his appreciation of the cultural value of the symptoms, he had been unable to decipher the hidden motivation for the retention of symptoms.

Furthermore, due to the relative lack of mobility in the social system prevailing in the district, the role-assigning process within the family has been observed to be extremely therapeutic, and family participation advocated in the Kali form of healing has been utilized to great advantage by the service.

## WESTERN THERAPEUTIC MODALITIES EMPLOYED BY THE PSYCHIATRIC SERVICE AT THE MENTAL HOSPITAL AND PSYCHIATRIC CLINICS

Comprehensive mental health care, as it is generally conceived in the Western world, has had to be modified in the absence of trained staff. The service was geared to the economic realities of the situation, and remained at the level of "emergency psychiatric measures"; the objectives were mainly preventing chronicity, providing symptomatic relief, and lowering the in-patient population to reduce hospitalization cost. Toward this end, ECT and drugs were the main therapeutic measures employed. These measures seemed well-adapted to the situation because the majority of the patients belonged to the lower educational and socioeconomic group, and seemed to have their awareness of self based mainly at the sensory level rather than at the symbolic level. Complaints of "feeling broken up," "me head a worry me, like things crawling inside," and "me skin a tremble and me burn all over" are presented by depressives as well as by schizophrenics. The expectations therefore of having their "weak nerves" and "bad blood" relieved by somatic procedures were well conditioned by the culture to help them respond to the procedures forced upon the psychiatrist by the circumstances. The focus of effort was directed toward the following goals: (1) Early detection of psychotic processes by admonishing the general practitioners to refer at their cases' beginning stages and treating these cases as intensively as possible with electrotherapy and drugs. (2) Discharging patients to their families as early as possible; this was done to minimize feelings of rejection. The promotion of readaptation rather than institutionalization was also encouraged. There is a tremendous stigma attached to hospital "madness" in Guiana and families fear being identified as having madness in the family lest their other children lose their opportunities to get married. The short hospitalization, therefore, can easily be explained as "nervousness needing a rest cure" and the stigma is avoided. (3) Keeping admission rates at a minimum by encouraging daycare, whenever this was possible. (4) Improving the living conditions of the hospitalized

patients and intensifying occupational and recreational activity programs; this helped to improve the atmosphere of the place very much.
The enhanced self-image resulting from the patients' awareness of
their productivity as well as the reawakening of their interest in their
environment created a social milieu that proved more therapeutic
than originally anticipated. (5) Persuading the custody-oriented staff
to accept the open wards which were introduced. (6) Holding group
discussions centered on the in-patient occupational and recreational
activities, with occasional reference to difficulties in readaptation
upon discharge, in lieu of an organized psychotherapeutic program
which time would not permit. Outings for patients, organized by
religious leaders and individual families in the community were
encouraged in the absence of an organized readaptation and rehabilitation program. (7) Undertaking, at least occasionally, supportive, and
integrative, reality-oriented interviews with clinic patients in conjunction with drug therapy.

Due to the time limitation and the ever-increasing case demands
(which occurred as hope of recovery for the mentally ill broke down
the social stigma attached to seeking psychiatric help), the Kali
healers' help became very important to provide the much needed
culturally oriented psychotherapeutic assistance.

The indigenous Kali healers of Guiana relieve symptoms through
private and public rituals. They do not use herbal medicines as a
rule, and patients usually see the Western-trained physician before
going to the native healer. The healers' diagnoses are related to
specific, stereotyped dreams, and are "working diagnoses" concerned
with "reality" problems and treatment. Motivation of the patient and
his sincerity in coming for aid are an important prerequisite for his
acceptance into therapy. Little or no attention is paid to the differential subtleties of the diagnosis regarding the patient's behavior. This
approach prevails, because outside of motivation, prognosis does not
depend on diagnostic shadings in Kali work, which is basically concerned with emotional disorders associated with attitudinal maladapta-
tion, as expected in the culture, and the Mother Goddess Kali.

The healer does not make any prognosis. He does not accept the
principal responsibility. His job is to assist in the devotion by his
encouragement and his understanding of the resources available in
ritual and devotion for combating emotional deprivation among the
devotees. Occasionally, as in the Kali Puja, which is the public healing
ceremony, he will invoke the gods. A clear distinction is made between
invoke and devote. When the mother is invoked, she must help. She

then moves through the body of the healer, who is in a trance. The mother must now speak and say what is wrong. The people devote. The effectiveness of the therapy is always the patient's responsibility. Thus, the patient participates directly and WORKS ACTIVELY IN HIS THERAPY. His contribution depends on his sincerity and zeal at reintegrating his values; it has nothing to do with his material offering, i.e. his gifts to the temple, which are given after the devotee (patient) gets better. Because of the nature of the transaction, the healer is never manipulated. He does not make promises and is not "bribed" or "bought." This therefore places the responsibility for emotional or life-style modification where it properly belongs.

There is no overt counter-transference. The transference is to the mother, Kali. The healer is only the agent. Together, the healer and the patient both beg the mother and are ready to "regress," i.e. to prostrate themselves before the mother, assume temporary dependency to proceed along the path of accepted cultural functional evolution. Guilt is always turned inwards, unless this could be displaced to the bad spirits. In any case, the patient is always at fault in the performance of his "devote," which can never be perfect. There is introjection of the good object (spirit) in the ingestion of the food prescribed by the healer, blessed by the mother, and cooked and eaten by the patient.

Family members are encouraged to participate in the fasting, the confession of their shortcomings, the renunciation of their bad habits, and in devoting. In the process of sharing the work, a better understanding of the role-assigning and role-assuming process within the family often comes about.

INDIGENOUS HEALER — PSYCHIATRIST COLLABORATION

As a result of growing experience in the collaborative efforts in therapy, a group of problems and situations were identified as showing good response to Kali healing methods and their modifications described above. These situations and problems have these features in common. (1) The patients must be sensorially intact, so that they can be aware of and respond to the rituals. (2) The patients have defined their goals to the psychiatrist and healer in relation to what they would do for themselves should their affliction be healed. (3) The patients of the rural areas are more responsive (irrespective of diagnostic category). (4) The patients are usually consciously and/or unconsciously embracing the Hindu value system. (5) Patients' families are willing to participate in the patients' treatment.

## DIAGNOSTIC CATEGORIES

In relation to Western diagnostic categories, the following types of cases have shown good responses, as indicated by the data on cases that were followed up.

### Neurotic Depressive Reactions Occurring During and After the Involutional Period

A typical case is that of a fifty-seven-year-old widow, Sumitra, who became depressed after her son and daughter married and left her home. Her illness developed rather abruptly; she had symptoms of insomnia, shakiness and weakness, loss of appetite, and loss of interest in her surroundings to the extent that she became bedridden for about two weeks before she was admitted to the hospital.

On admission, she showed psychomotor retardation and marked inattention, which caused her to give many irrelevant answers; she also suffered from severe depression, which was expressed by feelings of hopelessness and uselessness.

A course of six bilateral ECTs was given with good results. The patient recovered her appetite; her sleep improved, and she became active in the ward and joked and laughed with other patients.

She was discharged after twelve days of hospitalization, and placed in the care of her son and daughter-in-law. As an outpatient, she was maintained on Tofranil 25 milligrams and Librium 10 milligrams four times daily.

On her third visit to the clinic (twelve weeks after discharge) the patient again showed psychomotor retardation and had difficulty sleeping as well as a poor appetite; the daughter-in-law complained that the patient was very "passionate" (meaning easily provoked) and would get very angry, would curse, and threaten to harm herself.

The Kali healer was consulted and, after a joint interview with the patient, in which her relationship with her relatives and, particularly, her resentment of the fact that her married son had set up an independent household (contrary to Hindu tradition) were discussed, the patient was encouraged to report to the healer.

Subsequent follow-ups (one every four weeks) revealed steady improvement in the patient. She was again taking care of her garden and poultry, her daughter-in-law became more appreciative of her, and her medication was reduced to 10 milligrams of Librium in the evenings. When last seen, a year after her initial symptoms, she appeared to be contented and enthusiastic; she looked years younger, and contributed voluntary work at the Kali temple.

Of sixteen cases of this nature that were referred in 1964 to the Kali healer, about 40 percent of the patients, (of all those who went for Kali treatment) showed complete recovery, as in the case cited above. Another 40 percent showed marked improvement, although in those cases the patients had to be maintained on antidepressant medications periodically. (Some had to report back to the healer.) The remaining 20 percent did not return to the clinic.

Most of the patients who showed recurrences of symptoms were those whose families showed little or no interest in participating in the Kali treatment.

*Neurotic Reactions with (Hysterical) Conversion Manifestations, Usually with Hyperventilation*

This condition is fairly common among the young, unmarried girls of the rural areas of Berbice and the Corentyne. A typical case is that of Elena, an orphaned East Indian girl of seventeen who was living with her aunt in Albion village. The girl experienced several attacks in which she would scream, curse, and then stiffen up and be temporarily withdrawn and unresponsive for a few minutes. This started about two months after her only brother died. She saw several physicians, all of whom prescribed tranquilizers (Librium, Valium, Chlorpromazine), and sedatives (phenobarbital), etc., but these gave her no relief. The patient became progressively more irritable and erratic; and the attacks became more frequent.

When seen at the Fort Canje clinic, this tall, well-developed, attractive girl appeared withdrawn and gave only monosyllabic responses. She was well oriented to time, place, and person. She expressed grief over her brother's accidental death, and was vague about her plans for herself. She described her relationship with her brother as a close one, although her brother had been strict with her, especially in her relationships with the opposite sex. She denied having any steady boyfriend, and said this was not a problem because her aunt was "reasonable." There was no gross thinking difficulty noted. The patient, however, appeared anxious and expressed fear over developing the "attacks," which she described as giving her very "bad feelings." She could not relate the attacks with any specific event or thoughts, although she said that she became irritable just prior to the attacks, and would cry, scream, and feel "short of breath." This would be followed by coldness and stiffness of the extremities, light-headedness, "bad feelings all over," and a sense of fading away and being confused, "like me head go swing me, and me can go out of me sense." An impression of hyperventilation syndrome associated with anxiety was made; and the possibility of a predisposition to seizures was entertained. The patient was placed on sodium amytal 65 milligrams, Mysoline 250 milligrams, and Librium 10 milligrams, three times daily.

A week later, the aunt brought the patient for admission because her erratic behavior and attacks persisted. On admission the patient showed tremendous emotional lability and had to be sedated with sodium amytal 250 milligrams intramuscularly (g.i.d.) for two days (neurological examination proved negative). She was maintained on sodium amytal 65 milligrams (g.i.d.) during the succeeding days of hospitalization and was encouraged to participate in the recreational and occupational activities. There was no recurrence of the attacks during her ten days of hospitalization. Her aunt, who visited her almost daily, then requested the patient's discharge so she could participate in the "Kali Puja," with which she was familiar.

After discharge, the patient reported regularly at the clinic for her pills, which were changed to Librium 10 milligrams at bedtime (just to keep track of her progress). There was no recurrence of the "attacks" reported during the subsequent year, and the patient's behavior stabilized. She was studying dressmaking and was quite content with her life with her aunt when last seen.

Many cases of this nature have been referred to the Kali healer for treatment and generally have shown remarkable improvement.

## Compulsive Neurotic Reactions

Patients troubled by compulsive promiscuity and compulsive drinking, usually in response to restrictive authority or restrictive situations or physical handicaps, also respond well to Kali healing practices.

The case of Drupatie illustrates the condition referred to above as compulsive promiscuity. This girl was brought by her parents, who "begged" the psychiatrist to admit the girl because she brought shame to the family. Drupatie appeared as a very shy youngster although she was physically well developed for her fourteen years. The parents reported that the girl would run away from home and live with one man after another until she was located and brought back by the family. The mother revealed that Drupatie had always been a submissive and obedient little child. However, since the girl's menarche at age twelve and a half, she had become rebellious, and despite the parents' warning about doing "what black girls do" (meaning being flirtatious and going out with boys to dances as Negro girls like to do), Drupatie would run away and do these very things. As the restrictions were intensified, her behavior became worse.

The psychiatrist's interview with the patient was most unproductive, all she would do was cry and remain mute. An impression of compulsive neurosis was made, and the parents were made to understand that their restrictive attitude revealed to the girl that they anticipated this "bad" behavior. It was suggested that if they could show her more trust and discuss with her the consequences of her behavior, it would enable her to make up her own mind about what would be a more beneficial course of action for herself and she would be less likely to be "mannish" (meaning wild).

Two weeks later the patient was again brought to the psychiatrist by her parents for the same reason. Because it was hard to establish a good rapport with this uncommunicative patient, it was decided that admission was worth a trial. During her two-week stay at the hospital, she cried continually, begging to return to her parents. She said that she did not know why she behaved as she did, that she was sorry because she knew it was not to her benefit.

On one of the parents' visits they brought the Kali healer, whom they had contacted for help. The healer examined the girl, placed his thumb upon the girl's forehead, and looked steadily into her eyes. The girl looked away, cried, and ran back into the ward. The healer diagnosed the girl as being possessed by "bad spirits due to a spell cast upon her by a black boy." (The girl always ran away with Negro boys.) Arrangements were then made to have the girl taken by her parents to the healer for a series of treatments extending from Thursday to Sunday for seven successive weeks. Discharge from the hospital was effected the following Wednesday and treatment by the healer began.

Two months later the patient reported back to the hospital clinic to "repeat her tablets" which consisted of Mellaril 50 milligrams, two times daily. The parents at this time reported that the patient was behaving better and that the family regularly participated in the Kali temple rituals. Medication was reduced to one dose at bedtime; and the patient was encouraged to report back to the clinic every three months. When last seen, seven months after the initiation of treatment with the Kali healer, the parents reported her to have been "behaving good." Later, arrangements were made for her marriage according to the accepted Hindu custom of having the parents choose the husband.

Of the seven cases of this nature referred to the healer, only three reported, and of these, two showed rapid improvement. The other one did not report regularly and eventually was lost track of.

The case of Bob Kisson, who was a twenty-eight-year-old married epileptic, exemplified a case of compulsive drinking. This patient was originally seen by the healer for "convulsive seizures" which started at the time of puberty after the patient suffered a severe head injury and was unconscious for about two hours. He was referred for evaluation from the Kali Temple where he sought help for his "fits" on the advice of the anthropologist, who was at that time studying the Kali healing practices.

The patient's history revealed that he had seen several physicians and that the attacks had diminished to twice a month instead of ten to sixteen times per month. A neurological examination revealed no lateralizing sign; therefore, the patient's medication was increased to Dilantin 100 milligrams and Meberal 100 milligrams four times daily. Within six weeks the seizures ceased. The patient was strongly advised to take his tablets regularly, which he did. However, within another six weeks the patient reported recurrence of the fits again.

Despite a further increase in his anticonvulsant doses to five times daily, the fits continued, and the patient was noted to be depressed. Personal history showed that the patient had been unemployed since his marriage at age nineteen because of his frequent "fits." This forced his wife to work to support the family. The patient felt very badly about this; and because he was certain that nobody would employ him because of his work record, he felt he was a burden to his family.

His wife revealed that the patient had been a compulsive drinker since two years after their marriage. She also said that when he drank a lot, he would get very mean to her and would develop "fits" within the next twenty-four hours.

At the patient's next visit to the clinic he was confronted with his having failed to follow instructions to avoid alcohol. The patient cried and discussed his feeling of futility because of his "fits." He was reassured that he could return to work if his fits were controlled; but he would have to stop drinking. He was advised to report to the Kali healer to get treatment for his compulsive drinking.

During succeeding visits, no fits were reported, and within six months the patient was reported by his wife as having completely controlled his need to resort to alcohol. He was certified as fit to return to work, and has been symptom free since.

There have been many compulsive drinkers who have sought help at the various psychiatric clinics operated by the psychiatrist. Two of these have consented to report to the Kali healer and both have done well.

*Acute Schizophrenic Reactions Manifesting Marked Dissociation and Paranoid Ideation*

Many such patients have been referred to the healer for therapy. A typical example is the case of Danny (a young married man of mixed East Indian and Negro background). He was brought to the mental hospital for treatment by his brothers, who described the patient as "talking stupidness." The illness started about two weeks before admission with sleeplessness, bizarre ideation, and erratic, irrational behavior. Gradually, the patient became withdrawn, suspicious, and more irrelevant in his responses. An interview revealed the patient to be anxious, suspicious, and grossly dissociated. He was given a course of unilateral ECTs, and, because he came from the area close to the Kali temple, the brothers were advised to contact the healer to help in the follow-up care, which they did.

Within two weeks, the patient was discharged much improved and was transferred to the out-patient clinic for continuation of drug therapy, which consisted of Stelazine 8 milligrams and Chlorpromazine 50 milligrams three times daily and 100 milligrams of Chlorpromazine at night. The patient also reported to the Kali healer.

Within six months the patient was completely withdrawn from medication. His performance as a farmer and head of a family exceeded his morbid norm, and he was not seen again until about ten months later when after hearing that the psychiatrist was leaving the country, he came to bid him farewell.

About sixty similar cases have been referred to the healer. Of these only two have had recurrence of attacks within fourteen months. Six have been completely withdrawn from medication; the rest were still reporting to the clinic for maintenance drug treatment at the time of the psychiatrist's departure from Guiana.

*Phobic Reactions*

These cases received the same treatment from the Kali healer as the schizophrenics with paranoid tendencies. They responded well to the exorcism of the Dutchman spirit in their bodies. Of four cases of phobic reactions that performed the Kali "work," two showed significant relief.

The case of Sookchan, a thirty-year-old married school teacher, is typical. He had a long history of being afraid of crowds. He would avoid meetings and would enter his classroom long before the class would start, so as to avoid being with people in the corridor. He managed to continue with his work by taking Libraxin continuously over a period of years.

When interviewed, the patient showed tremendous anxiety and expressed resentment over his father's lack of support of the patient's academic goals. He described himself as having always been a perfectionist and being overly concerned about what people thought of him. He showed a great sense of obligation toward his wife because she contributed to the family economy by working as a clerk at the town hall.

Many drugs were tried to reduce the symptoms. The combination of Librium and sodium amytal proved most efficacious. However, significant relief was experienced only after the patient underwent treatment at the Kali temple.

THE "WESTERN" PSYCHIATRIC DIAGNOSTIC CONFERENCE

A traditional, contemporary, Western, open-ended diagnostic conference in a teaching hospital may last between sixty and ninety minutes. The conference participants are usually the patient's assigned psychiatrist, a psychiatric resident or residents, sometimes a third- or fourth-year medical student on the psychiatry clerkship, the psychiatric social worker who first interviewed the patient, and now-adays other members of the staff, students, other behavioral scientists including anthropologists, all of whom are jammed behind a one-way mirror and pretending invisibility. Relatives will usually NOT be present, either at the interview or behind the mirror. The rationale sometimes given for the exclusion is that the patient would not be frank if kin were present.

The history-taking is conducted by the patient's assigned psychiatrist; this may last about forty-five minutes or less depending upon whether or not there has been a previous history. The psychiatrist's supervisor may ask the patient questions. Other members of the staff may ask questions. The patient is then asked to leave the conference room. Then a discussion usually starts with the question of degree of rapport established between the patient and the psychiatrist assigned to the case. Other areas discussed will usually include the patient's complaints, the revealed and discerned life pattern of the patient, and speculations about the presentation of self by the patient before the professional group. Another element in the diagnostic conference is an evaluation of the patient's mental status, which is designed to "test" whether the patient perceives reality, reasons adequately, and uses good judgement. A discussion usually then follows in order to determine where the patient's pathology lies in relation to his "pre-morbid personality." A diagnosis is then usually proffered, discussed, and concensus sought from the rest of the therapeutic team.

Lastly, there will be a discussion of the therapeutic "management" of the patient. Usually, the concern here is to be "supportive," and there will be discussion of therapeutic "modalities" insofar as they concern "management" decisions over use of chemotherapy, electro-convulsive therapy [ECT], and various forms of psychotherapy.

## DIAGNOSTIC CONFERENCE WITH INDIGENOUS HEALER

The patient (East Indian) is usually accompanied by relatives, including mother, father, mother-in-law, elder brother or other collateral, who almost always are overwhelmingly concerned and sympathetic. Generally, he will be brought to the psychiatric clinic NOT because of some overt act of behavioral deviancy, contrary to the norms of the larger community or the police, but because his immediate rel-atives have come to the conclusion that the patient needs sympathy and specialized help. In the course of the conference, the relatives play a useful role in CONFRONTING the patient with his behavior. Far from this being taken amiss, it serves to articulate the actual behavior causing concern. Usually, the only other professional personnel present are the Kali healer (Jamsie Naidoo) and the anthropologist.

In contrast to the Western psychiatric conference, this may be called a SELECTIVE DIAGNOSTIC CONFERENCE, lasting between five and fifteen minutes. It is primarily meant to help the psychiatrist understand the cultural reality problems, to get the input of the indigenous healer into the patient's problems, and to point out to (teach) the healer how emotions, as well as cultural realities, may be utilized by the patient to withdraw from coping normally with reality. HISTORY TAKING is brief and pointed and is concerned with the patient's chief complaint, its onset, and its development; how the patient spends his time now as contrasted to "before"; "now" aspirations contrasted to "before"; and when it was that the patient noticed in himself a change in his own ideas about the purpose of his life.

In the process of this history taking, the psychiatrist may "lose" his patient because of difficulties in phrasing. For example: the patient talks about changes in his life plans at about the age of twenty-five. The psychiatrist believes this may be related to the fact that he unwillingly married at that time due to family pressures. The psychiatrist says:

Sometimes, when one assumes responsibilities, one has to give up certain things, and sometimes it is quite painful.

[Deep silence follows. At this point the healer will intervene.]

You must answer Doctah or he cannot help you. What Doctah wants to know is you getting plenty, much too plenty pickny [children] now and things you like to sport before with sweet gyal and so on, you not able sport now!

The invariable effect of the healer's translation-intervention is to appropriately culturally force the patient to respond and verify the psychiatrist's inferences.

Thus, we can see that unlike the traditional psychiatric history, this history is undisguisedly directive and authoritarian. For example, based on the approach and interventiors of the composite psychiatrist-healer, an interview would proceed as follows:

Psychiatrist: What you feel now?
Patient:     Doctor, me head a swing me, me nah know what me can do
             with meself. Sometime me feel me body atremble. Me don't
             care for eat and me got too much passion [irritation, agression].

Psychiatrist: Tell me when it is you notice feeling like this.
Patient:      [Repeats same list of complaints and is interrupted].
Psychiatrist: How many weeks you now feel like this?
Patient:      Two-three weeks.
Psychiatrist: Before this, you feel allright?
Patient:      Me used to get this bad feeling and me head swinging two years now.
Psychiatrist: What you mean couple years now? Since you get you first pickny or since you got you last pickny? Answer truth. Nah be frightened!
Patient:      Since me second pickny born.
Psychiatrist: Well, how much pickny you got?
Patient:      Me got six.

[and so on].

The healer's specific interventions are made when asking details of the couple's sexual relations or of relations between the patient and the mother-in-law. If the healer cannot get the desired information from the patient, he will get it from the mother-in-law, who is usually present. He asks and receives frank answers to candid questions, such as: "When you husband go sporting and get drunk, does he beat you?" The wife will usually maintain a shamed, hung-head silence, but the mother-in-law will now tell her complaints about the son-in-law or daughter-in-law. She expects that the psychiatrist-healer (whom she sees as one authority) will support the traditional authoritarian cultural norms.

When a patient does not directly or indirectly know of the healer, the psychiatrist will introduce him as "Uncle Jamsie Kali Mai Pujari. We work together." In this way, the psychiatrist is no longer perceived as a stranger-foreigner, and the healer at the same time is the recipient of some of the charisma of the doctor.

When the patients know the healer, they usually speak freely. Occasionally, a younger man will say, "Doctah. Me nah believe in Kali puja. Why you bring this man?" The healer responds by saying, "Me come to learn from Doctah." This is usually accepted and problems are then freely discussed.

The healer will also frequently give a credentials boost to the psychiatrist in some of the remoter clinic areas by saying to the patient:

Me been with Doctah to Port Mourant [a well-known village associated in the minds of most East Indians as the birthplace of Cheddi Jagan] and everybody me and Doctah see is feeling better now.

The significance of this psychiatrist-healer interaction is to improve rapport with the patient, who sees the healer associating himself with "Doctah Work," and who perceives the psychiatrist according professional respect to the "Bush Doctah" in his performance of "Kali work."

After the history is completed, the psychiatrist asks the healer's opinion, in the presence of the patient and family, about why the patient feels the way he does. This results in the healer giving a cultural interpretation, or, if he feels he needs more information, giving him an opportunity to ask direct questions such as:

You does dream anyone comes to you when you sleep? You mess up you shorts [wet dream]? You got desire for you wife [husband]? You make enough money to circulate in the house? What you going to do when you get better?

These are standard questions put by the healer. It is interesting that they reflect cultural concern with dreams, sex, work, money, and future.

After the healer has asked his questions, he will tell the patient he will get well if he goes to "doctah" and takes the prescribed "tablets." This is supportive and prognostic, which is directly contrary to Kali therapy ("work"), in which no prognosis is made and only the assurance of effort is made. The basis on which the healer feels he can offer prognostic assurance in the psychiatric setting is his understanding that the patient wants to get well and his future orientation, learned from the psychiatrist — "What you going to do when you get well?"

At the Kali Puja itself there is no prognosis; this is due to the fact that the patient may not necessarily be motivated because Kali Puja is a community, cultural participation, and not just a place to get well. Also, it may be a place of "last resort," where, after having been to many doctors, a patient finally goes without expecting to get well.

The character of the Kali Puja has gradually changed and now emphasizes the therapeutic aspect as well as the community cultural performance. Very often, because of the press of time, the psychiatrist and healer will interrupt the patient's discursiveness to force direct answers. Discursiveness, open-ended spontaneity is NOT encouraged. In short, the diagnostic conference is a CULTURALLY DEDUCTIVE session meant to test the reality of the cultural assumptions. This is very different from the Western psychiatric diagnostic conference, in which questions are phrased AS IF there are no assumptions, but in which the *Diagnostic statistical manual* labels are very much in the forefront of the minds of the physician, psychiatric social worker, etc.

The patient's basic assumptions, in turn, and his presentation of self involve his desire to have the psychiatrist believe he is a poor unfortunate with absolutely no other resources. In order to reinforce this posture of helpless dependence, he will often present to the psychiatrist a letter of referral, given to him for a usual fee of four dollars from a Western-trained physician, which testifies to the fact that the patient's condition is chronic and nonorganic.

After the patient has left, usually with tablets (medication) and a follow-up appointment with the psychiatrist, there will often be a brief consultation between the psychiatrist and the healer. The healer may observe that the patient does not want to get well, and the psychiatrist observes that it is a matter that must involve the entire family. Together, they will agree that the entire family will be asked to go to the Kali temple where the work performed — prayer-devotion, anointing, circumambulation, and the cooking and eating of the sacred food — will be a family affair. All of this Kali "work" will often be performed, although not always, while the patient's emotional response is influenced by the drugs. At least, that is the theory.


## THE MANAGEMENT-REEVALUATION CONFERENCE [M-RC] BETWEEN PSYCHIATRIST AND HEALER

Traditionally, in Western psychiatric settings the management conference follows the diagnostic conference and involves cases in active therapy. There are reasons for calling a management conference. It may be standard operating procedure in child guidance centers or community mental health centers after all reports and evaluations are turned in from the various specialists such as psychiatrists, psychologists, social workers, and others. It will follow an initial evaluation and two or more preliminary therapeutic sessions with the assigned psychiatrist. The M-RC in a psychiatric training institution is usually built into the continuous case conference, in which the interactions between therapist and patient are minutely examined. The M-RC in state hospitals takes the form of progress reports usually submitted every two weeks to the clinical director; these contain the recommendations made by the submitting psychiatrist.

Presumably a diagnostic conference is also a management conference. The major difference, however, is that the management conference constitutes a reevaluation, not in terms of diagnostic categories, but more in terms of "ego needs." The objective is to utilize the therapeutic relationships that presumably have come to be established between the therapist and the patient, the family and the patient, the family and the social worker and all the rest of the therapeutic human and institutional armamentarium, including the nurse and the hospital milieu.

In the case of the psychiatrist and the indigenous healer, there were three kinds of cases involved:

1. those brought to the psychiatrist by the healer for consultation and/or hospital admission;

2. cases seen together at out-patient clinics by the psychiatrist and the healer;

3. cases up for discharge from the hospital.

The greatest difference between the M-RC conducted with the healer, as distinguished from the Western approach, is that it was rarely "scheduled"; it was spur-of-the-moment and reflected process rather than bureaucratic organization and scheduled predictability.

For example, the healer might just "drop in" unannounced at the hospital or a clinic, alone or with a patient. He might inquire, as an interested friend and coprofessional, about the progress of patients with whom he had been involved. Should the healer come by the hospital in the morning, he would make rounds with the psychiatrist and possibly discuss some of the dynamics about particular patients at that time. If the healer arrived at the hospital in the afternoon, he would make his own ward rounds.

In all cases, patients who wished to might "devote" for a few minutes with the healer and make arrangements to be brought to the Kali temple for more intense devotions (and therapy) on Sundays.

During his time in the ward, the healer makes his own judgments which he then later reports to the psychiatrist. The healer's primary concern here is whether the patient seems to be sufficiently integrated to perform the simple Kali devotions and "work" at the temple. In summary, the following elements are present in the M-RC:

1. Psychiatrist and healer confer;

2. Healer and patient confer in the ward;

3. Psychiatrist and healer discuss healer's evaluation of the patient and knowledge of the family;

4. A decision may be made to discharge the patient and inform the family that they are all expected to go to the Kali temple for "work."

What is most unusual here, as contrasted with the Western-style M-RC, is that the healer plays a triple role — social worker, peer therapist, and cultural mediator-interpreter. As a result of his sustained contact with the psychiatrist, the healer has learned to evaluate patients behaviorally. For example, in the beginning he tended to be symptom-oriented, and to report that "this man complain all the time," but later he described behavior, such as "this man is now working. He do not run after sweet gyal, but he live good with he wife and money circulate in the house."

As of this writing, the cooperation with the Mental Hospital has broken down due to the deterioration of psychiatric services in Guiana. There is now no psychiatrist in charge of the Mental Hospital. However, the reputation established by the healer has continued to grow through the years and he estimates that on an average Sunday he personally sees between thirty and fifty patients. Also, he normally sees a number of persons every evening, after work, at his home. As always, no fee is charged.

## REFERENCES

SINGER, P., *et al.*
  1967 Integration of indigenous healing practices of the Kali cult with Western psychiatric modalities in British Guinana. *Revista Interamericana de Psicología* 1:103—113.

# A Peruvian Curandero's Séance: Power and Balance

DOUGLAS SHARON

Northern Peru has long been reputed to be a major region for *curanderismo* [shamanistic folk healing] as practiced by mestizo *curanderos* [folk healers] in night healing séances involving the use of hallucinogens, elaborate and culture-specific psychotherapy, and syncretistic religious symbolism in which Indian beliefs and folk Catholicism are functionally blended. Since the 1960's such practices have been attracting increasing attention from scholars (cf. Friedberg 1959, 1960, 1963; Chiappe 1967, 1968, 1969a, 1969b; Dobkin de Ríos 1968, 1968–1969, 1969a, 1969b; Seguin 1969, 1970; Rodríguez Suy Suy 1970; Sharon 1972). This paper is meant to contribute to our growing knowledge of northern *curanderismo* by concentrating on the dynamics of the night séance of one *curandero*. It is based upon ethnographic data gathered during two field seasons (summer, 1970, and fall, 1971) of apprenticeship to the *curandero* Eduardo Calderón. The focus will be on the central goal of Eduardo's séances, balance of power, as expressed in the symbolism of his curing rituals.

Studies by Gillin (1945), Cruz Sánchez (1948, 1950), Friedberg (1960, 1963), Chiappe (1968), Dobkin de Ríos (1968), and Sharon (1972) have independently verified that the focal point of all northern Peruvian night healing séances to cure witchcraft is the *mesa* [table], an altar-like arrangement of power objects laid out on the ground. Eduardo also works with a *mesa*. As with other *curanderos*, the power objects of his *mesa* have all been acquired under special circumstances during his years of practice as a *curandero*. Each object has a personal significance to him and embodies a special "account" or story representing a projection of his own inner psychic power. This account becomes activated together with the accounts of the other power objects on the *mesa* whenever they are manipulated at night under the catalytic influence of the psychedelic San Pedro cactus, imbibed in liquid form (mixed with black tobacco juice or alone) by the *curandero*, his two assistants, patients, and accompanying friends. Taken as a whole, the *mesa* symbolizes the duality of the worlds of man and nature — a veritable microcosmos duplicating the forces at work in the universe.

Eduardo's *mesa* is divided into two major (though unequal) zones, called *campos* [fields], which are kept apart by a third neutral *campo* between them. The left, and smaller, side of the rectangular *mesa* is called the *Campo Ganadero* [Field of the Sly Dealer (Satan)]. It contains artifacts associated with the forces of evil, the underworld, and negative magic, mainly fragments of ancient ceramics and stones from archaeological ruins, along with cane alcohol, a deer foot, and a triton shell. This zone is covered by Satan, whose negative powers are concentrated in three staffs, called Satan's Bayonet, Owl Staff, and the Staff of the Single Woman. These are placed upright in the ground behind the artifacts of the *Campo Ganadero*. A sorcerer would use this negative zone for witchcraft or for lucrative curing; a benevolent curer needs it for consultation in cases of witchcraft, adverse love magic, or bad luck, because this is the realm responsible for such evils, and consequently it is also capable of revealing their sources. The number thirteen is associated with this zone.

The right, and larger, side of the *mesa* — called the *Campo Justiciero* [Field of the Divine Judge, or Divine Justice] — contains artifacts related to the forces of good or positive magic, including images of saints, crystals, shells, a dagger, a rattle, three perfumes, holy water, wild black tobacco, sugar, sweet lime, and a five-gallon can of San Pedro infusion. This zone is governed by Christ — considered as the center or axis of the *mesa* and Lord of all three fields — whose positive powers are focused in the crucifix at the center of the *mesa* as well as in eight staffs (called Swordfish Beak Staff, Eagle Staff, Greyhound Staff, Hummingbird Staff, Staff of the Virgin of Mercy, Sword of St. Paul, Saber of St. Michael the Archangel, and Sword of St. James the Elder). These staffs and swords are placed upright in the ground behind the artifacts of the *Campo Justiciero*. The sacred number twelve (for the twelve apostles and the signs of the zodiac) is associated with this field. The crucifix is the focal point for the 12,000 accounts of the *Campo Justiciero*, as well as for the sacred number seven (the "perfect" number of Christianity and the symbol of seven "justices" or miracles of Christ).

The Middle Field *(Campo Medio)* between the other two fields contains artifacts of a neutral nature in which the forces of good and evil are evenly balanced. This zone is governed by St. Cyprian (a powerful magician who was converted to Christianity), whose neutral powers are focused in a Serpent Staff, the Staff of Moses. The neutral or balanced objects are: a bronze sunburst, a stone symbolizing the sea and the winds, a glass jar containing magic herbs that Eduardo considers to be his spiritual alter ego, a statue of St. Cyprian seated on a deck of Spanish divining cards with divinatory runes at his feet, a "fortune stone," and a crystal "mirror" with a cat amulet on top of it. The sacred number twenty-five — i.e. twelve plus thirteen — is associated with this Middle Field. The artifacts of the Middle Field are symbolic of forces in nature and the world of man which can be used for good and for evil, depending on the intention of the individual. For Eduardo, who is a "white" shaman, the emphasis is on good, in accord with the pact he made when he was initiated. This commitment is further emphasized by the fact that the *Campo Justiciero* is the largest field of the *mesa*. Here is how Eduardo explains what the concept of balance governing the *Campo Medio* means to him:

The *Campo Medio* is like a judge in this case, or like the needle in a balance, the controlling needle between those two powers, between good and evil. The *Campo Medio* is where the chiefs, the guardians, those who command, those who govern, present themselves since it is the neutral field — that is, the dividing field between two frontiers where a war can occur over a dispute. That is the place where one has to put all, all, all his perseverence so that everything remains well controlled.

The Middle Field represents the core of Eduardo's philosophy, for the opposing forces of the universe — as manifest in this microcosmos known as a *mesa* — although giving birth to the struggle between good and evil in the world, are not conceived of as irreconcilable. Rather, they are seen as complementary, for it is their interaction which creates and sustains all life. The Middle Field, in addition to symbolizing the concept of balance or the complementarity of opposites, also provides guidance for practical action because it is the focal point of the *curandero*'s supernatural vision or sixth sense, which is activated by the San Pedro infusion. It is this vision or capacity to "see" that distinguishes the *curandero* from other men and permits him to divine and cure. The Middle Field, as a neutral, balanced area, helps focus the *curandero*'s supernatural faculties on the problem at hand, thus making possible his therapy.

A night healing session is the event which provides the proper environment for the focusing of the *curandero*'s vision and the manipulation of the forces of the *mesa* in order to solve the patients' problems. There are two parts to the session: ceremony and curing. The ceremonial division lasts from about 10 P.M. until midnight and consists of a series of prayers, rituals, and songs or chants (including whistling) performed to the rhythmic beat of the *curandero*'s rattle. At periodic intervals a mixture of boiled San Pedro cactus and wild black tobacco juice is taken through the nostrils by the *curandero* and his two assistants. Nasal imbibing is called "raising," which Eduardo defines as a libation, offering, or tribute to the cosmos intended to "clear the mind." The first division of the seance terminates with the drinking (at midnight) by all of a cup of pure San Pedro infusion. The purposes of the ceremonial division of the session are to invoke the forces of nature and guardian spirits, to balance the opposing forces operating within man and the cosmos, to make the patient susceptible to therapy, and to focus the *curandero*'s vision on the problems at hand. The following are the phases of the ceremonial division of the séance as observed by the author and later explained by Eduardo from taped replays:

1. Opening of the account of the entire *mesa*. Between invocations to the forces of nature and the "four winds and four roads" — i.e. the cardinal points — the *curandero* orally sprays the *mesa* twelve times with substances from the *Campo Justiciero*. This same phase is repeated at the end of the entire séance to close the account.

2. Prayers addressed to God, the Virgin Mary, Christ, and the saints of the Roman Catholic faith.

3. Invocations to sacred hills, lagoons, archaeological shrines of pre-Columbian Peru, the ancients, and other *curanderos*, alive and dead.

4. "Raising" the seven justices of Christ and the 7,000 accounts. The *curandero* nasally imbibes seven servings of boiled San Pedro cactus mixed with wild black tobacco juice. Each time he holds his dagger, rattle, and the crucifix from the center of the *mesa* over his head. The *curandero*'s two assistants "raise" the same mixture one time only, and do not handle the crucifix. These acts activate the center or axis of the *mesa*.

5. Chant addressed to the personages of the Christian tradition — i.e. Jesus, the Virgin Mary, the apostles, saints, angels — and to miraculous events in their lives, sung to the rhythmic beat of the rattle and interspersed with whistling.

6. "Raising" the 12,000 accounts of the *mesa*. The *curandero* nasally imbibes four servings of San Pedro and tobacco. His assistants imbibe one serving. These acts activate the *Campo Justiciero*. Twelve symbolizes the eleven faithful disciples of Christ plus Paul, who replaces Judas.

7. Chant relating the life of Christ (birth, deeds, death, and resurrection). It is intended to invoke his presence in spirit.

8. Imitation of the mass. The *curandero* lifts a mixture of perfume and holy water above his head and then drinks it.

9.  "Raising" the 25 and 250,000 accounts. Only the *curandero*'s two assistants perform this operation, imbibing one portion of San Pedro and tobacco each. Twenty-five in *curandero* symbology is obtained by adding the twelve disciples of Christ (the eleven faithful plus Paul) to thirteen — i.e. the eleven faithful plus Paul and Judas. In this act the two assistants activate not only the Middle Field governed by the sacred number twenty-five but also the *Campo Ganadero* governed by the number thirteen. However, the negative accounts of the *Campo Ganadero* are carefully balanced by the Middle Field.

10.  Chant addressed to all the forces of nature and the "ancients" (Indian and Christian). This chant is addressed to the activated collective forces of both *campos, Justiciero* and *Ganadero*.

11.  "Raising" the San Pedro remedy. The two assistants nasally imbibe three servings of San Pedro and tobacco in the name of the San Pedro brew. Each portion is literally raised along the side of the container of San Pedro. Then the sign of the cross is made over the brew before it is imbibed. After the assistants have "raised" the brew, everyone else present must perform the same operation. The *curandero* abstains from this operation.

12.  "Raising" and purification of the *curandero* and San Pedro brew. The *curandero* stands up, holding the herb jar — his alter ego from the *Campo Medio* — as well as his dagger, rattle, and a cup of pure San Pedro — all from the *Campo Justiciero*. Then his two assistants raise individual portions of San Pedro and tobacco from his feet to waist, waist to neck, and neck to the crown of the head before imbibing. While this is being done, the *curandero* chants a song in his own name.

13.  "Raising" the San Pedro remedy. This is performed one time only, and by the *curandero*. He then drinks the first cup of pure San Pedro brew. When he is finished, everyone else present is allowed to drink the pure brew. The two assistants are the last ones to drink.

14.  Cleansing of all present. While one assistant holds his seat before the *mesa*, the *curandero* steps out in the open beyond the staffs at the head of the *mesa*. One by one, all present must be rubbed down with the *curandero*'s rattle. Finally the *curandero* rubs himself. The stage is now set for the curing acts.

In sum, opening prayers and invocations lead to the activation of the center or axis associated with the number seven — i.e. the crucifix. Next, the right side of the *mesa*, associated with the forces of good and the number twelve, is activated. Then the neutral Middle Field, associated with the number twenty-five, is activated by the two assistants. In the latter process the smaller left side of the *mesa*, associated with the forces of evil and the number thirteen, is also brought to life through the balanced mediation of the Middle Field. After this the two assistants activate the forces of the San Pedro brew. Then they "center" the *curandero*, which allows him to give the San Pedro brew a final activation and initiate its consumption at midnight. Finally the *curandero* cleanses all participants in the séance, including himself.

A shorthand formula for the numerical buildup of power involved in the activation of the accounts of the *mesa* is: $3 + 4 = 7 + 5 = 12 + 13 = 25$. Eduardo gives the following explanations for these numbers: 3 represents the trinity of Christianity, the three planes of the cosmos (hell, earth, and heaven), the pyramid, the triangle, and the tripartite division of man into body, mind, and spirit; 4 represents the four cardinal points, the "four winds and roads," and the four elements of nature; 7 represents the seven "justices" or miracles of Christ, the seven seas, the seven rungs of Jacob's ladder, the seven virgins, the seven churches of early Christianity, the seven seals on the book of life mentioned in Revelation, the seven angels, the seven planets, the seven martyrs, the seven metals, the seven capital sins, the seven spirits, the seven hours required for the preparation of San Pedro before the session, the seven somersaults performed to exorcise attacking evil spirits in serious crises during the curing acts, the four cardinal points plus the three planes of the cosmos, and the center or axis of the *mesa*, i.e. Christ; 5 represents the five senses of man, and the four corners of the mesa united to a central fifth point (the crucifix) via the "four roads"; 12 represents the twelve disciples (with Judas replaced by Paul), the twelve hours of the day, the twelve signs of the zodiac, the twelve months of the year, completion, unity, and the *Campo Justiciero*; 13 represents the eleven loyal disciples plus Paul and Judas, as well as the *Campo Ganadero*; 25 represents the twenty-five balanced accounts of the *Campo Medio* in which polar opposites are united.

In the ninth phase of the ceremonial acts, i.e. "raising" the twenty-five and the 250,000 accounts of the *Campo Medio*, the balancing of the forces of evil or darkness implied in the number twenty-five involves a skillful power play. According to *curandero* folklore, St. Paul, the great lawyer of Christianity who replaced Judas and thus restored balance to the "incomplete" ranks of the eleven disciples through the "complete" number twelve, gathers the positive forces of the *Campo Justiciero* (particularly the Virgin of Mercy, patron of the military forces of Peru, and St. Michael, the commander of the celestial armies). Then, through the balancing power of the *Campo Medio*, he moves into the *Campo Ganadero* to remove Judas temporarily from the domain of Satan. The rationale behind this process is that Judas, as one who has fallen from grace, has a certain affinity with the forces of light — despite his residence in hell — which makes him the most likely candidate to serve as "informer" regarding the evils performed in the *Campo Ganadero* which he knows so well. But the power of the number twelve, by itself and as part of the number thirteen (i.e. $12 + 12 + 1 = 25$), is required to concentrate enough force to perform this balancing act.

There seems to be an apocalyptic undertone to this numerical symbolism and repetitive increase of sacred power. A review of the mystical experiences of St. John the Divine contained in the Book of Revelation in the New Testament confirms this. For example, the idea of the "four winds" and the four cardinal points, although having Indian antecedents, probably received some reinforcement from the following passage: "And after these things I saw four angels standing on the four corners of the earth, holding the four winds of the earth, that the wind should not blow on the earth, nor on the sea, nor on any tree" (Revelation IV: 1). There are also four beasts — a lion, a calf, an animal with a man's face, and a flying eagle — corresponding to the Four Apostles, around the throne of God, which provides a central fifth point, like the crucifix of the *mesa* in relation to the four cardinal points. We also have the Four Horsemen of war, destruction, hunger, and death.

The number seven is found throughout the whole book — i.e. the seven churches of early Christianity symbolized by seven golden candlesticks surrounding Christ, seven stars in Christ's right hand symbolizing the seven angels of the seven churches, the seven seals on the book of life as held by the seventh angel, the seven angels with seven trumpets who usher in the Millennium, seven plagues, the red dragon with seven heads and crowns, and the beast from the sea also with seven heads. But the following passage gives us a clear indication of the number's use in association with Christ, the sacrificed Lamb of Christianity: "And I beheld, and lo, in the midst of the throne of the four beasts and in the midst of the elders, stood a Lamb as it had been slain, having seven heads and seven eyes, which are the seven spirits of God sent forth into all the earth" (Revelation V: 6).

Six is found in the number 666 used to mark the followers of the devil on their right hands or foreheads. The following passage may indicate where the idea of multiplying the accounts of the *mesa* by thousands comes from: "And I beheld, and I heard the voice of many angels round about the throne and the beasts and the elders: and the number of them was ten thousand times ten thousand, and thousands of thousands" (Revelation V: 11).

Twelve is very clearly an important number associated with completion or salvation, for Jerusalem, the holy city in heaven promised to the elect after the Millennium, embodies the number: twelve gates (three at each cardinal point) associated with twelve pearls, guarded by twelve apostles, and named after the twelve tribes of Israel; twelve foundations of twelve precious stones named after the twelve apostles; and a wall 12,000 furlongs in length, height, and breadth. In addition, at the end of the book, the tree of life, nurtured by the water of the river of life flowing from the throne of God, has twelve fruits which are replenished every month. A power buildup is associated with the number twelve when it is squared (12 × 12) in reference to the 144,000 elect. This is the number of servants of God sealed on their foreheads with the seal of the living God by a fifth angel, ascending in the east from among the four angels at the four corners of the earth just before the destruction of the world. Finally, we have twenty-four elders surrounding the throne of God, which provides the central, "balanced" number twenty-five, the sacred number governing the Middle Field.

It is interesting to note the number of times the *curandero* and his assistants "raise" San Pedro and tobacco through their nostrils during the ceremonial division of the seance, as summarized in Table 1.

Table 1.   Summary of "raisings" during the séance

| "Raisings" | | Number of incidences | |
| | | *Curandero* | Assistants |
| --- | --- | --- | --- |
| *Mesa*, 7,000 accounts | | 7 | 1 |
| *Mesa*, 12,000 accounts | | 4 | 1 |
| | Total | 11 | |
| *Mesa*, 25 and 250,000 accounts | | 0 | 1 |
| San Pedro (by 2 assistants, patients) | | 0 | 3 |
| | | | Total  6 |
| *Curandero* (by 2 assistants) | | 0 | 1 |
| San Pedro (by *curandero*) | | 1 | 0 |
| | Total | 12 | Total  7 |

From Table 1, it can be seen that the *curandero* is "centered" — that is, he "raises" the symbol of the center seven times early in the session Then he "raises" himself to an incomplete number (eleven, the number of disciples after the betrayal by Judas) or state of imbalance (in terms of completion, or twelve). After performing the mass he maintains the dynamic tension of this imbalance by abstaining from the next two "raising" rites (for twenty-five and San Pedro). Because the herb jar in the *Campo Medio* is the *curandero*'s spiritual alter ego, it is understandable that he abstains from the "raising" of the number twenty-five (symbol of the *Campo Medio*), for in effect he is overseeing the delicate task of "raising" his own soul as well as activating the negative forces of the *Campo Ganadero* and, because the *mesa* is a projection of his own inner powers, those of his own nature, both balanced by the *Campo Medio*. While he maintains this detachment, the assistants also "raise" themselves to an incomplete number (six, the number of the devil in Revelation) or state of imbalance in terms of the center, or seven. They escape this dilemma by imbibing for the seventh time while "raising" the *curandero*'s corporeal self as he holds his activated alter ego, the herb jar. They thus center themselves and establish their capacity to do this for the patients later on in the curing rituals. Now that both his alter ego and corporeal self are "raised," the *curandero* is finally in a position to complete or integrate himself by "raising" the San Pedro infusion and then drinking it at the twelfth hour of clock time, midnight. This climactic culmination of events leads to activation of all his personal powers at the birth of a new day, realized by balancing the opposing forces of the microcosmic *mesa* and of his own psyche.

Thus the ceremonial division of the séance consists of a balanced power buildup. This power is then applied in the second part of the session, which lasts from midnight until 4 to 6 A.M. and consists of the actual curing acts. During the curing division of the séance, each person present must take a turn before the *mesa* while the *curandero* chants a song in his name. Then everyone concentrates on the staffs and swords placed upright in the ground at the head of the *mesa*. One of these artifacts is supposed to vibrate, because it is the focal point of the forces affecting the patient. It is given to the patient to hold in his left hand and over his chest, while the *curandero* chants the song of the staff to activate its account and cause its powers to become manifest. While everyone now concentrates on the patient, the *curandero* begins a long divinatory discourse in which he relates what he "sees." Sometimes others present see the same things as the *curandero*. According to Eduardo, the purpose of the discourse is to get the patient's subconscious to release whatever blockages are causing his problem. Once terminated, two assistants (one behind the patient and one in front) "raise" the patient from foot to waist, waist to neck, and neck to crown with a liquid provided by the *curandero* (usually the San Pedro and tobacco mixture, but other liquids — often a perfume — may be chosen) while he chants a final song. Then the patient must nasally imbibe a liquid provided by the *curandero* while holding the staff by one end over his head. This is called "raising the staff." Finally an assistant or the *curandero* rubs the patient with the staff, sprays it orally with whatever liquid is indicated, and returns it to the head of the *mesa*. After all present have had a turn before the *mesa*, the *curandero* closes the account with a final invocation to the "four winds and four roads" combined with a ritual purification of the *mesa* — performed by spraying it twelve times with substances from the *Campo Justiciero*. Thus the number twelve associated with Christ can be seen as an apt symbol for completion and the saying "I am Alpha and Omega, the beginning and the ending ..." (Revelation I: 8). Before departing, each person must be orally sprayed with a mixture of water, lye, and white corn flour while the *curandero* makes the form of a cross in the ground where the *mesa* stood and sprinkles the four corners of the area and the outlines of the cross with the same white corn flour mixture.

In conclusion, analysis of the spatial arrangement of power objects on Eduardo's *mesa* and the structure of the curing séance reveal the symbolic expression of his major goal: balance of power. Through ritual and the mediation of the Middle Field, the opposing forces of the *mesa* — and of the *curandero* — are activated and brought into meaningful, balanced interaction. The power generated by the ritual manipulation of power objects is then applied in solving patients' problems. The creative synthesis between aboriginal shamanism and Christian symbology manifest in Eduardo's art seems to be directly relevant to those who seek his services. It appears that shamanism in northern Peru may be more than a colorful relic left over from the Indian past.

## REFERENCES

CHIAPPE, MARIO
1967   Alucinógenas nativas. *Revista del Viernes Médico* (Lima) 18:293–299.
1968   Psiquiatría folklórica peruana: el curanderismo en la costa norte del Perú. *Anales del Servicio de Psiquiatría* (Lima) 11.
1969a  El curanderismo con alucinógenas de la costa y la selva del Perú. *Psiquiatría Peruana* (Lima) 1:318–325.
1969b  El sindrome cultural de "daño" y su tratamiento curanderil. *Psiquiatría Peruana* (Lima) 1:330–337.

CRUZ SÁNCHEZ, GUILLERMO
1948   Informe sobre las aplicaciones populares de la cimora en el norte Perú. *Revista de Farmacología y Medicina Experimental* (Lima) 1:253–259.
1950   Estudio folklórico de algunas plantas medicamentosas y tóxicas de la región norte del Perú. *Revista de Medicina Experimental* (Lima) 9:159–166.

DOBKIN DE RÍOS, MARLENE
1968 Trichocereus pachanoi — a mescaline cactus used in folk healing in Peru. *Economic Botany* 22:191–194.
1968–1969 Folk curing with a psychedelic cactus in north coast Peru. *International Journal of Social Psychiatry* 15:23–32.
1969a Curanderismo psicodélico en el Perú: continuidad y cambio. *Mesa Redonda de Ciencias Prehistóricas y Antropológicas* 1:139–149.
1969b Fortune's malice: divination, psychotherapy, and folk medicine in Peru. *Journal of American Folklore* 82:132–141.

FRIEDBERG, CLAUDINE
1959 Rapport sommaire sur une mission au Pérou. *Journal d'Agriculture Tropicale et de Botanique Appliquée* (Paris) 6:439–450.
1960 "Utilisation d'un cactus à mescaline au nord du Perou," in *Proceedings of the Sixth International Congress of Anthropological and Ethnological Sciences* 2(2): 21–26.
1963 Mission au Pérou — Mai 1961–Mars 1962. *Journal d'Agriculture Tropicale et de Botanique Appliquée* (Paris) 10: 33–52, 245–258, 344–386.

GILLIN, JOHN
1945 *Moche: a Peruvian coastal community.* Smithsonian Institution 3.

RODRÍGUEZ SUY SUY, VICTOR ANTONIO
1970 "La medicina tradicional en la costa norte del Perú actual," in *Proceedings of the Thirty-ninth International Congress of Americanists.* Lima.

SEGUIN, CARLOS ALBERTO
1969 Psiquiatría folklórica. *Psiquiatría Peruana* (Lima) 1:154–159.
1970 "Folk psychiatry," in *World biennial of psychiatry and psychotherapy,* volume one. Edited by S. Arieti, 165–177. New York: Basic Books.

SHARON, DOUGLAS
1972 "The San Pedro cactus in Peruvian folk healing," in *Flesh of the gods: the ritual use of hallucinogens.* Edited by Peter T. Furst, 114–135. New York: Praeger.

# SECTION FOUR

# Esoteric Rituals in Japanese Traditional Secret Societies: A Study of the Death and Rebirth Motif

TSUNEO AYABE

This paper is an analysis of the initiation rites of traditional esoteric groups in Japan to see how the death and rebirth motif is embodied in them. However, it is necessary first to explain the term "secret society," which is a rather vague notion.

Perhaps secrecy exists in some degree in any organization. However, not all societies that do not wish to be overt are secret societies. Secret societies can be divided roughly into political secret societies and esoteric secret societies. It is the latter — esoteric societies — that are the subject of this paper. Such societies have a grading system and a series of secret rituals, with increasing secrecy as one proceeds from the initiation to the higher grades. Secret societies of this sort, with secret rituals, may well take advantage of their secrecy to engage in political activities, or there may be secret societies which conceal their activities and membership with the intention of instigating rebellion or subversion against the political power. It is characteristic of such secret societies that they naturally disappear when their purpose has been achieved, or when the cause that gave rise to the organization no longer exists.

The outstanding characteristic of secret societies is that they have mysteries. The initiation, which forms the center of the mysteries in specialized secret societies, generally includes the following three factors:

(1) Through initiation there is realized the psychological advancement of an initiate's spirit from what is viewed as a lower level to a higher level. In other words, the goal of the initiation ceremony is to change a profane individual into a reborn person. This rebirth is considered possible only through the initiation rites of the various secret organizations.

(2) Initiation rites are always accompanied by ordeals. Since the purpose

of the initiation rites is to impress a feeling of death and rebirth upon the spirit of the initiate, he undergoes various material and spiritual ordeals in the course of his installation in which he goes symbolically through the process of having died and been reborn after overcoming the ordeal of death. Most such initiation rites are exclusive, and an initiate has to swear that he will not betray the secret. Only in rare cases are the rites performed in public, as they are in primitive societies.

(3)   An initiate cannot arrive at once at the level of completeness. In order to reach the best and perfect state of mind he has to go through a long, hard process requiring great effort. As a result, most secret societies have not only an initiation but also a graded hierarchy of rites corresponding to each stage in the progression. The Scottish rite, for example, which is one of the main institutions of Freemasonry, has thirty-three steps (Gist 1940; Jones 1967; Ferguson 1937).

The above are the characteristics of initiation in specialized secret societies. In many unspecialized primitive secret societies the initiation rites include a visiting deity rite related to harvest festivals, in addition to the rites of death and rebirth connected with the initiation ceremony into adulthood (Oka et al. 1958: 75–78). In these secret societies, a group wearing exotic costumes and with masked members disguised as deities, ancestral spirits, and the dead, appears in the village on certain nights during the year. Sometimes the disguised members perform a quaint mythical dance, or visit and threaten each house in the village. They also give sanction to acceptable deeds or warning against unacceptable deeds of the uninitiated. This implies that many secret societies of primitive and folk communities are inseparably connected with the life and social structure of the community, and the order within the secret society forms a substantial part of the order of the entire community (Mendelson 1967: 20–37). Whereas the specialized secret societies of modern communities set as the central goal of their initiation rites the renovation of the personality through existential experience (or through the drama of "death and rebirth" — a kind of denial of the self), many secret societies in primitive or folk communities have not only this goal but also the goal of serving as an influential organ of the entire community, including the uninitiated (Webster 1932; Loeb 1929).

## DEATH AND REBIRTH IN JAPANESE TRADITIONAL ESOTERIC ORGANIZATIONS

Among the traditional Japanese esoteric groups are a group of *Yamabushi* called *Shugendo;* the *Shingon Tachikawaryu*, persecuted as heretics by the

*Shingon* sect of Buddhism; the *Kakushi-nenbutsu* of northeastern Japan; the *Shingosho* of the Saga Prefecture of Kyushu; the *Kakure Kirishitan* [hidden Christian] of the western coast of Kyushu; the *Renmonkyo;* the *Omotokyo;* the *Hitonomichi;* etc. There are also some right-wing groups, like the *Tenkento*, that may be equivalent to secret societies. A hunters' group called *Matagi*, located deep in the mountains of northeastern Japan and maintaining unique beliefs and customs concerning bear hunting (Suzuki 1964); the *Miyaza*, with mysteries concerning shrines (Higo 1941); and an esoteric society called *Akamata-Kuromata* in the southwestern islands of Japan would also fall into this category of secret society.

In the following sections I will discuss four such groups, namely, the rather archaic *Akamata-Kuromata;* the shamanistic *Kakushi-nenbutsu* and *Shingosho;* and *Shugendo*, to show that the motif of death and rebirth is embodied embryonically in each of these unique societies. The *Kakushi-nenbutsu* and *Shingosho* will be treated in the same section because of their similarity.

A.  *Akamata-Kuromata*

The name denotes both the custom of wearing masks and other disguises to celebrate the festival of certain deities, and also the esoteric group that carries out these observances, found only in several hamlets on the islands of Panari and Ishigakijima (the center being in the hamlet of Komi, Iriomote Island). *Akamata-Kuromata* is the popular name — the natives use the formal name, *Niirukito*. *Niiru* is an abbreviation of *Niraikanai*, a paradise beyond the sea that brings happiness to this world. Deities from this paradise visit people, and it is said that fire and rice seeds were brought to them from there. It is really the deities that people mean by *Akamata-Kuromata* — the deities in masks and other disguises who come from the *Niraikanai* in August to visit each house and wish the people prosperity and good harvest during the two days of *puru* (the harvest festival in Yaeyama Archipelago, generally performed after reaping rice). As will be mentioned later, the deities have another kind of birthplace — in paradise on the one hand, and in the sanctuary in the village on the other (Sumiya 1964a: 6–13).

At the festival of Panari in 1963, for example, celebrated on the sixth, seventh, and eighth of August, a family of four deities appeared: *Akamata* (male), *Kuromata* (female), child *Akamata*, and child *Kuromata*. The festival begins on the fifth of August, when a person disguised as the goddess who administers the festival confines himself in the sanctuary of the sacred Bitaku Mountain. The first day, called *onpuru* (August 6), is the day when people thank the deity for the good harvest of the past year, and the lion dance is performed in the garden of the shrine that night. The *Akamata-Kuromata* appear on the night of August 7. In masks and other disguises, they appear in front of the villagers and threaten women and children in the audience, and then visit each house in a certain order. At dawn on the eighth, at the first cockcrow, the villagers say goodbye to the *Akamata-Kuromata*, who return to the sacred Bitaku Mountain.

The ceremony of *Akamata-Kuromata* is kept completely secret, and is performed only by a certain group of qualified villagers who have passed screening. Therefore, those who take part in this ceremony constitute an exclusive group.

Enrollment in this *Akamata-Kuromata* esoteric group is called *umutu-iri* in Komi Village, and *nabindo-iri* in Miyara Village. According to Miyara (1973: 133–134), in order to join this society, one has to have the following qualifications:

1. PRINCIPLE OF AGE   One has to have reached a certain age — in Komi, seventeen; in Kohama, fourteen, after graduation from middle school.

2. PRINCIPLE OF RESIDENCE   Not only does one have to have been born in the village and still live there, but also one's parents have to have citizenship in the village. In the case of a *grebo-fa* [wife's son] — a person whose father is from some other village but whose mother is from this village, he is likely to be admitted a little later than the fully qualified boys.

3. PRINCIPLE OF PERSONALITY   One has to be a young man of good conduct.

In Panari, an *Akamata-Kuromata* scout is called a *Shinka*. Fourteen- and fifteen-year-old boys (nowadays, they enter middle school at twelve or thirteen) are automatically enrolled in the ranks of the *Shinka*, who follow the children *Akamata-Kuromata* when they appear at the *gomapuru* (the millet harvest festival in July). However, they are not fully qualified to be members of the *Shinka* at the *mazupuru*, or rice harvest festival in August, when the boys are put through a more stringent screening. The screening committee meets in a secret corner somewhere on the sacred mountain. At this time all of the applicant's conduct since childhood is taken into consideration, and he has to undergo severe physical ordeals in order to pass the screening. Usually all the boys in the village at the age of fourteen or fifteen apply for *Shinka*. At the screening, the opinions of the junior group (*Bahamono*) are respected above those of the senior group (*Nahatze*) or the O.B.'s (*Uyaninzu*, those over forty), so that it is possible for the *Bahamono* group to make the final decision. The novices are called *Shintsukya*. They wear headbands made from miscanthus, a tall green grass, and wait on the older members.

The age-group stratification of the *Akamata-Kuromata* Society of Panari Village is as follows:

| | |
|---|---|
| *Shintsukya* (novice) | 14–15 years |
| *Sampu* (servant) | 14 or 15–21 years |
| *Bahamono* (junior) | 21–26 years |
| *Nahatze* (senior) | 26–40 years |
| *Uyaninzu* (O.B.) | over 40 years |

The structure of the *Akamata-Kuromata* Society given above seems to reflect their age principle, but it should be thought of rather as a stratification according to year of enrollment.

Sumiya (1964b: 93) summarizes the characteristic features of *Akamata-Kuromata* as follows:

Positive aspects:
1. The group is structured on the principle of age grade, like the junior and the senior.
2. At the screening, the applicant's moral quality proven by his conduct is highly relevant.
3. The members have to keep the mysteries of *Akamata-Kuromata* secret throughout their lives.
Negative aspects:
1. The group is not structured STRICTLY on the age-grading principle.
2. Ranking of house is not reflected in the stratification within the group.
3. Women are excluded from the group.

Incidentally, although the fundamental rule is that only men can join the *Akamata-Kuromata* Society, in some villages the wives of the members can also join.

Members of the *Akamata-Kuromata* must not talk about their secrets even among themselves, except during the festival. The history of the *Niiru* deities and the songs for the festival are taught only during the festival, so that those with poor memories cannot learn them even after many years. Therefore, the more complex verbal traditions and deeper secrets are transmitted only to the more able members, who learn and accumulate secrets of higher degree as the years go by. As a result, only a few able senior members are granted the highest leadership. Such leaders are called *Uya* (the equivalent of "parent"), and they have absolute authority not only over matters concerning *Akamata-Kuromata*, but also over all aspects of life in the village.

The research on Komi Village is most detailed concerning the initiation rite of the *Akamata-Kuromata* Society.

In Komi, the *Kuromata* group meets on the second and third day of the harvest festival at the house of the black *tunimutu* (a certain lineage that presides over the festival), while the *Akamata* and *Shiromata* (Komi happens to have this third divinity) groups meet at the house of the red *tunimutu*. The boys who have just accomplished *umutu-iri* or enrollment in the society are called *uitabi*, the second-year novices are called *matatabi*, and the still older ones are called *giramunu*. When the *giramunu* and the senior members have gathered, the applicants are ordered to sit straight with their feet neatly tucked in (called *pentukibiti*) in the garden of the *tunimutu* under the glaring sun for a long time (about an hour at present) and are told to perform repeatedly the action of keeping their arms straight out and wide open and then, with the arms still extended, slowly bringing the two hands together in front of them until the palms meet. If any *uitabi* falls into poor posture, he is either hit with a stick or gets a bucket of water poured over him. After this ordeal, the *uitabi* takes up a wine cup and sways it from right to left from left to right to the rhythm of the *yunta*, or working song. The final stage of the initiation is *mamari*, or confession of the name of the girl the novice happens to like. If he utters the name of a girl deemed unsuitable for him (say if she is much older than he), he is ordered to repeat all of the ordeals. So he is careful to name a girl of his own age or younger.

Thus, it is clear that the custom called *Akamata-Kuromata* includes both the festival for the *Akamata-Kuromata* deities and the esoteric society that carries out the festival. A kind of initiation rite is also observed when one joins this society (Miyara 1962: 347-352; Sumiya 1964b: 85–99).

### B.  *Kakushi-nenbutsu* and *Shingosho*

There are esoteric groups called *Kakushi-nenbutsu* in the Tohoku area, and *Shingosho* in the Saga Prefecture on Kyushu Island. Although they have no direct relationship with each other, they fall into the same category of folk religion with Buddhist elements.

1.  KAKUSHI-NENBUTSU    The *Kakushi-nenbutsu* do not use the ordinary

Buddhist temples as their gathering place. Their gatherings and ceremonies are conducted at the homes of their members by a leader called *Zenchishiki* and his assistant, *Wakiyaku*, without professional priests. *Kakushi-nenbutsu* stems from the *Shingon* (a Buddhist sect) mystery, and is said to have spread in Tohoku in the middle of the Edo period (1603-1867). Before it permeated to Tohoku, the folk religions in the area had a magical basis, and *Kakushi-nenbutsu* seems to be a kind of syncretism between them.

In Iwate Prefecture, in the ceremony called *Oshichiya*, the following rituals are observed: *omotozuke, otoriage, hōe,* and *kaishoku,* in this order. The first two rituals, *omotozuke* and *otoriage,* are most important as mysteries. *Omotozuke* is a simple ritual for an infant held in its parent's arms, to whom *Zenchishiki* reads the Buddhist scriptures while he strokes the infant's head with them. The infant is told by *Zenchishiki* that he will undergo the *otoriage* ritual in the future, and will become a formal member of the group. *Otoriage* is an initiation ceremony for a child at about the age of seven, and is the most important ritual in *Kakushi-nenbutsu.* Children who are about to undergo the initiation ceremony of *otoriage* are guided to a place where they are seated in front of an image of Amitabha and other saints. *Zenchishiki* sits on the left side and *Wakiyaku* on the right side of the Buddhist altar, and they announce various rituals to the children. Then, after the children chant *namiamidabutsu* and *tasuketamae* [please help me], they are told to make a sign of ecstasy and joy with the help of *Wakiyaku,* and are asked to shout *ta,* the first syllable of *tasuketamae,* repeatedly with all their hearts. *Zenchishiki* observes the faces of the children shouting *ta* and decides according to the degree of a child's ecstasy whether or not he will be permitted to become a member of the group. A basis for permission to join the group is said to be whether or not in one breath he can puff off worldly concerns, along with impurity, and reach the ecstatic state. After this ritual the children are forced to take an oath that they will never tell others about the rituals of *Kakushi-nenbutsu,* will set the day of *otoriage* as their day of death, and will come to pray at the altar for their whole life. This means that a child who has undergone the initiation ceremony has died once and has then been reborn. For this reason, children who are going to undergo the *otoriage* ritual are called dead men. Children who have died once and have departed from the secular world have been born again as men of a spiritually higher state. Children who pass the rites of *otoriage* are permitted to be grownup members of the group. There is the same characteristic in the rituals for adulthood, attaching importance to frantic ecstasy in wishing to fuse into one with the Buddha to whom they minister.

Having this character, *Kakushi-nenbutsu* has been suppressed by the government, which has prohibited the conduct of mysteries. The characteristics of *Kakushi-nenbutsu* are exactly contrary to the government policy, which has ordered people to register in officially recognized sects, so that movements of popular unrest may be kept under supervision. In 1754, in the records of Iwate Prefecture, punishment for engaging in *Kakushi-nenbutsu* practices included death of the leader (one), exile (three), banishment (seventeen). As a result of these suppressions, *Kakushi-nenbutsu* has become a secret society, and it has survived to this day (Takahashi 1956, 1966; Naito 1971: 154–160).

2.   SHINGOSHO   This secret society is found around the eastern area of Tosu city and Kiyama-cho in Saga Prefecture. The initiation ceremony of *Shingosho* is divided into (a) *haragomino-gojoju*, (b) *ochomon*, and (c) *gojoju*.

a.   *Haragomino-gojoju* has the purpose of letting an embryo listen to Buddhist scriptures before birth so as to avoid being buried in the dark by death or miscarriage, without getting the mercy of Buddha in this world. *Goza* is performed for the embryos twice a year, in spring and autumn, when people make offerings to the departed spirits.

b.   *Ochomon* is also performed at the same time, for an infant or for an adult who has not gone through the ritual. In this ritual a member of the *Shingosho* takes a position of *sazukeyaku* and chants a special scripture attached to this position.

c.   *Gojoju* is the most important and decisive ritual in *Shingosho*. The ritual is in principle for a child before elementary-school age, and is held at a place called the *hōzo*, which is constructed especially for the ritual. A person who has undergone this ritual and is known as a man who possesses the mercy of Buddha, is recognized as a formal member of the group. In this ceremony a member called *mitodoke* sits in front of Buddha's image, which is put in the center of the altar in the *hōzo*. Opposite this *mitodoke* sits an initiate with his patron, while an assistant member called *osusume* advises the initiate to cling to Buddha with all his mind, or ask Buddha to help him. The initiate follows this advice and chants *namiamidabutsu* and *tasuketamae* [please help me] repeatedly. In the meantime, several initiates attain a state of ecstasy. *Mitodoke* observes this state of ecstasy of the initiates and announces that they have got Buddha's mercy. In order to gain membership in *Shingosho* it is necessary to pass the above-mentioned three rituals. In some groups of *Shingosho*, however, some of the rituals are not observed. New members who have gone through the rituals may participate in various ordinary services for the dead, as well as in mysteries. The rite of *goza* is performed at each service. A unit of *goza* consists of chants by the participants and *sata*. *Sata* is a sermon recited in a special rhythm in the state of ecstasy, and it takes about thirty minutes to complete one round. The place where *goza* is done is called *yado*. As to the organization of the *Shingosho*, generally speaking, a group is divided into the following three classes; *kyakujin* (the leader of the ritual), *sewanin* (the leader of the organization), and *dogyo* (the ordinary member). The status of *kyakujin* is not hereditary, and it has several statuses within it. The leader of *Shingosho* is required to have a special quality of so-called charisma (Hiroo 1970: 125–126; Koga 1972: 65–80).

Thus, we can observe shamanistic elements of ecstasy or orgy in *Kakushi-nenbutsu* and *Shingosho*. And more important, they have characteristics that distinguish them from other esoteric societies in that initiation is centered mainly on the embryo, infant, and child.

Incidentally, in the case of the *Kayakabe* belief (also a kind of hidden Buddhism) found around Yokokawa-cho in Kigoshima Prefecture, the rituals are performed secretly at midnight. The group is composed of both men and women. *Kayakabe* emphasizes rituals for ancestors and wishes for happiness after death. Rites of passage at the time of conception, birth, adulthood, and marriage are also performed by the group. However, whether or not the motif of death and rebirth is observed at the initiation ceremony is still unknown to the outsider. An important characteristic of the group is that there is a food taboo against chicken, as it is a messenger of the deity. Also, marriage of a member with a heretic is prohibited (Chiba 1970: 31–60).

## C. *Shugendo*

*Shugendo* is a kind of religion in which one acquires magical power with which he carries out magico-religious activities. It grew out of many different "religions" such as Japanese folk beliefs (mountain worship, in particular), Shintoism, and esoteric Buddhism, all syncretized into one. Its origin can be seen in the folk Buddhism of the Nara period (710–794), the disciples of which lived in the mountains and sought to acquire magical power through asceticism, chanting the Saddharma Pundarika Sutra (one of the Buddhist scriptures). *Shugendo* has no creed or scriptures.

In the Heian period (794–1192), the disciples of esoteric Buddhism also practiced austerities. In the course of time several different groups of disciples gradually formed the religious group called *Shugen*.

In the Kamakura period (1192–1338), two separate groups appeared, the *Honzan* group, with its center in Kumano, and the *Tozan* group, with its center in Yoshino, each of which had its own way of ascetic practice in the mountains.

In the Muromachi period (1338–1573), the content of ascetic practice such as abstinence, purification, and other details became further elaborated.

In the Edo period (1603–1867), asceticism finally developed into an authorized practice of the group. Novices participated in the religious society's ascetic practice, and they could ascend to a higher rank by being "baptized."

In 1873 *Shugendo* was abolished by the Meiji Government, resulting in a temporary decline of ascetic practices by the group as a society, but it still continued its existence under the leadership of grass-roots believers.

After World War II, each sect of *Shugendo* became independent, but the most important activity in each sect has continued to be the ascetic practice in the mountains.

This paper is concerned with how the motif of death and rebirth is treated in *Shugendo*. Each sect has its own goal, such as the acquisition of magical power or various other magico-religious purposes, and in the case of the autumn ritual held on Haguro Mountain, the motif of death and rebirth is clearly apparent. The first practice is initiation into the rank of *yamabushi* [novice]. It is performed during the week of August 24 – 31 in Kotaku Temple. Several ranks intervene between the first step of *yamabushi* and the highest rank, *daisendachi*, and each step is accompanied by mysteries. When a *yamabushi* becomes *shinkyaku* [member of the second rank], the mystery is called the practice in the world of the womb.

The novices carry on their backs a container called *oi*, an object of worship for them. On the night of August 24, in the garden of Kotaku Temple, they observe a rite called *oikaraksa*, which means "funeral." On the twenty-fifth, the novices come out of the temple carrying a big magical stick, and march in line to a pavilion at the foot of the mountain. Here the *daisendachi*, or the holder of the highest rank, knocks down the stick in the direction toward the center of the temple. This is said to symbolize conception. In the world of esoteric Buddhism, the world is divided into the male sphere and the female sphere, the former being called the *Kongokai* and the latter, *Taizokai*. The meaning of *taizo* is "the inside of the womb of the goddess of the earth," "underworld," and "the world of the dead." Knocking down the magical stick signifies farewell to this world and entry into the womb of the goddess, which is actually achieved by going into Kotaku Temple. For the practice of this ritual, symbols of the blood vessels and bones of the goddess of the earth are placed in all corners of the room. Ascetic practice in Kotaku Temple has three stages (the first lodge, the second lodge, and the third lodge), and each stage is accompanied by mysteries.

In the first lodge (August 25 – 27) the novices are assigned to "smoking off," abstaining from both food and water, etc. Also observed at this stage is a symbolic rite of intercourse and conception under a torch light.

In the second lodge (August 28), confession before the *daisendachi*, and a special rite of wrestling called *tenguzumo*, are observed.

In the third lodge (August 29 – 31) there are no more ordeals, but only preaching and the teaching of magical words. Before leaving the mountain on the thirty-first, the novices dedicate their final prayer, leave the temple, go down the valley where they engage in further ascetic practice, pass in front of a waterfall, and then go to Motohaguro, the most sacred spot on this mountain, where they go through the mystery of taking the oath. After all this they line up to march to Haguro Shrine to pray, and then the *daisendachi* leads the chorus of "*wooo...*," when all the novices squeeze out a big cry in the squatting posture. This is called *denari*, or the symbol of the second birth. After this, they run down the mountain toward Tamuke Village which lies at its foot, jump over a fire made in front of the lodge of the *daisendachi*, and finally go into the lodge to receive a new title (Murakami 1943; Miyake 1970; Hori 1955).

To sum up the rituals, the novices first die, and then perform ascetic practices within the mother goddess' womb — in other words, they pass through "conception" and gradual formation into man, which symbolizes death and rebirth.

The titled ascetics are usually engaged in incantations and prayer. In order to become an independent ascetic, one should not only pray, but also be able to experience union with god. This is an important doctrine in this mystery, expressed as "God comes into me and I go into God." The secular person dies, then he is fertilized in the womb of the goddess Dainichinyorai, and is born again in front of Haguro Shrine; such is the mystery of eternal return.


CONCLUSION

The following is a list of the characteristics of each of the three Japanese esoteric societies described:

*Akamata-Kuromata*
1.  Worship of deities,

2. Deity visits the village from a faraway land (although he may be born in the sacred mountain near the village),
3. Esoteric ritual related to agrarian rites,
4. Members of the esoteric society in masks and disguises,
5. Threats to women and children,
6. Initiation accompanied by ordeals,
7. Initiate made to confess his girlfriend's name,
8. Graded ranks,
9. The society's helping to maintain order in the village,
10. No connection with other existing religions.

*Kakushi-nenbutsu* and *Shingosho*
1. Ecstasy,
2. Embryos and infants are the subject of the initiation,
3. Ascetic practice,
4. Graded ranks,
5. Elements of a kind of orgy,
6. Shamanistic elements,
7. A territorial connection between the esoteric society and the community,
8. A connection with the existing religion (Buddhism).

*Shugendo*
1. Mountain worship,
2. Embryological factors,
3. Sacred marriage,
4. Elaborate ascetic practices,
5. Graded ranks,
6. Incantations and prayer,
7. Ecstasy,
8. A connection with existing religions (Buddhism and Shintoism).

We have already seen that the three above kinds of esoteric societies have no relation among themselves, and that they have different characteristics. On the other hand, if we consider that esoteric secret societies presuppose the existence of the "death and rebirth" motif, then it is also true that these three societies fall into one single class.

The "death and rebirth" motif in the *Akamata-Kuromata* society of Yaeyama Archipelago is somewhat less clear than in the other cases, although when one takes into consideration the fact that one of the important factors in the mystery is that the deity is born in a mountain sanctuary, it seems reasonable to classify it with other societies that have the "death and rebirth" motif. The existence of a farmer's role in the mystery leads us to believe that the deity is an agrarian deity presiding over the harvest.

Generally speaking, initiation can be divided into puberty rites and specialized initiations (Eliade 1958: 128). Initiation in the *Akamata-Kuromata* belongs to the former type, while that in the *Kakushi-nenbutsu* and *Shugendo* belongs to the latter. Puberty rites are further divided into personal rites and group rites. In the *Akamata-Kuromata* they are group rites, as almost all of the youngsters in the community participate. The *Akamata-Kuromata* society, which worships the *Akamata-Kuromata* deity, or the agrarian deity of fertility, is deeply rooted in the social structure of the community. The threatening of women and children and the reproaching of nonmembers when they are guilty of undesirable conduct seem to serve as important social sanctions in maintaining order in the community. Although the *Kakushi-nenbutsu* and *Shingosho* may also have a strong connection with their communities, they never have any public pageant such as that of the *Akamata-Kuromata* society; all of their rituals are carried on away from the eyes of the public.

Shamanistic elements are strongly apparent in the ecstasy and orgies of the *Kakushi-nenbutsu* and *Shingosho*. In these societies, people qualified as shamans or people having charisma are held in higher esteem. In *Shugendo*, the element of ecstasy is present also, but not the shamanistic elements.

Some comments concerning the sex factor may be added here. In *Shugendo* women are strictly excluded, whereas they are included in *Kakushi-nenbutsu* and *Shingosho*. In the case of the *Akamata-Kuromata* society, membership is limited to young men, although they do have a female deity (*Akamata* is a male deity, *Kuromata* a female deity); and in the harvest festival which has a strong connection with the *Akamata-Kuromata* mystery, a female medium called *tsukasa* plays the central role. There is a paradox here: on the one hand they exclude females, while on the other hand their central motif is the productivity bestowed only upon females. *Shugendo*, with its strong embryological character, also falls into this paradox: the members first die, then, through a symbolical rite of conception, go into the womb of the goddess of the earth, and only after this can they become completely new people. It is not easy to determine just why in *Akamata-Kuromata* each of the initiates is made to confess his girlfriend's name, but it reminds us of a passage from the works of H. Schultz concerning age-grade and free love, referring to "*Versteigerung oder öffentliches Ausrufen der Mädchen*" (Emori 1954: 177–221). The masks and other disguises of *Akamata-Kuromata*, together with the threatening of women and children, can be compared with the practices of the *Duk-Duk* of Melanesia, particularly on New Britain Island.

Let us return to the "death and rebirth" motif. Although the three societies are similar in that they all have this motif, it would be more reasonable to consider them as having no connection among themselves. Since puberty rites exist all over the world, even where there are no esoteric societies, it may well be that puberty rites were merely added to the initiation rites of esoteric societies and then further refined. In this sense, the *Akamata-Kuromata* society, in which the characteristics of puberty rites are most clearly seen, may be considered as maintaining its original form more than the other societies. However, in a country like Japan, with a complex compound of various cultures formed through her long history, there are many factors that militate against an evolutionist explanation of what influenced what. It would be more appropriate to say that *Akamata-Kuromata*, *Kakushi-nenbutsu*, and *Shugendo* have coexisted in Japan with no interrelations whatsoever. If it is true that as culture becomes more complex, initiation rites become more refined (Eliade 1958: 131), then *Shugendo* may be considered the most elaborate among the esoteric societies in both rituals and organization.

## REFERENCES

CHIBA, NONITAKA
1970   "Kayakabe no genkyo [The contemporary state of Kayakabe]," in *Kayakabe*. Edited by Ryukoku University, 31–60. Kyoto: Hozonkan.
ELIADE, MIRCEA
1958   *Birth and rebirth: the religious meanings of initiation in human culture.* Translated from the French by W. R. Trask. New York: Harper and Bros.
EMORI, ITSUO
1954   Nenrei-kaiteisei narabini jiyurenai ni kansuru H. Schurtz no gakusetsu ni tsuite [On the theory of H. Schurtz concerning age-grades and romantic love]. *Shakaigaku Kenkyu* [Study of Social Sciences] 4:177–221.
FERGUSON, CHARLES W.
1937   *Fifty million brothers.* New York: Farrar and Rinehart.
GIST, P.
1940   Secret societies. *The University of Missouri Studies* 1 (XV).
HIGO, KAZUO
1941   *Miyaza no kenkyu* [A study of Miyaza]. Tokyo: Kobundo.
HIROO, KAZUNORI
1970   Saga-ken Kiyama chiiki ni okeru tokushu shukyo shudan ni tsuite [On the special religious groups in Saga Prefecture]. *Nishi-nihon Shukyo-gaku Zasshi* [Western Japanese Journal of Religion] 1:125–126.

HORI, ICHIRO
1955   *Wagakuni minkan-shinko-shi no kenkyu* [A study of the history of Japanese folk religion], two volumes. Tokyo: Sogensha.

JONES, MERVYN
1967   "Freemasonry," in *Secret societies*. Edited by Norman Mackenzie, 152–177. New York: Holt, Rinehart and Winston.

KOGA, KAZUNORI
1972   Kiyabu chiho ni okeru Shingosho no kenkyu [A study of *Shingosho* in the Kiyabu area]. *Nishi-nihon Shukyo-gaku Zasshi* [Western Japanese Journal of Religion] 2:65–80.

LOEB, EDWIN M.
1929   *Tribal initiations and secret societies*. Berkeley: University of California Press.

MENDELSON, E. MICHAEL
1967   "Primitive secret societies," in *Secret societies*. Edited by Norman Mackenzie, 20–37. New York: Holt, Rinehart and Winston.

MIYAKE, JUN
1970   *Shugendo girei no kenkyu* [A study of rituals in *Shugendo*]. Tokyo: Shunju-sha.

MIYARA, TAKAHIRO
1962   Yaeyama-gunto ni okeru iwayuru himitsukessha ni tsuite [On the secret societies in the Yaeyama Islands]. *Japanese Journal of Ethnology* 27:347–352.
1973   "Yaeyama-gunto [Yaeyama Islands]," in *Okinawa no minzokugakuteki kenkyu* [Ethnological studies of Okinawa]. Edited by T. Obayahi, 117–140. Tokyo: Japanese Society of Ethnology.

MURAKAMI, TOSHIO
1943   *Shugendo no hattatsu* [The development of *Shugendo*]. Tokyo: Unebi.

MURATAKE, SEIICHI
1964–1965   Dualism in the Southern Ryukyus. Offprint from *Archiv für Völkerkunde* 19:120–128.

NAITO, MASATOSHI
1971   "Kakushi-nenbutsu [Hidden Buddhism]," in *Dento to Gendai* [Traditional and modern] 10:154–160.

OKA, M., *et al.*
1958   *Nihon-minzoku no Kigen* [Origin of Japanese]. Tokyo: Heibonsha.

SUMIYA, KAZUHIKO
1964a   Akamata-Kuromata. *Misuzu* 56:6–13.
1964b   "*Geheimkult* in Southwestern Islands," in *Ishida Eiichiro kyoju kanreki kinen ronbunshu* [Special articles dedicated to Professor E. Ishida's sixtieth birthday], 85–90. Tokyo: Kadokawa.

SUZUKI, MITSUO
1964   "Matagi no yamakotoba [special vocabularies of Matagi]," in *Ishida Eiichiro kyoju kanreki kinen ronbunshu* [Special articles dedicated to Professor E. Ishida's sixtieth birthday]. Tokyo: Kadokawa.

TAKAHASHI, BONSEN
1956, 1966   *Kakushi-nenbutsuko* [A study of *Kakushi-nenbutsu*], two volumes. Tokyo: Nihon Gakujutsu Shinkokai.

TAKAHASHI, TOICHI
  1970   Miyaza no shakaijinruigakuteki chosa [A social anthropological study of Miyaza]. *Bulletin of the Institute for Asian and African Studies, Tokyo University*, 29–56.
WEBSTER, HUTTON
  1932   *Primitive secret societies*. New York: Macmillan.

# Ritual, Myth, and the Murdered President

DOROTHY WILLNER

I. John F. Kennedy, thirty-fifth President of the United States, was slain by an assassin on November 22, 1963 in his forty-sixth year of life and in his third year as head of state and government. As the murder of the young President swiftly became known, historic time intersected with mythic time throughout most of his land and beyond. The intersection of these contrasting representations of time corresponded to the concurrence of different rituals sharing common properties.

Three sets of rituals were called forth by the news that President Kennedy had been shot and, soon afterwards, by the news that he was dead. These were: rituals of the Catholic church for its dead son, rituals of the state and nation for its fallen chief, and rituals of the state for the accession to its highest office and for the continuity of orderly government.

The basic ceremony in this last set of rituals was the swearing-in of Lyndon Johnson as thirty-sixth President of the United States. This occurred at 2:38 P.M. Central Standard Time on November 22, 1963. This was two hours and about eight minutes after President Kennedy had been shot (between 12:30 and 12:31 P.M.) and one hour and thirty-eight minutes after he had been pronounced dead (at 1:00 P.M.).

The enumeration of these timed events demonstrates the defining attributes of historic time. It is linear and irreversible; it records the occurrence of unique events and their succession and it measures the intervals between them. However, historic time is itself measured, and it is measured by reference to recurrent sequences: the revolutions of the earth around its axis and around the sun and the resulting periodicity of natural phenomena such as day and night and the seasons (Leach 1961). Counting transforms the repetitive intervals by which time is measured into an irreversible succession of such units and cycles of units. Historic time is bound to dates ( Lévi-Strauss 1966).

Mythic time, in contrast, is time without measure or finitude. "On the one hand, a myth always refers to events alleged to have taken place in time . . . long ago. But what gives the myth an operative value is that the specific pattern described is everlasting; it explains the present and the past as well as the future" (Lévi-Strauss 1955: 403). If "a myth remains the same as long as it is felt as such" (Lévi-Strauss 1955: 435), it follows that events occurring in historic time, including the immediate past and present, "can become endowed with the quality of myth if they fit or can be fitted into the pattern of a traditional myth" (Willner and Willner 1965: 83). Mythic time is forever within a cultural or semantic system (Maranda 1972).

If myths and rituals associated with one another communicate the same message (Leach 1954, 1968), the occurrence of one without the other presumably is sufficient to transmit a communication, provided that its idiom is understood. The three sets of rituals called forth by the murder of President Kennedy are not equally associated with myths. Only the rituals of the Catholic church are explicitly related to myth, predominantly the myth that Jesus Christ was the Son of God, crucified to redeem mankind from sin. The rituals of the Catholic church are replete with symbolism and the Church provides explanations of its symbols.

In contrast, the rituals of the United States for a dead chief of state are not associated with myths but may evoke mythic images through their symbolism, much of which is military. The messages communicated by "ritual symbols" (Turner 1964) include those associated with any mythic images evoked.

Unlike the death in office of a President of the United States, the installation of the duly elected President and Vice-President is an event which recurs every four years, conforming to the term of office stipulated in the Constitution of the United States (Article II, Section I.1). Inaugurations traditionally are rich in pageantry, except in times of war, and in ritual symbols of the powers of the highest office in the United States. Nonetheless, the only essential legitimating rite is the presidential oath of office decreed in the Constitution. It states: "Before he enter on the Execution of his Office, he shall take the following Oath or Affirmation: 'I do solemnly swear (or affirm) that I will faithfully execute the Office of President of the United States, and will to the best of my ability, preserve, protect and defend the Constitution of the United States' " (Article II, Section 1.8). Before the President is sworn in, the Vice-President takes a similar oath in regard to his office.

Constitutional provisions for succession to the presidency between inaugurations are, however, ambiguous. A source of ambiguity, prior to the adoption of Article XX (1933), was the statement: "In case of the Removal of the President from Office, or of his Death, Resignation, or Inability to discharge the Powers and Duties of the said Office, the Same shall devolve on the Vice-President" (Article II, Section 1.6). "The Same" can denote either the office of President or only its powers and duties. This ambiguity was resolved and precedent established upon the first death of an incumbent President, William Henry Harrison, in 1841. John Tyler, his Vice-President, then assumed the office of President, although there were claims that he lacked the right to do so, and could only be acting President. Despite his oath as Vice-President, which he maintained was sufficient for the succession, John Tyler had the oath of President administered to him "as doubts may arise, and for greater caution" (Manchester 1967: 226).

This act served as precedent not only for the accession of later Vice-Presidents upon the death of an elected President but also for their being sworn in as soon as possible. It is not legally established that the presidential oath is necessary for succession to the presidency under such circumstances (Manchester 1967: 224–227). Nonetheless, the seven Vice-Presidents since John Tyler who have acceded to the presidency upon the death of an incumbent President have all taken the presidential oath.[1] It apparently has become established as the rite legitimating occupancy of the highest office in the United States.

If this is an example of history giving rise to the myth that a rite is essential for legitimate succession to the position of head of state, it is a paradigmatic example of "the part played by ceremony and ritual, not only in the conferment of office but also in its maintenance

---

[1] The Vice-Presidents of the United States who succeeded to the presidency on the death of a President are as follows: John Tyler, who succeeded William Henry Harrison in 1841; Millard Fillmore, who succeeded Zachary Taylor in 1850; Andrew Johnson, who succeeded Abraham Lincoln in 1865; Theodore Roosevelt, who succeeded William McKinley in 1901; Calvin Coolidge, who succeeded Warren G. Harding in 1923; Harry S. Truman, who succeeded Franklin Delano Roosevelt in 1954; and Lyndon Baines Johnson, who succeeded John Fitzgerald Kennedy in 1963. Presidents Lincoln, Garfield, and McKinley, as well as President Kennedy, were assassinated.

and exercise" (Fortes 1962: 61). The death of a President of the United States, especially by assassination, assaults the body politic and the moral order. Ritual installation of his designated successor, repetition of the essential rite in the periodic inauguration of a President, reasserts the rule of law.

Thus, the three sets of rituals evoked by the slaying of President Kennedy all share elements of both transition (van Gennep 1960) and perpetuity. The rituals of the Catholic church — extreme unction and the requiem mass — are sacraments which confer sanctifying grace on, respectively, those whose afflicted bodies are in danger of death and the souls of those who have departed from this world to eternal life. The rituals of the United States for a dead President pay honor not only to a particular fallen warrior, Commander-in-Chief, before his death, of the armed forces of the United States; they also pay honor to the office, which does not die, and they assert its precedence in the land (Pitt-Rivers 1968). The accession of a Vice-President on the death of his elected President signifies the passing on of the office and its powers, the change of status from Vice-President to President and also the durability of constitutional rule.

II.   John F. Kennedy was the eighth President of the United States to die in office, the fourth to be slain, and the first whose televised presence could be followed to the grave by his people. Within ten minutes after the President was shot in Dallas, radio and television bulletins transmitted the news to the nation and the world (Mayo 1967: 15–16). Within half an hour, according to surveys (Schramm 1964: 15), over two-thirds of the people of the United States had heard this news. By then the national television and radio networks had discontinued their scheduled programs to report on the President's condition and on the appalling events of the day. With the announcement of President Kennedy's death, no story unconnected with it was transmitted by the national networks for the rest of Friday, November 22, 1963, the weekend which followed, and Monday, November 25, the day of the murdered President's funeral and a day of national mourning. A nationwide congregation participated in the rituals for its fallen chief as the adult population of the United States watched and listened to the media for an average of eight hours on Friday, ten hours on Saturday, eight hours on Sunday, and eight hours on Monday (Sheatsley and Feldman 1964: 159).

The assassination of President Kennedy evoked not only shock and sorrow among most of the people of the United States but also personal grief, as if an intimate had died (Sheatsley and Feldman 1965: 168 ff.). Such emotions can be attributed to some extent to the death, particularly the slaying, of a President of the United States, head of state and government and embodiment of the nation's sovereignty (Neustadt 1968). But no small part of the emotions elicited by the murder of the young President may have been invoked by its mythic overtones, its resonance of the doomed heroes of myth.

The rites of farewell for John F. Kennedy embodied three intersecting sets of myths and of ritual and mythic symbols. These were: myths of the sacrifice of Christ and the Christian martyrs; symbolic representations of Abraham Lincoln, the preeminent mythic figure in United States history; and symbols, some reputedly going back to ancient Rome, of the fallen warrior, the hero and commander cut down.

The slaying of President Kennedy brought into the closest proximity rituals of church and state; holders of the highest public offices linked civic duty to prayer. The earliest confirmation that the President was dead came from the priest who had administered the last rites of the Roman Catholic church to the slain man. Less than half an hour later, NBC television showed the White House flag flying at half-staff.[2] United Nations Ambassador Adlai Stevenson issued a public statement saying: ". . . At such a moment we can only turn to prayer . . . May God help us."[3] As the presidential plane arrived in Washington, D. C., from Dallas, television transmissions showed the waiting Navy ambulance and Army pallbearers, the casket containing President Kennedy's body lowered by his aides, his widow in her blood-stained clothes met by Attorney General Robert F. Kennedy, Lyndon Johnson making his first public appearance and statement as President of the United States. A silent public of thousands was on hand. Films of mourners praying in a Chicago church followed on NBC television within the hour.

Postmidnight viewers of NBC saw a tape of a requiem mass for President Kennedy held earlier Friday evening in a church in Philadelphia. Early morning viewers on Saturday saw the interior of Saint

---

[2]   Of the two National Broadcasting Company publications consulted, *There Was a President* includes pictures reproduced from NBC kinescope and film. All references to the timing of what was shown on television during this period come either from this source or from Mayo (1967). Timing and the description of the events themselves were cross-checked with Manchester (1967).

[3]   The public statements of public figures that are quoted can be found in the National Broadcasting Company publications and in *The New York Times*, November 23, 1963, November 24, 1963, and November 25, 1963.

Patrick's Cathedral in New York prepared for a solemn requiem mass, also televised, at 10:00 A.M. An hour earlier a television tape showed the first view of the East Room of the White House where the flag-draped casket holding President Kennedy's body lay in state, a crucifix at its foot, four candles burning, one at each corner and, beyond them, a four-man Honor Guard composed of one man from each of the Armed Forces of the United States, standing at attention. In issuing his first proclamation that afternoon, President Johnson not only declared the day of President Kennedy's funeral a day of national mourning but also recommended that "the people . . . assemble on that day in their respective places of divine worship, there to bow down in submission to the will of Almighty God. . . ."

This ritual juxtaposition of symbols of church and state brought into the majority of American homes a series of correspondences between Christian sacrifice and the death of a ruler dating from the early development of medieval political theology (Kantorowicz 1957). During the tenth and eleventh centuries, the Christian king was associated with the image of Christ and with His representation as the Son on the Altar (1957: 90–93). The distinction between the "king's two bodies" — between the office of king, seen as immutable and enduring, and his mortal person — was equated with the two natures of Christ. The Christian king, when annointed, "became the *christomimētēs* — literally the 'actor' or 'impersonator' of Christ" (1957: 47), "human by nature and divine by grace" (1957: 87). Although by the twelfth century this equivalence had become obsolete, a new set of correspondences was established in the thirteenth century. ". . . the Prince, being the head of the mystical body of the state and sometimes even that body itself, paralleled Christ who was both the head of the mystical body of the Church and that body itself; also, just as Christ laid down his life for his corporate body, so was the Prince supposed to sacrifice his life for the commonweal" (1957: 268).

These correspondences can be diagrammed as follows:

Christ ～ Sacrifice on the Altar → consecrated ruler;

Christ: Church ～ ruler: state

Sacrifice (Christ) → Sacrifice (ruler).

These correspondences have retained potency in the United States. A biographer of Abraham Lincoln, John Hay, who also became Theodore Roosevelt's Secretary of State, called Lincoln "the greatest character since Christ" (Hofstadter 1948: 92). After reviewing Memorial Day sermons and other utterances in a New England town before and after World War II, Warner (1953: 15) concluded: "From the day of his death, thousands of sermons and speeches have demonstrated that Lincoln, like Christ, died that all men might live and be as one in the sight of God and man. Christ died that this might be true forever beyond the earth; Lincoln sacrificed his life that this might be true forever more on earth."

In a sample of sermons preached around the country following the assassination of John F. Kennedy (Stewart and Kendall 1964), the young President was frequently compared to Lincoln. Moreover, his murder, on a Friday, was compared not only to that of Lincoln, also on a Friday, but to the crucifixion of Christ on a Friday hallowed by Christianity.

Comparisons of John F. Kennedy with Abraham Lincoln occurred not only in sermons but also in the news media. These comparisons were furthered by similarities in ritual arrangements for the two slain Presidents. Descriptions and sketches, almost a century old, of the East Room of the White House when Abraham Lincoln's body lay there in state were drawn on by the Kennedy family and aides as they prepared the same room to receive the body of John F. Kennedy (Manchester 1967: 418–420, 436–438): the catafalque which supported President Kennedy's coffin duplicated that which had supported President Lincoln's coffin and was similarly draped; the crucifix at the foot of President Kennedy's bier followed the model of a cross at the foot of President Lincoln's; the chandeliers of the East Room, enveloped in crepe when President Lincoln lay in state, were bordered with crepe for President Kennedy. The catafalque on which President Kennedy's coffin lay in the rotunda of the Capitol was the same one on which President Lincoln's casket had lain.

If these duplications of ritual symbols helped associate the murder of John F. Kennedy with the myth of Abraham Lincoln, this association was furthered by correspondences between the careers of the two Presidents as well as between their deaths. One component of the Lincoln myth is that of the man of humble origins who rose to the highest office in the United States (Hofstadter 1948; Warner 1953). John F. Kennedy not only was the first Catholic to achieve this office; he also was the great-grandson of a penniless immigrant from Ireland whose grandson became one of the richest men in the land. The career of Abraham Lincoln reinforced the American myth of the self-made man to whom no achievement is impossible; the career of the Kennedy family held out this myth to those denied it, who could now imagine a grandchild as President.

However, Abraham Lincoln had saved the Union and emancipated the slaves. In contrast, John F. Kennedy's brief tenure as President produced no towering accomplishments.[4] The legend of Abraham Lincoln offers "a drama in which a great man shoulders the torment and moral burdens of a blundering and sinful people, suffers for them, and redeems them with hallowed Christian virtues — 'malice toward none and charity toward all'" (Hofstadter 1948: 92). Those who had admired and loved John F. Kennedy in life apparently sought to endow the tragic glamour of his figure in death with the aura of Abraham Lincoln, to extend to a truncated career the tragic grandeur of the Republic's most venerated figure.

The correspondences diagrammed earlier can be extended to illustrate the sacrificial character of the myths invoked by the rituals of farewell for John F. Kennedy:

Sacrifice (Christ) → Sacrifice (Lincoln) ∼ Sacrifice (Kennedy)
Abraham Lincoln → John F. Kennedy.

The metaphor of sacrifice indicates the continued vitality of another correspondence of medieval political theology: that between the Christian martyr and, initially, the knight who offered up his life fighting for the Church, then the crusader fallen for the faith and, by the thirteenth century, the soldier slain in the service of the state (Kantorowicz 1957: 234–244). "The Christian martyr . . . [who] had died for his divine Lord *pro fide,* was to remain — actually until the twentieth century — the genuine model of civic self-sacrifice" (Kantorowicz 1957: 234–235).

While the myths of Christ and Christian sacrifice dominate the rituals of the Catholic church, the state rites for a dead member of the Armed Forces of the United States are relatively devoid of institutionalized myths. As Commander-in-Chief of the Armed Forces slain while in office, President Kennedy received in death the most elaborate state rituals that can be performed for a citizen of the United States. However, much of the symbolism of a state funeral is repetitive and its most basic ritual symbols are those of any United States military funeral.[5]

[4] President Kennedy seems to have worried ". . .that time might run out on him. One night at the White House, he joined other Administration thinkers . . . in talk with a Civil War historian about Abraham Lincoln. Abe was lucky, somebody argued, to be assassinated before his greatness could be battered by the evil confusions of Reconstruction. Yes, answered the 35th President of the United States, but what if Lincoln had been shot two years earlier. He would have died an uncertain failure and never made known the greatness that was in him" (Harris 1964: 64).
[5] Information on state and military funerals has been derived from U. S. Bureau of Naval Personnel (1971) and U. S. Department of the Army (1965; 1970). The

The minimum symbols of such a funeral are: the nation's flag covering the coffin; honors, at least a hand salute rendered by honorary pallbearers and other military escort each time the coffin is moved; a vehicle, traditionally a caisson, to bear the body to the cemetery; a procession to the grave with the coffin carried by military pallbearers, traditionally six in number; graveside honors which include three volleys by a firing squad after graveside services have been said and then "Taps" sounded by a bugler. After the body has been carried to and placed over the grave, the pallbearers hold the flag which covered it waist-high over the coffin until "Taps" has been played; they then fold the flag ceremonially and present it to the officer in charge of the funeral who then presents it to the next of kin to the dead. A military funeral also includes a religious service and a graveside committal service. In the funeral for an enlisted man, a hearse is currently used rather than a caisson (U.S. Bureau of Naval Personnel 1971: 2).

However, ritual symbols for dead officers in the Full Honor military funeral include not only a horse-drawn caisson but also a ceremonial band, a military escort and a color detail which march ahead of the coffin in this order in the funeral procession. The band plays predetermined military honors according to the rank of the deceased, and/ or a hymn each time the coffin is moved. Rank also determines the size of the military escort. Those officers whose high military rank entitled them to a cannon salute receive it in death just before the graveside religious service concludes with the benediction. Then, after this is recited, the three volleys and "Taps" follow. The musical honors accorded such deceased ranking officers include the number of ruffles (on drums) and flourishes (on bugles) prescribed for their rank.

In state and special military funerals (U.S. Department of the Army 1965), additional symbols are introduced. If the deceased was of flag rank, the appropriate flag is carried immediately behind his coffin. Behind the flag may be led a riderless horse, boots thrust in the stirrups backwards. A formation of aircraft flies past in the funerals of officers of stipulated rank in the Air Force and persons in positions of command over the ensemble of the Armed Forces. The bodies of persons granted state funerals — Presidents and past Presidents, a President-elect and anyone designated by the President — may lie in state in the Capitol rotunda on the day before the funeral. The

---

state funeral of President Kennedy is described in *The New York Times*, November 24, 1963, November 25, 1963, and November 26, 1963, and in Manchester (1967).

Joint Chiefs-of-Staff of the Armed Forces or their representatives are part of the military escort preceding the coffin. In the cortege of mourners following the coffin, designated officials, beginning with the President of the United States, have places after the family. Servicemen from all the forces line the route such a funeral procession takes.

Some of these rites and ritual symbols are explicitly associated with explanations or legendary justifications. Covering the coffin with a flag is reputed to have originated on the battlefield where the flag might serve as a pall in which to wrap the corpse for burial (*The officer's guide* 1972: 65). Now the flag on the coffin officially symbolizes that the deceased served in the armed forces and that the "Nation regards the burying of its military dead as a solemn and sacred obligation" (U.S. Bureau of Naval Personnel 1971: i). The use of the caisson to bear the dead is also supposed to have originated on the battlefield (*The officer's guide* 1972: 64–65). Several legends are offered to account for the three volleys after graveside services: one is that the custom was practiced during the seventeenth century but had its origins in the Roman practice of throwing dirt three times on a coffin, calling the deceased by name and bidding him good-bye three times (1972: 64); another legend refers the volleys to the three cheers or chords sounded for departing crusaders (1972: 64); and, in a government publication, the custom is attributed to "ancient belief" about frightening away evil spirits (U.S. Bureau of Naval Personnel 1971: i).

The symbolism of "Taps" can be traced historically. General Daniel Butterworth of the Army of the Potomac is said to have composed the call in July 1862 and subsituted it for the three volleys to avoid enemy knowledge of the frequency of burials (*The officer's guide* 1972: 82). "Taps" afterwards became the last bugle call sounded at night in military encampments and installations. Its use in military funerals was decreed in 1891 (*The officer's guide* 1972) and the symbolism now given for this usage is that of "the last long sleep" and "hope and confidence in an ultimate reveille to come" (*The officer's guide* 1972: 65; U.S. Bureau of Naval Personnel 1971: 1). If the account of the origin and the sequence in which "Taps" was put to use is correct, then its current symbolism in military funerals derives from its symbolism as a final bugle call at night which, in turn, derives from its initial use as a salute at the burial of military dead. Such transpositions of meaning are common in the symbolism of rituals.

In contrast, legend is invoked in the meaning of the riderless horse, which represents a fallen warrior. The use of the riderless horse is at tributed to the Mongols, who also purportedly sacrificed the horse on the death of its master. The reversal of boots in the stirrup signifies that a commander is dead.[6]

The vapidity of some of the meanings attributed to the ritual symbols, the perfunctoriness with which their meanings are mentioned, in contrast to the detailed description of their performance and the number of ritual elements to which no meaning beyond "Honors" is attached suggest that the rituals themselves encode and reiterate a very few basic messages of military life. One of them is that exchanges take place within the military hierarchy and between the military and society; another is that honors and privileges are distributed according to the distribution of power by rank.

The flag on the coffin, never here or in other situations allowed to touch the ground, not only symbolizes the nation but also the subordination to command of the serviceman under the flag. In exchange for his submission and his services, he receives total if graded subsistence in life and honors in death, as well as a box and a grave for his remains. He is armed while alive; volleys of arms salute his body. The caisson which carried the gun also carries the gunsman. The more arms his rank can command, the heavier the artillery that sounds at his passing. The escalation of funeral symbolism and honors according to rank corresponds to the hierarchical command over power. The man on a horse looks down on and can ride down the unmounted; the horse and boots symbolize the commander.

However, the Commander-in-Chief is the President, elected by the nation according to the constitutional principle of sovereignty vested in the people. The President designates who, besides holders of the same office, is to receive a state funeral, but only Congress can make the Capitol rotunda available. The President is Commander-in-Chief but wars must be authorized by Congress, which appropriates allocated funds for military expenditure. The constitutional separation of powers finds expression even in funerals of state. The Vice-President follows the President, unless other heads of state and government attend and are placed between them in the procession of mourners; the Speaker of the House, next in line for the presidency after the Vice-President, then follows together with the justices of the Supreme Court.

The nation, its offices of power and its Armed Forces survive the passing of any individual. The corporate continuity of the state and its Armed Forces is symbolized not only in funerals of state but in the minimal honors rendered in the humblest military funeral. The band or bands which lead the funeral processions of those of rank sound

[6]  *The New York Times*, November 25, 1963.

their former privileges and powers. But some military escort accompanies and salutes the body of anyone given a military funeral. At least three volleys are fired; a single bugler sounds "Taps" over the grave; and the next of kin receive the flag.

The procession which bore President Kennedy's body to the Capitol on Sunday, November 24, the even more splendid procession which bore it the next day from the White House to Saint Matthew's Cathedral for the requiem mass and then to Arlington National Cemetery, were the most elaborate in the nation's history. But half an hour before the media transmitted across the nation and abroad the beat of muffled drums in the march to the Capitol, the huge NBC audience saw Lee Harvey Oswald, who had been charged with the President's murder, shot down at police headquarters in Dallas. The motivation of that act may never be fully determined. But it can be associated with symbols in the funeral rituals for the dead President, with the power of arms and with sacrifice.

III.   The mighty of the world, some of them uniformed and with swords, followed President Kennedy's beautiful young widow and his youthful and handsome brothers, as they marched behind the riderless horse to Saint Matthew's Cathedral. Cardinal Cushing in his robes and miter awaited the dead President in his coffin on the steps of the cathedral. The televised pageantry of the rituals of the Catholic church succeeded the televised pageantry of the state procession on November 25, 1963.

After the requiem mass, Cardinal Cushing cried out the last prayer — with its reiteration of the themes of sacrifice — in English: "May the angels, dear Jack, lead you into Paradise. May the martyrs receive you at your coming. May the spirit of God embrace you and mayest thou, with all those who made the supreme sacrifice of dying for others, receive eternal rest and peace."[7] The dead President's image of youthfulness also was reiterated as his three-year-old son,

---

[7]   Manchester (1967: 589). This is a slight modification of the *In paradisum* antiphon which, in Catholic countries, is read as priests accompany a funeral procession to the cemetery. It is one of the prayers which could be recited in the vernacular after the Requiem Mass when Latin was still the obligatory language for Church rites. One English translation of the prayer reads: "May the angels lead thee into Paradise; at thy coming may the martyrs receive thee and bring thee to Jerusalem the holy city. May the choirs of angels receive thee, and, with Lazarus once a beggar, mayest thou have eternal rest" (Sullivan 1942: 285). The complete Catholic funeral rite is described by Fortescue and O'Connell (1962: 388–395). Funeral ceremonies in the United States are discussed in an appendix (Fortescue and O'Connell 1962: 418).

standing next to his mother in front of the cathedral after the service, saluted his father's body as it was placed on the caisson for the procession to the grave. There military honors alternated with the Catholic graveside rites until the blessing and lighting of the eternal flame — a final symbol requested by the President's widow — brought the funeral to an end.

Shortly after John F. Kennedy's life and presidency had ended, the metaphor of his administration as Camelot came into use. President Kennedy had seen and was supposed to have enjoyed the musical [8] of that name, a retelling of the myth of King Arthur and his court and of their end. The musical concludes with a "reprise" in which the king sings to a young follower, a mythical Sir Thomas Malory:

Think back on all the tales that you remember
Of Camelot.
Ask every person if he's heard the story
And tell it strong and clear if he has not
That once there was a fleeting wisp of glory
Called Camelot.
Don't let it be forgot
That once there was a spot
For one brief shining moment
That was known as Camelot.[9]

The appearance of the musical was timely and its concluding song more than apt for linking John F. Kennedy and his presidency to the chivalry of Arthurian legend. However, the musical glosses over not only the Christian myths encompassed in the medieval and modern versions of the legend but also one of its most awesome themes. In the twentieth-century recreation of the legend by T. H. White (1966) from which the musical was derived and which, in turn, was modeled on Malory's fifteenth century version, the theme is reiterated with clarity. Mordred, King Arthur's illegitimate son, who made war on the king and brought down the King and his realm, had been begotten on Morgause, Arthur's half-sister.[10] She was one of the daughters of Igraine, Arthur's mother, and her husband, the Earl of Cornwall. Arthur himself had been begotten on Igraine by Uther Pendragon, the king, three hours after he had slain the earl:

---

[8]   *Camelot*, book and lyrics by Alan Jay Lerner, music by Frederick Loewe.
[9]   Copyright by Alan Jay Lerner and Frederick Loewe. Chapel and Company owns publication and allied rights.
[10]   Malory makes her the sister of Igraine.

This pedigree is a vital part of the tragedy of King Arthur. It is why Sir Thomas Malory called his very long book the *Death* of Arthur. Although nine tenths of the story seems to be about knights jousting and quests for the holy grail and things of that sort, the narrative is a whole and it deals with the reasons why the young man came to grief at the end. It is the tragedy, the Aristotelian and comprehensive tragedy, of sin coming home to roost (White 1966:312).

White ends his reworking of the legend on the eve of the fatal battle between Arthur's forces and those of Mordred and thus before the full culmination of the tragedy, according to Malory: Arthur slays his son and Mordred fatally wounds his father.

John F. Kennedy was the second son of Joseph Patrick Kennedy, multimillionaire and one-time Ambassador to Great Britain and to the English court. President Kennedy's grandfathers on both sides had been Boston Irish politicians. This pedigree was vital to launching the President's political career as Congressman from the district in which his grandfathers had held sway (see Whalen 1964: 393–395). His father's wealth and flaming ambition for his sons were a vital part of President Kennedy's triumphant fight for the highest office of the United States. But if the tragedy of the glorious Arthur of myth was conceived in incestuous sin, what sin can be adduced to transform the tragedy of John F. Kennedy into mythic retribution?

The Arthurian legend, as told by Malory and White, with its themes of incest and of the slaying of the father by the son, calls to mind the epitome of Greek tragedy, Sophocles' *Oedipus the king*. The tragedy of *Oedipus the king* begins with a speech in which the hero characterizes himself as "I, Oedipus, renowned of all." The priest of Zeus then says to him: "We beg your help regarding you not as one equated to the gods but as the first of men." But as Knox (1955) says of Sophocles' Oedipus at the beginning of the play, "the magnificent figure set before us in the opening scenes, *tyrannos*, the man of wealth and power, first of men, the intellect and energy which drives on the search . . . can address the chorus . . . with godlike words" (1955: 12, 14). Knox uses the term *tyrannos* as a ruler who has not inherited his power but "succeeds by brains, force, influence" (1955: 8). Oedipus, at the beginning of Sophocles' tragedy, presents the image of *hubris,* of the man who "thought himself 'equated to the gods'" (Knox 1955: 11).

The myth of Arthur resembles that of Oedipus through correspondences of incest and patricide leading to the fall of a hero and ruler. But the *hubris* of ancient Greek thought corresponds with the Christian mortal sin of pride. The opening scenes of John F. Kennedy's presidency, his inauguration and inaugural address, can be mapped into the image of Oedipus in the opening scenes of Sophocles' play.

But are patricide and incest entirely absent from the correspondences between the tragedy of Oedipus and the tragedy of John F. Kennedy?

The perfect plot of tragedy must have a single issue; the change in the hero's fortunes . . . from happiness to misery; and the cause of it must lie not in any depravity, but in some great error on his part . . . The finest tragedies are always on the story of some . . . houses . . . that may have been involved as either agents or sufferers in some deed of horror (McKeon 1941:1467).

If the entire Kennedy family is viewed as the subject of tragedy, a different protagonist comes into view: Joseph P. Kennedy, the father who willed that a son would be President. His first-born, cast for this role, died a hero in World War II. The political destiny of his dead brother then passed to John, also a hero of World War II. The father's ambition was fulfilled but also led to the slaying of the son. When Robert F. Kennedy, the next brother, bid for the presidency in 1968, he, too, was murdered. The messages of myth, as Leach has noted (1962), are repeated; this repetition allows the message to be deciphered. The *hubris* of the father can be viewed as the Aristotelian cause of the slaying of the sons. The patricide of Oedipus is inverted into filicide.

Oedipus leaves Thebes in exile at the end of the play, blinded by his own act so as not to behold more horrors. A stroke made Joseph P. Kennedy paralyzed and speechless at the end of his son's first year in the presidency. He was still alive when his third son was killed.

Joseph P. Kennedy had been a vigorous and rich man in his middle sixties when John F. Kennedy and Jacqueline Bouvier were married in 1953. Mrs. Kennedy was beside the President when he was shot in Dallas; her comportment during the next few hours and days made her the heroine of the nation and "Her American Majesty" (Manchester 1967: 644) to admirers abroad. She married a vigorous and rich man in his sixties in the fall of 1968.[11]

Jocasta, the widow of Laius who was the father of Oedipus, unknowingly became the wife of her own son. Overwhelmed by the knowledge of the true identity of Oedipus, she then put an end to her life. In contrast when the widow of the slain President married Aris-

[11] M. Erik Wright, professor of psychology at the University of Kansas, suggested the equivalence of Aristotle Onassis to Joseph P. Kennedy.

totle Onassis, she put an end only to her queenly image. The tragedy of Jocasta is inverted into the worldly comedy of the celebrities, "Jackie O." and "Daddy O."

The symbolic correspondences between Oedipus and the Kennedys are based on inversion: patricide inverted to symbolic filicide; marriage between son and mother inverted to marriage between daughter and symbolic father. The correspondence that is not inverted is that between Oedipus at the beginning of Sophocles' tragedy and President Kennedy, his brother Robert, and their father at the beginning of the Kennedy administration: "the man of pride plunges down into doom" (Knox 1955: 12).

The correspondences between Oedipus and Arthurian legend do not involve either *hubris* or the Christian sin of pride. The myths of Oedipus and Arthur, as summarized by Raglan (1934), share sixteen of the twenty-two characteristics of the pattern of the "hero of tradition" which Raglan sets forth. However, it is not correspondences between the heroes' careers but between their tragedies that are relevant here. The tragedies of Oedipus and Arthur meet in the figure of the fallen ruler, doomed by incest and patricide. The murder of his father by Oedipus becomes the mutual slaying of father and son in *Le morte d'Arthur* yet it is not certain that Arthur died, according to either White or Malory. He may return as future king. The myth of Christ and the Resurrection can be transformed into that of Arthur, anointed Christian king.

The transformation is both by equivalence and inversion. In Christian myth, the Son is sacrificed to the Father to redeem mankind from sin. The Father has His Son conceived in order to be a sacrifice. In Malory's Arthurian legend, the father begets a son and slays him not just once but twice. This repeated transmission of the mythic message first occurs soon after Mordred's birth when Arthur sets him adrift in a boat with other babies born the same day. They die; he is rescued. The story is recounted by White as well as by Malory. The son, begotten in sin, seeks as an adult to slay his father, the anointed king, and force marriage on his father's queen; he succeeds in destroying Arthur's Round Table. The father finally succeeds in slaying the son and may reign again.

Christian mythology provides its own inversions of the myth of Christ instead of the anti-Christ; and the Prince of Darkness also can be viewed as the first son of God. The legend of Arthur can be accommodated to a series of equivalences and inversions within Christian myth and counter-myth, while also offering correspondences to

Celtic mythology from which it sprang and the myths of ancient Greece. The semantic system of a tradition gives meaning to the myths it generates and the tragedies it seeks to explain.

Christian myth, juxtaposed with military symbols in the funeral of President Kennedy, is fused with the warrior code of chivalry in Arthurian legend. The association of President Kennedy and his administration with Camelot and the Round Table may have been inspired by the musical *Camelot* and its final song. However, Arthurian legend does present themes of sin and sacrifice and the hero of White's recounting of the legend suffers tragic doom. The correspondences between Arthur and his court and John F. Kennedy's presidency are not just those of the "brief shining moment" but those of Aristotelian tragedy.

IV. By Tuesday, November 26, 1963, most of the people of the United States resumed their daily activities and the media returned to normal programming. The four-day focus of the nation on the life and death of its late President may have made it into a community of mourners sharing "collective ties" and a "generalized social bond" (Turner 1968: 576, 1969: 96). But this "liminal period" (ibid.) was over. The four days "arousing pity and fear" had accomplished a "catharsis of such emotions" in Aristotelian terms.[12]

If President Kennedy passed into history, he also passed into myth. As Sapir suggested (1934), the condensation of meanings in symbols can saturate them with emotions derived from the unconscious. The condensation of symbols and myths in the figure of the slain young President brings him into a company of mythic heroes whose power over the imagination is one of the most potent concepts in the traditions of Western civilization.

REFERENCES

FORTES, MEYER
1962   "Ritual and office in tribal society," in *Essays on the ritual of social relations*. Edited by Max Gluckman, 53–88. Manchester: Manchester University Press.

[12] Verba (1965) discusses how the media made possible shared mourning and collective rededication to the norms of the American political system. Mindak and Hursh (1965) present findings from interviews with a random sample of Minneapolis residents illustrating that watching television during the four days provided people with a way of dealing with the feelings produced by the assassination.

FORTESCUE, ADRIAN, J. B. O'CONNELL
1962   *The ceremonies of the Roman rite described.* Westminster, Maryland: Newman.

HARRIS, T. GEORGE
1964   Eight views of JFK: the competent American. *Look* (November 17):52–64.

HOFSTADTER, RICHARD
1948   *The American political tradition: and the men who made it.* New York: Alfred Knopf.

KANTOROWICZ, ERNST H.
1957   *The king's two bodies: a study in mediaeval political theology.* Princeton, New Jersey: Princeton University Press.

KNOX, BERNARD
1955   "Sophocles' Oedipus," in *Tragic themes in Western literature.* Ed. by Cleanth Brooks, 7–29. New Haven: Yale University Press.

LEACH, E. R.
1954   *Political systems of Highland Burma.* Cambridge: Harvard University Press.
1961   "Two essays concerning the symbolic representation of time," in *Rethinking anthropology,* 124–136. London School of Economics: Athlone.
1962   "Genesis as myth," in *Myth and cosmos: readings in mythology and symbolism.* Edited by John Middleton, 1–13. New York: Natural History Press.
1968   "Ritual," in *International encyclopedia of the social sciences,* 520–526. New York: Macmillan.

LÉVI-STRAUSS, CLAUDE
1955   "The structural study of myth," in *Myth: a symposium.* Edited by Thomas A. Sebeok, 81–106. Bloomington: Indiana University Press.
1966   *The savage mind.* Chicago: University of Chicago Press.

MALORY, SIR THOMAS
1954   *The works of Sir Thomas Malory.* London: Oxford University Press.

MANCHESTER, WILLIAM
1967   *The death of a President.* New York: Harper and Row.

MARANDA, PIERRE
1972   "Introduction," in *Mythology.* Edited by Pierre Maranda, 7–20. Harmondsworth: Penguin.

MAYO, JOHN B., JR.
1967   *The president is dead: the story of John F. Kennedy's assassination as covered by radio and T.V.* New York: Exposition Press.

MC KEON, RICHARD, editor
1941   *The basic work of Aristotle.* New York: Random House.

MINDAK, WILLIAM, GERALD D. HURSH
1965   "Television's functions on the assassination weekend," in *The Kennedy assassination and the American public: social communication in crisis.* Edited by Bradley S. Greenberg and Edwin B. Parker, 130–141. Stanford, California: Stanford University Press.

NATIONAL BROADCASTING COMPANY
1966 *Seventy hours and thirty minutes.* New York: Random House.

NATIONAL BROADCASTING COMPANY, NBC NEWS
1966 *There was a president.* New York: Random House and Ridge Press.

NEUSTADT, RICHARD E.
1968 "Presidential power," in *International encyclopedia of the social sciences,* 12:451–456. New York: Macmillan.

*Officer's guide, The*
1973 Thirty-sixth edition. Harrisburg, Pennsylvania: Stackpole Books.

PITT-RIVERS, JULIAN
1968 "Honor," in *International encyclopedia of the social sciences,* 503–511. New York: Macmillan.

RAGLAN, LORD
1934 The hero of tradition. *Folklore* 45:212–231.

RANK, OTTO
1932 "The myth of the birth of the hero," in *The myth of the birth of the hero and other writings.* Edited by Philip Freund, 3–96. New York: Alfred Knopf.

SAPIR, EDWARD
1934 "Symbolism," in *International encyclopedia of the social sciences,* 492–495. New York: Macmillan.

SCHRAMM, WILBUR
1964 "Introduction: communication in crisis," in *The Kennedy assassination and the American public: social communication in crisis.* Edited by Bradley S. Greenberg and E. B. Parker, 1–25. Stanford, California: Stanford University Press.

SHEATSLEY, PAUL P., JACOB J. FELDMAN
1964 "A national survey of public reactions and behavior," in *The Kennedy assassination and the American public: social communication in crisis.* Edited by Bradley S. Greenberg and Edwin B. Parker, 149–177. Stanford, California: Stanford University Press.

STEWART, CHARLES J., BRUCE KENDALL, *editors*
1964 *A man named John F. Kennedy: sermons on his assassination.* Glenrock, New Jersey: Paulist Press.

SULLIVAN, JOHN F.
1942 *The externals of the Catholic church: her government, ceremonies, festivals, sacramentals, and devotions.* New York: P. J. Kennedy and Sons.

TURNER, VICTOR
1964 "Symbols in Ndembu ritual," in *Closed systems and open minds.* Edited by Max Gluckman, 20–51. Chicago: Aldine.
1968 "Myth and symbol," in *International encyclopedia of the social sciences* 10:576–582. New York: Macmillan.
1969 *The ritual process: structure and antistructure.* Chicago: Aldine.

U.S. BUREAU OF NAVAL PERSONNEL
1971 *Naval funerals at Arlington National Cemetery.* Washington, D.C.: Government Printing Office.

U.S. DEPARTMENT OF THE ARMY

1965   *State, official and special military funerals.* Washington, D.C.: Government Printing Office.

1970   *Salutes, honors and visits of courtesy.* Washington, D.C.: Government Printing Office.

VAN GENNEP, ARNOLD

1960   *The rites of passage.* Chicago: University of Chicago Press.

VERBA, SIDNEY

1965   "The Kennedy assassination and the nature of political commitment," in *The Kennedy assassination and the American public: social communication in crisis.* Edited by Bradley S. Greenberg and Edwin B. Parker, 348–360. Stanford, California: Stanford University Press.

WARNER, W. LLOYD

1953   *American life: dream and reality.* Chicago: University of Chicago Press.

WHALEN, RICHARD J.

1964   *The founding father: the story of Joseph P. Kennedy.* New York: The New American Library.

WHITE, T. H.

1966   *The once and future king.* Berkley Medallion Edition.

WILLNER, ANN RUTH, DOROTHY WILLNER

1965   The rise and role of the charismatic leader. *Annals of the American Academy of Political and Social Science* 358:77–88.

# SECTION FIVE

# Pandharpur Priesthood: Its Changing Role, Functions, and Future

G. V. DINGRE

Pandharpur and its sacred Vaishnavite shrine in Maharashtra, India, is well-known as the "Vithal temple" and provides a constant source of inspiration to Hindus. Vaishnavism rose in the center and south and then reached gradually into the rest of India, as Bhandarkar (1913) points out. Three or four different deities were included in this sect by the beginning of the Christian era. Narayan seems to be the name of an old deity mentioned in Mahabharata. Vishnu was a minor god in the Vedas, but assumed greater importance in post-Mahabharata times. Krishna Vasudev, an allegedly historical personality, became a cult hero and then a god. Lastly, there was a cowherd god who killed many demons and established a cult of cow worship in defiance of older Vedic gods. All these various gods have been known in the post-Christian era. The sect came to be called the Bhagavat from the Sanskrit word *bhagavā* for god. The god Vithal, the river Bhima (also known as Chandrabhaga) and the devotee Pundalik are sacred to the followers of the Bhagavat sect, popularly known in Maharashtra as "Varkari Sampradaya." Karve (1968) observes that, "The worship of Vishnu in the forms of Vithal of Pandharpur has played a very important role in the cultural history of Maharashtra."

## VITHAL TEMPLE AND THE PRIESTHOOD

*The Significance of an Anthropological Query and Related Problems*

Many problems in relation to the origin, location, and antiquity of the

temple town of Pandharpur and the Vithal temple remain unsolved
even today. Scholars have tried to approach the problems from various
angles, viz. mythological, iconographical, epigraphic, etc. Yet nothing
which can be called a final and firm answer is forthcoming.

*Pandharpur: History and Antiquities*

The town of Pandharpur is the headquarters of a subdivision (Taluka)
of the same name, in the Sholapur district of the Maharashtra State
(India). This district lies in the basins of the Nira, Bhima, and Sina
Rivers. The town, with a latitude of 17°41' north and longitude of
75°26' east, is situated on the southern bank of the Bhima at a distance of about 44 miles to the south of Sholapur by road and 152 miles
to the southeast of Poona by rail. Pandharpur is bounded on the north
and east by the Bhima River.

The Bhima rises in the 19°4' north latitude and 73°34' east longitude, in the Sahyadris in the Khed subdivision of Poona. The source of
the river is adorned by the sacred shrine of Bhimashankar, which is
one of the twelve sacred Shiva shrines (Jyotirlingas) in India.

*Pre- and Proto-History*   The banks of the Bhima River around Pandharpur were inhabited by early Stone-Age man. Stone tools of this
period were discovered about half a mile upstream, by Sankalia, in
1968. These might go back a million years or so. Mate and Dhavalikar
(1970) (of the Department of Archaeology, Deccan College Postgraduate and Research Institute, Poona), who were assigned the work
of "Pandharpur Excavation" in 1968–1969, have given evidence about
"habitation of early and medieval man around Bhima banks." According to them, the primary goal of the excavations was generally to ascertain the antiquity of Pandharpur through systematic excavations; and
from the available evidence the earliest layers of occupation debris uncovered in the trench might go back to the thirteenth century.

*Chalcolithic Period*   From the ranges of Sahyadri, the Bhima River
runs southeast through the Poona, Nagar, and Sholapur districts before
it flows around Pandharpur. The Bhima flows between high alluvial
and tilled banks. Its breadth varies from 500 to 1500 feet. In some
places it is rocky. The Bhima flows in a curved, almost crescent-shaped
bed and this probably gives her the name Chandrabhaga (half-moon-
shaped curve). Around the modern township of Pandharpur and up-

stream, in the region now known as "Panchganga Beta" (mini island created due to the five streams of the sacred river sources), extremely rolled stone tools (known to archaeologists as Series II and dateable to around 50,000 years back) and a few microlithic blades were discovered. The latter are assigned to a period 25,000 years ago. From this remote past one comes to the Chalcolithic period, dated around 1200 B.C. From the Chalcolithic period (circa 1200 B.C.) to the beginning of the early Rastrakuta period (A.D. 516), which comes within proto-historic and historic periods, we have neither excavations nor inscriptions which can shed light on the Vithal temple.

### Hindu Shrines and the Pandharpur Vithal Temple

According to Alain Danielou (1964): "All religions, all religious philosophies, are ultimately an attempt at finding out the nature of the perceptible world — and of ourselves who perceive it — the process of the world's manifestation and the purpose of life, so that we may discover the means of fulfilling our destiny." A Hindu temple is a symbol or rather synthesis of various symbols, as Krishna Deva (1963) observes; he further argues that to the Hindu the temple is the abode of God, who is the spirit immanent in the Universe. The deity dwelling in the temple symbolizes the King of Kings and is consequently offered regal honor, consistent with the concept of God as the supreme ruler of the Universe.

We have already seen that there is a gap between 1187 B.C. and A.D. 516, for which we have no authentic and almost insignificant ethnographic data about the Vithal temple and about the habitation of its different categories of people (the worshipers, priests of the believers, and the devotees living in the vicinity of modern Pandharpur). And this is one problem of academic interest to the anthropologist, as well as to the ethnologist, that warrants further attention and efforts.

"The anthropologist is working within a body of theoretical knowledge and he makes his observations to solve problems which derive from it." If this observation by Evans-Pritchard (1967) is to be applied for ascertaining and interpreting the facts and problems connected with the theme of this article, then the changing roles, functions, and problems of priests and devotees could be classified and presented. But before that we would like to present a picture and a short résumé about the organization of the cult and the origin and organization of the priests who guard this tradition of about five centuries.

*The Deity, Devotees, and Priests*

An early reference to the deity and to the sacred place is in a devotional verse supposed to have been composed by the first "Sankaracarya" (circa A.D. 788–820). These verses are known as "Sri Pandurangashtak." The first verse of this hymn contains significant mention of several things. The meaning of the verse, originally composed in Sanskrit, is as follows: In the great seat of Yoga on the banks of Bhimrathi (Bhima River) stands the source of all Joy, "Pandurang." The Brahmalinga (whose other name) "Pandurang" I worship. He had come with great sages to this place to bless Pundalik.

The Pundalik or Paundrika mentioned in the verse above was connected with the God Vithoba in the thirteenth century by the first saint-poet, Namdev (1270–1350), of Maharashtra.

*Inscriptional Record*   There are various inscriptions which mention the town of Pandharpur and the Vithal temple. These were carved in A.D. 1236, 1248, 1249, and 1311 and are known respectively by the name or title: Pandarage, Hebbalil, Bendigere, Chouryansi or the inscription known as the writing of 84, and the Chokhamela inscription. A number of scholars in India have reviewed and studied them. Khare (1945), Deleury (1960), Tulpule (1965), and Bendre (1962) have consistently given their impressions while writing about the organization of the Bhagavat sect and the cult of Vithal and while reviewing the epigraphic sources of the development of Marathi literature, Vithal *sampradaya*, and such other related topics.

*Priests of the Deity Vithal — Earliest References*   Pandharpur temple, as it might have been originally constructed and later on renovated, establishes an admixture of Dravidian style, Hemadpanthi art, and Deccan pattern. The present priesthood of the Vithal temple has existed since the early sixteenth century. From the way in which their duties, functions, and privileges are mentioned in the historical document known as "Watanzada" (composed during the Adilsahi Regime of Bijapur), we can surmise the existence of the same priesthood for at least a century or two before A.D. 1519. An inscription, apparently belonging to a smaller Vithal temple before the bigger one was built, mentions seven types of chief, probably priestly, positions.[1] This in-

---

[1]   In the inscription a mention is made of seven chief persons to be responsible for the temple worship and ritual. The sixteenth-century record indicating "the rights and privileges of the temple priests," though, is the first document to specifically refer to temple priests.

scription from 1189 is known as "Pandharpur Vithal Devacha Shila lekh Sak 1111."

*Sociological Significance of the Profession of Priesthood*

The term "priest" used in the sociological literature represents one type of religious authority. The term priest is also used for a person who is authorized to preside over the celebration of traditional ceremonies. In the Weberian sense (1965), Hinduism, however, is exclusive — like a sect. But in the Hindu religion the office of the priest is not the same as it is in Christianity. In Hindu society the term priest is applied to certain ministrants of ritual functions. In India, and particularly in Maharashtra, many terms are in vogue for the people who follow the occupation of priesthood or are related in one way or another to priestly duties and functions. Those who are born in communities such as Brahmin, Lingayat, or Gurav and are connected with some temple, Math, or sectarian branch through inheritance could be eligible for training for the profession of priesthood — provided that they have hereditary functions connected with performance, responsibilities, or assignment in the daily and occasional worship performed through ritual, and that they have some kind of tradition of continuity or dedication for preservation of the priestly role.

According to Sarma (1966), "A well-organized ritualism in a religion has many important functions — social, historical, psychological, aesthetic, and mystical — the most important of which is the mystical."

In India, all famous Hindu temples were and still are being managed and administered by some type of authority or organization, and in them the priests usually perform the key roles and occupy the significant positions. The temple priesthood at Pandharpur caters to the ritual routine by which a great deity is expected to be served. It also helps in keeping before the people, in a sense devotees, the idol in its expected magnificence. These are, however, the formal and external requirements of a religion. Max Weber demonstrated the role of religion as an independent causal element influencing action throughout history. Six different functions are discussed by Thomas O'Dea (1969) in his interpretation of the sociology of religion. Out of these six functions the first, the fifth, and the last could be tested in light of the "Varkari sect" in Maharashtra and the convictions and belief system of millions of its followers.

The Varkari devotees are interrelated and keep their identity with subsectarian affinities towards the Math tradition, connected with the Vithal temple, while the common devotees of the god visit Pandharpur for consolation, reconciliation, or support which they hope to gain through the temple priest's worship and performance of ritual, when he feels it convenient and possible for him to do. The sectarian chiefs or successors of the Maths, who are connected with the cult of the god Vithal and who are known in Marathi as "Maharaj," are keeping the link between the traditions, scriptures, and teachings of the saint-poets through their discourses and litanies, and they are in turn honored and respected by the temple priests. Thus, the ceremonies of worship and the functions of transcendental relationship through cult are being kept in high esteem at Pandharpur.

*Temple Priests: Internal Organization*

The temple priests are subdivided into three categories namely (1) BADVES, (2) SEVADHARIS, and (3) UTPATS.
1. The Badves belong to the Brahmin caste of the Maharashtrian Deshastha and the inheritors of Kashyapgotra within the Kanva branch of Shukla Yajurveda. The Kanva Brahmins are one of the ten endogamous units of the Maharashtra Brahmins, anthropometrically studied by Malhotra (1966). In 1966, there were 82 families of Badves divided into four groups, each inheriting its succession from the original four brothers by whose names the four groups are identified and are divided for performing various roles and functions according to a rotation system. The names of these four groups and the number of families belonging to each in 1966 are as follows: Tanba-24, Timman-27, Sharma-15, and Malhar-15 (and according to legend, they are all descendants of the four brothers). In the course of time, the number in the original four families increased to 100 by the beginning of twentieth century. In 1972, there were more than 200 male members qualified to retain their functions and profession.
    The entire community of the Badves in its representative capacity is qualified to perform the temple rituals, on behalf of the devotee, through the ritual functionaries, the "Sevadharis." The Badves look after the temple management and are guardians of the deity. They have performed significant roles in historical times and were instrumental in protecting and preserving the icon of the god, from the attack of an army of the Mogu generals. In this, the Sevadharis and Utpats had also assisted them. There are various historical documents which shed

light on these events, and which are now in the custody of the Director of Archives, Government of Maharashtra, and with the temple priests at Pandharpur. The changing roles and functions of the Badves will be reviewed later in this article.

2. The Sevadharis, consisting of seven groups with different specialized functions and privileges, perform the actual worship of the god according to a set ritual. They are responsible for the daily and occasional worship performed and conducted in the temple on behalf of the devotees. The seven groups of Sevadharis are known by the surnames below. The figures indicate the total number of their respective families in 1968. In all there were 128 families of Sevadharis.

| | |
|---|---|
| Pujari-8 | Benari-22 |
| Paricharak-24 | Dingre-22 |
| Haridas-48 | Dange-1 |
| Diwate-3 | |

Out of these, the Pujari, Benari, Dingre, and Diwate belong to the Brahmin caste of the Maharashtrian Deshasthas but are the inheritors of the Koushik, Bharadwaja, Goutam, and Atri *gotra*s, respectively, within the Kanva branch of Shukla Yajurveda; while Dange priests belong to the Madhyandin branch of Yajurveda and are the inheritors of the Gargya *gotra*. The Paricharak are the inheritors of the Atri *gotra* and are followers of Rigveda.

Each male member, by inheriting the above family surnames, qualifies for occupying his specific role and function in the temple ritual and for worship as soon as his thread ceremony is performed. Unless seven members, each representing one of the seven groups, are assembled, temple worship is not started. Therefore, all seven groups are responsible to each other and are interdependent for the functioning and conducting of temple ritual according to the set tradition. Besides, they are always in communication with the Badves, who have been given the functions of temple management and guardianship for the last seventy-five years.

The roles and functions of the Badves and Sevadharis are defined in their duties and rights, and a huge record is available from the sixteenth century which indicates their disputes and rivalries over details connected with their honor, position, income, and succession. Throughout the past four centuries, the two organizations of priests connected with the management and routine ritual performance and conduct of daily and occasional worship, namely the Badves and Sevadharis, have maintained the tradition of the temple worship and ritual. But, for this they have had to pay a high price. They have lost money and energy in quarrels and disputes among themselves — which were sometimes caused by a decision of the King's Court or Court of the Political Powers, such as during the Adilsahi regime, by the Marathi and Peshwa Courts, and by the British Courts.

3.   The Utpats, all having the same surnames, also belong to the Deshastha caste of the Maharashtra Brahmins, and are followers of Rigveda and inherit the succession of the Vashistha *gotra*. In 1966, there were 71 Utpat families. The Utpats in their representative capacity are held responsible for the management, ritual and worship, and guardianship of the Rukmini temple, which is in the precinct of the main temple but located at a distance. The goddess Rukmini is treated as the consort of the god Vithal. Generally in the temples of Hindu gods like Vishnu or Ram, there is an image of the consort by the side of the god. But, in Pandharpur, there are two temples for the goddess Rukmini exclusively. The first being the above temple and the other known as the "Rukmini," alias "Lakhubai," temple which is situated near the western bank of the river Bhima. But the Utpats are not related to that second temple. The Utpats, like the Badves and Sevadharis, have been associated with the temple since the sixteenth century. At that time, they were involved in disputes with the Badves over issues of income and privileges in the Rukmini temple.

The Badves and Sevadharis have no rights or powers in relation to the administration and performance of temple ritual nor to the conduct of daily and occasional worship at the Rukmini temple. Therefore, the Utpats occupy an exclusive status and eminence as far as the Rukmini Temple is concerned. There are four divisions among the Utpats and the number of families in each division are as follows: Khedkar-33, Barbhai-17, Damu Anna-12, and Undegaonkar-9.

The Utpats are the chief priests, trustees, and managers of the Rukmini temple. They manage the temple and take the surplus income after defraying the expenses of ritual, consisting of the daily *pujas* and *upcārs* and the administrative expenses of the Rukmini temple. There is no priesthood corresponding to the Sevadharis in the Rukmini temple. The Utpats auction among themselves the right to the monthly income received before Rukmini, and they give the auction to the highest bidder, as do the Badves. The entire body of Utpats elects members to represent them in the year's management of the temple. The representatives enjoy privileges and income according to their status.

## Changing Roles and Functions of the Temple Priests

The thousands of devotees who flock to Pandharpur for the monthly fairs, may not all be considered as the followers of the "Varkari" cult. Some of them visit the town for various other reasons or functions; while a considerable number of them visit occasionally or regularly to offer their homage to the deity and perform sacred acts and rituals, such as the thread ceremony, marriage, vow taking, and fulfillment celebrations. Secondly, the aim of a Pandharpur pilgrimage is to obtain some personal merit (*punya* or *apurva*).

Besides the priesthood of the Vithal and Rukmini temples, there is a minor priesthood of the many small temples of the different Vaishnava saints in Pandharpur. Besides the Badves, Sevadharis, and Utpats, there are two other organizations functioning as town priests who possess the hereditary tradition. They are known as the Kolis and Kshetropadhyes. The Kolis are non-Brahmins, while the Kshetropadhyes are an organization of 35 families from various *gotra* and *shakha* origins of Rigveda and Yajurveda and have different surnames. The members of these two organizations cater to the needs and requirements of the devotees and visitors, as their guides and as managers of their lodging and boarding during their stay at Pandharpur.

*Traditional Roles of the Badves, Sevadharis, and Utpats as Priests and Guides*   In the polytheistic religion which is institutionalized here and there in India, but not everywhere, all people worship many gods and owe different allegiances to these gods. The pattern of belief and worship changes from region to region because of historical causes. In Maharashtra, most of the people believe in and pay respect to such gods as:

Vaishnavite gods: Vishnu, Ram, Krishna, Vithal

Saivaite gods: Shiva, Kartikeya, Ganesh

Mother goddesses: Amba, Bhavani, Renuka, Ekvira, Maha-Laxmi, a number of minor village goddesses

Other deities and spirits: Mhasoba, Biruba, Rokdoba

At Pandharpur, in the main temple there are several subsidiary sacred icons, and in the town there exist images of some saint-poets which have been established by the priests; or else priests have been assigned to perform rituals in some temple on behalf of the devotees. Thus, the priests have performed the traditional role as mediator between the deity and the devotee, not only in the main temple but also in the town.

*Tradition and Transition: Ritual Worship and the Litigations of the Temple Priests*   Among the Hindus, the family ritual, which includes daily worship of gods at home and the worship of the god at shrines, forms two separate aspects of religious life. In worship by the family or by the individual, four types of deities were grouped and discussed by the author (Dingre 1968) while analysing the priest's relationship with the god and the devotees.

Because the roles and functions of the Badves, Sevadharis, and Utpats are connected to protracted litigations and court judgments and records, one can find interesting phases of change in their priesthood occupations. Their efforts to preserve tradition and thereby keep their rights of worship undisturbed were consistent throughout the eighteenth and nineteenth centuries. The decisions handed down by the state authorities or the Court of Justice in 1753, 1790, 1838, 1879, 1886, 1888, 1890, and 1892–1896, were responsible for increasing spirit, awareness, and consciousness among the Badves, Sevadharis, and Utpats. Their duties and privileges in connection with performing the ritual by conducting and presiding over the temple worship, were precisely defined by the judges, and a sort of legal sanction was accorded to their status and functions through the court judgements, which have confirmed customary rights and have sanctioned hereditary duties.

*Phases of Change*

1.   The forefathers of the present temple priests used to offer various services to the devotees as part of their hereditary profession of priesthood. These included guidance and assistance for the temple rituals and provision and arrangement of sacred feasts (to be offered as "Naivedya" to the god and learned Brahmins). This sacred role, in the course of time, was changed as the number of devotees increased. The limitations of time and an element of preference indirectly compelled the temple priests to change the trends and practices connected with preservation of the contacts and understanding which they once had established with their clients.

2.   Throughout the eighteenth and nineteenth centuries, the temple priests received money for the meals they provided to their client devotees (Yajmans). The Yajmans also asked the priests to prepare and offer Naivedya to the god and to feed the Brahmins. Some Yajmans have given away lands to the priests; out of the income of the lands concerned, the priests were to daily provide Naivedya to the god. In

this period, the temple priests followed the profession of "Puranik and Kirtankar," but their descendants could not maintain the scholarship and these supplementary occupations gradually have been abandoned in the last sixty years.

3.   The temple priests and the Kshetropadhyes have always kept a record of the people who have lodged and boarded with them. Some of the oldest records go back to the early seventeenth century. The oldest record is called the "Lekha." In former times, the devotees used to reside with either the temple priests or town priests. But during the nineteenth and first half of the twentieth centuries, the Math tradition and the complex connected with the tradition of the Varkari cult and literature were enlarged, and an additional area was found and constructed to provide lodging and boarding facilities for devotees. These actions consequently reduced the income of the priests.

4.   The fast-changing sociopolitical scene in India, which has been in the offing since the freedom agitation and throughout the winds of social reforms in the country, is indirectly a powerful stimulant to the phase of change. The introduction of road and rail transport in Pandharpur and nearby regions has been another factor, enlarging the number of pilgrims and devotees visiting Pandharpur from thousands to millions. In the last sixty years, the temple town has gradually developed a reputation as the meeting center of north and south Indian pilgrims and travelers. And the resultant introduction of amenities and facilities has created additional problems to be faced and solved. The profession and very existence of the priests is being challenged by sociopolitical change, particularly in the last two decades.

5.   The Badves, Sevadharis, and Utpats have maintained and preserved voluminous records about the tradition, customary rights, and genealogies of the devotees and pilgrims visiting Pandharpur periodically and staying with them. Details are kept of rituals performed during such visits, of names and kin relations of the pilgrim party, of dates of departure, etc. This record, in other words, is their ancestral property and is carefully kept. In former times, the majority of devotees would request their ancestral priest to write the details of their visit to the town, and the priest would record it and take the signatures or thumb impressions of the chiefs or elder members of the visiting party. The town priests, Kshetropadhyes, have also imitated this art. More than 2,000 record books with the handwriting, thumb impressions, and details of day, month, and year, according to the Hindu calendar, of various generations of devotees and worshipers of the god Vithal are kept by the priests of **Pandharpur.**

6. These records are interesting and valuable from the ethnographic and anthropometric viewpoint. The thumb impressions and handwriting of devotees within one family and belonging to three to seven generations could never be seen or traced except at Pandharpur in Maharashtra. At other sacred places, such records are maintained but none are as old and vivid as those of Pandhurpur. (Unfortunately, these records are gradually being affected by natural processes.) Among other things, a proposed legislative measure, to be adopted soon by the Maharashtra Legislative Assembly and Council, aims to abolish the hereditary rights and privileges of those Pandharpur priests who are associated with the management, worship, and ritual administration of the Vithal and Rukmini temples. The measure intends to appoint the government as administrator and thus threatens the traditional profession of priesthood in Pandharpur.

7. In the last ten years, efforts and agitations for this legislation have been made in Pandharpur and throughout Maharashtra. Because of the enlarged number of pilgrims, there are inadequate or insufficient facilities and amenities for the devotees and pilgrims during the four big fairs (July, November, February, and April) at Pandharpur; temple management and administration are disturbed during the fair times. Conscientious and educated devotees have also increased. In the last six years, there have been consistent efforts at various levels all over Maharashtra, which have compelled the Government of Maharashtra to appoint the Commission of Enquiry regarding "Pandharpur Temples" (according to the Commissions of Enquiry Act, 1952).

8. The Commission, with B. D. Nadkarni (retired District Judge) as chairman and G. V. Huprikar (Deputy Charity Commissioner) as secretary, started its work on October 21, 1968, and after detailed investigations submitted its report, along with a draft of proposed legislation and explanatory notes, in January 1970 (Nadkarni 1970).

9. The appointment and functioning of the commission created a great stir not only in Pandharpur but throughout Maharashtra. After the publication of its report a wave of criticism and hatred spread, and the temple priests and the Government of Maharashtra both became the targets of public criticism. The press in Maharashtra has also played a role, and a series of articles and news reports was published by all dailies and weeklies in Maharashtra. The tension in the minds of those who will be affected adversely is still mounting, while those who advocate a change, and insist it be implemented as soon as possible, have failed to suggest adequate measures. The atmosphere created in Pandharpur is full of distrust, rivalry, and some panic.

*Possible Repercussions and the Future*

1.   The "Nadkarni" Commission has recommended abolition of hereditary rights. In Chapter 18 of its report, the recommendations of the commission are given: "The Commission feels that hereditary rights of Badves and Utpats, both of management and service, and of all other Sevadharis, who have only the rights of service, should be abolished. Needless to say, preservations of any one of the two hereditary rights, viz. of management or service in Badves and Utpats, would be a source of constant trouble because possession of one is liable to be used as a lever or means to gain the other." The Government of Maharashtra has already accepted the report of the commission, and the draft of the bill is already on the floor of the House of the Legislature. The two legislatures of the Maharashtra State in the current monsoon session are likely to settle this issue. Ample efforts are being made, and the parties involved have concentrated their strength to obtain some kind of assurance from the Government of Maharashtra regarding their future position through legislative sanction.

2.   Because the public opinion in Maharashtra is divided on the issue of "Pandharpur temple administration and its proposed change," the temple priests are not keen about presenting their stand to the public. They feel that it will further contribute to the present wave of criticism and hatred against them or will be likely to curtail their chances of the desired compromise at negotiation level (if the state justice minister and concerned officials feel it necessary to open a fresh dialogue with the representatives of the Badves, Sevadharis, and Utpats before the legislature is moved for third reading and approval of the bill).

3.   It is the author's opinion that the change in the present setup of the Vithal temple, though desired and urgently required, should not be implemented merely by saying that this is the demand of the people of the state and that the state intends to honor it. It should be realized that this stand will further create an atmosphere of distrust and suspicion as soon as the priests' traditional position and established rights are abolished through the state act.

4.   The Badves have already approached the eminent advocates of the Supreme Court and are likely to present a written petition to the Supreme Court as soon as their hereditary rights are abolished by the state act. It has been learned that they have been assured there is a good chance of sanctioned legislative relief through a stay of execution from the Supreme Court. The Sevadharis are also likely to adopt the same measure, while the Utpats' stand is not yet finalized.

5.   Thus, coming action by the Maharashtra Government will determine the future of an estimated 350 priestly families, and their existence will be the subject of the policies of the government administrator to be appointed by the state act. Of these families, nearly one third could survive by finding some sort of secondary income source as a substitute for their traditional profession; one tenth could afford to continue using their acquired means and property; while the remainder will be placed at the mercy of the government and its bureaucrats.

## REFERENCES

BENDRE, D. R.
   1962   *Sri Vithal Sampradaya.* New Delhi: Publication Division, Government of India.
BHANDARKAR R. G.
   1913   *Vaishnavism, Saivism and minor religious systems.* Strassburg: Karl J. Trubner.
DANIELOU, A.
   1964   *Hindu polytheism.* London: Routledge and Kegan Paul.
DELEURY, G. H.
   1960   *The cult of Vithoba.* Poona: Deccan College Postgraduate and Research Institute.
DINGRE, G. V.
   1968   "A study of a temple town and its priesthood." Unpublished doctoral thesis, Poona University.
EVANS-PRITCHARD, E. E.
   1967   *Social anthropology* (reprint edition). London: Cohen and West.
KARVE, I.
   1968   *Maharashtra: land and its people:* Maharashtra State Gazetteers, General Series, Government of Maharashtra. Bombay.
KHARE, G. H.
   1945   *Sri Vithal ani Pandharpur.* Poona: Bharat Itihas Samshodhak Mandal.
KRISHNA DEVA
   1963   *Temples of north India.* New Delhi: National Book Trust.
MALHOTRA, K. C.
   1966   "Anthropometric measurements and blood groups of Maharashtrian Brahmins." Unpublished doctoral thesis, Poona University.
MATE, M. S., M. K. DHAVALIKAR
   1970   Pandharpur excavation: 1968, a report. *Bulletin of the Deccan College Research Institute* 29:76–117.
NADKARNI, B. D.
   1970   *Report of the Commission of Enquiry regarding Pandharpur temples.* Bombay: Government Central Press (R 151/1970).
O'DEA, T. F.
   1969   *Sociology of religion.* New Delhi: Prentice-Hall of India.

SARMA, D. S.
  1966 *Hinduism in a nutshell.* Madras: Higginbothams.
TULPULE, S. G.
  1965 *Prachin Marathi Koriv Lekha.* Poona: University of Poona.
WEBER, MAX
  1965 *The sociology of religion.* London: Methuen.

# An Anthropomorphic Shamanic Musical Instrument from the Eighth to Twelfth Centuries A.D.

A. KRALOVÁNSZKY

## DESCRIPTION OF THE OBJECT

The investigated object is a wind instrument made of clay, representing a man's head, unearthed in the early 1920's in a sandpit near the Cseke lake at Tata-Tóváros, Komárom county, Transdanubia, Hungary, while using a sand screen, i.e. at a secondary site (see Plates 1 and 2). Since then it has been preserved in the private collection of Mrs. György Zilahi in Budapest.

The circumstances of the uncovering have been confirmed by the workers who did it. The measurements of the finely polished, hand-shaped object baked to a brick red are: length — 119 millimeters, maximum width — 80 millimeters, largest horizontal circumference — 272 millimeters. Its whole surface is finely worn. The eyes, the ears, the open broad lips and the thick undulating moustache have been applied to the plastically formed face separately, while the broad and flattened nose, the bulging broad cheek region and the chin (perhaps beard?) protrude from the basic surface. The hairless skull of the man is broad and short, his occiput flattened vertically. On the left part of his forehead, near the median-sagittal line there is a definite, small, circular, artificial impression. On the whole, the male face is very expressive, suggesting strength.

The object is hollow. The protrusion representing the neck has two

I wish to thank Dr. V. Diószegi, Professor E. Dudich, Dr. H. Feriz, Professor R. Soós and Professor T. Tchernetzow for their thoughtful communications. I also thank Professor Gy. Bónis for the English translation, Dr. L. Kállay for the photos and Mr. Gy. Zilahi for allowing me to publish the find.

openings of irregular shape, the upper one is larger, the lower one smaller. The third orifice, a small circular one, is situated behind the left ear. If we blow the lower opening of the neck and we close the upper one simultaneously, we get an ocarina-like voice, the tone and rhythm of which may be regulated by opening and closing the orifice under the ear.

On the outer and inner surfaces of the object one may see the remains of calcified sea fauna and flora; these are, according to the expert opinion of the zoologist Dudich and the botanist Soós, of a worldwide type, thus unsuitable to a close topographical definition. The thickness of the deposit led the two professors to the conclusion that the object may have lain in sea water for one month at the most.

## DATE AND PLACE OF MANUFACTURE, ETHNICAL RELATIONS

In order to define the date and place of manufacture of the Tata find, I have studied the scientific literature without having discovered any direct analogy of purpose and portrayal. Only the Central American Indian material has furnished an anthropomorphic instrument similar in principle to the investigated find, i.e. a clay one; this is, however, naturally quite different from the Tata find genetically. We have also sought the opinion of a first-rate expert on such problems, the Dutch musicologist and ethnologist H. Feriz; having studied the photographs and data about the object in question, he stated that it is quite unknown in the tropical cultures. Its parallels may be looked for in Asia or among those exposed to Asian cultural influence (personal communication 1965). The Tata find was investigated by the Soviet ethnologist Tchernetzow and his Hungarian colleague Diószegi, both historians of religion; for all their wide experience they could not furnish a direct analogy to the find either (personal communication 1961). It has an extraordinary importance in our view, nevertheless.

We could find a partial analogy only in a publication by Gábori (Gábori 1960: 84). It is a baked clay tablet depicting a human face, unearthed from a Turkish (?) princely tomb of the sixth to eighth centuries A.D. in Mongolia (see Plate 3). Both finds are identical in the portrayal of an open mouth, the emphasis laid on the male characteristics (a large moustache and a strong nose), and are of the same material (baked clay). From the resemblance of the two portraits we may draw the inference that both examples may have tried to follow an ancestral and eventually obligatory iconographic model on one hand, and that we may be faced by a partial identity of function on the other.

The emphasis on the pronounced cheek region might indicate a certain Mongoloid anthropological feature in both cases. This is contradicted, however, by the thick moustache and the fleshy lips, these being rather Europoid characteristics. Thus we may imagine that the iconographic model may have belonged to a mixed Euro-Mongoloid type anthropologically, or that the original may have been modified toward the Europoid or the Mongoloid direction.

A slow infiltration of the Mongoloid racial elements from Asia began as early as the Iron Age in the East European regions, namely in the territory west and south of the Ural mountains. However, the appearance of significant Mongoloid anthropological components in the East European steppe zone may be reckoned with since the fourth century of our era, the time of the westward march of the Central Asian Huns (Debets 1948). Then this was reinforced by consecutive waves of Avars, Bulgarians, Hungarians, Petchenegs, Comans and at last in the thirteenth century Tartars, extending Mongoloid, mixed Euro-Mongoloid and naturally Europoid racial elements from southern Russia to the Viennese Basin. Consequently the shaping of an eventual Mongoloid or Euro-Mongoloid male face may be assumed in the eastern half of Europe only in the period between the fourth and thirteenth centuries of our era.

A more exact chronological and ethnic definition may be based on the circular and artificial impression on the forehead of the find's cranium, depicting a symbolic trepanation in our view. As is known, the symbolic trepanation is a ritual operation on the surface of the skull without penetrating the *tabula interna*, and its shape is most frequently circular (Nemeskéri, Ery, and Kralovánszky 1960: 30–32). According to scientific literature symbolic trepanation is found principally among the Volga and Danube Bulgarians of the eighth to the eleventh centuries, and among the Hungarians in the Carpathian Basin in the tenth and eleventh centuries, in the latter case especially in great frequency (Boev 1968: 127–131; Tóth 1962: 249–253; Nemeskéri, Kralovánszky, and Harsányi 1965: 413–437).

The investigation of the material of the find indicates the same period. The structure of the material, its degree of levigation, the mixing ratio and the resulting color are all typical of the products of sixth- to thirteenth-century pottery.

On the basis of our investigations as to the material and the portrayal of our object the date of its origin may be put between the eighth and the twelfth centuries, while the place of its manufacture may have been southern Russia or the Carpathian Basin. With regard to the historical data as well, we reach the most probable conclusion if we connect

the find with the conquering Hungarians who reached the Carpathian
Basin at about 900 A.D.

## INTERPRETATION OF THE FIND

In our view the interpretation of our object can be raised to the level of a
probable hypothesis only if we succeed in harmonizing the four main
characteristics: musical instrument, human portrayal, remains of maritime fauna and flora, symbolic trepanation.

Before attempting to solve the problem, we should note the following:

a.   It is common knowledge that in the early periods of history music
and also musical instruments were used primarily in religion and ritual.
As such, they occupy a special place in the life of society. With regard
to the estimated period of manufacture and use, we may state that the
society of the find was in all probability dominated by shamanism rather
than Christianity.

b.   The artistic and also religious elements of human portrayal are
equally recognized. Generally anthropomorphic design is very rare among
people believing in shamanism, since it almost falls under a taboo. Only
mythical ancestors and spiritual beings are portrayed in this manner
(Moschinskaja 1963: 101–110). Accordingly the human portrayal of
the object, the suggestive character of the design, the open mouth and
the use as a musical instrument are both special and important from the
artistic and the religious points of view.

c.   Ethnological research reveals that both professional (shaman) and
nonprofessional (popular) healing methods are used in explaining the
reasons and origins of illness (disease-demon, mysterious forces). The
cure is a science of mystical application of counter-magic and ritual acts
to cure the disease. One of its main methods is the carrying off, the
exorcism of the disease spirit and its casting to a place whence it cannot
return, e.g. digging it into the soil, throwing it into water, casting it into
the fire or in the wind (Szendrey and Szendrey 1939: 228–244).

d.   Finally it is known that the cure is connected with the person of the
shaman primarily (Diószegi 1962: 9).

Considering all this, an attempt to interpret the object in question must
follow certain guidelines:

1.   According to Tchernetzow (personal communication 1961) the successor of the dead shaman exercises his craft, i.e. healing, with the help
of the skull of the deceased shaman or of its copy until the strength and
knowledge of the shaman ancestor, centered in his head, is transmitted

to him. There are shamans who practice this all their lives.

2.   The purest and most perfect geometrical form is the circle, being the symbol of a series of ideas: the sun, the light, reason, health, etc. Consequently the bearer of this sign comes under the protection of the forces standing behind those ideas in a magical way; he becomes similar to them (Lips 1956: 67; Fettich 1958: 115–125). The symbolic trepanation visible on the dome of the investigated object is circular, like those observed on other investigated historical anthropological objects. There is both an ideological and causal relation with the phenomena of the diadem, the crown, the soul-hole, the halo, the tonsure, the *ushnisha* and *yati mukuti* of Hinduism and the seventh *chakra* of Tantrism. Their common origin and interpretation must be looked for in a belief rooted in the hitherto undiscovered depths of the human mind (Nemeskéri, Kralovánszky, and Harsányi 1965: 362). It is certain that the symbolic trepanation was executed by the shamans; its use is surely connected with shamanism in this period.

3.   Shamanic acts were always accompanied by instrumental music, usually a drum. But we know a Hungarian folk poem, sunk today to the level of children's games but reflecting an earlier living practice, related to cures; in this verse the Hungarian child heals the foot of the stork, hurt by the Turkish child, by whistle, drum and reed violin

Stork, stork, stork,
Why is your foot bloody?
The Turkish child has cut it.
The Hungarian child heals it.
By whistle, drum and reed violin (Solymossy 1939: 418).

In the 1950's, in the region beyond the Ural two living examples of healing by reed violin were found by Tchernetzow (personal communication 1961). Shamanic acts by whistle are, however, unknown in all Eurasia, except in the above-mentioned Hungarian folklore. As for the investigated object, it is similar to an ocarina sounded by blowing. The ocarina is a feature of maritime cultures and in Europe of the Mediterranean culture (Falk 1961: 36). This instrument of southern origin may have been connected to northern and eastern shamanism through the pre-Hungarians or the conquering Hungarians (maybe Petchenegs or Bulgarians?); this is why we lack this instrument in the north and the east among the peoples believing in shamanism. But we have to note that the Votyaks attach such importance to blowing in magic acts that they call the shaman "blower" and his performance "blowing" (Munkácsi 1910: 309).

4.   In the *Kalevala* Weinemöinen asks the virgin of Death, the mermaid

Disease, to throw the pains into the water and to cast them into the sea, so that they torment stones and crumble cliffs (Rune 45). Casting into the water is a cure not only among the Finns but also among the remaining related peoples, the Vogouls and Ostyaks (Pápay 1900: 272–276; Munkácsi 1910: 412).

This is why a sixteenth-century Hungarian document gains special importance: in a discussion with Catholic clergymen a Protestant pastor accuses them of healing in a heathen manner, because they chase the spirit of illness dwelling in the sick man into the sea in God's name, in order to overturn the sand, to disturb the foam and to break the stones by the sea (Bornemissza 1955 [1578]: 134–136). It is evident that such a sending of the spirit of the disease into the sea is a heathen custom of ancient origin; even its words may be regarded as original ones. It is also evident that this heathen custom was followed by clerics and laity alike, thus it was a practice known all over the land. Ideologically the clerics brought the demands and practice of the people into harmony with their own biblical ideology, since we read in the Apocalypse that the Devil organizes his army against the Church on the sand of the sea, the same sand from which a Beast rises, personifying all powers against God (The New Testament, Revelation 12: 13–18; 13: 1–10).

Finally we have to mention one more feature of the investigated object: it shows remains of a fauna and flora of cosmopolitan character, not to be derived from any specific sea topographically. Our object was not placed into the water of the sea without reason but by analogical thinking: having been in the sea, it should be able to return (Kralovánszky 1966: 97).

## CONCLUSION

1.  The investigated object was manufactured and used between the eighth and the twelfth centuries, most probably in the tenth or eleventh;
2.  It is connected with shamanism;
3.  It was unearthed in the Carpathian Basin, at the site of shamanic rites or from the grave of a shaman;
4.  It depicts a symbolically trephined shaman;
5.  It is a wind instrument which, when blown, caused by its sound the spirit of illness to be chased into the sea, where the object itself was for a while.

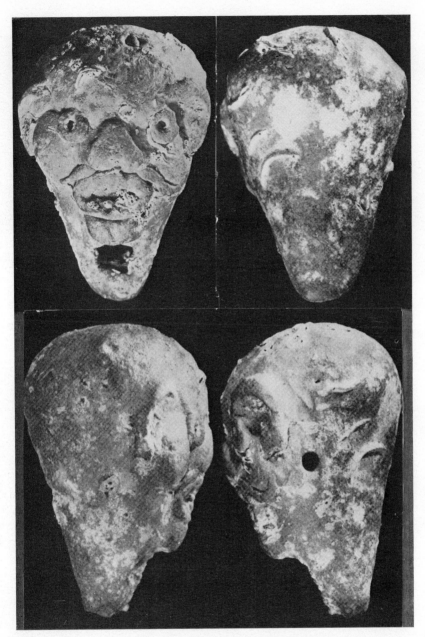

Plate 1.

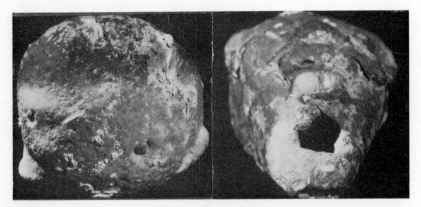

Plate 2.

Plate 3.

# REFERENCES

BOEV, PETER
1968 Die symbolischen Trepanationen. *Anthropologie und Human-genetik*, 127–135.

BORNEMISSZA, PÉTER, SÁNDOR ECKHART
1955 [1578] *Devilish ghosts*. (1955 edition by Sándor Eckhart.) Budapest.

DEBETS, G. F.
1948 "Paleoantropologia SSSR," in *Trudi Instituta Etnografii AN SSSR*, n.s. 4. Moscow-Leningrad.

DIÓSZEGI, VILMOS
1962 *Shamanism*. Budapest.

FALK, MARGARETHA
1961 Altindianische Musikinstrumente aus Costa Rica. *Atlantis* 33:36–38.

FETTICH, NÁNDOR
1958 Über den Sinn der prehistorischen Ornamente. *Acta Arch. Hung.* 9:115–125.

GÁBORI, MIKLÓS
1960 Report on the 1958 study trip in Mongolia. *Archaeologiai Értesítő* 87:83–86.

KRALOVÁNSZKY, ALÁN
1966 Anthropological data for the shamanistic belief of the conquering Hungarians. *Anthropologiai Közlemények* 10:91–98.

LIPS, EWA
1960 *Das Indianerbuch*. Budapest.

MOSCHINSKAJA, W.
1963 "Über einige alte anthropomorphe Darstellungen aus Westsibirien," in *Glaubenswelt und Folklore der sibirischen Völker*. Edited by V. Diószegi, 101–110. Budapest.

MUNKÁCSI, BERNÁT
1910 *Collection of Vogoul folk-lore*. Budapest.

NEMEKÉRI, JANOS, KINGA ÉRY, ALÁN KRALOVÁNSZKY
1960 Symbolically trephined skulls in Hungary. *Anthropologiai Közlemények* 4:3–32.

NEMESKÉRI, JÁNOS, ALÁN KRALOVÁNSZKY, LÁSZLÓ HARSÁNYI
1965 Trephined skulls from the tenth century. *Acta Arch. Hung.* 15: 413–437.

PÁPAY, JÓSZEF
1900 *A collection of Ostyak folk-lore*. Budapest.

SOLYMOSSY, SÁNDOR
1939 The ancestral belief of Hungarians. *Hungarian Ethnography* 4:402–449.

SZENDREY, ZSIGMOND, ÁKOS SZENDREY
1939 Customs. *Hungarian Ethnography* 4:228–244.

TÓTH, TIBOR
1962 Paleoanthropological finds from the Valley Hudjirte (Noin Ula, Mongolia). *Acta Arch. Hung.* 14:249–253.

# Rousalia: The Ritual Worship of the Dead

F. K. LITSAS

## INTRODUCTION

A sizable body of information has been compiled on ritual worship of the dead. Special emphasis and scholarly attention have been directed to the study of the ancient Greek burial rituals and to their survival in present-day customs. Most of the research in similarities of the ideas of the dead's return on earth between the ideas of the ancient Greeks and that of their modern counterparts has been conducted by Greek scholars.

The major objective of this paper is to describe the development and the character of the modern Greek feast of Rousalia. A determining factor in the choice of this topic is that the Rousalia Rituals are not only widely practiced, but are the most representative of the celebrations honoring the dead prevalent in Greece today.

Even though Rousalia is performed throughout the country, this essay will be restricted to the area of the southwestern Peloponnesus, and in particular the county of Triphylia. A considerable amount of information and research will also be included about the cities of Koróni and Messenia, closely situated near Triphylia, and Velvendós and Kozáni in western Macedonia.

A number of thoughtful people helped me in the undertaking and writing of this paper. Their moral support and constant encouragement were always with me. However, special recognition and thanks are extended to Vassilios Stavropoulos of Triphylia and J. Hatziharissis of Velvendós who aided me in gathering the material. Professor Robin E. Reed of Eastern Michigan College was also very helpful with his editorial comments.

The names Koróni, Triphylia, and Velvendós appear in text citations to show particular localities where the data given were found to be applicable.

## THE IDEA OF IMMORTALITY IN ANTIQUITY

The idea of the immortality of man's soul and its return to the earth from the underground is very common in antiquity (Farnell 1921; Lawson 1964). The literary sources and the archaeological finds throughout all the prehistoric kingdoms of the eastern Mediterranean support ancient notions of those ideas (Mylonas 1966: 176 ff.; Mercer 1947; Farnell 1911).

Prehistoric Greek burial situations give us serious evidence to verify their belief about man's immortality (Jevons 1895: 297 ff.). From the sixteenth century B.C., at least, Mycenaeans developed a close contact with Egyptians and learned their basic ideas about life beyond the grave (Mylonas 1966). Their burial monuments provide substantial proof of their convictions about immortality.

In Greek literature and archaeological sources as well as in oral traditions many elements of the idea of immortality and the return of the dead to the earth upon the occurrence of desirable circumstances have survived. Since the time of Homer (*Odyssey*, Book II, *Iliad*, Book 23) through all Greek and Roman antiquity and then throughout Christianity the idea of the dead's return has come down to our times unchanged in its general features.

If we presume that religious myths or stories from metropolitan Greece and abroad were used as a basis for Homeric poems, it seems to be beyond doubt that Greek ideas regarding spirits, the dead, and their reappearance to the living were formulated by influences from Sumerians, Babylonians, Egyptians and other races of the Near East (Mercer 1947; Farnell 1911; Nilson 1933: 119 ff.). Later, numerous elements of the religious myths came to be adopted from the Greek folk into the official rituals which have retained their general features (Politis 1871: 74).

Greek antiquity established an official worship for the deceased as exalted spirits who might return to haunt and molest the disrespectful and the negligent. Without these rites, performed by the survivors, the deceased were not accepted in the underworld, or "House of Hades" (Gulick 1927).

We can mention the famous Oracle of the Dead of Acheron in Epirus or the Aornon Oracle in Italian Kyme (Rohde 1907). There several ceremonies and rituals were performed in order to communicate with the deceased, to recall their spirits or to worship their souls. One can observe the entire absence of priestly ritual, or anything that resembles religious services for the deceased. In contrast, Christianity brought the mourner, through the deceased, closer to the church and to the consolation which through the hope of resurrection the church held out to her bereaved (Whisley 1931: 377 ff.).

Ancient Greek folk established under several names, such as Anthesteria, Nekysia, Epitaphia, etc. (Gulick 1927), certain cults and annual celebrations to honor the deceased. Anthesteria is one of them that appears to have many similarities with the modern celebration of Rousalia Day.

Although the Anthesteria was a festival of Dionysus (Harrison 1955: 32 ff. and 74 ff.), one of its days was devoted to the deceased. On this day, it was assumed that the spirits returned to earth to visit the living. It is notable that the gifts to the dead, such as the *panspermies* [various seed offerings], *enagismata* [sacrifices], *melitoussae* [honey-pies], and *chytroi* [cooked food] were offered and put at the graves on this day (Farnell 1921: 345 ff.; Harrison 1955: 173).

This festival, like the public celebration of Nekysia, is considered to be the antecedent of the later Rousalia (Kurtz and Boardman 1971: 147 ff). The basic beliefs and rituals were maintained by the same peoples — by the Romans, the most devoted pupils of Greek heritage; by the Christians; and by the Byzantine folk, the natural successors of Greek tradition until today.

## THE IDEA OF IMMORTALITY AMONG GREEKS TODAY

Today, Greek as well as many Balkan folk perform almost the same rituals, and their convictions seem to come directly from antiquity through the uninterrupted oral tradition (Karolides 1925: IV, 254 ff.)[1]

Moreover, the Orthodox Church that enriched her own tradition through many Greek elements, adopted the idea of the immortality of man's soul according to Jesus' instruction (The New Testament, Luke 16: 19 ff.) that the dead live eternally in another world. They are separated into the righteous and the iniquitous and are waiting for their final judgment (The New Testament, Matthew 25: 31 ff.).

Under those ideas the Orthodox Church must perform memorial services in order to help the souls of the dead before the divine judgment. Thus, after death at least five memorial services must be performed.[2]

[1] From the term Rousalia probably came the Russian word *rusalka* ["water sprite," also "scarecrow"]. One can meet it in Russian literature: Pushkin's poem, "Rusalka," and Gogol's story, "May Night of the Drowned Girl."
[2] The third, ninth and fortieth day and the sixth and twelfth month after death (see also Lawson 1964: 534).

Furthermore, memorial services are formally performed four times a year for all dead, the *psychosabbata* [All Souls' Saturdays]. Observing these memorial services from the common people's point of view one can note the obvious similarities between the modern and ancient Greek memorial celebrations. The same idea exists that the dead need to have our prayers, offerings, and help (Rouse 1902: 4 ff.; Lekatsas 1957: 410).

On the other hand, the popular written version of the idea of the dead's return to earth was contributed by a Byzantine *hagiologion* or *synaxarion* [book of the saints' lives].³ This book states that some time in the past the Virgin Mary visited Hell and because of the severe tortures of the sinners, she pitied their souls and pleaded that her Son be merciful with them. And so Christ allowed all souls to come to the earth for fifty days, from Easter Day to Pentecost (Mercer 1947: 314).

Greek common people today believe that for these fifty days the dead live as we do; they come up to the earth and get together with the living, visit their favorite places and try to enjoy their time of freedom. Thus, the living try to make them happier, to give them offerings and worship them by rituals.


ORIGIN OF THE ROUSALIA FESTIVAL

The festival of Nekysia⁴ is one among many ancient Greek celebrations for the dead. It was performed annually during the Attic month Boethromion, from mid-September to mid-October (Harrington and Tolman 1897: 3). The folk believed that the dead returned to the earth during this time. They brought offerings and sacrifices to the dead and various rituals were performed (Farnell 1921: 344 ff.). In the later years Lucian described the celebration ironically (Harmon 1953: 440 ff.):

CHARON: Why is it, then, that those people are putting garlands on the stones and anointing them with perfume? There are others also who have built

³ *Book of the lives of saints.* This book is popular among Greek common people. It is usually called *to filladaki tes panaigas* ["the Virgin's book" or "the apocalypse of the Holy Virgin Theotokos"]. It was published by J. Gidel from a manuscript in the Paris Library. Gidel found that the original text, written before the eleventh century A.D. was epitomized and interpreted in a vulgar Greek idiom by Sofronius, a sixteenth-century monk and subsequently adopted by the folk. One can easily obtain the sixteen-page book in front of the churches in Aeolou Street in Athens as well as in other towns and monasteries.

⁴ Sometimes called Nemesia (Nekysia from the word *nekys* [corpse or dead one]). Lucian of Samosata calls the festival ironically *thanatousia* from *thanatos* [death]. In Crete the eleventh month of the year was called *Nekysios* (Detternberger 1915–1924).

pyres in front of the mounds and have dug trenches, and now they are burning up those fine dinners and pouring wine and mead, as far as one may judge, into the ditches? ...

HERMES: I don't know what good these things are to men in Hades; they are convinced that the Souls, allowed to come up from the underworld, get their dinners as best they may by flitting about in the smoke and steam and drink, when their skulls are dry as tinder?

CHARON: You know whether they can come back to earth when they have once gone underground! I should be in a fine predicament, Hermes, and should have no end of trouble if I were obliged not only to bring them down but to bring them up to drink! What folly, the idiots! ... They do not know what an impassable frontier divides the world of the dead from the world of the living ....

The Greek festival of Nekysia seems to be very close to the Roman celebration of Lemouria.[5] It was performed on one of the days between 9 and 13 May. This period was dedicated to the dead, and other activities and wedding ceremonies were prohibited from being performed.

Another Roman feast, known as Floralia, Rosaria, or Rosalia, was also celebrated during the same period of May (Bianchi 1877: 136; Lawson 1964: 45). It was basically a festival to celebrate the emergence of spring and the renewal of plant life. Flowers were used extensively in adorning homes, public locations, and, occasionally, graves.

The Lemouria and the Rosalia festivals were held simultaneously. Through the evolution of time, the melancholia of the Lemouria feast slowly overshadowed the relatively carefree, lighthearted character of the Rosalia. As a result, the people became more absorbed in floral decorations of the graves. Many plants, particularly roses (Frazer 1927: 399 ff.), were planted on the graves and many sacrifices were offered there to the dead. Furthermore, the mournful character of the Lemouria and the lighthearted Rosalia were joined into one and became a new form containing the background of both. Then, the Christians[6] and the Byzantines[7] modified the feast further by the new Christian practices,[8]

[5] Lemouria or Remouria (Lemoures or Remoures were named by the Romans to honor the dead), was a festival established to honor Remus who was killed by his brother Romulus (Harrington and Tolman 1897: 3ff.; Harrison 1955: 35ff.).
[6] It is believed that the Christian Agapes (joint dinners and celebrations performed on the martyrs' graves) are similar customs (Lekatsas 1957: 407ff.).
[7] The Byzantine people called the celebration Rosalia, Rousalia or Rothismos (Koukoules 1937–1952: II, 29ff.; Pouqueville: II, 170).
[8] Emperor Julian the Apostate (A.D. 361–363) influenced by the suggestions of St. Theodore the Tyron and Patriarch Eytychios, consecrated Rousalia Day as a Christian feast.

but the original name of the celebration was retained⁹ until today.


## ROUSALIA DAY: BELIEFS AND RITUALS

Rousalia Day belongs among those kinds of celebrations, that, by their ethnological characteristics, give us the measure of the Greek peasants' attitude toward death. The terms that characterize the celebration and the offerings, beliefs, and rituals that are performed on this day are described below.


### The Offerings

TERMS USED

The purposes of the offerings usually determine the names given to them (Lawson 1964: 529 ff.):

1. *To sychorio, e sychoresi* [forgiveness] (Triphylia).
2. *To psychoponio* [compassion for the dead].
3. *To psychouthi, psychomertiko, mertiko tou pethamenou* [portion of the dead].
4. *To prosphorata* [offerings], ideally a loaf of bread with the seal of the church (Megas 1939: III, 80).

KINDS OF OFFERINGS

1. *Ta kollyba* [cooked wheat mixed with seeds]. As stated by an informant: "We use seeds such as pomegranate, raisins, walnuts, almonds and smashed sesame, all of them mixed with the wheat as well as sugar and parsley pieces well-shaped in trays or bowls" (field notes; also Lawson 1964: 535 ff.).
2. *Ta psychokeria* [souls' candles]. A small torch made from cotton thread dipped into melted beeswax (field notes; Megas 1939: I, 136).
3. Liquids such as wine, olive oil, the blood of a sacrificed animal, water "that must be poured on the graves, or tears of the people that must weep profusely upon them" (Triphylia, Koróni, Velvendós).¹⁰

---

⁹ The sixty-second canon of the Sixth Ecumenical Synod in its discussion on secular customs referred to the Rousalia in the following manner: "Then, Rousalia and Broumalia that existed by now [seventh century A.D.] after the Holy Easter, performed by the coeval peasants likely as was performed by Greeks for Dionysus sometime in the past" (Vlastaris 1888: VI, 43ff.).
¹⁰ Among primitives the blood is considered a very important offering (see Lekatsas 1957: 397ff.).
On this day in Triphylia each family usually sacrifices a goat or a specially fed

4.  Food, such as meat, cheese, beverages, or pies. In Triphylia people make the *rousalopitta* [honey pie]. Compare the ancient Greek *melitoussa* (Whisley 1931: 595).

5.  Flowers that are placed or planted on graves, such as roses (compare Frazer 1927: 399 ff.). Also placed there are seeds of wheat or other cereals, referred to in Greek as *demetriakoi karpoi* or *demetrakides* to symbolize the dead (Triphylia). Compare also with the ancient Greek *Demetrioi* (Harrison 1955: 267 and 599 ff.; Farnell 1921: 347; Lekatsas 1957: 101).

## The Rousalia Day Feast

TERMS USED

1.  *To psychosabbato tou mae, to megalo psychosabbato* [the great All Souls' Day] (field notes).

2.  *To psychosabbato stis peninta* [the All Souls' Saturday, fifty days after Easter] (field notes).

3.  *To psychosabbato stis gonatistis* [the All Souls' Saturday of kneeling], when people must kneel on the graves or at the church on such a day or on the coming Sunday that is popularly called "the Sunday of kneeling" (field notes; see also Megas 1939: III, 98 and 132).

4.  *Tou myriothanatou* [the anniversary of the innumerable dead] (Megas 1939: III, 132).

5.  *T' Aipsychou, Apsychou* [the anniversary of the Saint Soul] (field notes, Megas 1939: III, 132 ff.).[11]

6.  *Tou Mayopsychou* [the Soul's May anniversary] (Megas 1939: III, 132).

7.  *T' Ai-rousaliou, Arousaliou, tou Rousalione* [the Rousalia Day feast], or [the Saint's Rousales anniversary] (field notes).

---

lamb called "Rousalites." The water is an important offering "because the deceased is always thirsty in his grave" (field notes; see also Lekatsas 1957: 400). Perhaps a similar meaning is symbolized in the picture of the gold seal of Tyrins picturing the Procession of Ta-Ourt Demons or *Dipsion* ["the thirsty ones" or "the dead"] (see Marinatos 1960: 173a, Plate 207; Palmer 1965: 136ff.).

Compare also the coeval belief: "The poor deceased are always thirsty. Therefore we must cry, because the deceased need to drink the tears to be refreshed" (field notes; also Lekatsas 1957: 403).

[11] In Byzantine times people unconsciously modified the simple names in saints' names, as *Agiou Psykhou* [Saint Soul] and *Agio Rousales* [Saint Rousales] (see Megas 1939: III, 133). It is notable that in Triphylia there are place names such as Ai-Rousalē̄,ē, Arousalē̄,ē, Ai-Roúsalē̄,ē (Georgacas and McDonald 1967: 98).

RITUALS BEFORE THE ACTUAL DAY

One can find some common beliefs and rituals that are expressed before the Rousalia Day, such as the feast of the three All Souls' Saturdays before Easter. Closely connected with the Rousalia celebration are some rituals that are performed on Good Friday and Easter Friday. On all those days, especially on the Saturday before the Resurrection, offerings for the dead are put on their graves.[12]

Easter is the greatest religious celebration for Greeks. In the afternoon of this day they perform the *tis agapis* or *apokerasia* [the taste of Christian love]. In some places such a ceremony is celebrated in the cemeteries. In the city of Chora Triphylias this ceremony is performed in the old cemetery of the city and attended by clerical authorities of the entire area (field notes).

On the Monday of Easter the children of Megara-Attikis sing a kind of carol called the *Roysalia* (Megas 1939:3:173; Megas 1958: 187ff.). Some relevant rituals are also performed on Ascension-Day, forty days after Easter (Megas 1939:III, 130).

RITUALS ON ROUSALIA DAY

Common people consider the Rousalia Day as the last day of happiness for the dead. The next day they must return to the underground to continue passing their time in the unblissful life of Hades, "the fields of forgottenness" or "the tortures of Hell." Rousalia Day is their last opportunity to enjoy the happiness of life on the earth.

According to these beliefs the living try to do their best to make their beloved deceased as happy as possible. The offerings used on such a day by the people have been stated above. The rituals that are usually performed on this day are the following:

1. In Triphylia "They go to the cemeteries bearing offerings and kneel on the graves singing the songs of death and waiting for the deceased to come and eat . . ." In Velvendós they believe "that deceased dash in as falcons and eat or lick the offerings . . ." The living are accustomed to cover their eyes with rose leaves "purposely, to be not recognized by the deceased and make them sad . . ." (field notes).

2. "They collect oregano plants and put wreaths of them on the

---

[12] "Deceased must have their cookies, their red eggs, and their white torch to celebrate their resurrection with Christ. Before the resurrection of Christ the deceased come out from their graves and live together with the living for fifty days. They are invisible and they look like white flies or white bees or butterflies. Only the purified people can see them . . ." (field notes; Megas 1939: I, 3, 97, 140; Harrison 1955: 200ff.; Lekatsas 1957: 82).

graves to keep them pure from vampires ..." (Triphylia, Velvendós; see also Whisley 1931: 595).

3. In Athens "on the Rousalia Day people present their sick children to the deceased to ask their blessings for good health ... (Megas 1939: III, 133).

4. On such a day they make prognostications by using the offerings to the dead, especially the *kollyba* [cooked wheat].[13]

5. They comb their hair all day and spread it in the air "to help deceased passing the hair-bridge ..." It is commonly believed that "the deceased go back to the underworld by passing through *tes trichas to giofiri* [this hair-made bridge]; underneath this bridge the tortures of Hell are located" (field notes; see also Mercer 1947: 327; Frazer 1927: 224).

6. They plant flowers on the graves, especially roses, and cereals.

7. One can also refer to some activities that are held on the Rousalia Day, such as athletic games, performances with ethical overtones and fairs full of amusement.[14]

BELIEFS

Common beliefs for this day are the following:

1. Any work is strictly prohibited on such a day. "People must be free to help or entertain the deceased" (field notes).

2. In Velvendós "priests mustn't conduct any memorials because today both living and deceased are mixed all together ..."

3. In Triphylia "the elders must keep awake all day, even overnight

---

[13] In Triphylia "one can take three or seven or nine seeds of the cooked wheat, put them underneath his pillow together with a black piece of material and a black-handled knife. Thus, he can predict, by dreaming, anything he likes ...." In Velvendós, "they feed the sheep with cooked wheat. If sheep eat them it is good; if the sheep do not eat them, the coming year will be horrible ..." (field notes; see also Megas 1939: III, 70, 793).

[14] In Koróni "the youth play *tès amathes* [a hop-scotch game] and they also throw the discus. The winners of such a game are considered to be very lucky persons ...." The same custom exists in some villages of Triphylia. In the evening of the same day many families eat dinner together, drink the *psychozoumi* or *hagiozoumi* [cooked wheat juice], and sometimes sing and dance (field notes).

In some mountainous villages of Triphylia, called Soulimochoria, all the people would concentrate in front of the cemetery chapel. They would stand there in order of seniority — first the priest, then the elders, and so forth. They would forgive each other by a kiss, and then dance again, in order of their ages and authority. They would sing the song of Rousalia Day (field notes).

Also from mountainous Triphylia comes information that "years before, the celebration of Rousalia Day was a great fair, eight or ten days long, and was performed with songs, dance and amusement. People dressed in their best attire, would roast meat, every family would kill a specially fed lamb called the Rousalites, imbibing and dancing for Saint Rousales" (field notes; see also Dragoumes 1917: II, 255ff.).

to the coming Sunday, because some deceased might carry their souls with them to the underworld" (see also Megas 1939: III, 139).

4. "Nobody must be near the sea on such a day, because the waters are troubled" (Koróni).

5. "Nobody must wash his head this day; he might become deaf" (Triphylia, Koróni; see also Megas 1939: III, 80).

6. "No woman must spin on this day, because the cereals will be burned by the sun" (Triphylia).

7. "Sewing as well as driving nails is strictly prohibited, because the eyes of the deceased will be pierced" (Triphylia, Koróni).

8. "Digging and working in farms is also prohibited, because nobody must be involved with soils on such a day; the deceased hate soils . . ." (Triphylia, Koróni, Velvendós).

9. "The cutting of the tender branches of grape trees is prohibited on this day because the deceased are said to sit on these branches . . ." (Triphylia, Koróni).

10. "Freshly washed clothes were not allowed outside to dry after sunset because the deceased might sit on them and soil them . . ." (Triphylia, Koróni).

11. Large fires, flames and smoke are prohibited because "deceased are everywhere and might be burned; the fireplace should also be extinguished because one of the dead might step upon it . . ." (Triphylia, Koróni). Exception: the smoke of burning meat that the deceased like.

12. During the Rousalia Day "people must be very generous. Their first obligation should be to charities. Doing so, people deliver their beloved deceased ones from their sins . . ." (Triphylia, Koróni).

RITUALS AFTER THE ROUSALIA DAY

The Rousalia Saturday is rather more carefree than serious in character, but the coming Sunday (Sunday of Pentecost) is very somber and mournful. Saturday is the last day of the dead on the earth but on Sunday they must take the path of return to their unhappy habitation.

The common people perform additional rituals on this day in the following manner:

1. Kneeling: The orthodox kneel formally at the church during an extraordinary ceremony from which the name "Sunday of kneeling" originated. The people also kneel on the graves in honor of the departing dead.

2. Special usage of flowers or tree branches: "People go to the church, holding a tree branch and kneel praying for the deceased . . ." (Velvendós; see also Megas 1939: III, 131). "On the day of Pentecost,

while the people are kneeling, they chew mint leaves, rose stems or cooked lupine seeds" (Triphylia).[15]

In Velvendós "people kneel at the church or at the graves, put flowers in front of themselves and light a soul candle to enable the deceased to see better in their return to the underworld . . ." (Triphylia). "On the Sunday of kneeling people beat each other with walnut tree branches or leaves in order that they may have health for the rest of the year . . ." (Megas 1939: III, 134). "People kneel on the graves and cover their eyes with rose leaves or walnut tree leaves, because the deceased may see them and become sad or out of their position on the path to the underworld" (Triphylia; Megas 1939: III, 133).

3. Offerings: "On the Sunday of Pentecost, the old ladies distribute honey pies to the people and put some pieces on the trees or paths with which the deceased may treat the dog keeper of Hades . . ." (Triphylia, Koróni; see also Lekatsas 1957: 243ff.). "On the Sunday of Pentecost the people also bring to the church milk pies and other foods; they distribute them to each other and ask for the 'forgiveness' of the deceased . . ." (Triphylia).

## EXHUMATION OF REMAINS

One custom of the modern Greeks is to exhume the dead. The time of exhumation must occur in the third, fifth or seventh year after death.[16] Saturday is the preferable day (field notes; see also Megas 1939: I, 139ff.).

In the Greek language the common terms for exhumation are: *xechoma, xechomatiasma, xechomata; xechoniasma; vgalsimo, na ton evgaloume* (Lekatsas 1957: 213; see also Lawson 1964: 485ff.).

Before opening the grave the dead's relatives must bring to the grave some offerings[17] such as clean water, wine, a small basket, a

---

[15] Ancient Greeks would chew the *ramnos* [white thorn, briar] in the Nekysia festival (Rohde 1907: I, 237).

[16] "The years should be in odd, not even numbers, because death must not be duplicated" (Triphylia). It should be one month before the third year exactly or on the Rousalia Day after the third year" (Velvendós). "The exhumation should be held before three years, because the soil oppresses the deceased . . ." (Koróni; see also Megas 1939: I, 139ff.).

[17] "They must bring water to the grave in a clean and new urn, if possible; they might bring also a pitcher of wine. The bearer must be silent and be dressed in white . . ." (Triphylia, Koróni; see also Note 14). The family also bring digging tools such as *o kasmas* [a mattock], *e axina* [a spade], and *to ftiari* [a shovel]. These three words are of the three grammar genders – masculine, feminine and neuter – and thereby represent the influence of death upon everyone: men, women, children (field notes).

cotton bag or a pillow case, preferably white and unused, a *prospho-ron* [offering], and digging equipment.

In the beginning, the priest reads some prayers on the grave, then thrusts the spade into the soil[18] just four times. After that the workers continue digging until they hit the coffin. "Only men can participate in digging and excavation of the grave; woman must stay out of this matter" (Koróni).

After carrying the soil away, they open the coffin and observe the remains of the dead, and act in accordance with one of the following conditions:

1. If the body is decomposed, the process of exhumation is continued normally.

2. If the body "is covered by a white sheet or shadow" or at the first glance the remains look as though there is no decay, the people present must wait a few moments for the shadow to disappear . . .[19]

3. If the body is not decomposed (*Alyotos pethamenos*), the relatives must perform extra rituals and exorcisms.[20]

All bones are cautiously collected and washed with water or wine, are placed in the bag, put into the basket and taken to a small table at the church in front of the royal gates until the following Sunday when, after Divine Liturgy is served, a memorial service is performed for the deceased. At this time, everyone kisses the skull which is in the basket and "is usually decorated with flowers." The bones are then replaced or buried in a predetermined location in the cemetery "for the eternal rest."[21]

---

[18] "One might communicate with the deceased, if he touches this disturbed soil and throws some in front and behind himself" (field notes; see also Megas 1939: I, 139).

[19] The meaning of "shadow" might be explained by a shadowy figure of the dead, momentarily perceived just prior to the instant of disintegration. Compare also similar information from archaeology (see Schliemann 1878: 340, Figure 454; Marinatos 1960: 82; Ceram 1954: 20ff.).

[20] "In such a case, people must proclaim the *"Kyrie eleison"* until the phenomenon disappears" (Triphylia, Velvendós). In Velvendós, people believe that this phenomenon indicates the kindness of the dead and is called *anthè* [flowers] or *thymiama* [incense]. Relevant common terms: *athexios* [the iniquitous one] (Koróni); *then ton thechtike è ye* [one whom the earth did not accept] (Triphylia, Velvendós; Megas 1939: I, 140). The general idea of such a situation is that a non-decayed body belongs to a sinner, or to one excommunicated. The popular curse, "for one to be found not decayed" is considered the worst one (field notes).

[21] "They must perform a seven-priest litany or liturgy" (Koróni, Triphylia, Velvendós), "must call the Bishop to kneel on the grave" (Triphylia), "must carry the remains out and pass it from forty churches for forty days" (Megas 1939: I, 140), or "must bury the body again, until it has been decomposed" (Velvendós). Relatives bring offerings as in regular memorial services. In Triphylia "no flowers,

## MAGICAL OBSERVATIONS OF HUMAN REMAINS

After exhumation of the body, the people observe the remains, especially the bones. While observing the remains many prognostications are made concerning the future and past of the dead as well as of the living (Lekatsas 1957: 326ff.). These observations could be classified as follows:[22]

BONE OBSERVATIONS CONCERNING THE DEAD
1. "White bones means that he was a good man."
2. "Dark bones, he was a villain."
3. "Yellowish bones, he was very religious" (Triphylia, Koróni).
4. "Broken bones, his soul had many problems."
5. "The zig-zag suture lines that connect its particular bones mean letters that describe the dead's personality" (Triphylia, Velvendós).

BONE OBSERVATIONS CONCERNING THE LIVING
1. "Crossed calf bones means long life for the rest of the living" (Triphylia, Koróni).
2. "Dark shoulder-blade bone means miseries for the deceased's family" (Triphylia, Koróni, Velvendós).

GENERAL OBSERVATIONS CONCERNING THE DEAD
1. "Remains upside down means that the deceased's soul had problems."
2. "If the decomposition of the body is up on time, he was a good man" (field notes).
3. "If his hands are not decayed, he was a perjurer" (Triphylia; Megas 1939: I, 140).
4. "If his hair is not decayed, he was a slanderer."
5. "If his jawbone is down, as in an opened mouth, he was left hungry."

---

or decorations are permitted." The usual location of bones is a small building in a corner of the cemetery called bone place. The usual Greek terms for such a place are: *kokkalistra* [bone place], *honefteri* [melting or vanishing prace, crucible], *liostra* [crushing place], *Lemori*, which may have come from the same root as Lemoures (see Note 5).

[22] In Velvendós "people observe the remains curiously and cautiously, but only the elders know how to explain the indications, and how to predict the future." In Koróni "one, who knows how to read the bones, watches the future on the skull or the shoulder-blade bone of the deceased" (field notes).

GENERAL OBSERVATIONS CONCERNING THE LIVING

1. "If some flesh remains on the shoulder bone, someone else will die."

2. "If the skull is facing to the right, an abundance of goods will flood his family."

3. "If the skull is facing to the left, bad weather will occur."

4. "If the jawbone is down, as in an opened mouth, the prognostications are very bad."

5. "If his palms are still crossed, someone in his family will be married."

6. "If the skull is especially white, the first to touch it will be very lucky this year."


ELEGIES

The following are elegies performed in the course of Rousalia Day rituals.

1.

Let all Saturdays come, come and go,
But Rousalia Saturday must not come, must not pass . . .

Let all Saturdays come, come and go,
But let Rousalia Saturday neither pass nor come again . . .

A curse on those who were working on the All Souls' Saturdays,
The meat feast, the cheese feast, and the feast of Saint Theodore . . .

A curse on those who were working on the All Souls' Saturdays,
The first of Lent, the Feast of Saint Theodore and Rousalia Saturday . . .

Bless all those who were merciful on the All Souls' Saturdays,
The Feast of Lent, the Feast of Saint Theodore, and Rousalia Saturday . . .

2.

. . . If only the graves could be opened and the deceased allowed to come out,
A mother could see her child, even for but a day and night,
And if only the day were a May day and the night a year . . .

**3.**

Oh . . . , come, let us weep for all who have died,
All those of the last year and of this, even those, the forgotten ones,
So that our tears may form a river . . .

. . . . River, move on, O river, to the underworld,
That the drowsy may be revived that the thirsty may be refreshed,
And that the scholar may reawaken his pen.

**4.**

Now, when we get up from the soil and the black earth,
Please send some clothing for elders, handkerchiefs for youth,
wreaths for newlyweds, flowers for brides,
And for little children, baptismal gowns,
That we might be dressed and go to the Souls' Feast . . .

**5.**

I've told you, beloved Mother, what I desire: Send me
for Good Friday a candle, for Easter Sunday a white torch,
And for the *Apokerasia,* please send me my suit,
That I might be combed and dressed in my best attire . . .

**6.**

THE DECEASED:
I would like there to come a night of greeting,
To be with you at your table and console you,
But I have an earthy breath and an underground smell.

THE LIVING:
Even if you have the odor of the earth I want you,
Even any stench I love you,
If you could come back from the black earth, please . . .

**7.**

I am headed, I decided to move to the underworld . . .
. . . If anyone has a message to send or any letters, give them to me,
If anyone has an unarmed son, let me take him his weapons,
If anyone has an unadorned daughter, let me take her her ornaments,
And if any mother has a child ready for school, let me bear him his
books,

For I am headed to move to the underworld . . .

8.

My child, you departed for the underground,
Leaving your mother grievous and death-stricken . . .
. . . My little child, where might I place your sorrow? . . .
. . . If I place it on pavements, pedestrians will waste it,
And if I place it on trees, birds will peck at it . . .
. . . Where could my tears drop because of your departure? . . .
If they drop on the black earth, grass will not grow there,
If they drop into a stream, the stream will become arid,
If they drop into the sea, ships will drown,
Yet, if I enclose them in my heart, we'll meet each other soon . . .

9.

O Father, go to see her . . .
The deceased have a great feast tonight,
And are rising from their graves,
Ornately dressed as newlyweds,
To eat their offerings . . .
. . . When midnight comes and roosters crow,
Go and wait alone near the cypress,
Today is All Souls' Day, Rousalia,
She will come to your bosom
For your kisses . . .
. . . He went behind the Holy Chapel and waited,,
Midnight came, the graves shivered all at once,
And Maria, dressed in white, came up . . .

10.

Musket fire rends the air
And the Syrtzi mountains roar,
Some deceased youths group
When pine trees groan and whistle.
. . And all gather from about
At a lonely chapel on a ridge,
To decorate their graves with palm branches,
To sing songs of heroism and battle
    At Rousalia Day's dawning, after their rest
The Dead Souls descend to the underground,

But to George's grave no mother goes.
There, the only sound is their carefree songs . . .

## SUMMARY

The concept of the dead returning to the earth from the underworld is universal and popular among both primitive and more civilized peoples. This concept is one of the most emotionally expressed beliefs of human beings and demonstrates the mystery and the unbroken relationship between the living and the dead.

The belief that the dead live eternally, need food, are pleased by receiving offerings and experience a strong desire to communicate with the living explains the emotional basis of the existence of all those rituals and celebrations. Furthermore, their actual manifestation aims at the perception of life beyond the grave and bridging the abyss between life and death. It also aims at the comprehension and articulation of the mysterious association between the living and the deceased, the past with the present and the invisible with the visible yet uncertain human world.

The Rousalia Feast is an example of such a celebration and by its ethnological characteristics gives us the measure of the Greek common people's attitude toward death. By studying this celebration, one can distinguish the above-mentioned elements and trace their development from the classical times of Greece to the present.

From one point of view the exhumation of the dead's remains is related to the feast of the Rousalia Day. The description of the exhumation, as well as the magical observations on the dead's remains create a composite framework by which the background of these activities becomes more understandable.

## REFERENCES

BIANCHI, G. H., *editor*
  1887   *The mythology of Greece and Rome.* London: Chapman and Hall.
CERAM, C. W.
  1954   *Gods, graves and scholars* (English translation by G. B. Garside).
         New York: Alfred Knopf.
DETTERNBERGER, W.
  1915–1924   *Sylloge inscriptionum Graecarum* (fourth edition). Leipzig.
DRAGOUMES, N.
  1917   *Historic memories.* Athens: Stochastes.

FARNELL, L. R.
1911   *Greece and Babylon.* Edinburgh: T. and T. Clark.
1921   *Greek hero cults and the idea of immortality.* Oxford: Clarendon.
FRAZER, J. G.
1927   *The belief in immortality and the worship of the dead* (second edition). London: Macmillan.
GEORGACAS, D. G., W. A. MC DONALD
1967   *Place names of the southwest Peleponnesus.* Athens.
GULICK, C. B.
1927   *Modern traits in old Greek life.* New York: Longmans, Green.
HARMON, A. M.
1953   *Lucian.* Cambridge: Harvard University Press.
HARRINGTON, K. P., H. TOLMAN
1897   *Greek and Roman mythology.* Boston: Leach, Shewell and Sanborn.
HARRISON, J.
1955   *Prolegomena to the study of Greek religion.* New York: Meridian Books.
JEVONS, F. B.
1895   Greek burial laws and folklore customs. *Classical Review* 9:247–250.
KAROLIDES, P.
1925   *Paparregopoulos' history of the Greek nation* (second edition). Athens: Eleutheroudakes.
KOUKOULES, F.
1937–1952   *Byzantine life and civilization.* Athens: Institut Français d'Athènes.
KURTZ, D. C., J. BOARDMAN
1971   *Greek burial customs.* Ithaca: Cornell University Press.
LAWSON, J C.
1964   *Modern Greek folklore and ancient Greek religion: a study in survivals.* New York: University Books.
LEKATSAS, P.
1957   *The psyche: the idea of soul and its immortality and the customs of death.* Athens: Ecdoticon Institouton Athenon.
MARINATOS, S.
1960   *Crete and Mycenae.* New York: H. N. Abrams.
MEGAS, G. A.
1939   *Zitimata Ellenikis laographias.* Reprint from the Epetiris of Iaographicon archeion. Athens: Academia Athenon.
1958   *Ellenicai fortai* (Greek calendar customs). Athens: Prime Minister's Offices.
MERCER, S. A. B.
1947   *The religion of ancient Egypt.* London: Luzac.
MYLONAS, G. E.
1966   *Mycenae and the Mycenaean age.* Princeton: Princeton University Press.
NILSON, M. P.
1933   *Homer and Mycenae.* London: Methuen.

PALMER, L. R.
1965   *Mycenaeans and Minoans* (second edition). London: Faber and Faber.

POLITIS, N. G.
1871   *Modern Greek mythology.* Athens: Sakellariou.

POUQUEVILLE, F. C. H. L.
1820–1821   *Voyage de la Grèce,* five volumes. Paris: Didot.

ROHDE, E.
1907   *Psyche: Seelenkult und Unsterblichkeitsglaube,* two volumes. Tü-bingen: J. C. B. Mohr.

ROUSE, W. H. D.
1902   *Greek votive offerings.* Cambridge: Cambridge University Press.

SCHLIEMANN, H.
1878   *Mycenae.* London: J. Murray.

VLASTARIS, M.
1888   *Constitution of the holy canons.* Athens.

WHISLEY, L. A.
1931   *Companion to Greek studies.* Cambridge: Cambridge University Press.

# Personifications of Capes and Rocks in the Hellenic Seas

DEMETRIOS LOUKATOS

A look at the map of Greece will show us at a glance the great range of this country's coastline, from the islands of Corfu and Epirus to Taenarum and Crete, from Patras to the Sunium Cape, from Piraeus to Samos, from Mount Athos to Euboea, and from Thrace to Rhodes and to Cyprus.

It has been estimated that if all the coasts of the mainland and islands of Greece were put in a straight line, their length would total approximately 15,000 kilometers. One cannot miss the rich variety of gulfs and promontories rising from a sea strewn with islands and rocks in the eastern part of the Mediterranean.

It is well known that, since ancient times, Hellenistic mythology has originated, for the most part, in this sea. Hesiod, in his *Theogony,* speaks especially of the Nereids and Oceanids and of events occurring in the waters. Homer, in the *Odyssey,* speaks a great deal of rocks and of seas, and in the *Iliad* he similarly refers to the sea which borders the city of Troy.

In historical time, there was great interest in the Aegean Sea, with the coming and going of the Persians and the Greeks, as well as in the Ionian Sea, with the expedition to Sicily. In descriptions given by Herodotus and Thucydides, the islands, gulfs, harbors, capes, and promontories are presented in a familiar fashion, playing a role as important as that of the mainland.

It is with the same familiarity that neo-Hellenic mythology has continued to preserve the spirit of ancient tradition, as well as the majority of names and legends of the coasts. It is evident that, under new historical and cultural conditions, many elements have been changed.

But geographic and natural influences remain the same for the people of the country. Under the transparent light of the Hellenic Mediterranean sky, the people's imagination always creates legends which try to explain, in an anthropomorphic or zoomorphic fashion, the perceived silhouettes.

This phenomenon is well known in the maritime folklore of different countries. The more varied the coastline (cliffs, rocks, promontories, points, caverns, islets), the more frequent become the personifications and legendary narrations. We find interpretations of certain of these cases in James Frazer's *The golden bough*, especially in the ninth volume *The scapegoat*: 1–169) and in the fifth volume (the word "cape": 102) and we find evidence of their international presence in Stith Thompson's *Motif-index of folk-literature*, under the words: "canoe" (D 454.10.2); "leap" (A 972.5.2); "personifications" (Z 110); "petrifications" (M 458); "rock" (D 2153.1); "sea" (V 11.2); "stone" (C 961.2, D 231, D 425.1.1, D 429.2.2, D 432.1, D 442.1, D 1524.3.1, F 841.1.1, V 242.3); and "transformations" (A 974).

For the European coasts, however, I find that the descriptions of Paul Sebilllot in his *Folklore de France* (volume two: *La mer*; Paris, 1905) are the most representative. A native Breton, Sebillot has been able to describe in detail all that the famous Breton sailors conceived and practiced in their eminently coastal country.

To collect all the legends, names, and popular beliefs centering on the Hellenic coastline would be a worthwhile achievement for Greek maritime folklore. Many linguistic works on the toponymy of these regions offer some of these elements. In the same way, some regional folklore collections and anthologies of legends, such as that of N. Politis (1904), serve as proof of the rich folklore of these coasts. Equally frequent are monographs which study certain cases. But, as yet, we have no comprehensive work on the maritime or coastal folklore in Greece.

I shall limit myself here to the folklore of two features (the most impressive on the coast): the capes and the rocks, which, by their very presence and their projections into the deserted sea, excite the imagination and are most frequently personified.

I would like, at this point, to express my opinion that all personification imposed upon any inanimate object is (apart from any other magic or religious explanation) especially due to man's need for a milieu of "human-like" beings, and to his fear of solitude. Always avoiding isolation in nature, man everywhere creates imaginary beings in the form of men or animals in order to populate his sur-roundings. It is much the same need that led him in ancient times to the conception of the many divinities who filled his solitude on earth.

This is best illustrated in deserted places and on the seas, where travelers (hunters and shepherds in the former) and navigators (fish-ermen and sailors in the latter) have personified the mountains and rocks, the islands and cliffs, putting themselves in relation to them and even relating legendary histories about them.

For the capes and the rocks of the sea, we can say that during the long voyages of former times (by oar, by sail, or by steam) the sailors strongly felt the need to be accompanied by "human-like" mytho-logical beings. It was of no importance whether the boat's crew was numerous or not. The boat itself was all alone on the sea. Thus, the personifications were extremely necessary. The capes, promontories, rocks, and islets, because of their strange forms or of the caprice of the seas, became either friends or enemies of the sailors, and some-times, veritable monsters to be avoided. But, in merciless solitude, any animated presence is acceptable, even if it is an agent of the devil.

My folklorist colleagues, especially those native to maritime coun-tries, will more easily understand my point of view and my descrip-tions.

A. Since antiquity the Greek capes have been highly respected by the people for their importance in navigation, so vital to that epoch. They were either consecrated to the divinities (e.g. Poseidon, Nymphaeon, Artemisium, Dion) or personified as human beings or as animals, su-pernaturally conceived (e.g. Claucus, Kynaeon, Ierax [falcon], Krios [goat], etc.).

We do not know in detail the names of all the capes (and their coast-al locations) of antiquity. Thus, the toponymers have shown no sys-tematic interest in them. (It is in the *"Ethnika"* of Stephanos Byzan-tios — sixth century A.D. — that we find the names of the capes given separately.) But in the collections of neo-Hellenic toponymies, we find much that will concern us here. There are also capes dedicated to the Virgin Mary and to the Saints (especially to Saint Nicholas and the Archangels), as well as many capes personified as legendary old men and women.

B. The rocks in the Greek seas are sometimes gigantic. Their forms and their locations have inspired, since antiquity, the imagination of people who have made mythological personifications of them. (We are thinking of Homer's stories in the *Odyssey:* 12, 234, about the rocks of Scylla and Charybdis and the Scyronian Rocks near Megara.)

Today, the majority of rocks bear names which derive either from direct personifications or from references to other persons who resided in or frequented these places.

I shall give the principal categories of the different names that are assigned to the capes and rocks in neo-Hellenic folklore and which indicate the motifs of the popular imagination as well as the different aspects of personification.

There is almost always a little legend which accompanies each name (easily guessed, by the way) that I shall not cite here. Rather, I shall make a brief classification for every case which is common in international maritime folklore.

## CAPES AND PROMONTORIES

1. Capes bearing the names referring to human beings (direct personifications): the Old Man, the Old Woman, the Monk, the Nun, the Cyclops, the Janissary, the Cavalier, the Moor, the Two Brothers, etc. (also vestiges of the time of legends about giants).

2. Names of capes indicating a single part of the human body: the Nose, the Neck, the Head, the Tongue, the Old Man's Knee, the Two Heads, etc. (reminiscences also of the giant legends).

3. Capes named for personages who had visited or lived there (indirect personifications): the Widow's Cape, the Turk's Cape, the Monk's Point (hermitage), the Cape of Michael, of Nicholas, of the Deaf Man, of the Washerwoman, etc.

4. Capes with favorable or hostile names: among the former, the Gentleman, the Good Woman, the Good Cape, the Favorable, etc.; among the latter, the Assassin, the Drowner, the Ship Swallower, the Black, the Cursed, the Dog, the Sow.

5. Capes bearing animal names: the Lion, the Wild Boar, the Goat, the Fox, the Billy Goat, the Pig, the Dog, the Cat, the Snake, the Bird, the Cock, the Falcon, etc.

6. Capes whose names refer to the supernatural: the Demoniacal, the Sorcerer, the Nereid, the Saracens (the word having often replaced that of demon), the Ghost. The belief that demons or ghosts frequent the promontories is often encountered in Greece.

7. Capes personified by Saints' names: St. Andrew, St. Archangel, St. Helen, the Panagia (All Saints), St. Nicholas, St. Savior [Sostis], the Blessed Virgin, etc.

## ROCKS AND ISLETS

1.   Names of anthropomorphic conceptions: the Monk, the Nun, the Old Man, the Old Woman, the Couple, the Young Girl, the Pregnant Woman, the Tailor, the Slaves, George, Nicholas, the Stiff Neck, the Red-Bottomed Fellow, etc.

2.   Names referring to individuals who frequented the rocks (indirect personifications): the Passage of Manoussos, the Post of Yannis (the fisherman), the Cripple's Bench, Rock of Constantine, the Cliff of the Three Brothers, the Brigand's Rock, Helen's Precipice.

3.   Rocks known by legendary episodes:

a.   Leaps (motifs of Sappho and of giants): the Old Woman's Leap (very frequently used for rocks which are opposite an islet), the Old Man's Leap, the Leap of the Beautiful Woman (at Leucatas), of the Ogre, etc.

b.   Exploits of giants (cosmogonic legends): the Old Woman's Apron (a pile of rocks in the sea which have fallen, it is said, from the apron of a female giant), the Rocks of Samson (at Chios), the Rock of Diogenes (at Cyprus), the Devil's Hole, the Dragon's Crevice, the Ogre's Foot, etc.

c.   Petrifications: the Monk or the Pope (a priest who fishes on Sundays), the Petrified Girls (petrified from fear of being seized by pirates), the Fiancée (who was petrified while waiting by the sea for the return of her betrothed), the Laundry (linen petrified on the rocks).

d.   Petrified Ships (the motif of the Phaeacians' boat [Odyssey, 13, 163], a very widespread legend in the Hellenic seas): the Frigate, the Galleys, the Algerians' Boat, the Boat Rock (*Pétrokasavo*), etc. These are usually rocks or islets, resembling boats in rough sea. The legend says that they belonged to pirates, and that God or a patron saint petrified them at the moment of their raids.

4.   Zoomorphic Appellations: the Donkey, the Ox, the Ewes (little islets or rocks), the Camels, the Owl, the Pig, the Raven, the Ants, the Piglets, the Louse, the Wild Boar, the Turtle. Similarly, as in antiquity, the Fox's Tail, the Donkey's Jawbone.

5.   Favorable or hostile rocks: among the former are the Welcome, the Good Stones, the Good Harbor, the Old Grandmother, the Benevolent, etc. (one frequently finds a euphemistic spirit here). Among the latter are the Curses, the Wild Cat, Charon's Rock, the Infidels, the Vipers.

6.   Rocks named after their patron saints: some little white chapels on the rocks give their names to the coast. This is especially true of

Saint Kalé (the Good Woman) who is venerated in these rocks. It appears that she replaced an idolatrous spirit (Romeos 1953). Small churches dedicated to the Virgin are also found, from which the names of many rocks are derived, such as "Saint Thalassini" [Saint of the Seas].

## GENERAL OBSERVATIONS

1.   The study of the coastline of any maritime country reveals an imaginative and mythological psychology of great importance. The sailors are inspired in a cosmogonic way by the morphology of the coasts, and many ancient beliefs are revived through their inspiration.

2.   Personifications of every type of rock and cape are due principally, as we have already stated, to the need of navigators not to be alone in the solitude of the sea. This explains, I believe, all the toponymic mythology of the sea, which has created legendary place-names, such as the Bosphorus [passage of the ox], the Hellespont, the Isle of Icarus, and the Icarian Sea.

3.   The capes and the rocks in the Hellenic seas have had since antiquity a mythological and religious significance. The Hellenic seas are not always calm; there are periods of extremely violent storms. The coasts then become inaccessible and it was necessary to pray and make offerings so that the "spirits" of the sea would behave favorably. This is why not only were sanctuaries erected above the promontories but pagan offerings were also given — bread, cheese, and other foods, which were thrown into the sea to assure the kindness of the "divinity" (or demon) of the cape (Politis 1904; Romeos 1953).

4.   The almost universal superstition which says that the promontories and points are the dwellings of demons is also found in Greece. A characteristic example is the Taenarum Cape, at the far south of the Peloponnesian peninsula, which was considered the gate to hell in antiquity. It is still believed that in its cavern reside the souls of the deceased which the Archangel Saint Michael leads in or carries off, according to their sins (Politis, legend no. 989). Similarly, it is believed that the inevitable storms at Cape Malea are provoked by the demons that live there.

5.   The more time passes, the more the anthropomorphic appearances of the coastline are effaced by the waters and the storms. The names remain, however, and the people still use them, even when they have forgotten the legend. But new means of navigation depend less on these excellent guides and companions of former days. Moreover,

modern occupations and installations (tourism, the beach, factories, shipyards) alter, to some degree, the eternal face of the coast. This is one more reason for us to hasten to collect the toponymies and legends concerning the coastline, the folklore of which is an excellent summary of the freshest and freest imagination of any people.

# REFERENCES

AMANTOS, CONSTANTIN
  1964   *Etudes linguistiques* (in Greek). Athens: Publications de la revue *Athena.*
BAYAKAKOS, DIKÉOS
  1962–1964   Esquisse sur les études toponymiques et anthroponymiques en Grèce, 1833–1962 (in Greek) *Athena* (Athens) 66:301–424; 67:144–369.
BYZANTIOS, STEPHANOS
  1849   *"Ethnicorum" quae supersunt, ex recensione Augusti Meinekii.* Berolini: Reimeri.
DELATTE, ARMAND
  1947   *Les portulans grecs.* Liège: Bibliothèque de la Faculté de Philosophie et de Lettres de l'Université de Liège.
EVANGELIDIS, TRYPHON
  1909   *L'île de Seriphos et les îlots autour d'elle* (in Greek). Hermoupolis de Syra.
FRAZER, SIR JAMES GEORGE
  1936   *The golden bough,* volume nine: *The scapegoat* (third edition). London: Macmillan.
GEOGRAPHI GRAECI MINORES
  1855–1861   *E codibus recognovit Carolus Mullerus,* two volumes. Paris: Firmin Didot.
IMELLOS, STEPHANOS
  1968   *La légende sur les pirates en Grèce* (in Greek). Athens: Bibliothèque de la Société "Philekpédeftiki."
GEORGACAS, DEMETRIUS, WILLIAM MC DONALD
  1967   *Place names of southwest Peloponnesus. Register and indexes.* Athens.
KRETIKOS, PANAYOTIS
  1961   *Toponymies de Patmos* (in Greek). Athens: Spyropoulos.
KOUKOULES, PHEDON
  1952   "La vie maritime," in *Vie et civilization des Byzantins* (in Greek), five volumes, 344–386. Collection de l'Institut français d'Athènes.
LOUKATOS, DEMETRIOS
  1969   Légendes maritimes des îles Ioniennes (in Greek). *Actes du 3e Congrès Panionien* 2:58–68. Athens.
MENARDOS, SIMOS
  1970   *Études toponymiques et folkloriques* (in Greek). Nicosia (Cyprus): Publications du Centre de Recherches Scientifiques.

MOUSOURIS, SPYROS
1959   *Les toponymies et les noms de famille de l'île d'Ithaque* (in Greek).
        Athens: Imprimerie Ekdotiki.
PERDIKA, NIKI
1940   "Le périple de l'île," in *Skyros* (in Greek), volume one, 29–48.
        Athens: Pyrsos.
POLITIS, N. G.
1904   *Légendes populaires* (in Greek), two volumes. Athens: Biblio-
        thèque Marasli.
RICAS, GEORGES A.
1968   "Toponymies," in *Culture populaire de l'île de Skiathos* (in Greek),
        fascicle three, 239–259. Thessaloniki: Société d'Études Macé-
        doniennes.
ROMEOS, CONSTANTIN
1953   "La vieille femme, figure mythologique ancienne," in *Prosfora,
        dediée à Stilpon Kyriakidis* (in Greek), 561–580. Thessaloniki:
        Société d'Études Macédoniennes.
SEBILLOT, PAUL
1905   *Le folklore de France*, volume two: *La mer*. Paris: Maisonneuve.
        (Reprinted 1968.)
THOMOPOULOS, JEAN A.
1963   *Étude toponymique de L'île de Kéa* (in Greek), volume three.
        Separatum de l'Annuaire de la Société d'Études Cycladiques.
        Athens.
THOMPSON, STITH
1955–1958   *Motif-index of folk-literature*, six volumes. Bloomington:
        Indiana University Press.

# Historical Reality and Russian Supernatural Beings

FELIX J. OINAS

It is customary for people to project their own mode of life onto the spirits supposed to live in their immediate neighborhood. This holds true for Russians and other East Slavic peoples as well, whose supernatural world mirrors their own society.

Forest, water, house, and other spirits in Russia are thought to be married and to carry on a regular family life like humans, though some of them do not always have good moral conduct. Following are some excerpts from beliefs about them:

Forest spirits live in forests with their wives, children, fathers, and mothers. They have separate dwellings for each family in a separate forest. They rigorously protect their dwellings, and for this purpose they keep dogs. They also have their cattle (Kolchin 1899: 19).

Water spirits live like real property owners; they have big stone mansions built in whirlpools, among reeds and sedge; they have herds of horses, cows, sheep, and pigs, which they drive out of the water at night and graze in adjacent meadows. . . . The water spirits are almost always married and have many children; they marry water girls [*vodianye devy*], who are known among the Slavs under various names [*moriany, vodianitsy, wodne, żony, dunavki, rusalki* . . .] (Afanas'ev 1868: 238–239).

Water spirits marry drowned or cursed girls (Afanas'ev 1868: 239). Both the forest spirits and water spirits practice kidnapping. They kidnap women and live with them as if they were their wives (Tokarev 1957: 83; Haase 1939: 146).

The figure of the house spirit stands out from the rest by his positive features. This is caused by the fact that the tradition of the house spirit is maintained primarily by the master and mistress of the house, who endow him with all human, master-like traits. This appears especially clearly in the Belorussian tradition. There, the house spirit is, on the whole, a strict monogamist. After his wife dies, the house spirit can marry up to four times, but not his relatives. If he violates this rule, he must give up his house spirit's status and become a forest, water, or swamp spirit. The house spirit's sons become spirits of new houses, and their daughters are married off to house spirits, though some of them may remain single (Nikiforovskij 1907: 48).

The house spirit in Belorussia plays the role of the painstaking master of the house. At night he occasionally lights the lantern, goes to the granary, and dries the grain, strewing it with his hands. He looks into the barn and gives food to the horses and cows, strokes and flatters them. A close relative of his, the kiln spirit, sweeps the floor of the kiln, winnows the grain, and, for the "experienced" masters, even threshes grain in the morning (Bogdanovich 1895: 66–70). In Russia, the house spirit likes the families who live in harmony and the masters who care for their property and keep their houses clean and in fine order. If a good master of a house forgets his duties, such as feeding the cows and horses, then the house spirit does them for him. However, the house spirit does not always behave irreproachably. Mischievous and frolicsome by nature, he occasionally plays pranks on the people and domestic animals, especially during the night. If the house spirit does not like the color of a certain animal, he bothers and tortures it ceaselessly, so that the animal must finally be sold (Maksimov 1903: 34–41).

Beliefs recorded in Belorussia show that the life of the house spirits is adjusted completely to the life of the people of the house. The time of their meals, sleeping, and work is arranged in accordance with the routine of the house. The house spirits, thrifty as good peasants, endeavor to have the weddings of their children at the same time as the weddings of the children of the house, so as not to have to spend extra money for musicians. The dowry of their daughters is comparable to that of the daughters of the masters. The house spirits, following the Bible, avenge misdeeds against them up to the fourth generation. When the master invites the house spirit to appear before him on Easter midnight, the spirit comes in the image of the master (Nikiforovskij 1907: 48–49).

According to one source of information (Dobrovol'skij 1908: 5–6), the house spirit (referred to, obviously erroneously, as "the forest spirit") in Smolensk province has exactly the same ideas as a respectful peasant. Here are some of the house spirit's ideas:

... the people have to pray after breakfast; when going to bed, the sign of the cross must be made; and the children have to be put to bed with the sign of the cross; both the master and mistress must be orderly and clean; the flour for bread must be sieved; the bread must be treated with care and special reverence; it wouldn't do any harm to strain the water when making bread; bread should be put on the table and not on the bench. It is recommended that the grain in the corn bins be covered with a lid so that it will not get dusty. If the food is tasty and is prepared well, the house spirit [given as "forest spirit"] may taste it, but from bad food he turns away, makes a wry face, and leaves.[1]

These ideas are actually those of the God-fearing Russian master and mistress of the house. They are as if taken from *Domostroj*, a collection of household rules and religious practices of the Russian family in the sixteenth century.

There is information from Russia that the house spirit would punish those who violated the norm of good behavior. If a married woman went out bareheaded, the house spirit would pull her by her hair up to the garret. He would also punish a woman who would, against the accepted custom, spin on Friday (Tokarev 1957: 96).

The figures of the forest and water spirits of the East Slavs are by far not as idealized as that of the house spirit. Forests, rivers, and lakes with their dangers represented hostile environments for peasants. The attitudes of the people, the suspicion and apprehension that they had toward forests and bodies of water, were carried over to the masters of these settings — the forest and water spirits. The water spirit became generally identified with the devil, which is due to the intense fear and the feeling of insecurity that the peasants had toward waters (Paulson 1961: 280). Thus, the in-group attitude that the people had toward the house spirit is contrasted by the out-group attitude toward the forest and water spirits.

As in human society, the Russian forest and water spirits are imagined to have their superiors, who are called tsars or *atamans*. The forest tsar may differ from the normal forest spirit by his height; he is huge, higher than a forest (Dobrovol'skij 1908: 3). According to one source of information, the forest tsar lives in a big forest, into which the people very rarely go (Neustupov 1902: 116). The greatest dignitary among Russian forest spirits is called Musail-les (Rybnikov 1867: 224). The figure of the water tsar (*vodianoj tsar*) is much less distinct than that of

---

[1] This description is, according to Dobrovol'skij, said to refer to the forest spirit (*leshij*). This is, however, impossible, since the forest spirit has — in the beliefs of the East Slavs — nothing to do with life in the house. Here either the informant or the recorder has confused the house spirit with the forest spirit.

the forest tsar. He is master and ruler of a lake, and he is cared for and obeyed by the spirits of the rivers and brooks that flow into this lake, and by the spirits of small lakes which are connected with the big lake. There are also beliefs that the water tsar lives in the sea where he has his throne. Since people are inclined to refer euphemistically to the forest and water spirits as "forest tsar" and "water tsar," the term "tsar" occasionally denotes the rank and file spirits (Kharuzin 1894: 318; Neustupov 1902: 116).

It is believed in Russia that forest spirits form their armies by conscription and that they frequently wage wars. They fight with old trees torn up by the roots and with huge rocks broken off from boulders. Forests destroyed by storms and rocks broken into pieces testify to their fierce fights. When a war breaks out between peoples of different countries, forest spirits, too, have their war. The armies of the spirits and of their animals come together to fight between themselves until the war of the humans ends. People have noticed migrations of animals, especially of squirrels, before wars, and they interpret them as signs that the forest spirits are preparing to wage war and are raising their armies (Afanas'ev 1868: 334–335; Rybnikov 1867: 224; Kulikovskij 1898: 52).

Some spirits in Russia have different classes based on the model of Russian society in the past. A complicated class system of devils has been established, as Nikiforovskij tells us, among the Belorussians. Under the overlordship of his highness, the absolute autocrat *Liutsýpur* [Lucifer], are the classes of free demons (*shéshki*), of those who have lost their freedom (*pekél'niki*), of laborers working for other demons (*prákhi*), or invalids who are completely neglected (*kadukí*), and others (Nikiforovskij 1907: 34 ff.).

Spirits in Russia may temporarily lose their free status. We are told that the water spirit of Kushtozero — a small tsar or princeling — used to play a game of bones with the powerful tsar of Onega Lake. The latter was more skilled in this game, and therefore the princeling from the god-forsaken Kushtozero lost to him every time they played for high stakes.

All these [games for] stakes ended in such a way that he lost both his water and fish, and then even got himself into bondage. Having lost everything, he goes to the tsar of Onega Lake to make up for his losses and lives there as a laborer, until he has cleared himself. When the time set by the agreement is past, he will return to his den with its water and will provide himself with new fish (Maksimov 1903: 94).

The situation in Russia is reflected in this ordeal of the Kushtozero water spirit. Adam Olearius, a German traveler in Russia in the 1630's, tells that if a debtor in Russia was unable to pay his debts and if even imprisonment and flogging did not help, he became the slave of his creditor and had to serve him. There were various types of non-hereditary bondage in Muscovite Russia from the fifteenth to the seventeenth century, into which the debtors could fall or go voluntarily (Olearius 1967: 23; Hellie 1967: 233 ff.).

Some features of the spirits' outer appearance may find their explanation in the actual practices in Russia in the past. The forest spirit (and, by extension, also the house spirit) is called in Russian, among other things, *karnaukhij* (phonetic spelling for *kornaukhij* [one whose ear has been cut off]) and is said to have no right ear (Tokarev 1957: 80; Maksimov 1903: 33, 72). Also the devil is, among his numerous designations, called *karnoukhij*, and K. Moszyński tells that "one of his ears either has an incision or was cut off (*przycięte lub obcięte ucho*), hence *kornoukhij*" (Moszyński 1934: 617).

This detail, which can be classed with the asymmetric features of the supernaturals, evidently has deeper roots. It reminds us of the Russian legal practice of cutting off the ear or ears of robbers. The Russian official code of law of 1649 stipulates that, in the case of the robber's first crime, he had to be tortured, flogged, and his left ear was to be cut off, after which he would be imprisoned for two years. If he committed a second crime, he again was to be tortured, flogged, and his right ear was to be cut off. Then he was to be put into prison for four years. After he had served his term, he was to be sent to a city in the borderlands at the discretion of the tsar (Tikhomirov and Epifanov 1961: 266–267).

The same practice is also discussed by Adam Olearius. Olearius gives some details of how the punishment was actually meted out: "If this is his [the robber's] first offence, he is beaten with the knout all along the road from the Kremlin to the great square. Here the executioner cuts off one of his ears . . . ." If he is caught a second time, the robber loses his other ear in the same way (Olearius 1967: 229).

It seems plausible that the lack of one ear as a characteristic of the spirits and devils has been taken over from one-eared robbers, who had escaped from prison or exile or had served their prison term. However, a discrepancy calls for a comment: the robber punished for the first time lost his left ear, but the forest spirit is said to have lacked his right ear. As is generally known, the left side and the left parts of the body are considered to be ill-omened and in one way or another are associated with evil. When people happened to get a glimpse of one-eared criminals, whom they identified with spirits, they were naturally inclined to see them as having no right ear.

In Karelia, both the Finnish Karelians and the Russians visualized the forest and other spirits as having military attire with large gleaming buttons. In a special study (Oinas 1969: 202 ff.), I attributed these and other military features of the spirits to fugitive soldiers, who had fled from the long Russian military service, which until 1834 — and, actually, until the middle of the nineteenth century — lasted for twenty-five years. The fugitive soldiers, together with robbers and other criminals, found shelter in forests, and with their unusual appearance influenced the ideas of the local population concerning supernatural beings. The close connection that the spirits had with the criminal elements appears also in the efforts of the spirits to avoid being seen and recognized by the people. S. V. Maksimov tells that the one-eared forest spirit (*karnoukhij*) is in the habit of concealing his face when he sometimes comes to the campfire of the woodcutters to warm himself (Maksimov 1903: 72).

A curious mixture of the world of the spirits and that of the saints and worldly authorities appears in the people's complaints about the misdeeds attributed to spirits. If a spirit had done someone harm — hidden his cattle in the forest or caused a mysterious sickness — a complaint (oral or written or both) was made to the spirit's superior asking him to restore the original state of affairs; he was further warned that if the request was not fulfilled, still higher authorities would be notified and punitive actions requested. Here are some examples of such complaints:

a.  A letter of complaint written to several tsars of spirits goes as follows:

I am writing to the forest tsar and forest tsaritsa with their small children; to the earth tsar and earth tsaritsa with their small children; to the water tsar and water tsaritsa with their small children. I inform you that the servant of God [so and so] has lost a dark brown [or whatever color] horse [or a cow or another animal, distinctive marks to be given]. If you have it, send it back, without delaying an hour, a minute or a second. If you do not comply with my wish, I will pray against you to the great martyr God Egorij [i.e. St. George] and tsaritsa Aleksandra.

Usually only the beginning of this letter was written, from left to right, on a birch bark in three copies, whereas the remainder was said orally. One copy was fastened to a tree in the forest, the second buried in the earth, and the third thrown with a stone into the water. After that the lost animal was supposed to come home by itself (Vinogradov 1909: 75; cf. Haase 1939: 136).

b. If a sickness was believed to have been caused by water, a charm was read over water before an icon. The complaint (the text of which is somewhat corrupt) was addressed to a girl, "the viper's sister," who was lying on a bed under an oak-tree, on the sea, on the ocean, on the island Kurgan, telling her that her Pilates had eaten his cattle [*sic*], and if she did not soothe the pains [of the sufferer], a complaint would be made to Nikolaj the Intercessor and Nikolaj of Thessalonica. Upon this the petitioner himself answered slyly in the name of the girl: "No, do not complain, God's servant, I myself will soothe them, I will drive the sickness out of his sinews, out of his bones..." (Majkov 1869: 488).

c. P. N. Rybnikov tells that in Olonets, in case of a persistent sickness, a person wishing to find out where someone got his sickness from would go to the forest. He first armed himself with sticks of rowan wood so as to have a more ominous look and then began to complain to Musail, the forest tsar, about the forest spirit. He asked Musail to restore health to the sick person. "Otherwise," he continued, "I'll go to Mos . . . (probably Moscow) and will petition our Emperor the Tsar against you, and two regiments of musketeers (*strel'tsy*) will come from Moscow, a regiment from Novgorod, two regiments of Cossacks from Azov; and if you'll not save this honorable man [insert name], you will be cut down to the tree stump." This had to be written down in a letter and left in the rowan tree (Rybnikov 1867: 224, 250–251).

Complaints (a) and (b) reveal the strong influence that the Christian church had upon the belief in spirits. Some saints, such as St. George and Nikolaj the Intercessor, came to be recognized as the highest authorities for the supernatural forces inhabiting the forests and waters (Romanov 1891: 47; Loorits 1955: 39, 41, 92; Maksimov 1903: 441–442). Complaint (c) shows that even the all-powerful Russian tsar was believed to possess the same authority over the supernatural beings that he had over his subjects. Since the tsar was known to send detachments of musketeers and Cossacks to quell rebellions, the peasants believed that he could use the same forces against the willful spirit. The musketeers (*strel'tsy*), the first permanent armed forces in Muscovy, were formed during the reign of Ivan the Terrible in the middle of the sixteenth century, and they were disbanded by Peter the Great after their uprising in 1698. The Azov Cossacks became generally known because of their taking of Azov from the Turks in 1637 and their defense of it in 1641.

The supernatural world of the Russian spirits has been created, as we have seen, in the image of human society. The ideas about the house spirit reflect those of the Russian peasant family. The house spirit in his behavior not only follows that of the peasants but also sets the norm for good conduct. The forest and water spirits, belonging to the out-group, represent malevolent forces for the peasants. There is the tendency to identify them with the outcasts of the society — serfs, robbers, and fugitive soldiers. To hold them in check, both spiritual and worldly powers are brought in.

For some time, a debate has been going on over the trustworthiness of oral tradition as a source of history. Robert Lowie and Lord Raglan have questioned the value of folklore for history. Richard M. Dorson, on the other hand, has spearheaded a group of scholars viewing oral tradition as a source for popular attitudes, prejudices, and stereotypes that affect history. Dorson correctly cautions against making blanket judgments on the historical truth of traditions and suggests that the historical content of traditions should be judged in conjunction with testimony gained from other fields, such as archaeology, ethnology, and physical anthropology, with support from mnemonic devices, etc. The application of these criteria in combination has led to some rewarding results (Dorson 1968: 32–35; Dorson 1971: 129–144).

Our study of Russian demonology has disclosed popular attitudes toward the spirits held at the turn of the last century. The historical reality that emerges in these beliefs reaches back to sixteenth- and seventeenth-century Russia. The beliefs in spirits testify to the kind of historical traditions found suited to the peasant society, and to the ability of the collective memory to preserve them for centuries.

## REFERENCES

AFANAS'EV, A. N.
   1868   *Poeticheskie vozzrenija slavian na prirodu*, volume two. Moscow: K. Soldatenkov.
BOGDANOVICH, A. E.
   1895   *Perezhitki drevnego mirosozertsanija u belorussov*. Grodno: Gubernskaia tipografiia.
DOBROVOL'SKIJ, V.
   1908   Nechistaia sila v narodnykh verovaniiakh. *Zhivaia Starina* 17, 1:1–16.
DORSON, RICHARD M.
   1968   "The debate over the trustworthiness of oral traditional history," in *Volksüberlieferung: Festschrift für Kurt Ranke zur Vollendung des 60. Lebensjahres*. Edited by Fritz Harkort et al., 19–35. Göttingen: Otto Schwartz.

1971 *American folklore and the historian.* Chicago and London: University of Chicago Press.

HAASE, FELIX
1939 *Volksglaube und Brauchtum der Ostslaven.* Wort und Brauch 26. Breslau: G. Märtin.

HELLIE, RICHARD, *editor*
1967 *Readings for introduction to Russian civilization: Muscovite period.* Chicago: Syllabus Division, The College, University of Chicago.

KHARUZIN, N. N.
1894 Iz materialov, sobrannykh sredi krest'ian Pudozhskogo uezda, Olonetskoj gubernij. *Olonetskij Sbornik* 3:302–346.

KOLCHIN, A.
1899 Veroveniia krest'ian Tul'skoj gubernij. *Etnograficheskoe Obozrenie* 11, 3:1–60.

KULIKOVSKIJ, GERMAN
1898 *Slovar' oblastnogo Olonetskogo narechiia.* St. Petersburg: Otdelenie Russkogo Iazyka i Slovesnosti Imperatorskoj Akademij Nauk.

LOORITS, OSKAR
1955 *Der heilige Georg in der russischen Volksüberlieferung Estlands.* Veröffentlichungen der Abteilung für slavische Sprachen und Literaturen des Osteuropa Instituts (Slavisches Seminar) an der Freien Universität Berlin 7.

MAJKOV, L. N.
1869 Velikorusskie zaklinanija. *Zapiski Imperatorskogo Russkogo geograficheskogo Obshchestva po Otdeleniiu Etnografii* 2:417–580, 747–748.

MAKSIMOV, S. V.
1903 *Nechistaia, nevedomaia i krestnaia sila.* St. Petersburg: Tovarishchestvo R. Golike i A. Vil'borg.

MOSZYŃSKI, KAZIMIERZ
1934 *Kultura ludowa Slowian,* volume two: *Kultura duchowa.* Cracow: Polska akademja umie jętności.

NEUSTUPOV, A. D.
1902 Verovaniia krest'ian Shapshenskoj volosti, Kadnikovskogo uezda. *Etnograficheskoe Obozrenie* 14, 4:118–120.

NIKIFOROVSKIJ, N. IA.
1907 Nechistki. *Vilenskij Vremennik* 2:3–103.

OINAS, FELIX J.
1969 *Studies in Finnic–Slavic folklore relations.* Folklore Fellows Communications 205. Helsinki: Academia Scientiarum Fennica.

OLEARIUS, ADAM
1967 *The travels of Olearius in seventeenth-century Russia.* Translated and edited by Samuel H. Baron. Stanford, California: Stanford University Press.

PAULSON, IVAR
1961 *Schutzgeister und Gottheiten des Wildes (der Jagdtiere und Fische) in Nordeurasien.* Stockholm Studies in Comparative Religion 2. Stockholm: Almqvist and Wiksell.

484 FELIX J. OINAS

ROMANOV, E. R.
1891  *Belorusskij sbornik* 5. Vitebsk: Tipo-litografija G. A. Malkina.
RYBNIKOV, P. N.
1867  *Pesni sobrannye P. N. Rybnikovym* 4. St. Petersburg: Imperators-
kaja Akademija Nauk.
TIKHOMIROV, M. N., P. P. EPIFANOV
1961  *Sobornoe ulozhenie 1649 goda.* Moscow: Moskovskij Universitet.
TOKAREV, S. A.
1957  *Religioznye verovanija vostochnoslavianskikh narodov XIX na-
chala XX veka.* Moscow and Leningrad: Akademija Nauk SSSR.
VINOGRADOV, NIKOLAJ
1909  *Zagovory, oberegi, spasitel'nye molitvy i proch.* 2. St. Petersburg:
Tipografija Ministerstva Putej Soobshchenija (Tovarishchestva I.
N. Kushnerev).

# Some Findings Concerning the Nomenclature and Functions of Certain Lacandon Mayan Deities

JAROSLAW THEODORE PETRYSHYN

This paper is an account of certain important and rather intricate facts concerning nomenclature of the Lacandon Mayan deities.[1] It represents an effort to fill a gap not covered by other available materials.

In perusing the long list of the Lacandon gods, one becomes cognizant of relatively many duplications of divine names. Table 1 tabulates these. Because the tabulation of the names alone would not serve a serious Mayalogist adequately, other rubrics have been added.

[1]  The Mayas who call themselves Hach Winik [literally, the real, or the true people] in their own idiom, that is to say, in *hash t'aan* [the real, or the true, language], constitute one of many Mayan groups. Presently the Hach Winik live in the rain forest of Eastern Chiapas and in the western portion of Peten. To outsiders the Hach Winik have been known as Lacandons, Caribs, Masséwal (or Maséwal), etc. In the literature, Lacandon seems to be the term preferred by writers and most familiar to readers. This is one of the reasons why this term is also used in the article. I am, however, fully aware that the name Lacandon: (1) was coined by outsiders in the form in which it is applied by them and has been used in referring to various Mayan inhabitants on both sides of the Usumacinta River, particularly to the historical Chols and to today's Hach Winik, as well as, according to the writer's recent findings, to some non-Mayas (see von Sivers 1861: 291; also Stoll 1884: 78); (2) is linguistically distorted, its original form being *lacam tun* [large rock], according to some recent opinions (Scholes and Roys 1968: 40; Villa Rojas 1967: 29), or *lacan tun* [stone standard] (Brasseur de Bourbourg 1866: 2), the name of the river in the rain forest of Chiapas known as Lacantun (Sapper 1897: 258; Seler 1960: III, 582), according to the views expressed mostly in the nineteenth century; (3) abounds in all its well-known confusing connotations from the historical position; (4) when used in reference to various groups and inaccurately interpreted in certain cases, implies unjust and irresponsible accusations directed against the forebears of the Hach Winik; (5) has never been accepted or used by and has no meaning to the autochthons, to my knowledge. I propose the usage of the term Hach Winik instead of Lacandon in anthropology as well as in politics (Petryshyn i.p.; 1972: 272a).

The latter are diagramed to supply information on: (1) divine functions associated with various aspects in which those Lacandon deities appear, (2) residence of the deities in the Lacandon universe, (3) their membership in the divine patrilineal clans (*onen*), and (4) their origin, i.e. their birth, either from *baknikté* [2] or from their divine parents. (For a *tableau vivant* of the Lacandon pantheon see Petryshyn 1972: Addendum I.) [3] For practical reasons, all the duplicated names of the gods are diagramed in alphabetical rather than hierarchical order, so that they may be located with ease.

Because of cultural diversity within the Lacandon group,[4] it should be emphasized that statements on the Lacandon people are applicable at this time only to the natives at Nahá who were the subject of this study (Plates 1–6). Only after further investigations will it be possible to propose with confidence a single schema of classification for the Lacandon Mayas and their varied cultural manifestations.

There has been far too much speculation concerning the Lacandon people. My objective in these Lacandon studies is to provide an

[2]   *Baknikté* is a small white flower. In its blossom season (that is, in spring) one can see it quite frequently in the *koor* (Yucatec *kool*), a cultivated clearance in the jungle which is used by the Hach Winik to grow corn and other plants. *Baknikté* is the only plant that is never cut. The forest dwellers venerate it. They would never show it to any outsider whom they do not trust. *Baknikté* is the only flower created by K'akoch, the supreme deity in the Lacandon hierarchy. All other flowers, including *nikté shtabay*, from which Kisin was born, were created by Hachakyum, the most admired and loved god, the most meaningful divine being in the daily life of the Hach Winik, although not the first in the pantheon's hierarchy. *Baknikté* is the flower from which some important gods derive. A flower called *ix bac nicté* is mentioned in Chilam Balam de Chumayel (Roys 1967: 33), and is translated by Roys (1967: 104) as "the little flower". Its cultural meaning in the Lacandon tradition, however, is definitely different from that of *baknikté*. Is *ix bac nicté* of Chilam Balam botanically the same as the Lacandon *baknikté*? It appears to be impossible to answer this question at this time, because the Yucatec Mayas of today do not have *ix bac nicté*, at least not in their vocabulary. My attempt for nearly twenty years to trace that name in the Yucatec tongue, sometimes in the most remote areas, has failed completely. Tozzer (1907: 93) asserts that "the two flowers *chaknikté* (*Plumeria rubra*) and *saknikté* (*Plumeria alba*) are the father and mother respectively of Nohochakyum." That is not so. Both flowers are well known in Yucatán. The Hach Winik in Eastern Chiapas are familiar with *chaknikté*. In the Lacandon mythology, however, *chaknikté* (*Plumeria rubra*) has absolutely nothing to do with the creation of gods.
[3]   The following sources are recommended for purposes of comparison: Amram 1942: 15–30; Anders 1963: 239–242 and Chapter 4: passim; Baer and Baer 1952: 230–330; Bruce 1967: 93–108; Cline 1944: 107–115; Duby and Blom 1969: 292–296 and Figures 16, 17, and 18; Petryshyn 1969: 169–176 and Plates I–III; Seler 1960: III, 578–589; Thompson 1970: 202–327, 344–346, passim; Tozzer 1907: 79–150 and appropriate plates.
[4]   See, for example, Amram 1937: 33–35; Helmuth 1970: xiv; G. Soustelle 1947: 408–418; Tax 1951: 148; and some other articles by this writer and by J. Soustelle.

empirically-based perspective at the ethnographic level in the hope of contributing to the still relatively meager store of reliable information on the Lacandon people.

Ethnographic materials included here were obtained on several expeditions to Nahá in the Lacandon rain forest. They have been verified time and again with the native informants, particularly with Chankin.[5] The most recent reexamination of the data took place in August 1972.

---

[5] Chankin is one of the oldest Hach Winik in the Chiapas rain forest. His name literally means "small sun" (*chan* "small," *k'in* "sun"). Chankin is the son of the late Hach Winik named Boor, the main informant of Alfred M. Tozzer at the beginning of this century. Chankin grew up at Arena and then moved to the settlement of Nahá, where he has lived for many years. He says about himself, "*Ten ch'ihaan* [I am *ch'ihaan*]." *Ch'ihaan* literally means "grown," by extension, "old," a designation describing Chankin's age level in a society that views old age as culturally important and meaningful. As all Hach Winik belong to patrilineal clans, so does Chankin. His clan is called *Máash-Kásyaho. Máasch* means "monkey," *kásyaho* cannot be easily explained and /or reliably translated at this time.

Table 1.   Nomenclature of Lacandon Mayan deities

| Deity | Aspect associated with the deities | Residence | Onen | Origin | Remarks |
|---|---|---|---|---|---|
| Bo(o)r Hachakyum | Preparing *baché* for Hachakyum in two sacred dugouts: *u-chem-il-u-ka-ha-bi'-sukar* and *u-chem-il-baché* | Fourth, i.e. Hacha-kyum's heaven (Ukaaninhacha-kyum); also Chi-shyokradjatoch-hachakyum [The Residence of Our Very Lord on the Usumacinta River], or Yachilan known to outsiders as Yaxchilan | Máash-Kásyaho | Born from *baknikté* | *Máash* means monkey *Kásyaho* does not originate in any Mayan language |
| Bo(o)r K'akoch | Preparing *baché* for K'akoch | Second, i.e. K'akoch's heaven (Ukaanink'akoch) | Máash-Kásyaho or K'ek'en-Kóho (?) | ,, ,, | K'akoch belongs to the K'ek'en-Kóho *onen* K'ek'en means wild boar; Sp. *jabalí* *Koh* may mean puma or tooth. Here it is puma |
| Chembek'uh or Chemberk'uh | Living in the dark heaven that does not have any sun; receiving the souls (*pishan*) of Hach Winik in their heaven at the end of the world after Barum, Kotikan, Hapbikan (the same as K'uk'ulkan mentioned in the literature), and K'ishk'ek'en living presently in Hachakyum's heaven, devour them | First, i.e. Chembek'uh's heaven | (?) K'ek'en-Kóho (?) | ,, ,, | One deity |

| | | Terrestrial | K'ek'en-Kóho (?) | | There are some 20–30 Chembek'uh |
|---|---|---|---|---|---|
| Chembek'uh or Chemberk'uh | Protecting Hach Winik; eating Hach Winik; causing Hachakyum to dislike them because of their malevolence toward Hach Winik; possessing snakes (*kan*), jaguars (*barum*), and dogs (*pek*) that are not dogs in reality; making rain; appearing as young men | | | | |
| Hachakyum | Creating the second sun that illuminates the earth by day and the underworld by night; creating the moon, all the stars, fire, trees (jungle); functioning as father of Hach Winik; guarding the whole world; and his brother Kyanthó's creating water, sea, lagoons, and fish; creating the first man Nushi; maize, beans, sugar cane, rice, tobacco, snakes, dogs, cats and horses; former residence at Palenque called U-la'-atoch-hachakyum (The Old Residence, or House, of Our Very Lord); praying and offering to his god K'akoch; visits with his older brother Sukunkyum, the supreme lord of the underworld; and his wife's creating raiment, temples, and houses; and Ok'inchob's constructing a very large boat in the period of flood, thus saving some male and female humans and animals as well as seeds; guarding that boat on the other side of the sea; creating eyes, *koor* [cornfield], and musical instruments | Fourth, i.e. Hachakyum's heaven (Ukaaninhachakyum); also Chishyokradjatochhachakyum [The Residence of Our Very Lord on the Usumacinta River] known also as Yatochhachakyum [The Residence, or House, of Our Very Lord] or Yachilan | Máash-Kásyaho | Born from *baknikté* | |
| Hachakyum K'akoch | Working for his god K'akoch; praying to K'akoch and offering him *hachpom*, one of three kinds of incense | Second, i.e. K'akoch's heaven (Ukaanink'akoch) | „ | | „ |

Table 1. (Continued)

| Deity | Aspect associated with the deities | Residence | Onen | Origin | Remarks |
|---|---|---|---|---|---|
| Itsana K'akoch | Helping K'akoch and working with him | Second, i.e. K'akoch's heaven | Máash-Kásyaho | Born from *baknikté* | |
| Itsana Hachakyum | Working for Hachakyum; protecting neighbors; sending fever; being prayed to | Fourth, i.e. Hachakyum's heaven | ,, | ,, | Pillars in the underworld are stone columns. There are 100 of them, according to the native belief |
| Itsana | Working for Sukunkyum; guarding pillars (*yokmanluum*) which support the world, in company with Sukunkyum and Sakapuksukunkyum | Underworld, i.e. Yalam (or Yalan) Luum U Sukunkyum | ,, | ,, | |
| Itsanohk'uh | Helping Mensabok in his divine functions; guarding *pethá* called Itsanohk'uh; guarding fish; being prayed to for good weather beneficial to corn; providing rain for the jungle | Terrestrial | K'ek'en-Kóho | ,, | *Pethá* or *pétdah* means lagoon, lake |
| Isanohk'-uhmeebat | Sending hail (*ba(a)t*), little rain, and creating cold weather; being prayed to in case of excessive hail; being offered ("paid") *baché* and asked for good crop of corn | Terrestrial | ,, | ,, | |
| K'a(a)k K'akoch | (?) | The second, i.e. K'akoch's heaven | (?) Yuk-Kého or K'ek'en-Kóho (?) | ,, | Hach Winik do not pray to K'a(a)k K'akoch; not Booray *Yuk* means kid, *Mazama pandora* Merriam. *Keh* means deer |
| K'a(a)k Hachakyum | Painting "houses" (temples) with the food (*k'iik*) of Hach Winik in earlier days; painting *ishikur* [tunic-like garment] of Hach Winik with blood in ancient times | (?) | Máash-Kásyaho | ,, | Not Booray |

| | | | | | |
|---|---|---|---|---|---|
| K'a(a)k Mensabok | Hunting with the traditional weapon (bow and arrow); success in hunting; killing deer and eating it; killing jaguar but not eating it; cave residence on the lagoon of the same name; being prayed to for good weather and success in *koor* [cornfield] | Terrestrial | Yuk-Kého | " " | Just the name; definitely not the god of fire! Other name of this deity is Booray (*boor, pay*) — indicative of offerings ("payments") made to this lord, according to Chankin |
| K'a(a)k Sukunkyum | Gathering firewood; working in the *koor* [cornfield] for Sukunkyum, the supreme lord of the underworld | Underworld | (?) Yuk-Kého or Máash-Kásyaho (?) | " " | Not Booray because no offerings are made to him |
| Kanank'ash | Guarding the jungle and protecting Hach Winik from jaguars (*barum*) and snakes (*kan*); shielding chickens (*kaash*) from nocturnal monkeys (*akmash*; Sp. *mico de noche*); guarding pheasants (*k'ambur*) and peccary (*kitam*); being prayed to in his temple near Sival (Sib); appearing as jaguar (*barum*) or human (*winik*) | Terrestrial (old Mayan ruins called Kanank'ash near Sival (Sib) | K'ek'en-Kého | " " | Not to be confounded with U Djum K'ash, a malevolent god who used to eat people. His name literally means Lord of the Jungle. He lives in a cave and does not leave it frequently. He walks through the jungle alone without companions and kills wild boar with his bow and arrow |
| Kanank'ash | Guarding the jungle and protecting people from snakes; taking precaution so as to prevent dryness of rivulets; being prayed to for good crop of tobacco | Terrestrial (near Capulin) | K'ek'en-Kého | " " | |

Table 1. (Continued)

| Deity | Aspect associated with the deities | Residence | Onen | Origin | Remarks |
|---|---|---|---|---|---|
| K'ay(y)um K'akoch (also K'ay(y)om) | Playing and singing | Second, i.e. K'akoch's heaven | (?) Máash-Kásyaho or K'ek'en-Kóho (?) | Born from baknikté | |
| K'ay(y)um Hachakyum | Playing on hachhub [a large seashell with pointed tip cut off], sacred drum called also k'ay(y)um, and singing, thus calling gods to take baché; playing on hachhub to call K'akoch for drinking baché with Hachakyum in the latter's house | Fourth, i.e. Hacha-kyum's heaven; also at Chishyokra-djatochhachakyum the Residence of Our Very Lord on the Usumacinta River | Máash-Kásyaho | " " | |
| K'in K'akoch | (?) | Second, i.e. K'akoch's heaven | (?) Máash-Kásyaho or K'ek'en-Kóho | " " | |
| K'in Hachakyum | Preparing incense (hachpom, pom, and/ or k'iik) and offering it to K'akoch | Fourth, i.e. Hacha-kyum's heaven; also Chishyokradja-tochhachakyum | Máash-Kásyaho | " " | Hachakyum has wlakilk'uh [literally "bowl of god" or "divine bowl, dish"] of K'akoch known to outsiders as brasero |
| Kurer K'akoch | Working for K'akoch | Second, i.e. K'akoch's heaven | (?) Máash-Kásyaho or K'ek'en-Kóho (?) | " " | |

| Deity | Function | Location | | Notes |
|---|---|---|---|---|
| Kurer Hachakyum | Cleaning Hachakyum's house | Fourth, i.e., Hachakyum's heaven; also Chishyokradja-tochhachakyum (Yachilan) | Máash-Kásyaho | |
| Kushtey K'uh Hachakyum | Working in the cornfield | Celestial; also Chishyokradja-tochhachakyum (Yachilan) | (?) | Kushtey K'uh are lesser deities who provide livelihood. They work in cornfields (*koor*) for the following gods: Hachakyum, Itsana Hachakyum, Sakapuk Hachakyum, Kyanthó', Mensabok, K'ak Mensabok, Tsibana, and Sukunkyum |
| Kushtey K'uh Itsana Hachakyum | " | " | (?) | |
| Kushtey K'uh Sakapuk Hachakyum | " | " | (?) | |
| Kushtey K'uh Kyanthó' | " | Terrestrial | K'ek'en-Kóho | |
| Kushtey K'uh Mensabok | " | " | " | |
| Kushtey K'uh K'ak Mensabok | " | " | " | |
| Kushtey K'uh Tsibana | " | " | " | |
| Kushtey K'uh Sukunkyum | " | The underworld of Sukunkyum (U Djalam Luum U Sukunkyum) | (?) | |

Table 1.  (Continued)

| Deity | Aspect associated with the deities | Residence | Onen | Origin | Remarks |
|---|---|---|---|---|---|
| Kyanthó' | Advanced age level reflected in his appearance as an old man, according to Chankin's grandfather; and Hachakyum's creating the first man Nushi; and Hachakyum's creating water, sea, lagoons, maize, beans, sugar cane, rice, tobacco, fish, snakes, dogs, horses, and cats; guarding sea; liking rain if not excessive; disliking too strong winds damaging cornfields (*koor*); dwelling situated at the north (very far on the other side of the sea); being prayed to and/or thanked for good health and abundant harvest as well as for a successful journey; creating airplanes, automobiles, non-Lacandon foodstuffs, and such objects as *manta*, etc.; creating non-Lacandons | Terrestrial | Máash-Kásyaho | Born from *baknikté* | Kyanthó' is Hachakyum's and Sukunkyum's brother. He is the highest ranking god on earth followed hierarchically by another terrestrial deity called Mensabok. He is the only lord in the Lacandon pantheon who has two wives (*ka-tro-u-lak*). In the literature there is a statement that Mensabok has two wives. That is not so |
| Kyanthó' K'akoch | Working with K'akoch and helping him | Celestial (Second, i.e. K'akoch's heaven) | Máash-Kásyaho | Born from *baknikté* | The title *t'o'ohil* given to Chankin by one contemporary writer may rather go to Kyanthó' K'akoch according to Chankin |
| Mensabok | Sending rain for cornfields; guarding the lagoon at Mensabok and Nahá; dwelling in a cave on the lagoon called Mensabok | Terrestrial | K'ek'en-Kóho | ,, | |
| Mensabok K'akoch | Working for K'akoch | Celestial (Second, i.e. K'akoch's heaven) | ,, | ,, | |

| Name | Function | Location / Heaven | Parents | Origin | Notes |
|---|---|---|---|---|---|
| Mensabok Sukunkyum | Working in the cornfield (*koor*) for Sukunkyum | The underworld of Sukunkyum (U Djalam [or Djalan] Luum U Sukunkyum) | " | " | The initial "o" in "Ok'inchob" is a sound between "o" and "a" — closer to the first |
| Ok'inchob K'akoch | Working with K'akoch and helping him | Second, i.e. K'akoch's heaven | Máash-Kásyaho | Born from his divine parents | Ok'inchob Hachakyum is son-in-law of Hachakyum. *Ok'inchob* probably means "the priest of maize." *O'in*, Yucatec *ah k'in*, means priest. The second part of the word reminds the writer of "chob" in "Chakchóben," which may be a distorted form of "Chakchobil," "the place of red maize," name of a small *pueblito* near the lagoon Bacalar, to which José Agapito Xiu from Oxkutzcab Yucatán, called the writer's attention many years ago |
| Ok'inchob Hachakyum | Guarding Hach Winik and their possessions upon Hachakyum's and Kyantho's order; being prayed to in case of fever and other illnesses as well as injuries inflicted by a snake; protecting from snakes and malevolent gods; knowledge of curing; shielding native families from illnesses; helping to kill snakes; protecting cornfields from destructive winds; calling on Hachakyum in the event of bad harvest and lack of corn; being prayed to that the sun may not die; image of a young male | Fourth, i.e. Hachakyum's heaven; also Yachilan | " | " | |

Table 1. (Continued)

| Deity | Aspect associated with the deities | Residence | Onen | Origin | Remarks |
|---|---|---|---|---|---|
| Ok'inchob Sukunkyum | Working in the cornfield; providing seeds of maize for the souls of animals | Underworld | ,, ,, | ,, ,, | |
| Sakapuk K'akoch | Working with K'akoch | Second, i.e. K'akoch's heaven | (?) | Born from baknikté | |
| Sakapuk Hachakyum | Working with Hachakyum; calling on Hachakyum and praying that "I may not die," according to a native informant | Fourth, i.e. Hachakyum's heaven; also Yachilan | Máash-Kásyaho | ,, ,, | This god does not live in the house of Hachakyum. He has his own residence |
| Sakapuk Sukunkyum | Working with Sukunkyum; guarding pillars that support the world, in company with Sukunkyum and Itsana Sukunkyum | Underworld | ,, ,, | ,, ,, | There are 100 (hun buka winik) pillart (yokmanluum) |
| Shkareosh Hachakyum | Preparing meals from corn | Fourth, i.e. Hachakyum's heaven; also Yachilan | K'ek'en-Kóho | (?) | Other names of this goddess: U-k-na-il-hachakyum, Our Lady of Our Very Lord; Oshnuk ("o" in this name is a sound between "o" and "a" — closer to the first), Lady, a designation implying affection. She is Hachakyum's wife |
| Shkareosh Ok'inchob | ,, | ,, | ,, | Born from her divine parents | Hachakyum's daughter and Ok'inchob's wife |

| | | | | | |
|---|---|---|---|---|---|
| Shkareosh Sukunkyum | " | Underworld | (?) | | Sukunkyum's wife. In the Lacandon mythology, the Shkareosh aspect must not be confounded with other aspects, as was the case in the literature recently. Corn is the key word in the Shkareosh aspect |
| Shtabay | Attractive appearance and intimate relations with some male deities | Terrestrial; close to the ruins of Kanak'sh near Sival (Sib) | Máash-Kásyaho | Born from their divine mother | There are many Shtabay. This name must not be confounded with *nikté shtabay*, a small flower created by Hachakyum, from which Kisin was born. It has been stated in the literature that Shtabay is Kisin's wife, a confusion that, it is hoped, has been clarified now |

# REFERENCES

AMRAN, DAVID W., JR.
1937   Eastern Chiapas, Mexico. *Geographic Review* 27:30–36.
1942   The Lacandon, last of the Maya. *El México antiguo* 6:15–30.
ANDERS, FERDINAND
1963   *Das Pantheon der Maya*. Graz: Akademische Druck- und Ver-
       lagsanstalt.
BAER, PHILLIP, MARY BAER
1952   *Materials of Lacandon culture of the Pethá (Pelhá) region*. Micro-
       film Collection of Manuscripts on Cultural Anthropology, sixth
       series, 34. Chicago: University of Chicago.
BRASSEUR DE BOURBOURG, CHARLES ÉTIENNE
1866   *Monuments anciens du Mexique, Palenqué et autres ruines de
       l'ancienne civilisation de Mexique*. Paris.
BRUCE, ROBERTO D.
1967   Jerarquía maya entre los dioses lacandones. *Anales del Instituto
       Nacional de Antropología e Historia*. 18:93–108. Mexico City.
CLINE, HOWARD
1944   Lore and deities of the Lacandon Indians, Chiapas, Mexico. *Jour-
       nal of American Folklore* 57:107–115.
DUBY, GERTRUDE, FRANS BLOM
1969   "The Lacandon," in *Ethnology*, part one. Edited by Evon Z. Vogt,
       276–297: *Handbook of Middle American Indians*, volume seven.
       Edited by Robert Wauchope.
HELLMUTH, NICHOLAS M.
1970   *A bibliography of the 16th – 20th century Maya of the Southern
       Lowlands: Chol, Chol Lacandon, Quejache, Itza, and Mopan*.
       Greeley, Colorado: Museum of Anthropology, University of
       Northern Colorado.
MAUDSLAY, ALFRED P.
1883   "Explorations in Guatemala and examination of the newly dis-
       covered Indian ruins of Quiriguá, Tikal, and the Usumacinta," in
       *Proceedings of the Royal Geographical Society and Monthly
       Record of Geography*, new monthly series, 5(4):185–204.
PETRYSHYN, JAROSLAW T.
1968   *El panteón maya de los lacandones en Najá*. San Cristóbal de Las
       Casas, Chiapas, Mexico. Privately printed.
1969   Ein lakandonischer Gottesdienst in der Höhle des Gottes Tsibaná
       am Heiligen Sie von Mensabok in den tropischen Urwäldern von
       Chiapas. *Archive für Völkerkunde* 23:165–176, Tafel I–III.
1972   "Worship in the rain forest: ritual sites of the Lacandon Mayas,"
       in *Proceedings of the Shevchenko Scientific Society in Canada*
       12:231–272.
i.p.   Sukunkyum and Kisin only? *Nineteenth Annual Meeting of the
       American Society for Ethnohistory*.
ROYS, RALPH L.
1967   *The Book of Chilam Balam of Chumayel*. Norman, Oklahoma:
       University of Oklahoma Press.

SAPPER, KARL
1897   Das nördliche Mittel-Amerika nebst einem Ausflug nach dem Hochland von Anahuac. Braunschweig.
1907   "Chols und Chorties," in Congrès International des Americanistes, XVe Session tenue à Quebec en 1906 2:423–465.

SCHOLES, FRANCES V., RALPH L. ROYS
1968   The Maya Chontal Indians of Acalan-Tixchel. Norman, Oklahoma: University of Oklahoma Press. (Reproduced from the first edition published in 1948.)

SELER, EDWARD
1960   Gesammelte Abhandlungen zur amerikanischen Sprach- und Altertumskunde. Graz: Akademische Druck- und Verlagsanstalt.

SOUSTELLE, GEORGETTE
1947   "Notes sur le rituel religieux chez les Lacandons du Chiapas," in Proceedings of the twenty-seventh International Congress of Americanists, Mexico 1939 2:408–418.

STOLL, OTTO
1884   Zur Ethnographie der Republik Guatemala. Zürich.

TAX, SOL
1951   Lacandon nasal ornament. American Anthropologist 53:148.

THOMPSON, J. ERIC S.
1970   Maya history and religion. Norman, Oklahoma: University of Oklahoma Press.

TOZZER, ALFRED M.
1907   A comparative study of the Mayas and the Lacandones. New York: Macmillan.

VILLA ROJAS, ALFONSO
1967   Los lacandones: su origen, costumbres y problemas vitales. América Indígena 27:25–53.
1968   Los lacandones: sus dioses, ritos y creencias religiosos. América Indígena 28:81–137.

VON SIVERS, JÉGOR
1861   Über Madeira und die Antillen nach Mittelamerika. Leipzig.

Plate 1. In their temple, two Hach Winik perform acts of worship together, including singing, burning incense, and other rituals. A temple, which may be individual or communal, is one of the three kinds of sites in which the Hach Winik of Nahá worship

Plate 2. A Hach Winik from Nahá prepares for a ritual in worship in the ruins of an ancient ceremonial center, another kind of place in which the jungle dwellers conduct their religious celebrations. This site, near the Tzettal Mayan settlement Sival (Sib), is named for the god Kanank'ash

Plate 3.   This is a ceremony in progress in a sacred cave, the third type of site in which the Hach Winik pray and bring offerings to their gods. The photograph is of the cave of the god Tsibana on the lagoon of the same name. Of the three kinds of worship sites the sacred caves appear to be the most secret. Outsiders are rarely permitted to see the interior of the caves. To the writer's knowledge, he was the first outsider who was privileged to be invited to cave ceremonies

Plate 4. This *wlakilk'uh* (*u* 'his'; *lak* 'bowl,' 'dish,' 'cup'; *il* 'of'; *k'uh* 'god') is a bowl of fired clay and the god Mensabok. The attached head is called *uhoork'uh* (*u* 'his'; *k'uh* 'god'; *hoor* 'head'). *Wlakilku'h* are made for sundry gods but by far not for all. Information on the name of *wlakilk'uh* can be obtained from the maker of *wlakilk'uh* only. In addition to using it for burning incense (*hachpom, pom,* or *k'iik, hachpom* pleasing the Lacandon deities more than *pom* or *k'iik*), the Hach Winik also apply those bowls to offer to their gods small quantities of agricultural products in liquid form, placing them upon the protruding lip of the deity. The only *wlakilk'uh* that is produced but placed in grass outside the temple and never used is that of Sukunkyum, the supreme lord of the underworld

Plate 5. This *wlakilk'uh* of the goddess who is Mensabok's wife, shows different patterns than those shown on bowls made for male deities

Plate 6.  The author's principal informant at Nahá stands in front of a "tunnel" cut out in the jungle with *maská'* (Yucatec *maskáb*; Mexican machete)

# The Moon-Mythical Character of the God Yü-huang

JOHN TU ER-WEI

Throughout the ages Chinese culture has been built on the three pillars of Confucianism, Buddhism, and Taoism. Each of these is still a living reality. Together they continue to exert a profound influence on today's religious concepts, customs, and behavior. Our subject here is Taoism, and the Taoist supreme god Yü-huang (*Yü* [jade] + *huang* [emperor]).

Yü-huang is a familiar name. But what of his cult? What is the effect of this cult? How, above all, has the Yü-huang concept been formed? This paper aims at answering such questions.

## THE TRADITION OF YÜ-HUANG AND ITS EXPLANATION

The mother of Yü-huang is named Pao-jo-kuang [Precious Moonlight]. She brought forth the child on the ninth midday of the first lunar month of the Ping-Wu year. Upon his arrival into the world, Yü-huang emitted light and shone forth. As a youth, he abdicated the prince's throne and distributed all his wealth, personal property, and valuables. He even cut his own body's flesh and gave it as medicine to the poor (*The Yü-huang Classic*).

Some explanation is necessary. This account of Yü-huang is surely moon-mythical. His mother's name is moonlight. He emitted light and shone forth. So, he is something luminous. A Taoist classical book (*Kao Shang Yü-huang Pen-ching ching-sui*) tells us that the body of Yü-huang is the body of the Tao himself. In the study of the *I-Ching* (Tu Er-wei 1960) we showed that Tao, being luminous, is "moon."

Yü-huang was born at midday on the eighth or ninth of the lunar month when the moon rises in the east. The moon of two days is in its first quarter. In this sense, both, the ninth and the eighth day have the same meaning. There is another version in the *Funk and Wagnalls' standard dictionary of folklore, mythology, and legend*: on the birthday of Yü-huang, the eighth of the first lunar month, the people make offerings to the god. The fact that at his first arrival in the world Yü-huang emitted light also helps us to believe that the birth of Yü-huang was symbolized by the rising moon at midday of the eighth or ninth. The mythical birth story almost always corresponds to that of the moon (Ehrenreich 1910: 81).

Yü-huang's cutting of his own body's flesh, giving it as medicine to the poor, is a description based on that of the Buddha (*Maharat-nakuta-sutra*). In fact the whole life story of Yü-huang consists of imitations of the Buddha (*Buddhacarita*).

A very important account (*Lieh-sheng pao-kao*) pictures Yü-huang, the creator and conservator of the universe, living in the Yellow Gold Palace or the White Jade Capital. Riding on the back of a dragon, he always travels in the heavens, varies in form, and governs the thirty-six heavens and the three thousand worlds. To this the following (*Yu-shu han san-miao ching*) should be added: Yü-huang subjugates the twenty-eight constellations and those stars which do injuries to the people. One can be certain that what is involved is the "moon extinguishes the stars" myth.

That the moon-myth character of Yü-huang cannot hide itself is also proved by the word *Yü* [jade]). *Yü-huang* means "the Jade Emperor" or "the Jade Sovereign." Somebody named Tsai Chien-yu "saw the jade building in the moon" (*Wang-chia shih-yi chi*). A poem phrase of Pai Chü-yi says: "The moon sets as a jade ring falls." The Ch'u-tz'u says: "I ascend to the Künlün (moon) mountain, where my food is the jade-flower." Again we have the Huai-nan-tzu classic: A certain jade, even if it should be burnt in the stove for three days and three nights, would not lose its beautiful luster. Here the moon is regarded as the jade and this moon-jade disappears for three days and three nights; afterwards it appears again as a new one. Even today, the popular belief still is that Yü-huang's residence is the Jade Palace. Surely, Yü-huang was so named because his residence was the Jade Capital.

## THE CULT OF YÜ-HUANG, HIS MERCY AND PROTECTION

On the ninth of the first lunar month people celebrate the anniversary of the birth of Yü-huang. The famous temples dedicated to him are Yü-huang Kung and Tien-kung Tan in Tai-nan, Taiwan; Yuan-ching Kuan in Chang-huru and Yü-tzuen Kung, as well as Pai-yuan shan-tzu in Taipei. Popularly, Yü-huang is also called *Tien-kung* [the Lord of Heaven]. In the Taoist classics his honorific appellation is Yü-huang Shang-ti (*Yü-huang* [the Jade Emperor], *Shang-ti* [the High Emperor]).

In Taiwan, the offerings to Yü-huang on his birthday are pigs, chickens, hens' eggs, duck, and fish. In addition, incense and paper money are burnt, and firecrackers are set off. The people bow their heads to the ground in reverence (*kowtow*). The acts of worship begin on the evening of the eighth and last until midnight. Most of the families keep vigil through the night and repeatedly implore the mercy of Yü-huang or Tien-kung. What the god can do for them is referred to below.

In the *Yü-huang Classic* there is a eulogy to Yü-huang. The residence of Yü-huang is the Jade Palace or the Golden Mansion. He is merciful and benevolent; his energy and force are irresistible; and he controls all the harmful demons. Yü-huang is pure because of his sanctity and round form. He delivers the masses from the *samsara* [the valley of tears]. In the same classic Yü-ti (Yü-huang) is the great luminous sovereign, his majesty is incomparable; he can exterminate the cruel demons, absolve the people from sins and crimes, and make the people morally pure. He protects the country and delivers the masses from the *samsara*. According to another classic (*Yü-huang Shang-ti hung-tzu chiu-chieh pao-ching*) Yü-huang is infinitely merciful and will deliver the masses from the *Kalpas* [long period]. Yü-huang can change his body's form, he can take a round shape.

The precepts of Yü-huang (of *Yü-huang Shang-ti hung-tzu chiu-chieh pao-ching*) are no killing, no egoism, no concupiscence, not doing harm, no flattering, no slander but mercy, filial piety, and faithfulness to the sovereign of the state.

Yü-huang wants penitence from the people who have sinned. He can absolve them from sin. Even those who are punished in the Ten Hells can be delivered by Yü-huang, if they do penance.

As to those punished in the hells and their salvation, we cannot omit the *Yü-li* (*Yü-li pao-ch'ao*). The *Yü-li* is a very popular book. The author of the book is believed to be Yü-huang himself, who wrote it and gave it to mankind for salvation. In it are depicted the terrible torments and tortures of the Ten Hells over which the Ten Kings rule, three of whom, including the famous Yamaraja, are adopted from

Buddhism. The Ten Kings are under the direction of the Buddhist Kshitigarbha, who, however, is inferior to Yü-huang; here he is the president of the hells. Yü-huang, the first authority, hears the reports from Kshitigarbha or directly from the Ten Kings.

According to the *Yü-li*, Yü-huang is very merciful and agrees that the punished who are penitent can come out of the hells to be reborn in this world, or to be immediately admitted into the Pure Land (Paradise), if they become penitent on one of the Ten Kings' birthdays, who, together with Kshitigarbha, are all Bodhisatvas.

The Taoist belief in hells is, of course, like that of Buddhism. The *Yü-li* is a salvation book. The people are conscious that penitence is salvation (*Yü-li pao-ch'ao*).

## THE MAGIC POWER OF THE *YÜ-HUANG CLASSIC*

The *Yü-huang Classic* is wonderful and marvelous in itself. He who keeps the *Classic* and reads it over once can exorcise devils, resist the evil stars which injure the people by emitting lights over them, escape from the dangers of beasts and bandits, and deliver the innocent from prison. Furthermore, he can earn great wealth and treasures and obtain high office for himself and his descendants. He who keeps the *Classic* is free from the calamities of wars, floods, and famines. His harvests are always good; he can live in prosperity always, and his country is peaceful.

The keeper of the *Classic* deserves to become a pure man, a saint, who is absolved from his sins. He has no fear of being reborn in hells; on the contrary, when he dies, he sees a group of the so-called Jade Girls of the Heavenly Palace, who descend with banners in their hands and receive him into the Heavenly Paradise.

The great sinners and criminals are absolved, if only they meet a keeper of the *Classic* whose shadow touches their bodies. The same thing happens if they hear such a keeper's voice.

If the keeper of the *Classic* makes a banner and thereon writes the name "Yü-huang" and hangs it on a high pole, then all the people who live in the direction toward which the wind blows the banner, win victories and are absolved from all their sins.

If the keeper of the *Classic* writes the name "Yü-huang" on the ceremonial clock, cymbals, copper or wooden ring, etc. and one of them is shaken (even by winds), all the people who hear the sound so caused are absolved from their sins. Finally, if the keeper of the

*Classic*, as a hermit in retirement, gazes from the mountain peak at a lot of near and distant places, in all these places, so gazed upon by him, all sins are extinguished, i.e. sins of the people as well as of the animals and plants, if these were culpable too. How much more are the sins of those who accept and keep the *Classic* forgiven (*Yü-huang Classic*)! How much more are the sins of the worshippers of Yü-huang himself forgiven! Here we have a good example of magic coming later than religion. The *Yü-huang Classic* at most is a book of the Sung Dynasty (A.D. 960–1278). All sins can be taken away by Yü-huang, with the exception of that of "destroying" the *Classic's* doctrine (*Yü-huang Shang-ti hui-hao pao-she*). The wrath of Yü-huang is so rare that such an instance is not easy to find.

## EXPLANATION OF THE YÜ-HUANG CLASSIC

The author of this *Classic* (whose name is lacking) may be a Taoist of the Sung dynasty, a period in which people no longer understood the old moon mythology. He has composed the stories along the traditional lines of Taoism and Buddhism and was unconscious that he was influenced by the culture currents of the old moon mythology.

Yü-huang here is compared to the moon. In myths this planet is also compared to the gazing eye (here of the hermit); where the eye (moon) gazes, there the sins (stars) are extinguished. The moon is regarded as a mythical clock, ring, and cymbals, the sounds of which all can extinguish the sins (stars). The stars which are close to the moon are extinguished. So, the sins of the people (stars), who live in the direction toward which the wind blows the banner (moon), are extinguished. Absolved are the sinners (stars), who meet a bearer of the *Yü-huang Classic* (moon). Therefore it is said, too, that such a bearer deserves to become a pure man ('the moon in myths is pure and can make one pure). Only pure men can be admitted into the Pure Land (moon), namely, Paradise (which in primitive mythology becomes the moon).

The keeper of the *Yü-huang Classic* (moon) represents the moon, can dissipate the devils, beasts, and bandits (evil stars) (*Yüan-shih tien-tsun shuo Pei-fang chen-wu miao-ching*).

The good harvests caused by the *Yü-huang Classic* are the stars (crops) which are very bright, flourishing when the moon is waning. Famines mean scarce stars in heaven when the moon is full and quite bright. The myth says: the moon recedes and so causes the appearances of the stars (crops). Stars also mean wars (soldiers); when the moon comes, the stars cease to appear; then the (heavenly) country is peaceful (without star soldiers).

The *Yü-huang Classic* (or Yü-huang, the moon) says plainly: "The keeper of the *Classic* can resist or extinguish the harmful stars." That Yü-huang (the moon) can deliver the innocent (stars) from prison (a certain number of stars have the form of a prison) means again that where the bright moon comes, there the stars disappear.

Such explanations are based on the primitive mythical traditions (see Tu Er-wei 1965, 1966).

## THE BOOK'S DISTRIBUTION

In addition to what we have described concerning the *Yü-huang Classic*, is the custom of book distribution (donation) in this island province of Taiwan. The custom is, of course, a mirror which reflects the customs of all Taoist and Buddhist people everywhere.

The well-to-do pious people have some religious books or booklets printed and donate the copies to others. The merit of doing so is believed to be very considerable. The people will often not give up the opportunity to acquire the merit. The procedure is as follows: they contribute a small sum of money to the Taoist or Buddhist temple which undertakes to have two items reprinted, and so they get a number of the copies which they donate to others. There are variously titled books (or parts of books) or booklets so reprinted, among which, for instance, we have *Yü-li* or the *Yü-li* in vernacular, and the Buddhist *Paramita* (practically a part of it). A person does good and induces others to do good; a person worships Yü-huang or the Buddha and induces others to do so; thus one truly leads a life of a missionary.

Usually in the temple there are several kinds of copies, from which one can choose at will. So the cult of Yü-huang is propagated in a popular way. Today, Taoism cannot compete with Buddhism, but its vigor remains among the common people and in their hearts.

## THE COMPOSITE ELEMENT OF YÜ-HUANG

The concepts of Yü-huang are composed of various elements, almost all of which are moon-mythical.
1. From the point of view of Taoism:
a. The Primordial Heavenly Sovereign should have been the imme-

diate precursor of Yü-huang. True, the two are two entities in the Taoist classics, but, in practice, the two are often regarded as one and the same godhead. The reason for this confusion is that close similarities exist: (1) both live in the Jade Capital; (2) both live in the mythical land, called Fuli (*Ku-shen-pien*). *Fuli = buli = bulan*, an Austronesian word for "moon"; (3) both are in heaven and make the circuit of heaven (*Tai-shang chu-tien ling-shu tu-ming miao-ching*); (4) both emit the great light and illuminate the heavenly worlds; and (5) both promulgated the classics. Both are moon-gods. There is a tra- dition that the Primordial Heavenly Sovereign once closed the light of heaven for three days and three nights so that at that time the light disappeared. The heavenly light which disappears for the inter- val can only be the moon. So here what is in question is the moon god.

b. Taoism as a philosophy, which is very old, has an immense influence on Taoism as a religion. The Yü-huang god is also believed to be Tao himself (or itself) who is the moon-mythologized divinity. The original meaning of the word *Tao* is moon (for moon-god) (see Tu Er-wei 1960). That I have discovered the original meaning of the Chinese word *Tao* is a source of great gratification to me.

2. From the point of view of Buddhism.

The father of the Buddha is Suddhodana [the Pure Food]. The father of Yü-huang is Ching-te [the Pure Virtue]. The latter name also contains within it the word "pure." The mother of the Buddha is Maya (this word is a moon-myth one, as we have proved elsewhere (Tu Er-wei 1965); Yü-huang has, as his mother, Pao-yo-kuang [The Precious Moonlight]. Here again there is parallel. The birth of the Buddha was symbolized by the moonrise (Tu Er-wei 1965), as is also that of Yü-huang. Both left home life and became devotees; both gave up the prince's dignity; both are said to be luminous; both were very merciful and so compassionate that they not only gave all they had as alms, but also cut the flesh from their own bodies and dis- tributed it as medicine to cure the patients. Both were also spiritual saviors and wanted to liberate the people from the *samsara* bondage. Both are the central objects of the most important cults of their respec- tive religions. Taoism then needed a godhead as great as Yü-huang, because plans were made for it to compete with Buddhism. Buddhism held a strong attraction for the people, but it stressed the afterlife too much and did not permit the facing of real difficulties. That the par- ticular solemn official cult started in the Sung Dynasty had much to do with the politics of that period in which hostilities from the northern enemies had to be faced. The political authorities felt themselves in need of new energy and new consolation from the new godhead (Yü-huang).

The essential difference between Yü-huang and Buddha is that the former, in and after this life, always retained his personality, while the latter entered Nirvana (Extinction) and lost his personality.

3. From the point of view of Confucianism:

The fundamental composite element of Yü-huang is also the ancient Chinese Tien-Ti concept. Sometimes it is even clearly said that Yü-huang is Ti or Shang-ti (*Lee-yu, Sung-ch'ao-shih-shih*). Up to now Yü-huang has been called Yü-huang Shang-ti, or Tien-kung [The Lord of Heaven], the latter being kept for the highest god by the people today. Tien-kung can signify two things: (1) Tien-Ti (the classical *Huang-tien Shang-ti*) and (2) Yü-huang. Tien-kung is very anthropomorphic. Already in the Tang Dynasty, the respect for Tien-kung was declining. For instance the poem of Li-pai reads: "Tien-kung, when he saw the Jade Girls, laughed ceaselessly for joy." This shows no respect for Tien-kung. Here both Tien-kung and the Jade Girls are, no doubt, moon-mythical.

Of course, the difference between Yü-huang and Tien is very considerable: Tien does not speak in a voice, Yü-huang does; Tien is in heaven, Yü-huang is in the Jade Capital, although this is also in heaven. The sacrifice to Tien takes place at the winter solstice, that to Yü-huang in the first lunar month. Tien is autogenous, Yü-huang has his parents. The Tien religion is without a talisman, the Yü-huang religion is full of them.

The essential composite elements of Yü-huang are the Tien-Ti godhead of Confucianism, the Primordial Heavenly Sovereign and the Tao Absolute, and the Buddha, especially as described by the Buddhist canon *Buddhacarita*. But the whole and integral concept of Yü-huang is neither that of the Tien-Ti, nor that of the Primordial Heavenly Sovereign, nor that of Tao, nor that of the Buddha; it is a mixture of the four. In other words, it is a characteristic case of Sino-Indian culture confusion. It is wrong to think that Yü-huang is a facsimile of Sakradevanam Indra; the truth is that he was depicted like Buddha. Yü-huang is also called "the Ancient Buddha of Charity and Justice" (*Hsuan-ling Yü-huang pao-ching*). The *Classic* (*Tai-Shang sheng-huan hsiao-tsai hu-ming miao-ching*) takes the Primordial Heavenly Sovereign not only for Yü-huang but also for Buddha. Yü-huang's name, residence, attributes, and relations to the Tao absolute, and to Buddha prove his moon-myth character. Above all, the influences of Buddhism on him are immense, though they cannot be enumerated here.

Finally, we are not allowed to omit the fact that the Tao religion is henotheistic: Tien or Shangti, Tao and Yuan-shih Tien-tsun; Lao-tzu and Yü-huang, each of them can be the supreme divinity.

## CONCLUSION

From all points of view, Yü-huang is a moon-mythical god. The primitive culture currents of moon mythology are perpetually strong and do not dry up. The traditions of Yü-huang, although this god arose in a much later period, were formed in these currents. In folklore today we find many culture elements of the present which are connected with primitive moon-mythological materials. It is no wonder that a number of the divinities are moon-mythological. All of Buddhism and Taoism is based on the moon-mythology systems, the utilization, investigation, and explanation of which formed and constituted the religions of both, and guided the development of their religious and philosophical doctrines. Only the moon-mythological key can solve the fundamental problems of Buddhism and Taoism which, otherwise, have been unintelligible till now.

## REFERENCES

*Books*

EHRENREICH, P.
1910   *Die allgemeine Mythologie und ihre ethnologischen Grundlagen.* Leipzig.
LEACH, MARIA, *editor*
1949–1950   *Funk and Wagnalls' standard dictionary of folklore, mythology, and legend.* New York.
TU ER-WEI, JOHN
1960   *Discovery of the original meaning of the I-Ching.* Taipei: Hua Ming Press.
1963   *Discovery of the original meaning of Buddhism.* Taipei: Hua Ming Press.
1965   *The original meaning of the Buddhist canon.* Taipei: Commercial Press.
1966   *The four divine animals: phoenix, unicorn, tortoise, and dragon.* Taipei.
1968   *The beliefs of Confucianism, Buddhism and Taoism.* Tapei: Hua Ming Press.

*The Taoist Collection* (1962, Taipei: I-wen Press)

*Kao Shang Yü-huang Pen-ching ching-sui*
*Ku-shen-pian*
*Yuan-shih tien-tsun shuo Pei-fang chen-wu miao-ching*
*The Yü-huang Classic (Kao Shang Yü-huang Pen-ching Chi-ching)*
*Yü-huang Shang-ti hui-hao pao-sheh*


*Popular Literature*

*Hsuan-ling Yü-huang pao-ching*
*Lieh-sheng pao-kao*
*Tai-shang chu-tien ling-shu tu-ming miao-ching*
*Yü-huang Shang-ti hung-tzu chiu-chieh pao-ching*
*Yü-li pao-ch'ao* (Shanghai: Hung-ta-Shan Press).

# Was Espingo (Ispincu) of Psychotropic and Intoxicating Importance for the Shamans in Peru?

S. HENRY WASSÉN

When the early Spanish chroniclers in South America wrote about *hechiceros* and their use of certain drugs, etc., we cannot always identify them with shamans or medicine men. The best translation seems to be "sorcerer." Among the Inca:

... the sorcerers (*omo*) claimed to speak directly with the spirits. They usually dressed differently from ordinary people, and wore their hair long or cut in some special way. They were usually consulted to find lost or stolen articles or to learn what was happening at a distance. They talked to the spirits in the dark, and theirs and the spirits' voices could be heard but not understood (Rowe 1946: 302).

Other words for *hechicero* are diviner and witch doctor. Rowe continues his text by saying that "some diviners summoned the spirits by saying a spell and drawing lines on the ground, others drank them-

I am deeply grateful to my Swedish friends, Dr. Victor Hasselblad, Gothenburg, and Dr. Herbert Tigerschiöld, Stockholm, who, with their liberal view of the importance of international scientific cooperation, have given their financial support so that I might accept the invitation of the President of the Organizing Committee of the IXth International Congress of Anthropological and Ethnological Sciences.

I have friends both in Sweden and in the United States of America who have taken a keen interest in this paper and participated scientifically. My sincere thanks to all of them: in Stockholm, Dr. Wolmar E. Bondeson, Professor Bo Holmstedt, M.D., Dr. Eskil Hultin, Dr. Jan-Erik Lindgren, and Dr. Benkt Sparre; in Gothenburg, Professor Gunnar Harling; and, in the United States, Professor José Cuatrecasas, Washington, D.C., and Professor Richard Evans Schultes, Cambridge, Massachusetts.

Mrs. Sharlie Otterström, an American living in Gothenburg, has very kindly helped with translation and text correction, and Miss Maj-Britt Berglund of the Gothenburg Ethnographic Museum, has typed the manuscript. To both of them my best thanks.

selves into insensibility and gave their answers when they recovered"
(Rowe 1946: 302). He also refers to Cobo's statement that the latter
"put the juice of the *wil'ka,* a berry also used as a purge, into their
*chicha* to give it more strength." This has been treated more in detail
by Siri von Reis Altschul (1967: 307) in her paper, "Vilca and its
use":

Around 1571, Polo de Ondegardo reported that the witch doctors of the
Incas foretold the future by speaking with the devil in some dark place by
means of various ceremonies, for which office they intoxicated themselves
with an herb called *Vilca,* pouring its juice into *chicha* or taking it another
way. The reporter stated that, although only old women were reputed to
practice this craft, in fact its use was widespread but concealed among men
and boys, as well.

The same author has also mentioned several other sources in which
we find references to *vilca* as a purgative, as a stimulant, etc. During
her herbarium search at Harvard University, two specimens labeled
*Vilca* were found. Both belonged to *Anadenanthera colubrina,* one
was from southern Peru, the other from east of La Paz. "These data
indicate that *A. colubrina* indeed is identifiable with *Vilca,* but they
do not insure that *Vilca* is referable exclusively to this plant" (von
Reis Altschul 1967: 308).

I have quoted this passage especially for the fact that in the old
literature we find another plant product used by sorcerers as an
admixture to *chicha* which no one seems to have taken interest in until now. What I am thinking of is *espingo,* seeds, that obviously were
used in old Peru in the same way as the above-mentioned *vilca,*
namely, as an added ingredient to *chicha,* with effects the chroniclers
described as in part purely medicinal, and in part quite drastic, plainly
with psychotropic effects. "They became crazy from it" is a common
phrase. I therefore consider that learning about *espingo* can add to
our knowledge of the different means used by South America's medicine men.

With respect to pursuing my research on *espingo,* I wish to acknowledge my gratitude to an Argentine-born friend and colleague, Dr. Ana
María Mariscotti de Görlitz, now of Marburg, Germany. It was she
who, in connection with a scientific correspondence between us on the
burning of *khoa* or *khoba* (*Mentha pulegium,* of the family *Labiatae*)
during the so-called *señaladas* or traditionally old offering ceremonies
to Pachamama (see Wassén 1967: 276-277), insisted that I should not
lose track of *espingo.* She kindly gave me some references to the

literature — e.g. to de Arriaga's *Extirpación*, where we find the following report:

*Espingo* is a little, dry fruit with round kernels (*al modo de unas almendras redondillas*), with a very intense smell, although not particularly good. One gets it from the Chachapoyas,[1] and it is said to be very medicinal [to be used] for stomach pains, stool bleedings (*cámaras de sangre*) and other sicknesses, and that it is taken in powder form and is expensive to buy. It was usually sold for these purposes. In Jaén de Bracamoros[2] not too many years ago, the Indians paid their tribute with *espingo*. The previous archbishop forbade, on risk of excommunication, that it be sold to the Indians, since he knew it was a question of an extraordinary offer to *huacas*,[3] especially in the flatlands, where there is no one who does not have *espingo*, since all who have been visited there have *conopas*[4] (de Arriaga 1920: 46).

A similar but shorter piece of information appears in the work *Exortaciones* written by the sixth archbishop of Lima, Pedro de Villagomes (1585–1671). He says, concerning what the Indians offer, only the following: "*Espingo, es una rutilla seca, al modo de unas almendras redondillas de muy vehemente olor, aunque no muy bueno, y no hay quien no tenga espingo teniendo conopa*" (Villagomes 1919; 165–166). He continues, as de Arriaga did, to tell of *aut*, another little, dry fruit, not dissimilar to *espingo*. He himself has explained that he had de Arriaga as a source as well as other chroniclers (see Urteagas' preface to the edition used here of de Arriaga's *Extirpación:* XIV).

I return to the beginning of de Arriaga's fourth chapter, where he declares those who used *espingo* to be sorcerers, and describes some of its effects. His reports are in translation: "On the plains from Chancay and downwards, the *chicha* that was presented to the *huacas* was called *yale*.[5] It is made of *zora*[6] mixed with chewed corn and

---

[1] Chachapoya would seem here to be one of the tribes from "deep in the Andean valleys of the upper Marañón River in North Central Perú," and who "apparently had diverse languages and Tropical Forest cultures" (Steward and Métraux 1948: 614–615).

[2] Jaén de Bracamoros was a "city" founded by Diego Palomino (in 1549?) near the junction of the Chinchipe and Marañón Rivers (see Steward and Métraux 1948: 616).

[3] *Huaca*, sacred shrine.

[4] *Conopa*, sacred image.

[5] *Yale*, possibly from the Chancay language, "once spoken on the Chancay river, department of Lima" (Loukotka 1968: 272).

[6] *Zora, sora,* or *jora*. According to Friederici (1947: 570), "malted Indian corn used for preparing a very strong *chicha*, the use of which, according to Garcilaso, was forbidden by the Incas." In Garcilaso's original text (1943: 177, *libro octavo,* 9): "Algunos indios más apassionados de la embriaguez que la demás comunidad echan la cara en remojo, y la tienen assí hasta que echa sus raízes; entonces la muelen toda como está y la cuezen en la misma agua con otras cosas, y, colada, la guardan hasta que se sazona; házese un brevaje fortíssimo, que embriaga repen-

powder of *espingo* is put into it. It [the *yale*] is made very strong and thick and then one gives of it what one considers suitable to the *huaca*; the sorcerers drink the rest and they are driven crazy (de Arriaga 1920: 42).[7]

De Arriaga has also reported on nocturnal sessions of "*hechiceros, chupadores de sangre*": "During these sessions the devil appears, sometimes in the figure of a lion, other times as a tiger, and as he sits down very furiously, resting on his forearms, they worship him" (de Arriaga 1920: 40–41).[8] This reference to the mighty felines (puma and jaguar) in the sphere of conjuring Indian sorcerers or shamans is evidently of great interest, specially if we think of the nearly pan-American distribution of jaguar figures in combination with the *alter ego* motif.[9]

Cobo is another chronicler who mentions *espingo*. According to him:

... the gentle Indians of the Andean provinces in Peru used to get from the peoples of their frontier some small capsules [Cobo uses the word *vainillas*] as *algarrobas*, of a dark, tawny color, the curdled substance of which is like *Sangre de Drago* (*Pterocarpus draco*), however brilliant with a shade of black, and of a mild and intense smell. These "*vainillas*" are produced by a tree called *Espingo*, found in those regions. The rude Indians bring forth these capsules as a precious thing to barter them for knives, scissors and other trifles which they highly value; and this they obtain easily from the Spaniards as these capsules are held to be very medicinal.

Cobo continues to tell how the powder, taken in different ways, cures various forms of serious bleeding (Cobo 1891: 95–96).

There are some more references to *espingo* in various sources. Murúa (1946: 306) says that it was the *trébol* (Latin *Trifolium*) which was called *espinco*, and that the Indians connected this plant with various superstitions. The same information, but without mention of

---

tinamente: llámanle *uiñapu*, y en otro lenguaje *sora*. Los Incas lo prohibieron, por ser tan violento para la embriaguez; después acá, me dizen, se ha buelto a usar por algunos viciosos."

[7] In Spanish: "En los llanos desde Chancay a baxo la chicha que ofrecen a las Huacas se llama Yale, y se haze de Zora mezclada con maís mascado, y le hechan polvo de Espingo, hazen la muy fuerte y espesa, y después de aver hechado sobra la Huaca lo que les parece, beven la demás los Hechiceros, y les buelve como locos."

[8] In Spanish: "En estas juntas se les aparece el Demonio, vnas vezes en figura de León, otras vezes en figura de Tigre, y poniéndose asentado, y estrivando sobre los braços muy furioso, le adoran."

[9] Dr. Ana María Mariscotti de Görlitz observing this wrote to the author: "Allí tiene su alter ego!"

*trébol,* is found in Antonio Ricardo's Quechua vocabulary from 1586 (1951), where it is said that *Yspincu* is a certain plant and fruit which is fragrant and used for various bewitchments.[10]

Lastres (1961: 305) also gives *espingo (ispunku)* as botanically *trébol.* According to the Peruvian Quechua Indian, Dr. Salvador Palomino Flores (who, at this writing, is at the University of Copenhagen), the correct spelling should be *ispunku; espingo* could, however, be a phonetic variation of the word in the Quechua of Bolivia (letter of January 30, 1973). As meaning *trébol,* Lastres (1951: 305) also quotes the names *chullku* and *cchikmu. Trébol,* however, cannot be the source for the samples treated here, and we must draw the conclusion that the Indian word has been used for several plants, or seeds from several plants. Thus we do not know which *espingo* Lastres (1951: 250) is referring to when he, without any indication of his source, reports that *chicha,* prepared from Indian corn and *espingo,* was used as an offering to the *huacas* during the great Inca ceremonial feasts Raimi, Citua, and Aymoray. The same is the case when he mentions (1951: 291) a medicinal use of *espingo* powder.

What we have determined thus far, from the testimony of the original written sources, is that *espingo* is used as an admixture with *chicha;* it is said to have medicinal uses, and was even used for certain purposes by the shamans. It soon became clear that knowledge of *espingo* was minimal, and really, from a scientific point of view, nonexistent. Neither La Barre (1938) nor Hartmann (1958), writing about alcoholic beverages among the natives of South America, named the *espingo* additive to *chicha* in old Peru. On the other hand, the Bolivian ethnobotanical specialist, Enrique Oblitas Poblete (1969) listed *asango-espingo* together, explaining that the *callahuayas* receive these remedies from Cajamarca, Peru; that they are used in cases of neuralgia and muscular pains; and, taken with *agua de llantén*[11] and wine, also are used for curing *cámaras de sangre* (Oblitas Poblete 1969: 80). If the information presented by Oblitas Poblete was received from modern *callahuayas,* it would mean that the traditions about the use of *espingo* for certain BLEEDINGS, etc., has been carried on from the time of its discovery.

As I wanted to find out what *espingo* really was, I started a correspondence with Dr. Oblitas Poblete, and one reason for going to La Paz in the summer of 1970 was the *espingo* problem. When we

---

[10] The original text (93): "*Yspincu,* cierta yerua y fruto oloroso con que se hazen muchos hechizos."

[11] *Llantén, Plantago* species.

met in La Paz, Dr. Oblitas Poblete gave me two seeds of *asango* (possibly from the Family *Rubiaceae*), and two quite different seeds, about one centimeter long and half a centimeter wide, of *espingo,* without, however, knowing anything about the botanical names for the plants producing these seeds. We also went to the Bolivian capital's historical museum, Casa de Murillo, with its collection of medicinal plants, seeds, etc., and among the specimens on exhibit were some *espingo* seeds of exactly the same appearance as those I had received that day. When Oblitas Poblete gave me the two samples, he also left a little note saying (in translation): "Seeds of a small tropical plant from the Department of Loreto, Peru. It is used antiseptically (against stomach disorders) and it is taken pulverized or it has to be chewed." [12] The *espingo* samples had and still have a fragrant smell, as stated in the old sources. This curious odor has been referred to as being similar to that of fenugreek, typical for all species of *Quararibea.* [13]

On my way back to Sweden, the samples were left in the hands of Dr. Richard Evans Schultes, director of the Botanical Museum at Harvard University. Dr. José Cuatrecasas of the Smithsonian Institution also inspected the *espingo* samples and suggested they might originate from the family *Lauraceae.* When Schultes was in Gothenburg in September 1971, he, however, considered the *espingo* samples to represent a *Quararibea,* in this case of the family *Bombacaceae.* This determination was confirmed in 1973 by Dr. Benkt Sparre of the Botanical Section of the Natural History Museum, Stockholm, and by Professor Gunnar Harling, Gothenburg University's Institution for Systematic Botany, Sweden.

Two small samples (one of the seeds weighing 0.4470 gram) constitute too limited a supply for a real investigation of the chemical compounds found in the *espingo* seeds (Collection 71.35.2a-b in the Gothenburg Ethnographic Museum), but I have submitted the material anyway to Professor Bo Holmstedt for chemical research and to Dr. E. Bondeson for a pharmacognostical examination (see Wassén 1973: Appendix).

As Cajamarca in Peru was referred to in connection with *espingo,* I got in touch with Dr. Luís Ibérico Mas of the Universidad Técnica de Cajamarca. He kindly sent a considerable quantity of a Peruvian

[12] Original text: "Semilla de una planta pequeña de zona tropical, departamento Loreto, Perú. Aplicación antiseptical (para desarreglos estomacales). Se toma pulverizado o se masca."
[13] Letter from Dr. Richard Evans Schultes, Cambridge, Massachusetts, March 14, 1973.

plant called *ishpingo* (Collection 71.36. in the Gothenburg Ethnographic Museum). Samples were forwarded to Dr. José Cuatrecasas in Washington, D.C., via Dr. R. E. Schultes, and according to a written statement of August 30, 1971, Dr. Cuatrecasas has determined the *ishpingo* material (leaves and stalks, no seeds) to be *Gnaphalium dysodes* Spreng. This plant, however, has nothing to do with the plant *espingo* of a *Quararibea* species.

Valdizán and Maldonado (1922: II: 397) have included *ishpingo* in a list of popular names for plants used medicinally, but botanically unknown. The reference seems to be from the region of Madre de Dios, and they present this *ishpingo* as a tree with very fragrant seeds, useful for curing dysentery and other diseases.

As has already been pointed out, both American and Swedish botanical experts have reached agreement on a *Quararibea* as the mother plant to the *espingo* seeds. My collaborator, Wolmar Bondeson, Stockholm, has therefore been able to send me a list of not fewer than twelve species, that according to MacBride (1951-56) are known from the Department of Loreto. Furthermore, the list names four additional Peruvian *Quararibea* species (Bondeson, personal communication, March 7, 1973).

We must now go on to further botanical clarity, and above all, through chemical-pharmacological research, to find out if the old sources spoke the truth when they described the psychotropic effect of *espingo*. Dr. Eskil Hultin of Stockholm, in a letter written January 9, 1973, considered some form of folk-etymological idea association: "*à la absinthe* with the fragrant scented addition of *Artemisia*." Perhaps the Indians' intoxication on strong beer, with the addition of *espingo*, was what the Spaniards disliked?

Lévi-Strauss (1950: 483, 1948: 368) has mentioned "the rosin of certain *Bombacaceae* as a magical poison," with references to the *Nambicuara* (the rosin of the barrigudo tree). We do not know, however, if this last idea could have a direct connection with the use of *espingo* as an added ingredient to beer and a means of magic in Ancient Peru.[14]

---

[14]   To quote La Barre (1972: 277):
"Whether shaman alone, or shaman and communicants, or communicants alone imbibe or ingest *Ilex* drinks, *Datura* infusions, tobacco in whatever form, native beers and wines, peyote cactus, ololiuqui or morning-glory seeds, mushrooms, narcotic mint leaves or coca, the ayahuasca 'vine of the dead spirits' (*Banisteriopsis caapi*) or any of the vast array of Amerindian psychotropic plants, the ethnographic principle is the same. THESE PLANTS CONTAIN SPIRIT POWER."

# REFERENCES

COBO, BERNABÉ
1891   *Historia del nuevo mundo*, volume two. Seville: E. Rasco.
DE ARRIAGA, PABLO JOSEPH
1920   *La extirpación de la idolatría en el Perú.* Collección de libros y documentos referentes a la historia del Perú 1, second series. Lima.
DE MURÚA, MARTÍN
1946   *Historia del origen y genealogía real de los reyes incas del Perú.* Madrid: Consejo Superior de Investigaciones Científios.
DE VILLAGOMES, PEDRO
1919   *Exortaciones e instrucción acerca de las idolatrías: del arzobispado de Lima.* Collección de libros y documentos referentes a la historia del Perú 12. Lima.
FRIEDERICI, GEORG
1947   *Amerikanistisches Wörterbuch.* Hamburg: Cram, De Gruyter.
GARCILASO DE LA VEGA
1943   *Comentarios reales de los incas*, volume two. Buenos Aires: Emecé.
HARTMANN, GÜNTHER
1958   *Alkoholische Getränke bei den Naturvölkern Südamerikas.* Berlin.
LA BARRE, WESTON
1938   Native American beers. *American Anthropologist*, n.s. 40:224–234.
1972   "Hallucinogens and the shamanic origins of religion," in *Flesh of the gods: the ritual use of hallucinogens.* Edited by Peter T. Furst, 261–278. New York, Washington: Praeger.
LASTRES, JUAN B.
1951   *Historia de la medicina peruana*, volume five (1): *La medicina incaica. Lima:* Santa María.
LÉVI-STRAUSS, CLAUDE
1948   "The Nambicuara," in *Handbook of South American Indians*, volume three, 361–370. Bureau of American Ethnology Bulletin 143. Washington, D.C.
1950   "The use of wild plants in tropical South America," in *Handbook of South American Indians*, volume six, 465–466. Bureau of American Ethnology Bulletin 143. Washington, D.C.
LOUKOTKA, ČESTMÍR
1968   *Classification of South American Indian languages.* Edited by Johannes Wilbert. Los Angeles: Latin American Center.
MAC BRIDE, J. FRANCIS
1951–1956   *Flora of Peru.* Field Museum of Natural History Publication 351. Chicago.
OBLITAS POBLETE, ENRIQUE
1969   *Plantas medicinales de Bolivia.* Cochabamba.
RICARDO, ANTONIO
1951 [1586]   *Vocabulario y phrasis en la lengua general de los indios del Perú, llamada Quichua* (1951 edition). Edited by Guillermo Escobar Risco. Lima: Instituto de Historia de la Facultad de Letras.

ROWE, JOHN HOWLAND
1946  "Inca culture at the time of the Spanish conquest," in *Handbook of South American Indians*, volume two, 183–330. Bureau of American Ethnology Bulletin 143. Washington, D.C.
STEWARD, JULIAN H.
1948  "Tribes of the montaña: an introduction," in *Handbook of South American Indians*, volume three, 507–533. Bureau of American Ethnology Bulletin 143. Washington, D.C.
STEWARD, JULIAN H., ALFRED MÉTRAUX
1948  "Tribes of the Peruvian Ecuadorian montaña," in *Handbook of South American Indians*, volume three, 535–636. Bureau of American Ethnology Bulletin 143. Washington, D.C.
VALDIZÁN, HERMILIO, ANGEL MALDONADO
1922  *La medicina popular peruana*, volume two. Lima.
VON REIS ALTSCHUL, SIRI
1967  "Vilca and its use," in *Ethnopharmacologic search for psychoactive drugs*, 307–314. Workshop Series of Pharmacology 2. Washington, D.C.: National Institute of Mental Health.
WASSÉN, S. HENRY
1967  "Anthropological survey of the use of South American snuffs," in *Ethnopharmacologic search for psychoactive drugs*, 233–289. Workshop Series of Pharmacology 2. Washington, D.C.: National Institute of Mental Health.
1973  *Ethnobotanical follow-up of Bolivian Tiahuanacoid tomb material, and of Peruvian shamanism, psychotropic plant constituents, and espingo seeds* (with an appendix by Wolmar E. Bondeson: Anatomical notes on *espingo* and seeds of *Quararibea*). Göteborgs Etnografiska Museum Årstryck 1972. Gothenburg, Sweden.

# Epilogue

SAMARENDRA SARAF

So rich an intellectual harvest of ethno-anthropological literature has been presented in the foregoing pages that an exhaustive recapitulation seems impossible. Proceeding selectively though, an attempt is nevertheless made to thresh and husk the crop in order to get to the grains.

The ethnographic information displayed in these presentations is both wide in its coverage and representative of nearly every major culture area that has ever arrested the attention of students of the supernatural — including what seems bizarre to the lay or the noniniate. Whereas the descriptive sections supply meticulous details and fill up gaps in the ethnographic atlas, the analytical sections offer rigorous treatment of data while arriving at conceptual formulations and insights, often with sharp and precise delineations.

The methodological repertoire or the ethno-anthropological stock-in-trade, as exploited by the participants, also tells its tale. Whereas few scholars are given to evolutionist dogmatism, and only a small number are guided by the patron saint of historicalism — the diffusionist predilections of the latter remaining confined to the working out of culture areas and the mapping of culture history — those following the structuralist-functionalist methodological orientation far outnumber them; the synchronic outweighs the diachronic perspective.

The contours that are delineated in these papers present conventional themes in strikingly unconventional treatment. Even a topical listing of the areas of exploration and their current emphases would validate this characterization. For instance, rituals, beliefs, religious movements, and shamanism persist as foci of attention, though their treatment has departed significantly from that of the older generation of pioneer researchers. This departure could perhaps be explained in terms of new disciplinary orientations and cross-disciplinary approaches that are gaining ground. The rigidly defined frontiers of every discipline are now being continually blurred, effecting merger and accelerating the emergence of an interdisciplinary perspective.

In order to pool these disciplinary orientations and their conceptual framework, a thematic and topical recapitulation must be attempted. I shall concentrate on these major representative themes: shamanism, religious communities and/or movements, rituals, and myths.

Kralovánszky has tapped insights offered by the history of religion, anatomical science, and the ethnology of the northwestern group of the Ural-Altaic, or Finno-Ugric, people, while addressing himself to the task of interpreting the archaeological specimen under study — a musical instrument unearthed from a trans-Danubian site in Hungary. Because the musical wind instrument is modeled in the shape of a human head sporting "a big, open mouth with a moustache, a flat nose, thin ears, and round eyes," symbolic trepanation on the skull as well as several foramens serving as ventages, surrounded by remnants of indefinable marine flora and fauna, Kralovánszky summoned the aid of the disciplines involved to conclude that the human head shape of the instrument is that of a shaman or the Demon of Illness. The dialectics of the researcher run thus: the humanoid head form is expressive of virility and prowess so characteristic of a shaman; the Mongoloid or Euro-Mongoloid ethnic features of the iconographic specimen are suggestive of the ethnic waves over a period of about a millennium; the marine floral and faunal incrustations are reminiscent of the belief in driving out the Demon of Illness and chasing it down to the bottom of the sea; and the symbolic trepanation on the forehead suggests an accompanying ritual of the shamanistic trade. The folk belief about causation and cure of disease, the functional relevance of music to ritual, and the symbolism of trepanation reveal the meaning of the iconographic instrument. Unlike the dialectics of a poet (John Keats's "Ode on a Grecian Urn"), those of Kralovánszky are founded, hopefully, on interdisciplinary methodology.

An exercise in folk typonymy, Loukatos's paper addresses itself to the origin of the Hellenistic mythology, wherein the perception of coastal gulfs and promontories rising from a sea strewn with islands and rocks has taken anthropomorphic and zoomorphic characteristics. Loukatos proposes the hypothesis that the human mind, especially the seafarer's, often turns the unfamiliar into the familiar by peopling the precarious nautical environment:

... all personification imposed upon any inanimate object is (except for any other magic or religious explanation) especially due to man's need for a milieu of humanlike beings, and to his fear of solitude.

Loukatos's notion of the role of nature in Hellenic mythology recalls Max Muller's somewhat faded dictum:

Nature was the greatest surprise, a terror, a marvel, a standing miracle. ... It was that vast domain of surprise, of terror, of marvel, of miracle, the unknown, as distinguished from the known ... the infinite, as distinct from the finite. ... Religion really commences only at the moment when these natural forces are no longer represented in the mind in an abstract form. They must be transformed into personal agents, living and thinking beings, spiritual powers or gods ... (1891: 119–120, 128).

The shaman's psychopathology now generates interest comparable to that in yogic *samadhi* or the ecstatic state of a mystic. Referring to "this uncharted realm of mental activity [which] has been neither systematically explored nor adequately conceptualized" (the realm which has been variously designated as "dissociational states," "altered states of consciousness," "altered awareness," "peak experiences," and the like), Goodman postulates it as the condition in which "a person [is] divorced from awareness of the ordinary reality surrounding him ... A CAPACITY COMMON TO ALL MEN" (emphasis mine). In a similar vein, Long likewise categorically rejects the generally held assumption that *psi* events are either a separate reality as a class of phenomena or that they are embedded in different, perhaps inferior, planes of reality. His hypothesis is that trance and possession states of the shaman, the sorcerer, and the witch doctor — whether such states be induced by invocation or by hallucinogens — belong to the same plane of psychic reality as that of the ordinary man.

Starting with the aforesaid hypothesis, Long has rather convincingly discussed the prospects of a fruitful utilization of the impressive array of electronic gadgets and other sophisticated tools in the study of psychical events. Devices like ideographs, electronic encephalographs, and Kirlian photography may serve well in the data-collection and data-verification stages. Long recommends the utilization of precision tools apparently because he views the human psychic level of existence on a cybernetic model. The central thrust of his advocacy could perhaps best be summarized by a passage from Lex: "Laboratory experiments on the physiology of dissociational states [can] close the gap between speculation and knowledge."

Viewing ritual as "a means for achieving altered states of consciousness," Lex highlights the functional significance of a roster of North

Iroquoian rituals, spotlighting the role of kinesics, music, intense vocalizations, and the stoic endurance tests that are geared to the common goal of intensifying dissociational states.

Wassén's focus of interest is directed towards the *espingo* seed and its myriad kith and kin which, according to chronicler Cobo, "the rude Indians [once traded in the form of] capsules as a precious thing, to barter them for knives, scissors, and other trifles which they highly valued." The indigenous herbal capsules are reported to have therapeutic use for the laity and a psychotropic quality for the shaman in Peru. Wassén's paper combines a quest for ethnobotanical taxonomy with chemico-pharmacological enquiries. Wassén does not mention emics and etics and he is probably not acquainted with these terms, but his paper displays a strategy not too far removed from that of the "new ethnography" closer home.

Prince Peter of Greece and Denmark proceeds on the assumption of the schools of culture-historians in his study of the Tibetan oracles (*Chos-sKyong* or *Chos-rgyal*). Viewing the institution of Tibetan oracles as a variant of shamanism and as rooted in the dim, hoary, prehistoric past, he has placed it close to its Asiatic and Arctic parallels, taking into account the spatial distribution of the institution of shamanism: "They are pre-Buddhistic and certainly closely connected with the Central Asian and Arctic shamans." Non-Tibetologists notice that an "oracle" is a person, not an event in this context.

Attracting his reader's attention to the coexistence of oracles with the highly formalized Lamaist church (their gradations resulting from vertical extension from the village to the state levels in pre-occupation Tibet) and to their enjoyment of popular and official esteem, the Prince points to the parallel existence of "little" and "great traditions" in Tibetan culture, but without labeling either the oracles as lesser specialists and carriers of a little tradition or the Lama priests as higher specialists and carriers of a great tradition. Neither did he spell out transcommunication and symbiosis between the two traditions which appear to polarize the folk and elite elements. The Tibetan oracles as a local variant of Asiatic-Arctic shamans are of interest; their symbiotic functions must be assigned some territory in the Lamaist tradition in the manner in which Marriott (1961) analyzed his Indian data a while ago.

Viewing the man-supernature communication continuum against the backdrop of Hindu beliefs, Wadley has worked out two broad patterns: an upward communication process from man to the supernatural, such as the suppliant priest invokes; and a downward communication process from the supernatural to man, such as in the case of the oracle, the exorcist, and the "victims." Suggesting a dichotomy of spiritual beings into benevolent and malevolent or "the good guys and the bad guys," Wadley further attempts "two broad patterns of possession" where the good guys "come" to the oracles, the bad guys "ride" the victims. The typology of the dextral/sinistral spirits and their visitation on the oracle/exorcist-victim as the mediums respectively imply the differences that underlie the phenomena of spirit "coming" and spirit "riding" as well as the contingent manipulative modes or behavioral patterns, as marked by supplication in the former instance and exorcism in the latter. Wadley succeeds in creating a refined typology which carries her beyond the point where Dumont, Pocock, and others had let things rest.

Basilov and Potapov follow the line of the Prince insofar as they treated shamanistic studies as a means to the same end: reconstruction of the ethnocultural history of the Siberian people. The former illustrates his concept of ethnic history through the paradigm of shamanism by delineating the Turkic and Tajik shamanistic complexes and by explaining differences in the two complexes as rooted in ethnocultural history. Potapov likewise explains why the Russian scholars, who have collected a wealth of literature and who established scientific archives, continue to study shamanism: "The study of Siberian shamanism, especially the attributes of the shamanistic cult, is of great value as a historical key to the ethnic history, the ethnocultural and ethnogenetic ties of the Siberian peoples with one another and with peoples of other neighboring countries."

Manning views shamanism as a profession, since it carries characteristic traits as recruitment, initiation, training, specialization, role playing, and status position. He posits two models of "profession," i.e. professionalization and professionalism, deriving these models from "European-type" professions.

Nachtigall places his emphasis in shamanistic studies on what he considers the core of the matter: how shamans are trained and how they are buried. The period of training of the Siberian shaman and the mode of his burial form the central theme of Nachtigall's exploration. The twin processes of metamorphosis and metempsychosis (from whose matrix the shaman proceeds) are seen by him as rooted in the symbolism of death, "skeletonization," and reincarnation. Self-mortification through taboos, self-torture and privations — a method of "skeletonization" — paves the stoic way to mystic attainments. Nachtigall's interpretation of skeletonization as a process of the symbolic devouring of the flesh of the novice by the spirits and of a symbolic reincarnation of the shaman perfected by the spirits brings out the *raison d'être* of the symbolic burial of a shaman.

Litsas presents a graphic account of the *Rousalia* rituals as "the most representative of the celebrations mourning the dead" prevalent in the southwestern Peloponnesian peninsula and the county of Triphylia. Motivated by belief in the immortality of the soul and the return of the dead to the earth, the Greeks make offerings, performing at least five memorial services to the exalted spirits of the departed lest they "might return to haunt and molest the disrespectful and the negligent." The spirits tend to act this way if they are refused entry into the underworld or "the house of Hades" because the survivors neglected to perform these memorial services.

By pointing out the configurational aspect of Greek *Rousalia* and its Roman parallel *Lemouria* or *Remouria* (*lemoures* and *remoures* being the Roman words for the dead), Litsas contrasts "the melancholia of the *Lemouria* feast [with] the carefree, lighthearted character of the *Rousalia*." In time, the *Lemouria* apparently outweighed the *Rousalia*. Syncretic Graeco-Roman beliefs and rituals, as well as subsequent Christian and Byzantine accretions, shaped the feast into its extant form. In the *Rousalia* feast (as a culture complex wherein beliefs and rituals, offerings and sentiments, prescriptions and prohibitions, exhumation and prognostication intertwine), Litsas illustrates the functional significance of the feast as a bridge between the living and the deceased, the past and the present, the invisible yet certain and the visible yet uncertain human world.

Despite the fragmentary historical accounts, Aiyappan has proceeded as a cultural historian, opening his paper with "some hints about the probable nature of popular religion in Kerala in the centuries preceding Sámkara." Highlighting the theological beliefs and mortuary rituals of the Kurchiyas of Wynad, the author has employed the Kurchiya conception of a triadic linear continuum (human, spiritual, and divine beings) in his explanation of "the Hindu monistic concept of identity of the individual soul with the Universal Spirit (*Brahman*) as a development from the tribal archetype of man-god continuum."

Aiyappan emphatically endorses (like Marriott 1961) the orthogenetic view of the growth of Hindu culture:

... the germ of the idea of [Hindu] monism, namely — the continuity of men with god, is likely to be found among the primitive substratum of India's population. *Anyway, the idea could not have been a sudden discovery of the Upanishadic philosopher but should have been vaguely in the popular mind at its sensitive, creative, myth-making level* (emphasis added).

Preoccupied with a folklorist's predilection, Aiyappan has nearly overlooked the elite tradition of classical Hinduism and the fact that the classical literati have also resorted to zoomorphism, dendromorphism (Keith 1925; MacDonell 1963; Max Muller 1891), neuromorphism (Rele 1931), and sonomorphism (Woodroffe 1963).

Related to the extended theme of dissociational states, Goodman's study throws light on the question why in the Pentecostal (or Apostolic) churches in Yucatán congregations either grew or declined. The total acoustic effect produced by such rhythmic manipulations as singing, clapping, and accentuation of musical instruments apparently furthers the charismatic effect of the glossolalial utterances of the priest. Glossolalia is often interpreted as the evidence of possession by the Holy Spirit, as is a possession trance. The shaman-minister in the Pentecostal church becomes the chosen practitioner of the masses only because, in his armamentarium, he has and can activate psychologically adaptive mechanisms or "psychological strategy for relieving the anxiety, stress, and tension characteristically produced by situations of overwhelming cultural distortion." He thereby moves large audiences.

Addressing himself to symbolism and dynamism in a north Peruvian séance, Sharon singles out the preparatory, the prophetic, and the therapeutic phases in the ritual where Eduardo Calderón plays the *curandero* [folk healer], with his *mesa* [altarlike arrangement of power objects] as his ritual paraphernalia and with the San Pedro cactus and wild black tobacco as the psychedelic ingredients. The author takes his reader on a discussion of the polar opposition of the worlds of men and nature, on the one hand, and of the dextral and sinistral forces, on the other, which resolves itself in the "Middle Field" as represented by the ritual go-between. The entire dramatization boils down to the *curandero's* twin symbolic roles: his power buildup as effected by his periodic imbibing of cactus-tobacco juice (and, later, in the consumption of pure San Pedro by all the participants), and his balancing role as activating a meaningful rapport between the polarized worlds and forces.

Rituals, myths, symbols, and dreams constitute the complex of supranatural experiences and its expression. In her interpretation of the funeral services of the Catholic Church for the murdered president — "the figure of John F. Kennedy [who] became endowed with the quality of myth because his life and death invoke some of the most powerful myths in the traditions of the United States and of Western Civilization" — Willner detects a link between the Christian and the civic sacrifice. Willner views the myth of the assassinated president as the theme of the fallen warrior and hero, with the pomp of a state funeral and the accession of his successor to the highest office in the land — a service in which "the nation [was turned] into a community of mourners engaged in shared rites." She thus demonstrates how the mortuary rites "helped bridge a national crisis," partly through ritual dramatization and partly through constitutional *rites de passage* — thereby symbolizing the transition and continuity of the enduring power of the state.

P. Singer takes up the case history method to illustrate how, from the traditional role of a passive mediator of supernatural power, an indigenous, illiterate Kali-cult healer (who is a laborer on a sugar cane plantation in Guiana), could arrive at the modern role of a therapist and community social worker, this phenomenal transformation of roles resulting from his year-long association with a psychiatrist and anthropologist. Singer's optimism takes wing when he proceeds to visualize the possible utilization of such indigenous therapy for the purpose of community psychiatry, especially in the emerging countries.

Placing shamanism against the changing Siberian context, Vdovin invokes economic determinism in order to explain such change: "Religious consciousness of a people is closely connected with, even dependent on, the level of development which its production forces and production relations have attained." The economic determinist argues how in the late nineteenth and early twentieth centuries the forces of economic development have invaded the Siberian precincts, bringing differing religious consciousness and promoting radically changed notions about nature and society. Variations of economic development at different levels — national, tribal, clan, or patriarchal family — are bound to produce impulses for change in the selection of cults and in the social roles of shamans.

Fornaro takes up an extremely interesting, equally contemporaneous, highly complex problem: the neo-Hindu humanist and missionary (rather than proselytization) movement as an alternative to the "lost generation" of a "sick society" — the American youth who lived by psychedelic drugs or psychotropic alkaloids, treating them as fundamentals of their "spiritual life-style." The moral fabric and the new way of life of the psycho-pathological practitioners of such "instant chemical religion," "many thousands of [whom] were actively experimenting with a wide variety of drugs for an even wider variety of reasons," have aroused widespread concern among social workers and in official circles in the United States of America.

Because Fornaro has confined his research to "significant cognitive and behavioral changes" generated by the neo-Hindu acculturation of the American youth, he views the emergent counter-culture as a phase of youth activism that is eagerly seeking a base for a search for identity along both sacred and secular pathways. The neo-Hindu "devotees" are erstwhile victims or rebels who, obeying the call to "turn on, tune in, and drop out," busied themselves in their "quest for a drug-oriented mystical experience [that] only led them to rapid physical deterioration and disillusionment." Collected methodically through participant observation and structured interviews, Fornaro's data are as systematic as they are neat in presentation. What the paper lacks is the rigorous analytical frame of reference against which the neo-Hindu acculturation movement has to be conceptualized. The "instant chemical religion" presents a model of religion where indigenous and exotic traits intertwine into a flexible complex. As a cocktail of alkaloids, wild and ecstatic music, intense vocalizations and vigorous kinesics, esoteric cults and eclectic espousal of Oriental philosophies, it presents a "libertine" model. Of the two Hindu models, the "ascetic" and the "nonascetic" (Bharati 1970a, 1970b), only the former is offered by the cultural ambassadors of neo-Hinduism. From the way the neo-Hindu devotees are taking to a neo-Hindu model, as Fornaro reports, it is evident that a "compromise" model is preferred and promoted. The phenomenon of neo-Hindu acculturation is, thus, a shift from the "libertine" to the "compromise" model.

Shamanism, rituals, myths, and religious communities/movements are broad areas of academic interest which have evoked a variety of researches with highly diverse emphases and orientations. The shaman-oracle, for example, has been viewed as a profession by some, a process by others, a psychic syndrome by yet some others, and as a ritualistic medium by still others. In the case of religious movements, varying emphases have been laid on the nature, course, and direction of change, its agents, and the universe. However, in all these fields, whatever the scholastic predilection or orientation of the researcher — history, economic determinism, psychology, sociology, or ritualism — one common perspective seems to underlie every presentation: the perspective of positivism.

## REFERENCES

BHARATI, AGEHANANDA
   1970a *The ochre robe.* New York: Doubleday.
   1970b *The Tantric tradition.* New York: Doubleday.
HOEBEL, E. ADAMSON
   1958 *Man in the primitive world.* New York: McGraw-Hill.

KEITH, A. B.

1925   *Religion and philosophy of the Vedas and Upanishads.*Cambridge, Mass.: Harvard Oriental Series.

MAC DONELL, A. A.

1963   *The Vedic mythology.* Varanasi, India: Indological Book House.

MARRIOTT, MC KIM

1961   "Little communities in an indigenous civilization," in *Village India.* Edited by McKim Marriott. Bombay: Asia Publishing House.

MULLER, MAX

1891   *Physical religion.* London: Longmans, Green.

RELE, V. G.

1931   *The Vedic gods as figures of biology. Bombay: D. B.*Taraporavala.

WOODROFFE, SIR JOHN

1963   *The garland of letters: studies in the* Mantra Shastra. Madras: Ganesh.

# Biographical Notes

AYINIPALLI AIYAPPAN (1905– ), born in Kerala, was educated at Madras and the London School of Economics, London University, under Professor B. Malinowski and Sir Raymond Firth. He worked as Curator for anthropology and later as Director at the Government Museum, Madras (1929–1958); as Professor of Anthropology, Utkal University, Orissa (1958–1966); as U.G.C. Professor in the Andhra University, Andhra State; as Vice-Chancellor, Kerala University (1968–1970), and as Special Officer, Tribal Research and Training Institute, Calicut, Kerala State (1970–1972). His publications are: *Social revolution in a Kerala villaga* (Asia); and *Travas and culture change* (Madras Government Press). His main interests include anthropology of the tribes of southern India and social change.

ENRIQUE ARANETA (1925– ) is a physician and Professor of Psychiatry, University of Florida, Gainesville, and Assistant Chief, Psychiatric Services, Veterans Administration Hospital, Gainesville, Florida. He was born in the Philippines and was educated both in the Philippines and in the United States. He is a Diplomate of the American Board of Psychiatry and Neurology and Adjunct Professor of Behavioral Sciences (Psychiatry), Allport College of Human Behavior, Oakland University, Rochester, Michigan. He served as Head of all Mental Health Services, Ministry of Health, Guyana, South America.

TSUNEO AYABE (1930– ) is Professor of Anthropology at Kyushu University, Fukuoka, Japan. He received his Ph.D. (1966) from Tokyo Metropolitan University with a dissertation on the structural analysis of traditional society in Thailand. He was Research Fellow at the University of California (1960–1961), Program Specialist in UNESCO (1963–1965), and also Visiting Professor of the the University of Pennsylvania and Stanford University (1967–1968). His special interests include the comparative study of voluntary associations and secret societies, initiation ceremonies, rites of passage, and the application of the idea of unconsciousness to the study of culture.

VLADIMIR NIKOLAJEVICH BASILOV (1937–　) is Scientific Secretary of the Ethnography Institute (Academy of Sciences, U.S.S.R.), Moscow, where he has been working since 1959. After graduating from the Moscow Government University, he received his Ph.D. in 1967, with a thesis on "The cult of Muslim saints in Turkmenia." His special interests primarily include the ethnography of Central Asian peoples and the history of religions, especially problems of shamanism.

AGEHANANDA BHARATI (1923–　), born in Vienna, has been a U.S. citizen since 1968. He studied ethnology and Indology at Vienna University and moved to India in 1947 where he was ordained a Hindu monk. He obtained the Acharya (Ph.D.) degree at the Samnyasi Mahavidyalaya in Varanasi, India, in 1951. He was Reader in Philosophy (1951–1953) at Benares Hindu University, India; Visiting Professor at the Royal Buddhist Academy in Bangkok, 1956; at the Universities of Tokyo and Kyoto in 1957; Research Associate in the Far Eastern Institute at the University of Washington, Seattle, 1957–1961 and joined the Department of Anthropology at Syracuse University in 1961, where he is now Chairman and Professor of Anthropology. His special fields are South Asian languages and cultures, religious behavior, and cognitive systems. He is a Fellow of the American Anthropological Association, a Fellow of the Royal Anthropological Institute of Great Britain and Ireland, a Fellow of the Society for Applied Anthropology, and a Member of the Association for Asian Studies. The following books are among his numerous publications: *The ochre robe* (Doubleday, New York, 1970; *The Tantric tradition* (Rider, London, 1969); *A functional analysis of Indian thought and its social margins* (Benares, 1964); The *The Asians in East Africa: Jayhind and Uhuru* (Chicago, 1972).

G. V. DINGRE (1939–　) received his B.A. in Economics (1960), his M.A. in Sociology (1962), and his Ph.D. in Sociology and Cultural Anthropology (1969) from Poona University. He was associated with the Department of Sociology and Anthropology, Deccan College, and the Research Institute, Poona, in various capacities and worked with the late Professor Irawati Karve in the project entitled "Bio-Cultural and Social Investigations among the Shepherd (Dhangar) Community of Maharashtra" from 1969 to 1970. Since August, 1970, has has been working as Senior Lecturer at the Department of Social Work and Social Sciences, Sholapur College. He has a life membership with the Indian Anthropological Association. His special interests include Hindu temples and priesthood tradition, population studies, and nomadism.

ROBERT FORNARO (1941–    ) was born in Utica, New York. He studied at the Maxwell Graduate School of Citizenship, Syracuse University. He received his Ph.D. in Social Science in 1969 with a dissertation on Sivananda and the Divine Life Society. His major research interest is the growing number of neo-Hindu religious societies in the United States and the effect they are having on the traditional American cultural patterns. Since 1969 he has held a post as Assistant Professor of Anthropology at DePauw University with part-time teaching assignments at Indiana University. His specific interests include acculturation and cultural change in religion.

FELICITAS D. GOODMAN (1914–    ) was born in Budapest, Hungary. She received her diploma from the University of Heidelberg in Interpretation and Translation (1936), an M.A. from Ohio State University in Linguistics (1968) and a Ph.D. in Anthropology (1971). She taught at Ohio Wesleyan University and at Ohio State University and has been Professor of Anthropology and Linguistics at Denison University since 1968. Her principal interests are religion, altered states of consciousness, and culture change. She published numerous articles in these areas, as well as *Speaking in tongues: a cross-cultural study of glossolalia* (1972) and, with Jeannette Henney and Esther Pressel, *Trance, healing, and hallucination: three field studies in religious experience* (1974).

DOUGLAS A. JACKSON (1946–    ) received his B.A. in Psychology from the University of California, Riverside, and his M.A. in Family Social Science from the University of Minnesota. He is currently working toward the Ph.D. in Family Social Science and is studying to be a marriage counselor. His recent scholarly work deals with various aspects of grief and mourning.

A. KRALOVÁNSZKY. No biographical data available.

BARBARA W. LEX (1941–   ) was born in Buffalo, New York. She studied anthropology at Syracuse University (B.A., 1964; M.A., 1968; Ph.D., 1969); her dissertation is an ethnography of low-income white inhabitants of a St. Louis, Missouri, residential district. She was Research Associate in the Washington University Social Science Institute from 1966 to 1968, Lecturer in Anthropology at Utica College of Syracuse University from 1968 to 1969, Assistant Professor of Anthropology at Lehigh University from 1969 to 1970, and has been Assistant Professor of Anthropology and Social Science at Western Michigan University since 1970. She has studied Iroquois ritual intermittently since 1966 and was Visiting Research Anthropologist at the Langley Porter Neuropsychiatric Research Institute in 1973. Her current interests include a neurobiological approach to ritual trance, shamanism, and native therapies.

FOTIOS CONSTANTINE LITSAS (1943–   ) was born in Greece. He studied Greek literature and archaeology at the University of Athens (B.A., 1966) and Greek history and religion at the University of East Michigan (M.A., 1973). He taught at several schools in Greece and in the U.S. As a Curriculum Consultant for a Multi-Ethnic Program at Michigan, he did special research on Greek-Americans and their culture. He is now working on a Ph.D. program at the University of Chicago. His special interests include Byzantine history and culture in relation to antiquity and modern times, Greek cultural aspects and development, and the survival of ancient culture among the modern Greeks. Most of his publications are on the same or related subjects.

LAURENCE D. LOEB.   No biographical data available.

JOSEPH K. LONG (1937–   ) was born in Greenville, Kentucky. He received his Ph.D. in Medical Anthropology and Epidemiology at the University of North Carolina in 1973. He has taught at the University of Kentucky, the University of Wisconsin, and Southern Methodist University and is currently Professor of Sociology at Plymouth College of the University of New Hampshire. His fieldwork in the U.S., Jamaica, and Mexico are reflected in publications on applied anthropology, ecology, psychosomatic medicine, and genetics and evolution. His current research focuses on deviance and the folk-urban exchange in the context of tourism.

DEMETRIOS LOUKATOS (1908–   ) was born in Cephalonia, Greece. He studied philosophy and ancient literature at the Athens University (diploma in 1930) and ethnology and folklore at the Paris University (Docteur ès lettres, 1950). There he also studied museography, with training in the archives of the Musée de l'Homme and the Musée des Arts et Traditions Populaires. He has worked in Greek high schools (1931–1937), in the Research Center of Greek Folklore of the Academy of Athens (1938–1963), and, as Professor of Folklore (Laography), at the University of Jannina (1964–1969). He has published books and studies, and papers in Congresses, on Greek anthropology, particularly on popular religion and proverbs. Since 1965 he has been a member of the Editorial Committee of *Proverbium* (Helsinki). He also contributes to Greek and foreign ethnological reviews.

LAKSHMAN KUMAR MAHAPATRA (1929– ) has been Professor of Anthropology at Utkal University, Bhubaneswar, India, since 1967. Formerly, he has Visiting Professor in Anthropology, Indology, and Sociology at Hamburg University in 1968 and Reader in Social Anthropology at Karnatak University (1962–1964) and delivered National Lectures in Anthropology in 1970. He received his M.A. from Calcutta in 1952 and his Ph.D. from Hamburg University in 1960. He has had field experience in Orissa, Bihar, U.P., Assam, N.E.F.A. (Arunachal Pradesh), and Mysore (Karnatak). His present interests include the study of the tribes and peasantry of India and Southeast Asia and their relations with gods, temples and kings. Recent publications include: *Folklore of Orissa* (National Book Trust of India) and (editor) *Man in society* (1973–1974, inaugural volume).

ROY OTHWORT MANNING. No biographical data available.

LORNA MCLAUCHLAN MCDOUGALL (1942– ), born in Edingburgh, is currently teaching at Pitzer College, The Claremont Colleges, Claremont, California. She received her B.A. from the Honours School of Modern Languages, Trinity College, Dublin; pursued the study of anthropology at the Institute of Social Anthropology at Oxford; and, in 1969, received her B.Litt. with a dissertation, "Comparative analysis of the symbolism of numbers." Her special interests include several aspects of symbolization, classification, and cognition.

EUGENE L. MENDONSA (1942– ) received his B.A. in anthropology in 1968, his M.A. in sociology in 1969 from Brigham Young University, and his Ph.D. in social anthropology from the University of Cambridge,

England in 1974. His fieldwork was among the Sisala people of northern Ghana and his doctoral dissertation concerns their system of divination. He is presently on leave from the University of Wisconsin-Fdl for two years (1974–1976) to lecture in sociology at Ahmadu Bello University, Zaria, Nigeria and to carry out research among the Hausa.

HORST NACHTIGALL (1924–  ) has been Professor of Ethnology at the University of Marburg/Lahn since 1963. He received his Ph.D. in 1950 from the University of Mainz and wrote his habilitation in 1957. He was Head of the Archaeological Department of the Instituto Colombiano de Antropología in Bogotá during the academic year 1952–1953. From 1961 to 1962 he was Visiting Professor of Ethnology at the University of Buenos Aires. He has participated in much ethnological and archaeological fieldwork and is the author of seven books as well as more than a hundred articles contributed to various publications on ethnology, social anthropology, and archaeology.

JAMSIE NAIDOO (1900?–  ) has just retired as a sugar estate plantation worker in Albion, Guyana. He is the *Pujari* of the Kali Mai church in Albion, Guyana, and has been a Visiting Professor of Behavioral Sciences (Indigenous Healing) at the Allport College of Human Behavior, Oakland University, Rochester, Michigan. His area of specialization as a healer is "kali work" (or functional disorders) as distinguished from "doctor work" (or organic disorders). His parents came to Guyana from South India as indentured laborers. In Guyana, he is presently continuing to supervise Allport College Oakland University students doing fieldwork in traditional healing. In the past, he has also supervised medical students and psychiatric residents from the Albany Center Medical Hospital, New York. His illiteracy proved no bar to his cooperation as coauthor of the chapter in this volume.

EDWARD NORBECK.   No biographical data available.

FELIX JOHANNES OINAS (1911–  ) was born in Tartu, Estonia, and naturalized in the United States in 1955. He received his M.A. from Tartu State University (1938), did graduate study at the University of Heidelberg (1946–1948), and received his Ph.D. from Indiana University (1952). He was Lecturer in Finno-Ugric languages at the University of Budapest (1938–1940), Lecturer in Estonian Language at the Baltic University, Hamburg (1946–1948), and Lecturer (1951–1952), Instructor (1952–1955), Assistant Professor (1955–1961), Associate Professor (1961–1965), and Professor of Slavic and Finno-Ugric Languages (1965 to the present) at Indiana University. Among his publications are: *Language teaching today* (Editor, 1960: Indiana University Research Center); *The development of post-positional cases in Balto-Finnic languages* (1961: Finno-Ugric Society); *Studies in Finnic-Slavic folklore relations* (Editor with Stephen Soudakoff, 1969: Finnish Academy); and *The study of Russian folklore* (1972, Slavic Department: Indiana University).

GOTTFRIED OOSTERWAL (1930–   ), born in Rotterdam, received his B.A. from John Calvin College (1950), his Ph.D. from the University of Utrecht (1956) in Comparative Religion and Theology, and a D. Litt. from the Universities of Utrecht and Cambridge (1961) in Anthropology. He was President of the West Irian Training College, Sukarnapura, Indonesia (1960–1963), Advisor on Nutrition and Native Affairs for the National Bureau of Native Affairs, Dutch Colonial Government (1962–1963), Dean of the College of Liberal Arts at Philippine Union College, Manila (1964–1966), and has been Director of the Institute of World Mission at Andrews University, Berrien Springs, Michigan, since 1968. Among his publications are: *People of the Tor* (1961, Assen: Van Gorkum); *Muremarew: a dual organized village on the Mamberamo* (1967, Ithaca, Djakarta); *Mission: possible* (1972, Nashville: Southern Publishing Association); "A cargo cult in the Mamberamo area" (1963, *Ethnology*); "West Irian: population patterns and problems" (1966, *Asian Studies* 4: 291–302); and "Crisis movements — a discussion" (February 1971, *Current Anthropology*).

RAPHAEL PATAI (1910–   ) was born in Budapest, Hungary. He studied at the University of Budapest (Ph.D., 1933) and the Hebrew University of Jerusalem (Ph.D., 1936). He is Professor of Anthropology at Fairleigh Dickinson University, Rutherford, N.J. He specializes in the study of Middle Eastern and Jewish culture and is the author of more than two dozen books, the latest being: *The Hebrew goddess* (1967), *Society, culture and change in the Middle East* (1971), *Tents of Jacob: the diaspora yesterday and today* (1971), *Myth and modern man* (1972), *The Arab mind* (1973), *The myth of the Jewish race* (with Jennifer P. Wing, 1975), and *The Jewish mind* (1976).

JAROSLAW THEODORE PETRYSHYN (1917–   ) was born in Austria. After graduating from a classic gymnasium in the western Ukraine, he studied at several European universities. In his doctoral work he dealt with the

Ukrainians from the position of anthropological psychology. He became a resident of the United States in 1949, and is presently Associate Professor of Anthropology at the City Colleges of Chicago. He has done extensive fieldwork among the Lacandon Mayas (Hach Winik) for for many years, primarily in the rain forest of the Usumacinta River in Eastern Chiapas, Mexico. He met the Lacandons for the first time in Guatemalan Western Peten in the mid-1950's. His studies have been focused on supernatural beliefs of the contemporary Lacadons and his current research includes analysis of eighteenth-century Spanish manuscripts reporting on their ancestors. His museum collections obtained in various parts of the Mayan area also contain many ethnographic objects from the Lacandon country.

L. P. POTAPOV.    No biographical data available.

H.R.H. PRINCE PETER OF GREECE AND DENMARK (1908–   ), born in Paris, was educated at the Lycée Janson de Sailly. He received his Ll.D. from the Law School of Paris University. He studied anthropology from 1935 to 1936 at the London School of Economics with Dr. Malinowski and Sir Raymond Firth and received his Ph.D. from London University in 1959 with a thesis on polyandry in Ceylon, India, and Tibet. He is the author of *The science of anthropology* (1968) and of numerous contributions to scientific, anthropological publications. He is presently engaged in a study of Tibetan oracles in exile.

ALFRED K. QUARCOO (1923–   ), a Ghanaian, graduated with honors in sociology at the University of Ghana in 1963, where he later obtained his M.A. degree in African Studies in 1965. He was appointed Research Fellow in Visual Art at the Institute of African Studies at the University of Ghana in 1965. From 1969 to 1970, he was at the University of Edinburgh where he was awarded a Ph.D. in Anthropology. The range of his numerous publications covers the fields of social organization, government and politics, social control, art history, the sociology of art, religion, and philosophy. His current special interest is in the sociology of art and religion.

PAUL C. ROSENBLATT (1938–   ) received a B.A. in Psychology from the University of Chicago in 1958 and a Ph.D. in Psychology from Northwestern University in 1962. After teaching psychology, sociology, and anthropology at the University of Missouri, Columbia, and psychology and anthropology at the University of California, Riverside, he moved to the University of Minnesota, where he is now Professor in the Departments of Family Social Science and Psychology. His principal scholarly interests are close social relations and theory translation. His recent publications, many of them coauthored with students or former students, deal with such topics as the development of close social relations, the effects of children and childlessness on families, sex differences and birth-order differences in cross-cultural perspective, and coping with anger and aggression in mourning.

FRANK A. SALAMONE (1939– ) was born in Rochester, New York. He received his B.A. from the St. John Fisher College, his M.A. from the University of Rochester, and his Ph.D. from the State University of New York, Buffalo. Currently, he is Assistant Professor of Anthropology at St. John's University, New York. His Ph.D. concerned religious and ethnic change in Yauri, northern Nigeria, and his numerous publications have dealt with religious and ethnic problems. A member of a number of national and international organizations, he is presently doing research on symbolism and ethnicity.

SAMARENDRA SARAF (1931– ) received his education at the University of Saugar (Madhya Pradesh, India), where he graduated in anthropology (M.A., 1959) and law (Ll.B., 1957), receiving his Ph.D. (1971) with a dissertation on "Hindu caste system and the ritual idiom." He is presently working as Reader in Anthropology at the University. In 1965 he participated in the International Development Seminar at the East-West Center, Hawaii. His publications include research papers on Hindu ritual idiom, sociology of religion, and communication; those awaiting publication include his doctoral thesis, an anthology of published and unpublished research papers entitled "Hindu ritual idiom: perspectives and orientations," and a collection of essays, memoirs, and satires.

DOUGLAS SHARON (1941– ) was born in Quebec City. He worked in archaeological exploration (Mexico and Peru) with the Andean Explorers Club from 1957 to 1967. He studied cultural anthropology at the University of California, Los Angeles, where he received his B.A. (1971), an M.A. (1972), and a Ph.D. (1974), the latter with a dissertation on north Peruvian shamanism. He is currently a Postdoctoral Scholar at the Latin American Center, UCLA, and Member of the editorial board of *Folklore Americas*. His special interests include shamanism, symbolic anthropology, comparative religion, ethnohistory, and ethnographic film. Recent publications are: "The San Pedro cactus in Peruvian folk healing" (1972), "Eduardo the healer" (1972), and "Shamanism in Moche iconography" (1974). His first book, *Wizard of the four winds*, is in press.

PHILIP SINGER (1925–    ) is Professor of Anthropology and Behavioral Sciences at the Allport College of Human Behavior, Oakland University, Rochester, Michigan, and Member of the International Committee on Traditional Medical Therapy. His special interests include medical anthropology, ethnopsychiatry, community development, and pharmacognosy. He has worked for the United Nations and the Albany Medical Center Hospital and College, New York. His fieldwork has been conducted in America, India, Guyana, and Nigeria.

MITSUO SUZUKI.    No biographical data available.

JOHN TU ER-WEI (1914–    ), born in Hopei, China, is Professor of Anthropology at the National Taiwan University, Taipei, where he began teaching in 1955. He received his B.A. from Fu-Jen University, Peiping, in 1946 and his Ph.D. in Anthropology from the University of Fribourg, Switzerland, in 1953, with a doctoral thesis on "Funeral customs in Vietnam and China." His research interests are history of religions and primitive mythology, and he is perhaps the only one who has discovered that the Buddhist and Taoist doctrines are wholly based on primitive lunar mythology. He is also interested in the Moon-mythological System of China and America. Among his publications are: *Discovery of the original meaning of Buddhism* (1963, Taipei: Hua-Ming Press); *The religious system of ancient* China (1960, Tapei); *The beliefs of Confucianism, Buddhism and Taoism* (1968, Tapei); and *The original meaning of the name China* (1973, Tapei: The Commercial Press).

I. S. VDOVIN.    No biographical data available.

SUSAN S. WADLEY (1943–    ) received her B.A. from Carleton College and her Ph.D. in Anthropology from the University of Chicago. Since 1970, she has been Assistant Professor of Anthropology at Syracuse University where she is also affiliated with the South Asia Program. Her special interests are religion, semantic analysis, and oral traditions.

R. PATRICIA WALSH (1945–    ) received her B.A. in Psychology from the University of Maryland and her Ph.D. in Psychology from the University of Minnesota. Currently she is Assistant Professor of Psychology at Loyola University in Los Angeles. Her recent scholarly work deals with the desire to have children, the attribution of personality traits, and grief and mourning.

S. HENRY WASSÉN (1908– ) has been Professor, Director emeritus of the Gothenburg Ethnographic Museum, Sweden, since September, 1973. He received his academic training at the University of Gothenburg and held the positions of Assistant, Curator, and Director at the Gothenburg Ethnographical Museum since 1930. He did repeated seasons of fieldwork in South America and Central America. His special interest is in Americanistic research and his speciality is Latin America's Amerindian cultures, including use of medicines and hallucinogenic drugs. Bibliographies of his scientific publications can be found in the *Årstryck* [Annual Reports] of the Göteborgs Etnografiska Museum since 1930.

DOROTHY WILLNER. No biographical data available.

# Index of Names

# Index of Subjects